The Globalization Reader

Edited by

Frank J. Lechner

and

John Boli

BLACKWELL
Publishers

First published 2000

Reprinted 2000 (twice), 2001 (twice)

Blackwell Publishers Inc.
350 Main Street
Malden, Massachusetts 02148
USA

Blackwell Publishers Ltd
108 Cowley Road
Oxford OX4 1JF
UK

Library of Congress Cataloging-in-Publication Data

The globalization reader / edited by Frank J. Lechner and John Boli.
    p.   cm.
  Includes bibliographical references and index.
  ISBN 0–631–21476–3 (hb.). — ISBN 0–631–21477–1 (pb.)
  1. International economic relations. 2. International economic relations—Social aspects. 3. International economic integration.
  I. Lechner, Frank. II. Boli, John, 1948- .
  HF1359.G59 1999
  337—dc21   99-39722
                                     CIP

British Library Cataloguing in Publication Data

A CIP catalogue record for this book is available from the British Library.

Typeset in 10½ on 12 pt Sabon
By Best-set Typesetter Ltd., Hong Kong
Printed in Great Britain by T.J.International Ltd, Padstow, Cornwall.

This book is printed on acid-free paper.

Contents

Sources and Acknowledgments

The authors and publishers gratefully acknowledge the following for permission to reproduce copyright material:

Albrow, Martin, "Travelling Beyond Local Cultures" from John Eade (ed.), *Living the Global City: Globalization as a Local Process* (Routledge, 1997);

Amnesty International, "AI on Human Rights and Labour Rights," 1998, courtesy of Amnesty International;

Appadurai, Arjun, "Disjuncture and Difference in the Global Cultural Economy," *Public Culture*, Vol. 2, No. 2 (Spring 1990);

Barber, Benjamin, "Introduction" from *Jihad vs. McWorld* (Times Books, 1995). Benjamin R. Barber is Whitman Professor of Political Science and Director of the Walt Whitman Center at Rutgers University and the author of many books including *Strong Democracy* (1984), *Jihad vs. McWorld* (Times Books, 1995) and *A Place for Us* (Farrar, Straus & Giroux, 1998).

Beneria, Lourdes and Savitri Bisnath, "Gender and Poverty: An Analysis for Action," United Nations Development Programme, 1996;

Berkovitch, Nitza, "The Emergence and Transformation of the International Women's Movement" excerpted from *Constructing World Culture: International Nongovernmental Organizations Since 1875*, edited by John Boli and George Thomas with the permission of the publishers, Stanford University Press. Copyright © 1999 by the Board of Trustees of the Leland Stanford Junior University;

Boli, John and George Thomas, "World Culture in the World Polity: A Century of International Non-Governmental Organization," *American Sociological Review* (April 1997), courtesy of American Sociological Association, Washington D.C.;

Burtless, Gary, Robert Z. Lawrence, Robert E. Litan and Robert J. Shapiro, *Globaphobia: Confronting Fears about Open Trade*, Brookings Institution, 1998;

Cassen, Bernard, "To Save Society" from *Le Monde Diplomatique*, May 1997;

Diamond, Larry, "The Globalization of Democracy" reprinted from *Global Transformation and the Third World*, edited by Robert O. Slater, Barry M. Schutz and Steven R. Dorr. Copyright © 1993 by Lynne Rienner Publishers, Inc. Reprinted with permission of the publisher;

Fishman, Ted C., "The Joys of Global Investment," from *Harper's*, February 1997;

Friedland, Lewis A., excerpt from *Covering the World*, Twentieth Century Fund, 1992;

Fuller, Bruce, "Strong States, Strong Teachers?" from *Growing Up Modern: The Western State Builds Third-World Schools* (Routledge, 1991);

Garrett, Geoffrey, "Introduction" from *Partisan Politics in the Global Economy* (Cambridge University Press, 1998);

Greider, William, "Wawasan 2020" from *One World, Ready or Not* (Simon & Schuster, 1997);

Haeri, Shahla, "Obedience versus Autonomy: Women and Fundamentalism in Iran and Pakistan" from Martin E. Marty and R. Scott Appleby (eds.), *Fundamentalisms and Society* (University of Chicago Press, Chicago, 1993);

Halimi, Serge, "When Market Journalism Invades the World" from *Le Monde Diplomatique*, May 1997;

Hannerz, Ulf, "Scenarios for Peripheral Cultures" from *Culture, Globalization and the World-System*, Anthony D. King (ed.) (State University of New York, Binghamton, 1991);

Harvey, David, "Time–Space Compression and the Rise of Modernism as a Cultural Force" from *The Condition of Postmodernity* (Blackwell, Oxford, 1990);

Hobsbawm, E. J., "The World Unified" from *The Age of Capital 1848–1875* (Weidenfeld and Nicolson, 1975);

Huntington, Samuel P., "The Clash of Civilizations?" from *Foreign Affairs*, Vol. 72, No. 3, 1993, reprinted by permission of *Foreign Affairs*, 1993;

Iyer, Pico, "Bali: On Prospero's Isle" and "The Philippines: Born in the U.S.A." from *Video Night in Kathmandu*. Copyright © 1988 by Pico Iyer. Reprinted by permission of Alfred A. Knopf, Inc.;

Karliner, Joshua, "Grassroots Globalization: Reclaiming the Blue Planet" from *The Corporate Planet: Ecology and Politics in the Age of Globalization* (Sierra Club Books, 1997);

Keck, Margaret E. and Kathryn Sikkink, "Environmental Advocacy Networks" from *Activists Beyond Borders: Advocacy Networks in International Politics*. Used by permission of Cornell University Press, 1998;

Keohane, Robert O. and Joseph S. Nye, "Realism and Complex Interdependence" from *Power and Interdependence*. Copyright © 1989 by Robert O. Keohane and Joseph S. Nye. Reprinted by permission of Addison-Wesley Educational Publishers Inc.;

Korzeniewicz, Miguel, "Commodity Chains and Marketing Strategies: Nike and the Global Athletic Footwear Industry" from Gary Gereffi and Miguel Korzeniewicz (eds.), *Commodity Chains and Global Capitalism*. Copyright © 1993 by Greenwood Press. Reproduced with permission of Greenwood Publishing Group, Inc., Westport, CT;

Küng, Hans, excerpt from *A Global Ethic for Global Politics and Economics* (Oxford University Press, 1998);

Lechner, Frank J., "Global Fundamentalism" from William H. Swatos (ed.), *A Future for Religion?*, pp. 27–32. Copyright © 1993 by Sage Publications Inc. Reprinted by permission of Sage Publications;

MacBride, Sean and Colleen Roach, "The New International Information Order" from *International Encyclopedia of Communcations*, 4 volumes, edited by Erik Barnouw. Copyright © 1989 by Trustees of the University of Pennsylvania. Used by permission of Oxford University Press, Inc.;

Martin, Peter, "The Moral Case for Globalisation" from *Financial Times*, May 1997;

McNeely, Connie L., "The Determination of Statehood" from *Constructing the Nation-State: International Organization and Prescriptive Action*. Copyright © 1995 by Greenwood Press. Reproduced with permission of Greenwood Publishing Group, Inc., Westport, CT;

Mayer, Ann Elizabeth, "The Fundamentalist Impact on Law, Politics, and Constitutions in Iran, Pakistan, and the Sudan" from Martin E. Marty and R. Scott

Appleby (eds.), *Fundamentalisms and the State* (University of Chicago Press, Chicago, 1993);

Meyer, John W., John Boli, George M. Thomas, and Francisco O. Ramirez, "World Society and the Nation-State," *American Journal of Sociology*, 1997;

Nederveen Pieterse, Jan, "Globalization as Hybridization" from Mike Featherstone et al. (eds.), *Global Modernities* (Sage Publications Ltd, London, 1995);

Ogata, Sadako, "Peace, Security and Humanitarian Action," United Nations High Commissioner for Refugees, 1997;

Ohmae, Kenichi, excerpt from *The End of the Nation State: The Rise of Regional Economies* (Free Press, New York, 1995);

Roberts, Adam and Benedict Kingsbury, "Introduction: The UN's Roles in International Society Since 1945" from *United Nations, Divided World: The UN's Roles in International Relations* (Clarendon Press, Oxford, 1993);

Robertson, Roland and JoAnn Chirico, "Humanity, Globalization, and Worldwide Religious Resurgence" from *Sociological Analysis*, Fall 1985;

Rodrik, Dani, excerpt from *Has Globalization Gone Too Far?*, Institute for International Economics, 1997;

Sassen, Saskia, "Introduction: Whose City Is It? Globalization and the Formation of the New Claims" from *Globalization and Its Discontents* (The New Press, 1998);

Sinclair, John, Elizabeth Jacka and Stuart Cunningham, "Peripheral Vision" from *New Patterns in Global Television: Peripheral Vision*, John Sinclair et al. (eds.) (Oxford University Press, Oxford, 1996);

Sklair, Leslie, *Sociology of the Global System*, pp. 59–63 & passim. Copyright © 1995 The Johns Hopkins University Press;

Slaughter, Matthew J. and Phillip Swagel, "Does Globalization Lower Wages and Export Jobs?" International Monetary Fund, 1997;

Smith, Jackie, "Building Political Will after UNCED: EarthAction International" from *Transnational Social Movements and Global Politics: Solidarity Beyond the State*, Jackie Smith, Charles Chatfield and Ron Pagnucco (eds.) (Syracuse University Press, Syracuse, 1997). Used by permission of the publisher;

Tehranian, Majid, "Islamic Fundamentalism in Iran and the Discourse of Development" from Martin E. Marty and R. Scott Appleby (eds.), *Fundamentalisms and Society* (University of Chicago Press, Chicago, 1993);

Tomlinson, John, excerpt from *Cultural Imperialism: A Critical Introduction* (Pinter Publishers, 1991);

United Nations Fourth World Conference on Women, Beijing Declaration, 1995;

United Nations Conference on Environment and Development, excerpt from "Rio Declaration on Environment and Development" and "Agenda 21," 1992;

Wallerstein, Immanuel, "The Rise and Future Demise of the World Capitalist System: Concepts for Comparative Analysis" from *Comparative Studies in Society and History*, 16, 1974;

Wapner, Paul, "Greenpeace and Political Globalism." Reprinted by permission of the State University of New York Press, from *Environmental Activism and World Civic Politics* by Paul Wapner. Copyright © 1996, State University of New York. All rights reserved;

Wolf, Martin, "Why This Hatred of the Market?" from *Financial Times*, May 1997;

World Commission on Environment and Development, excerpt from *Our Common Future* (Oxford University Press, Oxford, 1987);

World Trade Organization, "10 Common Misunderstandings about the WTO," 1998;

Yergin, Daniel and Joseph Stanislaw, excerpt from *The Commanding Heights: The Battle Between Government and the Marketplace that is Remaking the Modern World* (Simon & Schuster, New York, 1998).

The publishers apologize for any errors or omissions in the above list and would be grateful to be notified of any corrections that should be incorporated in the next edition or reprint of this book.

General Introduction

At the end of the twentieth century, globalization became an all-purpose catchword in public and scholarly debate. Government officials could attribute their country's economic woes to the onslaught of globalization, business leaders justified downsizing of their companies as necessary to prepare for globalization, environmentalists lamented the destructive impact of unrestrained globalization, and advocates for indigenous peoples blamed the threatened disappearance of small cultures on relentless globalization. As different parties used the term in highly disparate ways and the concept itself became a global symbol, its meaning became inflated. Globalization risked becoming a global cliché. One purpose of this reader is to show that, worn though it may be, the concept still usefully captures significant worldwide changes. Indeed, underlying the various nuances of the term, as used strategically by various groups, is a shared awareness that the world itself is changing. We think that awareness is correct. The end of the twentieth century has witnessed the consolidation of a new world society. The selections compiled in this reader aim to describe and explain the course of globalization and the shape of its outcomes.

What does globalization involve? After World War II, the infrastructure for communication and transportation improved dramatically, connecting groups, institutions, and countries in new ways. More people can travel, or migrate, more easily to distant parts of the globe; satellite broadcasts bring world events to an increasingly global audience; the Internet begins to knit together world-spanning interest groups of educated users. Such links are the raw material of globalization. They are molded into new organizational forms as regional institutions go global or new ones take shape on the world stage. Increasing international trade and investment bring more countries into the global capitalist system; democracy gains strength as a global model for organizing nation-states; numerous international organizations take on new responsibilities in addressing issues of common concern. These institutions, in turn, are crystallizing into a comprehensive world society. The world is becoming a single place, in which different institutions function as parts of one system and distant peoples share a common understanding of living together on one planet. This world society has a culture; it instills in many people a budding consciousness of living in a world society. To links and institutions we therefore add culture and consciousness. Globalization is the process that fitfully brings these elements of world society together.

Is globalization new? Many scholars point to sixteenth-century Europe as the original source of globalization. After all, the Europeans established worldwide trade connections on their own terms, brought their culture to different regions by settling vast areas, and defined the ways in which different peoples were to interact with each other. Economically and culturally, the modern world system already existed nearly five centuries ago. Others point to the late nineteenth century as a period of intense globalization, when millions migrated, trade greatly expanded, and new norms and organizations came to govern international conduct. At the beginning of the twentieth century, such scholars would stress, the movement of people, goods, and finance across national borders was at least as free and significant as it is today. We agree that globalization has been happening for a long time. We also agree that specific features of world society have their roots in earlier periods. We add, however, that the second half of the twentieth century is a significant period of globalization in its own right. World War II gave globalization a new impetus. Obscured by Cold War divisions, the transformation of world society in the past five decades – in terms of linkages, institutions, and culture and consciousness – was nevertheless profound. This reader includes selections from scholars skeptical of this claim, but it also illustrates by many examples that globalization has entered a new phase.

Is globalization driven by the expanding market? The pursuit of economic opportunity has long sent merchants around the globe, and powerful states have supported their profit-seeking activities. Capitalism knows no bounds, as Marx noted more than a century ago. Marx expected the European economy to become a truly global system, and in many ways it has. In recent years, the integration of financial markets has added a new level of interdependence. To us, this does not mean that globalization is first and foremost an economic project. While an economic system operating along capitalist lines now encompasses most regions of the world, and economic motives always have been important in creating global linkages, globalization takes place in many spheres for many reasons. The economy may be a driving force in global change in some periods, but its effects depend on what happens outside of world markets. To understand the world economy, then, one also needs to understand world society. Accordingly, this reader presents a comprehensive picture of globalization, covering economic, political, cultural, and experiential dimensions.

Does globalization make the world more homogeneous? This question would seem to answer itself: If certain activities or institutions are to become global, they must displace existing, locally variable activities and institutions. If there are more global linkages, global institutions, and global values, presumably this means that more people will have more in common. To many critics of globalization, this seemingly neutral description is nefarious. Globalization is the work of the West, they argue. Markets set western rules for economic activity; one kind of western state has taken hold around the world; by controlling information flows, western media companies shape global consciousness; the popular culture of "McWorld" is of mostly western origin. Globalization thus entails cultural imperialism.

We agree that some things become more similar around the world as globalization proceeds. There is only one World Trade Organization and it enforces one set of free trade rules; there is only one kind of bureaucratic state that societies can legitimately adopt. But we do not think this leads to a homogeneous world, for three reasons. First, general rules and models must be interpreted in light of local circumstances. Thus, regions respond to similar economic constraints in different ways; countries still have great leeway in structuring their own polities; the same television program means different things to different audiences; McDonald's adapts its menu and marketing to local tastes. Second, growing similarity provokes reactions. Advocates for many cultures seek to protect their heritage or assert their identity – witness the efforts of fundamentalists to reinstate what they consider orthodoxy, the actions of indigenous peoples to claim their right to cultural survival, and the attempt of Asian leaders to put forth a distinctive Asian model of human rights. Third, cultural and political differences have themselves become globally valid. The notion that people and countries are entitled to their particularity or distinctiveness is itself part of global culture. The tension between homogeneity and heterogeneity is integral to globalization, and this reader illustrates it in several ways.

Does globalization determine local events? In 1998, an Indonesian dictator stepped down and poor Indonesians got poorer; in the United States, gas prices plummeted while Asian products flooded western stores; in the Hague, a war crimes tribunal handed down convictions for atrocities committed on different sides of the war in Bosnia. Around the world, local events bear the imprint of global processes. It would be easy to infer that local autonomy and local tradition must fall by the wayside, but globalization is not a one-way street. To be sure, local and global events become more and more intertwined. But the local feeds into the global as well: the Asian crisis was compounded by domestic policy errors in various Asian countries, the Bosnian war provoked the innovative establishment of a war crimes tribunal to enforce global principles. Yet, even if globalization does not "determine" local events, there is no escaping it. As world society integrates, individuals become conscious of being enveloped in global networks, subject to global forces, governed by global rules. Some of our selections concretely illustrate this local–global connection.

Is globalization harmful? Implicit in the questions we have raised is a widespread sense that globalization may be harmful to the well-being of individuals, countries, and cultures. If the market is the driving force in globalization, many fear it is bound to exacerbate inequality by creating winners and losers. If globalization makes the world more homogeneous, others fear many cultures are in trouble. Loss of local autonomy may mean that more people will be vulnerable to economic swings, environmental degradation, and epidemics. For these and other reasons, globalization has become an extremely contentious process. Indeed, the debate about the merits and direction of globalization is itself an important component of global culture. As we indicated above, we are skeptical of the most sweeping critiques of globalization. But our purpose in this reader is not to offer definite judgments; the subject is too complex for a clear-cut assessment in any case. Rather, we present a variety of perspectives that convey the thrust of actual debates and ongoing research so readers can understand the varied consequences of globalization and make their own informed judgments.

The Globalization Reader aims to convey the complexity, importance, and contentiousness of globalization. This is an exciting time in social science scholarship, as many creative minds try to discern the outlines of a new era. The reader includes some of their best work. But making sense of globalization is not just a task for scholars and students. It is a public concern. We hope this reader will assist a diverse audience in understanding the patterns and problems of globalization, which is likely to be a dominant concern of the twenty-first century.

Note on selections
Footnotes, citations, and sources of quoted passages have been excised. Omitted text is indicated by "[. . .]".

Part I

Debating Globalization

Introduction

When the Cold War drew to a close in the late 1980s, some in the West proclaimed the "end of history": from now on, there would be no more deep conflicts about how to organize societies, no more ideological divisions in the world. In the "new world order" heralded by an American President, George Bush, countries would cooperate peacefully as participants in a single worldwide market, pursuing their interests while sharing commitments to basic human values. These triumphant responses to the new world situation heartily embraced global liberalization and the prosperity and democratization it supposedly entailed. As global trade and investment expanded, more and more people could share in the bounty of a growing world economy. Economic and political interdependence would create shared interests that would help prevent destructive conflict and foster support for common values. As vehicles of globalization, international organizations could represent such common values for the benefit of humanity. Globalization, in this rosy scenario, created both wealth and solidarity. The spread of market-oriented policies, democratic polities, and individual rights promised to promote the well-being of billions of people.

This influential perspective on globalization has been challenged by critics who see globalization as a juggernaut of untrammeled capitalism. They fear a world ruled by profit-seeking global corporations. They see economic interdependence as making countries more vulnerable to the destructive impact of market shifts. The social fabric – the ties between people all across the globe – is strained when winners in the global game become disconnected from losers. "By allowing market values to become all-important," said George Soros, himself a significant player in world financial markets, in 1998, "we actually narrow the space for moral judgment and undermine public morality . . . Globalization has increased this aberration, because it has actually reduced the power of individual states to determine their destiny." The process, other critics add, is lopsided because it imposes the political and cultural standards of one region of the world, namely the West, on all other regions. Globalization is westernization by another name. It undermines the cultural integrity of other cultures and is therefore repressive, exploitative, and harmful to most people in most places.

Our selections in this part illustrate the major positions in the global debate about the merits and direction of globalization. We start with articles by Martin Wolf and Peter Martin, two British journalists, insisting on the economic and moral benefits that flow from economic interdependence in a free global market. Bernard Cassen and Serge Halimi, two of their French counterparts, respond with alarmed concern about globalization, expressing views widely shared in France. Because unrestrained market expansion threatens to undermine the social fabric and humane values of societies, this form of globalization must be resisted. Benjamin Barber, an American political scientist, similarly questions the benefits of economic globalization. He espies an increasingly homogeneous "McWorld," in which American-inspired popular culture overwhelms all others and societies have lost the capacity to govern themselves democratically. He emphasizes that McWorld calls forth a defense of indigenous national or religious traditions around the world, producing a variety of movements he captures with the label of "Jihad." Pushing Barber's ideas still further, Samuel Huntington, another American scholar, argues that the defense of distinct cultural values is not merely reactive; rather, he points out, the globe is now divided into several civilizations with often irreconcilable world views. Resisting incorporation into one world society, these civilizations struggle with one another in profound conflicts that ultimately will reduce the influence of the West.

While Barber and Huntington sketch culturally divisive responses to globalization, Joshua Karliner, an American environmentalist, and Hans Küng, a German theologian, hold out hope for a more unifying or universal resolution of the problems created by globalization. They envision a world society that serves common human interests. Karliner argues that, through concerted efforts, communities of the underprivileged can rein in destructive corporations, thus "reclaiming the blue planet." Küng proposes a global ethic, consisting of principles potentially shared by all human beings, as a moral restraint on states and markets and as a foundation for a global "civil society."

The critics of globalization thus share a fear of the unrestrained capitalist system. Some lament its imperious obliteration of cultural distinctions and advocate preserving or reviving traditional cultural distinctions. Others are most concerned about the impact on solidarity within societies and advocate stronger self-governance in democratic states. Still others worry most about the economic, political, and cultural divisions that result from globalization and advocate the cosmopolitan pursuit of a unified but just world. Such critical views of globalization themselves affect the course of the process. The increasingly deliberate efforts from many quarters to define the proper shape of world society also contribute significantly to its formation. At the very least, the debate expresses a common global consciousness, though not, of course, a global consensus.

1 Why this Hatred of the Market?

Martin Wolf

Globalisation is the great economic event of our era. It defines what governments can – and should – do. It explains what is happening to the world economy. But what is globalisation? And why is it so desirable?

In a splendid discussion in its latest World Economic Outlook, the IMF describes it as "the growing economic interdependence of countries worldwide through the increasing volume and variety of cross-border transactions in goods and services and of international capital flows, and also through the more rapid and widespread diffusion of technology."

Between 1930 and 1990, average revenue per mile in air transport fell from 68 US cents to 11 cents, in 1990 dollars; the cost of a three-minute telephone call between New York and London fell very substantially; and between 1960 and 1990, the cost of a unit of computing power fell by more than 99 per cent. Improved communications have led to an organisational innovation – the multinational company, a superb mechanism for transferring technology across frontiers.

Technology makes globalisation feasible. Liberalisation makes it happen. Liberalisation there has been: between 1970 and 1997, for example, the number of countries that eliminated exchange controls affecting imports of goods and services jumped from 35 to 137.

True, in certain respects, the world economy is less integrated than before the first world war. The UK's capital outflow, for example, was 9 per cent of gross domestic product at its pre-1914 peak, twice as big a share of GDP as outflows from Germany and Japan in the 1980s. The world then effectively operated with a single currency – gold. Likewise, in the early part of the century, the number of workers moving across frontiers was greater than now.

Yet, on balance, globalisation has gone further than ever before. Global ratios of exports to output returned to 1918 levels by 1970, but have since risen from 12 to 17 per cent, financial markets are highly integrated; technology is being transferred at unprecedented rates; and governments are increasingly bound by multilateral agreements.

Why have so many governments chosen – or been forced – to open up to the world economy? Lessons of experience is the answer. States may imprison their citizens, but they cannot force those imprisoned to show the initiative of free people.

Contrast West and East Germany, South and North Korea or Taiwan and Maoist China. In every case, the second of these pairs chose – or were forced to choose – isolation, while the first adopted international economic integration. Over some 40 years, ratios of real incomes per head became three to one or more.

These are the closest to the controlled experiments that economic history affords. Their results explain why China liberalised, the Soviet empire disappeared, communism collapsed and Mr Tony Blair calls his party "New Labour."

Original publication details: Wolf, Martin, "Why This Hatred of the Market?" from *Financial Times*, May 1997.

Those who believe the liberalisation of today is incomprehensible or unreasonable are purblind. Yet many do. They have three motivations: hatred of markets; fear of foreigners; and concerns about wages, jobs and economic activity. The first two attitudes are pathological. The last is at least rational.

In advanced economies over the past two decades there have been big increases in wage differences between the skilled and unskilled, or growth in unemployment of the unskilled, or both. This has happened even though the relative supply of skilled workers has risen. Many blame this development on rising competition from low-wage countries. This is indeed conceivable. The evidence suggests, however, that it is largely untrue.

The theory is simple. Imports from countries that have a relative abundance of unskilled labour should lower the prices of products that use such labour relatively intensively. This will shift production in advanced countries towards products that are intensive in skilled labour, increasing demand for skilled labour and lowering demand for unskilled labour. This shift will be manifested either in a growing wage gap between skilled and unskilled workers or in rising unemployment of the latter.

The theory is elegant. But empirical evidence suggests the relative prices of goods produced by unskilled labour have not fallen, probably because imports from countries like China have replaced imports from countries like South Korea, rather than production in advanced countries. Morever, merchandise imports from developing countries equal only 9–8 per cent of total output in advanced economies. In an IMF working paper, the Effect of Globalisation on Wages in Advanced Economies, Mr Matthew Slaughter of Dartmouth College and Mr Phillip Swagel of the IMF conclude: "increased trade accounts for only about 10 to 20 per cent of the changes in wages and income distribution in the advanced economies."

In every advanced economy, the share of the labour forces employed in manufacturing has been falling: in the European Union it has dropped from above 30 per cent in 1970 to 20 per cent in 1994; in the US the share has fallen from 28 per cent in 1965 to 16 per cent in 1994. These falls parallel declines in the share of manufacturing in GDP at current prices, suggesting that the reason for the diminished role of manufacturing in employment is the failure of output to grow.

Appearances are misleading. At constant prices there has been very little decline in the share of manufacturing in total output. The faster rate of growth productivity in manufacturing than in services is, instead, leading to a reduction of relative prices of manufactured output, as well as of employment in manufacturing per unit of output.

Thus, between 1971 and 1994, output of manufacturing rose at 2.5 per cent a year in advanced economies, but output per person at 3.1 per cent. For services, the figures were 3.3 and 1.1 per cent respectively. The share of employment in manufacturing was bound to decline, as it has long done in agriculture.

The damage that globalisation has been alleged to cause to some people in advanced countries is largely mythical. What is not mythical, however, has been the opportunity offered by economic integration to poor countries.

Between 1965 and 1995, for example, the real incomes per head of the Asian newly industrialised economies rose seven times, while their share in world trade increased more than fourfold. Similarly, China's period of rapid development can be dated to its decisions to liberalise agriculture and open up to the world economy. Where trade led, capital flows followed: in 1996, capital flows to China were larger than to all developing countries combined in 1989.

Globalisation was not inevitable. Nor does it merely reflect the march of technology. It marks the successful worldwide spread of the economic liberalisation that began nearly 50 years ago in western Europe with the Marshall Plan. It is now bringing unprecedented opportunities to billions of people throughout the world.

Inevitably, those who fear markets and foreigners clamour against it. Their voices must be ignored. What is needed, instead, is a careful consideration of what governments can – and should – do when the market is global, but their sway is merely local.

2   The Moral Case for Globalization

Peter Martin

The discussion of globalisation usually focuses on the economic issues involved. I would like here to address the profoundly moral case for globalisation. It can be summarised in a single sentence: the accelerated integration of previously marginalised societies is the best thing that has happened in the lifetime of the post-war generation.

This process is a true collaboration across borders, across societies, across cultures – not the false collaboration of spurious North–South dialogues and bureaucratic elites. Not only has it undermined the evil empire of the Soviet Union, it is also starting to achieve the same effects in China. But even without these directly political effects it would still have been an extraordinarily positive process. It has produced an enormous degree of improvement in human happiness in those countries which have taken advantage of the opportunities it provides.

This transformation will produce exactly the opposite of the effects that its left-wing critics claim. It will lead to an irreversible shift of power away from the developed countries to the rest of the world. It is the desire to avoid this at all costs that underlies the critics' view of the world. In my view, the critics base their arguments on a visceral desire to preserve the status quo, to retain the hegemony of their profoundly conservative ideology.

The anti-globalisation argument is, I believe, profoundly immoral. It is profoundly immoral to exclude third-world aspirations merely to preserve the convenience of a particular pattern of western work. The critics of this process allege that there are many more losers than winners from globalisation. This is simply untrue, both in relative and in absolute terms, as any study of economic statistics over the post-war period will show.

The more sophisticated critics admit that millions of jobs have been created. But these are not real jobs, they say – they are in sweatshop conditions. Tell that to the educated work-forces of Hong Kong, Singapore, Malaysia, Thailand – the electronics workers at Samsung, the car-workers at Daewoo. Tell it to the workers of southern China who have escaped from back-breaking agricultural misery and are making their way, through sweatshop conditions it is true, to genuine prosperity and independence of living. I exult in the aspirations of the third-world poor – their desire for wealth, prosperity and freedom. What would the critics say to such people? That they cannot have the future they want because we Europeans cannot adjust rapidly enough to permit it? Where is the morality there?

It is possible to opt out of globalisation, but the price that is paid is not merely an economic one. It is also a political one, because the desire to repress globalisa-

Original publication details: Martin, Peter, "The Moral Case for Globalisation" from *Financial Times*, May 1997.

tion leads to an inevitable extension of the powers of the state and a loss of individual freedom. It requires the suppression of natural desires of individuals, an ever more elaborate web of regulation, legislation, the criminalisation of natural economic activity, the politicisation of routine decisions – and we have seen all that in many European countries over the past 20–30 years. It requires a fundamental undermining of democratic rights, including that most precious right, the right to be left alone.

You may have your own views about whether the freedom to choose between 30 different types of breakfast cereal is a valuable freedom. That is a matter of opinion. What is not a matter of opinion but rather a matter of bitter experience is that the extension of state power required to eliminate the cross-border choice offered by globalisation is damaging and deeply anti-democratic.

It is sometimes said that free trade must cede precedence to more elevated values. Surely there is no more elevated value than delivering billions of people from poverty, creating opportunities for choice and personal development, and reinforcing democracy all round the world? The liberal market economy is by its very nature global. It is the summit of human endeavour. We should be proud that by our work and by our votes we have – collectively and individually – contributed to building it.

3 To Save Society

Bernard Cassen

Free markets ("laissez-faire") and free trade ("laissez-passer"): these are the two age-old articles of faith of the doctrine of ultraliberalism. And, as inevitably happens with articles of faith, they take precedence, whatever the circumstances, over other considerations or values at issue. The *Financial Times*, which is a firm believer, frequently provides examples of this.

For instance, the columns of the *Financial Times* describe as a "dilemma" of great significance the risks of a trade "war" between the European Union and the United States – this on account of the appallingly insanitary conditions in which poultry is slaughtered in the US and then exported to Europe. The "dilemma" is how to reconcile genuine public interest with free trade. Free trade – at best a means – is the only stable point of reference and is not open to discussion. It is for the public interest – an end – to adjust to free trade and, moreover, to prove that it is indeed a genuine public interest. And so the means becomes the end.

Reversing the order of precedence in this way does not bother the ideologists of free trade one jot. It is they who hold pride of place in the media, the universities, the major international economic and financial organisations. More particularly, since the conclusion of the GATT Uruguay Round in 1993 we have experienced truly global brainwashing designed to give credence to the notion that deregulation of trade and total market freedom are bound to produce a general rise in standards of living and societies that are fairer for all. These are allegedly the miraculous results of globalisation. The facts tell a very different story.

To begin with, instead of reducing inequalities, globalisation of trade exacerbates them and does so both between and within nations. In the so-called rich countries and above all the champions of free trade – the United States and the United Kingdom – no-one disputes the ever-widening income and poverty gap. Even the OECD puts on a show of concern from time to time. The fact is that this gap is no longer a matter of real concern for leaders, some of whom actually argue that inequalities are an essential factor for growth.

This polarisation is also typical of relations between countries themselves. As was clearly shown in a recent report by the United Nations Development Programme, the poorest countries are getting poorer, both in relative and absolute terms. There is, in effect, no correlation between need and investment. In Africa, where infrastructure of all kinds is cruelly lacking, direct investment fell by 27 per cent between 1994–95 and accounts for just $2.1 billion, that is 3 per cent of total world investment. It is no use counting on the international financial markets to fund new schools or dispensaries . . .

In deference to the structural adjustment policies of the World Bank and the IMF, which require countries to "open up" to the world market, public spending is

Original publication details: Cassen, Bernard, "To Save Society" from *Le Monde Diplomatique*, May 1997.

slashed and consequently, and more particularly, the number of teachers is cut dramatically, and so we are back to square one. All the statistics show that, since the early 1990s, the percentage of poor people has increased in Latin America, the Caribbean and Africa. Who is going to sing the praises of globalisation to them?

We are told that wages and employment can only benefit from generalised liberalisation. That is not the experience of American workers, among others. Those who failed to leave their secondary education with a diploma have seen their average hourly pay fall by a third in 20 years: from $11.85 to $8.64 between 1973–93. Sociologists have had to invent a new category for them: the "working poor", workers who get poorer as they work and whose numbers have been substantially swollen in the UK with the help of Mrs Margaret Thatcher and Mr John Major. In France we have five million unemployed, and in Germany, where industrialists have decided that their compatriots have become too expensive for them, the situation is scarcely any better.

The ultraliberals counter these situations with other ones – always the same: the "tigers" of eastern Asia with growth rates sometimes in two figures. But they completely fail to grasp that these examples dramatically undermine their theories. Neither South Korea nor Taiwan – still less China – founded their industrial and commercial power on the precepts of Adam Smith or David Ricardo. Massive US government aid – in the interests of the cold war – in the case of South Korea and Taiwan; absolute protectionism to preserve their developing industries; managed trade (the Chinese make no secret of this); and, generally speaking, an economically omnipresent state. These are the real ingredients of the much-vaunted and very real "export-driven growth" of these countries.

We also need to mention the political and social repression, from which Taiwan alone is now free in the region. The fact is that a totalitarian regime which bans free trade unions (China, South Korea, Singapore and Indonesia etc.) can achieve "miracles" and create a "climate propitious" to business. It is nonetheless astounding that "liberals" should assess fundamental freedoms in terms of profits and losses in this way and, more serious from their point of view, that they should close their eyes to the distortion of competition brought about by the daily intervention of police states that are often corrupt into the bargain. Indeed, they never stopped praising the Chilean "miracle" in the days of General Augusto Pinochet.

Instead of getting up in arms about the introduction of "social clauses" into international trade, the liberals should welcome it, in the interests of fair competition and "transparency" of price formation mechanisms. It seems perfectly natural that the "ticket" allowing goods or services access to an export market should take into account compliance with a minimum of the standards of the International Labour Organisation (trade union freedom, ban on forced labour and the exploitation of children etc.) that apply in the country concerned.

These social clauses are designed to improve the situation of workers in the newly industrialised countries. Failure to comply with them has an adverse effect on workers in the developed countries, and is not directed against the South. Far from it, in the South, the clauses are being called for by the NGOs and trade unions, and it is abundantly clear that they possess a quite different legitimacy to protect their own people than do the spokesmen for the multinationals.

What applies to the social sphere also applies to the environment. It is actually not possible to "green up" total free trade: it inevitably encourages the delocation of centres of production to those sites where environmental standards impose the least constraints and where, generally speaking, the least fuss is made about workers' rights. We cannot accept, as so many "comparative advantages," the destruction of the natural environment, pollution of the air, water and the land. Instead of being "externalised," that is to say borne by the global community in its entirety, the environmental cost must be fully "internalised" within prices. If not, then it must be incorporated into the "ticket" giving access to those markets in which the relevant standards are in force. Plainly, if we have the intellectual honesty to reject "liberalism" on the variable geometry model, that ignores all factors other than the right of "global" companies to be predatory, then the principles underlying the liberal theory provide excellent arguments for social and environmental clauses.

In the final analysis, it is democracy itself which is the prime victim of free trade and globalisation. The way in which they operate actually widens the physical gap separating the centres of decision-taking and those affected by those same decisions: between producers and consumers of goods and services and of fantasy. Alienation in the extreme. Taking responsibility and being obliged to be accountable are the touchstones of democracy. On the assumption that it is their intention to work for the good of all their fellow citizens, what happens when elected representatives and governments are less and less in control of the real decision-makers, who have no direct link with their territory, that is to say the financial markets and the vast conglomerates? There is no need to seek further the main factor in the disintegration of societies. Moreover, it is becoming increasingly inappropriate to describe them as "societies," since they are being subjected to the kind of treatment that is antithetical to the very notion of the common good.

Mrs Margaret Thatcher was fond of saying that she only knew individuals and had not the slightest idea of what a society was. It is high time to act to stop that cry from the heart becoming a self-fulfilling prophecy. And if we are to do that, we need to have a radical rethink of the principles and practices of globalisation now under way.

4 When Market Journalism Invades the World

Serge Halimi

What *should* we – journalists, intellectuals – do in a world where 358 billionaires have more assets than the combined incomes of nearly half of the planet's population? What should we do when Mozambique, where 25 percent of children die before the age of five from infectious diseases, spends twice as much paying off its debt as it does on health and education? What should we do in a world where, according to the UNDP administrator, "*if present trends continue, economic disparities between industrial and developing nations will move from inequitable to inhuman*"? What should we do when, within democratic countries themselves, money dominates the political system until it becomes the system, those who write the checks write the laws and ask the questions, and increasingly citizens seem to be replaced with investors?

But *can* we still, as journalists and intellectuals, denounce this situation and suggest remedies when so many of these billionaires – the Bill Gates, Rupert Murdochs, Jean-Luc Lagardères, Ted Turners, Conrad Blacks of the world – own the papers in which we write, the radios on which we speak, the television networks in which we appear? When so much of the news and culture that is fed into developing nations comes from industrial countries and so little of the news the industrial countries ever hear about seeps in from developing nations? When those who write the checks and write the laws and ask the questions and invest and divest and downsize, are also our employers, our providers of advertising revenue, our trend-setters, our decision-makers, our news-makers?

In other words, can we even think of doing what we *must* in this global world, doing what we *should*, as journalists and as intellectuals, comforting the afflicted and afflicting the comfortable, being a counter-power, a voice for the voiceless, when so many of us are as much a part of the ruling class as the business elite itself? When so many of us echo the speeches of the powerful and blame the attitudes of the poor?

Unfortunately, if the questions are necessary, the answers are obvious. Most of us cannot, most of us will not do what they must. And this too is the result of the type of globalization we have let happen. Although I do not believe this globalization to be inevitable, the media are trying to make it seem inevitable and to pretend it to be desirable. And no one – least of all us journalists and intellectuals – should deny the power of the ideas which we disseminate and back to the drumbeat of around-the-clock propaganda in a sleepless and borderless world.

Two and a half years ago, at *Le Monde diplomatique*, we called this propaganda "pensée unique." The expression caught on so fast that within a month, candidate

Original publication details: Halimi, Serge, "When Market Journalism Invades the World" from *Le Monde Diplomatique*, May 1997.

Jacques Chirac used it to re-ignite his sputtering presidential campaign. And three months later, he had become president of France. Needless to say, the sense of the expression has lost a lot with its new popularity . . . So what is "pensée unique," or more precisely what was it before its meaning became so blurred? And why should we oppose it?

It is the ideological translation of the interests of global capital, of the priorities of financial markets and of those who invest in them. It is the dissemination through leading newspapers of the policies advocated by the international economic institutions which use and abuse the credit, data and expertise they are entrusted with: such institutions as the World Bank, the IMF, the OECD, the World Trade Organization.

Easy to spot in most countries, and in constant expansion because of globalization, this new orthodoxy results in submitting democratically-elected governments to the one and only policy claimed to be sustainable, that which has the consent of the rich. Speaking of this, and trying to sound rational and Anglo-Saxon, a French essayist, Alain Minc explained:

> The totalitarianism of financial markets does not please me. I find it alienating. But I know it is there. And I want everyone in the elite to know it too. I am like a peasant who does not appreciate hail and yet he knows he will have to live with it. What I mean is simple: I don't know whether the markets think right. But I know one cannot think against the markets. If you do not respect a certain number of canons, as rigorous as those of the Church, the 100,000 illiterates who make the markets will blow the whole economy away. Experts have to be the propagandists of that reality.

When he said "experts," he also implied "journalists" of course. And, in this respect, he is served well enough.

But should one accept this nice vignette of "pensée unique," this suave legitimation of a new dictatorship, that of financial markets, politics will amount – and it largely does – to little more than a pseudo-debate between parties of government shouting out the minuscule differences that separate them and silencing the significant convergences that unite them. Electoral dissaffection will be, is already, the result of this non-debate.

In the United States, where foreign companies heavily invested in the White House "coffees" funding the President's reelection – thereby blurring even further the line between national politics and global commerce – only 48.8 percent of the eligible voters went to the polls last November, the lowest number since 1924. This indifference almost amounted to a quiet expression of civil disobedience.

But I would like to take another example, this one from Greece, and see how the mainstream press, in this instance *The Washington Post*, reacted to it by drilling into our brains the major postulates of what we, at *Le Monde diplomatique*, also like to call "market journalism." Last December, as Greek peasants were barring the roads in protest of austerity measures threatening their survival, one of them complained: *"The only right we have is the right to vote and it leads us nowhere."* An election had been held, leading to the victory of a pro-business socialist party. And when it happened, *The Washington Post* had concluded: *"This was the first truly modern election in the history of the birthplace of democracy . . . The two parties essentially agree on most of the major issues."*

Can we, as journalists, as intellectuals, accept the idea that a "modern democracy" is one in which the major parties agree on most issues? And if we do, as is too often the case, how dare we bemoan the rise of so-called "extremism" and "populism" when it is but the mere consequence of the legitimate anger that comes from a truncated political debate in a socially polarized society? We all make fun of the tendency, especially in America, to be "politically correct." But don't *we* fall in the trap of being economically correct – cheerleaders for the stock market, asleep at the switch when Robert Maxwell was robbing his companies, or maybe just too busy then writing fawning profiles of Carlos Salinas's "economic miracle". . . ?

"*In three years, the new millennium,*" "*a bridge to the 21st century*": the definition of modernity and of its opposite is, I believe, one of the most telling instances of the weight of this "pensée unique." When one listens to the mass media, "modernity" is almost invariably equated with free trade, strong currencies, deregulation, privatizations, communication (of those who have the means to communicate with each other in the virtual "communities" they create), Europe (insofar as it is that of free trade, strong currencies, privatizations, and communication).

"Outdated notions," on the other hand, are almost invariably associated with the welfare state, government in general (unless it shrivels into a lean and mean law-and-order machine), unions (which are said to defend "special interests," unlike those of, say, big business), the nation-state (guilty of fostering "nationalism"), the people (always likely to be entranced by "populism").

Then let me say this: their modernity is archaic. It is as old as the steam machine. And their outdated notions have never been more necessary. Too often, we journalists pretend the opposite. So, yes indeed we must oppose globalization and its logical consequences. And, most of all, we must fight the belief that it is inevitable. In this respect, *Le Monde diplomatique* and the *Financial Times* cannot but be allies. Because, what, at *Le Monde diplomatique*, could we add to the excellent analysis of Martin Wolf in an article he wrote two years ago. The article was entitled: "The Global Economy Myth" and it said: "*Global economic integration is far from irresistible. Governments have chosen to lower trade barriers and eliminate foreign exchange controls. They could, if they wished, halt both processes.*" They must. Let us help them.

But, clearly, this is not the sense of the comments we have just heard. Because, what strikes me in the discourse of the apostles of the market and of globalization is its extremism, its oblivion of the notion of healthy doubt. It's the analogy one easily can draw with the cant of communists thirty or forty years ago.

According to Wolf and Martin, markets have to be a great model for humankind, and so does globalization. And when these don't quite work out, we hear: "Give us more time," "Let's go one more step," "Change is always painful," "What we've seen wasn't quite pure enough," "If only the people were better, more pliable, things would have worked beautifully."

Social inequalities? Let's deny their existence or claim they exist because . . . we don't have enough markets. Not enough school or hospital vouchers. Not enough enterprise zones. Not enough tax breaks. Not enough pension funds. Not enough competition within the civil service. Like with Stalinism before, every stumble in the march toward a pure, radiant, bountiful market society is explained by the timidity of the march, not by its direction. And, like with Stalinism before, the critics of your model have to be irrational, in need of a reeducation program or of a mental treatment?

Well, it might be – just might be – that the market is a model that doesn't work well for most people; that markets can be a great wealth-creating machine, but not so great when it comes to building a human, just, and decent society for most of us. And what will it take us to learn that? How many people living in poverty? How many people sealed out of what Mr Alan Greenspan, the Chairman of the Federal Reserve, called the *"irrational exuberance of the market"*? How many people sealed out of the gated communities of the rich? How many people behind bars? How many riots? And which proportion of us convinced that democracy is not for them?

If the fall of communism and of its related certainties about the nature of mankind have taught us anything, it should not be the need for another totalitarianism, for another tyranny – that of financial markets. But the value of doubt and the need for dissidents.

Let us all relearn the value of doubt.

5 Jihad vs. McWorld

Benjamin Barber

History is not over. Nor are we arrived in the wondrous land of techné promised by the futurologists. The collapse of state communism has not delivered people to a safe democratic haven, and the past, fratricide and civil discord perduring, still clouds the horizon just behind us. Those who look back see all of the horrors of the ancient slaughterbench reenacted in disintegral nations like Bosnia, Sri Lanka, Ossetia, and Rwanda and they declare that nothing has changed. Those who look forward prophesize commercial and technological interdependence – a virtual paradise made possible by spreading markets and global technology – and they proclaim that everything is or soon will be different. The rival observers seem to consult different almanacs drawn from the libraries of contrarian planets.

Yet anyone who reads the daily papers carefully, taking in the front page accounts of civil carnage as well as the business page stories on the mechanics of the information superhighway and the economics of communication mergers, anyone who turns deliberately to take in the whole 360-degree horizon, knows that our world and our lives are caught between what William Butler Yeats called the two eternities of race and soul: that of race reflecting the tribal past, that of soul anticipating the cosmopolitan future. Our secular eternities are corrupted, however, race reduced to an insignia of resentment, and soul sized down to fit the demanding body by which it now measures its needs. Neither race nor soul offers us a future that is other than bleak, neither promises a polity that is remotely democratic.

The first scenario rooted in race holds out the grim prospect of a retribalization of large swaths of humankind by war and bloodshed: a threatened balkanization of nation-states in which culture is pitted against culture, people against people, tribe against tribe, a Jihad in the name of a hundred narrowly conceived faiths against every kind of interdependence, every kind of artificial social cooperation and mutuality: against technology, against pop culture, and against integrated markets; against modernity itself as well as the future in which modernity issues. The second paints that future in shimmering pastels, a busy portrait of onrushing economic, technological, and ecological forces that demand integration and uniformity and that mesmerize peoples everywhere with fast music, fast computers, and fast food – MTV, Macintosh, and McDonald's – pressing nations into one homogenous global theme park, one McWorld tied together by communications, information, entertainment, and commerce. Caught between Babel and Disneyland, the planet is falling precipitously apart and coming reluctantly together at the very same moment.

Some stunned observers notice only Babel, complaining about the thousand newly sundered "peoples" who prefer to address their neighbors with sniper rifles

Original publication details: Barber, Benjamin, "Introduction" from *Jihad vs. McWorld* (Times Books, 1995); Benjamin R. Barber is Whitman Professor of Political Science and Director of the Walt Whitman Center at Rutgers University and the author of many books including *Strong Democracy* (1984), *Jihad vs. McWorld* (Times Books, 1995) and *A Place for Us* (Farrar, Straus & Giroux, 1998).

and mortars; others – zealots in Disneyland – seize on futurological platitudes and the promise of virtuality, exclaiming "It's a small world after all!" Both are right, but how can that be?

We are compelled to choose between what passes as "the twilight of sovereignty" and an entropic end of all history; or a return to the past's most fractious and demoralizing discord; to "the menace of global anarchy," to Milton's capital of hell, Pandaemonium; to a world totally "out of control."

The apparent truth, which speaks to the paradox at the core of this book, is that the tendencies of both Jihad *and* McWorld are at work, both visible sometimes in the same country at the very same instant. Iranian zealots keep one ear tuned to the mullahs urging holy war and the other cocked to Rupert Murdoch's Star television beaming in *Dynasty*, *Donahue*, and *The Simpsons* from hovering satellites. Chinese entrepreneurs vie for the attention of party cadres in Beijing and simultaneously pursue KFC franchises in cities like Nanjing, Hangzhou, and Xian where twenty-eight outlets serve over 100,000 customers a day. The Russian Orthodox church, even as it struggles to renew the ancient faith, has entered a joint venture with California businessmen to bottle and sell natural waters under the rubric Saint Springs Water Company. Serbian assassins wear Adidas sneakers and listen to Madonna on Walkman headphones as they take aim through their gunscopes at scurrying Sarajevo civilians looking to fill family watercans. Orthodox Hasids and brooding neo-Nazis have both turned to rock music to get their traditional messages out to the new generation, while fundamentalists plot virtual conspiracies on the Internet.

Now neither Jihad nor McWorld is in itself novel. History ending in the triumph of science and reason or some monstrous perversion thereof (Mary Shelley's Doctor Frankenstein) has been the leitmotiv of every philosopher and poet who has regretted the Age of Reason since the Enlightenment. Yeats lamented "the center will not hold, mere anarchy is loosed upon the world," and observers of Jihad today have little but historical detail to add. The Christian parable of the Fall and of the possibilities of redemption that it makes possible captures the eighteenth-century ambivalence – and our own – about past and future. I want, however, to do more than dress up the central paradox of human history in modern clothes. It is not Jihad and McWorld but the relationship between them that most interests me. For, squeezed between their opposing forces, the world has been sent spinning out of control. Can it be that what Jihad and McWorld have in common is anarchy: the absence of common will and that conscious and collective human control under the guidance of law we call democracy?

Progress moves in steps that sometimes lurch backwards; in history's twisting maze, Jihad not only revolts against but abets McWorld, while McWorld not only imperils but re-creates and reinforces Jihad. They produce their contraries and need one another. My object here then is not simply to offer sequential portraits of McWorld and Jihad, but while examining McWorld, to keep Jihad in my field of vision, and while dissecting Jihad, never to forget the context of McWorld. Call it a dialectic of McWorld: a study in the cunning of reason that does honor to the radical differences that distinguish Jihad and McWorld yet that acknowledges their powerful and paradoxical interdependence.

There is a crucial difference, however, between my modest attempt at dialectic and that of the masters of the nineteenth century. Still seduced by the Enlightenment's faith in progress, both Hegel and Marx believed reason's cunning was on the side of progress. But it is harder to believe that the clash of Jihad and McWorld will issue in some overriding good. The outcome seems more likely to pervert than to nurture human liberty. The two may, in opposing each other, work to the same ends, work in apparent tension yet in covert harmony, but democracy is not their beneficiary. In East Berlin, tribal communism has yielded to capitalism. In Marx-Engelsplatz, the stolid, overbearing statues of Marx and Engels face east, as if seeking distant solace from Moscow: but now, circling them along the streets that surround the park that is their prison are chain eateries like TGI Friday's, international hotels like the Radisson, and a circle of neon billboards mocking them with brand names like Panasonic, Coke, and GoldStar. New gods, yes, but more liberty?

What then does it mean in concrete terms to view Jihad and McWorld dialectically when the tendencies of the two sets of forces initially appear so intractably antithetical? After all, Jihad and McWorld operate with equal strength in opposite directions, the one driven by parochial hatreds, the other by universalizing markets, the one re-creating ancient subnational and ethnic borders from within, the other making national borders porous from without. Yet Jihad and McWorld have this in common: they both make war on the sovereign nation-state and thus undermine the nation-state's democratic institutions. Each eschews civil society and belittles democratic citizenship, neither seeks alternative democratic institutions. Their common thread is indifference to civil liberty. Jihad forges communities of blood rooted in exclusion and hatred, communities that slight democracy in favor of tyrannical paternalism or consensual tribalism. McWorld forges global markets rooted in consumption and profit, leaving to an untrustworthy, if not altogether fictitious, invisible hand issues of public interest and common good that once might have been nurtured by democratic citizenries and their watchful governments. Such governments, intimidated by market ideology, are actually pulling back at the very moment they ought to be aggressively intervening. What was once understood as protecting the public interest is now excoriated as heavy-handed regulatory browbeating. Justice yields to markets, even though, as Felix Rohatyn has bluntly confessed, "there is a brutal Darwinian logic to these markets. They are nervous and greedy. They look for stability and transparency, but what they reward is not always our preferred form of democracy." If the traditional conservators of freedom were democratic constitutions and Bills of Rights, "the new temples to liberty," George Steiner suggests, "will be McDonald's and Kentucky Fried Chicken."

In being reduced to a choice between the market's universal church and a retribalizing politics of particularist identities, peoples around the globe are threatened with an atavistic return to medieval politics where local tribes and ambitious emperors together ruled the world entire, women and men united by the universal abstraction of Christianity even as they lived out isolated lives in warring fiefdoms defined by involuntary (ascriptive) forms of identity. This was a world in which princes and kings had little real power until they conceived the ideology of nationalism. Nationalism established government on a scale greater than the tribe yet less cosmopolitan than the universal church and in time gave birth to those intermediate, gradually more democratic institutions that would come to constitute the nation-state. Today, at the far end of this history, we seem intent on re-creating a world in which our only choices are the secular universalism of the cosmopolitan market and the everyday particularism of the fractious tribe.

In the tumult of the confrontation between global commerce and parochial ethnicity, the virtues of the democratic nation are lost and the instrumentalities by which it permitted peoples to transform themselves into nations and seize sovereign power in the name of liberty and the commonweal are put at risk. Neither Jihad nor McWorld aspires to resecure the civic virtues undermined by its denationalizing practices; neither global markets nor blood communities service public goods or pursue equality and justice. Impartial judiciaries and deliberative assemblies play no role in the roving killer bands that speak on behalf of newly liberated "peoples," and such democratic institutions have at best only marginal influence on the roving multinational corporations that speak on behalf of newly liberated markets. Jihad pursues a bloody politics of identity, McWorld a bloodless economics of profit. Belonging by default to McWorld, everyone is a consumer; seeking a repository for identity, everyone belongs to some tribe. But no one is a citizen. Without citizens, how can there be democracy? [. . .]

Jihad is, I recognize, a strong term. In its mildest form, it betokens religious struggle on behalf of faith, a kind of Islamic zeal. In its strongest political manifestation, it means bloody holy war on behalf of partisan identity that is metaphysically defined and fanatically defended. Thus, while for many Muslims it may signify only ardor in the name of a religion that can properly be regarded as universalizing (if not quite ecumenical), I borrow its meaning from those militants who make the slaughter of the "other" a higher duty. I use the term in its militant construction to suggest dogmatic and violent particularism of a kind known to Christians no less than Muslims, to Germans and Hindis as well as to Arabs. The phenomena to which I apply the phrase have innocent enough beginnings: identity politics and multicultural diversity can represent strategies of a free society trying to give expression to its diversity. What ends as Jihad may begin as a simple search for a local identity, some set of common personal attributes to hold out against the numbing and neutering uniformities of industrial modernization and the colonizing culture of McWorld.

America is often taken as the model for this kind of benign multiculturalism, although we too have our critics like Arthur Schlesinger, Jr., for whom multiculturalism is never benign and for whom it signals the inaugural logic of a long-term disintegration. Indeed, I will have occasion below to write about an "American Jihad" being waged by the radical Right. The startling fact is that less than 10 percent (about twenty) of the modern world's states are truly homogenous and thus, like Denmark or the Netherlands, can't get smaller unless they fracture into tribes or clans. In only half is there a single ethnic group that comprises even 75 percent of the population. As in the United States, multiculturalism is the rule, homogeneity the exception. Nations like Japan or Spain that appear to the outside world as integral turn out to be remarkably multicultural. And even if language alone, the nation's essential attribute, is made the condition for self-determination, a count of the number of languages spoken around the world suggests the community of nations could grow to over six thousand members.

The modern nation-state has actually acted as a cultural integrator and has adapted well to pluralist ideals: civic ideologies and constitutional faiths around which their many clans and tribes can rally. It has not been too difficult to contrive a civil religion for Americans or French or Swiss, since these "peoples" actually contain multitudes of subnational factions and ethnic tribes earnestly seeking common ground. But for Basques and Normans? What need have they for anything but blood and memory? And what of Alsatians, Bavarians, and East Prussians? Kurds, Ossetians, East Timorese, Quebecois, Abkhazians, Catalonians, Tamils, Inkatha Zulus, Kurile Islander Japanese – peoples without countries inhabiting nations they cannot call their own? Peoples trying to seal themselves off not just from others but from modernity? These are frightened tribes running not to but from civic faith in search of something more palpable and electrifying. How will peoples who define themselves by the slaughter of tribal neighbors be persuaded to subscribe to some flimsy artificial faith organized around abstract civic ideals or commercial markets? Can advertising divert warriors of blood from the genocide required by their ancient grievances? [. . .]

McWorld is a product of popular culture driven by expansionist commerce. Its template is American, its form style. Its goods are as much images as matériel, an aesthetic as well as a product line. It is about culture as commodity, apparel as ideology. Its symbols are Harley-Davidson motorcycles and Cadillac motorcars hoisted from the roadways, where they once represented a mode of transportation, to the marquees of global market cafés like Harley-Davidson's and the Hard Rock where they become icons of lifestyle. You don't drive them, you feel their vibes and rock to the images they conjure up from old movies and new celebrities, whose personal appearances are the key to the wildly popular international café chain Planet Hollywood. Music, video, theater, books, and theme parks – the new churches of a commercial civilization in which malls are the public squares and suburbs the neighborless neighborhoods – are all constructed as image exports creating a common world taste around common logos, advertising slogans, stars, songs, brand names, jingles, and trademarks. Hard power yields to soft, while ideology is transmuted into a kind of videology that works through sound bites and film clips. Videology is fuzzier and less dogmatic than traditional political ideology: it may as a consequence be far more successful in instilling the novel values required for global markets to succeed.

McWorld's videology remains Jihad's most formidable rival, and in the long run it may attenuate the force of Jihad's recidivist tribalisms. Yet the information revolution's instrumentalities are also Jihad's favored weapons. Hutu or Bosnian Serb identity was less a matter of real historical memory than of media propaganda by a leadership set on liquidating rival clans. In both Rwanda and Bosnia, radio broadcasts whipped listeners into a killing frenzy. As *New York Times* rock critic Jon Pareles has noticed, "regionalism in pop music has become as trendy as microbrewery beer and narrowcasting cable channels, and for the same reasons." The global culture is what gives the local culture its medium, its audience, and its aspirations. Fascist pop and Hasid rock are not oxymorons; rather they manifest the dialectics of McWorld in particularly dramatic ways. Belgrade's radio includes stations that broadcast Western pop music as a rebuke to hard-liner Milosevic's supernationalist government and stations that broadcast native folk tunes laced with antiforeign and anti-Semitic sentiments. Even the Internet has its neo-Nazi bulletin boards and Turk-trashing Armenian "flamers" (who assail every use of the word *turkey*, fair and fowl alike, so to speak), so that the abstractions of cyberspace too are infected with a peculiar and rabid cultural territoriality all their own.

The dynamics of the Jihad–McWorld linkage are deeply dialectical. Japan has, for example, become more culturally insistent on its own traditions in recent years even as its people seek an ever greater purchase on McWorld. In 1992, the number-one restaurant in Japan measured by volume of customers was McDonald's, followed in the number-two spot by the Colonel's Kentucky Fried Chicken. In France, where cultural purists complain bitterly of a looming Sixième République ("la République Américaine"), the government attacks "franglais" even as it funds EuroDisney park just outside of Paris. In the same spirit, the cinema industry makes war on American film imports while it bestows upon Sylvester Stallone one of France's highest honors, the Chevalier des arts et lettres. Ambivalence also stalks India. Just outside of Bombay, cheek by jowl with villages still immersed in poverty and notorious for the informal execution of unwanted female babies or, even, wives, can be found a new town known as SCEEPZ – the Santa Cruz Electronic Export Processing Zone – where Hindi-, Tamil-, and Mahratti-speaking computer programmers write software for Swissair, AT&T, and other labor-cost-conscious multinationals. India is thus at once a major exemplar of ancient ethnic and religious tensions and "an emerging power in the international software industry." To go to work at SCEEPZ, says an employee, is "like crossing an international border." Not into another country, but into the virtual nowhere-land of McWorld.

More dramatic even than in India, is the strange interplay of Jihad and McWorld in the remnants of Yugoslavia. In an affecting *New Republic* report, Slavenka Drakulic told the brief tragic love story of Admira and Bosko, two young star-crossed lovers from Sarajevo: "They were born in the late 1960s," she writes. "They watched Spielberg movies; they listened to Iggy Pop; they read John le Carré; they went to a disco every Saturday night and fantasized about traveling to Paris or London." Longing for safety, it seems they finally negotiated with all sides for safe passage, and readied their departure from Sarajevo. Before they could cross the magical border that separates their impoverished lane from the seeming sanctuary of McWorld, Jihad caught up to them. Their bodies lay along the riverbank, riddled with bullets from anonymous snipers for whom safe passage signaled an invitation to target practice. The murdered young lovers, as befits émigrés to McWorld, were clothed in jeans and sneakers. So too, one imagines, were their murderers.

Further east, tourists seeking a piece of old Russia that does not take them too far from MTV can find traditional Matryoshka nesting dolls (that fit one inside the other) featuring the nontraditional visages of (from largest to smallest) Bruce Springsteen, Madonna, Boy George, Dave Stewart, and Annie Lennox.

In Russia, in India, in Bosnia, in Japan, and in France too, modern history then leans both ways: toward the meretricious inevitability of McWorld, but also into Jihad's stiff winds, heaving to and fro and giving heart both to the Panglossians and the Pandoras, sometimes for the very same reasons. The Panglossians bank on EuroDisney and Microsoft, while the Pandoras await nihilism and a world in Pandaemonium. Yet McWorld and Jihad do not really force a choice between such polarized scenarios. Together, they are likely to produce some stifling amalgam of the two suspended in chaos. Antithetical in every detail, Jihad and McWorld nonetheless conspire to undermine our hard-won (if only half-won) civil liberties and the possibility of a global democratic future. In the short run the forces of Jihad, noisier and more obviously nihilistic than those of McWorld, are likely to dominate the near future, etching small stories of local tragedy and regional genocide on the face of our times and creating a climate of instability marked by multimicrowars inimical to global integration. But in the long run, the forces of McWorld are the forces underlying the slow certain thrust of Western civilization and as such may be unstoppable. Jihad's microwars will hold the headlines well into the next century, making predictions of the end of history look terminally dumb. But McWorld's homogenization is likely to establish a macropeace that favors the triumph of commerce and its markets and to give to those who control information, communication, and entertainment ultimate (if inadvertent) control over human destiny. Unless we can offer an alternative to the struggle between Jihad and McWorld, the epoch on whose threshold we stand – postcommunist, postindustrial, postnational, yet sectarian, fearful, and bigoted – is likely also to be terminally postdemocratic.

6 The Clash of Civilizations?

Samuel P. Huntington

The Next Pattern of Conflict

World politics is entering a new phase, and intellectuals have not hesitated to pro-liferate visions of what it will be – the end of history, the return of traditional rival-ries between nation states, and the decline of the nation state from the conflicting pulls of tribalism and globalism, among others. Each of these visions catches aspects of the emerging reality. Yet they all miss a crucial, indeed a central, aspect of what global politics is likely to be in the coming years.

It is my hypothesis that the fundamental source of conflict in this new world will not be primarily ideological or primarily economic. The great divisions among humankind and the dominating source of conflict will be cultural. Nation states will remain the most powerful actors in world affairs, but the principal conflicts of global politics will occur between nations and groups of different civilizations. The clash of civilizations will dominate global politics. The fault lines between civilizations will be the battle lines of the future.

Conflict between civilizations will be the latest phase in the evolution of conflict in the modern world. For a century and a half after the emergence of the modern international system with the Peace of Westphalia, the conflicts of the Western world were largely among princes – emperors, absolute monarchs and constitutional mon-archs attempting to expand their bureaucracies, their armies, their mercantilist eco-nomic strength and, most important, the territory they ruled. In the process they created nation states, and beginning with the French Revolution the principal lines of conflict were between nations rather than princes. In 1793, as R. R. Palmer put it, "The wars of kings were over; the wars of peoples had begun." This nineteenth-century pattern lasted until the end of World War I. Then, as a result of the Russian Revolution and the reaction against it, the conflict of nations yielded to the conflict of ideologies, first among communism, fascism-Nazism and liberal democracy, and then between communism and liberal democracy. During the Cold War, this latter conflict became embodied in the struggle between the two superpowers, neither of which was a nation state in the classical European sense and each of which defined its identity in terms of its ideology.

These conflicts between princes, nation states and ideologies were primarily conflicts within Western civilization, "Western civil wars," as William Lind has labeled them. This was as true of the Cold War as it was of the world wars and the earlier wars of the seventeenth, eighteenth and nineteenth centuries. With the end of the Cold War, international politics moves out of its Western phase, and its cen-terpiece becomes the interaction between the West and non-Western civilizations and among non-Western civilizations. In the politics of civilizations, the peoples and governments of non-Western civilizations no longer remain the objects of history as

Original publication details: Huntington, Samuel P., "The Clash of Civilizations?" from *Foreign Affairs*, Vol. 72, No. 3, 1993, reprinted by permission of *Foreign Affairs*, 1993.

targets of Western colonialism but join the West as movers and shapers of history.
[. . .]

Why Civilizations Will Clash

Civilization identity will be increasingly important in the future, and the world will
be shaped in large measure by the interactions among seven or eight major civilizations. These include Western, Confucian, Japanese, Islamic, Hindu, Slavic-
Orthodox, Latin American and possibly African civilization. The most important
conflicts of the future will occur along the cultural fault lines separating these civilizations from one another.

Why will this be the case?

First, differences among civilizations are not only real; they are basic. Civilizations are differentiated from each other by history, language, culture, tradition and,
most important, religion. The people of different civilizations have different views
on the relations between God and man, the individual and the group, the citizen
and the state, parents and children, husband and wife, as well as differing views of
the relative importance of rights and responsibilities, liberty and authority, equality
and hierarchy. These differences are the product of centuries. They will not soon
disappear. They are far more fundamental than differences among political ideologies and political regimes. Differences do not necessarily mean conflict, and conflict
does not necessarily mean violence. Over the centuries, however, differences among
civilizations have generated the most prolonged and the most violent conflicts.

Second, the world is becoming a smaller place. The interactions between peoples
of different civilizations are increasing; these increasing interactions intensify civilization consciousness and awareness of differences between civilizations and commonalities within civilizations. North African immigration to France generates
hostility among Frenchmen and at the same time increased receptivity to immigration by "good" European Catholic Poles. Americans react far more negatively to
Japanese investment than to larger investments from Canada and European countries. Similarly, as Donald Horowitz has pointed out, "An Ibo may be . . . an Owerri
Ibo or an Onitsha Ibo in what was the Eastern region of Nigeria. In Lagos, he is
simply an Ibo. In London, he is a Nigerian. In New York, he is an African." The
interactions among peoples of different civilizations enhance the civilization-
consciousness of people that, in turn, invigorates differences and animosities stretching or thought to stretch back deep into history.

Third, the processes of economic modernization and social change throughout
the world are separating people from longstanding local identities. They also weaken
the nation state as a source of identity. In much of the world religion has moved in
to fill this gap, often in the form of movements that are labeled "fundamentalist."
Such movements are found in Western Christianity, Judaism, Buddhism and Hin-
duism, as well as in Islam. In most countries and most religions the people active
in fundamentalist movements are young, college-educated, middle-class technicians,
professionals and business persons. The "unsecularization of the world," George
Weigel has remarked, "is one of the dominant social facts of life in the late twentieth century." The revival of religion, "la revanche de Dieu," as Gilles Kepel labeled
it, provides a basis for identity and commitment that transcends national boundaries and unites civilizations.

Fourth, the growth of civilization-consciousness is enhanced by the dual role of
the West. On the one hand, the West is at a peak of power. At the same time,

however, and perhaps as a result, a return to the roots phenomenon is occurring among non-Western civilizations. Increasingly one hears references to trends toward a turning inward and "Asianization" in Japan, the end of the Nehru legacy and the "Hinduization" of India, the failure of Western ideas of socialism and nationalism and hence "re-Islamization" of the Middle East, and now a debate over Westernization versus Russianization in Boris Yeltsin's country. A West at the peak of its power confronts non-Wests that increasingly have the desire, the will and the resources to shape the world in non-Western ways.

In the past, the elites of non-Western societies were usually the people who were most involved with the West, had been educated at Oxford, the Sorbonne or Sandhurst, and had absorbed Western attitudes and values. At the same time, the populace in non-Western countries often remained deeply imbued with the indigenous culture. Now, however, these relationships are being reversed. A de-Westernization and indigenization of elites is occurring in many non-Western countries at the same time that Western, usually American, cultures, styles and habits become more popular among the mass of the people.

Fifth, cultural characteristics and differences are less mutable and hence less easily compromised and resolved than political and economic ones. In the former Soviet Union, communists can become democrats, the rich can become poor and the poor rich, but Russians cannot become Estonians and Azeris cannot become Armenians. In class and ideological conflicts, the key question was "Which side are you on?" and people could and did choose sides and change sides. In conflicts between civilizations, the question is "What are you?" That is a given that cannot be changed. And as we know, from Bosnia to the Caucasus to the Sudan, the wrong answer to that question can mean a bullet in the head. Even more than ethnicity, religion discriminates sharply and exclusively among people. A person can be half-French and half-Arab and simultaneously even a citizen of two countries. It is more difficult to be half-Catholic and half-Muslim.

Finally, economic regionalism is increasing. The proportions of total trade that were intraregional rose between 1980 and 1989 from 51 percent to 59 percent in Europe, 33 percent to 37 percent in East Asia, and 32 percent to 36 percent in North America. The importance of regional economic blocs is likely to continue to increase in the future. On the one hand, successful economic regionalism will reinforce civilization-consciousness. On the other hand, economic regionalism may succeed only when it is rooted in a common civilization. The European Community rests on the shared foundation of European culture and Western Christianity. The success of the North American Free Trade Area depends on the convergence now underway of Mexican, Canadian and American cultures. Japan, in contrast, faces difficulties in creating a comparable economic entity in East Asia because Japan is a society and civilization unique to itself. However strong the trade and investment links Japan may develop with other East Asian countries, its cultural differences with those countries inhibit and perhaps preclude its promoting regional economic integration like that in Europe and North America.

Common culture, in contrast, is clearly facilitating the rapid expansion of the economic relations between the People's Republic of China and Hong Kong, Taiwan, Singapore and the overseas Chinese communities in other Asian countries. With the Cold War over, cultural commonalities increasingly overcome ideological differences, and mainland China and Taiwan move closer together. If cultural commonality is a prerequisite for economic integration, the principal East Asian economic bloc of the future is likely to be centered on China. This bloc is, in fact, already coming into existence. As Murray Weidenbaum has observed,

Despite the current Japanese dominance of the region, the Chinese-based economy of Asia is rapidly emerging as a new epicenter for industry, commerce and finance. This strategic area contains substantial amounts of technology and manufacturing capability (Taiwan), outstanding entrepreneurial, marketing and services acumen (Hong Kong), a fine communications network (Singapore), a tremendous pool of financial capital (all three), and very large endowments of land, resources and labor (mainland China)... From Guangzhou to Singapore, from Kuala Lumpur to Manila, this influential network – often based on extensions of the traditional clans – has been described as the backbone of the East Asian economy.

Culture and religion also form the basis of the Economic Cooperation Organization, which brings together ten non-Arab Muslim countries: Iran, Pakistan, Turkey, Azerbaijan, Kazakhstan, Kyrgyzstan, Turkmenistan, Tadjikistan, Uzbekistan and Afghanistan. One impetus to the revival and expansion of this organization, founded originally in the 1960s by Turkey, Pakistan and Iran, is the realization by the leaders of several of these countries that they had no chance of admission to the European Community. Similarly, Caricom, the Central American Common Market and Mercosur rest on common cultural foundations. Efforts to build a broader Caribbean-Central American economic entity bridging the Anglo-Latin divide, however, have to date failed.

As people define their identity in ethnic and religious terms, they are likely to see an "us" versus "them" relation existing between themselves and people of different ethnicity or religion. The end of ideologically defined states in Eastern Europe and the former Soviet Union permits traditional ethnic identities and animosities to come to the fore. Differences in culture and religion create differences over policy issues, ranging from human rights to immigration to trade and commerce to the environment. Geographical propinquity gives rise to conflicting territorial claims from Bosnia to Mindanao. Most important, the efforts of the West to promote its values of democracy and liberalism as universal values, to maintain its military predominance and to advance its economic interests engender countering responses from other civilizations. Decreasingly able to mobilize support and form coalitions on the basis of ideology, governments and groups will increasingly attempt to mobilize support by appealing to common religion and civilization identity.

The clash of civilizations thus occurs at two levels. At the micro-level, adjacent groups along the fault lines between civilizations struggle, often violently, over the control of territory and each other. At the macro-level, states from different civilizations compete for relative military and economic power, struggle over the control of international institutions and third parties, and competitively promote their particular political and religious values.

The Fault Lines between Civilizations

The fault lines between civilizations are replacing the political and ideological boundaries of the Cold War as the flash points for crisis and bloodshed. The Cold War began when the Iron Curtain divided Europe politically and ideologically. The Cold War ended with the end of the Iron Curtain. As the ideological division of Europe has disappeared, the cultural division of Europe between Western Christianity, on the one hand, and Orthodox Christianity and Islam, on the other, has reemerged. The most significant dividing line in Europe, as William Wallace has suggested, may well be the eastern boundary of Western Christianity in the year 1500. This line runs along what are now the boundaries between Finland and Russia and between the Baltic states and Russia, cuts through Belarus and Ukraine separating the more Catholic western Ukraine from Orthodox eastern Ukraine, swings westward separating Transylvania from the rest of Romania, and then goes through Yugoslavia almost exactly along the line now separating Croatia and Slovenia from the rest of Yugoslavia. In the Balkans this line, of course, coincides with the historic boundary between the Hapsburg and Ottoman empires. The peoples to the north and west of this line are Protestant or Catholic; they shared the common experiences of European history – feudalism, the Renaissance, the Reformation, the Enlightenment, the French Revolution, the Industrial Revolution; they are generally economically better off than the peoples to the east; and they may now look forward to increasing involvement in a common European economy and to the consolidation of democratic political systems. The peoples to the east and south of this line are Orthodox or Muslim; they historically belonged to the Ottoman or Tsarist empires and were only lightly touched by the shaping events in the rest of Europe; they are generally less advanced economically; they seem much less likely to develop stable democratic political systems. The Velvet Curtain of culture has replaced the Iron Curtain of ideology as the most significant dividing line in Europe. As the events in Yugoslavia show, it is not only a line of difference; it is also at times a line of bloody conflict.

Conflict along the fault line between Western and Islamic civilizations has been going on for 1,300 years. After the founding of Islam, the Arab and Moorish surge west and north only ended at Tours in 732. From the eleventh to the thirteenth century the Crusaders attempted with temporary success to bring Christianity and Christian rule to the Holy Land. From the fourteenth to the seventeenth century, the Ottoman Turks reversed the balance, extended their sway over the Middle East and the Balkans, captured Constantinople, and twice laid siege to Vienna. In the nineteenth and early twentieth centuries as Ottoman power declined Britain, France, and Italy established Western control over most of North Africa and the Middle East.

After World War II, the West, in turn, began to retreat; the colonial empires disappeared; first Arab nationalism and then Islamic fundamentalism manifested themselves; the West became heavily dependent on the Persian Gulf countries for its energy; the oil-rich Muslim countries became money-rich and, when they wished to, weapons-rich. Several wars occurred between Arabs and Israel (created by the West). France fought a bloody and ruthless war in Algeria for most of the 1950s; British and French forces invaded Egypt in 1956; American forces went into Lebanon in 1958; subsequently American forces returned to Lebanon, attacked Libya, and engaged in various military encounters with Iran; Arab and Islamic terrorists, supported by at least three Middle Eastern governments, employed the weapon of the weak and bombed Western planes and installations and seized Western hostages. This warfare between Arabs and the West culminated in 1990, when the United States sent a massive army to the Persian Gulf to defend some Arab countries against aggression by another. In its aftermath NATO planning is increasingly directed to potential threats and instability along its "southern tier."

This centuries-old military interaction between the West and Islam is unlikely to decline. It could become more virulent. The Gulf War left some Arabs feeling proud that Saddam Hussein had attacked Israel and stood up to the West. It also left many feeling humiliated and resentful of the West's military presence in the Persian Gulf, the West's overwhelming military dominance, and their own apparent inability to shape their destiny. Many Arab countries, in addition to the oil exporters, are reaching levels of economic and social development where autocratic forms of government become inappropriate and efforts to introduce democracy become stronger. Some openings in Arab political systems have already occurred. The principal beneficiaries of these openings have been Islamist movements. In the Arab world, in short, Western democracy strengthens anti-Western political forces. This may be a passing phenomenon, but it surely complicates relations between Islamic countries and the West. [. . .]

The West versus the Rest

The west is now at an extraordinary peak of power in relation to other civilizations. Its superpower opponent has disappeared from the map. Military conflict among Western states is unthinkable, and Western military power is unrivaled. Apart from Japan, the West faces no economic challenge. It dominates international political and security institutions and with Japan international economic institutions. Global political and security issues are effectively settled by a directorate of the United States, Britain and France, world economic issues by a directorate of the United States, Germany and Japan, all of which maintain extraordinarily close relations with each other to the exclusion of lesser and largely non-Western countries. Decisions made at the UN Security Council or in the International Monetary Fund that reflect the interests of the West are presented to the world as reflecting the desires of the world community. The very phrase "the world community" has become the euphemistic collective noun (replacing "the Free World") to give global legitimacy to actions reflecting the interests of the United States and other Western powers. Through the IMF and other international economic institutions, the West promotes its economic interests and imposes on other nations the economic policies it thinks appropriate. In any poll of non-Western peoples, the IMF undoubtedly would win the support of finance ministers and a few others, but get an overwhelmingly unfavorable rating from just about everyone else, who would agree with Georgy Arbatov's characterization of IMF officials as "neo-Bolsheviks who love expropriating other people's money, imposing undemocratic and alien rules of economic and political conduct and stifling economic freedom."

Western domination of the UN Security Council and its decisions, tempered only by occasional abstention by China, produced UN legitimation of the West's use of force to drive Iraq out of Kuwait and its elimination of Iraq's sophisticated weapons and capacity to produce such weapons. It also produced the quite unprecedented action by the United States, Britain and France in getting the Security Council to demand that Libya hand over the Pan Am 103 bombing suspects and then to impose sanctions when Libya refused. After defeating the largest Arab army, the West did not hesitate to throw its weight around in the Arab world. The West in effect is using international institutions, military power and economic resources to run the world in ways that will maintain Western predominance, protect Western interests and promote Western political and economic values.

That at least is the way in which non-Westerners see the new world, and there is a significant element of truth in their view. Differences in power and struggles for military, economic and institutional power are thus one source of conflict between the West and other civilizations. Differences in culture, that is basic values and beliefs, are a second source of conflict. V. S. Naipaul has argued that Western civilization is the "universal civilization" that "fits all men." At a superficial level much of Western culture has indeed permeated the rest of the world. At a more basic level, however, Western concepts differ fundamentally from those prevalent in other civilizations. Western ideas of individualism, liberalism, constitutionalism, human rights, equality, liberty, the rule of law, democracy, free markets, the separation of church and state, often have little resonance in Islamic, Confucian, Japanese, Hindu, Buddhist or Orthodox cultures. Western efforts to propagate such ideas produce instead a reaction against "human rights imperialism" and a reaffirmation of indigenous values, as can be seen in the support for religious fundamentalism by the younger generation in non-Western cultures. The very notion that there could be a "universal civilization" is a Western idea, directly at odds with the particularism of most Asian societies and their emphasis on what distinguishes one people from another. Indeed, the author of a review of 100 comparative studies of values in different societies concluded that "the values that are most important in the West are least important worldwide." In the political realm, of course, these differences are most manifest in the efforts of the United States and other Western powers to induce other peoples to adopt Western ideas concerning democracy and human rights. Modern democratic government originated in the West. When it has developed in non-Western societies it has usually been the product of Western colonialism or imposition.

The central axis of world politics in the future is likely to be, in Kishore Mahbubani's phrase, the conflict between "the West and the Rest" and the responses of non-Western civilizations to Western power and values. Those responses generally take one or a combination of three forms. At one extreme, non-Western states can, like Burma and North Korea, attempt to pursue a course of isolation, to insulate their societies from penetration or "corruption" by the West, and, in effect, to opt out of participation in the Western-dominated global community. The costs of this course, however, are high, and few states have pursued it exclusively. A second alternative, the equivalent of "band-wagoning" in international relations theory, is to attempt to join the West and accept its values and institutions. The third alternative is to attempt to "balance" the West by developing economic and military power and cooperating with other non-Western societies against the West, while preserving indigenous values and institutions; in short, to modernize but not to Westernize. [. . .]

Western civilization is both Western and modern. Non-Western civilizations have attempted to become modern without becoming Western. To date only Japan has fully succeeded in this quest. Non-Western civilizations will continue to attempt to acquire the wealth, technology, skills, machines and weapons that are part of being modern. They will also attempt to reconcile this modernity with their traditional culture and values. Their economic and military strength relative to the West will increase. Hence the West will increasingly have to accommodate these non-Western modern civilizations whose power approaches that of the West but whose values and interests differ significantly from those of the West. This will require the West to maintain the economic and military power necessary to protect its interests in relation to these civilizations. It will also, however, require the West to develop a more profound understanding of the basic religious and philosophical assumptions underlying other civilizations and the ways in which people in those civilizations see their interests. It will require an effort to identify elements of commonality between Western and other civilizations. For the relevant future, there will be no universal civilization, but instead a world of different civilizations, each of which will have to learn to coexist with the others.

7   Grassroots Globalization: Reclaiming the Blue Planet

Joshua Karliner

We are not a market; first and foremost we are a people.
> La Falda Declaration, from the Second Meeting of Chemical and Paper
> Industry Workers of the South American Common Market (MERCOSUR)

Every local community equipped with rights and obligations constitutes a new global order for environmental care.
> Vandana Shiva, Indian Environmentalist

As dawn bathes Mexico City's central plaza, or Zócalo, in a hazy light, hundreds of *campesinos* and indigenous people from the faraway state of Tabasco arise. They roll up their makeshift bedding, assemble in rows of three and begin a procession toward Los Pinos, the residence of President Ernesto Zedillo. They have come from more than 600 miles away, marching for forty days and finally camping in the Zócalo to protest electoral fraud and to demand, in their words, "democracy, liberty and social justice."

As they pass by the National Stock Exchange – one of the country's primary links with the global economy – the peasants suddenly switch targets. They stop and then rush the doors, blocking all entrances just one half-hour before the day's transactions are to begin. The Exchange is forced to shut down for nearly two hours. News and police helicopters hover overhead and riot squads equipped with tear gas assemble. The newspaper *La Jornada* reports from the scene, describing the clash of two very different Mexican realities:

> The businessmen yuppies, with their Hermes Italian silk ties, Armani suits . . . Florsheim shoes . . . Burberry's shirts, and Ralph Lauren aftershaves . . . are exasperated by the demonstration. Meanwhile, the Chontal Indians and peasants remain seated, sandals off, *itacates* at one side. Their dark bodies give off the smell of various days' sweat. Their stern faces observe the executives and brokers who may have never before been so close to people from the Mexican countryside – or perhaps only know them from TV.

With police surrounding them, and the director of the Exchange pleading with the protesters to allow one hundred people into the building "to begin transactions," one of the group's spokespeople, leftist opposition leader Andrés Manuel Lopez Obrador, explains why they are there. The Stock Exchange, he says, "is the clearest example of the practices that have sunk Mexico and its people." Asserting that

Original publication details: Karliner, Joshua, "Grassroots Globalization: Reclaiming the Blue Planet" from *The Corporate Planet: Ecology and Politics in the Age of Globalization* (Sierra Club Books, 1997).

the liberalization of the Mexican economy has caused *campesinos* to lose their land, workers to lose their jobs and those employed to have their buying power drop to levels of sixty years ago, Lopez continues: "In the last twelve years of hunger and sacrifice, in which the workers and peasants have been forced to survive in inhumane conditions, we have seen the corporate profits on the Exchange grow."

As tensions mount and the police prepare to move in, the protesters clear out, avoiding a violent confrontation. But they have made their point, not only to President Zedillo, but also to corporations and investors from around the world who hold a stake in Mexico.

The Mexico City protest, which took place in June 1995, is one of a growing number of grassroots mobilizations around the world against the impacts of globalization. As the centers of political and economic power shift from the nation-state toward an international economic system increasingly dominated by transnational corporations, shifting also are the strategies, tactics and targets of movements working for social and environmental justice. The presidential palace, center of power in the universe of Mexico's one-party state, is less and less relevant. Increasingly pertinent – and vulnerable – is the National Stock Exchange, which, since it was opened to international investors, has become a symbol of Mexico's growing subordination to the prerogatives of the corporate-driven world economy.

The specter of disenfranchised peasants blockading, even briefly, Mexico's access to international capital and international capital's access to Mexico, provides us with a glimpse of the future. It presents the prospect of a world in which those seeking social justice and ecological sanity on the national and even local levels take their demands into the global arena. The old 1960s slogan "Think globally, act locally" is no longer sufficient as a guiding maxim. Rather, taking a cue from the peasants of Tabasco, civil society – popular movements, non-governmental organizations, labor unions, academics, doctors, lawyers, artists and others around the world – must confront the essential paradox and challenge of the twenty-first century by developing ways of *thinking and acting both locally and globally at the same time*. For without a host of fresh, innovative and coordinated international approaches firmly anchored in a diversity of local realities, the world's social and environmental movements will be rendered increasingly ineffective before the transnational power and mobility of the global corporations in the age of globalization.

Such collaborative initiatives are emerging in a scattershot fashion across the globe. Communities and organizations are increasingly working together across national boundaries to combat corporate abuses. Groups throughout the world are campaigning jointly around a diversity of issues ranging from Mitsubishi's deforestation to Union Carbide's ongoing denial of accountability for the Bhopal gas disaster. Indigenous peoples from Nigeria to British Columbia are increasingly working together to save the natural and cultural integrity of their resources from corporate and governmental intervention. Some organizations, such as the Pesticide Action Network, have secretariats in every continent dedicated to collaborative efforts to phase out some of the world's deadliest agricultural chemicals. Other organizations, such as Greenpeace and Friends of the Earth, have offices in dozens of countries working on coordinated campaigns aimed at curbing corporate-led destruction of the global environment. Similar international efforts are also emerging from the South. The recently created Ecuador-based group Oil Watch works with activists throughout the Third World to combat the abuses of transnational oil corporations in the tropics. And the Malaysia-based Third World Network, whose representatives operate in various countries in Asia, Africa and Latin America, has helped lead the critique of GATT and the World Trade Organization as new structures for global corporate governance.

The kinetic activity in all of these areas begins to provide a picture of a somewhat dispersed but burgeoning process of grassroots globalization. Communities the world over are breaking their isolation and entering into direct contact and collaboration with one another. As a document entitled *From Global Pillage to Global Village* – the product of a post-NAFTA meeting of more than seventy United States-based grassroots organizations – optimistically declares:

> The unregulated internationalization of capital is now being followed by the internationalization of peoples' movements and organizations. Building peoples' international organizations and solidarity will be our revolution from within: a civil society without borders. This internationalism or "globalization from below" will be the foundation for a participatory and sustainable global village.

Unfortunately, the current level of organization and approach of most of those working to build grassroots globalization still comes up well short. Corporate globalization continues apace, and civil society has so far been unable to significantly slow or change, let alone reverse, its destructive course. Even many examples of successful international collaboration have been thwarted by the mobility that transnationals enjoy in the world economy. For instance, when Mitsubishi responded to international pressure by shutting its rare earth processing plant in Malaysia, it immediately subcontracted that work to two companies in China. Despite sporadic triumphs at the local, national and even international levels, the Corporate Planet continues to appropriate the Blue Planet for its profit-driven motives. [. . .]

The New Anticolonialism

While the process of economic globalization has propagated a new form of colonialism, or what Indian journalist Chakravarthi Rhagavan has referred to as "recolonization," one of the ways social movements the world over have responded to this dynamic is by harkening back to anticolonial movements of the past. Such is the case in Mexico, where the Zapatista insurgents not only built on five centuries of indigenous resistance to colonialism, but also took up the banner of Emiliano Zapata, a hero of the Mexican Revolution. By doing so, they positioned themselves as guardians of a deeply ingrained tradition of revolution that is counterposed to foreign domination and in favor of local self-government and land reform.

The situation in India is similar. There, burgeoning peoples' movements against globalization and the growing control of the country's economy by transnational corporations and international lending institutions are reaching back to the relatively recent history of the country's movement for independence against British colonialism. And while resistance to globalization in India is still by no means as broad or powerful as was the anticolonial movement led by Mahatma Gandhi and Jawaharlal Nehru, it is clear, says leading opposition figure George Fernandes, that "for the first time [since 1948] there is a genuine feeling that our independence is at stake."

In response to the waning economic and political sovereignty of the Indian state, organizers are drawing on the country's rich history of nonviolent protest for political independence and local self-sufficiency. "This is the land of *Satyagraha*.* This country produced Mahatma Gandhi and nonviolently threw out the colonizers. And we are very confident of throwing out all of the powers that are trying to colonize

India now," asserts M. D. Nanjundaswamy, who led a movement of hundreds of thousands of farmers against the Cargill corporation's agricultural forays into central India.

In some cases the transnationals seem to be obliging their Indian critics by following the well-worn paths of history. Cargill, for example, which in a few short years has become one of the largest traders of agricultural commodities in India, moved in 1992 to initiate a massive salt-mining enterprise in the Kutch region of the state of Gujarat – home of Mahatma Gandhi. This struck a powerful chord for many, as salt was one of the issues upon which India's independence movement was forged. Gandhi himself led the famous salt *Satyagraha* civil disobedience march in 1930 and the ensuing campaign aimed at making India self-sufficient in salt, a basic commodity it was forced to import under British rule.

So when the New Delhi government gave Cargill its blessing to move in and begin producing salt for Japan and the East Asian market (salt is a key input for, among other things, chlorine production), it touched a raw nerve. Labeling Cargill the "New East India Company," activists launched a "second salt *Satyagraha*" in 1993. In addition to pursuing a legal strategy to protect small-scale salt producers in the region from the US transnational, tens of thousands of people, including members of parliament, students and youth, trade union leaders, representatives of other popular movements, non-governmental organizations and local salt manufacturers, participated in a series of protests, including a march that followed the reverse route of Gandhi's famous *Satyagraha*. With the protest building toward a planned blockade of the port of Kutch and Gandhi's simple, powerful words "We will make salt" echoing across the land, Cargill pulled out.

From the corporate perspective, Cargill was wise to quit the fight when it did. The salt issue, carrying with it as deep an historical and symbolic resonance as the Boston Tea Party does for the United States, or perhaps as the nationalization of oil does for Mexico, could have catalyzed a significant backlash not only against Cargill, but against the opening of the Indian economy in general. Yet while Cargill bailed out before the *Satyagraha* built into a national movement, it was an important moment. As the New Delhi-based Public Interest Research Group observes, this victory marked "the beginning of the larger struggle against the new economic policies of the government which strike at the very roots of a self-reliant and socially oriented economy."

Since that time, one of the most vibrant movements in the world against the negative impacts of globalization has emerged in India. Millions of farmers, fisherfolk, union workers, urban dwellers and others have engaged in various forms of protest against the growing transnational corporate penetration of the Indian economy. And to a large degree they base their organizing on their country's recent struggle against colonialism, including the principles of *Satyagraha*, *swadeshi* (economic independence) and *charkha* (self-sufficiency).[†] As the *Sunday Times of India* reports, "Their philosophy . . . must seem like heresy to the champions of globalisation." Yet for these organizations, which serve as a voice for the hundreds of millions of people who subsist on the country's natural resources, "*swadeshi* is an imperative, much

* Literally translated as "truth" (or "soul") "force," *Satyagraha* was the essence of Gandhi's philosophy and strategy of nonviolent civil disobedience. In his words, *Satyagraha* aimed at the "vindication of truth, not by infliction of suffering on the opponent, but on one's self."
[†] *Swadeshi* was also a term popularized by Gandhi. *Charkha* is the spinning wheel that Gandhi used as a symbol of the *swadeshi* campaign to create homespun cotton cloth in order to free India from its dependence on the cotton mill trade with Great Britain.

more so today than 50 years ago. For in this period a process called 'development' has deprived more and more people of direct control over their immediate environment and means of livelihood." [. . .]

Reclaiming the Blue Planet

As the world moves into the twenty-first century, corporate globalization has become the dominant economic – and to some degree political – paradigm. In response, various social movements are emerging to challenge its reign, presenting both danger and opportunity. The danger is that the xenophobic nationalist reaction will arise as the foremost voice of opposition. The opportunity is that the nascent forces of grassroots globalization, which are weaving an emerging web of activism and building networks across the Earth, have a chance to step forth with alternatives to both the Corporate Planet and its neofascist detractors.

Reclaiming the Blue Planet from the clutches of corporate globalization will not be a simple task. It must be achieved by creating and implementing mechanisms for democratic control over corporations and economies. Such democratization involves redefining both the concept of corporate accountability and the concept of "the corporation" itself. Corporate accountability is presently understood by many people as a corporation's nonbinding response to the demands of those affected by its activities. It is variously defined as a transnational's responsibility to its investors, the responsiveness of a corporation to the demands of its workers or of a local community in which it is operating, or as a company's voluntary reporting of environmental information. Indeed, corporate accountability is increasingly confused with corporate self-regulation.

True corporate accountability, however, is something much broader and more profound than the above definitions. It means that a company can be held strictly accountable to the laws and democratic processes of communities, governments and the global framework in which it operates. At the heart of such democratic governance should lie the concept that corporations do not have any inherent right to exist, but rather are granted that right by "the people" and therefore must answer to the public. Thus the people, through a process of democratic political representation, should have the right to define "the corporation" – what it is, and what it can and cannot do. If a company knowingly sells defective products or consistently violates the law, the public should be able to petition the government to revoke its charter and dismantle it by liquidating its assets.

With corporations under more democratic control, their power can be curbed. Monopolies can be broken up. Economies could become focused more on sustainability. Such a climate could foster a decentralized, ecologically oriented market economy based on the development of alternative clean technologies, organic agriculture, worker-controlled enterprises, small businesses, municipal corporations, alternative trade associations, banks that are truly dedicated to the eradication of poverty, community empowerment and greater equity between North and South, and more.

Building such a vision – one that would dismantle global capitalism as we know it – may seem to be a Quixotic quest, a tilting at skyscrapers of sorts. Yet many interim steps can be taken at the local, national and international levels to build democratic control over corporations while fostering alternative economic development. [. . .]

8   A Global Ethic as a Foundation for Global Society

Hans Küng

An ethical consensus – an agreement on particular values, criteria, attitudes – as a basis for the world society that is coming into being: is that not a great, beautiful illusion? In view of the differences which have always existed between nations, cultures and religions; in view of the current tendencies and trends towards cultural, linguistic and religious self-assertion; in view even of the widespread cultural nationalism, linguistic chauvinism and religious fundamentalism, is it possible to envisage any ethical consensus at all, let alone in global dimensions? However, one can also argue in the opposite direction: precisely in view of this oppressive situation, a basic ethical consensus is necessary.

Challenges and Responses

Key questions and principles

(1)   We live in a world and time in which we can observe new dangerous tensions and polarizations between believers and non-believers, church members and those who have been secularized, the clerical and the anti-clerical – not only in Russia, Poland and Germany but also in France, in Algeria and Israel, in North and South America, Asia and Africa.

My response to this challenge is: there will be no survival of democracy without a coalition of believers and non-believers in mutual respect!

However, many people will say: do we not also live in a period of new cultural confrontations? That is true.

(2)   We live in a world and a time in which humankind is threatened by what S. Huntington has called a "clash of civilizations", for example between Muslim or Confucian civilization and Western civilization. However, we are threatened not so much by a new world war as by every possible conflict between two countries or within one country, in a city, even a street or school.

My response to this challenge is: There will be no peace between the civilizations without a peace between the religions!

And there will be no peace between the religions without a dialogue between the religions.

However, many people will object: are there not so many dogmatic differences and obstacles between the different religions which make a real dialogue a naive illusion? That is true.

Original publication details: Küng, Hans, excerpt from *A Global Ethic for Global Politics and Economics* (Oxford University Press, 1998).

(3)   We live in a world and a time when better relations between the religions are often blocked by every possible dogmatism, which can be found not only in the Roman Catholic Church but in all churches and religions and also in modern ideologies.

My response to this challenge is: There will be no new world order without a new world ethic, a global or planetary ethic despite all dogmatic differences.

What should the precise function of such a global ethic be? I can only repeat that a global ethic is not a new ideology or superstructure; it does not seek to make the specific ethics of the different religions and philosophies superfluous. Thus it is no substitute for the Torah, the Sermon on the Mount, the Qur'an, the Bhagavadgita, the discourses of the Buddha or the sayings of Confucius. The one global ethic does not mean a single global culture, far less a single global religion. To put it positively, a global ethic, a world ethic is none other than the necessary minimum of common human values, criteria and basic attitudes. Or, to be more precise: the global ethic is a basic consensus on binding values, irrevocable criteria and basic attitudes which are affirmed by all religions despite their dogmatic differences, and which can indeed also be contributed by non-believers. [. . .]

A First Formulation of a Global Ethic

To avoid misunderstandings I should repeat here: a global ethic does not mean a new global ideology, far less a uniform world religion beyond all existing religions; least of all does it mean the domination of one religion over all others. As I have indicated, a global ethic means a basic consensus on binding values, irrevocable criteria and personal basic attitudes, without which any community is sooner or later threatened with anarchy or a new dictatorship. But if the question is one of a basic ethical consensus, I will certainly be expected not to keep to universal programmatic words (truth, justice, humanity) and the Golden Rule, but to define the content of this consensus more closely. However, if one is to make the global ethic more concrete, first of all the formal question must be clarified. [. . .]

How should a global ethic be made specific? Content

For the first time in the history of the religions, the Council of the Parliament of the World's Religions, which met for the first time in Chicago between 28 August and 4 September 1993 with the participation of 6,500 people from every possible religion, ventured to commission and present a declaration on a global ethic: the author of this book had the honour and the burden of drafting this declaration and has given an account of the whole history of its origin and the broad international and inter-religious process of consultation in a publication of his own. As was only to be expected, this declaration provoked vigorous discussions during the Parliament. But the welcome thing was that at a time when so many religions are entangled in political conflicts, indeed in bloody wars, adherents of very different religions, great and small, made this declaration their own by signing it, as representatives of countless believers on this earth. This declaration is now the basis for an extensive process of discussion and acceptance which will certainly last a long time. It is to be hoped that despite all the obstacles the discussion will take place in all religions. For of course this first declaration on human obligations – like the first Declaration on the Rights of Man in 1776 in connection with the American Revolution – is not an end but a beginning.

One of the many hopeful signs for this acceptance is the firm confirmation of the Chicago Declaration by a report of the InterAction Council of former Presidents of State and Prime Ministers under the chairmanship of the former German Federal Chancellor Helmut Schmidt. This report was discussed under the title *In Search of Global Ethical Standards* in Vienna from March 22–24, 1996 with experts from the various religions, and approved in a plenary assembly of the InterAction Council in Vancouver on May 22, 1996.

Of course these statesmen are also aware of the negative role which the religions have often played and still play in the world: "The world is also afflicted by religious extremism and violence preached and practised in the name of religion." But that does not prevent them from also taking note of the positive role of the religions, particularly in respect of a common human ethic: "Religious institutions still command the loyalty of hundreds of millions of people," and do so despite all secularization and all consumerism: "The world's religions constitute one of the great traditions of wisdom for humankind. This repository of wisdom, ancient in its origins, has never been needed more." The minimal standards which make a collective life possible at all are important. Without an ethic and self-restraint humankind would revert to the jungle. "In a world of unprecedented change humankind has a desperate need of an ethical base on which to stand."

The statements on the priority of ethics over politics are encouragingly clear: "Ethics should precede politics and the law, because political action is concerned with values and choice. Ethics, therefore, must inform and inspire our political leadership." In response to the epoch-making change that is taking place, our institutions need a rededication to ethical norms: "We can find the sources of such a rededication in the world's religions and ethical traditions. They have the spiritual resources to give an ethical lead to the solution of our ethnic, national, social, economic and religious tensions. The world's religions have different doctrines but they all advocate a common ethic of basic standards. What unites the world's faiths is far greater than what divides them."

The InterAction Council positively adopted the Chicago Declaration on a Global Ethic: "We are therefore grateful that the Parliament of the World's Religions, which assembled in Chicago in 1993, proclaimed a Declaration towards a Global Ethic which we support in principle." The legal and ethical levels are clearly distinguished, and it is emphasized that what the United Nations proclaimed in its Declaration on Human Rights and the two supplementary conventions is confirmed and deepened by the Declaration of the World's Religions from the perspective of human responsibility: the full realization of the intrinsic dignity of the human person, the inalienable freedom and equality in principle of all humans, and the necessary solidarity and interdependence of all humans with each other, both as individuals and as communities. The statesmen are also convinced "that there will be no better global order without a global ethic".

Of course the politicians are also very well aware that a global ethic is no substitute for the Torah, the Gospels, the Qur'an, the Bhagavadgita, the Discourses of the Buddha or the Teachings of Confucius and others. It is concerned simply with "a minimal basic consensus relating to binding values, irrevocable standards and moral attitudes which can be affirmed by all religions despite their dogmatic differences, and can also be supported by non-believers". The alliance of believers and non-believers (also including that of theologians, philosophers, religious and social scientists) in the matter of an ethic is important. What is it aimed at?

The core of a global ethic

The basic ethical demand of the Chicago Declaration is the most elementary that one can put to human beings, though it is by no means a matter of course: true humanity: "Now as before, women and men are treated inhumanely all over the world. They are robbed of their opportunities and their freedom; their human rights are trampled underfoot; their dignity is disregarded. But might does not make right! In the face of all humanity our religions and ethical convictions demand that every human being must be treated humanely! That means that every human being without distinction of age, sex, race, skin colour, physical or mental ability, language, religion, political view, or national or social origin possesses an inalienable and untouchable dignity."

In this way, modern men and women with their "will to power" are shown quite clearly that even in our time they in no way stand "above good and evil", that rather the criterion of humanity has to be respected by all: "Everyone, the individual as well as the state, is therefore obliged to honour this dignity and protect it. Humans must always be the subjects of rights, must be ends, never mere means, never objects of commercialization and industrialization in economics, politics and media, in research institutes, and industrial corporations. No one stands 'above good and evil' – no human being, no social class, no influential interest group, no cartel, no police apparatus, no army, and no state. On the contrary; possessed of reason and conscience, every human is obliged to behave in a genuinely human fashion, to do good and avoid evil!"

Would not only Woodrow Wilson, but also Hans Morgenthau, who had endured so much inhumanity in his life and at the same time was always in search of universal criteria, have been in agreement with such basic demands? At all events it is a sign of the times that today a body of proven and completely realistic statesmen have expressly adopted as the basis of a global ethic the two basic principles:

- Every human being must be treated humanely!
- What you wish done to yourself, do to others.

These two principles should be the irrevocable, unconditional norm for all spheres of life, for family and communities, for races, nations and religions. Moreover on the basis of them the InterAction Council also affirms four irrevocable directives on which all religions agree. (Here they can be given only by title, without further elaboration; one could also render them, recalling the demonstrators in Prague or Rangoon, with ethical imperatives like "justice", "truth", humanity or whatever):

- Commitment to a culture of non-violence and respect for all life: the age-old directive: You shall not kill! Or in positive terms: Have respect for life!
- Commitment to a culture of solidarity and a just economic order: the age-old directive: You shall not steal! Or in positive terms: Deal honestly and fairly!
- Commitment to a culture of tolerance and a life of truthfulness: the age-old directive: You shall not lie! Or in positive terms: Speak and act truthfully!

- Commitment to a culture of equal rights and partnership between men and women: the age-old directive: You shall not commit sexual immorality! Or in positive terms: Respect and love one another! [. . .]

Human rights and human obligations: The International Commission on Global Governance

The report by The Commission on Global Governance appointed by UNO bears the title *Our Global Neighbourhood*. The term "global governance" can be misunderstood as indicating a "global government"; such a thing is neither realistic nor worth striving for. It would be all too remote from the citizens of the world, nor could it be legitimated democratically. Moreover a world government is already firmly ruled out by the co-chairmen of the distinguished twenty-five member commission, the former Swedish Prime Minister Ingvar Carlsson and the former Commonwealth General Secretary Shridath Ramphal, in their introduction: "We are not proposing movement towards world government"; this could lead to "an even less democratic world than we have", indeed to "one more accommodating to power". But on the other hand the goal is not a "world without systems or rules"; this would be "a chaotic world" and "it would pose equal or even greater danger". So the challenge is "to strike the balance in such a way that the management of global affairs is responsive to the interests of all people in a sustainable future, that it is guided by basic human values, and that it makes global organization conform to the reality of global diversity." Indeed, the growing number of people who are committed to a global ethic will find themselves supported by this report: "This is a time for the international community to be bold, to explore new ideas, to develop new visions and to demonstrate commitment to values in devising new governance arrangements."

The phenomenon of globalization in all its dimensions forms the starting point for this analysis of "a new world" which takes several hundred pages: "Never before has change come so rapidly, on such a global scale, and with such global visibility." This is true:

- of the military transformations and the total change in the strategic setting: a new arms race, the arms trade, the rise in civil conflict, widespread violence;
- of the economic trends, in which the economic rise of several developing countries is distracting attention from the still rising number of the poorest of all;
- of the social and environmental change, in which people are beginning to assert their right to participate in their own governance; this urgently calls for an enlightened leadership which represents all countries and peoples and not just the most powerful.

After this analysis of the situation in the first chapter of the report, there follow a wealth of analyses, reflections and proposals on the great problem areas of a policy for world governance today:

- the advancement of global security (avoiding, recognizing and settling crises);
- the management of economic interdependence;
- the strengthening of the rule of law world-wide (international law);
- the reform of the United Nations.

What is surprising here from the perspective of a global ethic is that before all these problem areas, immediately after the analysis of the situation, in a whole chapter the question of "values for the Global Neighbourhood" is raised and in view of the increased neighbourhood tensions in all spheres, a "neighbourhood ethic" is called for. Why? Without a global ethic the frictions and tensions in life together in the one world would multiply: "Without leadership (a courageous leadership infused with that ethic at all levels of society) even the best-designed institutions and strategies will fail." There is then the terse comment that "global values must be the cornerstone of global governance". And anyone who asks doubtfully whether enough of today's political leaders are steeped in this ethic is given hope by the remark that "many people world-wide, particularly the young, are more willing to respond to these issues than their governments, for whom the short term in the context of political expediency tends to take preference".

But let us leave aside speculation as to which politicians in particular will stand out in respect for the "ethical dimension of the world political order". More important is the question how it can be made concrete. And here, too, it is amazing that this document gives the Golden Rule as the main basic principle: "People should treat others as they would themselves wish to be treated." On this foundation the basic values of respect for life, freedom, justice, mutual respect, readiness to help, and integrity are developed: "All these values derive in one way or another from the principle, which is in accord with religious teaching around the world, that people should treat others as they would themselves wish to be treated."

And the report goes very much further in explicitly requiring "these values to be expressed in the form of a global civic ethic with specific rights and responsibilities", in which "all citizens, as individuals and as members of different private groups and associations, should accept the obligation to recognize and help protect the rights of others". This ethic should be incorporated into the developing "fabric of international norms". For such a global ethic "would help humanize the impersonal workings of bureaucracies and markets and constrain the competitive and self-serving instincts of individuals and groups". Indeed, without this global ethic the new wider global civil society which is coming into being could "become unfocused and even unruly".

It would be hard to think of a finer confirmation of the global ethic project than these statements by the commission. Finally, the commission even makes an explicit request. The authors were presumably unaware that, as I remarked earlier, it had already been made in a discussion in the Revolutionary Parliament of 1789 in Paris, but could not be met at that time: "Rights need to be joined with responsibilities." For the "tendency to emphasize rights while forgetting responsibilities" has "deleterious consequences". "We therefore urge the international community to unite in support of a global ethic of common rights and shared responsibilities. In our view, such an ethic – reinforcing the fundamental rights that are already part of the fabric of international norms, would provide the moral foundation for constructing a more effective system of global governance."

It cannot be repeated often enough that all human beings have rights, human rights: the right to a secure life, equitable treatment, an opportunity to earn a fair living and provide for their own welfare, the definition and preservation of their differences through peaceful means, participation in governance at all levels, free and fair petition for redress of gross injustices, equal access to information and to the global commons.

But hardly ever has it been stated in an official international document that concrete responsibilities, human responsibilities, are associated with human rights: "At the same time, all people share a responsibility to:

- contribute to the common good;
- consider the impact of their actions on the security and welfare of others;
- promote equity, including gender equity;
- protect the interests of future generations by pursuing sustainable development and safeguarding the global commons;
- preserve humanity's cultural and intellectual heritage;
- be active participants in governance; and
- work to eliminate corruption."

Moreover it is remarkable that this fundamental section of the UN Commission Report on a civil ethic ends with a very concrete hope, that "over time, these principles could be embodied in a more binding international document – a global charter of Civil Society – that could provide a basis for all to agree on rules that should govern the global neighbourhood". [. . .]

Questions

1   The expansion of world markets is often justified in terms of a set of ideas labeled "neoliberalism." According to neoliberals, free trade and competition will lead to greater growth and prosperity. They believe a smaller role for government will make markets more efficient and enhance individual well-being. They view globalization mainly as "the great economic event of our era." What arguments do Wolf and Martin offer in support of such neoliberalism? In what different ways do Cassen, Halimi, Barber, Karliner, and Küng object to it?

2   Do these contributions to the debate about globalization express or illustrate distinct views of the "ideal" world society? How would you describe your own ideal?

3   What are the key features of "McWorld" and "Jihad"? How does McWorld provoke and support Jihad? What does Barber find most threatening about globalization?

4   What is new about world politics today, according to Huntington? Does his image of a world embroiled in clashes of civilizations contradict the conventional view that globalization is a process that creates new bonds across cultural boundaries? Does he demonstrate that civilizations are now the primary organizing units in world society?

5   What is "grassroots globalization"? How can local groups create a global network? What should be their objective, according to Karliner?

6   Why does the world need a "global ethic," according to Küng, and what does it consist of? Do you think people around the world can agree on such an ethic?

Part II

Explaining Globalization

Introduction

How can we best explain globalization? Simple answers will not suffice because globalization is so complex, with many layers and dimensions. A good explanation must come to grips with this complexity. In addition, a new world society, still being formed, presents a moving target, so any theory must be adaptable in defining globalization itself, in identifying its object. And explanation is all the more difficult because, as globalization recreates the world, tools once used to make sense of earlier historical periods may no longer be adequate. The "global age," Martin Albrow argues in his book by that title, calls for new theory – new thinking and new departures in social science, especially if the discontinuity between old and new is as profound as many observers claim. In this part, we illustrate important work in progress on these issues drawn from four major perspectives.

Each of these perspectives proposes a different account of globalization. We can illustrate the differences between them by comparing their answers to a hypothetical question (taken from the excerpt by John Meyer et al.): How would a newly-discovered island society be incorporated into world society? One group of scholars would reply that corporations would stake a claim to the island's natural resources, send engineers to create infrastructure, and build plants to take advantage of cheap labor. Another group of scholars would argue that representatives of major powers would assist the society in building a capable state and tempt it to form alliances; international organizations would provide support and advice so that the society can be a stable participant in global politics. A third group of scholars would stress that the island would be invaded by advisors to help it build the institutions any proper state must have so that it can function like any other society. A final group would focus on the way the society would balance its own heritage against the intrusions of world culture, aided by organizations concerned about preserving its unique culture. Incorporation can thus take the form of economic exploitation, political agreements and alliances, institutional reform according to global models, or self-reflexive cultural identification. The selections show that such answers derive from different views on the motive forces and characteristic features of globalization.

1 World-system theory

To scholars inspired by Marx, globalization is the expansion of the capitalist system around the globe. The selection by Eric Hobsbawm sets the stage with historical evidence of the unification of the globe around the middle of the nineteenth century. Networks of communication and economic exchange were thickening. A world economy, guided by western liberal philosophy with global aspirations, constituted a single world that since has grown more integrated and standardized. Immanuel Wallerstein, author of the landmark multivolume study of *The Modern World-System*, puts this historical evidence in context. What happened in the mid-nineteenth century, he implies, was a phase in a centuries-old process. The capitalist world-system originated in the sixteenth century, when European traders established firm connections with Asia, Africa, and the Americas. From the outset, this system consisted of a single economy – a market and a regional division of labor – but many states. In the "core" of the system, the dominant classes were supported by strong states as they exploited labor, resources, and trade opportunities, most notably in "peripheral" areas. The "semiperiphery" lessened polarization between core and periphery and thus helped to account for the remarkable stability of the system. Sklair complements the Wallersteinian perspective by stressing the role of transnational corporations and classes as the prime movers in the contemporary global system. He argues that a global con- sumerist ideology supports the exploitative structure command by transna- tional corporations and helps the dominant transnational class get ever stronger. Sassen adds that the global economy "materializes in a worldwide grid of strategic places," that is, world cities. Those who run the world economy from world cities are less and less subject to political control or influenced by local cultures – the economy is loosened from its local moorings. Yet particular places are bound to experience the effect of global structures; in major cities, for example, inequality between global elites and low-skilled workers increases.

2   *Neorealism/Neoliberal Institutionalism*

The states that play a supporting role in Wallerstein's world-system analysis move center stage in the work of students of international relations. In the classic neorealist view, the focus is on independent states pursuing their inter- ests – security and power – constrained only by the power of others. Many scholars now think this "realistic" picture is too simple. As Keohane and Nye illustrate, globalization produces a more complex system of interdependent states in which transnational rules and organizations have gained influence. States pursuing their interests are still a major force, and study of this global system must still focus on the way states respond to constraints. But in an inter- dependent system, new organizations besides states critically influence world politics, no clear hierarchy of issues common to all states exists, and the use of force has become less effective. World society therefore contains many centers of power and has no single power hierarchy. Even as power disperses and goals diverge, new common rules for dealing with issues gain strength. "Complex interdependence" is but one label for the more nuanced picture that emerges.

3   *World polity theory*

Other scholars agree that states are an important component of world society but draw greater attention to the global context in which states are immersed. What is new in world society, they argue, is the all-encompassing "world polity" and its associated world culture, which supplies a set of cultural rules or scripts that specify how institutions around the world should deal with common problems. Globalization is the formation and enactment of this world polity and culture. One of the world polity's key elements, as John Meyer and his colleagues explain, is a general, globally legitimated model of how to form a state. Guided by this model, particular states in widely varying circumstances organize their affairs in surprisingly similar fashion. Because world society is organized as a polity with an intensifying global culture, new organizations spring up to enact its precepts. As carriers of global principles, these organizations then help to build and elaborate world society further.

4   World culture theory

In this perspective, world culture is indeed new and important, but it is less homogeneous than world-polity scholars imply. Globalization is a process of relativization, as Roland Robertson and JoAnn Chirico argue. Societies relate to a single system of societies, while individuals relate to a single sense of humanity. World society, thus, consists of a complex set of relations among multiple units. This society is not governed by a particular set of values but by the confrontation of different ways of organizing these relationships. Globalization compresses the world into a single entity, and people necessarily become more and more aware of their new global existence. But what is important about this process is the problem of "globality": how to make living together in one global system meaningful or even possible. Not surprisingly, then, religious traditions take on new significance insofar as they address the new global predicament that compels societies and individuals to "identify" themselves in new ways. The responses to this predicament, Jan Nederveen Pieterse suggests, will be many. Unlike world polity theorists, he sees globalization as producing a jumble of world views and organizational forms, all becoming available for use in necessarily "hybrid" mixtures.

As even this brief sketch of theories makes clear, scholars thus far have offered different views on the key dimensions, sources, and consequences of globalization. These theories have made substantial advances in accounting for transformations of the world. They all express a distinctly global point of view, even though they also still rely on ideas familiar from earlier social theory. As orienting perspectives, they guide much current research. But explaining globalization is necessarily work in progress, a collective effort to clarify the problems posed by the rise of a new world society as much as an attempt to produce one satisfying account of how the world has become a global whole.

9 The World Unified

E. J. Hobsbawm

> The bourgeoisie, by the rapid improvement of all instruments of production, by the immensely facilitated means of communication, draws all, even the most barbarian nations into civilisation . . . In one word, it creates a world after its own image.
>
> K. Marx and F. Engels, 1848

> As commerce, education, and the rapid transition of thought and matter, by telegraph and steam have changed everything, I rather believe that the great Maker is preparing the world to become one nation, speaking one language, a consummation which will render armies and navies no longer necessary.
>
> President Ulysses S. Grant, 1873

> "You should have heard all he said – I was to live on a mountain somewhere, go to Egypt or to America."
>
> "Well, what of it?" Stolz remarked coolly. "You can be in Egypt in a fortnight and in America in three weeks."
>
> "Whoever goes to America or Egypt? The English do, but then that's the way the Lord God made them and besides, they have no room to live at home. But which of us would dream of going? Some desperate fellow, perhaps, whose life is worth nothing to him."
>
> I. Goncharov, 1859

I

When we write the "world history" of earlier periods, we are in fact making an addition of the histories of the various parts of the globe, but which, in so far as they had knowledge of one another, had only marginal and superficial contacts, unless the inhabitants of some region had conquered or colonized another, as the west Europeans did the Americas. It is perfectly possible to write the earlier history of Africa with only a casual reference to that of the Far East, with (except along the west coast and the Cape) little reference to Europe, though not without fairly persistent reference to the Islamic world. What happened in China was, until the eighteenth century, irrelevant to the political rulers of Europe, other than the Russians, though not to some of their specialized groups of traders; what happened in Japan was beyond the direct knowledge of all except the handful of Dutch merchants who were allowed to maintain a foothold there between the sixteenth and the mid-nineteenth centuries. Conversely, Europe was for the Celestial Empire merely a region of outer barbarians fortunately remote enough to pose no problem of assessing the precise degree of their undoubted subservience to the Emperor, though raising some minor problems of administration for the officials in charge of some ports. For that matter, even within the regions in which there was significant

Original publication details: Hobsbawm, E. J., "The World Unified" from *The Age of Capital 1848–1875* (Weidenfeld and Nicolson, 1975).

interaction, much could be ignored without inconvenience. For whom in western Europe – merchants or statesmen – was it of any consequence what went on in the mountains and valleys of Macedonia? If Libya had been entirely swallowed by some natural cataclysm, what real difference would it have made to anybody, even in the Ottoman Empire of which it was technically a part, and among the Levant traders of various nations?

The lack of interdependence of the various parts of the globe was not simply a matter of ignorance, though of course, outside the region concerned and often within it, ignorance of "the interior" was still considerable. Even in 1848 large areas of the various continents were marked in white on even the best European maps – notably in Africa, central Asia, the interior of South and parts of North America and Australia, not to mention the almost totally unexplored Arctic and Antarctic. The maps which might have been drawn up by any other cartographers would certainly have shown even vaster spaces of the unknown; for if the officials of China or the illiterate scouts, traders and *coureurs de bois* of each continental hinterland knew a great deal more about some areas, large or small, than Europeans did, the sum total of their geographical knowledge was much more exiguous. In any case, the mere arithmetical addition of everything that any expert knew about the world would be a purely academic exercise. It was not generally available: in fact, there was not, even in terms of geographical knowledge, *one* world.

Ignorance was a symptom rather than a cause of the lack of the world's unity. It reflected both the absence of diplomatic, political and administrative relations, which were indeed slender enough, and the weakness of economic links. It is true that the "world market", that crucial pre-condition and characteristic of capitalist society, had long been developing. International trade had more than doubled in value between 1720 and 1780. In the period of the Dual Revolution (1780–1840) it had increased more than threefold – yet even this substantial growth was modest by the standards of our period. By 1870 the value of foreign trade for every citizen of the United Kingdom, France, Germany, Austria and Scandinavia was between four and five times what it had been in 1830, for every Dutchman and Belgian about three times as great, and even for every citizen of the United States – a country for which foreign commerce was only of marginal importance – well over double. During the 1870s an annual quantity of about 88 million tons weight of seaborne merchandise were exchanged between the major nations, as compared with 20 million in 1840. Thirty-one million tons of coal crossed the seas, compared to 1.4 million; 11.2 million tons of grain, compared to less than 2 million; 6 million tons of iron, compared to 1 million; even – anticipating the twentieth century – 1.4 million tons of petroleum, which had been unknown to overseas trade in 1840.

Let us measure the tightening of the net of economic interchanges between parts of the world remote from each other more precisely. British exports to Turkey and the Middle East rose from 3.5 million pounds in 1848 to a peak of almost 16 million in 1870; to Asia from 7 million to 41 million (1875); to Central and South America from 6 million to 25 million (1872); to India from around 5 million to 24 million (1875); to Australasia from 1.5 million to almost 20 million (1875). In other words in, say, thirty-five years, the value of the exchanges between the most industrialized economy and the most remote or backward regions of the world had increased about sixfold. Even this is of course not very impressive by present standards, but in sheer volume it far surpassed anything that had previously been conceived. The net which linked the various regions of the world was visibly tightening. [. . .]

Indeed, what we call the "explorers" of the mid-nineteenth century were merely one well-publicized, but numerically not very important, sub-group of a very large body of men who opened the globe to knowledge. They were those who travelled in areas in which economic development and profit were not yet sufficiently active to replace the "explorer" by the (European) trader, the mineral prospector, the surveyor, the builder of railway and telegraph, in the end, if the climate were to prove suitable, the white settler. "Explorers" dominated the cartography of inner Africa, because that continent had no very obvious economic assets for the west between the abolition of the Atlantic slave-trade and the discovery, on the one hand of precious stones and metals (in the south), on the other of the economic value of certain primary products which could only be grown or collected in tropical climates, and were still far from synthetic production. Neither was yet of great significance or even promise until the 1870s, though it seemed inconceivable that so large and under-utilized a continent should not, sooner rather than later, prove to be a source of wealth and profit. (After all, British exports to sub-Saharan Africa had risen from about 1.5 million pounds in the late 1840s to about 5 million in 1871 – they doubled in the 1870s to reach about 10 million in the early 1880s – which was by no means unpromising.) "Explorers" also dominated the opening of Australia, because the interior desert was vast, empty and, until the mid-twentieth century, devoid of obvious resources for economic exploitation. On the other hand, the oceans of the world ceased, except for the Arctic – the Antarctic attracted little interest during our period – to preoccupy the "explorers". Yet the vast extension of shipping, and above all the laying of the great submarine cables, implied a great deal of what can properly be called exploration.

The world in 1875 was thus a great deal better known than ever before. Even at the national level, detailed maps (mostly initiated for military purposes) were now available in many of the developed countries: the publication of the pioneer enterprise of this kind, the Ordnance Survey maps of England – but not yet of Scotland and Ireland – was completed in 1862. However, more important than mere knowledge, the most remote parts of the world were now beginning to be linked together by means of communication which had no precedent for regularity, for the capacity to transport vast quantities of goods and numbers of people, and above all, for speed: the railway, the steamship, the telegraph.

By 1872 they had achieved the triumph chronicled by Jules Verne: the possibility of travelling round the world in eighty days, even allowing for the numerous mishaps which dogged the indomitable Phileas Fogg. Readers may recall the imperturbable traveller's route. He went by rail and channel steamer across Europe from London to Brindisi and thence by boat through the newly opened Suez Canal (an estimated seven days). The journey from Suez to Bombay by boat was to take him thirteen days. The rail journey from Bombay to Calcutta should, but for the failure to complete a stretch of the line, have taken him three days. Thence by sea to Hong Kong, Yokohama and across the Pacific to San Francisco was still a long stretch of forty-one days. However, since the railroad across the American continent had been completed by 1869, only the still not wholly controlled perils of the West – herds of bison, Indians etc. – stood between the traveller and a normal journey of seven days to New York. The remainder of the trip – Atlantic crossing to Liverpool and railway to London – would have posed no problems but for the requirements of fictional suspense. In fact, an enterprising American travel agent offered a similar round-the-world trip not long after.

How long would such a journey have taken Fogg in 1848? It would have had to be almost entirely by sea, since no railway lines as yet crossed the continent, while virtually none existed anywhere else in the world except in the United States, where they hardly yet went further inland than two hundred miles. The speediest of sailing ships, the famous tea clippers, would most usually take an average of 110 days for the journey to Canton around 1870, when they were at the peak of their technical achievement; they could not do it in less than ninety days but had been known to take 150. We can hardly suppose a circumnavigation in 1848 to have taken, with anything but the best of fortunes, much less than eleven months, or say four times as long as Phileas Fogg, not counting time spent in port. [. . .]

II

We are today more familiar than the men of the mid-nineteenth century with this drawing together of all parts of the globe into a single world. Yet there is a substantial difference between the process as we experience it today and that in the previous century. What is most striking about it in the later twentieth century is an international standardization which goes far beyond the purely economic and technological. In this respect our world is more massively standardized than Phileas Fogg's, but only because there are more machines, productive installations and businesses. The railroads, telegraphs and ships of 1870 were not less recognizable as international "models" wherever they occurred than the automobiles and airports of 1970. What hardly occurred then was the international, and interlinguistic standardization of culture which today distributes, with at best a slight time-lag, the same films, popular music-styles, television programmes and indeed styles of popular living across the world. Such standardization did affect the numerically modest middle classes and some of the rich, up to a point, or at least in so far as it was not brought up against the barriers of language. The "models" of the developed world were copied by the more backward in the handful of dominant versions – the English throughout the Empire, in the United States and, to a much smaller extent, on the European continent, the French in Latin America, the Levant, and parts of eastern Europe, the German–Austrian throughout central and eastern Europe, in Scandinavia and also to some extent in the United States. A certain common visual style, the overstuffed and overloaded bourgeois interior, the public baroque of theatres and operas, could be discerned, though for practical purposes only where Europeans or colonists descended from Europeans had established themselves. Nevertheless, except in the United States (and Australia) where high wages democratized the market, and therefore the lifestyles, of the economically more modest classes, this remained confined to a comparative few.

There is no doubt that the bourgeois prophets of the mid-nineteenth century looked forward to a single, more or less standardized, world where all governments would acknowledge the truths of political economy and liberalism carried throughout the globe by impersonal missionaries more powerful than those Christianity or Islam had ever had; a world reshaped in the image of the bourgeoisie, perhaps even one from which, eventually, national differences would disappear. Already the development of communications required novel kinds of international coordinating and standardizing organisms – the International Telegraph Union of 1865, the Universal Postal Union of 1875, the International Meteorological Organization of 1878, all of which still survive. Already it had posed – and for limited purposes solved by means of the International Signals Code of 1871 – the problem of an internationally standardized "language". Within a few years attempts to devise artificial cosmopolitan languages were to become fashionable, headed by the oddly named *Volapük* ("world-speak") excogitated by a German in 1880. (None of these succeeded, not even the most promising contender, *Esperanto*, another product of the 1880s.) Already the labour movement was in the process of establishing a global organization which was to draw political conclusions from the growing unification of the world – the International.

Nevertheless international standardization and unification in this sense remained feeble and partial. Indeed, to some extent the rise of new nations and new cultures with a democratic base, i.e. using separate languages rather than the international idioms of educated minorities, made it more difficult, or rather, more circuitous. Writers of European or global reputation had to become so through translation. And while it is significant that by 1875 readers of German, French, Swedish, Dutch, Spanish, Danish, Italian, Portuguese, Czech and Hungarian were able to enjoy some or all of Dickens's works (as Bulgarian, Russian, Finnish, Serbo–Croat, Armenian and Yiddish ones were to before the end of the century), it is equally significant that this process implied an increasing linguistic division. Whatever the long-term prospects, it was accepted by contemporary liberal observers that, in the short and medium term, development proceeded by the formation of different and rival nations. The most that could be hoped was that these would embody the same type of institutions, economy and beliefs. The unity of the world implied division. The world system of capitalism was a structure of rival "national economies". The world triumph of liberalism rested on its conversion of all peoples, at least among those regarded as "civilized". No doubt the champions of progress in the third quarter of the nineteenth century were confident enough that this would happen sooner or later. But their confidence rested on insecure foundations.

They were indeed on safe ground in pointing to the ever-tightening network of global communications, whose most tangible result was a vast increase in the flow of international exchanges of goods and men – trade and migration. Yet even in the most plainly international field of business, global unification was not an unqualified advantage. For if it created a world economy, it was one in which all parts were so dependent on each other that a pull on one thread would inevitably set all others into movement. [. . .]

All these developments affected only that sector of the world which was already drawn into the international economy. Since vast areas and populations – virtually all of Asia and Africa, most of Latin America, and quite substantial parts even of Europe – still existed outside any economies but those of purely local exchange and remote from port, railway and telegraph, we ought not to exaggerate the unification of the world achieved between 1848 and 1875. After all, as an eminent chronicler of the time pointed out, "The *world economy* is only at its beginning"; but, as he also added, correctly, "even these beginnings allow us to guess at its future importance, inasmuch as the present stage already represents a truly amazing transformation in the productivity of humanity". [. . .]

10 The Rise and Future Demise of the World Capitalist System

Immanuel Wallerstein

We take the defining characteristic of a social system to be the existence within it of a division of labor, such that the various sectors or areas within are dependent upon economic exchange with others for the smooth and continuous provisioning of the needs of the area. Such economic exchange can clearly exist without a common political structure and even more obviously without sharing the same culture.

A mini-system is an entity that has within it a complete division of labor, and a single cultural framework. Such systems are found only in very simple agricultural or hunting and gathering societies. Such mini-systems no longer exist in the world. Furthermore, there were fewer in the past than is often asserted, since any such system that became tied to an empire by the payment of tribute as "protection costs" ceased by that fact to be a "system", no longer having a self-contained division of labor. For such an area, the payment of tribute marked a shift, in Polanyi's language, from being a reciprocal economy to participating in a larger redistributive economy.

Leaving aside the now defunct mini-systems, the only kind of social system is a world-system, which we define quite simply as a unit with a single division of labor and multiple cultural systems. It follows logically that there can, however, be two varieties of such world-systems, one with a common political system and one without. We shall designate these respectively as world-empires and world-economies.

It turns out empirically that world-economies have historically been unstable structures leading either towards disintegration or conquest by one group and hence transformation into a world-empire. Examples of such world-empires emerging from world-economies are all the so-called great civilizations of pre-modern times, such as China, Egypt, Rome (each at appropriate periods of its history). On the other hand, the so-called nineteenth-century empires, such as Great Britain or France, were not world-empires at all, but nation-states with colonial appendages operating within the framework of a world-economy.

World-empires were basically redistributive in economic form. No doubt they bred clusters of merchants who engaged in economic exchange (primarily long-distance trade), but such clusters, however large, were a minor part of the total economy and not fundamentally determinative of its fate. Such long-distance trade tended to be, as Polanyi argues, "administered trade" and not market trade, utilizing "ports of trade".

Original publication details: Wallerstein, Immanuel, "The Rise and Future Demise of the World Capitalist System: Concepts for Comparative Analysis" from *Comparative Studies in Society and History*, 16, 1974.

It was only with the emergence of the modern world-economy in sixteenth-century Europe that we saw the full development and economic predominance of market trade. This was the system called capitalism. Capitalism and a world-economy (that is, a single division of labor but multiple polities and cultures) are obverse sides of the same coin. One does not cause the other. We are merely defining the same indivisible phenomenon by different characteristics.

How and why it came about that this particular European world-economy of the sixteenth century did not become transformed into a redistributive world-empire but developed definitively as a capitalist world-economy has been explained elsewhere. The genesis of this world-historical turning-point is marginal to the issues under discussion in this paper, which is rather what conceptual apparatus one brings to bear on the analysis of developments within the framework of precisely such a capitalist world-economy.

Let us therefore turn to the capitalist world-economy. We shall seek to deal with two pseudo-problems, created by the trap of not analyzing totalities: the so-called persistence of feudal forms, and the so-called creation of socialist systems. In doing this, we shall offer an alternative model with which to engage in comparative analysis, one rooted in the historically specific totality which is the world capitalist economy. We hope to demonstrate thereby that to be historically specific is not to fail to be analytically universal. On the contrary, the only road to nomothetic propositions is through the historically concrete, just as in cosmology the only road to a theory of the laws governing the universe is through the concrete analysis of the historical evolution of this same universe.

On the "feudalism" debate, we take as a starting-point Frank's concept of "the development of underdevelopment", that is, the view that the economic structure of contemporary underdeveloped countries is not the form which a "traditional" society takes upon contact with "developed" societies, not an earlier stage in the "transition" to industrialization. It is rather the result of being involved in the world-economy as a peripheral, raw material-producing area, or as Frank puts it for Chile, "underdevelopment . . . is the necessary product of four centuries of capitalism itself".

This formulation runs counter to a large body of writing concerning the under-developed countries that was produced in the period 1950–70, a literature which sought the factors that explained "development" within non-systems such as "states" or "cultures" and, once having presumably discovered these factors, urged their reproduction in underdeveloped areas as the road to salvation. [. . .]

What was happening in Europe from the sixteenth to the eighteenth centuries is that over a large geographical area going from Poland in the northeast westwards and southwards throughout Europe and including large parts of the Western Hemisphere as well, there grew up a world-economy with a single division of labor within which there was a world market, for which men produced largely agricultural products for sale and profit. I would think the simplest thing to do would be to call this agricultural capitalism.

This then resolves the problems incurred by using the pervasiveness of *wage*-labor as a defining characteristic of capitalism. An individual is no less a capitalist exploiting labor because the state assists him to pay his laborers low wages (including wages in kind) and denies these laborers the right to change employment. Slavery and so-called "second serfdom" are not to be regarded as anomalies in a capitalist system. Rather the so-called serf in Poland or the Indian on a Spanish *encomienda* in New Spain in this sixteenth-century world-economy were working for landlords who "paid" them (however euphemistic this term) for cash-crop production. This is a relationship in which labor-power is a commodity (how could it ever be more so than under slavery?), quite different from the relationship of a feudal serf to his lord in eleventh-century Burgundy, where the economy was not oriented to a world market, and where labor-power was (therefore?) in no sense bought or sold.

Capitalism thus means labor as a commodity to be sure. But in the era of agricultural capitalism, wage-labor is only one of the modes in which labor is recruited and recompensed in the labor market. Slavery, coerced cash-crop production (my name for the so-called "second feudalism"), share-cropping, and tenancy are all alternative modes. It would be too long to develop here the conditions under which differing regions of the world-economy tend to specialize in different agricultural products.

What we must notice now is that this specialization occurs in specific and differing geographic regions of the world-economy. This regional specialization comes about by the attempts of actors in the market to avoid the normal operation of the market whenever it does not maximize their profit. The attempts of these actors to use non-market devices to ensure short-run profits makes them turn to the political entities which have in fact power to affect the market – the nation-states. (Again, why at this stage they could not have turned to city-states would take us into a long discursus, but it has to do with the state of military and shipping technology, the need of the European land-mass to expand overseas in the fifteenth century if it was to maintain the level of income of the various aristocracies, combined with the state of political disintegration to which Europe had fallen in the Middle Ages.)

In any case, the local capitalist classes – cash-crop landowners (often, even usually, nobility) and merchants – turned to the state, not only to liberate them from non-market constraints (as traditionally emphasized by liberal historiography) but to create new constraints on the new market, the market of the European world-economy.

By a series of accidents – historical, ecological, geographic – northwest Europe was better situated in the sixteenth century to diversify its agricultural specialization and add to it certain industries (such as textiles, shipbuilding, and metal wares) than were other parts of Europe. Northwest Europe emerged as the core area of this world-economy, specializing in agricultural production of higher skill levels, which favored (again for reasons too complex to develop) tenancy and wage-labor as the modes of labor control. Eastern Europe and the Western Hemisphere became peripheral areas specializing in export of grains, bullion, wood, cotton, sugar – all of which favored the use of slavery and coerced cash-crop labor as the modes of labor control. Mediterranean Europe emerged as the semi-peripheral area of this world-economy specializing in high-cost industrial products (for example, silks) and credit and specie transactions, which had as a consequence in the agricultural arena share-cropping as the mode of labor control and little export to other areas.

The three structural positions in a world-economy – core, periphery, and semi-periphery – had become stabilized by about 1640. How certain areas became one and not the other is a long story. The key fact is that given slightly different starting-points, the interests of various local groups converged in northwest Europe, leading to the development of strong state mechanisms, and diverged sharply in the peripheral areas, leading to very weak ones. Once we get a difference in the strength of the state-machineries, we get the operation of "unequal exchange" which is enforced by strong states on weak ones, by core states on peripheral areas. Thus capitalism involves not only appropriation of the surplus-value by an owner from a laborer, but an appropriation of surplus of the whole world-economy by core areas. And this was as true in the stage of agricultural capitalism as it is in the stage of industrial capitalism.

In the early Middle Ages, there was to be sure trade. But it was largely either "local", in a region that we might call the "extended" manor, or "long-distance", primarily of luxury goods. There was no exchange of "bulk" goods, of "staples" across intermediate-size areas, and hence no production for such markets. Later on in the Middle Ages, world-economies may be said to have come into existence, one centering on Venice, a second on the cities of Flanders and the Hanse. For various reasons, these structures were hurt by the retractions (economic, demographic, and ecological) of the period 1300–1450. It is only with the creating of a *European* division of labor after 1450 that capitalism found firm roots.

Capitalism was from the beginning an affair of the world-economy and not of nation-states. It is a misreading of the situation to claim that it is only in the twentieth century that capitalism has become "world-wide", although this claim is frequently made in various writings, particularly by Marxists. Typical of this line of argument is Charles Bettelheim's response to Arghiri Emmanuel's discussion of unequal exchange:

> The tendency of the capitalist mode of production to become worldwide is manifested not only through the constitution of a group of national economies forming a complex and hierarchical structure, including an imperialist pole and a dominated one, and not only through the antagonistic relations that develop between the different "national economies" and the different states, but also through the constant "transcending" of "national limits" by big capital (the formation of "international big capital", "world firms", etc. . . .).

The whole tone of these remarks ignores the fact that capital has never allowed its aspirations to be determined by national boundaries in a capitalist world-economy, and that the creation of "national" barriers – generically, mercantilism – has historically been a defensive mechanism of capitalists located in states which are one level below the high point of strength in the system. Such was the case of England *vis-à-vis* the Netherlands in 1660–1715, France *vis-à-vis* England in 1715–1815, Germany *vis-à-vis* Britain in the nineteenth century, the Soviet Union *vis-à-vis* the US in the twentieth. In the process a large number of countries create national economic barriers whose consequences often last beyond their initial objectives. At this later point in the process the very same capitalists who pressed their national governments to impose the restrictions now find these restrictions constraining. This is not an "internationalization" of "national" capital. This is simply a new political demand by certain sectors of the capitalist classes who have at all points in time sought to maximize their profits within the real economic market, that of the world-economy.

If this is so, then what meaning does it have to talk of structural positions within this economy and identify states as being in one of these positions? And why talk of three positions, inserting that of "semi-periphery" in between the widely-used concepts of core and periphery? The state-machineries of the core states were strengthened to meet the needs of capitalist landowners and their merchant allies. But that does not mean that these state-machineries were manipulable puppets. Obviously any organization, once created, has a certain autonomy from those who pressed it into existence for two reasons. It creates a stratum of officials whose own

careers and interests are furthered by the continued strengthening of the organization itself, however the interests of its capitalist backers may vary. Kings and bureaucrats wanted to stay in power and increase their personal gain constantly. Secondly,
in the process of creating the strong state in the first place, certain "constitutional"
compromises had to be made with other forces within the state-boundaries and these
institutionalized compromises limit, as they are designed to do, the freedom of
maneuver of the managers of the state-machinery. The formula of the state as "executive committee of the ruling class" is only valid, therefore, if one bears in mind
that executive committees are never mere reflections of the wills of their constituents,
as anyone who has ever participated in any organization knows well.

The strengthening of the state-machineries in core areas has as its direct counterpart the decline of the state-machineries in peripheral areas. The decline of the
Polish monarchy in the sixteenth and seventeenth centuries is a striking example of
this phenomenon. There are two reasons for this. In peripheral countries, the interests of the capitalist landowners lie in an opposite direction from those of the local
commercial bourgeoisie. Their interests lie in maintaining an open economy to maximize their profit from world-market trade (no restrictions in exports and access to
lower-cost industrial products from core countries) and in elimination of the commercial bourgeoisie in favor of outside merchants (who pose no local political
threat). Thus, in terms of the state, the coalition which strengthened it in core countries was precisely absent.

The second reason, which has become ever more operative over the history of
the modern world-system, is that the strength of the state-machinery in core states
is a function of the weakness of other state-machineries. Hence intervention of outsiders via war, subversion, and diplomacy is the lot of peripheral states.

All this seems very obvious. I repeat it only in order to make clear two points.
One cannot reasonably explain the strength of various state-machineries at specific
moments of the history of the modern world-system primarily in terms of a genetic-
cultural line of argumentation, but rather in terms of the structural role a country
plays in the world-economy at that moment in time. To be sure, the initial eligibility for a particular role is often decided by an accidental edge a particular country
has, and the "accident" of which one is talking is no doubt located in part in past
history, in part in current geography. But once this relatively minor accident is given,
it is the operations of the world-market forces which accentuate the differences,
institutionalize them, and make them impossible to surmount over the short run.

The second point we wish to make about the structural differences of core and
periphery is that they are not comprehensible unless we realize that there is a third
structural position: that of the semi-periphery. This is not the result merely of establishing arbitrary cutting-points on a continuum of characteristics. Our logic is not
merely inductive, sensing the presence of a third category from a comparison of
indicator curves. It is also deductive. The semi-periphery is needed to make a capitalist world-economy run smoothly. Both kinds of world-system, the world-empire
with a redistributive economy and the world-economy with a capitalist market
economy, involve markedly unequal distribution of rewards. Thus, logically, there
is immediately posed the question of how it is possible politically for such a system
to persist. Why do not the majority who are exploited simply overwhelm the minority who draw disproportionate benefits? The most rapid glance at the historic record
shows that these world-systems have been faced rather rarely by fundamental
system-wide insurrection. While internal discontent has been eternal, it has usually
taken quite long before the accumulation of the erosion of power has led to the

decline of a world-system, and as often as not, an external force has been a major factor in this decline.

There have been three major mechanisms that have enabled world-systems to retain relative political stability (not in terms of the particular groups who will play the leading roles in the system, but in terms of systemic survival itself). One obviously is the concentration of military strength in the hands of the dominant forces. The modalities of this obviously vary with the technology, and there are to be sure political prerequisites for such a concentration, but nonetheless sheer force is no doubt a central consideration.

A second mechanism is the pervasiveness of an ideological commitment to the system as a whole. I do not mean what has often been termed the "legitimation" of a system, because that term has been used to imply that the lower strata of a system feel some affinity with or loyalty towards the rulers, and I doubt that this has ever been a significant factor in the survival of world-systems. I mean rather the degree to which the staff or cadres of the system (and I leave this term deliberately vague) feel that their own well-being is wrapped up in the survival of the system as such and the competence of its leaders. It is this staff which not only propagates the myths; it is they who believe them.

But neither force nor the ideological commitment of the staff would suffice were it not for the division of the majority into a larger lower stratum and a smaller middle stratum. Both the revolutionary call for polarization as a strategy of change and the liberal encomium to consensus as the basis of the liberal polity reflect this proposition. The import is far wider than its use in the analysis of contemporary political problems suggests. It is the normal condition of either kind of world-system to have a three-layered structure. When and if this ceases to be the case, the world-system disintegrates.

In a world-empire, the middle stratum is in fact accorded the role of maintaining the marginally-desirable long-distance luxury trade, while the upper stratum concentrates its resources on controlling the military machinery which can collect the tribute, the crucial mode of redistributing surplus. By providing, however, for an access to a limited portion of the surplus to urbanized elements who alone, in pre-modern societies, could contribute political cohesiveness to isolated clusters of primary producers, the upper stratum effectively buys off the potential leadership of coordinated revolt. And by denying access to political rights for this commercial-urban middle stratum, it makes them constantly vulnerable to confiscatory measures whenever their economic profits become sufficiently swollen so that they might begin to create for themselves military strength.

In a world-economy, such "cultural" stratification is not so simple, because the absence of a single political system means the concentration of economic roles vertically rather than horizontally throughout the system. The solution then is to have three *kinds* of states, with pressures for cultural homogenization within each of them – thus, besides the upper stratum of core-states and the lower stratum of peripheral states, there is a middle stratum of semi-peripheral ones.

This semi-periphery is then assigned as it were a specific economic role, but the reason is less economic than political. That is to say, one might make a good case that the world-economy as an economy would function every bit as well without a semi-periphery. But it would be far less *politically* stable, for it would mean a polarized world-system. The existence of the third category means precisely that the upper stratum is not faced with the *unified* opposition of all the others because the *middle* stratum is both exploited and exploiter. It follows that the specific economic role is not all that important, and has thus changed through the various historical stages of the modern world-system.

Where then does class analysis fit in all of this? And what in such a formulation are nations, nationalities, peoples, ethnic groups? First of all, without arguing the point now, I would contend that all these latter terms denote variants of a single phenomenon which I will term "ethno-nations".

Both classes and ethnic groups, or status-groups, or ethno-nations are phenomena of world-economies and much of the enormous confusion that has surrounded the concrete analysis of their functioning can be attributed quite simply to the fact that they have been analyzed as though they existed within the nation-states of this world-economy, instead of within the world-economy as a whole. This has been a Procrustean bed indeed.

The range of economic activities being far wider in the core than in the periphery, the range of syndical interest groups is far wider there. Thus, it has been widely observed that there does not exist in many parts of the world today a proletariat of the kind which exists in, say, Europe or North America. But this is a confusing way to state the observation. Industrial activity being disproportionately concentrated in certain parts of the world-economy, industrial wage-workers are to be found principally in certain geographic regions. Their interests as a syndical group are determined by their collective relationship to the world-economy. Their ability to influence the political functioning of this world-economy is shaped by the fact that they command larger percentages of the population in one sovereign entity than another. The form their organizations take have, in large part, been governed too by these political boundaries. The same might be said about industrial capitalists. Class analysis is perfectly capable of accounting for the political position of, let us say, French skilled workers if we look at their structural position and interests in the world-economy. Similarly with ethno-nations. The meaning of ethnic consciousness in a core area is considerably different from that of ethnic consciousness in a peripheral area precisely because of the different class position such ethnic groups have in the world-economy.

Political struggles of ethno-nations or segments of classes within national boundaries of course are the daily bread and butter of local politics. But their significance or consequences can only be fruitfully analyzed if one spells out the implications of their organizational activity or political demands for the functioning of the world-economy. This also incidentally makes possible more rational assessments of these politics in terms of some set of evaluative criteria such as "left" and "right".

The functioning then of a capitalist world-economy requires that groups pursue their economic interests within a single world market while seeking to distort this market for their benefit by organizing to exert influence on states, some of which are far more powerful than others but none of which controls the world-market in its entirety. Of course, we shall find on closer inspection that there are periods where one state is relatively quite powerful and other periods where power is more diffuse and contested, permitting weaker states broader ranges of action. We can talk then of the relative tightness or looseness of the world-system as an important variable and seek to analyze why this dimension tends to be cyclical in nature, as it seems to have been for several hundred years. [. . .]

11   Sociology of the Global System

Leslie Sklair

The Conceptual Space for Transnational Practices (TNP)

The global system, at the end of the twentieth century, is not synonymous with the global capitalist system, but the driving forces behind global capitalism are the dominant though not the only driving forces behind the global system. My argument is that the primary agent and institutional focus of economic transnational practices is the transnational corporation.

However, there are others. The World Bank, the IMF, commodity exchanges and so on are mostly driven by the interests of the TNCs. The underlying goal of keeping global capitalism on course is in constant tension with the selfish and destabilizing actions of those who cannot resist system-threatening opportunities to get rich quick or to cut their losses. It is, however, the direct producers, not the capitalist class who usually suffer most when this occurs as, for example, the tin miners of Bolivia and the rest of the world found out when the London Metal Exchange terminated its tin contract in 1985.

The primary agents of the political and cultural-ideological TNPs may be somewhat more contentious. The theory of the global system being developed here proposes that the primary agent in the political sphere is a still-evolving *transnational capitalist class*. The institutions of the *culture-ideology of consumerism,* as expressed through the transnational mass media, are the primary agents in the cultural-ideological sphere.

It may be helpful to explain this in terms of what each of these three primary agents typically produces, the results of its practices. TNCs produce commodities and the services necessary to manufacture and sell them. The transnational capitalist class produces the political environment within which the products of one country can be successfully marketed in another. The culture-ideology of consumerism produces the values and attitudes that create and sustain the need for the products. These are analytical rather than empirical distinctions. In the real world they are inextricably mixed. TNCs get involved in host country politics, and the culture-ideology of consumerism is largely promulgated through the transnational corporations involved in mass media and advertising. Members of the transnational capitalist class often work directly for TNCs, and their lifestyles are a major exemplar for the spread of consumerism. Nevertheless, it is useful to make these analytical distinctions, particularly where the multiple strands of data are difficult to disentangle.

The thesis on which this conceptual apparatus rests and on which any viable theory of the global system depends is that capitalism is changing qualitatively from an inter-national to a global system. This is the subject of a very lively debate in

Original publication details: Sklair, Leslie, *Sociology of the Global System*, pp. 59–63 & passim. © 1995 The Johns Hopkins University Press.

academic, political and cultural circles. The idea that capitalism has entered a new global phase, whether it be "organized" or "disorganized", clearly commands a good deal of support, though, unsurprisingly, there are considerable differences on the details. The conception of global capitalism appears to me to be very sound in its analysis of the situation in the First and Third Worlds, and their argument that the emergence of global capitalism is facilitated by a series of technological revolutions (primarily in transportation, communications, electronics, biotechnology), provides a key support to the global system theory being elaborated here. My focus on transnational corporations draws on a large and rich literature on the "global corporation", again full of internal disputes, but based on the premise that "the production processes within large firms are being decoupled from specific territories and being formed into new global systems".

From the business periodical literature there are literally hundreds, probably thousands, of examples of the impact of globalization to choose from to fortify the thesis. The cover feature on "The stateless corporation" in *Business Week* (14 May 1990, pp. 98–106) was influential in this context, and in one of its regular forays into the big questions, *Fortune* magazine identified "globalization" as the first of four business revolutions happening simultaneously, the other three being computers, flexible management and the information economy. So, while some industrial and social phenomena seem to resist globalization and the nation-state has obviously not disappeared there is sufficient general support for the thesis that capitalism is entering something like a global phase to justify this inquiry.

It may seem to be a contradiction in terms, but much of the most stimulating "global" theory and research comes from those who hold what I have labelled "state-centrist" points of view. There is a struggle going on within global capitalism between inner-oriented modernizers and outward-oriented globalizers and this is reflected in research. Essentially state-centrist though they may be, Dicken's analysis of "global-local tensions", Sadler's notion of the "global region" and Teltscher's research on "small trade and the world economy", for example, throw considerable light on the globalizing tendencies of contemporary capitalism. One task that this book does set itself is to show how the political and the culture-ideology institutions of global capitalism complement the economic globalization that so many have identified and thereby demonstrate the limitations of state-centrism for a genuine theory of the global system.

This theory of the global system, then, revolves around the perceived necessity for global capitalism to continually increase production and international trade, to guarantee the political conditions for this to occur uninterruptedly all over the world, and to create in people the need to want to consume all the products that are available, on a permanent basis. There are, of course, other forces at work in the global system, and in some respects global capitalism has had to come to terms with these, particularly when they become opposing forces. This can be illustrated by looking more closely at the economic, political and cultural-ideological spheres.

Economic Transnational Practices

Economic transnational practices are economic practices that transcend national boundaries. These may be entirely contained within the borders of a single country even though their effects are transnational. For example, there may within one country be a consumer demand for a product which is unavailable from domestic supply. The retailer places an order with a supplier who fills the order from a foreign source. Neither the retailer nor the consumer needs to know or care where the product comes from, though some countries now have "country of origin" rules making mandatory the display of this information. There may be a parallel situation in the supplier country. Local producers may simply sell their products to a domestic marketing board or wholesaler and neither know nor care who the final consumers will be. The transnational corporation enters the scene when sellers, intermediaries and buyers are parts of the same global organization in ever-increasing networks of global commodity chains.

One important consequence of the expansion of the capitalist world economy has been that individual economic actors (like workers and entrepreneurs) and collective economic actors (like trade unions and TNCs) have become much more conscious of the transnationality of their practices and have striven to extend their global influence. Over recent years imports and exports have been vested with great political and cultural-ideological significance, and it is very likely that increasing numbers of consumers now register the country of origin of what they are buying, and producers now register the destination of what they are producing, and this knowledge may affect their actions. The volume of economic transnational practices has increased phenomenally since the 1950s, as evidenced by the tremendous growth of foreign trade, and this means that even some quite poor people in some poor countries can now distinguish many consumer goods in terms of their origins and the status-conferring advantages that some origins have over others. [. . .]

Global system theory predicts that the transnational capitalist class is growing stronger and more united and, as I shall go on to argue, this can be best explained within the context of the culture-ideology of consumerism.

The Transnational Capitalist Class

The transnational capitalist class is not made up of capitalists in the traditional Marxist sense. Direct ownership or control of the means of production is no longer the exclusive criterion for serving the interests of capital, particularly not the global interests of capital. The *international managerial bourgeoisie* is defined as: "a socially comprehensive category, encompassing the entrepreneurial elite, managers of firms, senior state functionaries, leading politicians, members of the learned professions, and persons of similar standing in all spheres of society". This is a very useful formulation, all the more so because it echoes another one, developed quite independently from a case study of the Mexico–US border. The membership of the "political cliques" that assisted the entrepreneurs in running the Mexican Border Industrialization Programme in its first decade is described as:

> a local government official, lawyer, accountant, banker, customs broker, labor contractor and in most cases the owner of factory land and buildings. US businessmen from industrial development committees and chambers of commerce from nearby US cities also usually form part of this clique.

The most important elements specifically missing from both of these formulations are the professional purveyors of the culture-ideology of consumerism, the mass media and promotional personnel whose task it is to sell the consumerist goals of the global capitalist system to the masses. These goals have to be sold to producers, citizens and consumers.

The transnational capitalist class (TCC) is transnational in at least three senses. Its members tend to have global rather than local perspectives on a variety of issues; they tend to be people from many countries, more and more of whom begin to consider themselves "citizens of the world" as well as of their places of birth; and they tend to share similar lifestyles, particularly patterns of luxury consumption of goods and services. In my formulation, the transnational capitalist class includes the following groups of people:

1 TNC executives and their local affiliates;
2 globalizing state bureaucrats;
3 capitalist-inspired politicians and professionals; and
4 consumerist elites (merchants, media).

This class sees its mission as organizing the conditions under which its interests and the interests of the system (which usually but do not always coincide) can be furthered within the national and local context. The concept of the transnational capitalist class implies that there is one central transnational capitalist class that makes system-wide decisions, and that it connects with the TCC in each locality, region and country.

The political practices of the transnational capitalist class will be analysed in terms of two issues. First, how the TCC operates to change the nature of the political struggle between capital and labour. This can be measured in terms of its local and transnational political organization, direct and indirect TNC interference in host country politics and the extent to which these constrain and are constrained by the local and/or transnational labour movement. Second, the transnational capitalist class aims to downgrade certain domestic practices by comparison with new and more glamorous transnational practices and to create a "comprador" mentality. This can be measured by the local and in some cases international brain drain from indigenous to transnational enterprises, mainly but not exclusively TNCs. The people who make up this brain drain are the backbone of the transnational capitalist class, the class whose political role is to persuade co-nationals that their interests are identical with, or at least best served by, those of the TNCs. [. . .]

Bagdikian characterizes those who control this system [world media] as "the lords of the global village". They purvey their product (a relatively undifferentiated mass of news, information, ideas, entertainment and popular culture) to a rapidly expanding public, eventually the whole world. Bagdikian argues that national boundaries are growing increasingly meaningless as the main actors (five groups at the time he was writing) strive for total control in the production, delivery, and marketing of what we can call the cultural-ideological goods of the global capitalist system. Their goal is to create a "buying mood" for the benefit of the global troika of media, advertising and consumer goods manufacturers. "Nothing in human experience has prepared men, women and children for the modern television techniques of fixing human attention and creating the uncritical mood required to sell goods, many of which are marginal at best to human needs". Two symbolic facts: by the age of 16, the average North American youth has been exposed to more than 300,000 television commercials; and the former Soviet Union sold advertising slots on cosmonaut suits and space ships! In order to connect and explain these facts, we need to generate a new framework, namely the culture-ideology of consumerism.

The Culture-Ideology of Consumerism

The mass media perform many functions for global capitalism. They speed up the circulation of material goods through advertising, which reduces the time between production and consumption. They begin to inculcate the dominant ideology from an early age, in the words of Esteinou Madrid, "creating the political/cultural demand for the survival of capitalism". The systematic blurring of the lines between information, entertainment, and promotion of products lies at the heart of this practice. This has not in itself created a culture and ideology of consumerism, for these have been in place for at least the last century and perhaps longer in the First World and among comprador classes elsewhere. What it has created is a reformulation of consumerism that transforms all the public mass media and their contents into opportunities to sell ideas, values, products, in short, a consumerist worldview.

In all this the shopping mall has come to play a central role, both symbolically and substantively. As Crawford argues in "The world in a shopping mall", the merging of the architecture of the mall with the culture of the theme park has become the key symbol and the key spatial reference point for consumer capitalism, not only in North America but increasingly all over the world. What Goss terms "the magic of the mall" has to be understood on several levels, how the consuming environment is carefully designed and controlled, the seductive nature of the consuming experience, the transformation of nominal public space into actual private terrain. Although there are certainly anomalies between the decaying cities of the First World and the gleaming malls bursting with consumer goods that surround them, it is in the poorer parts of the Third World that these anomalies are at their most stark. Third World malls cater mainly to the needs and wants of expatriate TNC executives and officials and members of the local transnational capitalist classes. The integration of the medium of the mall and the message of the culture-ideology of consumerism has a formative influence on the trajectory of global capitalism. The medium *is* the message because the message, the culture-ideology of consumerism, has engulfed the medium. The problem, therefore, is not *Understanding Media* (the title of McLuhan's great if somewhat misconceived book) but *Understanding Global Capitalism*, the system that produces and reproduces both the message and the media that incessantly transmit it. [. . .]

The Theory of the Global System: A Summary

The theory of the global system can be summarized, graphically, as follows. The global system is made up of economic transnational practices and at the highest level of abstraction these are the building blocks of the system. The political practices are the principles of organization of the system. Their agents work with the materials on hand, but by manipulating the design of the system they can build variations into it. The cultural-ideological practices are the nuts and bolts and the glue that hold the system together. Without them, parts of the system would drift off into space.

In order to work properly the dominant forces in each of the three spheres have to monopolize the key resources for which there is great competition. The transnational corporations strive to control global capital and material resources, the transnational capitalist classes strive to control global power, and the transnational agents and institutions of the culture-ideology of consumerism strive to control the realm of ideas. Effective TNC control of global capital and resources is almost complete. There are few important national resources that are entirely exempt from economic transnational practices. Transnational capitalist classes rule directly, through national capitalist political parties or social democratic parties that cannot fundamentally threaten the global capitalist project, or they exert authority indirectly to a greater or lesser extent as the price levied on non-capitalist states as a sort of entrance fee into the global capitalist system. In the last resort, it is the global control of capital and labour that is the decisive factor for those who do not wish to be excluded from the system.

The control of ideas in the interests of consumerism is almost total. The ideas that are antagonistic to the global capitalist project can be reduced to one central counter-hegemonic idea, the rejection of the culture-ideology of consumerism itself. Without consumerism, the rationale for continuous capitalist accumulation dissolves. It is the capacity to commercialize and commodify all ideas and the material products in which they adhere, television images, advertisements, newsprint, books, tapes, films and so on, not the ideas themselves, that global capitalism strives to appropriate.

12 Whose City Is It? Globalization and the Formation of New Claims

Saskia Sassen

A New Geography of Centrality and Marginality

The global economy materializes in a worldwide grid of strategic places, from export-processing zones to major international business and financial centers. We can think of this global grid as constituting a new economic geography of centrality, one that cuts across national boundaries and across the old North–South divide. It signals the emergence of a parallel political geography of power, a transnational space for the formation of new claims by global capital. This new economic geography of centrality partly reproduces existing inequalities but also is the outcome of a dynamic specific to current types of economic growth. It assumes many forms and operates in many terrains, from the distribution of telecommunications facilities to the structure of the economy and of employment.

The most powerful of these new geographies of centrality at the interurban level binds the major international financial and business centers: New York, London, Tokyo, Paris, Frankfurt, Zurich, Amsterdam, Los Angeles, Sydney, Hong Kong, among others. But this geography now also includes cities such as São Paulo, Buenos Aires, Bangkok, Taipei, Bombay, and Mexico City. The intensity of transactions among these cities, particularly through the financial markets, trade in services, and investment, has increased sharply, and so have the orders of magnitude involved. At the same time, there has been a sharpening inequality in the concentration of strategic resources and activities between each of these cities and others in the same country. Global cities are sites for immense concentrations of economic power and command centers in a global economy, while traditional manufacturing centers have suffered inordinate declines.

One might have expected that the growing number of financial centers now integrated into the global markets would have reduced the extent of concentration of financial activity in the top centers. But it has not. One would also expect this given the immense increases in the global volume of transactions. Yet the levels of concentration remain unchanged in the face of massive transformations in the financial industry and in the technological infrastructure this industry depends on.

The growth of global markets for finance and specialized services, the need for transnational servicing networks because of sharp increases in international investment, the reduced role of the government in the regulation of international eco-

Original publication details: Sassen, Saskia, "Introduction: Whose City Is It? Globalization and the Formation of New Claims" from *Globalization and Its Discontents* (The New Press, 1998).

nomic activity and the corresponding ascendance of other institutional arenas, notably global markets and corporate headquarters – all these point to the existence of a series of economic processes, each characterized by locations in more than one country and in this regard transnational. We can see here the formation, at least incipient, of a transnational urban system.

The pronounced orientation to the world markets evident in such cities raises questions about the articulation with their nation-states, their regions, and the larger economic and social structure in such cities. Cities have typically been deeply embedded in the economies of their region, indeed often reflecting the characteristics of the latter; and generally they still do. But cities that are strategic sites in the global economy tend, in part, to become disconnected from their region and even nation. This conflicts with a key proposition in conventional scholarship about urban systems, namely, that these systems promote the territorial integration of regional and national economies.

Alongside these new global and regional hierarchies of cities and high-tech industrial districts lies a vast territory that has become increasingly peripheral, increasingly excluded from the major economic processes that fuel economic growth in the new global economy. A multiplicity of formerly important manufacturing centers and port cities have lost functions and are in decline, not only in the less developed countries but also in the most advanced economies. This is yet another meaning of economic globalization.

But also inside global cities we see a new geography of centrality and marginality. The downtowns of global cities and metropolitan business centers receive massive investments in real estate and telecommunications while low-income city areas are starved for resources. Highly educated workers employed in leading sectors see their incomes rise to unusually high levels while low- or medium-skilled workers in those same sectors see theirs sink. Financial services produce superprofits while industrial services barely survive. These trends are evident, with different levels of intensity, in a growing number of major cities in the developed world and increasingly in major cities of some of the developing countries that have been integrated into the global economy.

The Rights of Capital in the New Global Grid

A basic proposition in discussions about the global economy concerns the declining sovereignty of states over their economies. Economic globalization does indeed extend the economy beyond the boundaries of the nation-state. This is particularly evident in the leading economic sectors. Existing systems of governance and accountability for transnational activities and actors leave much ungoverned when it comes to these industries. Global markets in finance and advanced services partly operate through a "regulatory" umbrella that is not state centered but market centered. More generally, the new geography of centrality is transnational and operates in good part in electronic spaces that override all jurisdiction.

Yet, this proposition fails to underline a key component in the transformation of the last fifteen years: the formation of new claims on national states to guarantee the domestic and global rights of capital. What matters for our purposes here is that global capital made these claims and that national states responded through the production of new forms of legality. The new geography of centrality had to be produced, both in terms of the practices of corporate actors and in terms of the work of the state in producing new legal regimes. Representations that characterize the national state as simply losing significance fail to capture this very important dimension, and reduce what is happening to a function of the global/national duality – what one wins, the other loses.

There are two distinct issues here. One is the ascendance of this new legal regime that negotiates between national sovereignty and the transnational practices of corporate economic actors. The second issue concerns the particular content of this new regime, which strengthens the advantages of certain types of economic actors and weakens those of others. The hegemony of neoliberal concepts of economic relations with its strong emphasis on markets, deregulation, and free international trade has influenced policy in the 1980s in the United States and Great Britain and now increasingly also in continental Europe. This has contributed to the formation of transnational legal regimes that are centered in Western economic concepts of contract and property rights. Through the International Monetary Fund (IMF) and the International Bank for Reconstruction and Development (IBRD), as well as the General Agreement on Tariffs and Trade (GATT) (the World Trade Organization since January 1995), this regime has spread to the developing world. It is a regime associated with increased levels of concentrated wealth, poverty, and inequality worldwide. This occurs under specific modalities in the case of global cities, as discussed earlier.

Deregulation has been a crucial mechanism to negotiate the juxtaposition of the global and the national. Rather than simply seeing it as freeing up markets and reducing the sovereignty of the state, we might underline a much less noted aspect of deregulation: it has had the effect, particularly in the case of the leading economic sectors, of partly denationalizing national territory. In other words, it is not simply a matter of a space economy extending beyond a national realm. It is also that globalization – as illustrated by the space economy of advanced information industries – denationalizes national territory. This denationalization, which to a large extent materializes in global cities, has become legitimate for capital and has indeed been imbued with positive value by many government elites and their economic advisers. It is the opposite when it comes to people, as is perhaps most sharply illustrated in the rise of anti-immigrant feeling and the renationalizing of politics.

The emphasis on the transnational and hypermobile character of capital has contributed to a sense of powerlessness among local actors, a sense of the futility of resistance. But the analysis in the preceding sections, with its emphasis on place, suggests that the new global grid of strategic sites is a terrain for politics and engagement. Further, the state, both national and local, can be engaged. Although certain agencies within the state have contributed to the formation and strengthening of global capital, the state is far from being a unitary institution. The state itself has been transformed by its role in implementing the global economic system, a transformation captured in the ascendance of agencies linked to the domestic and international financial markets in most governments of highly developed countries and many governments of developing countries, and the loss of power and prestige of agencies associated with issues of domestic equity. These different agencies are now at times in open conflict.

The focus on place helps us elaborate and specify the meaning of key concepts in the discourse about globalization, notably the loss of sovereignty. It brings to the fore that important components of globalization are embedded in particular institutional locations within national territories. A strategic subnational unit such as the global city is emblematic of these conditions – conditions not well captured in the more conventional duality of national/global.

A focus on the leading industries in global cities introduces into the discussion of governance the possibility of capacities for local governmental regulation derived from the concentration of significant resources in strategic places. These resources include fixed capital and are essential for participation in the global economy. The considerable placeboundedness of many of these resources contrasts with the hypermobility of the outputs of many of these same industries, particularly finance. The regulatory capacity of the state stands in a different relation to hypermobile outputs than to the infrastructure of facilities, from office buildings equipped with fiber optic cables to specialized workforces.

The specific issues raised by focusing on the placeboundedness of key components of economic globalization are quite distinct from those typically raised in the context of the national/global duality. A focus on this duality leads to rather straightforward propositions about the declining significance of the state *vis-à-vis* global economic actors. The overarching tendency in economic analyses of globalization and of the leading information industries has been to emphasize certain aspects: industry outputs rather than the production process involved; the capacity for instantaneous transmission around the world rather than the infrastructure necessary for this capacity; the impossibility for the state to regulate those outputs and that capacity insofar as they extend beyond the nation-state. And the emphasis is by itself quite correct; but it is a partial account about the implications of globalization for governance.

The transformation in the composition of the world economy, especially the rise of finance and advanced services as leading industries, is contributing to a new international economic order, one dominated by financial centers, global markets, and transnational firms. Cities that function as international business and financial centers are sites for direct transactions with world markets that take place without government inspection, as for instance the euro-markets or New York City's international financial zone (i.e., International Banking Facilities). These cities and the globally oriented markets and firms they contain mediate in the relation of the world economy to nation-states and in the relations among nation-states. Correspondingly, we may see a growing significance of sub- and supranational political categories and actors.

Unmooring Identities and a New Transnational Politics

The preceding section argues that the production of new forms of legality and of a new transnational legal regime privilege the reconstitution of capital as a global actor and the denationalized spaces necessary for its operation. At the same time there is a lack of new legal forms and regimes to encompass another crucial element of this transnationalization, one that some, including myself, see as the counterpart to that of capital: the transnationalization of labor. However, we are still using the language of immigration to describe the process. Nor are there new forms and regimes to encompass the transnationalization in the formation of identities and loyalties among various population segments which do not regard the nation as the sole or principal source of identification, and the associated new solidarities and notions of membership. Major cities have emerged as a strategic site not only for global capital but also for the transnationalization of labor and the formation of transnational identities. In this regard they are a site for new types of political operations.

Cities are the terrain where people from many different countries are most likely to meet and a multiplicity of cultures come together. The international character of major cities lies not only in their telecommunication infrastructure and international firms, but also in the many different cultural environments they contain. One can no longer think of centers for international business and finance simply in terms of the corporate towers and corporate culture at their center. Today's global cities are in part the spaces of postcolonialism and indeed contain conditions for the formation of a postcolonialist discourse.

The large Western city of today concentrates diversity. Its spaces are inscribed with the dominant corporate culture but also with a multiplicity of other cultures and identities. The slippage is evident: the dominant culture can encompass only part of the city. And while corporate power inscribes these cultures and identifies them with "otherness" thereby devaluing them, they are present everywhere. For instance, through immigration a proliferation of originally highly localized cultures now have become presences in many large cities, cities whose elites think of themselves as cosmopolitan, as transcending any locality. Members of these "localized" cultures can in fact come from places with great cultural diversity and be as cosmopolitan as elites. An immense array of cultures from around the world, each rooted in a particular country, town, or village, now are reterritorialized in a few single places, places such as New York, Los Angeles, Paris, London, and most recently Tokyo.

I think that there are representations of globality which have not been recognized as such or are contested representations. Such representations include immigration and its associated multiplicity of cultural environments, often subsumed under the notion of ethnicity. What we still narrate in the language of immigration and ethnicity, I would argue, is actually a series of processes having to do with the globalization of economic activity, of cultural activity, of identity formation. Too often immigration and ethnicity are constituted as otherness. Understanding them as a set of processes whereby global elements are localized, international labor markets are constituted, and cultures from all over the world are de- and reterritorialized, puts them right there at the center along with the internationalization of capital as a fundamental aspect of globalization. This way of narrating the large migrations of the post-war era captures the ongoing weight of colonialism and postcolonial forms of empire on major processes of globalization today, and specifically those processes binding countries of emigration and immigration. Although the specific genesis and contents of their responsibility will vary from case to case and period to period, none of the major immigration countries are passive bystanders in their immigration histories.

Making Claims on the City

These processes signal that there has been a change in the linkages that bind people and places and in the corresponding formation of claims on the city. It is true that throughout history people have moved and through these movements constituted places. But today the articulation of territory and people is being constituted in a radically different way at least in one regard, and that is the speed with which that articulation can change. Martinotti notes that one consequence of this speed is the expansion of the space within which actual and possible linkages can occur. The shrinking of distance and the speed of movement that characterize the current era find one of its most extreme forms in electronically based communities of individuals or organizations from all around the globe interacting in real time and simultaneously, as is possible through the Internet and kindred electronic networks.

I would argue that another radical form assumed today by the linkage of people to territory is the unmooring of identities from what have been traditional sources of identity, such as the nation or the village. This unmooring in the process of identity formation engenders new notions of community, of membership, and of entitlement.

The space constituted by the global grid of cities, a space with new economic and political potentialities, is perhaps one of the most strategic spaces for the formation of transnational identities and communities. This is a space that is both place centered in that it is embedded in particular and strategic locations; and it is transterritorial because it connects sites that are not geographically proximate yet are intensely connected to each other. As I argued earlier, it is not only the transmigration of capital that takes place in this global grid, but also that of people, both rich (i.e., the new transnational professional workforce) and poor (i.e., most migrant workers), and it is a space for the transmigration of cultural forms, for the reterritorialization of "local" subcultures. An important question is whether it is also a space for a new politics, one going beyond the politics of culture and identity, though at least partly likely to be embedded in it.

Yet another way of thinking about the political implications of this strategic transnational space anchored in cities is the formation of new claims on that space. As was discussed earlier, there are indeed new major actors making claims on these cities over the last decade, notably foreign firms that have been increasingly entitled through the deregulation of national economies, and the increasing number of international businesspeople. These are among the new "city users." They have profoundly marked the urban landscape. Their claim to the city is not contested, even though the costs and benefits to cities have barely been examined.

The new city users have made an often immense claim on the city and have reconstituted strategic spaces of the city in their image: their claim is rarely examined or challenged. They contribute to changing the social morphology of the city and to constituting what Martinotti calls the metropolis of second generation, the city of late modernism. The new city of these city users is a fragile one, whose survival and successes are centered on an economy of high productivity, advanced technologies, and intensified exchanges.

On the one hand, this raises a question of what the city is for international businesspeople: it is a city whose space consists of airports, top-level business districts, top of the line hotels and restaurants – a sort of urban glamour zone, the new hyperspace of international business. On the other hand, there is the difficult task of establishing whether a city that functions as an international business center does in fact recover the costs for being such a center: the costs involved in maintaining a state-of-the-art business district, and all it requires, from advanced communications facilities to top-level security and "world-class culture."

Perhaps at the other extreme of legitimacy are those who use urban political violence to make their claims on the city, claims that lack the de facto legitimacy enjoyed by the new business city users. These are claims made by actors struggling for recognition and entitlement, claiming their rights to the city. These claims have, of course, a long history; every new epoch brings specific conditions to the manner in which the claims are made. The growing weight of "delinquency," for example, smashing cars and shop windows, robbing and burning stores, in some of these uprisings during the last decade in major cities of the developed world, is perhaps an indication of the sharpened inequality. The disparities, as seen and as lived, between the urban glamour zone and the urban war zone have become enormous.

The extreme visibility of the difference is likely to contribute to further brutalization of the conflict: the indifference and greed of the new elites versus the hopelessness and rage of the poor.

There are then two aspects of this formation of new claims that have implications for transnational politics. One is these sharp and perhaps intensifying differences in the representation of claims by different sectors, notably international business and the vast population of low-income "others" – African Americans, immigrants, and women. The second aspect is the increasingly transnational element in both types of claims and claimants. It signals a politics of contestation embedded in specific places but transnational in character.

Globalization is a process that generates contradictory spaces, characterized by contestation, internal differentiation, continuous border crossings. The global city is emblematic of this condition. Global cities concentrate a disproportionate share of global corporate power and are one of the key sites for its valorization. But they also concentrate a disproportionate share of the disadvantaged and are one of the key sites for their devalorization. This joint presence happens in a context where the globalization of the economy has grown sharply and cities have become increasingly strategic for global capital; and marginalized people have found their voice and are making claims on the city. This joint presence is further brought into focus by the increasing disparities between the two. The center now concentrates immense economic and political power, power that rests on the capability for global control and the capability to produce superprofits. And actors with little economic and traditional political power have become an increasingly strong presence through the new politics of culture and identity, and an emergent transnational politics embedded in the new geography of economic globalization. Both actors, increasingly transnational and in contestation, find in the city the strategic terrain for their operations. But it is hardly the terrain of a balanced playing field.

13 Realism and Complex Interdependence

Robert O. Keohane and Joseph S. Nye

One's assumptions about world politics profoundly affect what one sees and how one constructs theories to explain events. We believe that the assumptions of political realists, whose theories dominated the postwar period, are often an inadequate basis for analyzing the politics of interdependence. The realist assumptions about world politics can be seen as defining an extreme set of conditions or *ideal type*. One could also imagine very different conditions. In this chapter, we shall construct another ideal type, the opposite of realism. We call it *complex interdependence*. After establishing the differences between realism and complex interdependence, we shall argue that complex interdependence sometimes comes closer to reality than does realism. When it does, traditional explanations of change in international regimes become questionable and the search for new explanatory models becomes more urgent.

For political realists, international politics, like all other politics, is a struggle for power but, unlike domestic politics, a struggle dominated by organized violence. In the words of the most influential postwar textbook, "All history shows that nations active in international politics are continuously preparing for, actively involved in, or recovering from organized violence in the form of war." Three assumptions are integral to the realist vision. First, states as coherent units are the dominant actors in world politics. This is a double assumption: states are predominant; and they act as coherent units. Second, realists assume that force is a usable and effective instrument of policy. Other instruments may also be employed, but using or threatening force is the most effective means of wielding power. Third, partly because of their second assumption, realists assume a hierarchy of issues in world politics, headed by questions of military security: the "high politics" of military security dominates the "low politics" of economic and social affairs.

These realist assumptions define an ideal type of world politics. They allow us to imagine a world in which politics is continually characterized by active or potential conflict among states, with the use of force possible at any time. Each state attempts to defend its territory and interests from real or perceived threats. Political integration among states is slight and lasts only as long as it serves the national interests of the most powerful states. Transnational actors either do not exist or are politically unimportant. Only the adept exercise of force or the threat of force permits states to survive, and only while statesmen succeed in adjusting their interests, as in a well-functioning balance of power, is the system stable.

Each of the realist assumptions can be challenged. If we challenge them all simultaneously, we can imagine a world in which actors other than states participate

Original publication details: Keohane, Robert O. and Joseph S. Nye, "Realism and Complex Interdependence" from *Power and Interdependence*, Copyright © 1989 by Robert O. Keohane and Joseph S. Nye. Reprinted by permission of Addison-Wesley Educational Publishers Inc.

directly in world politics, in which a clear hierarchy of issues does not exist, and in which force is an ineffective instrument of policy. Under these conditions – which we call the characteristics of complex interdependence – one would expect world politics to be very different than under realist conditions.

We will explore these differences in the next section of this chapter. We do not argue, however, that complex interdependence faithfully reflects world political reality. Quite the contrary: both it and the realist portrait are ideal types. Most situations will fall somewhere between these two extremes. Sometimes, realist assumptions will be accurate, or largely accurate, but frequently complex interdependence will provide a better portrayal of reality. Before one decides what explanatory model to apply to a situation or problem, one will need to understand the degree to which realist or complex interdependence assumptions correspond to the situation.

The Characteristics of Complex Interdependence

Complex interdependence has three main characteristics:

1   *Multiple channels* connect societies, including: informal ties between governmental elites as well as formal foreign office arrangements; informal ties among nongovernmental elites (face-to-face and through telecommunications); and transnational organizations (such as multinational banks or corporations). These channels can be summarized as interstate, transgovernmental, and transnational relations. *Interstate* relations are the normal channels assumed by realists. *Transgovernmental* applies when we relax the realist assumption that states act coherently as units; *transnational* applies when we relax the assumption that states are the only units.

2   The agenda of interstate relationships consists of multiple issues that are not arranged in a clear or consistent hierarchy. This *absence of hierarchy among issues* means, among other things, that military security does not consistently dominate the agenda. Many issues arise from what used to be considered domestic policy, and the distinction between domestic and foreign issues becomes blurred. These issues are considered in several government departments (not just foreign offices), and at several levels. Inadequate policy coordination on these issues involves significant costs. Different issues generate different coalitions, both within governments and across them, and involve different degrees of conflict. Politics does not stop at the waters' edge.

3   Military force is not used by governments toward other governments within the region, or on the issues, when complex interdependence prevails. It may, however, be important in these governments' relations with governments outside that region, or on other issues. Military force could, for instance, be irrelevant to resolving disagreements on economic issues among members of an alliance, yet at the same time be very important for that alliance's political and military relations with a rival bloc. For the former relationships this condition of complex interdependence would be met; for the latter, it would not.

Traditional theories of international politics implicitly or explicitly deny the accuracy of these three assumptions. Traditionalists are therefore tempted also to deny the relevance of criticisms based on the complex interdependence ideal type. We believe, however, that our three conditions are fairly well approximated on some global issues of economic and ecological interdependence and that they come close to characterizing the entire relationship between some countries. One of our purposes here is to prove that contention and to try to convince you to take these criticisms of traditional assumptions seriously.

Multiple channels

A visit to any major airport is a dramatic way to confirm the existence of multiple channels of contact among advanced industrial countries; there is a voluminous literature to prove it. Bureaucrats from different countries deal directly with one another at meetings and on the telephone as well as in writing. Similarly, nongovernmental elites frequently get together in the normal course of business, in organizations such as the Trilateral Commission, and in conferences sponsored by private foundations.

In addition, multinational firms and banks affect both domestic and interstate relations. The limits on private firms, or the closeness of ties between government and business, vary considerably from one society to another; but the participation of large and dynamic organizations, not controlled entirely by governments, has become a normal part of foreign as well as domestic relations

These actors are important not only because of their activities in pursuit of their own interests, but also because they act as transmission belts, making government policies in various countries more sensitive to one another. As the scope of governments' domestic activities has broadened, and as corporations, banks, and (to a lesser extent) trade unions have made decisions that transcend national boundaries, the domestic policies of different countries impinge on one another more and more. Transnational communications reinforce these effects. Thus, foreign economic policies touch more domestic economic activity than in the past, blurring the lines between domestic and foreign policy and increasing the number of issues relevant to foreign policy. Parallel developments in issues of environmental regulation and control over technology reinforce this trend.

Absence of hierarchy among issues

Foreign affairs agendas – that is, sets of issues relevant to foreign policy with which governments are concerned – have become larger and more diverse. No longer can all issues be subordinated to military security. As Secretary of State Kissinger described the situation in 1975:

> progress in dealing with the traditional agenda is no longer enough. A new and unprecedented kind of issue has emerged. The problems of energy, resources, environment, population, the uses of space and the seas now rank with questions of military security, ideology and territorial rivalry which have traditionally made up the diplomatic agenda.

Kissinger's list, which could be expanded, illustrates how governments' policies, even those previously considered merely domestic, impinge on one another. The extensive consultative arrangements developed by the OECD, as well as the GATT, IMF, and the European Community, indicate how characteristic the overlap of domestic and foreign policy is among developed pluralist countries. The organization within nine major departments of the United States government (Agriculture,

Commerce, Defense, Health, Education and Welfare, Interior, Justice, Labor, State, and Treasury) and many other agencies reflects their extensive international commitments. The multiple, overlapping issues that result make a nightmare of governmental organization.

When there are multiple issues on the agenda, many of which threaten the interests of domestic groups but do not clearly threaten the nation as a whole, the problems of formulating a coherent and consistent foreign policy increase. In 1975 energy was a foreign policy problem, but specific remedies, such as a tax on gasoline and automobiles, involved domestic legislation opposed by auto workers and companies alike. As one commentator observed, "virtually every time Congress has set a national policy that changed the way people live . . . the action came after a consensus had developed, bit by bit, over the years, that a problem existed and that there was one best way to solve it." Opportunities for delay, for special protection, for inconsistency and incoherence abound when international politics requires aligning the domestic policies of pluralist democratic countries.

Minor role of military force

Political scientists have traditionally emphasized the role of military force in international politics. Force dominates other means of power: *if* there are no constraints on one's choice of instruments (a hypothetical situation that has only been approximated in the two world wars), the state with superior military force will prevail. If the security dilemma for all states were extremely acute, military force, supported by economic and other resources, would clearly be the dominant source of power. Survival is the primary goal of all states, and in the worst situations, force is ultimately necessary to guarantee survival. Thus military force is always a central component of national power.

Yet particularly among industrialized, pluralist countries, the perceived margin of safety has widened: fears of attack in general have declined, and fears of attacks *by one another* are virtually nonexistent. France has abandoned the *tous azimuts* (defense in all directions) strategy that President de Gaulle advocated (it was not taken entirely seriously even at the time). Canada's last war plans for fighting the United States were abandoned half a century ago. Britain and Germany no longer feel threatened by each other. Intense relationships of mutual influence exist between these countries, but in most of them force is irrelevant or unimportant as an instrument of policy.

Moreover, force is often not an appropriate way of achieving other goals (such as economic and ecological welfare) that are becoming more important. It is not impossible to imagine dramatic conflict or revolutionary change in which the use or threat of military force over an economic issue or among advanced industrial countries might become plausible. Then realist assumptions would again be a reliable guide to events. But in most situations, the effects of military force are both costly and uncertain.

Even when the direct use of force is barred among a group of countries, however, military power can still be used politically. Each superpower continues to use the threat of force to deter attacks by other superpowers on itself or its allies; its deterrence ability thus serves an indirect, protective role, which it can use in bargaining on other issues with its allies. This bargaining tool is particularly important for the United States, whose allies are concerned about potential Soviet threats and which has fewer other means of influence over its allies than does the Soviet Union over its Eastern European partners. The United States has, accordingly, taken advantage of the Europeans' (particularly the Germans') desire for its protection and linked the issue of troop levels in Europe to trade and monetary negotiations. Thus, although the first-order effect of deterrent force is essentially negative – to deny effective offensive power to a superpower opponent – a state can use that force positively – to gain political influence.

Thus, even for countries whose relations approximate complex interdependence, two serious qualifications remain: (1) drastic social and political change could cause force again to become an important direct instrument of policy; and (2) even when elites' interests are complementary, a country that uses military force to protect another may have significant political influence over the other country.

In North–South relations, or relations among Third World countries, as well as in East–West relations, force is often important. Military power helps the Soviet Union to dominate Eastern Europe economically as well as politically. The threat of open or covert American military intervention has helped to limit revolutionary changes in the Caribbean, especially in Guatemala in 1954 and in the Dominican Republic in 1965. Secretary of State Kissinger, in January 1975, issued a veiled warning to members of the Organization of Petroleum Exporting Countries (OPEC) that the United States might use force against them "where there is some actual strangulation of the industrialized world."

Even in these rather conflictual situations, however, the recourse to force seems less likely now than at most times during the century before 1945. The destructiveness of nuclear weapons makes any attack against a nuclear power dangerous. Nuclear weapons are mostly used as a deterrent. Threats of nuclear action against much weaker countries may occasionally be efficacious, but they are equally or more likely to solidify relations between one's adversaries. The limited usefulness of conventional force to control socially mobilized populations has been shown by the United States' failure in Vietnam as well as by the rapid decline of colonialism in Africa. Furthermore, employing force on one issue against an independent state with which one has a variety of relationships is likely to rupture mutually profitable relations on other issues. In other words, the use of force often has costly effects on nonsecurity goals. And finally, in Western democracies, popular opposition to prolonged military conflicts is very high.

It is clear that these constraints bear unequally on various countries, or on the same countries in different situations. Risks of nuclear escalation affect everyone, but domestic opinion is far less constraining for communist states, or for authoritarian regional powers, than for the United States, Europe, or Japan. Even authoritarian countries may be reluctant to use force to obtain economic objectives when such use might be ineffective and disrupt other relationships. Both the difficulty of controlling socially mobilized populations with foreign troops and the changing technology of weaponry may actually enhance the ability of certain countries, or nonstate groups, to use terrorism as a political weapon without effective fear of reprisal.

The fact that the changing role of force has uneven effects does not make the change less important, but it does make matters more complex. This complexity is compounded by differences in the usability of force among issue areas. When an issue arouses little interest or passion, force may be unthinkable. In such instances, complex interdependence may be a valuable concept for analyzing the political process. But if that issue becomes a matter of life and death – as some people thought oil might become – the use or threat of force could become decisive again. Realist assumptions would then be more relevant. [. . .]

The Political Processes of Complex Interdependence

Role of international organizations

Finally, the existence of multiple channels leads one to predict a different and significant role for international organizations in world politics. Realists in the tradition of Hans J. Morgenthau have portrayed a world in which states, acting from self-interest, struggle for "power and peace." Security issues are dominant; war threatens. In such a world, one may assume that international institutions will have a minor role, limited by the rare congruence of such interests. International organizations are then clearly peripheral to world politics. But in a world of multiple issues imperfectly linked, in which coalitions are formed transnationally and transgovernmentally, the potential role of international institutions in political bargaining is greatly increased. In particular, they help set the international agenda, and act as catalysts for coalition-formation and as arenas for political initiatives and linkage by weak states.

Governments must organize themselves to cope with the flow of business generated by international organizations. By defining the salient issues, and deciding which issues can be grouped together, organizations may help to determine governmental priorities and the nature of interdepartmental committees and other arrangements within governments. The 1972 Stockholm Environment Conference strengthened the position of environmental agencies in various governments. The 1974 World Food Conference focused the attention of important parts of the United States government on prevention of food shortages. The September 1975 United Nations special session on proposals for a New International Economic Order generated an intragovernmental debate about policies toward the Third World in general. The International Monetary Fund and the General Agreement on Tariffs and Trade have focused governmental activity on money and trade instead of on private direct investment, which has no comparable international organization.

By bringing officials together, international organizations help to activate potential coalitions in world politics. It is quite obvious that international organizations have been very important in bringing together representatives of less developed countries, most of which do not maintain embassies in one another's capitals. Third World strategies of solidarity among poor countries have been developed in and for a series of international conferences, mostly under the auspices of the United Nations. International organizations also allow agencies of governments, which might not otherwise come into contact, to turn potential or tacit coalitions into explicit transgovernmental coalitions characterized by direct communications. In some cases, international secretariats deliberately promote this process by forming coalitions with groups of governments, or with units of governments, as well as with nongovernmental organizations having similar interests.

International organizations are frequently congenial institutions for weak states. The one-state-one-vote norm of the United Nations system favors coalitions of the small and powerless. Secretariats are often responsive to Third World demands. Furthermore, the substantive norms of most international organizations, as they have developed over the years, stress social and economic equity as well as the equality of states. Past resolutions expressing Third World positions, sometimes agreed to

Table 13.1 Political processes under conditions of realism and complex interdependence

	Realism	*Complex interdependence*
Goals of actors	Military security will be the dominant goal.	Goals of states will vary by issue area. Transgovernmental politics will make goals difficult to define. Transnational actors will pursue their own goals.
Instruments of state policy	Military force will be most effective, although economic and other instruments will also be used.	Power resources specific to issue areas will be most relevant. Manipulation of interdependence, international organizations, and transnational actors will be major instruments.
Agenda formation	Potential shifts in the balance of power and security threats will set the agenda in high politics and will strongly influence other agendas.	Agenda will be affected by changes in the distribution of power resources within issue areas; the status of international regimes; changes in the importance of transnational actors; linkages from other issues and politicization as a result of rising sensitivity interdependence.
Linkages of issues	Linkages will reduce differences in outcomes among issue areas and reinforce international hierarchy.	Linkages by strong states will be more difficult to make since force will be ineffective. Linkages by weak states through international organizations will erode rather than reinforce hierarchy.
Roles of international organizations	Roles are minor, limited by state power and the importance of military force.	Organizations will set agendas, induce coalition-formation, and act as arenas for political action by weak states. Ability to choose the organizational forum for an issue and to mobilize votes will be an important political resource.

with reservations by industrialized countries, are used to legitimize other demands. These agreements are rarely binding, but up to a point the norms of the institution make opposition look more harshly self-interested and less defensible.

International organizations also allow small and weak states to pursue linkage strategies. In the discussions on a New International Economic Order, Third World states insisted on linking oil price and availability to other questions on which they had traditionally been unable to achieve their objectives. Small and weak states have also followed a strategy of linkage in the series of Law of the Sea conferences sponsored by the United Nations.

Complex interdependence therefore yields different political patterns than does the realist conception of the world. (Table 13.1 summarizes these differences.) Thus, one would expect traditional theories to fail to explain international regime change in situations of complex interdependence. But, for a situation that approximates realist conditions, traditional theories should be appropriate.

14 World Society and the Nation-State

John W. Meyer, John Boli, George M. Thomas, and Francisco O. Ramirez

This essay reviews arguments and evidence concerning the following proposition: *Many features of the contemporary nation-state derive from worldwide models constructed and propagated through global cultural and associational processes.* These models and the purposes they reflect (e.g., equality, socioeconomic progress, human development) are highly rationalized, articulated, and often surprisingly consensual. Worldwide models define and legitimate agendas for local action, shaping the structures and policies of nation-states and other national and local actors in virtually all of the domains of rationalized social life – business, politics, education, medicine, science, even the family and religion. The institutionalization of world models helps explain many puzzling features of contemporary national societies, such as structural isomorphism in the face of enormous differences in resources and traditions, ritualized and rather loosely coupled organizational efforts, and elaborate structuration to serve purposes that are largely of exogenous origins. World models have long been in operation as shapers of states and societies, but they have become especially important in the postwar era as the cultural and organizational development of world society has intensified at an unprecedented rate.

The operation of world society through peculiarly cultural and associational processes depends heavily on its statelessness. The almost feudal character of parcelized legal-rational sovereignty in the world has the seemingly paradoxical result of diminishing the causal importance of the organized hierarchies of power and interests celebrated in most "realist" social scientific theories. The statelessness of world society also explains, in good measure, the lack of attention of the social sciences to the coherence and impact of world society's cultural and associational properties. Despite Tocqueville's well-known analysis of the importance of cultural and associational life in the nearly stateless American society of the 1830s, the social sciences are more than a little reluctant to acknowledge patterns of influence and conformity that cannot be explained solely as matters of power relations or functional rationality. This reluctance is most acute with respect to global development. Our effort here represents, we hope, a partial corrective for it.

We are trying to account for a world whose societies, organized as nation-states, are structurally similar in many unexpected dimensions and change in unexpectedly similar ways. A hypothetical example may be useful to illustrate our arguments, and we shall carry the example throughout the essay. If an unknown society were "discovered" on a previously unknown island, it is clear that many changes would occur.

Original publication details: Meyer, John W., John Boli, George M. Thomas, and Francisco O. Ramirez, "World Society and the Nation-State," *American Journal of Sociology*, 1997.

A government would soon form, looking something like a modern state with many of the usual ministries and agencies. Official recognition by other states and admission to the United Nations would ensue. The society would be analyzed as an economy, with standard types of data, organizations, and policies for domestic and international transactions. Its people would be formally reorganized as citizens with many familiar rights, while certain categories of citizens – children, the elderly, the poor – would be granted special protection. Standard forms of discrimination, especially ethnic and gender based, would be discovered and decried. The population would be counted and classified in ways specified by world census models. Modern educational, medical, scientific, and family law institutions would be developed. All this would happen more rapidly, and with greater penetration to the level of daily life, in the present day than at any earlier time because world models applicable to the island society are more highly codified and publicized than ever before. Moreover, world-society organizations devoted to educating and advising the islanders about the models' importance and utility are more numerous and active than ever.

What would be unlikely to happen is also clear. Theological disputes about whether the newly discovered *Indios* had souls or were part of the general human moral order would be rare. There would be little by way of an imperial rush to colonize the island. Few would argue that the natives needed only modest citizenship or human rights or that they would best be educated by but a few years of vocational training.

Thus, without knowing anything about the history, culture, practices, or traditions that obtained in this previously unknown society, we could forecast many changes that, upon "discovery," would descend on the island under the general rubric of "development." Our forecast would be imprecise because of the complexity of the interplay among various world models and local traditions, but the likely range of outcomes would be quite limited. We can identify the range of possibilities by using the institutionalist theoretical perspective underlying the analysis in this essay to interpret what has already happened to practically all of the societies of the world after their discovery and incorporation into world society. [. . .]

Explanatory Models

Most analyses see nation-states as collective actors – as products of their own histories and internal forces. Figure 14.1 depicts such conventional models. We emphasize instead models of the sort depicted in figure 14.2.

Figure 14.2 presents the view that nation-states are more or less exogenously constructed entities – the many individuals both inside and outside the state who engage in state formation and policy formulation are enactors of scripts rather more than they are self-directed actors. The social psychology at work here is that of Goffman or Snow, emphasizing dramaturgical and symbolic processes in place of the hard-boiled calculation of interests assumed by rationalistic actor-centric approaches.

We have deliberately oversimplified figure 14.2 because the proposition we are examining focuses on the enactment dimension of world-societal development. Of course, states, organizations, and individuals also contribute to the content and structure of world culture, and much world-cultural change and elaboration occur within transnational organizations and associations independent of lower-level units. A more complete figure would depict recursive processes among the constituent parts of world society, but here we concentrate on enactment processes.

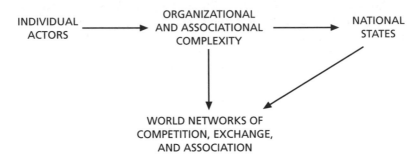

Figure 14.1   The world as aggregated action

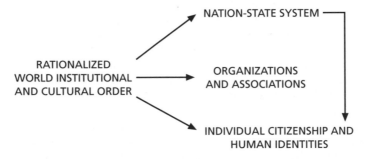

Figure 14.2   The world as enactment of culture

The exogenous cultural construction of the nation-state model makes it easy and "natural" for standard sociopolitical forms to arise in our island society. Models and measures of such national goals as economic progress and social justice are readily available and morally compelling. Also available are model social problems, defined as the failure to realize these goals, that make it easy to identify and decry such failures as inefficient production methods or violations of rights. Alongside these are prescriptions about standardized social actors and policies that are to be engaged in the effort to resolve these newly recognized problems. All this is widely known and ready for implementation. [. . .]

Isomorphism and Isomorphic Change

Given other perspectives' emphases on the heterogeneity of economic and political resources (realist theories) or on local cultural origins (microphenomenological theories), most lines of thought anticipate striking diversity in political units around the world and in these units' trajectories of change. Our argument accounts for the similarities researchers often are surprised to find. It explains why our island society, despite all the possible configurations of local economic forces, power relationships, and forms of traditional culture it might contain, would promptly take on standardized forms and soon appear to be similar to a hundred other nation-states around the world.

Take the example of women in higher education. Microrealist or functional actor-centric models suggest that female enrollments in universities would increase in developed economies much more than elsewhere. Macrorealist arguments imply that female enrollments would expand in the core much more than the periphery, while microphenomenological arguments point to rising female enrollments in Western but not Islamic countries. However, female enrollments have expanded rapidly everywhere, and in about the same time period – a period in which world societal discourse has emphasized female equality. This finding makes sense only if common world forces are at work.

Isomorphic developments leading to the same conclusion are reported in studies of many other nation-state features: constitutional forms emphasizing both state power and individual rights, mass schooling systems organized around a fairly standard curriculum, rationalized economic and demographic record keeping and data systems, antinatalist population control policies intended to enhance national development, formally equalized female status and rights, expanded human rights in general, expansive environmental policies, development-oriented economic policy, universalistic welfare systems, standard definitions of disease and health care, and even some basic demographic variables. Theories reasoning from the obviously large differences among national economies and cultural traditions have great difficulty accounting for these observed isomorphisms, but they are sensible outcomes if nation-states are enactments of the world cultural order. [. . .]

Processes of World Society's Impact on Nation-States

So far we have argued that the observable isomorphism among nation-states supports our proposition that these entities derive from models embedded in an overarching world culture. What processes in world society construct and shape these "actors" to produce such isomorphism? The usual approach to answering this question would seek to identify mechanisms whereby actors rationally pursuing their interests make similar choices and decisions. This approach implicitly assumes that actor definitions and interests are largely fixed and independent of culture. We find it more useful and revealing to focus on processes that produce or reconstruct the actors themselves. We identify three processes by which world-societal elements authorize and fashion national states: the construction of identity and purpose, systemic maintenance of actor identity, and legitimation of the actorhood of such subnational units as individuals and organized interests.

Construction of nation-state identity and purpose

World society contains much cultural material authoritatively defining the nation-state as the preferred form of sovereign, responsible actor. The external recognition and construction of sovereign statehood has been a crucial dimension of the Western system for centuries, with new claimants especially dependent on obtaining formal recognition from dominant powers. With the anticolonial and self-determination movements of the twentieth century, all sorts of collectivities have learned to organize their claims around a nation-state identity, and the consolidation of the United Nations system has provided a central forum for identity recognition that diminishes the importance of major states. Entry into the system occurs, essentially, via application forms (to the United Nations and other world bodies) on which the applicant must demonstrate appropriately formulated assertions about sovereignty and control over population and territory, along with appropriate aims and purposes.

More than 130 new nation-state entities have formed since 1945. They consistently proclaim, both internally and externally, their conformity to worldwide models of national identity and state structure. So, too, would our island society. But older states, too, have learned to adapt to changes in these models. Thus, through both selection and adaptation, the system has expanded to something close to universality of the nation-state form. Realist theories, grounding their analyses in each country's particular resources and history, would predict a much wider variety of forms, including the retention of older statuses such as formal dependency or indirect incorporation of small or weak entities.

World-cultural models of sovereign identity take concrete form in particular state structures, programs, and policies. As described above, worldwide models of the rationalized nation-state actor define appropriate constitutions, goals, data systems, organization charts, ministry structures, and policies. Models also specify standard forms for the cultural depiction of national identity. Methods of constructing national culture through traditions, museums, tourism, and national intellectual culture are highly stylized. Nation-states are theorized or imagined communities drawing on models that are lodged at the world level.

Often, copying world models or conventions amounts to simple mimesis that has more to do with knowing how to fill in forms than with managing substantive problems. For instance, to compile comparable educational enrollment data in the 1950s, UNESCO statisticians chose to report enrollments for a six-year primary level and three-year junior and senior secondary levels. In ensuing decades, many countries structured their mass schooling systems around this six-year/three-year/three-year model, generally without investigating whether it would best meet any of the presumed purposes of schooling.

Strang shows the extraordinary impact of the legitimized identity system on the survival and stability of states. Throughout modern history, dependent territories have moved to sovereign statehood at a steadily increasing rate that accelerated rapidly in the postwar period. Once sovereign, countries almost never revert to dependence. Even the breakup of the Soviet Union produced not dependent territories but formally sovereign nation-states, unprepared as some of the former republics were for this status. Thus, it is highly unlikely that our island society would be incorporated as a dependent territory of an extant nation-state; this would be too great a violation of the legitimized right to self-determination. Moreover, establishing the island society's sovereign status in the international system would stabilize its new state, though it would not preclude, and might even increase, instability in the state's government.

Orientation to the identity and purposes of the nation-state model increases the rate at which countries adopt other prescribed institutions of modernity. Having committed themselves to the identity of the rationalizing state, appropriate policies follow – policies for national development, individual citizenship and rights, environmental management, foreign relations. These policies are depicted as if they were autonomous decisions because nation-states are defined as sovereign, responsible, and essentially autonomous actors. Taking into account the larger culture in which states are embedded, however, the policies look more like enactments of conventionalized scripts. Even if a state proclaims its opposition to the dominant world identity models, it will nevertheless pursue many purposes within this model. It will develop bureaucratic authority and attempt to build many modern institutions, ranging from a central bank to an educational system. It will thereby find itself modifying its traditions in the direction of world-cultural forms.

Systemic maintenance of nation-state actor identity

If a specific nation-state is unable to put proper policies in place (because of costs, incompetence, or resistance), world-society structures will provide help. This process operates more through authoritative external support for the legitimate purposes of states than through authoritarian imposition by dominant powers or interests. For example, world organizations and professionalized ideologies actively encourage countries to adopt population control policies that are justified not as good for the world as a whole but as necessary for national development. National science policies are also promulgated as crucial to national development; before this link was theorized, UNESCO efforts to encourage countries to promote science failed to diffuse. As this example illustrates, international organizations often posture as objective disinterested others who help nation-states pursue their exogenously derived goals.

Resistance to world models is difficult because nation-states are formally committed, as a matter of identity, to such self-evident goals as socioeconomic development, citizen rights, individual self-development, and civil international relations. If a particular regime rhetorically resists world models, local actors can rely on legitimacy myths (democracy, freedom, equality) and the ready support of activist external groups to oppose the regime. Nation-state "choices" are thus less likely to conflict with world-cultural prescriptions than realist or microphenomenological theories anticipate because both nation-state choices and world pressures derive from the same overarching institutions.

Legitimation of subnational actors and practices

World-cultural principles license the nation-state not only as a managing central authority but also as an identity-supplying nation. Individual citizenship and the sovereignty of the people are basic tenets of nationhood. So too are the legitimacy and presumed functional necessity of much domestic organizational structure, ranging from financial market structures to organizations promoting individual and collective rights (of labor, ethnic groups, women, and so on). World-society ideology thus directly licenses a variety of organized interests and functions. Moreover, in pursuing their externally legitimated identities and purposes by creating agencies and programs, nation-states also promote the domestic actors involved. Programs and their associated accounting systems increase the number and density of types of actors, as groups come forward to claim newly reified identities and the resources allocated to them.

A good example is the rise of world discourse legitimating the human rights of gays and lesbians, which has produced both national policy changes and the mobilization of actors claiming these rights. As nation-states adopt policies embodying the appropriate principles, they institutionalize the identity and political presence of these groups. Of course, all these "internally" generated changes are infused with world-cultural conceptions of the properly behaving nation-state.

Hence, if a nation-state neglects to adopt world-approved policies, domestic elements will try to carry out or enforce conformity. General world pressures favoring environmentalism, for example, have led many states to establish environmental protection agencies, which foster the growth of environmental engineering firms, activist groups, and planning agencies. Where the state has not adopted the appropriate policies, such local units and actors as cities, schools, scout troops, and religious groups are likely to practice environmentalism and call for national action. Thus, world culture influences nation-states not only at their centers, or only in symbolic ways, but also through direct connections between local actors and world culture. Such connections produce many axes of mobilization for the implementation of world-cultural principles and help account for similarities in mobilization agendas and strategies in highly disparate countries.

Explicit rejection of world-cultural principles sometimes occurs, particularly by nationalist or religious movements whose purported opposition to modernity is seen as a threat to geopolitical stability. While the threat is real enough, the analysis is mistaken because it greatly underestimates the extent to which such movements conform to rationalized models of societal order and purpose. These movements mobilize around principles inscribed in world-cultural scripts, derive their organizing capacity from the legitimacy of these scripts, and edit their supposedly primordial claims to maximize this legitimacy. By and large, they seek an idealized modern community undergoing broad-based social development where citizens (of the right sort) can fully exercise their abstract rights. While they violate some central elements of world-cultural ideology, they nonetheless rely heavily on other elements. For example, religious "fundamentalists" may reject the extreme naturalism of modernity by making individuals accountable to an unchallengeable god, but they nevertheless exhort their people to embrace such key world-cultural elements as nation building, mass schooling, rationalized health care, and professionalization. They also are apt to reformulate their religious doctrine in accordance with typical modern conceptions of rational-moral discipline. In general, nationalist and religious movements intensify isomorphism more than they resist it. [. . .]

Conclusion

A considerable body of evidence supports our proposition that world-society models shape nation-state identities, structures, and behavior via worldwide cultural and associational processes. Carried by rationalized others whose scientific and professional authority often exceeds their power and resources, world culture celebrates, expands, and standardizes strong but culturally somewhat tamed national actors. The result is nation-states that are more isomorphic than most theories would predict and change more uniformly than is commonly recognized. As creatures of exogenous world culture, states are ritualized actors marked by extensive internal decoupling and a good deal more structuration than would occur if they were responsive only to local cultural, functional, or power processes.

As the Western world expanded in earlier centuries to dominate and incorporate societies in the larger world, the penetration of a universalized culture proceeded hesitantly. Westerners could imagine that the locals did not have souls, were members of a different species, and could reasonably be enslaved or exploited. Inhabiting a different moral and natural universe, non-Western societies were occasionally celebrated for their noble savagery but more often cast as inferior groups unsuited for true civilization. Westerners promoted religious conversion by somewhat parochial and inconsistent means, but broader incorporation was ruled out on all sorts of grounds. Education and literacy were sometimes prohibited, rarely encouraged, and never generally provided, for the natives were ineducable or prone to rebellion. Rationalized social, political, and economic development (e.g., the state, democracy, urban factory production, modern family law) was inappropriate, even unthinkable. Furthermore, the locals often strongly resisted incorporation by the West. Even Japan maintained strong boundaries against many aspects of modernity until the end of World War II, and Chinese policy continues a long pattern of resistance to external "aid."

The world, however, is greatly changed. Our island society would obviously become a candidate for full membership in the world community of nations and individuals. Human rights, state-protected citizen rights, and democratic forms would become natural entitlements. An economy would emerge, defined and measured in rationalized terms and oriented to growth under state regulation. A formal national polity would be essential, including a constitution, citizenship laws, educational structures, and open forms of participation and communication. The whole apparatus of rationalized modernity would be mobilized as necessary and applicable; internal and external resistance would be stigmatized as reactionary unless it was couched in universalistic terms. Allowing the islanders to remain imprisoned in their society, under the authority of their old gods and chiefs and entrapped in primitive economic technologies, would be unfair and discriminatory, even though the passing of their traditional society would also occasion nostalgia and regret.

Prevailing social theories account poorly for these changes. Given a dynamic sociocultural system, realist models can account for a world of economic and political absorption, inequality, and domination. They do not well explain a world of formally equal, autonomous, and expansive nation-state actors. Microcultural or phenomenological lines of argument can account for diversity and resistance to homogenization, not a world in which national states, subject to only modest coercion or control, adopt standard identities and structural forms.

We argue for the utility of recognizing that rationalized modernity is a universalistic and inordinately successful form of the earlier Western religious and post-religious system. As a number of commentators have noted, in our time the religious elites of Western Christendom have given up on the belief that there is no salvation outside the church. That postulate has been replaced by the belief among almost all elites that salvation lies in rationalized structures grounded in scientific and technical knowledge – states, schools, firms, voluntary associations, and the like. The new religious elites are the professionals, researchers, scientists, and intellectuals who write secularized and unconditionally universalistic versions of the salvation story, along with the managers, legislators, and policymakers who believe the story fervently and pursue it relentlessly. This belief is worldwide and structures the organization of social life almost everywhere.

The colossal disaster of World War II may have been a key factor in the rise of global models of nationally organized progress and justice, and the Cold War may well have intensified the forces pushing human development to the global level. If the present configuration of lowered systemic (if not local) tensions persists, perhaps both the consensuality of the models and their impact on nation-states will decline. On the other hand, the models' rationalized definitions of progress and justice (across an ever broadening front) are rooted in universalistic scientific and professional definitions that have reached a level of deep global institutionalization. These definitions produce a great deal of conflict with regard to their content and application, but their authority is likely to prove quite durable.

Many observers anticipate a variety of failures of world society, citing instances of gross violations of world-cultural principles (e.g., in Bosnia), stagnant development (e.g., in Africa), and evasion of proper responsibility (in many places). In our view, the growing list of perceived "social problems" in the world indicates not the weakness of world-cultural institutions but their strength. Events like political torture, waste dumping, or corruption, which not so long ago were either overlooked entirely or considered routine, local, specific aberrations or tragedies, are now of world-societal significance. They violate strong expectations regarding global integration and propriety and can easily evoke world-societal reactions seeking to put things right. A world with so many widely discussed social problems is a world of Durkheimian and Simmelian integration, however much it may also seem driven by disintegrative tendencies.

15 Humanity, Globalization, and Worldwide Religious Resurgence

Roland Robertson and JoAnn Chirico

We claim that serious social-scientific discussion of religious belief and practice in a global perspective must involve a basic concern with the crystallization of the modern global circumstances. More specifically, if the *Problemstellung* consists in accounting for the near-worldwide resurgence of religious fundamentalism, the extensive development of new religious movements (including liberational-theological movements within conventional churches and denominations), and the proliferation and sharpening of church–state tensions across much of the modern world, we must at least produce a theory sketch of the contours of and processes at work in respect of the globe as a sociocultural phenomenon. [. . .]

We will argue that, given the existence of a global complex which displays both bounded societal units and a widespread sense of global continuity, a theory sketch of that complex requires the following *basic* components: (a) *individual national societies*; (b) *a system of national societies*; (c) *individual selves*; (d) a category to which selves belong – *man/woman* (i.e. *mankind*). We will further argue that, at a more refined level of analysis, *relationships between* these four components (six sets of relationships in all) may be used to characterize in minimal terms "the modern global circumstance." The notion which best captures this overall conceptual patterning is that of the global-human system as an historically emergent and mutable phenomenon.

A Preliminary Positioning of Religion in the Global System

The virtually worldwide eruption of religious and quasi-religious concerns and themes cannot be exhaustively comprehended in terms of focusing on what has been happening sociologically *within* societies. The societies which have been affected by upsurges of religious expression during the past two decades or so are too diverse for that approach to suffice – although undoubtedly a number of *clusters* of relatively similar societies (for example, those in the North Atlantic area) may be sufficiently similar in sociological and historical terms for us to get a significant explanatory leverage by comparing societies within a cluster. Generally speaking, however, the worldwideness of the religious upsurge demands that we consider the global circumstances in totality.

The only other alternative (not, incidentally, precluding the comparative, intra-societal, or the global approaches) is the *diffusionist* perspective. That has at least one serious disadvantage. This is centered on the fact that the nearly global upsurge

Original publication details: Robertson, Roland and JoAnn Chirico, "Humanity, Globalization, and Worldwide Religious Resurgence" from *Sociological Analysis*, Fall 1985.

in religion of the last fifteen-to-twenty years has involved a large variety of religious doctrines. More specifically, the global revival consists in large part of movements which are sometimes indifferent and frequently hostile to the fortunes of each other. This factor largely precludes explanatory tacks which emphasize the diffusion of ideas among those with *shared interests*. It makes the recent cross-societal religious revival sociologically unlike, for example, the very widespread student movement of the late 1960s. In the latter case – quite apart from intra-societal determinants – there was clearly a sense of an international (or a transnational) movement, with students in one society or a group of societies emulating and influencing those in another society or other societies on the basis of a perceived *shared* – or, at least, shareable – set of interests. That is not, however, to say that shared interests – ideal and/or material – are entirely absent on a cross-societal basis in the present global religious revival. In the case of liberation-theological movements we can see something approaching the circumstances of shared, religiously expressed interests – now that liberation theologies have appeared, often collaboratively, on a number of continents. Another, perhaps very significant, form of modern linkage across national boundaries in relation to the revival of orthodoxies and fundamentalisms is that involving some of the fundamentalist evangelicals in the USA, on the one hand, and politicoreligious militants in Israel, on the other. In this particular case, we have a cross-national amplification of otherwise divergent religious worldviews – the primary basis for the mutual support being the dispensationalist theology of pre-millennial evangelicalism (with its emphasis upon the eschatological significance of the imminent fulfillment of Jewish congregation in Israel), on the one hand, and a perceived Israeli need for politicoreligious support in the USA beyond the Jewish American community, on the other.

The global approach has the advantage of being able to take both intra-societal and diffusional factors into account and of incorporating them into a higher level analytic. [. . .]

Source and Structure of Humanitic Concern

In the present perspective modern "humanitic concern" can be traced empirically to two major sources. First, there are aspects of the operation of modern – particularly Western – societies which generate a form of transcendence of society at the level of individuals. *The combination* of alienation from the state and the state's increasing concern – what we call a quasi-religious concern – with "deep" features of life (the definition of life, the organization of death, the "quality of life," aging, the regulation of religion, and so on) increasingly leads to explicitness about the attributes and *raison d'être* of human life beyond the particularities of social classification, voluntary religious involvement, even societal membership. The resurgence of "fundamentalistic" promotion of particularistic ideologies and doctrines (local, ethnic national, civilizational and regional) does not by any means constitute counter-evidence. For, as we will argue more fully later, the recent globe-wide assertion of particularistic ideas is heavily contextualized by the phenomenon of increasing *globality*.

The second major source of humanitic concern has to do with the relations *between* societies. On the inter-societal front there has been, in recent years, a considerable relativization of the image of the good society. While a few scholars argued quite a long time ago that the notion of societal modernization must, in order for

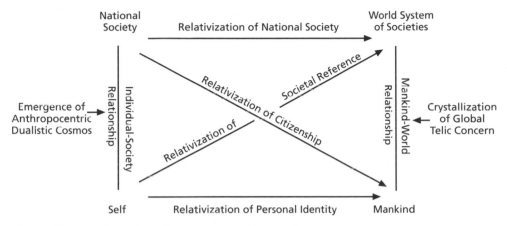

Figure 15.1 Trajectories of emergence of humanity

it to have any empirical purchase, involve a basically "relativistic" frame of reference, the fact remains that there is much to suggest that, until quite recently, the modern system of societies operated roughly in terms of two basic images of the good society – namely the liberal-democratic industrial society and the communistic industrial society. Moreover, even in that situation of two "northern" types of "good society" there was clearly considerable overlap. However, it became increasingly obvious during the 1970s that the situation of relatively stable and established images and directions of societal aspirations was rapidly breaking up. Now, in the mid-1980s it seems that there is global confusion about what constitutes the ideal-type of societal aspiration. If our diagnosis in this respect is cogent, it would inexorably follow – even without further empirical investigation – that there has to be "something" resembling what Parsons analytically pinpoints as telic concern of a trans-societal kind. In other words, in a situation in which there is very little stability or security in respect of what might be called model societies, then international discourse, including heavily politico-strategic discourse, often takes place in terms of ideas, however tacitly adhered to, concerning the ends of man.

We may now schematize our thinking, with particular – but not sole – reference to the emanation of humanitic concern in Western contexts. The most basic ingredient of that process is the linkage between a situation of "anthropocentric dualism," having to do with the relationship between individuals and societies, and a corresponding situation on a trans-societal scale. By anthropocentric dualism, we mean a human-centered world image involving a differentiation of life into two realms. On the one hand, there is the realm of *societal-systemic functionality*; on the other, there is the realm of individual and relational (if you will, life-world) *being*. As *anthropocentric*, this dualistic frame is pivoted upon *mankind*; it being an historical transformation of a theocentric dualism.

The linkages of which we have just spoken involve four processes of relativization, two having to do with the relativization of societies (trans-socialization) and two having to do with the relativization of persons, or selves (trans-personalization). By relativization we mean a process involving the placing of sociocultural or psychic entities in larger categorical contexts, such that the relativized entities are constrained to be more self-reflexive relative to other entities in the larger context (which does not mean that they will actually be "constructively" self-reflexive). The relativization of selves involves, along one dimension, the situating of selfhood in the more inclusive and fundamental frame of what it means to be of mankind; while the relativization of societies – along another, parallel dimension – involves the situating of concrete societies in the context of a world complex of societies – thus constraining particular societies to judge the extent to which they exemplify principles of "societal quality." These are the dominant processes of relativization. There branches from each a secondary process of relativization, one having to do with the relationship between concrete societies and the category of man, the other involving a connection between selves and the global complex of societies. [. . .]

Our major proposition at this point is that there is an intimate link between the development of what might be called asociality – the mode of individual, "mystical" concern with self – and the making available of individuals for concern with "man." In a sense this follows the line of argument of those who have spoken, in reference to the more "advanced" societies, of individuals growing out of the nation-state shell. On the other hand, our own contentions in this regard follow a Simmel–Durkheim line of reasoning. Galtung's argument rests on the detachment of the individual from national loyalty in trans- or cross-national mode, *via* ideologies of professionalism which are intolerant of national loyalties by virtue of cosmopolitanism and the universalism of technological-scientific values. This we find to be unpersuasive, certainly insufficient. The process of growing out of the (state-centered) society is a much more diffuse and "deep" process – having to do with a mixture of alienation from the state (and the economy) and a greater concern with selfhood in the mode of what is often called *psychological man*. The development of psychological man/woman at the same time raises issues concerning the phenomenal-categorical location of selves or persons. That process of locating tends in the direction of a concern with what it means to be human in the most general terms – hence our suggestion that what is primarily involved in this form of detachment from the state-centered society may be summarized under the conceptual rubric of *relativization of personal identity*. A significant aspect of the latter in broad, comparative-civilizational terms is that while we see the process as "Western-pulled," it is not confined to the "post-industrial" societies. The nature of the modern global system is such as to place constraints relevant to the process of relativization upon nearly all societies – hence, for example, the diagnosis of the intensification of narcissistic tendencies in *non*-Western contexts, as a response to industrialization in these contexts *relative to the global system*. In other words, although Third and Fourth World societies do have "problems" primarily centered upon incorporating individuals and primordial groups *into* the nation-state shell, the latter *diffusely* confronts the individual all over the contemporary world with at least some of the alienating characteristics of the modern Western model. This exacerbates the *other*-worldly mystical tendencies of some non-Western societies and makes the latter available as models for Western individuals, as exampled by the diffusion of non-Western religious ideas involving a monistic resistance to Western anthropocentric dualism. The upshot is a tendency toward a near-global conception of selfhood – or at least a thematization of potentially near-global scope of the latter issue.

The second *dominant* process – concerning the relativization of society – involves the thematization of such issues as: what *is* a society? what is the purpose of societies? what does "the good society" look like? In essence, this process of relativization – attendant upon the crystallization of a global system in which there appear to be no definite, or relatively permanent, models of "goodness" – involves the attenuation of historically taken-for-granted assumptions about society as a mode of coherence. As suggested previously, this questioning of society is at the core of the breakdown of the circumstance which prevailed up to the 1960s – namely the situation in which it was appropriate to talk of *modernization* as involving a rather definite trajectory, or a very small number of possible trajectories, of societal change. Increasingly during the 1970s modernization became relativized – to the point that by now the criteria of such are being thematized. By thematization in this respect we mean that rather than small clusters of societies being regarded as clearly *lead* societies or global epicenters there now obtains a situation in which the criteria for societal change themselves are matters of inter-societal, inter-continental, inter-civilizational, and inter-doctrinal interpretation and debate.

Each of our dominant processes has a secondary process. In the case of the process involving a shift along the axis self–mankind, we speak of the relativization of societal reference on the part of the individual. In the case of the shift involving relativization of society we speak of a secondary process having to do with a shift in the nature of "citizenly involvement." Let us consider relativization of societal reference first. In this respect detachment from society in the direction of the anthropic concern with the nature of man must also raise the question of the nature of orientation to the more concrete global system of inter-societal relationships. In other words, there arises the issue of the orientation on the part of individuals to societies other than their "own" and their participation – however *vicarious or empathic* – in the global complex of societies, which now becomes to all intents and purposes "the world" in the sense conveyed by theological traditions. In its extreme form, such relativization would involve looking at one's "own" society as *only* one among others, but at the same time retaining a sense of membership in one's "own" society.

The second branching process – relativization of citizenly involvement – has to do with what, in another context, has been called *tertiary mobilization*. Political scientists and political sociologists have tended to specify two phases of the process of political mobilization leading to the circumstance of citizenship inclusion. First, there is the phase of detachment from primordial loyalties of tribe, religion and so on – producing something like a loyalty to the political center. Second, there is a phase of secondary mobilization, involving the inclusion of individuals as citizens with respect to law, franchise and social security. (The second phase has often been studied as a series of subphases.) The analytical addition of a *third* phase of mobilization in an evolutionary perspective has to do with the process whereby citizenship is expanded so as to include both rights and duties developed in the second phase *and* a conception of the individual as human, with rights and needs (perhaps, ultimately, duties) which are not solely societal. Thus tertiary mobilization – the relativization of citizenly involvement – involves a realigning of the relationship between the concrete society and the individual in the form of an establishment of a new kind of differentiated attachment to man/woman. Here again our basic point of reference is the industrialized society. But we can also add that the process of political mobilization in other societies is certainly affected – in the sense that many individuals in those societies, for example Middle Eastern societies, are implicated in a globe–human context *at the same time as* they are oriented toward society-centered, primary or secondary processes of mobilization.

These analytical representations of trajectories of movement away from the historical circumstances of society-centered anthropocentric dualism are intended primarily, when taken as a schematic whole, to pinpoint significant aspects of the drift toward humanitic concern in the modern world. The overall scheme characterizes an evolutionary step beyond the usual type of evolutionary stage relating to society and relationships between individuals and societies. In "ideal-typical" form we have depicted a circumstance involving a set of processes of differentiation emanating from the anthropocentric–dualistic, individual–society context. It must be very strongly emphasized, however, that the crystallization of a new man–globe form of dualism does not entail elimination of that context. Rather, the individual–society relationship is contextualized by a much broader frame of humanitic concern. Thus, in highly ideal-typical terms, the two are coordinated in such a way that persons are both autonomous and yet implicated in no less than three other sets of circumstances, as are societies. Finally, it must be very strongly emphasized that, even though for *present* purposes we have schematically indicated processes of relativization in terms of one-way arrows, the implication of our discussion is that the global–human circumstance *per se* can be most fruitfully represented analytically in terms of an entire series of *two*-way arrows. [. . .]

The globalization process itself raises religious and quasi-religious questions. Theodical and eschatological questions – or successor questions to old theodical and eschatological queries – are high on the agenda of global discourse. Religion is centered in the process of globalization by virtue of both the religious or quasi-religious matters raised as a result of universalistic tendencies involving mankind and relations between societies *and* by the particularizing responses to the universalistic tendencies. In the latter regard the internal-societal development of fundamentalisms is pivoted upon the perceived need for societal integrity. The extent to which would-be or actual religiopolitical elites are *atavistic* in the sense of being reactionary relative to the globalization process is a matter in need of case-by-case discussion. Some fundamentalist movements which have recently staked their claims to interpret and control the sociocultural identities of their respective societies can, indeed, be viewed as reactionary – as sites for the expression of discontents – relative to the globalization process. At the opposite end of the spectrum, other fundamentalist movements may be viewed as merely offering – if often very militantly – new modes of particularistic societal identity relative to global universalism in more-or-less "concultural," relatively pluralistic mode.

There are many other aspects of the ideas which we have presented here which have a direct bearing on religion and religiosity across the modern world as well as upon arguments surrounding the secularization thesis. Our major goal here, however, has been to contribute to the task of seeing how religion may be discussed within the context of growing concern with the phenomenon of globality, which we see as a generalization and extension of the older *gemeinschaft–gesellschaft* problem. *Direct* discussion of globality and globalization is necessary before the distinctively religious aspects of such can be systematically analyzed. We should, however, emphasize in conclusion that we consider, and not only for the reasons already given, that globalization enhances, at least in the relatively short run, religion and religiosity.

16 Globalization as Hybridization

Jan Nederveen Pieterse

The most common interpretations of globalization are the ideas that the world is becoming more uniform and standardized, through a technological, commercial and cultural synchronization emanating from the West, and that globalization is tied up with modernity. These perspectives are interrelated, if only in that they are both variations on an underlying theme of globalization as Westernization. The former is critical in intent while the latter is ambiguous. My argument takes issue with both these interpretations as narrow assessments of globalization and instead argues for viewing globalization as a process of hybridization which gives rise to a global mélange.

Globalizations in the Plural

Globalization, according to Albrow, "refers to all those processes by which the peoples of the world are incorporated into a single world society, global society". Since these processes are plural we may as well conceive of globalizations in the plural. Thus in social science there are as many conceptualizations of globalization as there are disciplines. In economics, globalization refers to economic internationalization and the spread of capitalist market relations. "The global economy is the system generated by globalising production and global finance". In international relations, the focus is on the increasing density of interstate relations and the development of global politics. In sociology, the concern is with increasing world-wide social densities and the emergence of "world society". In cultural studies, the focus is on global communications and world-wide cultural standardization, as in Coca-Colonization and McDonaldization, and on postcolonial culture. In history, the concern is with conceptualizing "global history".

All these approaches and themes are relevant if we view globalization as a multidimensional process which, like all significant social processes, unfolds in multiple realms of existence simultaneously. Accordingly, globalization may be understood in terms of an open-ended synthesis of several disciplinary approaches. This extends beyond social science, for instance to ecological concerns, technology and agricultural techniques (for example, green revolution).

Another way to conceive of globalizations plural is that there are as many modes of globalization as there are globalizing agents and dynamics or impulses. Historically these range from long-distance cross-cultural trade, religious organizations and knowledge networks to contemporary multinational corporations, transnational banks, international institutions, technological exchange and transnational networks of social movements. We can further differentiate between globalization as policy

Original publication details: Nederveen Pieterse, Jan, "Globalization as Hybridization" from M. Featherstone et al. (eds.), *Global Modernities* (Sage Publications Ltd, London, 1995).

and project – as in the case of Amnesty International which is concerned with inter-nationalizing human rights standards – or as unintended consequence – as in the case of the "globalizing panic" of AIDS. *Globalism* is the policy of furthering or managing (a particular mode of) globalization. In political economy it refers to policies furthering or accommodating economic internationalization; or to the corporate globalism of transnational enterprises; and in foreign affairs, to the global stance in US foreign policy, in its initial post-war posture and its post Cold War stance.

These varied dimensions all point to the inherent fluidity, indeterminacy and open-endedness of globalizations. If this is the point of departure it becomes less obvious to think of globalizations in terms of standardization and less likely that globalizations can be one-directional processes, either structurally or culturally.

Globalization and Modernity

Modernity is a keynote in reflections on globalization in sociology. In several prominent conceptualizations, globalization is the corollary of modernity. It's not difficult to understand this trend. In conjunction with globalization, modernity provides a structure and periodization. In addition, this move reflects the general thematization of modernity in social science from Habermas to Berman. Together globalization and modernity make up a ready-made package. Ready-made because it closely resembles the earlier, well-established conceptualization of globalization: the Marxist theme of the spread of the world market. The timing and pace are the same in both interpretations: the process starts in the 1500s and experiences its high tide from the late nineteenth century. The structures are the same: the nation-state and individualization – vehicles of modernity or, in the Marxist paradigm, corollaries of the spread of the world market. In one conceptualization universalism refers to the logic of the market and the law of value, and in the other to modern values of achievement. World-system theory is the most well-known conceptualization of globalization in the Marxist lineage; its achievement has been to make "society" as the unit of analysis appear as a narrow focus, while on the other hand it has faithfully replicated the familiar constraints of Marxist determinism.

There are several problems associated with the modernity/globalization approach. In either conceptualization, whether centred on capitalism or modernity, globalization begins in and emanates from Europe and the West. In effect it is a theory of Westernization by another name, which replicates all the problems associated with Eurocentrism: a narrow window on the world, historically and culturally. With this agenda it should be called Westernization and not globalization. Another problem is that globalization theory turns into or becomes an annex of modernization theory. While modernization theory is a passed station in sociology and development theory, it is making a comeback under the name of globalization – the 1950s and 1960s revisited under a large global umbrella. Robertson takes issue with the prioritization of modernity, notably in Giddens' work. Robertson's approach to globalization is multidimensional with an emphasis on sociocultural processes. At the same time, his preoccupation with themes such as "global order" is, according to Arnason, "indicative of a Parsonian approach, transferred from an artificially isolated and unified society to the global condition". Neo-modernization theory and the contemporary re-thematization of modernity indicate the continuing appeal of modernization thinking, but the problems remain. [. . .]

Generally, questions of power are marginalized in both the capitalism and modernity perspectives. Another dimension which tends to be conspicuously absent from

Table 16.1   Timing of globalization

Author	Start	Theme
Marx	1500s	modern capitalism
Wallerstein	1500s	modern world-system
Robertson	1500s, 1870–1920s	multidimensional
Giddens	1800s	modernity
Tomlinson	1960s	cultural planetarization

modernity accounts is imperialism. Modernity accounts tend to be societally inward looking, in a rarefied sociological narrative, as if modernity precedes and conditions globalization, and not the other way round: globalization constituting one of the conditions for modernity. The implication of the modernity/globalization view is that the history of globalization begins with the history of the West. But is not precisely the point of globalization as a perspective that globalization begins with world history? The modernity/globalization view is not only geographically narrow (Westernization) but also historically shallow (1500 plus). The timeframe of some of the perspectives relevant to globalization is as shown in table 16.1.

Apparently the broad heading of globalization accommodates some very different views. The basic understanding is usually a neutral formulation, such as "Globalization can thus be defined as the intensification of worldwide social relations which link distant localities in such a way that local happenings are shaped by events occurring many miles away and vice versa". The "intensification of worldwide social relations" can be thought of as a long-term process which finds its beginnings in the first migrations of peoples and long-distance trade connections, and subsequently accelerates under particular conditions (the spread of technologies, religions, literacy, empires, capitalism). Or, it can be thought of as consisting only of the later stages of this process, from the time of the accelerating formation of global social relations, and as a specifically global momentum associated with particular conditions (the development of a world market, Western imperialism, modernity). It can be narrowed down further by regarding globalization as a particular epoch and formation – as in Tomlinson's view of globalization as the successor to imperialism (rather than imperialism being a mode of globalization), Jameson's view of the new cultural space created by late capitalism, and Harvey's argument where globalization is associated with the postmodern condition of time–space compression and flexible accumulation.

But, whichever the emphasis, globalization as the "intensification of worldwide social relations" presumes the prior existence of "worldwide social relations", so that globalization is the conceptualization of a *phase* following an existing condition of *globality* and part of an ongoing process of the formation of world-wide social relations. This recognition of historical depth brings globalization back to world history and beyond the radius of modernity/Westernization. [. . .]

Structural Hybridization

With respect to cultural forms, hybridization is defined as "the ways in which forms become separated from existing practices and recombine with new forms in new practices". This principle can be extended to structural forms of social organization.

It is by now a familiar argument that nation-state formation is an expression and function of globalization and not a process contrary to it. At the same time it is apparent that the present phase of globalization involves the relative weakening of nation-states – as in the weakening of the "national economy" in the context of economic globalism and, culturally, the decline of patriotism. But this too is not simply a one-directional process. Thus the migration movements which make up demographic globalization can engender absentee patriotism and long-distance nationalism, as in the political affinities of Irish, Jewish and Palestinian diasporas and émigré or exiled Sikhs in Toronto, Tamils in London, Kurds in Germany, Tibetans in India.

Globalization can mean the reinforcement of or go together with localism, as in "Think globally, act locally". This kind of tandem operation of local/global dynamics, global localization or *glocalization,* is at work in the case of minorities who appeal to transnational human rights standards beyond state authorities, or indigenous peoples who find support for local demands from transnational networks. The upsurge of ethnic identity politics and religious revival movements can also be viewed in the light of globalization. "Identity patterns are becoming more complex, as people assert local loyalties but want to share in global values and lifestyles". Particularity, notes Robertson, is a *global* value and what is taking place is a "universalization of particularism" or "the global valorization of particular identities".

Global dynamics such as the fluctuations of commodity prices on the world market can result in the reconstruction of ethnic identities, as occurred in Africa in the 1980s. State development policies can engender a backlash of ethnic movements. Thus, "globalisation can generate forces of both fragmentation and unification . . . globalisation can engender an awareness of political difference as much as an awareness of common identity; enhanced international communications can highlight conflicts of interest and ideology, and not merely remove obstacles to mutual understanding".

Globalization can mean the reinforcement of both supranational and sub-national regionalism. The European Union is a case in point. Formed in response to economic challenges from Japan and the United States, it represents more than the internal market and is in the process of becoming an administrative, legal, political and cultural formation, involving multiple Europes: the Europe of the nations, regions, "European civilization", Christianities, etc. The dialectics of unification mean, for instance, that constituencies in Northern Ireland can appeal to the European Court of Human Rights in Strasbourg on decisions of the British courts, or that Catalonia can outflank Madrid, and Brittany outmanoeuvre Paris by appealing to Brussels or by establishing links with other regions (for example, between Catalonia and the Ruhr area). Again there is an ongoing flow or cascade of globalization–regionalism–sub-regionalism. Or, "Globalization encourages macro-regionalism, which, in turn, encourages micro-regionalism".

> Micro-regionalism in poor areas will be a means not only of affirming cultural identi-
> ties but of claiming pay-offs at the macro-regional level for maintaining political sta-
> bility and economic good behaviour. The issues of redistribution are thereby raised
> from the sovereign state level to the macro-regional level, while the manner in which
> redistributed wealth is used becomes decentralised to the micro-regional level.

What globalization means in structural terms, then, is the *increase in the available modes of organization*: transnational, international, macro-regional, national, micro-regional, municipal, local. This ladder of administrative levels is being criss-crossed by *functional networks* of corporations, international organizations and non-governmental organizations, as well as by professionals and computer users. Part of this is what has been termed the "internationalization of the state" as states are "increasingly engaged in multilateral forms of international governance". This approximates Rosenau's conceptualization of the structure of *"post-international politics"* made up of two interactive worlds with overlapping memberships: a state-centric world, in which the primary actors are national, and a multi-centric world of diverse actors such as corporations, international organizations, ethnic groups, churches. These multi-centric functional networks in turn are nested within broader sprawling "scapes", such as finanscapes and ethnoscapes.

Furthermore, not only these modes of organization are important but also the informal spaces that are created in between, in the interstices. Inhabited by diasporas, migrants, exiles, refugees, nomads, these are sites of what Michael Mann calls "interstitial emergence" and identifies as important sources of social renewal.

Also in political economy we can identify a range of hybrid formations. The notion of articulation of modes of production may be viewed as a principle of hybridization. The dual economy argument saw neatly divided economic sectors while the articulation argument sees interactive sectors giving rise to mélange effects, such as "semi-proletarians" who have one foot in the agrarian subsistence sector. Counterposed to the idea of the dual economy split in traditional/modern and feudal/capitalist sectors, the articulation argument holds that what has been taking place is an interpenetration of modes of production. Uneven articulation has, in turn, given rise to phenomena such as asymmetric integration. Dependency theory may be read as a theory of structural hybridization in which dependent capitalism is a mélange category in which the logics of capitalism and imperialism have merged. Recognition of this hybrid condition is what distinguishes neo-Marxism from classical Marxism (in which capital was regarded as a "permanently revolutionizing force"): that is, regular capitalism makes for development, but dependent capitalism makes for the "development of underdevelopment". The contested notion of semiperiphery may also be viewed as a hybrid formation. In a wider context, the mixed economy, the informal sector, and the "third sector" of the "social economy", comprising co-operative and non-profit organizations, may be viewed as hybrid economic formations.

Hybrid formations constituted by the interpenetration of diverse logics manifest themselves in *hybrid sites* and spaces. Thus, urbanization in the context of the fusion of pre-capitalist and capitalist modes of production, as in parts of Latin America, may give rise to "cities of peasants". Border zones are the meeting places of different organizational modes – such as Free Enterprise Zones and offshore banking facilities (hybrid meeting places of state sovereignty and transnational enterprise), overseas military facilities and surveillance stations. Border lands generally have become a significant topos. The blurring and reworking of public and private spaces is a familiar theme. Global cities and ethnic mélange neighbourhoods within them (such as Jackson Heights in Queens, New York) are other hybrid spaces in the global landscape. The use of information technology in supranational financial transactions has given rise to a hyperspace of capital.

Another dimension of hybridity concerns the experience of time, as in the notion of *mixed times* (*tiempos mixtos*) common in Latin America, where it refers to the coexistence and interspersion of premodernity, modernity and postmodernity. A similar point is that "intrinsic asynchrony" is a "general characteristic of Third World cultures".

Globalization, then, increases the range of organizational options, all of which are in operation simultaneously. Each or a combination of these may be relevant in specific social, institutional, legal, political, economic or cultural spheres. What matters is that no single mode has a necessary overall priority or monopoly. This is one of the salient differences between the present phase of globalization and the preceding era from the 1840s to the 1960s, the great age of nationalism when by and large the nation-state was the single dominant organizational option. While the spread of the nation-state has been an expression of globalization, the dynamic has not stopped there.

The overall tendency towards increasing global density and interdependence, or globalization, translates, then, into the pluralization of organizational forms. Structural hybridization and the mélange of diverse modes of organization give rise to a pluralization of forms of co-operation and competition as well as to novel mixed forms of co-operation. This is the structural corollary to flexible specialization and just-in-time capitalism and, on the other hand, to cultural hybridization and multiple identities. Multiple identities and the decentring of the social subject are grounded in the ability of individuals to avail themselves of several organizational options at the same time. Thus globalization is the framework for the amplification and diversification of "sources of the self". [. . .]

Conclusion: Towards a Global Sociology

Globalization/hybridization makes, first, an empirical case: that processes of globalization, past and present, can be adequately described as processes of hybridization. Secondly, it is a critical argument: against viewing globalization in terms of homogenization, or of modernization/Westernization, as empirically narrow and historically flat.

The career of sociology has been coterminous with the career of nation-state formation and nationalism, and from this followed the constitution of the object of sociology as society and the equation of society with the nation. Culminating in structural functionalism and modernization theory, this career in the context of globalization is in for retooling. A global sociology is taking shape, around notions such as social networks (rather than "societies"), border zones, boundary crossing and global society. In other words, a sociology conceived within the framework of nations/societies is making place for a post-inter/national sociology of hybrid formations, times and spaces.

Structural hybridization, or the increase in the range of organizational options, and cultural hybridization, or the doors of erstwhile imagined communities opening up, are signs of an age of boundary crossing. Not, surely, of the erasure of boundaries. Thus, state power remains extremely strategic, but it is no longer the only game in town. The tide of globalization reduces the room of manoeuvre for states, while international institutions, transnational transactions, regional co-operation, subnational dynamics and non-governmental organizations expand in impact and scope.

In historical terms, this perspective may be deepened by writing diaspora histories of global culture. Due to nationalism as the dominant paradigm since the nineteenth century, cultural achievements have been routinely claimed for "nations" – that is, culture has been "nationalized", territorialized. A different historical record can be constructed on the basis of the contributions to culture formation and diffusion by diasporas, migrations, strangers, brokers. A related project would be histories of the hybridization of metropolitan cultures, that is a counter-history to the narrative of imperial history. Such historical inquiries may show that hybridization has been taking place all along but over time has been concealed by religious, national, imperial and civilizational chauvinism. Moreover, they may deepen our understanding of the temporalities of hybridization: how certain junctures witness downturns or upswings of hybridization, slowdowns or speed-ups. At the same time it follows that, if we accept that cultures have been hybrid *all along*, hybridization is in effect a tautology: contemporary accelerated globalization means the hybridization of hybrid cultures.

As such, the hybridization perspective remains meaningful only as a critique of essentialism. Essentialism will remain strategic as a mobilizational device as long as the units of nation, state, region, civilization, ethnicity remain strategic: and for just as long hybridization remains a relevant approach. Hybridity unsettles the introverted concept of culture which underlies romantic nationalism, racism, ethnicism, religious revivalism, civilizational chauvinism, and culturalist essentialism. Hybridization, then, is a perspective that is meaningful as a counterweight to the introverted notion of culture; at the same time, the very process of hybridization unsettles the introverted gaze, and accordingly, hybridization eventually ushers in post-hybridity, or transcultural cut and mix.

Hybridization is a factor in the reorganization of social spaces. Structural hybridization, or the emergence of new practices of social co-operation and competition, and cultural hybridization, or new translocal cultural expressions, are interdependent: new forms of co-operation require and evoke new cultural imaginaries. Hybridization is a contribution to a sociology of the in-between, a sociology from the interstices. This involves merging endogenous/exogenous understandings of culture. This parallels the attempt in international relations theory to overcome the dualism between the nation-state and international system perspectives. Other significant perspectives are Hannerz' macro-anthropology and his concern with mapping micro-macro linkages and contemporary work in geography and cultural studies.

In relation to the global human condition of inequality, the hybridization perspective releases reflection and engagement from the boundaries of nation, community, ethnicity, or class. Fixities have become fragments as the kaleidoscope of collective experience is in motion. It has been in motion all along and the fixities of nation, community, ethnicity and class have been grids superimposed upon experiences more complex and subtle than reflexivity and organization could accommodate.

Questions

1   How, and to what extent, did the world become "unified" in the mid-nineteenth century? Would Immanuel Wallerstein agree that this period marks a key stage in globalization?

2   What does the world of the twentieth century have in common with that of the sixteenth, according to Wallerstein? How does he explain the remarkable stability of an economically unequal and politically divided world-system? What concepts does he contribute to the study of globalization?

3   Although Sklair notes that the current global system is "not synonymous with the global capitalist system," he regards specific features of world capitalism as driving forces in globalization. What are these features, and what do they add to Wallerstein's analysis of world capitalism?

4   Globalization is sometimes described as a process that reduces geographic constraints on social life. How would Sassen challenge this notion? Whom does she depict as winners and losers in globalization? Does her description of globalization contradict or amplify Wallerstein's?

5   How does "complex interdependence" constrain the behavior of states interested in enhancing their power and security, according to Keohane and Nye? What traditional assumptions about world politics does this new situation call into question? How can international organizations transform world politics?

6   What do Meyer and his colleagues mean when they say that nation-states are not "collective actors"? What surprising similarities among nation-states do they note, and how do they account for them? Do they identify a driving force in globalization?

7   How does symbolic concern for our common humanity increase around the globe, according to Robertson and Chirico? Does the rise of this new value imply that individuals and societies will develop more similar identities? Why should globalization enhance religion and religiosity?

8   What does Nederveen Pieterse mean when he calls globalization "multidimensional"? Why does he argue that globalization does not necessarily make people and societies around the world more similar? What point does he make in quoting Robertson on the global value of particularity?

Part III

Experiencing Globalization

Introduction

As older residents of Hong Kong revel in the quality of Cantonese cuisine, their offspring avidly consume Big Macs, pizza, and Coca-Cola (as James Watson reported in *Golden Arches East*). Not long ago, travelers on British Rail's first class Pullman service could enjoy dishes from India, the Middle East, China, Greece, and so on (as Allison James reported in a volume on *Cross-Cultural Consumption*). From personal experience we can attest that, in urban areas of the American South, Thai cuisine successfully competes with traditional fare and supermarkets abound with produce from most continents. To be sure, these examples refer to privileged areas of the world. They are not unprecedented, as the earlier European adoption of New World potatoes and sugar demonstrates. Yet they illustrate one way in which globalization affects people concretely, namely, through changes in diet and taste. Such changes express new linkages, new transnational structures, a new global culture. More and more people can literally get a taste of what it means to be part of world society.

No one experiences globalization in all its complexity, but globalization is significant insofar as it is reshaping the daily lives of billions of people. Increasingly, the world is present in the everyday. This obviously applies to a Kofi Annan (the UN Secretary-General) or a Bill Gates (the Chairman of Microsoft), conscious contributors to globalization. It is also true for the Thai prostitutes, minions in a global industry, who are now suffering from AIDS. American textile workers know it as they feel the impact of intense foreign competition and outsourcing to overseas companies. Soccer fans regard it as routine when a large portion of the world's population directs its attention to the World Cup every four years. Business people traveling internationally see it daily in the media offerings in their hotel rooms.

Experiencing globalization, as some of these examples indicate, is not a one-way process, in the sense that large structural change is bound to overwhelm individuals. People participate and respond in different ways. They can shape, resist, absorb, or try to avoid globalization. They can seek opportunity in it, feel the harm of it, or lament the power of it. For some, globalization is a central reality; for others, it is still on the margins of their lives. In short, there is no one experience of globalization. That, in itself, is an important aspect of the process. The formation of a new world society does not involve all people in the same way; neither does it create the same texture in everyone's everyday life. But there are some commonalities in the global experience of globalization. To one degree or another, globalization is real to almost everyone. It transforms the prevailing sense of time and space, now globally standardized. It envelops everyone in new institutions. It poses a challenge, in the sense that even marginally affected groups must take a stance toward the world. And globalization, as we will see again in part VIII, raises identity problems for societies and individuals alike.

The selections in this section illuminate the experience of globalization from different vantage points. They show that the experience of globalization involves creative adaptation to global processes, new mixtures of cultural frameworks, and the growth of a variable global consciousness. On travels to Asia, Pico Iyer found that the West does not simply enter the East as a conquering culture. The island of Bali adapted to a global tourist industry while also maintaining its "exotic" tradition. Tourism and paradise, cliché and distinctive culture coexist. In Manila, he finds, American culture is transformed, and made local, through eerily faithful reproduction of popular songs. Martin Albrow studies the lives of various groups in London, showing that for many the place where they live is no longer connected to a sense of community through local culture. Rather, many groups, notably immigrants and their offspring, extend their relations and allegiances transnationally, as far as their resources can carry them. The global city thus harbors many global actors, and not only in the financial institutions emphasized by Sassen in part II. Bruce Fuller studies one aspect of globalization – the expansion of formal education as a world institution – as it unfolds in Malawi. In one of the poorest countries in the world, bureaucratically organized and classroom-based public education is regarded as the way to "become modern." Malawi tries to do what any proper state must. But as Fuller observed classes in action, he found that teachers trying to control large classes with few resources necessarily deviated from the global ideology that legitimates their position. David Harvey, finally, describes a global experience we have already alluded to, what he calls "time–space compression." He explains how this experience first affected many Europeans in the mid-nineteenth century. Their sense of history as a calmly progressive process was disturbed, as their social space had become more integrated and unified across national boundaries. New technologies made it possible to take part in events occurring far away; they made the globe decidedly "smaller." European artists, Harvey argues, came to represent this new awareness in new ways, but he implies that the challenge they faced has itself become globalized. All of us now face the experience of globalization.

17 Bali: On Prospero's Isle/The Philippines: Born in the USA

Pico Iyer

I had come into town the previous afternoon watching video reruns of *Dance Fever* on the local bus. As I wandered around, looking for a place to stay, I had noted down the names of a few of the stores: the Hey Shop. The Hello Shop. Easy Rider Travel Service. TGI Friday restaurant. And after checking into a modest guesthouse where Vivaldi was pumping out of an enormous ghetto blaster, I had gone out in search of a meal. I ran across a pizzeria, a sushi bar, a steak house, a Swiss restaurant and a slew of stylish Mexican cafés. Eventually, however, I wound up at TJ's, a hyper-chic fern bar, where long-legged young blondes in tropical T-shirts were sitting on wicker chairs and sipping tall cocktails. Reggae music floated through the place as a pretty waitress brought me my corn chips and salsa.

After dinner, I had made my way to a nearby café for a cappuccino. Next to the cash register were enough stacks of old copies of *Cosmo*, *Newsweek* and the London *Sunday Times* to fill six doctors' waiting rooms. Behind the counter was a backgammon set for customers and a homemade library of faded paperbacks – Erica Jong, Ken Follett, Alexandra Penney. From Casablanca, the showy, two-story singles bar across the street, Bruce Springsteen was belting out "Dancing in the Dark." Hungry-eyed girls in tiny skirts were cruising the place in pairs, while muscular guys with gold medallions dangling across their bronzed chests perched on the balcony, drinking beer.

After an unquiet sleep, I had woken up and walked around the three or four square blocks of the town. Most of the stores seemed to be trendy boutiques, across whose windows were splashed New Wave Japanese T-shirts and pretty sundresses in *Miami Vice* turquoise and pink. Surfaris. Tropical Climax. Cherry. Mariko. *An American Werewolf in London* was playing at the local cinema. The Narnia. Frenchy. Pancho's. The Pub. A few Men at Work songs were pouring out of cassette stores opened to the street, only to be drowned out by the roar of Suzukis erratically ridden by local boys in leopardskin shirts. Fatty. The Beer Garden. Depot Viva. The Duck Nuts. "Marijuana and hashish," whispered one man to me. "Hashish and cocaine," muttered his friend. Joe's. Lenny. Jerry. Elly's. Elice's. I walked back to my guesthouse – Van Morrison had now replaced Vivaldi on the system – and a couple of the boys there invited me to sit down over some guacamole and give them my opinion of Michael Landon and John McEnroe.

I was, of course, in Bali, the Elysian isle famous for its other-worldly exoticism, its cultural integrity, its natural grace.

Original publication details: Iyer, Pico, "Bali: On Prospero's Isle" and "The Philippines: Born in the U.S.A." from *Video Night in Kathmandu*. Copyright © 1988 by Pico Iyer. Reprinted by permission of Alfred A. Knopf, Inc.

Say Bali, and two things come to mind: tourism and paradise. Both are inalienable features of the island, and also incompatible. For as fast as paradises seduce tourists, tourists reduce paradises. Such are the unerring laws of physics: what goes up must come down; for every action there is an equal and opposite reaction. Hardly has a last paradise been discovered than everyone converges on it so fast that it quickly becomes a paradise lost.

Nowhere, however, had this struggle been so protracted or intense as in Bali, most pestered and most paradisiacal of islands. The first Westerners ever to land here, Dutch sailors in 1597, announced their discovery of Eden, and two of them decided never to leave. By 1619, Balinese girls were already fetching 150 florins in the slave markets of Réunion and by 1847, the first tract in the fertile field of Baliology was already being brought into print. And for more than half a century now, Bali had been perhaps the world's best-kept idyll and its worst-kept secret: a race of charmed spirits still danced in its temples, and a crush of foreigners kept pushing their way in for a view. Tourism hung around Bali like chains around a mermaid.

The animist Hindus who grace the island regard all of life as a battle between the spirits of light and darkness, and nearly every native dance plays out this unending elemental struggle in the form of a celebration or an exorcism. But Bali had also become the world's most popular stage for a subtler battle, and a less ethereal dance – between the colonizing impulse of the West and the resistant cultural heritage of the East. Like Prospero's isle, Bali was a kind of paradise crowded with wood nymphs and cave-hidden spirits. Like Prospero's isle, it was governed by a race of noblemen, artisans and priests that had been chased into exile across the seas. And like Prospero's isle, it was now being threatened by a new mob of aliens, who found themselves charmed by its virgin goddesses, made sleep-heavy by its unearthly music. Bali had thus become the magical setting on which the two forces were deciding destinies larger than their own: could Ariel, airy spirit and agent of the gods, disarm Antonio, worldly and usurping Duke of Milan, before it was too late?

Like Prospero's isle too, Bali offered all the amenities of Eden. Its regally graceful people dwelt in a lush Rousseauesque garden of snakes and tropical flowers. Young girls, careless of their loveliness, bathed in running streams, wore scarlet hibiscus in their hair and silken sarongs around their supple bodies; the soft-eyed local men seemed likewise gods of good health, dazzling smiles offsetting the flowers they tucked behind their ears. In Bali, even old women were slender creatures who moved with a dancer's easy grace. There was no friction in this land of song and dance, and nothing unlovely: children, taken to be angels of purity descended from the heavens, were never scolded or spanked, crime was unknown and even cremations were opulent festivals of joy. Nature had been charmed by Art. Everything was at peace.

In Bali, indeed, life itself, and everything in it, was taken to be sacrament and dance. The Balinese traditionally had no particular conception of "art," since every villager wove or danced or painted as a matter of course; every house, moreover, had its own shrine, and every village had three temples, open to the heavens and wrapped in white and golden sashes. Every day, as I arose, bare-shouldered women in sumptuous silks were sashaying through the early morning sunlight, stately and unhurried, piles of fruit on their heads to be placed as offerings before the gods. And every night, in village courtyards, radiant little girls, in gorgeous gold brocades, white blossoms garlanding the hair that fell to their waists, swayed together out of the darkness, their eyes rolling, twisting their hands like sorcerers, moving as one to the gongs and cymbals of the spellbinding gamelan. Like Prospero's isle, Bali was "full of noises, sounds and sweet airs . . . a thousand twangling instruments."

And the beauty, and the curse, of Bali was that a piece of this paradise was available to everyone who entered. For $2 a night, I was given my own thatched hut in a tropical courtyard scented with flowers and fruit. Each sunny morning, as I sat on my veranda, a smiling young girl brought me bowls of mangoes and tea, and placed scarlet bougainvillaeas on the gargoyle above my lintel. Two minutes away was the palm-fringed beach of my fantasies; an hour's drive, and I was climbing active volcanoes set among verdant terraces of rice. Along the sleepy village lanes, garden restaurants served tropical drinks and magic mushrooms, while a hundred stores offered giddy T-shirts, sixties paintings and cassettes galore. And all around were dances, silken ceremonies and, in a place scarcely bigger than Delaware, as many as 30,000 temples.

Thus the paradox remained: Bali was heaven, and hell was other people. Tourism had become the island's principal detraction. And the specter of commercialism shadowed every visitor from his first step to his last: one might debate the issue or demean it, but one could not ignore it. Sightseers were inclined not to say that Bali was beautiful or terrible, only that it had been raped or was still intact. " 'Isn't Bali spoiled?' is invariably the question that greets the returned traveler . . . meaning, is the island overrun by tourists?" wrote Miguel Covarrubias. He had written that in 1937. "This nation of artists is faced with a Western invasion, and I cannot stand idly by and watch its destruction," wrote André Roosevelt, in his introduction to a book on Bali, entitled (what else?) *The Last Paradise.* He had written that in 1930.

And after fifty years of such anxieties, Bali had, inevitably, become a paradise traduced by many tourists, the place that sophisticates hated to love: many of my British friends would rather have vacationed in Calais or Hull than submit to what they regarded as the traveler's ultimate cliché. Even those who adored the island found it more and more trying. For if it is the first vanity, and goal, of every traveler to come upon his own private pocket of perfection, it is his second vanity, and goal, to shut the door behind him. Paradise is a deserted island or a solitary glade. Bali, however, was a common paradise, a collective find and, as such, an insult to the imagination. For years, the island had swarmed with crowds desperate to get away from the crowds. "The thing I hate about Bali," an American in Hong Kong told me, "is that everyone on the island is American or Australian, but every one of them is ignoring all the others and pretending that he's the only foreigner who's discovered the place."

Yet still Bali remained unavoidable and irresistible. And what distinguished it most from its rivals for the Pyrrhic distinction of the world's loveliest paradise island – what set it apart from Mustique or Ios or even Tahiti – was the variety of its enticements. Bali had something for everyone. Some people traveled to pamper themselves, some to enjoy themselves, some to improve themselves; all of them came to Bali. And all of them, whether sun worshipper, antique collector or truth seeker, were guaranteed absolute satisfaction. For though the Indonesian government had wisely stuck by the Dutch policy of "Bali for the Balinese" and permitted tourists only in the eastern half of the island – the west remained virtually impenetrable – there was still a wealth of guidebook riches to be found here: pamphlet-perfect surf and sand for the beach bum; five-star resorts for the sybarite; myths and rituals in abundance for the culture vulture.

Through a miracle of convenience, moreover, the separate needs of the separate species of *Homo touristicus* were satisfied in three separate areas, located within a twenty-mile radius of one another. Along the western side of the super-developed southern peninsula was Kuta Beach, once a major rest stop for hippie gypsies on their way from Kathmandu to Cuzco, and now primarily a holiday camp for Australian surfers and their blondes; on the other side of the peninsula – ten miles, and a thousand worlds, away – was Sanur Beach, a strip of concrete, luxury hotels set along the sea, the Waikiki or Cannes of the East, where the international set came out to play; and at the apex of the compact triangle, set in the heart of Bali's magical middle kingdom, was the hillside village of Ubud, where trendy visitors came to study the native culture and foreign artists set up home and shop.

Even more conveniently, tourism in Bali was remarkably segregated. No self-respecting self-styled student of the local culture would ever be caught dead inside the discos and juice bars of Kuta, while few of the musclemen on the beach had time for the festivals and galleries of Ubud; both groups scorned the Sanur life they could not afford, and the Sanur settlers looked down on the basic conditions of Kuta and Ubud, which they found uncomfortably close to those of the Balinese they so admired. And everyone, in all three areas, shunned Denpasar, the noisy, traffic-choked town at the middle of the triangle, which had the unenviable task of under-writing the pleasures of Eden with practical facilities. [...]

The Philippines is not just the site of the largest US military installations in the world. It is also perhaps the world's largest slice of the American Empire, in its purest impurest form. The first time I landed in Hong Kong, I felt a thrill of recognition to see the pert red letterboxes, the blue-and-white road signs, the boxes of Smarties that had been the props of my boyhood in England; upon arriving in Manila, I felt a similar pang as my eye caught Open 24-Hour gas stations, green exit signs on the freeways, Florida-style license plates and chains of grocery stores called "Mom and Pop." The deejay patter bubbling from the radios, the Merle Haggard songs drifting out of jukeboxes, the Coke signs and fast-food joints and grease-smeared garages – all carried me instantly back home, or, if not home, at least to some secondhand, beat-up image of the Sam Shepard Southwest, to Amarillo, perhaps, or East LA.

Most of all, the Philippines took me back to the junk-neon flash of teen America, the rootless Western youth culture of drive-ins and jukeboxes, junior proms, cheap cutoffs, and custom dragsters. [...]

The most conspicuous institutions that America had bequeathed to the Philippines seemed to be the disco, the variety show and the beauty pageant. Perhaps the ideas and ideals of America had proved too weighty to be shipped across the seas, or perhaps they were just too fragile. Whatever, the nobility of the world's youngest power and the great principles on which it had been founded were scarcely in evidence here, except in a democratic system that seemed to parody the chicanery of the Nixon years. In the Philippines I found no sign of Lincoln or Thoreau or Sojourner Truth; just Dick Clark, Ronald McDonald and Madonna.

On a human level, of course, the relation between America and her former colony was altogether more complex, and best seen, I thought, just by watching the slow mating dances that filled the smoky country-and-western joints of Ermita every night.

As I entered Club 21 one rainy evening, a small and perky Filipina in a red-and-white-checked shirt and tight jeans – a kind of dusky Joey Heatherton – was leading a country band through songs of lost love and heartbreak. The minute the group struck up the opening chords of another sad song, one of the American GI types seated at the bar, a craggy man in his sixties, six feet tall perhaps, slowly stood up and extended his hand to a pretty teenage girl in a white frock and white pumps. "Today," drawled the singer, "is the darkest day of my life," and the pedal steel wailed and the man put one hand around the girl's tiny waist and the other on her shoulder and led her, with great courtliness, through a slow, slow dance.

As the next ballad began, the vocalist went into a perfect Dolly Parton rasp, and a man in a bushy ginger mustache with sad eyes behind his thick glasses stood up, hitched up his trousers and walked over to a table in the corner where eight young Filipinas were staring idly into the distance. Crouching down, he whispered something to a beautiful young lady in a yellow-and-red ruffled skirt and she followed him back to the bar. "What's your name?" he said softly as they sat down, extending his hand. "I'm an American."

A couple of barstools away, another old-timer was gently stroking the long hair of his doll-like companion. "Hey," he chuckled, looking over her head to a colleague. "I'm going to marry her in a minute." And the band went through another plaintive ballad, then vanished through a back door that said "George's Massage Special."

A man got up from the bar and walked out, and as the door slammed behind him, his sweet-faced companion stuck out her tongue at his memory, then straightened her skirt and went off to sit in another man's lap. The door swung open again, and a lady came in with a basket full of roses. A red-faced Australian hailed her from where he sat and bought ten flowers. Then, very slowly, he walked around the place and, very tenderly, presented a rose to every girl in the room. The band came back again, and sailed into more sad songs from the West. "I warned you not to love me," wailed the singer, "I'm not going to be here very long."

If I had closed my eyes, I could have believed myself in Tucumcari, New Mexico, or listening to some jukebox in Cheyenne. But my eyes were wide open and in front of me two couples were gliding around the dance floor, tiny arms wrapped around large backs as two pretty young girls, eyes closed, buried their silky heads in their partners' burly chests.

A couple of minutes later, the band went into a faster number. "Yee-hah," cried a man with the frame of a construction worker, standing up at the bar, shaking his fanny and pumping his elbows. He swirled a high school girl in high heels out onto the dance floor, and she flashed a smile back at him, shimmying like a dream. "Shake it," cried out the singer. "Yee-hah!" The dance floor started to get crowded. The Australian pulled his companion out onto the floor. Two girls in jeans began dancing together. A young girl in a flounced skirt swayed happily opposite an old girl with too much makeup. "Welcome to my world," sang the girls as they danced, smiling at their partners and clapping. "Welcome to my world." And as I went out, the singer was just breaking into a perfect replica of Loretta Lynn, while singing, with flawless anguish, "You know, it's only make-believe."

The professionalism of music in Manila had impressed me almost as soon as I arrived. But as I stayed longer in town, I was hit more forcibly by a different aspect of the local singing. It struck me first one night in Baguio, in one of the city's many "Minus One" sing-along pubs, where customers take turns coming onstage and delivering the latest hits, accompanied by a tape to provide backup instrumentation. "I would like to dedicate this song to a special someone," a girl was whispering huskily into the mike as I walked in. Then she adjusted the stand, put on her tape and proceeded to deliver a note-perfect version of Madonna's "Like a Virgin," absolutely identical to the original, down to the last pause and tic. Song complete, she whispered "Thank you" to the mike, sauntered offstage and went home with her special someone.

As the evening went on, the scene was repeated again and again and again and again. Almost everyone in the pub came up to deliver flawless imitations of some American hit. And almost everyone had every professional move down perfectly. They knew not only how to trill like Joan Baez and rasp like the Boss, but also how to play on the crowd with their eyes, how to twist the microphone wire in their hands, how to simulate every shade of heartbreak. They were wonderfully professional amateurs. But they were also professional impersonators.

When I walked into another pub down the street I got to witness an even greater display of virtuoso mimicry: the Chinese singer onstage was able to modulate his voice so as to muster a gruff warmth for a Kenny Rogers number, a high earnestness for Graham Nash, a kind of operatic bombast for Neil Diamond and a bland sincerity for Lionel Richie. His Paul Simon was perfect in its boyish sweetness. Yet what his own voice sounded like, and what his own personality might have been, were impossible to tell. And when it came to improvising, adding some of the frills or flourishes that his culture relished, making a song his own, he – like every other singer I had heard – simply did not bother.

"Sure," an American correspondent based in Manila told me when I mentioned this. "Music is definitely the single best thing here. But there's no way you're going to hear any local tunes, or variations on the recorded versions of the American hits. There's one singer in Davao they call the Stevie Wonder of the Philippines, because he sounds exactly – *exactly* – like Stevie Wonder. And there's another woman locally who's the Barbra Streisand of the Philippines. That's how they make it big here. You know one reason why the Filipinos love 'We Are the World' so much? Because it gives one member of the group the chance to do Michael Jackson, and another Cyndi Lauper and a third Bruce Springsteen. Some guy even gets to do Ray Charles."

Finally, in Baguio one night, I came upon a happy exception to the rule: a pudgy singer who slyly camped up Julio Iglesias's song "To All the Girls I Know" by delivering it in a perfect simulation of Iglesias's silky accent, while substituting "boys" for "girls." But then, a few days later, back in Manila, I heard another singer at the Hobbit House do exactly the same trick, with exactly the same words (and, a few months later, I was told, local minstrels were delivering the same song, in honor of the fallen Imelda, to the words: "To all the shoes I had before / I wore them once, and then no more"). Likewise, at a free public concert one afternoon I was surprised to hear a professionally trained singer transform the revved-up anarchy and energy of the Beatles' "Help" into a slow, soulful ballad of lovelorn agony. But then I heard the song delivered in exactly the same way, with exactly the same heartrent inflections, in a small club in Baguio, and then again at another bar: all the singers, I realized, were not in fact creating a new version, but simply copying some cover version quite different from the Beatles' original. All the feelings were still borrowed.

This development of musical mannequins struck me as strange, especially in a country that understandably regarded its musical gifts as a major source of national pride. I could certainly see how the Filipinos' brilliance at reproducing their masters' voices, down to the very last burr, had made them the musical stars of Asia – the next-best thing, in fact, to having a real American. But as a form of self-expression, this eerie kind of ventriloquism made me sad.

It was the same kind of sadness I felt when I read that the national hero José Rizal had described his home as "a country without a soul" or when I opened *What's On in Manila* to find the first ad in the personals section begin: "I would like to meet an American. Looks are not important but he must be kind and cheerful." It was the same kind of sadness I felt when I went to Pistang Pilipino, the capital's main tourist center, and found that the highlight of its show of local culture was a splashy Hollywood-style spectacular in which chorus lines of handsome young men whipped through some brassy choreography and six-year-old girls in bikinis performed acrobatics while a fat man with greasy hair in an open shirt crooned "House of the Rising Sun." Mostly, it was the sadness I felt, when an intelligent Filipino friend in New York told me, with a happy smile, "Every Filipino dreams that he will grow up to be an American."

While I was in Manila, there was plenty of token opposition to the US presence. Nationalists railed against the country's still justified image as the world's great center of mail-order brides and chambermaids. The Marcos-run paper, in a show of ill-considered braggadoccio, printed Manuel Quezón's famous cry: "I prefer to see a government run like hell by Filipinos than a government run like heaven by Americans." And when foreign newsmen flooded into town for the election a few months later, an opposition paper greeted them as "two-bit, white-skinned, hirsute, AIDS-predisposed visitors." But the "two-bit," I thought, said it all. In the Philippines, anti-American guerrillas drew up their strategies in Michael Jackson notebooks. And a respected newspaper greeted the suggested removal of the American bases with the headline "Bye, Bye, American Pie." [. . .]

18 Travelling Beyond Local Cultures

Martin Albrow

Globalization, Culture and Locality

In the last thirty years transformations of industrial organization in the advanced societies, accompanied by the acceptance of the ideas of post-industrialism and post-modernity, mean that the problem-setting for community analysis has shifted. In the last decade globalization theory has brought issues of time, space and territorial organization into the centre of the frame of argument. We have to look again at the way social relations are tied to place and re-examine issues of locality and culture.

Our data about people in one small area suggest that locality has a much less absolute salience for individuals and social relations than older paradigms of research allow. They live in a global city, London, which has already been the focus for much globalization research. However, research has largely focused on links with international finance, on urban development and on the more emphatically international lifestyles of jet-setters and yuppies. Scant attention has been paid to everyday life. Thus Knight and Gappert's useful volume on cities in a global society contains twenty-three papers, but not one considers everyday life in the city. Yet the volume already implies quite different patterns of living for those caught up in global processes and takes us far outside notions of locality as the boundary for meaningful social relations.

Yet the theorization of everyday life under global conditions effectively introduces a range of considerations which takes us beyond ideas of post-modernity and post-industrialism. These ideas evolved out of earlier mass society concerns and the notion of the fragmentation of industrial society. To that extent post-modernity theory lent credence to the idea of a dissolution of concepts without effectively advocating an alternative frame. Indeed very often the claim was implicit that the search for an alternative was a doomed project from the beginning.

Globalization theory, on the other hand, does commit itself to propositions about the trajectory of social change which do not envisage a collapse into chaos or a meaningless juxtaposition of innumerable and incommensurable viewpoints. It puts on the agenda a recasting of the whole range of sociological concepts which were forged for the period of nation-state sociology.

We do not have to begin from scratch. For our purposes in this chapter we can draw on a number of core propositions about globalization based on earlier work. In exploring their relevance for local social relations we will find that we develop them further and discover the need to advance additional ones. Our starting points to which we will return are:

Original publication details: Albrow, Martin, "Travelling Beyond Local Cultures" from John Eade (ed.), *Living the Global City: Globalization as a Local Process* (Routledge, 1997).

1   The values informing daily behaviour for many groups in contemporary society
    relate to real or imagined material states of the globe and its inhabitants
    (*globalism*).
2   Images, information and commodities from any part of the earth may be avail-
    able anywhere and anytime for ever-increasing numbers of people worldwide,
    while the consequences of worldwide forces and events impinge on local lives
    at any time (*globality*).
3   Information and communication technology now make it possible to maintain
    social relationships on the basis of direct interaction over any distance across
    the globe (*time–space compression*).
4   Worldwide institutional arrangements now permit mobility of people across
    national boundaries with the confidence that they can maintain their lifestyles
    and life routines wherever they are (*disembedding*).

We could add to this list but for the moment it is sufficient to permit us to turn to
our local studies and identify the patterns of social life which call out for new sociological conceptualizations. Before doing so we ought to add that while these propositions are associated with the general theory of globalization, the extent to which
they necessarily implicate the globe as a whole, or require the unicity of the world,
is open to an argument which does not have to be resolved here in order to show
their relevance for studies of local social relations.

Social and Cultural Spheres in an Inner London Locality

The transformations of the last sixty years now make it difficult to capture anything
in London like the picture of locality you will find in a study such as Hoggart's.
The paradigmatic equivalent of his account in empirical research was the work of
Willmott and Young at the Institute of Community Studies in 1957. But they were
capturing a world imminently dissolving. The variety of possibilities now evident
extend our conceptual capacities to the extreme. They certainly burst the bounds
of nation-state sociology.

   Our research on locality and globalization is based in the inner London borough
of Wandsworth, south of the river, west of centre, formed from the amalgamation
of seven or eight nineteenth-century villages, which give their names to the local
areas within what is a largely continuous residential belt. In terms of race politics headlines Wandsworth has led a quiet life in comparison with neighbouring
Lambeth. Its press image is mainly associated with the policies of the Conservative-
controlled local council which has been known as the "flagship" authority of the
Thatcher years for its advocacy of low local taxation, contracting out of local services and the sale of council houses.

   This image of tranquil continuity through change is maintained even for the area
of Tooting which has a large Asian immigrant population. Yet even a cursory visit
suggests that the concept of local culture is unlikely to fit new conditions. Given
that the task of reconceptualization and documenting new realities is long term,
I will not attempt to prejudge our findings by a premature characterization of
Tooting. However, if we turn to our respondents in Tooting and, instead of seeking
to fit them to pre-given sociological categories, listen to their own references to locality, culture and community, we already detect the possibility of new cultural
configurations occupying the same territorial area.

Adopting an individualistic methodology as one strategy for penetrating the new social relations, we can identify a range of responses which take us beyond the notion of local culture and community without suggesting any corollary of anomie or social disorganization as the old conceptual frames tended to assume. At this stage we are not offering a holistic account of social relations in this area of London, but we can already say that globalization theory is going to allow us to interpret our respondents in a quite different way from older sociologies which focused on place rather than space.

True we can find old-established "locals", benchmarks for analysis, but if we let them speak, the nuances of a new age come through. Take 73-year-old Grace Angel, who was born in Wandsworth and has lived in her house in Tooting for over fifty years, who met her husband when they carried stretchers for the injured during the air raids on London in the Second World War. He is now disabled but she benefits from the support of her own age group, mainly white women, who meet at a Day Centre three times a week. She engages in all the traditional activities of a settled life, visiting family, knitting and enjoying crafts. She rarely leaves Wandsworth; she enjoys the sense of community.

At the same time her life is not confined by the locality. She tells how she writes letters to France and the United States. She also wrote "to Terry Waite all the time he was held hostage and to his wife. I actually got a letter from him, thanking me for my support." Into her local frame enters a mass media symbol of the conflict between the West and militant Islam. We have to ask where that fits in with the concept of local culture, not simply an ephemeral image cast on a screen as diversion or even information, but a global figure who becomes a personal correspondent.

Mrs Angel would hardly recognize the image of Tooting another resident provides. True, Reginald Scrivens only moved to Tooting seventeen years ago but he has lived in London for thirty-two years and works in a City bank. He reads the broadsheet Conservative newspapers, has a drink with his colleagues after work and watches television with his wife in the evening. They don't socialize locally and he doesn't enjoy living in Tooting any more:

> It's very mixed these days, with the Asians and the blacks, and a lot of the area is quite run down. It's not a nice place to walk through. There isn't any real community either. I still know a few people along my street, but most of the people I used to know moved out, because Tooting got so bad. . . .
> Families come and go. Neighbours don't care about each other any more. The foreigners all stick together though. I'll say this about them – they look after their own. That's more than you can say about most of our lot these days.

His wife goes to local shops. He goes to a local church. They are not going to move. It is an easy journey to work in Central London.

Mr Scrivens lives in Tooting but is alienated from it, or rather Tooting falls short of an image of community which he thinks it might have had or ought to have. Yet it still is convenient enough to remain there. Convenience, however, can also combine with indifference. Forty-four-year-old Ted North came to Tooting from Yorkshire ten years ago and has worked as a traffic warden ever since, feels settled, belongs to the local Conservative club, rarely goes out of the area, but doesn't really notice whether there is a community as such.

A Londoner, who moved to Tooting three years ago at the age of 22 and became a postman, Gary Upton, is even more detached:

> Locality isn't all that important to me, but I don't really feel affected by the rest of the world either. I have my life to lead and I'll lead it wherever I am.

Even a much older man, Harry Carter, a 62-year-old taxi driver, who has lived in Tooting for twenty-two years, would move anywhere and feels community spirit has totally disappeared almost everywhere in London. For him globalization is "common sense" and "obviously happening". And if you are a young unemployed man like Dean Garrett, born in Tooting the year Harry arrived, living with your girlfriend and her parents, you are used to the Asians because you were brought up with them but stick with your own. You stay in Tooting and use its library and shops but not because of community feeling.

This indifference to place, however, can be transvalued into a positive desire for constant mobility and into an estimation of locality as a consumer good. Keith Bennett is 25, works in a shop and came to Tooting six months ago. He has travelled through the United States, his mother lives abroad, he has completed a degree, reckons travel has changed his life and would love to go all over the world. He has never had a sense of community but values Tooting:

> because it's got a mixed feel . . . it helps to make people aware of other people . . . it's close enough to fun places like Brixton and Streatham, and it's easy to get into town from here.

He is white but lives with an Asian family and has an Asian friend. His Asian friends tell him "that they have a good community feel among other Asians but not with the whites". For an older widow living alone, like 77-year-old Agnes Cooper, the issues of culture and community cannot be transvalued into spectacle as they are with Keith. She responds directly to their messages. The Asians are close-knit "with no room for outsiders" and she was plainly baffled by a Sikh who could not understand the meaning of hot cross buns at Easter when she tried to explain them to him. She has lived for fourteen years in Tooting and her social network and activity are as local as Grace Angel's, but she notices a lack of true community feeling. She remarked on people buying properties in the area just for resale.

Eight white residents of Tooting, each one with a different orientation to the local area, easily generalized into a different type, potentially raising a series of conceptual distinctions which render the question of the presence or absence of local community simplistic. This question makes more sense in the case of our older respondents, but their answers are quite different. For Grace it is there, Agnes is not sure, for Reginald it has gone and for Harry it went a long time ago everywhere in London. Ted is younger than them and came later. He does not know whether community is there and is unconcerned as he gets on with his local life.

Our three young men have different responses again. As with Ted "community" has lost salience, and locality has become facility. Globalist Keith finds Tooting a useful point from which to enjoy the world, for Gary its generalizable qualities are what counts, it could be anywhere and that suits him, while for Dean it's a question of necessity rather than values. There is nowhere else to go.

At one time a sociologist might have held that these were all different perspectives on the same phenomenon, partial points of view which could be composited into the social reality of Tooting. Later these views would have been held to justify a sociological relativism – perspectives which simply co-existed without any way of reconciling them. A later post-modernist view would find in them a fragmented, dislocated reality.

There is another (at least one) alternative. The Deans co-exist with the Agneses, the Reginalds with the Keiths. If they do not meet each other at least they encounter many others who are similar. These people inhabit co-existing social spheres, coeval and overlapping in space, but with fundamentally different horizons and time-spans. The reality of Tooting is constituted by the intermeshing and interrelating of these spheres. Grace's community is no more the authentic, original Tooting than is Ted's.

There is an additional vital point. Apart from Grace these white Tooting residents are all immigrants, they all moved into the area, respectively seventeen, ten, three, twenty-two, a half and fourteen years ago. It is an area which is always on the move and in that sense in- and out-migration is normal. Yet this does not preclude a sense of the "other" in Tooting, namely the Asians, often perceived as holding together, as constituting a community in the sense that the whites are not. To that extent we can see the Asian community acquires in the eyes of the whites the qualities which they consider themselves to have lost. Instead of seeking to assimilate the incoming ethnic group, which in any case has lived there longer than them, whites like Keith, with Asian friends and living in an Asian family, may seek to be assimilated themselves. We may then be tempted to apply the concept of local culture, not to the white residents but to the Asians.

Our oldest Asian respondent, Naranjan, is 65 years old and has lived in Tooting for nineteen years. She came from Tanzania but met her husband in India and nearly all her family live there apart from sons who live just outside London. She is in constant touch with her family in India and a sister in New York, usually by letter, and returns to India every year. Yet she and her husband are fond of Germany and Switzerland and she enjoys travelling. Otherwise she is very busy locally, sings in her temple, attends the elderly day centre and has friends in all ethnic groups.

Here the point which comes through strongly is that Indian culture is as much a family culture as a local one. Religious occasions encourage the maintenance of family ties across space. The disembedding Giddens associates with modernity effectively sustains pre-modern kin relations and permits a form of reverse colonization.

The same is the case with a much younger Pakistani woman, Zubdha, aged 26, born in Bradford, who came to Tooting three years ago. She is married and works in a social agency, maintains constant touch by telephone with family in Pakistan and visited over 120 friends and relatives there earlier in the year. However, she likes Tooting as a place where she is comfortable with her ethnic culture, can buy *halal* meat, has plenty of friends and no wish to leave.

For the white population, looking in from the outside, the Asians in Tooting appear to constitute a community. From the inside the orientations are varied. One thing is clear, racial segregation is apparent to both sides, but its meaning varies from person to person. In some cases it is a matter of feeling safer rather than any deep identification with an ethnic group. Such was the case with a 28-year-old shop owner, born in Birmingham, who moved to Tooting four years ago and who has no contact with aunts and uncles in India. His experience in both Birmingham and Tooting was that Asian youths stuck together for safety but he feels a sense of community in Tooting, too, which does not extend to cover blacks and whites. He thinks he will stay in Tooting so that his daughter can settle in somewhere. Settling seems a matter of contingent considerations rather than anything deeper.

A much more recent newcomer is Ajit, also 28 years old, who came to Tooting from Delhi three years ago and brought his wife, but has broken off relations with his family in India. He has set up a small business and his contacts are other businessmen. He notices no real community but has no intention of returning to India either. He sees signs of racial barriers breaking down for young people and considers this process as providing hope for the future.

These hopes might be borne out by the experience of 18-year-old Kuldeep, who helps in his parents' shop. He came to Britain from Bombay with them six years ago and says that he could not now return to India because he feels "too English". He considers most white people to be very open but his friends are almost all Asian and they spend a lot of time together out in clubs or playing football.

The same questioning of his Indian identity arises for a 35-year-old Asian pharmacist, Kishor, who was born in East Africa and has lived in Tooting for ten years. He finds no real community and strong racial segregation but he appreciates Tooting for its convenient location for work and his sports club. He has distant cousins in the United States whom he occasionally calls and when he has a holiday he usually goes to Portugal.

In sum, our Asian respondents have orientations to community as varied as those of the whites. They all acknowledge the barriers between Asian and white but their orientations to other Asians are not as the whites imagine. For a start the most intense felt identification with the Asian community comes from women and their local involvements are matched by the strength of their ties with the sub-continent. The men have a more instrumental relationship with other Asians, one of mutual protection and business opportunity, but not one which leads them to celebrate cultural difference.

Out of these interviews emerge both real differences in involvement in local culture and quite refined conscious distinctions about the nature of community. Most observant of all is possibly a Jamaican-born black community worker, Michael, who has lived with his parents in Tooting for eighteen years and works in Battersea, the other side of Wandsworth. For him nothing happens in Tooting which could be called community life. He contrasts it with Battersea, but even there what goes on he attributes to boredom rather than real involvement. His own friends are spread across London and everything he does revolves around the telephone. He calls Jamaica and the United States every week, and has been back to Jamaica every year for the last ten years. He sees Britain as just another American state but does not believe that the world is becoming a smaller place. Somehow for him the very strength of his Caribbean ties and the barriers coming down between people also push other people away.

New Concepts for Local/Global Conditions

We have cited individual cases at some length, not to confirm a general picture, nor to find a common thread. Indeed it would be possible to construct a different general type of orientation to living in the global city for each of our respondents. Equally we are not concerned to identify where some are right and others wrong. Our initial hypothesis is that each may be right for his or her own circumstances and social network.

Grace Angel and Naranjan both find active lives in a local community, one white the other Asian, and we have no reason to think that these are not reliable respondents. It is just that their worlds co-exist without impinging on each other.

Similarly the much-travelled Keith Bennett and Michael, the Jamaican community worker, agree that there is no community life in Tooting. Each finds it a convenient base for a London life and links with the rest of the world. But just because they agree there is no reason to take their view to be of more weight than anyone else's.

Let us suppose that this is not a matter of perspectives; rather that our interviews represent different realities, linked by their co-existence in a locality but not thereby creating a local culture or community. If that were the case the local area of Tooting would be characterized by a co-present diversity of lifestyles and social configurations. This diversity would then *constitute* the reality, not some average of a set of dispersed readings of the same phenomenon.

Yet this diversity would not represent chaos. Broadly there is no sense from our interviews of a collapsing world, even if there is regret for a world that is past. Each respondent makes sense of a situation, each relating in a different way to the local area. Certainly there is no sense of a Tooting community which comprises the population of the local area. Nor even is there a configuration in Elias' sense, except in so far as there is substantial agreement on the importance of the ethnic divide between whites and Asians. Yet ethnicity provides only one of the conditions for the lives of our respondents and in no sense creates an overall framework in the way Elias and Scotson's "established" and "outsiders" model encapsulates and co-ordinates the lives of the inhabitants of Winston Parva.

In other words our material is suggestive of a different order of things, which requires different conceptualizations from those available even only twenty years ago. Note the word "suggestive" – we are talking about empirical possibilities. Their realization is not yet demonstrated by these few interviews. Further research will need to adopt a variety of methodologies and take account of contextual factors, such as the possible effects of local state policies, before it can conclude that the globalized locality exists in Tooting. Moreover the impact of any future political mobilization can never be discounted. None the less, we have enough evidence to warrant the close examination of an alternative theoretical framework for future research.

We can make sense of these interviews by drawing on globalization theory. In particular by taking account of the different time horizons and spatial extent of our respondents' social networks we can specify the new elements of regularly constituted social relations in a locality in a global city. Let us now advance four new propositions about locality paralleling the four on globalization we set out above:

1   The locality can sustain as much globalist sentiment as there are sources of information for and partners in making sense of worldwide events.
2   A locality can exhibit the traces of world events (e.g. the expulsion of East African Asians) which remove any feeling of separation from the wider world.
3   The networks of individuals in a locality can extend as far as their resources and will to use the communications at their disposal. Time–space compression allows the maintenance of kin relations with India or Jamaica as much as with Birmingham or Brentford.
4   The resources and facilities of a locality may link it to globally institutionalized practices. It is convenient both to be there if you want to use the products of global culture and as good as anywhere else as a base from which to travel. As such both transients and permanent residents can equally make a life which is open to the world.

Let us now bring these four propositions about a globalized locality together. In sum they suggest the possibility that individuals with very different lifestyles and social networks can live in close proximity without untoward interference with each other. There is an old community for some, for others there is a new site for a community which draws its culture from India. For some Tooting is a setting for peer group leisure activity, for others it provides a place to sleep and access to London. It can be a spectacle for some, for others the anticipation of a better, more multicultural community. [. . .]

19 Strong States, Strong Teachers?

Bruce Fuller

My friend Chimtali, age 14, moved 10 kilometers from her small village nestled against the Zomba plateau to just outside the trading post of the same name. She had recently entered a government boarding school to pursue her secondary studies. She liked her teachers and her subjects. It was the foreign-seeming customs that she found amusing. Chimtali now was required to wear pajamas at night. And she was relearning how to eat. Growing up in the village she simply used her hands, but now she was required to use utensils imported from London. Nor was she allowed to eat fried *ngumbi*, those plentiful and tasty African bugs resembling winged roaches. While Chimtali obviously enjoyed becoming modern, she had not suspected that secondary school would require such deep changes in daily habits.

State Penetration of the School's Boundaries

Administrative rituals

State regulation of teacher action is often not very subtle within Malawi. Each teacher is expected to speak in English, or in the dominant tribe's language, after grade 4, to move through three textbooks page by page, to write down a lesson plan for each day's activities, and to hand this book over for inspection whenever requested by the headmaster (this is termed a "modern educational reform"). But the lack of subtlety I discovered that cool morning I sat in the back of a damp classroom outside Lilongwe was still surprising. Instructing grade 7 civics, the teacher was eliciting choral responses as pupils looked at a list written on the blackboard. He began with the question:

T: "How does government get money?"
Ps   (in unison): "Income tax, customs duties . . ."

Then, he asked individual children:

T: "What is the work of police?"
P1:   "To arrest kids."
P2:   "To protect houses."

Getting the attention of the class, the teacher (through his intonation) then elicited everyone to repeat what he said:

Original publication details: Fuller, Bruce, "Strong States, Strong Teachers?" from *Growing Up Modern: The Western State Builds Third-World Schools* (Routledge, 1991).

T: "The police work to maintain peace and order."

Ps (in unison): "To maintain peace and order."

The teacher then called on individual pupils to recite the six types of police in Malawi (as he wrote each type on the blackboard). Then reviewing each branch, he continued:

T: "If the PMF police came here, what will (*sic*) they do?"

P3: "They will deal with a riot or a strike."

T: "Now the special branch . . . when you go to public meetings and see well-dressed men, they are checking on whether the situation is okay. If it is not, they take away the leaders."

> My note: of the forty-seven pupils in the room, about ten are visibly fading from the conversation. The teacher then erases the six types of police, pro-ceeding to call on individual pupils asking the functions of each type. This serves to get the attention of previously disinterested youngsters.

The education ministry can not afford to write and publish a civics textbook for primary school pupils. Only in the past decade have texts become available for arithmetic, English, and Chichewa. But this factual material on police was pulled from a modest secondary school text which serves as this primary teacher's curriculum guide. [. . .]

Competing clubs: limits to the state's penetration

Political elites – with clear intent or through inadvertent mimicry of modern orga-nizing – shape the social rules and knowledge that are transmitted into the class-room. Yet how does the teacher respond to this pressure to construct bureaucratic social rules and to express modern symbols? I see three basic factors that limit the state's actual influence over the classroom teacher.

First, *the state's capacity to provide material resources is constrained*, which eats into the state's own authority. Despite limited resources, Third World governments have been very effective in constructing school buildings, often collaborating with traditional local leaders and drawing on villagers' eagerness to build even simple structures. But the second injection of resources, necessary for deepening the school's effect on children's achievement, either never comes or is very modest. In most Third World countries teachers remain in short supply. Our Malawi school survey found an average of 119 pupils enrolled in grade 1 classes (with about eighty-five attend-ing each day); attendance falls to about forty-five pupils per classroom by grade 6. Most primary school teachers in this African nation have not completed secondary school. Many come from families that are still engaged in subsistence farming. Almost two-thirds of the teachers we surveyed had no desks for pupils in their class-rooms. Over half the teachers received fewer than ten textbooks for their entire class each year. With this questionable level of teacher quality and extreme shortage of instructional materials, should we expect the state, via the school, to have much impact on children's learning?

On the other hand, the scarcity of instructional material may inadvertently strengthen the state's authority over what legitimate knowledge is presented to pupils. In the Third World, teachers must rely heavily on state-written textbooks. [. . .]

Books other than texts are rarely found in African classrooms; libraries in primary schools are non-existent. The central state's influence – in casting official knowledge and communicating modern symbols via textbooks – goes unchallenged. [. . .]

Second, the state's influence on teachers is constrained by the *inconsistent character of ideological messages emanating from political elites*. This is especially true as fragile (or stumbling) states struggle to rapidly build (or reinforce) institutions that will incorporate diverse groups. [. . .] Schools, for instance, can teach high-status languages, talk about math and science, and rhetorically link schooling to higher paying jobs. Of course, *signaling opportunity* to enter the modern world does not guarantee material gains for the masses. Where schooling expands more quickly than jobs in the cash economy, political elites must contend with disenchanted youths and parents. And if the state moves too quickly, ignoring tribal traditions and forms of authority, secular elites lose legitimacy.

The fragile state's tendency to emit mixed messages was crisply illustrated one day as I observed two energetic teachers in a southern Malawi primary school, close to the Mozambique border. Walking into the grade 4 classroom, I noticed that the day's attendance was written on the blackboard: "48 girls and 52 boys." A science teacher accompanied the regular teacher in presenting a talk on different types of soil. In large urban schools – this primary had over two thousand pupils attending each day – it is common to see a teacher with specific training in mathematics or science. The fact that a specialist joins the regular teacher adds to the status of the subject. And this specialist came with some hands-on material: canisters filled with five different types of dirt. In rapid succession, the two teachers gave each pair of children a dash of brown soil, red soil, sandy soil, and rain soil. The science teacher pursued tangents on how to read a rain gauge and on which soils would support more crops. The science teacher talked at this batch of one hundred pupils, eliciting choral pronunciation of terms in English: "milliliter," "this is clay soil," "rocks lay beneath this kind of soil."

The content of this lesson was quite relevant, especially to children who spent part of each day working on the family plot. Yet the pieces of knowledge (facts) were simply spoken at this densely packed group of children. This was science – a high-status topic that required a special authority to explain the topic in English. This modern set of codes was delivered within a mass setting. Dishing out dirt to one hundred kids must be done quickly; information is attached to each pile; children repeat these fragments of knowledge; the teacher moves on quickly to the next chunk of information. Marking the class period's end, the teacher ordered everyone to engage in quick calisthenics, "Stand up! . . . hands up, forward, side, sit down." All one hundred obediently responded, although several had to lift their drowsy heads off their desks before popping up. The science specialist launched into the next topic: "germs and pests that live in dirty houses."

Teachers' ideologies

When we examine teachers' own beliefs about schooling and socialization the third constraint on the state's local penetration arises. *Teachers' own beliefs and behaviors vary*, spawned either within the school's own institutional boundaries or determined by the state's mixed messages. [. . .]

Our initial findings on the educational ideologies of teachers in Malawi, as well as their perceptions of their classroom behavior are quite interesting. We asked teachers, for instance, about the importance they place on three possible goals of schooling. Seventy percent of the teachers reported that improving "pupils' ways of thinking" is a very important goal. Just 47 percent believed that assistance in getting a better job is very important. We also asked about more specific teaching practices related to how children should be socialized. Fifty-one percent said that they "strongly agreed" with the statement: "schools should teach children rules and how to fit into society." Fewer (38 percent) strongly agreed that "pupils learn more when they listen and ask fewer questions." But only 19 percent strongly agreed that "school should teach children how to pursue their own individual goals and interests." The greatest consensus was on a statement that fell between a liberal-individualistic versus a strong fitting-in view of socialization. Sixty percent of all teachers strongly agreed that "school should teach children to cooperate and respect other people." In short, ideologies held by the typical teacher are not clear-cut, often reflecting a mix of educational philosophy.

Mass Conditions and the Teacher's Pursuit of Authority

Romantic or functionalist beliefs are one thing. But when the teacher actually is faced with sixty or seventy children in the classroom, how does he or she structure action? Reports by teachers of what they do are not always reliable. Teachers' perceptions in Malawi, however, closely matched the observational findings from other work, including the recent studies in Nigeria and Thailand, and my ongoing work in Botswana (with Wes Snyder and David Chapman).

Teachers in Malawi report spending 45 percent of their class time lecturing and interacting with the entire class (including presentation of material, reading aloud from textbooks, asking for choral recitations, and asking questions of individual pupils while the class listens). Thirty percent of teachers' time was reportedly spent supervising pupils working silently on exercises (in Malawi, usually writing out arithmetic problems or short vocabulary lists in their exercise books). These teacher actions commonly occur in a thirty-five-minute sequence like that which I observed in a four-room school close to Lunzu:

- The fourth-grade teacher begins the period by writing a multiplication problem on the board (.252 kilograms times 3). (Note: since this is math, the teacher shifts to speaking English.)
- The teacher asks for a choral response (from all seventy-two pupils) to each calculation: "3 times 2 is? . . . 3 times 5 is? . . ." Whenever the response is not loud and crisp, the teacher speaks more sharply, "3 times 2 is what?!"
- After working through three such problems with the entire class, the teacher writes another problem on the board and directs all pupils to calculate it in their exercise books. (Note: all pupils have an exercise book and a pencil.)
- As pupils finish the problem they eagerly wave their books, remaining seated on the cold concrete floor. One by one the teacher circulates to each pupil, checking answers. Getting to seventy-two pupils requires only 20 minutes. (Note: pupil attention drifts as the teacher continues to circulate.)
- The teacher then goes back to the blackboard, asking individual pupils to stand and work through the problem. When a pupil makes a mistake, the teacher quickly interrupts and moves to another pupil, many of whom are emphatically waving their hands and snapping their fingers. Those pupils who made a mistake, four in all, remain standing until a correct answer is given.

This sequence of talking at the entire class, eliciting choral responses, then assigning an individually-performed exercise is quite common, regardless of the subject being taught. The important point here is that the *conditions of mass schooling* drive teacher action, not the more complex and diverse ideologies that teachers hold in their heads. This pedagogical sequence aims at keeping the attention of the entire class and demanding that each child work alone on an exercise (at least for a very brief time). [. . .]

Sounds of clashing symbols

Under the fragile state, the teacher is the arbiter between central elites seeking uniform socialization and plural tribes which resist or ignore this pursuit of hegemony. In attending to the classroom's "maintenance system" the teacher must accommodate these local differences. To build cohesion teachers must depart from the central state's socialization agenda. For instance, teachers in Malawi are expected to teach all subjects in English after grade 4. In addition, the language spoken by the dominant tribe – which controls the national government – is taught beginning in the first grade. Once you leave the towns and the central region dominated by the Chewa tribe, few children will understand Chichewa or English. So teachers commonly speak in Yao, Tumbuka, or one of the other thirty-five tribal languages spoken. Instruction in English holds enormous status among the political elite; but the teacher must obviously speak in the children's tribal language if any camaraderie is to be built inside the classroom.

In remote rural schools, headmasters are apologetic that Chichewa and English are not spoken by their teachers. These schools enroll children of subsistence farmers, living in sparsely populated villages often a day's walk from the nearest paved road. The only government official they see is the district education officer, once a month when he brings teachers' salaries in cash. If teachers pressed the language of a foreign tribe (be it the language of Chewa political elites or of British economic elites), children would understand little and the school would alienate parents. In this case the central government would be seen as too ideological and irrelevant. But by delivering subjects in the indigenous language, the state's socialization agenda appears less obtrusive.

At times, even the state will attempt to accommodate local forms of authority within textbooks and the curriculum. Early one morning we arrived at a primary school close to rural Dowa. The rains had come two weeks prior. The morning air was cool and damp. Entering the dark, stark classroom I saw just eleven youngsters, all sitting on the floor, which my butt soon told me was cold and wet. Embarrassed, the teacher flew out the door, returning with an old chair . . . a scarce but strong symbol of respect for his strange white visitor. The teacher continued reading a passage from the government's grade 7 English textbook ". . . Mkandawire, the local headman, sat talking to his fellow villagers. The rains had not come that season, and the villagers were worried about their crops and the health of their children. The headman had thought much about why the rain had not come. He was presenting possible explanations. . . ."

Interestingly, the story goes on to present several spiritual and traditional explanations for why the rains had not come. After reading the story, the teacher asked pupils questions in English, practicing their reading comprehension. But the traditional wisdom of village headmen continued to receive respect throughout the discussion. This section of the textbook provides a collection of traditional stories, at times blended with Western knowledge and symbols. One historical story deals with a woman who allegedly fools slave traders by pretending she's a witch. Another tells of a middle-class man who uses a clock to make sure he catches his bus on time, and features pictures of him jumping from bed dressed in pajamas running to the bus stop. Very few Malawians can afford to ride a bus, and fewer sleep in beds. Pajamas are seen as an incredibly funny artifact worn only by the British.

Many teachers are quite active within their classrooms. The life and pace of interaction between these teachers and their many pupils is remarkable. Their common lesson sequence does engage the majority of pupils: presenting a chunk of material, eliciting choral responses, assigning short twenty-minute exercises, then reviewing the material by working out the problems on the blackboard. The resulting cohesion maintains the teacher's authority and sanctions the discrete bits of information contained within the official curriculum. This routine also allows the teacher to demonstrate to the headmaster, in a standardized way, how far the class has progressed in the textbook. Whether this regimen effectively imparts literacy or useful social skills is rarely asked. The teacher's legitimacy is simply reinforced by following institutionalized rules for how he or she is supposed to act. There is ample faith that these actions will lead to desired socialization and academic outcomes.

Occasionally Malawian teachers set down social rules that contradict the otherwise mass structure of the classroom. Maintaining order and discipline remains a concern. Yet the teacher relinquishes control, encouraging pupils to engage in more complex individual activities or to work cooperatively in groups. This combination of high energy, engagement, and more lateral interaction among children was illustrated by the following sequence observed in one classroom not far from the capital city of Lilongwe:

- The teacher begins the Chichewa period (grade 3) by passing out textbooks. Few pupils own their own. I noted that on the blackboard was written, "67 on roll, 59 present." The teacher commanded all children to stand and touch their toes, raise their arms over their heads, and clap their hands. The morning is warm, but the children seem keen on getting off the concrete floor for a few moments. These sudden calisthenics signal the beginning of the next thirty-five-minute period.
- The teacher writes twelve Chichewa words on the board and begins pointing to each word. This prompts a wild waving of hands and snapping of fingers – a stylized snapping that results from a sharp simultaneous flicking of the wrist and fingers. Performed by this batch of kids, it sounds like a muffled orchestra of crickets. (I think to myself that Victorian missionary teachers would have been shocked to witness this audible African sign of eagerness in the classroom.)
- A five-sentence paragraph containing these new words is read by the teacher from the Chichewa text. She then bangs an aluminum pot with a broad stick . . . like a metal drum. This sends the children scurrying around, forming into familiar groups of three or four. As the dust (literally) settles, one child in each group begins reading the passage out loud to the other group members. The teacher circles around the class, listening to recitations within each group, for about 15 minutes.

- The teacher grabs the pot and stick once more; the same piercing percussion sends pupils back into their tidy columns, as if they were sitting one behind each other in desks (but in this classroom there are no desks).
- Again, the pupils are told to stand and run through their well-learned exercises. This round includes turning in circles, jumping up and down, pointing to the blackboard, the door, and the windows (where no glass remains). The names of these classroom features are shouted out in English.
- The teacher then reads ten Chichewa words which pupils write in their exercise books. They exchange books to read how their partner wrote the words. The teacher again circulates around to all fifty-nine, checking their spelling.

I recall my initial fright in seeing the instinctive compliance exhibited by these small children, quickly replying to the teacher's every command. But within the routine, children were encouraged to interact with each other. First, reading to each other. Later, reading their partner's written Chichewa words. The content and form of this cooperative action was certainly prescribed by the teacher. But this horizontal interaction between small groups or pairs of children departed strongly from the usual pattern where the teacher constantly interacts with the entire mass of pupils, or where pupils work in isolation from one another. [. . .]

The teacher's strong authority

Most African teachers are members of the small class of people who are literate and who receive a steady wage in cash. The teacher also holds the power to allocate forms of secular merit and virtue to children. Relatively few children persist through primary school and enter secondary school. But those that do persist gain a shot at entering the modern economic sector to make a steady wage. This institutionalized role as gate-keeper, legitimated by the state, brings enormous status to the teacher. Yet day to day in the classroom, many teachers feel that they must demonstrate their strict authority. This is particularly true in settings like Malawi, where colonial schools historically reflected deference to authoritarian officialdom, and the overcrowded conditions of mass schooling create uncertainty for which tight control appears to be an effective antidote.

Whenever a Malawian pupil must urinate, he or she is required to seek out the teacher, who is usually standing at the front of the class. Before all, the pupil bows down onto one knee, folds his or her hands, and requests a leave. Two or three children during each class period will typically go through this rather fluid motion, with little apparent embarrassment. But as a ritual, signaling control over the child's most basic movements, the exercise is significant.

Often when a thirty-five-minute class period has been completed, the teacher will signal to a pupil to pick up a rag and erase the blackboard, as the teacher moves to the back of the classroom. The teacher will just stand, scanning over the pupils, until the blackboard is spotless. This crisply signals the shift to a new subject, as well as the teacher's authority to assign a routine chore while he or she simply waits. Similarly, when the headmaster or a visitor enters the classroom, the teacher bows and clasps one wrist as they shake hands. The teacher is thereby displaying his or her deference to persons that are higher in the status order. I have often thought about how pupils, who are subordinated daily to the teacher's authority, view their own teacher's self-subordination to the headmaster or the occasional government representative.

These rituals reinforce the hierarchical form of authority found in the "modern" African school. In fact, the severe asymmetry of authority found in Malawian schools suggests that Dreeben's emphasis on achievement and individualism may not apply in many Third World settings. The modern state may preach the virtues of self-reliance, higher productivity, and entrepreneurial initiative. But the structure of authority and status previously found in colonial schools (be they operated by imperial administrations or by missions) continues to be reproduced. Here the liberal, romantic side of the Western state can not be operationalized in the face of classrooms spilling over with children. Note again, the *post-colonial* state is attempting to broaden opportunity to achieve higher status and higher income by opening access to the school institution. But the mass conditions and uncertainty which result inside the classroom push the teacher to seek control, and to engage in rituals that signal authority but which do very little to encourage learning. [. . .]

20 Time–Space Compression and the Rise of Modernism as a Cultural Force

David Harvey

The depression that swept out of Britain in 1846–7 and which quickly engulfed the whole of what was then the capitalist world, can justly be regarded as the first unambiguous crisis of capitalist overaccumulation. It shook the confidence of the bourgeoisie and challenged its sense of history and geography in profound ways. There had been many economic and political crises before, but most could reasonably be attributed to natural calamities (such as harvest failures) or wars and other geopolitical struggles. But this one was different. Though there were bad harvests here and there, this crisis could not easily be attributed to God or nature. Capitalism had matured by 1847–8 to a sufficient degree, so that even the blindest bourgeois apologist could see that financial conditions, reckless speculation, and over-production had something to do with events. The outcome, in any case, was a sudden paralysis of the economy, in which surpluses of capital and labour lay side by side with apparently no way to reunite them in profitable and socially useful union.

There were, of course, as many explanations of the crisis as there were class positions (and a good few more besides). The craft workers from Paris to Vienna tended to view it as the inevitable outcome of a rampant capitalist development process that was changing employment conditions, raising the rate of exploitation, and destroying traditional skills, while progressive elements in the bourgeoisie could view it as a product of the recalcitrant aristocratic and feudal orders who refused the course of progress. The latter, for their part, could attribute the whole affair to the undermining of traditional values and social hierarchies by the materialist values and practices of both workers and an aggressive class of capitalists and financiers.

The thesis I want to explore here, however, is that the crisis of 1847–8 created a crisis of representation, and that this latter crisis itself derived from a radical readjustment in the sense of time and space in economic, political, and cultural life. Before 1848, progressive elements within the bourgeoisie could reasonably hold to the Enlightenment sense of time ("time pressing forward" as Gurvitch would put it), recognizing that they were fighting a battle against the "enduring" and ecological time of traditional societies and the "retarded time" of recalcitrant forms of social organization. But after 1848, that progressive sense of time was called into question in many important respects. Too many people in Europe had fought on the barricades, or been caught up in the maelstrom of hopes and fears, not to appreciate the stimulus that comes with participant action in "explosive time." Baudelaire, for one, could never forget the experience, and came back to it again and again in

Original publication details: Harvey, David, "Time–Space Compression and the Rise of Modernism as a Cultural Force" from *The Condition of Postmodernity* (Blackwell, Oxford, 1990).

his explorations of a modernist language. In retrospect, it became easier to invoke some cyclical sense of time (hence the growing interest in the idea of business cycles as necessary components to the capitalist growth process that would connect back to the economic troubles of 1837, 1826, and 1817). Or, if people were mindful enough of class tensions, they might invoke, as Marx did in *The Eighteenth Brumaire of Louis Bonaparte*, a sense of "alternating time" in which the outcome of bitter struggles must always be seen as a precarious balance between class forces. But I think it true to say that the question "What time are we in?" came in upon the philosophical agenda after 1848 in ways that challenged the simple mathematical presuppositions of Enlightenment thinking. The sense of physical and social time, so recently brought together in Enlightenment thought, began once more to diverge. It then became possible for the artist and the thinker to explore the nature and meaning of time in new ways.

The events of 1847–8 also challenged certainties as to the nature of space and the meaning of money. Events proved that Europe had achieved a level of spatial integration in its economic and financial life that was to make the whole continent vulnerable to simultaneous crisis formation. The political revolutions that erupted at once across the continent emphasized the synchronic as well as the diachronic dimensions to capitalist development. The certainty of absolute space and place gave way to the insecurities of a shifting relative space, in which events in one place could have immediate and ramifying effects in several other places. If, as Jameson suggests, "the truth of experience no longer coincides with the place in which it takes place," but is spreadeagled across the world's spaces, then a situation arises "in which we can say that if individual experience is authentic, then it cannot be true; and that if a scientific or cognitive mode of the same content is true, then it escapes individual experience." Since individual experience always forms the raw material of works of art, this condition posed deep problems for artistic production. But this was not the only arena of confusion. Diverse local workers' movements suddenly found themselves swept up in a series of events and political shifts which had no obvious boundaries. Nationalist workers could exhibit xenophobia in Paris yet sympathize with Polish or Viennese workers struggling, like them, for political and economic emancipation in their particular spaces. It was in such a context that the universalist propositions of *The Communist Manifesto* made more than a little sense. How to reconcile the perspective of place with the shifting perspectives of relative space became a serious issue to which modernism was to address itself with increasing vigour up until the shock of the First World War.

European space was becoming more and more unified precisely because of the internationalism of money power. 1847–8 was a financial and monetary crisis which seriously challenged received ideas as to the meaning and role of money in social life. The tension between the functions of money as a measure and store of value, and money as a lubricant of exchange and investment had long been evident. But it was now registered as a downright antagonism between the financial system (the whole structure of credit moneys and "fictitious capitals") and its monetary base (gold and other tangible commodities that give a clear physical meaning to money). Credit money in effect came crashing down, leaving a shortage of "real money" and specie in 1847–8. Those who controlled specie controlled a vital source of social power. The Rothschilds used that power to great effect and, through their superior command over space, came to dominate the finances of the whole European continent. Yet the question of the true nature and meaning of money was not so easily resolved. The tension between credit and specie money loomed large in the subsequent years, eventually bringing even the Rothschilds into a banking world in which the credit system and "fictitious capital formation" became paramount. This in turn altered the meaning of time (investment times, rate of return, etc.) and other vital magnitudes to capitalism's dominant mode of conducting business. It was only after 1850, after all, that stock and capital markets (markets for "fictitious capital") were systematically organized and opened to general participation under legal rules of incorporation and market contract.

All of these shifts created a crisis of representation. Neither literature nor art could avoid the question of internationalism, synchrony, insecure temporality, and the tension within the dominant measure of value between the financial system and its monetary or commodity base. "Around 1850," writes Barthes, "classical writing therefore disintegrated, and the whole of literature, from Flaubert to the present day, became the problematics of language." It is no accident that the first great modernist cultural thrust occurred in Paris after 1848. The brushstrokes of Manet that began to decompose the traditional space of painting and to alter its frame, to explore the fragmentations of light and colour; the poems and reflections of Baudelaire that sought to transcend ephemerality and the narrow politics of place in the search for eternal meanings; and the novels of Flaubert with their peculiar narrative structures in space and time coupled with a language of icy aloofness; all of these were signals of a radical break of cultural sentiment that reflected a profound questioning of the meaning of space and place, of present, past and future, in a world of insecurity and rapidly expanding spatial horizons.

Flaubert, for example, explores the question of representation of heterogeneity and difference, of simultaneity and synchrony, in a world where both time and space are being absorbed under the homogenizing powers of money and commodity exchange. "Everything should sound simultaneously," he wrote; "one should hear the bellowing of the cattle, the whispering of the lovers, and the rhetoric of the officials all at the same time." Unable to represent this simultaneity with the requisite effect, Flaubert "dissolves the sequence by cutting back and forth (the cinematographic analogy is quite deliberate)" and in the final crescendo to a scene in *Madame Bovary* juxtaposes two sequences "in a single sentence to reach a unified effect". Frédéric Moreau, the hero of Flaubert's *L'Éducation Sentimentale*, moves from space to space in Paris and its suburbs, collecting experiences of quite different qualities as he goes. What is special is the way that he glides in and out of the differentiated spaces of the city, with the same sort of ease that money and commodities change hands. The whole narrative structure of the book likewise gets lost in perpetual postponements of decisions precisely because Frédéric has enough inherited money to enjoy the luxury of not deciding, even in the midst of revolutionary turmoil. Action is reduced to a set of paths that might have been but were not taken. "The thought of the future torments us, and the past is holding us back," Flaubert later wrote, adding, "that is why the present is slipping from our grasp." Yet it was the possession of money that allowed the present to slip through Frédéric's grasp, while opening social spaces to casual penetration. Evidently, time, space, and money could be invested with rather different significances, depending upon the conditions and possibilities of trade-off between them. Flaubert had to find a new language to speak of such possibilities.

These explorations of new cultural forms occurred in an economic and political context which in many respects belied that of the economic collapse and revolutionary upsurge of 1848. Even though, for example, excessive speculation in railroad construction triggered the first European-wide crisis of overaccumulation, the resolution to that crisis after 1850 rested heavily upon further exploration of temporal and spatial displacement. New systems of credit and corporate forms of organization, of distribution (the large department stores), coupled with technical and organizational innovations in production (increasing fragmentation, specialization, and de-skilling in the division of labour for example), helped speed up the circulation of capital in mass markets. More emphatically, capitalism became embroiled in an incredible phase of massive long-term investment in the conquest of space. The expansion of the railway network, accompanied by the advent of the telegraph, the growth of steam shipping, and the building of the Suez Canal, the beginnings of radio communication and bicycle and automobile travel at the end of the century, all changed the sense of time and space in radical ways. This period also saw the coming on stream of a whole series of technical innovations. New ways of viewing space and motion (derived from photography and exploration of the limits of perspectivism) began to be thought out and applied to the production of urban space. Balloon travel and photography from on high changed perceptions of the earth's surface, while new technologies of printing and mechanical reproduction allowed a dissemination of news, information, and cultural artefacts throughout ever broader swathes of the population.

The vast expansion of foreign trade and investment after 1850 put the major capitalist powers on the path of globalism, but did so through imperial conquest and inter-imperialist rivalry that was to reach its apogee in World War I – the first global war. En route, the world's spaces were deterritorialized, stripped of their preceding significations, and then reterritorialized according to the convenience of colonial and imperial administration. Not only was the relative space revolutionized through innovations in transport and communications, but what that space contained was also fundamentally re-ordered. The map of domination of the world's spaces changed out of all recognition between 1850 and 1914. Yet it was possible, given the flow of information and new techniques of representation, to sample a wide range of simultaneous imperial adventures and conflicts with a mere glance at the morning newspaper. And if that was not enough, the organization of a series of World Exhibitions, beginning with the Crystal Palace in 1851 and passing through several French efforts to the grand Columbian Exhibition in Chicago in 1893, celebrated the fact of globalism while providing a framework within which what Benjamin calls "the phantasmagoria" of the world of commodities and competition between nation states and territorial production systems might be understood.[. . .]

It was in the midst of this rapid phase of time–space compression that the second great wave of modernist innovation in the aesthetic realm began. To what degree, then, can modernism be interpreted as a response to a crisis in the experience of space and time? Kern's study of *The Culture of Time and Space, 1880–1918* makes such a supposition more than a little plausible.

Kern accepts that "the telephone, wireless-telegraph, X-ray, cinema, bicycle, automobile and airplane established the material foundation" for new modes of thinking about and experiencing time and space. While he is anxious to maintain the independence of cultural developments, he does argue that "the interpretation of phenomena such as class structure, diplomacy, and war tactics in terms of modes of time and space makes possible the demonstration of their essential similarity to explicit considerations of time and space in literature, philosophy, science, and art". Lacking any theory of technological innovation, of capitalist dynamics across space, or of cultural production, Kern offers only "generalizations about the essential cultural developments of the period". But his descriptions highlight the incredible confusions and oppositions across a spectrum of possible reactions to the growing sense of crisis in the experience of time and space, that had been gathering since 1848 and seemed to come to a head just before World War I. I note in parenthesis that 1910–14 is roughly the period that many historians of modernism (beginning with Virginia Woolf and D. H. Lawrence) point to as crucial in the evolution of modernist thinking. Henri Lefebvre agrees:

> Around 1910 a certain space was shattered. It was the space of common sense, of knowledge, of social practice, of political power, a space hitherto enshrined in everyday discourse, just as in abstract thought, as the environment of and channel for communication. . . Euclidean and perspectivist space have disappeared as systems of reference, along with other former "common places" such as town, history, paternity, the tonal system in music, traditional morality, and so forth. This was a truly crucial moment.

Consider a few aspects of this crucial moment set, significantly enough, between Einstein's special theory of relativity of 1905 and the general theory of 1916. Ford, we recall, set up his assembly line in 1913. He fragmented tasks and distributed them in space so as to maximize efficiency and minimize the friction of flow in production. In effect, he used a certain form of spatial organization to accelerate the turnover time of capital in production. Time could then be accelerated (speed-up) by virtue of the control established through organizing and fragmenting the spatial order of production. In that very same year, however, the first radio signal was beamed around the world from the Eiffel Tower, thus emphasizing the capacity to collapse space into the simultaneity of an instant in universal public time. The power of wireless had been clearly demonstrated the year before with the rapid diffusion of news about the sinking of the *Titanic* (itself a symbol of speed and mass motion that came to grief in much the same way that the *Herald of Free Enterprise* was to keel over to speedy disaster some seventy-five years later). Public time was becoming ever more homogeneous and universal across space. And it was not only commerce and railways, for the organization of large-scale commuting systems and all the other temporal co-ordinations that made metropolitan life bearable also depended upon establishing some universal and commonly accepted sense of time. The more than 38 billion telephone calls made in the United States in 1914 emphasized the power of intervention of public time and space in daily and private life. Indeed, it was only in terms of such a public sense of time that reference to private time could make sense. De Chirico appropriately celebrated these qualities by conspicuously placing clocks (an unusual gesture in art history) in his paintings of 1910–14.

The reactions pointed in many directions. James Joyce, for one, began his quest to capture the sense of simultaneity in space and time during this period, insisting upon the present as the only real location of experience. He had his action take place in a plurality of spaces, Kern notes, "in a consciousness that leaps about the universe and mixes here and there in defiance of the ordered diagramming of the cartographers." Proust, for his part, tried to recover past time and to create a sense of individuality and place that rested on a conception of experience across a space of time. Personal conceptions of time became a matter of public commentary. "The two most innovative novelists of the period," Kern continues, "transformed the stage of modern literature from a series of fixed settings in homogeneous space" (of the sort that realist novelists typically deployed) "into a multitude of qualitatively different spaces that varied with the shifting moods and perspectives of human consciousness."

Picasso and Braque, for their part, taking their cue from Cézanne who had begun to break up the space of painting in new ways in the 1880s, experimented with cubism, thus abandoning "the homogeneous space of linear perspective" that had dominated since the fifteenth century. Delaunay's celebrated work of 1910–11 depicting the Eiffel Tower was perhaps the most startling public symbol of a movement that tried to represent time through a fragmentation of space; the protagonists were probably unaware that this paralleled the practices on Ford's assembly line, though the choice of the Eiffel Tower as symbol reflected the fact that the whole movement had something to do with industrialism. It was in 1912, also, that Durkheim's *Elementary Forms of the Religious Life* was published with its explicit recognition that "the foundation of the category time is the rhythm of social life," and that the social origin of space likewise necessarily entailed the existence of multiple spatial visions. Ortega y Gasset, following Nietzsche's injunction that "there is *only* a perspective seeing, *only* a proper perspective knowing," formulated a new version of the theory of perspectivism in 1910 which insisted that "there were as many spaces in reality as there were perspectives on it," and that "there are as many realities as points of view." This put a philosophical nail in the coffin of rationalist ideals of homogeneous and absolute space.

I have cited just a few of the incidents that Kern records in order to convey a sense of the confusions rampant in social and cultural thought in the period 1910–14. But matters can, I think, be taken a step further, hinging an argument on an idea that Kern launches but makes very little of: "One response was a growing sense of unity among people formerly isolated in distance and lack of communication. This was not, however, unambiguous, because proximity also generated anxiety – apprehension that the neighbours were seen as getting a bit too close". How was this "ambiguity" expressed? Two broad and rather distinctive currents of thought can be identified depending upon the emphasis upon unity or difference.

Those who emphasized the unity between peoples also accepted the "unreality of place" within a fragmented relative space. Celebrating the annihilation of space through time, the task was to re-launch the Enlightenment project of universal human emancipation in a global space bound together through mechanisms of communication and social intervention. Such a project implied, however, spatial fragmentation through planned co-ordination. And how could that be done except through "pulverizing" pre-existing spaces in some manner? Ford had shown how social processes could be speeded up, and productive forces augmented, by the spatialization of time. The problem was to harness this capacity to human emancipation rather than to some narrow set of interests, such as those of capital. A German group proposed in 1911, for example, the creation of a "world office" that would "unify all the humanitarian tendencies that run in parallel but disorderly directions, and bring about a concentration and a promotion of all creative activities". It was only in such a context of rationalized and totally organized external and public space, that interior and very private senses of time and space could properly flourish. The space of the body, of consciousness, of the psyche – spaces kept too long repressed, given the absolute suppositions of Enlightenment thought, but now opening up as a consequence of psychological and philosophical findings – could be liberated only through the rational organization of exterior space and time. But rationality now meant something more than planning with the aid of the map and the chronometer, or subjecting all of social life to time and motion study. New senses of relativism and perspectivism could be invented and applied to the production of space and the ordering of time. This kind of reaction, which many were later to dub as exclusively modernist, typically entailed a whole set of accoutrements. Despising history, it sought entirely new cultural forms that broke with the past and solely spoke the language of the new. Holding that form followed function and that spatial rationality should be imposed on the external world in order to maximize individual liberty and welfare, it took efficiency and function (and hence the image of the metropolis as a well-oiled machine) as its central motif. It had a deep concern for purity of language, no matter whether it was in architecture, music, or literature.

It is an open question, of course, whether this response was a pure bowing down to the force of spatial and temporal restructuring of the period. Fernand Léger, the French cubist painter, certainly thought so, observing in 1913 that life was "more fragmented and faster moving than in previous periods" and that it was essential to devise a dynamic art to depict it. And Gertrude Stein certainly interpreted cultural events, such as the advent of cubism, as a response to the time–space compression to which everyone was exposed and sensitized. This in no way detracts, of course, from the importance of grappling with that experience in the field of representation in such a way as to enhance, support, and perhaps even command the processes that seemed to be escaping from all forms of collective control (as they were indeed set to do in World War I). But it does re-focus our attention on the practical ways in which that might be done. Le Corbusier was, in effect, merely following the Jeffersonian principles of land partition when he argued that the way to individual liberty and freedom lay through the construction of a highly ordered and rationalized space. His project was internationalist, and emphasized the kind of unity in which a socially conscious notion of individual difference could be fully explored.

The other kind of reaction bundled together a host of seemingly divergent responses built, however, around one central principle: that the more unified the space, the more important the qualities of the fragmentations become for social identity and action. The free flow of capital across the surface of the globe, for example, places strong emphasis upon the particular qualities of the spaces to which that capital might be attracted. The shrinkage of space that brings diverse communities across the globe into competition with each other implies localized competitive strategies and a heightened sense of awareness of what makes a place special and gives it a competitive advantage. This kind of reaction looks much more strongly to the identification of place, the building and signalling of its unique qualities in an increasingly homogeneous but fragmented world.

Questions

1   Does Iyer show that globalization means the westernization of Asian societies? Can Bali preserve its "cultural integrity" as an exotic "Eden"? Does the Manila music scene show that globalization is a one-way flow of symbols?

2   In what ways is everyday local life in metropolitan areas like London becoming more profoundly "global," according to Albrow? How does globalization affect people's attachment to their local community?

3   In what respects is the school experience of the students and teachers observed by Fuller similar to your own, and how does it differ from yours? What does their experience tell you about the difficulties developing countries face in implementing a global institution? Do schools in Malawi strengthen the state? Do they make individual students more independent thinkers?

4   What does Harvey mean by "time–space compression"? How did some Europeans first express their experience of it around the turn of the nineteenth century? How could this experience lead to both a greater sense of unity among peoples and a greater sense of fragmentation that causes people to identify more with particular places?

Part IV

Economic Globalization

Introduction

By 1997, most countries of Southeast Asia had become an integral part of the world economy. Successful exporters, they had enjoyed high growth rates for many years, and the promise of these "emerging markets" had attracted increasing amounts of foreign capital. Then, quite unexpectedly, the pattern reversed. As Japan's recession translated into diminished Japanese investment in and imports from the region, the growth prospects of other countries dimmed. In Thailand, South Korea, and Indonesia, banks and companies had trouble paying their debts. As foreign capital fled, even high interest rates could not prevent a slide in currencies, which further exacerbated the debt problems. With exports to Europe and the US absorbing only part of the excess production capacity in Asia, failing companies had to lay off workers. Since its own financial sector was burdened by bad debts, Japan could not be an engine for regional growth. The Asian "miracle" gave way to Asian "contagion."

Asia's problems had global ramifications. Western financial markets came under severe pressure as profit expectations declined. The Asian contagion contributed to a loss of confidence in Russia's economic reform efforts, halting though they were in any case. The ruble went into free fall, defaults on foreign debts ensued, and economic misery spread widely within Russia. Latin America was not immune either; its largest economy, Brazil, became the focus of an intense international effort to prevent the contagion from spreading there. As Asian demand declined, commodity prices fell in world markets, adding to the difficulties of countries dependent on raw material exports. In the United States, the contagion helped to dampen inflation; already low gasoline prices, for example, fell to their lowest levels since World War II.

The widespread use of the contagion metaphor indicated to worldwide audiences that the world indeed had become a single, integrated economy in which everyone had become dependent on everyone else. For government officials and business leaders, consumers and investors, Korean workers and IMF strategists, Russian farmers and Brazilian retirees, the Asian contagion represented globalization become real and dangerous. It was not the first shock to the world economy, since the oil crisis of the 1970s and the subsequent debt crisis in many developing countries had already exposed the extent of modern global interdependence. Yet in the decades prior to the Asian crisis, economic globalization had been generally welcomed. For many years, leaders and economists cheered as world trade grew faster than world GDP, foreign direct investment outstripped domestic investment, and the volume of international currency transactions increased exponentially. Many formerly marginal countries became growing, exporting tigers. The production of many goods once monopolized by the industrialized West spread across the globe, linking companies, workers and whole countries in transnational "commodity chains." Not only did actual economic exchanges intensify, they also were increasingly managed by international organizations, such as the GATT and its successor, the World Trade Organization, that relied on global rules. By many standards, then, economic integration had become a hallmark of globalization, deliberately promoted by governments, corporations, and international organizations alike. So closely intertwined had parts of the world economic system become that they now all became vulnerable to distant troubles.

At the same time, various skeptical voices challenged what had quickly become conventional wisdom among opinion leaders. Like Immanuel Wallerstein in part II, scholars question the uniqueness of the late twentieth century. The sixteenth and nineteenth centuries, they argue, already witnessed dramatic economic integration that set the stage for all subsequent developments. Financial markets may operate differently due to computer technology, and the geopolitical context may be different due to the demise of the Soviet Union, but these are not qualitative changes. Other skeptics, by contrast, argue not that capitalism has always been global but that it is not yet fully globalized. For example, they suggest that the real roots of economic troubles, from Asia to Russia to Brazil, lie in bad domestic decisions. International markets can exploit and aggravate such errors, but they are not the primary cause of a contagious crisis. The involvement of countries in the world economy varies greatly in any case. While some small economies, such as the Netherlands, are highly dependent on exports, for large countries, especially the USA, imports and exports still represent only a small portion of total GDP. The whole notion of integration is misleading for these skeptics, since the core of the world economy is only perhaps thirty of the world's 200 countries – a few countries of the Asian Pacific, western Europe, and North America, which account for the vast bulk of world capital and nearly all of the largest multinational corporations. Globalization, from this perspective, amounts to only modestly more intense ties among countries, corporations, and consumers in the industrialized democracies.

We think the skeptics make some good empirical points but underestimate the significance of recent qualitative changes. Our purpose, however, is not to settle these debates. Instead, we want to convey a sense of what is at stake with selections that focus on one dimension of economic globalization, namely, its implications for inequality. Parts I and II showed that this issue is important both to critics of globalization-as-market-expansion and to economically oriented theorists of globalization. This part adds a more empirical approach to the issue.

William Greider illustrates how Malaysia attracted investment by offering tax-free economic zones to foreign companies, notably in the semiconductor industry. While Malaysian growth accelerated as a result, Greider is concerned about the "global jobs auction" that such policies engender, as countries compete to provide the lowest-wage work force. He bemoans this "manic logic of capitalism," in the words of his book's subtitle. At the same time, he shows that Malaysian women who work at plants such as Motorola's derive real benefits from their new-found employment. Next, Miguel Korzeniewicz demonstrates how global production actually works in one prominent sector. The Nike corporation relied on Asian production and American marketing from the outset, but production in Asia diversified as Korean producers began to manage sites in Vietnam and Indonesia. The Nike commodity chain thus pulled in cheaper workers in new countries, while most profits still flowed to corporate owners in the West. In recent years, this disparity has motivated various groups to protest the treatment of Asian workers producing Nike shoes. Such humanitarian concerns should not enter into rational investment decisions, Ted Fishman implies with some irony. As he plans his family's finances, he bets that "Third World workers are going to work like hell." The pursuit of high returns leads him to chase misery. To be sure, foreign workers reap some benefits from their labors and, as a result, may eventually become fully competitive with Fishman's own children. In the short run, however, he counts on authoritarian governments to pacify their workers. To Lourdes Beneria and Savitri Bisnath, that priority seems completely misguided. The real problem in economic development, they argue, is that women are left out. They carry a heavy work load, but, due to lower education and family constraints, they cannot obtain well-paying jobs in most countries. When governments and organizations try to create economic opportunity for the poor, their focus is usually on men. Eradicating poverty, Beneria and Bisnath insist, requires specific policies to overcome the subordination of women.

Does globalization pose a risk to workers in western countries? In the United States, many union officials and politicians have long expressed concerns about the impact of imports on high-wage manufacturing jobs. After summarizing some evidence on global economic integration, Matthew Slaughter and Phillip Swagel address these concerns with data on US wages and jobs. While globalization coincides with unemployment and declining wages among the less skilled, they find that trade with developing nations did not play a large role in exacerbating inequality. Gary Burtless and his colleagues reinforce this message with evidence on the relationship between free trade and employment in America. The overall American picture runs counter to conventional fears: employment has expanded and the unemployment rate has dropped as the country has become more globally integrated. Burtless and colleagues point to gains from foreign trade and argue that shifts in the domestic economy have outweighed even possibly harmful external effects. Not surprisingly, they counsel against the temptations of "globaphobia."

While not directly disputing such economic analyses, the excerpt from Amnesty International expresses an increasingly global concern. Workers in many places, AI feels, are subject to ruthless competition and ill treatment precisely at a time when their governments have less leverage to improve their condition via social programs. Unions are often too weak and fragmented to present a united front against business interests. Activists interested in protecting worker interests, then, have a global task in creating solidarity across national boundaries. Treating labor rights as human rights, AI suggests, may aid in this effort.

21 Wawasan 2020

William Greider

The process of global economic integration is broadly driven by market forces, in particular the competitive price pressures to reduce costs, but the actual events of industrial movement depend crucially upon political transactions – irregular deals that often offend the reigning principles of free-market enterprise. When a multinational corporation seeks to shift production to low-wage labor markets, a process of political bargaining ensues with the governments competing for the new factories. Concessions are offered, deals are made, investment follows.

Given the worldwide thirst for economic development and the abundance of willing governments, these political arrangements are now so commonplace that almost everyone regards them as normal. The multinational companies usually have the leverage to stipulate terms for their capital investments, but the leverage is reversed in some important cases and nations can dictate terms to the firms.

A corporation's power is naturally strongest if it is dealing with a small, very poor country desperate for industrial development. The terms typically involve special political favors not available to others in commerce: state subsidies, exemption from taxation, government suppression of workers, special status as export enclaves free of import duties.

With these protective benefits, commerce is able to leap across the deepest social and economic divisions, bringing advanced production systems to primitive economies, disturbing ancient cultures with startling elements of modernity. Governments of developing nations may be nervous about the cultural disruption, but they usually suppress doubts and dissent. Starting from positions of weakness, the poor states hope this exchange will start them on an upward track toward higher levels of industrialization and an escape from general poverty. Some are succeeding in those terms and with spectacular results; many others eagerly offer themselves as the new greenfields for migrating production.

Even successful nations discover, however, that a basic insecurity lingers in their economic advance. A prosperity based on the strategies of multinational corporations remains hostage to them. If a country manages to graduate from low-wage status and establish a self-sustaining industrial base, its achievement may become permanent. But the very process of moving up also threatens to drive away the global investors. If capital does eventually move on, a relationship intended to be a mutually rewarding symbiosis may prove to have been parasitic.

An ironic and debilitating form of global convergence is under way between rich and poor: a global jobs auction. The irregular political leverage that commerce first employed in the weak countries is now being applied to the wealthy and powerful as well, especially the United States. Multinationals are, in effect, conducting a peripatetic global jobs competition, awarding shares of production to those who make the highest bids – that is, the greatest concessions by the public domain. If a poor

Original publication details: Greider, William, "Wawasan 2020" from *One World, Ready or Not* (Simon & Schuster, 1997).

country like Malaysia grants public favors to capital in exchange for scarce jobs, then so will Ohio or Alabama.

In the industrial zone at Petaling Jaya outside Kuala Lumpur, a line of dingy blue buses began delivering workers for the 2 P.M. shift change at the Motorola plant. Motorola's blue logo was visible from the freeway, along with some other celebrated names of electronics like Canon, Sanyo, Panasonic and Minolta. Its factory looked like a low-slung office building facing an asphalt parking lot that was bordered by palms and giant yews. The white facade was temporarily decorated with dozens of red paper lanterns and gilded banners in honor of the Chinese New Year. Above the front entrance, a billboard invited workers to enter the "Motorola 10 K Run," winners to compete at the US Austin marathon.

The arriving workers passed through glass doors and headed down a long gleam-ing corridor toward the changing room, past the library and health center and an automatic banking machine. All of them were women, and most were young, small and delicate by American standards. They were dressed in the modesty of Islam – flowing ankle-length dresses, heads and shoulders draped by the Muslim *tundjung*, silken scarves of pale blue, orange and brown. A few wore the fuller, more con-servative black veils that closely framed their faces like pale brown hearts and encased the upper body like shrouds.

"Good afternoon, ladies." Roger Bertelson, Motorola's country manager, was showing me around, and the two of us towered above the stream of women. They passed by, eyes down, barely nodding. Bertelson had brush-cut hair and a sunny American forwardness, like a taller version of Ross Perot. He was explaining the "I Recommend" board on the wall, a display covered with snapshots of employees who had made successful suggestions.

"We had to change the culture," Bertelson said, "because the Malay home does not encourage women to speak out. The daughter is supposed to have babies and take care of her husband. The idea was to break down the resistance to speaking out. We use positive reinforcement, just like you would work with schoolchildren. First, convince them that you are going to listen to them. Then have them stand up before their peers for recognition."

The automatic teller machine also disturbed the culture. "We had to change the pattern," he said. "She had to go home and tell her father: 'I'm not going to bring my money home in a pay envelope any more. It's going into the bank.'"

Farther along the hallway, the women passed by a collection of Norman Rock-well paintings – warm, nostalgic scenes of American life – each accompanied by an inspirational aphorism in English. "People Will Take Note of Excellent Work." "You'll Be Prepared for Anything with Enthusiasm." "What We Say Is as Impor-tant as How We Say It." It was hard to know what meaning these homey Ameri-can images might have in this setting.

At the changing room, the women removed shoes and veils and proceeded to the gowning room across the hall. A few minutes later they emerged cloaked in ghostly white jumpsuits, wearing surgical masks and hooded bonnets. They looked like otherworldly travelers, more chaste than they would appear in the most severe Islamic garments. At the air shower, blasts of purified air cleansed them of any remaining particles of dust. Then they entered the sealed operations room, where the rows of complex machines and monitors awaited the next shift.

Once inside, the women in space suits began the exacting daily routines of manu-facturing semiconductor chips. They worked in a realm of submicrons, attaching leads on devices too small to see without the aid of the electronic monitors. Watching the women through an observation window, Bertelson remarked: "She doesn't really do it, the machine does it."

The manufacturing process for semiconductors literally bounced around the world. Larger silicon wafers that included the circuitry for multiple chips had been designed and fabricated back in the States (or perhaps in Scotland, where the industry had also located a major production base). Then the wafers were flown by 747 to Malaysia (or perhaps Singapore or the Philippines or elsewhere in Asia) for final assembly – sawed into individual chips, wired, tested and packaged. The finished chips were shipped back to North America, Asia and Europe to become the functional guts of TV sets, computers, cars, portable phones, missile control systems and countless other products.

The spectacle of cultural transformation at Motorola was quite routine – three times a day, seven days a week – but it conveyed the high human drama of globalization: a fantastic leap across time and place, an exchange that was banal and revolutionary, vaguely imperial and exploitative, yet also profoundly liberating. In the longer sweep of history, the social intrusions of modern technology might be as meaningful as the economic upheavals. Motorola and the other semiconductor companies settled in Malaysia have managed to unite the leading edge of technological complexity with shy young women from the *kampong*, rural villages where destiny was defined as helping peasant fathers and husbands harvest the rice or palm oil.

At lunch in the company cafeteria, Bertelson and his management staff talked about the complexity. "We improve our productivity 15 percent a year, that's company policy," he said. "We have a road map for each one of our operations that calls for a 10x improvement by the year 2000, by automating and by improving worker efficiency. We will do that."

Malaysian production was not exempt from the same steep "learning curve" that drove price competition throughout the global industry, a standing assumption that costs and prices will fall by roughly 30 percent every time the volume doubles. To defend market share, every producer must continuously squeeze out more waste and imperfection or develop the new materials and production methods that could keep up with the curve. "Our technology, the miniaturization, is growing so fast that we really need to get the human element out of the process as fast as we can," Bertelson said.

Around the lunch table Bertelson's department managers looked like a visionary's ideal of multicultural cooperation. Chinese, Malay, Indian, black, yellow, pale brown, Christian, Buddhist, Muslim, Hindu. The only white guys were Bertelson and a Scottish engineer named Dave Anderson, hired from Singapore. Longinus Bernard, an Indian from Johore whose father had worked on colonial estates, described the early days in 1974 when Motorola started up. "We were so small, everybody knows everybody," he said. "It was really – how do you call it – a good feeling."

Hassim Majid, manager of government affairs, explained how the racial diversity had been achieved. "We were advised by the government to play an active role in restructuring the ethnic composition of the company," he said. "We were told to hire x number of Malay people like me, Chinese and Indians, just like your affirmative action in the United States. Motorola did well in meeting the government requirement."

The Kuala Lumpur operations, Motorola's largest outside the United States, had 5,000 employees, 80 percent Malay and 3,900 ladies, as the managers called them. The company had plans to double this facility, though not its employment. It represented one of the ripe anomalies of global economic revolution: while conservative ideologues in America fiercely contested the threat of multiculturalism, conservative American corporations were out around the world doing it. In the global context, the preoccupation of American politics with race and cultural superiority seemed ludicrous, out of touch and perhaps also dangerous.

At night, downtown Kuala Lumpur looked a little like a theme park celebrating postcolonial Asian prosperity. Some important buildings were fancifully lit with streamers of sparkling lights, giving outline to an eclectic collection of architecture. The clock tower of an old British administrative building was reminiscent of Westminster, but with oriental grace notes. The railway station looked like a Moorish fantasy imported from some other colonial outpost, as indeed its design was. Dozens of modern office towers formed a dense cluster that dwarfed remnants of the past. The city's oldest mosque, Bandaraya, one of its pale domes in collapse, sat at the foot of the thirty-story Bank Bumiputra.

By the river, the old central market hall had been renovated into artisans' stalls and tourist boutiques, with a US fast-food franchise nearby that sold "Prosperity Burgers." In the early evening, young professionals from the office towers gathered at the outdoor cafes for beer or tea. One night I watched six Malay boys entertaining the sidewalk patrons with an acrobatic hip-hop routine that seemed straight out of Compton, California, the lyrics in Bahasa.

On the headquarters building of the state-owned television station, the Malaysian national imperative – "2020" – was spelled out in huge red lights two stories high and framed by two glittering butterflies. The full slogan, "*Wawasan 2020,*" appeared frequently around the city and was otherwise embedded in everyday consciousness. It stood for the shared "vision" of what Malaysia intended to become: a self-sufficient industrial nation, with an economy that will grow eight times larger by 2020, with a people who will be, as Prime Minister Mahathir Mohamad often emphasized, "psychologically subservient to none."

To that end, the government in the last decade force-fed the development of a national car, the Proton Saga, a smart-looking sedan that relied heavily on Mitsubishi of Japan for design and components, but now claimed 70 percent local content. Mahathir rode in one with "2020" on the license plate. Proton was selling 102,000 cars a year at home and abroad, and has spawned an infant components industry. It was moving into Vietnam with a co-production venture, and a second national car, the Kancil, named for a small jungle deer, was planned with Daihatsu.

The essence of "*Wawasan 2020*" was rapid growth – 7 percent a year, every year for the next twenty-five years – and government industrial strategies to foster homegrown industries and a new middle class of talented managers and professionals. Per capita income was supposed to quadruple by 2020. Mahathir talked somewhat airily about launching ventures in telecommunications and aerospace, forming industrial consortia with Asian neighbors like Indonesia or Thailand that could become freestanding rivals to the most advanced economies.

That was the plan. It sounded improbably optimistic, even for the dynamic economies of Southeast Asia, and grandiose in some elements. But Malaysia had earned its self-confidence. Since 1971 its economy had expanded yearly at about the same phenomenal pace: GNP rose from 13 million ringgits in 1971 to 123 million twenty years later. Per capita income had exploded from an impoverished level of $410 a year to more than $3,000. In more basic terms, Malaysian life expectancy increased in two decades from 62.3 to 70.5 years.

In some ways Malaysia was the best-case illustration of globalization, though it was also unrepresentative because its development was more mature than others and the country was quite small, only twenty million people in territory the size of Florida and Georgia combined. The spectacular growth occurred under a one-party regime that Mahathir had led for nearly fifteen years. [. . .]

Malaysia, in order to secure its status as a major export platform, had offered the semiconductor industry, among other things, a lengthy holiday from taxes. Plants in the economic zones were given "pioneer" status for five to ten years. That meant no taxation on earnings in the country, exemptions from import duties and other forms of state subsidies. These tax holidays would eventually expire, but could be renewed and extended if a company made new investments. Other tax breaks kicked in later.

A more controversial benefit was the government's guarantee that electronics workers would be prohibited from organizing independent unions. Though organized labor functioned with some freedom in other sectors, including electrical manufacturing, the government decreed that the goal of national development required a union-free environment for the "pioneers" in semiconductors. The original restriction, supposedly temporary, was regularly protested by groups of workers, but nearly twenty-five years later the ban was still enforced. It now covered not just semiconductors but every other electronics product as well, including at the Japanese firms, which, unlike the American firms, were unionized at home.

Whenever the labor rights issue arose, leading companies professed not to care one way or the other, but the same message always got delivered to the government: unions will jeopardize investment. The government always backed off. On one occasion in the 1980s a delegation from American companies warned the minister of labor: "If unionization is forced upon them, some companies that are already operating here will close down their local operations while others would cease to continue investment, thereby moving to obsolescence."

In 1988, pressured by complaints from the AFL-CIO and the threat of trade sanctions, the labor minister announced an opening. Given the robust growth in Malaysia's electronics sector, he was lifting the restrictions and would recognize a new national union of electronics workers. Five hundred workers gathered from Kuala Lumpur factories to begin an organizing drive. A few days later a delegation from the Malaysian-American Electronics Industry Association met with the labor minister to express their disappointment. Simultaneously, US executives collared Mahathir at a trade conference he was attending in New York. The policy change was rescinded. The labor minister retired.

Instead of the national union, the government offered a weaker alternative, company-by-company "in-house unions." When workers organized one at Harris Electronics, the twenty-one leaders were fired and the new union evaporated. The French-owned Thomson Electronics, which had acquired elements of the old RCA from General Electric, inherited a factory with a union with three thousand members. It closed the plant and moved to Vietnam.

Bruno Petera, a forty-two-year-old supervisor at Harris and one of the union organizers who lost his job, thought the union movement would eventually persevere, regardless of the obstacles, as Malaysians became more confident about themselves. The nation was building not only a new middle class, but also a new working class. In time, he said, people would object to their own powerlessness.

"Once you meet your material needs, you want the dignity," Bruno said. "The dignity to ask a question, to file a complaint, to speak for yourself. It will happen, little by little. Nothing is given free without a struggle." [. . .]

The strategy of pursuing rapid growth was more plausible when only a limited number of Asian nations were pursuing it, but it became less so as the poker game was widened to take in many more players. Malaysia was now surrounded by struggling nations engaged in a fierce competition for capital, for any industries that would move them up the ladder.

Malaysia's economic vulnerability had two dimensions. First, the domestic shortage of labor put upward pressure on wages at all skill levels, despite one million foreign workers brought in temporarily from Indonesia and elsewhere. If wage levels were allowed to rise too rapidly, it would drive capital elsewhere. Yet reformers on the other end of the global system in America and Europe were pushing in that direction: campaigning for labor rights in countries like Malaysia in order to foster rising wages that might lessen the downward pressures on high-wage nations and also increase worldwide consumer demand for everyone's products.

In Malaysia, the low wages were frankly regarded as a national asset. Mahathir complained about the Western intruders: "They know very well this is the sole comparative advantage of the developing countries. They know that all the other comparative advantages – technology, capital, rich domestic markets, legal framework, management and marketing network – are with the developed countries."

Those qualities of advancement were the other dimension of Malaysia's vulnerability: the frustrating struggle to acquire higher levels of technological development for the domestic economy. The threat was crisply summarized in a December 1993 economics report cabled from the US Embassy: The "concern is waning foreign interest in Malaysia as a site for investment, especially in high-tech, capital intensive industries.... The issue is technology transfer. Unless Malaysia manages to attract increasingly sophisticated manufacturers, it risks getting caught in a medium-tech trap, finding itself saddled with a low-growth industrial base."

The poker game continued, but on a more sophisticated level. American companies like Motorola and Intel were regarded as cooperative players because they were locating software design centers in Malaysia and spreading technological competence to the local population. The Japanese, on the other hand, "are very, very difficult," Anwar said. "No technology transfers, no locals hired for management, no research centers. The Americans are very different."

Malaysia's supposed "comparative advantage" of cheap labor did not help much in the advanced fields. Malaysian engineers with master's degrees were in overabundance and cost only one fourth of US engineers. But the Indian engineers in Bangalore were twice as cheap as the Malaysians. There were too many bidders for too few jobs.

"These guys are competing for the best airports," Jeffrey Garten remarked in Washington. "It sounds crazy, but this is going to boil down to infrastructure and which country provides the most convenient modern airport for businesses."

In broader outline, the political insecurities of a Malaysia were not as different from Alabama or Ohio or industrial countries in general as people in those places wished to imagine. All were stuck in different aspects of the same poker game. The global revolution put labor wages in play, but it also put governments in play. The shift in power that drove the irregular bargaining was eroding the public realm, as well as private incomes, and stimulated a race to the bottom: lower wages, lower taxes, less accountability. To borrow an old cliché from the ideology of laissez-faire capitalism, the multinationals were freely pursuing beggar-thy-neighbor politics.

That debilitating process would continue until nations found the sovereign means to confront the marketplace or collaborated on asserting new terms for how commerce was allowed to function. Or the process would continue until the system broke down, destabilized by its own freewheeling behavior.

In the meantime, the major powers, led by the United States, promoted further liberalization of the global trading regime, encouraged the competence of their own multinationals and promoted the objective of greater globalization. Increasing numbers of citizens were unconvinced. The US government, among others, lacked a coherent, concrete vision of how this globalization was expected to benefit the general population.

The Malaysian government at least had its own "*Wawasan 2020*," a concrete plan for what the nation intended to become. Americans might ask, What was the American *wawasan*?

22 Commodity Chains and Marketing Strategies: Nike and the Global Athletic Footwear Industry

Miguel Korzeniewicz

The world-economic trends and cycles of the past two decades have made it increasingly apparent that the production and distribution of goods take place in complex global networks that tie together groups, organizations, and regions. The concept of commodity chains is helpful in mapping these emerging forms of capitalist organization. Most often, analysts depict global commodity chains (GCCs) by focusing primarily on production processes and their immediate backward and forward linkages. Less attention has been paid to the crucial role played by the design, distribution, and marketing nodes within a GCC. These nodes are important because they often constitute the epicenter of innovative strategies that allow enterprises to capture greater shares of wealth within a chain. Furthermore, a GCC perspective helps us understand how marketing and consumption patterns in core areas of the world shape production patterns in peripheral and semiperipheral countries. Thus an analysis of the design, distribution, and marketing segments within a commodity chain can provide unique insights into the processes through which core-like activities are created, and competitive pressures are transferred elsewhere in the world-economy.

To provide such an analysis, this chapter focuses on the distribution segment of a particular commodity chain: athletic footwear. In particular, this chapter examines the marketing strategy of one corporation within the global athletic shoe industry (Nike) to refine our understanding of the dynamic nature of global commodity chains. The example of athletic footwear is useful in exploring how commodity chains are embedded in cultural trends. The social organization of advertising, fashion, and consumption shapes the networks and nodes of global commodity chains. The athletic footwear case shows that the organization of culture itself is an innovative process that unevenly shapes patterns of production and consumption in core, semiperipheral, and peripheral areas of the world-economy.

The first section of the chapter highlights the phenomenal growth of the athletic shoe industry, and its economic and cultural importance in our society. Athletic footwear has experienced explosive growth over the past two decades. The meteoric popularity and success of athletic shoes as a consumer good is explained by a complex interaction of cultural and organizational innovations. The analysis of these innovations within a commodity chain's framework can help produce a

Table 22.1 Wholesale revenues in the US athletic footwear market, 1981–1990 (in millions of US dollars)

	All firms	Nike	Reebok
1981	1,785	458	1
1982	1,900	694	4
1983	2,189	867	13
1984	2,381	920	66
1985	2,989	946	307
1986	3,128	1,069	919
1987	3,524	877	1,389
1988	3,772	1,203	1,785
1989	5,763	1,711	1,822
1990	6,437	2,235	2,159

Source: NSGA, 1990.

more refined theoretical understanding of the relationship between economics and culture.

The second section examines the historical trajectory and organizational strategies of Nike Corporation. Nike provides a particularly clear example of how successful growth strategies by core enterprises generally entail constant upgrading, or a shift within the commodity chain toward control over more sophisticated and value-added service activities. This process of upgrading or innovation can best be appreciated by examining three periods that reflect different environmental constraints and response strategies on the part of Nike Corporation. This section examines each of these periods.

Trends in the US Athletic Shoe Market

The athletic footwear market in the United States has been characterized over the past two decades by phenomenal rates of growth. As indicated by table 22.1 and figure 22.1, wholesale revenues of athletic shoes in the United States tripled between 1980 and 1990. In the past six years, consumers in the United States more than doubled their expenditures on athletic shoes: In 1985 they spent $5 billion and bought 250 million pairs of shoes, whereas by the end of 1991 retail sales totaled $12 billion for nearly 400 million pairs of shoes. Three-fourths of all Americans bought athletic shoes in 1991, compared with two-thirds in 1988. In 1990, athletic shoes accounted for about a third of all shoes sold. The athletic footwear industry today generates $12 billion in retail sales, with at least twenty-five companies earning $20 million or more in annual sales. From the point of view of Schumpeterian innovations, the trajectory of the athletic footwear commodity chain over recent times provides valuable insights into the creation of a modern consumer market.

Retail markets for athletic shoes are highly segmented according to consumer age groups. Teenagers are the most important consumers of athletic shoes. A study sponsored by the Athletic Footwear Association found that the average American over twelve years of age owns at least two pairs of athletic shoes, worn for both athletic

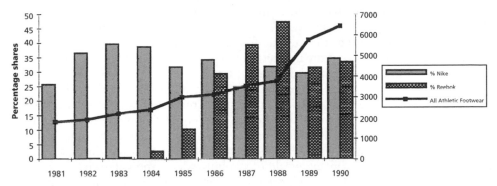

Figure 22.1 Total wholesale revenues of athletic footwear and Nike's and Reebok's shares, 1981–90
Source: NSGA.

and casual purposes. As experienced by many parents and youngsters during the 1980s and 1990s, athletic shoes have been constructed and often promoted among teenagers as an important and visible symbol of social status and identity.

The products in this commodity chain also are highly differentiated according to models and the particular sport for which they are purportedly designed. By 1989, Nike was producing shoes in 24 footwear categories, encompassing 300 models and 900 styles. Reebok sold 175 models of shoes in 450 colors, and planned to add 250 new designs. Adidas and LA Gear sell 500 different styles each. The two fastest-growing segments of athletic shoes in the late 1980s were basketball shoes and walking shoes, while the volume of sales for tennis and running shoes declined. In 1991, basketball shoes accounted for 22 percent of sales, and cross trainers for 14 percent of sales. Product differentiation provides an important vehicle both for competition among enterprises and price stratification.

Finally, the sports footwear market is highly segmented according to price. Indicative of this segmentation, the price distribution of athletic shoes has a very wide range. In 1989 the average cost of basketball, walking, and running shoes was between $40 and $47, while top-of-the-line shoes cost about $175. The bulk of production is oriented toward sales of the lower-priced shoes, while the market for the higher-priced commodities is substantially smaller. In 1990, more than 80 percent of athletic shoe purchases were priced under $35, with only 1.4 percent of shoes bought costing more than $65. Price rather than appearance or functionality often constitutes the primary matrix differentiating athletic shoes as status symbols.

Since displacing Adidas in the early 1980s, and after falling behind Reebok in the mid-1980s (see table 22.1), Nike Corporation has become the largest and most important athletic shoe company in the United States. Nike's sales have grown from $2 million in 1972 to $270 million in 1980, and to over $3 billion in 1991. Reebok, the number two brand in the United States today, experienced similar rates of growth – in fact, Reebok has been the fastest-growing company in the history of American business. Between 1981 and 1987, Reebok's sales grew from $1.5 million to $1.4 billion, experiencing an average annual growth rate of 155 percent. Similarly, LA Gear grew at a dazzling rate, from $11 million in 1985 to $535 million in 1989. Between 1985 and 1990, Nike's share of the athletic footwear market in the United States declined from 30 to 25 percent, Reebok's rose from 14 to 24 percent; LA Gear's increased from a minimal share to 11 percent, and Converse's share declined from 9 to 5 percent. These data suggest that a limited number of large firms compete within the athletic footwear market in the United States, but also that the organization of the market provides considerable permeability for successful entry and competition by new enterprises.

What are the factors that explain the enormous growth of the athletic shoe industry? The evidence suggests, in part, that the most important enterprises within this commodity chain have grown by increasing their control over the nodes involved in the material production of athletic shoes. The most fundamental innovation of these enterprises, however, has been the *creation* of a market, and this has entailed the construction of a convincing world of symbols, ideas, and values harnessing the desires of individuals to the consumption of athletic shoes. By focusing on the marketing and circulation nodes of a commodity chain, greater analytical precision can be gained in identifying the crucial features of these innovations.

Rather than analyzing the athletic footwear chain as a whole, the next section focuses on a single enterprise, Nike Corporation. Although a comparative analysis of other enterprises would yield greater insights into possible differences in organizational trajectories, the focus on a single firm allows a more detailed exploration of the innovative strategies that have characterized the athletic footwear commodity chain. This approach also highlights the relevance of world-systems theory, and the concept of commodity chains, to the study of economic and social processes at a microlevel of observation. Nike's rise to prominence has been based on its ability to capture a succession of nodes along the commodity chain, increasing its expertise and control over the critical areas of design, distribution, marketing, and advertising. This strategy also involved a fundamental reshaping of production and consumption, hence contributing to the recent transformation of the athletic footwear commodity chain.

Nike Corporation: Competition, Upgrading and Innovation in a Commodity Chain

The activities of Nike Corporation created a quintessential American product that has captured a large share of the giant US athletic footwear market. Nike Corporation increased its revenues tenfold in the past ten years, from $270 million in 1980 to an estimated $3 billion in 1991. Nike sells tens of millions of athletic shoes in the United States every year, yet all of the firm's manufacturing operations are conducted overseas, making the company an archetype of a global sourcing strategy. Nike Corporation never relocated domestic production abroad, as many American companies have done, because the firm actually originated by importing shoes from Japan. It has subcontracted nearly all of its production overseas ever since: currently, "all but 1 percent of the millions of shoes Nike makes each year are manufactured in Asia." In the United States, Nike has developed essentially as a design, distribution, and marketing enterprise.

Nike's successful implementation of its overseas sourcing strategy can best be understood as part of the firm's effort to retain control over highly profitable nodes in the athletic footwear commodity chain, while avoiding the rigidity and pressures that characterize the more competitive nodes of the chain. "We don't know the first thing about manufacturing," says Neal Lauridsen, Nike's vice-president for Asia-

Pacific. "We are marketers and designers." Nike's practice of overseas sourcing provides strategic and geographical mobility to the firm by developing a complex division of labor among the components of a global subcontracting network. The way these characteristics are linked to consumer demand and marketing strategies helps explain the tremendous growth and success of Nike.

Imports and distribution as a competitive strategy (1962–1975)

Nike Corporation originated in an enterprise called Blue Ribbon Sports. A founding member of the company was Philip Knight, who visited Japan in 1962 and claimed to represent an American distribution network for shoes that didn't really exist. In Japan, Philip Knight contacted the Onitsuka Company, manufacturers of a brand of athletic shoes (Tiger) whose image had been enhanced by the 1964 Tokyo Olympics. The timing of Knight's travel to Japan was fortunate because executives at the Onitsuka Company were beginning to realize the enormous potential of the US market. After preliminary contacts, and upon returning to the United States, Phil Knight and Bill Bowerman (an Oregon track and field coach) contributed $500 each to start a new enterprise, the Blue Ribbon Sports Company (BRS). In February of 1964, Phil Knight placed his first order for BRS, totaling $1,107, and a few months later they sold their first pairs of Tiger shoes at a state high-school track meet. By the end of 1967, the total revenues of Blue Ribbon Sports were $300,000. The company successfully developed a competitive market niche by targeting a small market of dedicated athletes, runners, and sports enthusiasts.

Tiger's marketing advantage in this early stage was based first and foremost on price competitiveness. The retail price of the very first shipment of Tiger shoes sold was $9.95, a few dollars below the price of the shoes made by Adidas. Later, when BRS began to market Nike shoes, the company's target once again was to undercut their main competitors (Adidas and now Tiger) by a few dollars. The distribution network of these early years centered mostly on a few BRS outlet stores and a painstakingly constructed network of contacts with independent sporting goods retailers. Shoes were promoted primarily at track meets and marathons through word of mouth and very elementary forms of athletic endorsements.

Through the 1960s and early 1970s, Blue Ribbon Sports remained a distribution company in charge of importing and distributing Tiger shoes. During the first few years of the partnership between Onitsuka company and BRS, the Japanese firm clearly held the upper hand because it was able to negotiate and bargain among several athletic footwear distributors in the United States. Trying to enhance its own bargaining position, BRS struggled to attain a contract granting it exclusive rights to distribute Tiger shoes in thirteen western states. Over time, a successful distribution strategy allowed BRS to enhance its leverage, and in 1966 Onitsuka Company granted BRS exclusive rights for the distribution of Tiger's shoes in the United States. Already in this partnership, BRS began to contribute design and performance innovations to Tiger's basic models. Within this arrangement, BRS remained vulnerable because of its financial dependence on Onitsuka Company. But until the late 1960s, the partnership worked as originally conceived: Onitsuka Company manufactured and delivered Tiger shoes, and BRS distributed them in the United States.

By 1968, as the market for athletic shoes underwent rapid growth, strains began to develop in the partnership between BRS and Onitsuka Company. Each of the two firms sought to enhance its share of profits by affirming greater control over new nodes in the commodity chain. Seeking to exploit new market opportunities, Onitsuka Company expanded its volume of shoe production, and apparently began to explore alternative distribution networks. BRS, doubting Onitsuka's commitment to maintaining exclusive arrangements, began identifying alternative supply sources. For this latter purpose, Phil Knight enlisted the services of Nissho Iwai, one of the largest Japanese trading companies, which offered to finance shipments of shoes for a 2 percent commission. Eventually Nissho Iwai became the importer of record, receiving a commission on all shipments, and BRS enjoyed financial backing. As tensions between Onitsuka and BRS simmered, the former attempted to take over BRS in 1971 by extending an ultimatum proposal that would in effect give Onitsuka control over 51 percent of the company.

In 1971 Knight went to Japan and placed his first independent order for 20,000 shoes, which included 6,000 pairs with the Nike "swoosh" pattern. Eventually, BRS entered into a longstanding relationship with two Japanese shoe manufacturers: Nippon Rubber and Nihon-Koyo. In 1971, BRS split with Onitsuka. In 1972 Onitsuka decided to stop shipments of shoes to BRS after finding shoes with Nike brands in one of BRS's stockrooms. Soon thereafter, both parties began lawsuits against each other. Onitsuka Company sued BRS in Japan for breach of contract. BRS sued for breach of contract, unfair competition, trademark infringement, and violation of the antitrust Clayton Act. In July of 1975, Phil Knight agreed to receive an out-of-court settlement of $400,000 after Onitsuka finally succumbed to pressure from the Tiger distributors to settle. By making a decision to design its own logo and produce its own brand of shoes, Nike Corporation emerged out of this conflict with greater control *vis-à-vis* its overseas suppliers in Japan. Its corporate image was enhanced as well, so that by the end of the 1970s the Nike Corporation had super-seded BRS.

During this initial period in the history of BRS/Nike, the company also began to delineate an innovative strategy regarding product design and promotion. Perhaps the one promotional idea that had the longest-lasting effect on the future of Nike Corporation was the choice of both the company's name (Nike is the name of the winged goddess of victory in Greek mythology) and the distinctive "swoosh" design on the side of the shoes. Although they later became promotional, the distinctive three stripes in the athletic shoes made by Adidas had primarily a functional purpose (additional bond between the upper and the sole). Nike's "swoosh," on the other hand, was designed solely on the basis of aesthetics. From that point on, anybody wearing Nike products was also advertising Nike shoes. Marketing and product design, in this sense, were closely related from the very beginning.

The Eugene, Oregon track and field Olympic trials in 1968 became the first major event where Nike developed its promotional efforts. Through its association with some of the best track and field athletes, who wore the company's newest models, Nike began to build a reputation as a new, specialized firm that focused on high-performance athletic shoes. The event convinced Nike that associating product promotion with athletes was a very effective form of advertising athletic shoes. For this reason, Blue Ribbon Sports initiated and maintained a program of subsidies for athletes and sponsorship of track meets throughout the 1970s. Later, Nike's strategy of associating its name with track and field athletes allowed the company's products to be viewed by consumers as associated with the development of first-class competitors for the 1980 Olympics, providing high visibility for Nike shoes.

Marketing as an upgrading strategy (1976–1984)

During this second period, Nike Corporation introduced major innovations in marketing, distribution, and subcontracting for the production of athletic footwear. First, between 1976 and 1984, Nike was shaped by (and helped to shape) the "fitness boom" – the phenomenal growth of jogging, running, and exercise as a common activity by millions of Americans. Nike was part of this phenomenon by implementing a marketing strategy that involved the development of a vast and visible network of endorsement contracts with basketball, baseball, and football players and coaches. Second, Nike's distribution network was enhanced by the establishment of a strategic alliance with Foot Locker, a rapidly growing chain of retail stores marketing athletic products. Finally, Nike Corporation sought to further enhance its control over subcontractors and lower production costs by shifting most manufacturing activities from Japan to South Korea and (to a lesser extent) Taiwan. Combined, these innovations provided a significant competitive edge to Nike Corporation.

Beginning in the mid-1970s, running, jogging, and exercise in general became part of mainstream American culture. Nike Corporation was in the right place at the right time to capitalize on this phenomenon by outperforming competing brands and becoming the most important athletic shoe company in the United States. But the ability to gain from this phenomenon required a major reorientation in the marketing of the company's products: Nike Corporation's main customer base had to shift, as one observer puts it, from "running geeks to yuppies." To achieve this shift, Nike's promotional efforts in the 1970s moved slowly but consistently away from amateur sports to professional sports, and from lesser-known track and field runners to highly visible sports figures. In 1977 and 1978 Nike developed a strategy to sign visible college basketball coaches; by 1979 it had signed over fifty college coaches. One measure of Nike's promotional success was the cover of *Sports Illustrated* of March 26, 1979, which showed Larry Bird (at the time a player in the NCAA tournament) wearing Nike shoes. In the late 1970s, Nike also began to promote heavily in baseball, and by 1980 a Nike representative had signed over fifty players in different baseball teams – as well as eight players in the Tampa Bay team that made it to the 1980 Super Bowl. This new marketing strategy enhanced Nike's image in its new market niche.

Nike's rise as the largest athletic shoe company in the United States also involved creating a more effective distribution network. Foot Locker, an emerging chain of sport equipment retailers, became the most important distributor of Nike shoes. As a way to solve inventory and financial bottlenecks, Nike people devised an advance-order purchase system they called "futures." The system required major distributors to commit themselves to large orders six months in advance, in return for a 5–7 percent discount and a guaranteed delivery schedule. Foot Locker was one of the first dealers to try the futures contracts, and to benefit from them, eventually becoming Nike's most important retailer. Another reason for Foot Locker's close relationship with Nike was the latter's flexibility, and its willingness to change design specifications on request from dealers. This responsiveness of Nike contrasted with Adidas' generally inflexible approach to their supply of shoes, and further extended the company's competitive edge.

Finally, the phenomenal growth in the demand for athletic shoes changed Nike's subcontracting patterns. Nike now needed larger outputs, lower labor prices, and more control over the manufacturing process. In 1974 the great bulk of BRS's $4.8 million in sales was still coming from Japan. Phil Knight, aware of rising labor costs in Japan, began to look for sourcing alternatives. One of these alternatives was the United States. In early 1974, BRS rented space in an empty old factory in Exeter, New Hampshire, and later opened a second factory in Saco, New Hampshire. Domestic facilities also fulfilled a critical R&D function that Nike would later use to gain greater control over production processes abroad. However, by 1984 imported shoes (mostly from Korea and Taiwan) rose to 72 percent of the US shoe market, and US-based factories were forced to close. The collapse of the US production base was due primarily to its limited manufacturing capacity and its economic implausibility. Product timelines lagged and American-based manufacturing found itself unable to compete with lower Asian labor costs.

While Nippon Rubber (Nike's Japanese supplier) reportedly made the decision to relocate part of its production to South Korea and Taiwan, Nike also began to look for new sources of its own. In October 1975, Phil Knight flew to Asia to search for alternative supply sources to lessen his dependency on both Nissho Iwai and Nippon Rubber without losing either company. In Japan, Knight met a Chinese trader who agreed to set up a Nike-controlled corporation called Athena Corporation that established production facilities in Taiwan. In South Korea the Sam Hwa factory of Pusan became the main partner, which began 1977 making 10,000 pairs of Nike shoes a month, and ending the year by making about 100,000 pairs a month. By 1980, nearly 90 percent of Nike's shoe production was located in Korea and Taiwan.

The consolidation of South Korea and Taiwan as the main geographical centers of manufacturing also involved the emergence of a complex system of stratification among Nike's suppliers. Donaghu and Barff identify three main classes of factories supplying Nike: developed partners, volume producers, and developing sources. "Developed partners" are the upper tier of Nike suppliers, responsible for the most innovative and sophisticated shoes. "Volume producers" are those that manufacture a specific type of product in large quantities. These factories are typically less flexible than developed partners in their manufacturing organization. Finally, "developing sources" are the newer factories that attracted Nike because of their low labor costs, entering into a series of tutelary arrangements both with Nike and the more experienced Nike suppliers.

The geographical dynamism of Nike's shifts in subcontracting arrangements interacted with this complex stratification system in interesting ways. As labor costs in Japan rose in the 1970s, Nike Corporation shifted production to emerging semiperipheral countries such as South Korea and Taiwan. As labor costs in the established semiperipheral supply locations began to rise in the 1980s, Nike tried to shift some of the labor-intensive, technologically less advanced segments of its production to new locations in peripheral areas (such as China). It is interesting to note, however, that linkages with developed partners remained critical for two reasons. First, several of Nike's more sophisticated models required the expertise and flexibility of older, more reliable partners. Second, the technological expertise and capital of the older partners was often necessary to bring newer production facilities up to Nike standards, leading to joint ventures between the older, more established sources and the newer ones. From this point of view, centralization and decentralization of subcontracting arrangements were constrained by marketing requirements.

Design, advertising, and the return to the semiperiphery (post-1985)

After 1985, Nike entered into another period of high growth, based on innovations in product design (the creation of the "Air Nike" models, which quickly became immensely popular) and advertising strategies (signing its most popular endorser, Michael Jordan). Also, Nike Corporation continued to target new market niches, entering the aerobics segment of the market, where Reebok had become increasingly dominant, and the growing and profitable athletic apparel markets. Finally, Nike Corporation altered its subcontracting arrangements, shifting important segments in the manufacture of Nike's athletic shoes to the People's Republic of China, Thailand, and Indonesia. However, the need for specialized and sophisticated production runs once again forced Nike to return to more experienced manufacturers in South Korea and Taiwan.

The ability to produce high-performance, sophisticated footwear models became critical to Nike because the company was able to pull out of its early 1980s stagnation through its "Nike Air" technological innovation. By 1984 the phenomenal growth of a mass market for jogging shoes began to stabilize, particularly in the men's segment of the market. Other companies, like Reebok and LA Gear, were becoming more effective in selling to the female and aerobics segments of the market. Nike Corporation, accustomed to years of high growth, was in crisis. Many endorsement contracts were canceled, the Athletics West program cut down its sponsored athletes from 88 to 50, and by the end of 1984, Nike had laid off 10 percent of its 4,000-person work force. Another indication of Nike's bad fortunes was its declining influence among sports coaches and agents. To reverse this decline, Nike Corporation once again turned toward introducing a drastic product innovation.

Nike's declining fortunes in the mid-1980s (see table 22.1) were reversed by the introduction of Air Nike (a new technology that allowed a type of gas to be compressed and stored within the sole) and by the phenomenal success of its "Air Jordan" line of basketball shoes, as well as the success of the endorser they were named after, Michael Jordan. In Nike's Los Angeles store, the first two shipments of Air Jordans sold out in three days. By 1985 it was clear that Air Jordan shoes were a huge success. Nike sold in three months what had been projected for the entire year. The first contract between Nike Corporation and Michael Jordan was worth $2.5 million over five years, and it included (among other things) a royalty to the athlete on all Air Jordan models sold by the company.

The several advertising campaigns featuring Michael Jordan highlight Nike's capacity to influence market demand for its shoes. Nike's video and print advertisements have been among the most innovative and controversial in recent years, adding to Nike's visibility and undoubtedly contributing to its phenomenal growth. Part of the appeal of Nike advertising is its success in tapping and communicating a consistent set of values that many people in the 1970s and 1980s identified with: hipness, irreverence, individualism, narcissism, self-improvement, gender equality, racial equality, competitiveness, and health.

But there also have been several allegations made that by targeting inner-city youths in its advertising and marketing campaigns, Nike has profited substantially from sales directly related to drug and gang money, showing little concern for the social and financial stability of the predominantly black, poor communities, where sales account for 20 percent of the total athletic footwear market. The relationship between the athletic footwear industry and drug money has become increasingly evident by the alarming rate of robberies and killings over expensive sports shoes. Some store owners claim that Nike is not only aware that drug money contributes heavily to its sales, but that Nike representatives adamantly encourage distributors in the inner cities to specifically target and cater to this market.

Nike commercials tend to be subtle. The trademark "swoosh" logo is often far more prominent than dialogue or a straightforward pitch. They are also controversial. Nike's use of the Beatles' song "Revolution" to advertise its new "Nike Air" was startling, and so has been its recent use of John Lennon's song "Instant Karma." Some of the most distinctive Nike advertisements contain themes that can best be described as postmodern: the rapid succession of images, image self-consciousness, and "ads-within-ads" themes. The "Heritage" Nike commercial, showing a white adult runner training in an urban downtown area while images of sports heroes are projected on the sides of buildings, is particularly striking because it seeks to identify the viewer with an idealized figure (the runner) who is in turn identifying with idealized figures (the sports heroes). This ninety-second advertisement cost over $800,000 to run once in its entirety during the 1991 Superbowl. Though there is no dialogue, the product is identifiable (it is seen almost subliminally several times), and the message of the commercial is clear. Postmodern theory, given its sensitivity to new cultural phenomena, can be helpful in understanding advertising as a crucial element in the athletic footwear global commodity chain. An understanding of consumption must be based on commodity aesthetics because consumption is increasingly the consumption of signs. Similarly, Featherstone has noted the increasing importance of the production of symbolic goods and images. In a sense, Nike represents an archetype of a firm selling to emerging postmodern consumer markets that rest on segmented, specialized, and dynamic features.

As in the previous periods, these drastic changes in marketing and distribution strategies were accompanied by shifts in the firm's subcontracting strategy. In 1980 Nike began a process of relocation to the periphery (particularly China, Indonesia, and Thailand) that most other companies would gradually follow in the course of the decade. This relocation was driven by cost advantages: "a mid-priced shoe made in South Korea which costs Nike US $20 when it leaves the docks of Pusan will only cost about US $15 to make in Indonesia or China." Nike Corporation was one of the very first companies to enter the People's Republic of China. In 1980, Phil Knight began to set up a manufacturing base in China. Soon an agreement between Nike Corporation and the Chinese government was finalized, and shoes began to be produced in the PRC. This rapid success can be explained by the fact that Nike used a Chinese-born representative (David Chang) who was thoroughly familiar with the local environment, which meant that proposals were quickly translated into Chinese and attuned to the negotiating style and objectives of the Chinese government. Also, Nike's objectives were long-term and the volumes of production being negotiated were significant, which coincided with the development priorities of the Chinese government at the time.

Just as Nike led the trend of entry into China, later in the mid-1980s it led a reevaluation of the benefits and disadvantages of associating directly with developing partners. By late 1984, production in Chinese factories totaled 150,000 pairs a month, one-seventh of the originally projected 1 million pairs a month. The early 1980s also signaled a slowdown in the rapid growth of conventional athletic footwear markets at a time when competition from other athletic footwear firms (LA Gear, Reebok) was increasing. By 1983 Nike terminated its subcontracting arrangement with the Shanghai factory, and in 1984 negotiated an early termination of its contract with the Tianjin factory.

In the mid-1980s Nike briefly considered shifting production back to established manufacturing sources in South Korea and Taiwan. The advantages of lower labor costs in the developing manufacturing areas had to be weighed against disadvantages in production flexibility, quality, raw material sourcing, and transportation. The development of a new shoe model from technical specifications to shoe production was four months in South Korea, compared to eight months in China. The ratio of perfect-quality (A-grade) shoes to aesthetically flawed, but structurally sound (B-grade) shoes was 99:1 in Korea, 98:2 in Taiwan, and 80:20 in China. While Taiwan and South Korea sourced 100 percent of the raw materials needed for production, China was only able to source 30 percent. Finally, shipping from Taiwan and South Korea was 20–25 days; from Shanghai it was 35–40 days.

The mid-1980s also marked the introduction of the "Nike Air" technology and especially the "Air Jordan" model. Being more sophisticated, secretive, and expensive, this model required more experienced and trustworthy suppliers of the "developed partners" type that had been developed in South Korea over the years. One Reebok executive argued that "as the complexity of our product increases, it continues to go to [South Korea]. The primary reason is that product development out of Korean factories is quick and accurate for athletic footwear, better than any place in the world." An observer concluded in the mid-1980s that after the trend of relocation to low-wage locations like Thailand, Indonesia, and China, "buyers are starting to return [to Pusan] after finding that the extra cost of doing business in South Korea is offset by reliability and the large capacity of its factories." This need for more established suppliers coincided with the adjustments that the Korean shoe producers themselves made in an effort to adapt to rising labor costs and the migration of many firms to other countries. Many Pusan firms shrunk in size but also increased the unit value of their production.

However, the relative importance of South Korean firms has continued to decline. Thus, "at least one-third of the lines in Pusan have shut down in the past three years. Only a handful of South Korean companies are expected to remain significant shoe exporters in a couple of years." Similar changes have affected shoe-producing firms in Taiwan, where "since 1988, the number of footwear companies has fallen from 1,245 to 745. Athletic shoe exports slipped from US$1.5 billion in 1988 to US$ 1 billion (in 1991)." Taiwanese and South Korean–based firms, on the other hand, are used for managing and mediating the relocation of production facilities to the periphery.

The shift of Nike's production to the periphery has become significant. "In the fiscal year to 31 May 1988, Nike bought 68 percent of its shoes from South Korea but only 42 percent in 1991–92. China, Indonesia and Thailand produced 44 percent of Nike's shoes last fiscal year; against less than 10 percent in 1987–88." This same trend is expected to continue in the future: "now, Vietnam looks like the next country on the list. Two major Taiwanese suppliers, Feng Tay and Adi Corporation, are interested in starting production in Vietnam if and when the U.S. trade embargo of its old adversary is lifted."

The advantages of Nike Corporation that have enabled it to become a powerful and profitable link in the athletic footwear commodity chain are the expertise of its designers in finding technological advances in shoe comfort and performance, the distribution networks built over the past twenty-five years, and the effectiveness of its marketing, promotion and advertising campaigns.

Overall assessment

To summarize the arguments made in this section, Nike's development of its twin strategies of overseas subcontracting and domestic marketing can best be understood as involving three distinct periods, each corresponding to different patterns of market demand, geographical locus of production, and marketing strategies. In the first period, between 1962 and 1975, Nike Corporation emphasized control over the import and distribution nodes of its commodity chain. Between 1976 and 1984, Nike Corporation enhanced its relative competitive position by extending control to marketing, and by redesigning its subcontracting strategy to take advantage of new opportunities in Southeast Asia (in South Korea and Taiwan initially, later in China, Thailand, and Indonesia). Finally, beginning in the mid-1980s, Nike Corporation successfully extended control to product design and advertising, further upgrading the firm's organizational structure. As a whole, these three periods suggest that Nike Corporation has sustained and enhanced its competitive edge through the implementation of frequent innovations in the nodes and networks of its commodity chain.

Conclusions

This chapter has examined the organizational strategies of Nike Corporation within the global athletic shoe industry. Nike's uncommon success and growth is due in part to social and cultural trends that have made leisure and fitness more important in our contemporary society. It is also the outcome of Nike's strategy of responding to these trends by accumulating expertise and control over the increasingly important service nodes of the athletic footwear commodity chain: import, distribution, marketing, and advertising.

Nike Corporation (and the athletic footwear industry in general) are excellent case studies of how goods emerge from complex, transnational linkages at different stages of production and distribution. Nike Corporation was born a globalized company. The study confirms a division of labor between core or postindustrial societies (that will presumably specialize in services over time) and noncore societies at different levels of industrialization (that will increasingly specialize in manufacturing). While Korean and Chinese firms are producing the actual shoe, US-based Nike promotes the symbolic nature of the shoe and appropriates the greater share of the value resulting from its sales.

Nike and the athletic shoe industry show that there are emerging patterns of consumption that have enormous consequences for social and economic organization. Linkages between consumption and production must be explored in greater detail. While a consensus has been building for some time that there are new patterns in the organization of production (alternatively called flexible specialization, flexible production, or post-Fordist production), we also need a better understanding of what may be called "post-Fordist consumption" – that is, the emerging patterns of consumption and distribution that are the counterpart to transformations in the realm of production.

23 The Joys of Global Investment

Ted C. Fishman

Last spring, when television hostess Kathie Lee Gifford was accused of endorsing a line of clothing made by thirteen-year-old Honduran girls working twenty-hour days, I found myself hard-pressed to choose which was the more remarkable, the media's ability to transmute celebrity into melodrama or the apparent wish of the American public to rescue Third World workers from an unnatural doom.

Here was Kathie Lee tearfully protesting that she was being unfairly maligned, and then (under the watch of her hastily engaged public-relations consultant) tear-fully demanding that something be done for these poor and suffering children. The well-televised image of her husband, Frank Gifford, handing out hundred-dollar bills to stunned laborers in a sweat-shop nicely complemented the announcement that his wife had discussed the complexities of the global economy with such wor-thies as New York governor George Pataki and Secretary of Labor Robert Reich. It was an ugly spectacle, not so much because we glimpsed the dark side of the coin of American celebrity – here was a woman who was paid $5 million and said that *she didn't know* – but because we saw how, given enough money and earnest cyn-icism, that coin can be turned back to its bright and proper side. All was more or less forgotten, Kathie Lee's smile continued to sell dishwashing liquid, and the viewers of the scandal were presumably relieved.

But I, for one, think that it was not Kathie Lee Gifford who misjudged the temper of the times but the American media, which arranged for her public flogging. And I'm glad she didn't have to cry for too long, because she was crying for me too – and perhaps for you as well.

The fact is that American investors, large and small, old and young, are, like Kathie Lee, hedging against what they anticipate will be the long-term relative decline of America by investing overseas. The pension and mutual-fund industries have led the exodus of cash, and together with universities, foundations, insurance companies, and private investors, they have changed the shape of the world equity markets. From 1980 to 1994, the movement of American money into stocks across borders jumped sixteenfold, to $1.5 trillion. Even though, as of this writing, the US stock market is up 70 percent over the last two years, with twelve new highs last November alone, the desire for international stocks remains so strong that nearly every American investor owns them – if not outright, then through a mutual fund or pension account. Overseas investments, in fact, account for one out of every eight dollars invested by American mutual funds and pensions. Most of the rise has come within the last three years, and the trend is accelerating. (The state of Connecticut, for example, wagered $400 million in the first six months of 1996.) Over the *next* three years, according to the consulting firm of Greenwich Associates, pensions alone will add $150 billion to their current $380 billion investment in foreign secu-

Original publication details: Fishman, Ted C., "The Joys of Global Investment," from *Harper's*, February 1997.

rities. That's a rousing commitment considering that until recently, US investors showed almost no interest elsewhere in the world.

Not surprisingly, the mutual-fund industry, ever willing to cater to each investment fad, has spawned two new products: global funds, which by mandate can buy stocks anywhere in the world; and international funds, which buy only abroad. By a fluke, my daughter's picture, sitting in a photographer's stock file, ended up last year on the cover of the prospectus for one such vehicle, the Stein Roe International Fund. Here's the message she unknowingly peddles: "Two decades ago, 30 percent of the world's equity investment opportunities were securities based outside the United States. Today that figure has more than doubled . . . as the economies of other countries continue to improve and develop, the long-term growth potential of global investments will continue to accelerate." When it was started, in 1994, the fund joined a crowded field. In 1984, global and international funds numbered 29; by last October, there were 658 of them. Over that same period, the assets of these funds grew from $5.2 billion to $264 billion. Investors poured in $40 billion in the first three quarters of 1996, much of it pulled out of traditional savings vehicles: bonds, money-market accounts, and mutual funds that invest in large US companies.

The strategy rests on the familiar principle that the safest and most profitable portfolios have the most varied assortment of investments. The trick is to fine-tune the mix of foreign assets so that a portfolio's investments don't all swing from expensive to cheap at the same moment. French stocks, for example, don't follow the thirty Dow Jones Industrials, and Malaysian and Japanese stocks act still more independently. At present, institutional investors want foreign stocks to make up as much as 15 percent of their holdings. In managing its portfolio, an institution will shift money around whenever one class of investment outperforms others by a wide margin. This process, known sacredly to money managers as "the readjust," has helped to drive the boom in international investments; because the US bull market has run so long, and weightings of US stocks have grown so heavy in institutional portfolios, managers have adjusted their asset mixes and poured money into foreign markets. Individual investors, usually operating less methodically, perform a reverse readjust; when the US stock market dropped last summer, the money flowing into domestic mutual funds slowed dramatically while money into international funds went up. And, even more complicatedly, foreign stocks attract money even when they are performing poorly, as some of the Asian markets have over the last year. The reasoning here is that American bull markets can't run forever. Money then goes to markets that look depressed but are poised for a bull run of their own. A headline in the "Forecast 1997" issue of *Money* magazine played to this one-two punch of greed and fear, urging readers to bail out of US stocks and into overseas winners: "Earn 20% Investing Abroad: Here's why foreign shares are poised to clobber US stocks in '97."

As American money pours into foreign markets, they pop up, sometimes literally. Stock exchanges are sprouting in places where they were once unthinkable, from the states of the former Eastern bloc and communist Asia to sub-Saharan Africa, including Uganda and soon, improbably enough, Mozambique. The value of the issues traded on Indonesia's Jakarta Stock Exchange has grown over 1,000 percent in the last five years to $90 billion, a third of which is in the hands of foreigners, mostly Americans. The internationalization of portfolio investing has fed a swell in the world's pool of exchange-listed securities. By the end of 1995 the total value of the world's equities was $18 trillion.

Although Americans investing abroad still favor such developed economies as Britain, Germany, Canada, and Japan, the real action is in the stocks of companies in the so-called emerging markets based in thirty-nine developing countries in Latin America, Eastern Europe, and all parts of Asia except Japan. Even financial calamities can't put investors off them for long: the chances for phenomenal returns are too great. In 1993 the average diversified emerging-market fund went up 38 percent. Even down years look good. In 1994, emerging markets overall slipped by 10 percent, dragged down by Mexico's financial crisis, yet in that same year nineteen of the twenty best-performing stock markets worldwide were emerging markets. South African stocks, for example, have outpaced the Dow Jones Industrial Average for the last five years, beating that index by 25 percent. In 1996, Mexican stocks were up 17 percent through early December; Philippine stocks, up 30 percent. Poland did well, too – up 77 percent. And then there was Russia, which despite Boris Yeltsin's heart troubles was up 153 percent.

Where there's collective greed, there's a market. But the same dynamic is true of collective fear. Much of the boom in American investment abroad derives from national and personal anxieties; reading the economic tea leaves, many of us believe that emerging economies threaten our jobs, our lifestyles, our prestige. While they take a piece of us, the logic goes, it's essential for us to stake a piece of them. The advertising copywriters working for the mutual funds have become adept at floating the euphemisms of dread. A press release from the large fund family Scudder, Stevens & Clark: "[I]t's clear that America's Baby Boom generation has developed over the past decade a strong appreciation for the importance of ensuring their future financial security," the release says left-handedly about the demographic group with the infamously low savings rate, "but to prepare prudently . . . they may wish to consider broadening their horizons, literally, given market conditions and expected developments both domestically and internationally."

My outlook is less abstract and more openly selfish: it involves my eight-year-old daughter and five-year-old son. Around them our house whispers for better returns – so that they may have a new computer, so that they may go to college, so that my wife and I are not a burden after we retire. In my view, my children live in a mature economy hamstrung by too many old people, ill-educated young people, and social problems that the government can't find the will to fix. When our economy, or the economies of Western Europe, grows 3 percent, economists call it a banner year, yet emerging markets are expected to have long-term growth rates surpassing 6 percent. Time, I believe, is running against my country.

In fact, the economic output of the developing world will soon outstrip that of developed countries and by the turn of the century will account for over 60 percent of everything the world produces. The hotly hyped promise of China is particularly fetching: its rate of growth has fluctuated between 4 percent and 14 percent over the last decade; the World Bank estimates that China will overtake the United States as the world's largest economy by the year 2020, just when my children are in the full swing of their working years. Taiwan, Thailand, Indonesia, and South Korea will rank higher than Great Britain. To be able to compete internationally, my children must be expensively prepared. With luck, private schools and top universities can provide my kids with skills that good students in Korea and India learn for free – or what will look free to me after I've sunk hundreds of thousands of dollars into my family's human capital over the course of the next twenty years. To make it that far, I'm betting a steady portion of my First World earnings that Third World laborers are going to work like hell. [. . .]

Remembering the uproar over Kathie Lee Gifford's Honduran girls, what do I know about my foreign portfolio, which is comprised of parts of twelve funds? Am I aware of all of my companies' labor or environmental practices? Am I aware of the social conditions in each country? Is the development model working in these places? Do I worry about what progress is being made? In a word, no. It's too much work to figure out how the funds I'm invested in have used my money; a quick look at the funds' annual reports shows that I own a piece of over 1,000 foreign companies in dozens of countries. I do know that I own shares in one of the fifteen or so funds that have a big stake in Daewoo and in two of the hundred-odd funds partial to Samsung. Both companies, among the world's largest, make or sell everything from semiconductors to lumber to insurance. Other big Korean conglomerates, called *chaebols*, are well represented, too. That's good. *Chaebols* control a huge portion of Korea's economy, with banks, government, and corporations combined so intricately that outsiders have little chance of learning how the influence and assets intertwine. For funds, the best bet is just to buy all the conglomerates and banks around, and that way get a piece of almost everything Korea is up to. As an investor, then, I am partners with the thirty families that control the Korean economy. These families are close to the country's former dictators, and our collective profits historically derive from a steady flow of government money (lured by hundred-million-dollar bribes), economic discrimination against competitors, and a police state that has brutalized Korean workers and enforced miserable working conditions.

Do I care that I am investing in tyranny, authoritarianism, and latter-day feudalism? Absolutely. I'm glad. What could be better for my get-rich-in-Asia strategy? To be perfectly honest, the fact that Korea is progressing socially at all unsettles me. Koreans tolerate corruption less and less these days, and workers organize more freely and earn higher wages. These changes fulfill the promises of the development model that Wall Street, Washington, and the international banks tout publicly, but also mean that doing business at home is tougher for Korean conglomerates, especially for those that built their market share on cheap exports.

Yet, as it turns out, conglomerates haven't lost their ability to exploit cheap workers; they've just exported that too. Officials at the US Trade Representative's office, human rights groups, and labor unions shudder when asked about Korea's foreign plants, now spread everywhere in the developing world. The practices at plants in Central and South America are the best documented, though hired security forces, cooperative police, and razor wire do a good job of keeping outsiders beyond the gates. The Korean government has tallied over two hundred Korean factories in the region, though it admits that many more exist. Most are assembly plants for Korea's garment industry; some assemble consumer electronics. Korean factories account for half of the clothing industry in both Guatemala and Honduras. In the Americas, Koreans can take advantage of free-trade privileges, dirt-cheap wages (as low as 11 cents an hour), and a near-total absence of unions.

The Kathie Lee Gifford episode shed some light on how these companies are returning value to people such as myself, their shareholders: the hires are mostly girls in their mid-teens, delivered to work on school buses. They presumably make ideal stitchers because they are at the peak of their manual dexterity. And they are easily managed, right down to their reproductive systems. Some plants pass out birth control pills daily but tell workers that they are vitamins. Given this atmosphere of coercion and threat, it's little wonder that labor-rights reports claim incidents of rape as well.

Thus does my money chase human misery. Although I don't know for certain which companies I own conduct business in this manner, Samsung and Daewoo do have garment plants in Latin America, and I take it on faith that either they or some other Korean company I hold is reaping the advantages of doing business there. I have tied my children's futures not only to rising Asia but to the backs of young girls working for a few dimes an hour. It's all good news for my portfolio, since my Korean holdings vested in Latin America bring me the residual diversification needed to put me in the middle of the two most dynamic trends in the global economy: the drive toward the top in Asian industrialization, and the drive toward the bottom in low-tech manufacturing.

The bottom, however, may turn out to be what I need most. Low wages and tough working conditions are nothing new in the garment industry, but now they are just as possible in more demanding high-tech fields. Girls with four years of school can now assemble sophisticated consumer electronics and computers as easily as they can Pocahontas pajamas. Automated manufacturing has shrunk the lag between the moment a product is state-of-the-art and when it is a low-tech commodity. Cheap workers are a necessary competitive advantage sooner in the life cycle of manufactured goods than ever before. In the life cycle of services, too. American multinationals farm out data processing to Third World workers who can't read English, and the programming of complex computer code, once handled by the graduates of American computer-science departments, is extracted on the cheap in Bangalore and Moscow. The companies that can push workers hardest win the drive to the bottom, and with the right stocks I will participate, I will win.

How fascinating, incidentally, that some of the burgeoning foreign stock funds actually end up investing in the United States. Formosa Plastics, a large Taiwanese chemical company, has long taken full advantage of Taiwan's hospitality toward polluters. The country's ruined landscape and toxic waters owe much to the plastics industry, in which Formosa Plastics ranks as the world's largest manufacturer of polyvinyl chloride. According to the latest study by the Council on Economic Priorities, Formosa Plastics USA is the largest producer of hazardous waste among America's midsized chemical companies and has, thankfully for its stock-holders, declined to participate in the chemical industry's voluntary waste-reduction program. Formosa is an attractive investment, and I'm glad that five funds can put the company in my portfolio.

Another investment that interests me is the DFA Pacific Rim Small Company Fund, which owns roughly a thousand stocks screened by a mathematical formula. It has a nice historical return. One of the companies that fits the fund's criteria is Poly Technologies, a mainland Chinese company owned largely by the Chinese military. Last June, the US Department of Justice charged Poly Technologies with attempting to smuggle two thousand AK-47s into the United States; the company is one of China's largest arms dealers and at the time was run by Deng Xiaoping's son-in-law. The military is pushing hard into mainstream business in China, and I'm glad, because stability, as everyone knows, is good for business, and who better to enforce it than an army that runs the economy? Next time Chinese soldiers bulldoze pro-democracy protesters, my family will benefit. [. . .]

24 Gender and Poverty: An Analysis for Action

Lourdes Beneria and Savitri Bisnath

Within the current global economy, poverty is being generated through other processes as well. Widespread economic restructuring has led to rapid increased levels of unemployment reaching crisis proportions in many countries, increased flexibilisation and insecurity in labour markets, informalisation, technological changes, the downsizing of the industrial workforce, and income polarisation. These processes can be observed in both high- and low-income countries. They have resulted in social polarisations and increased poverty for those who become unemployed and lack the necessary skills required by current labour markets.

Thus poverty is linked to the inability of the economic system to generate a sufficient number of jobs to absorb the unemployed and the underemployed. Again, these processes have specific gender dimensions, including higher levels of female *vis-à-vis* male unemployment, informalisation of work often performed by women, and increased participation of women in the precarious informal sector.

Poverty and Education

The precarious position of poor women in the global economy is in part related to low educational levels, including high levels of illiteracy, in many countries. According to the Human Development Report, in 1990 the illiteracy rate among women was approximately 19 percent in South East Asia and 17 percent in Latin America. High illiteracy rates are still prevalent in North and sub-Saharan Africa and South Asia. In countries with high illiteracy rates, "the illiteracy rate among women aged 15–24 is at least 25 percentage points higher than among young men."

During the last 20 years, combined female enrollment in primary and secondary schools increased across regions, but a significant proportion of the female population continues to have little or no access to educational institutions. For example, though the countries in the Middle East and North Africa almost doubled female enrollment in elementary and secondary schools from 32 percent in 1970 to 60 percent in 1992, approximately 40 percent of the female population continues to be uneducated. Similarly, sub-Saharan Africa has an enrollment rate of 49 percent and South Asia 55 percent. Overall illiteracy rates have decreased among adults in low-income countries but the percentage of illiterate women in the world is higher than the percentage of illiterate men.

Additionally, illiteracy rates for young women in rural communities are consistently two to three times higher than those of women in urban areas. Family preferences to educate boys, and the need for subsistence agricultural labour, are often

Original publication details: Beneria, Lourdes and Savitri Bisnath, "Gender and Poverty: An Analysis for Action," United Nations Development Programme, 1996.

cited as factors limiting the education of girls in rural communities. This point underlines the necessity for situation-specific analysis in order to formulate successful poverty eradication policies.

Gender and the Distribution of Work

Another dimension of women's well-being (or lack thereof) is related to the unequal distribution of work and leisure according to gender. Women work longer hours than men in most countries of the world and often carry a disproportionate share of the burden of coping with poverty. This is clearly seen in studies regarding women's and men's use of time. A comparison of time use for women and men in rural and urban communities reveals that women spend an average of 20 percent more time relative to men working in rural areas and 6 percent more in urban areas. This difference is often a result of women's reproductive roles, their greater responsibility for agricultural work in family-owned farms, and barriers to their entry in urban labour markets. A review of 31 countries indicates that:

- of the total work performed, women work an average of 55 percent more than men in low-income countries and 51 percent in high-income countries;
- of men's total work time in high-income countries, approximately 67 percent is spent in paid activities and one third in unpaid activities. For women, these statistics are reversed.

In low-income countries, more than 75 percent of women's work is in unpaid activities. Given that the system of national accounts (SNA) was designed to measure income and output – as produced, exchanged, and measured through the market – rather than human well-being, much of the non-market work performed in all societies remains statistically invisible. As a result, those who perform unpaid tasks are not economically rewarded, nor socially valued or recognised as productive members of society. This specifically erases and obscures the material reality of poor women who spend a high proportion of their time in subsistence activities. Within the context of economic restructuring, it also hides the costs and increasing privatisation of social reproduction. [. . .]

Gender Bias in Development Policy

Mainstream development theories, policies, and strategies have analysed poverty through what has been described as a gender-blind or gender-neutral lens. However, most approaches are in fact not neutral because they assume the male actor as the standard and representative of the human actor. Consequently, gender-neutral policies address women's lived experiences, needs, interests, and constraints only to the extent to which they conform to or overlap with the norms set by the male actor. Within the context of poverty analyses, this leads to misdiagnoses of poverty processes through the erasure of its gendered dimensions.

Additionally, policies and strategies developed to assist "the poor" have often focused on men's roles or on institutions such as the household or the family, with the assumption that women would benefit as equally as men. One such example is that of social investment funds that have been implemented in many low-income countries to assist "the poor" during the process of structural adjustment. Although some of the projects have been designed to assist women, the most common pre-supposition has been that women will benefit alongside men from project imple-mentation. The operationalisation of social investment funds has ignored women and proved unable to address the specific needs of women living in poverty. This is principally because the lived experiences of poor women are rarely conceptualised. When their material realities are theorised, women are primarily perceived in the roles of dependent wives and mothers and they are as a result incorporated into policies only in terms of these family roles.

Thus, when projects are implemented specifically for women, they are most often formulated from limited, stereotypical, and essentialist notions of femininity. They consequently reinforce women's subordinate positions within their households and communities, as with microenterprise projects that promote low-paid craft produc-tion for women without training them in marketing or other better-paid skills. Tra-ditional poverty eradication measures also prioritise the provision of "basic" goods and services (such as food, housing, health care, and education) to poor women and men without questioning the role(s) of economic, political, and social institutions and ideologies that are implicated in the production and perpetuation of poverty processes.

One such measure is a microenterprise development project in Cali, Colombia. This programme provides training and counseling in business administration and credit to existing microentrepreneurs. There is no economic literacy programme provided to the participants about SAPs or the impact of macroeconomic policy on their lives. Additionally, these programmes are not likely to get women out of poverty because they do not provide access to productive resources on a permanent basis. It is therefore important to integrate a gender perspective within these pro-grammes, an integration that should take place from the bottom up on the basis of needs and policies identified by women. The social investment funds in Latin America provide an interesting context for such an effort to integrate a gender per-spective since they have been operationalised through a process of decentralisation and have often encouraged a shift of initiatives to the community and/or local level.

Feminist scholars have provided alternative and more complete ways of analysing development from a gender perspective. Since the appearance of Ester Boserup's book "Women's Role in Economic Development" in 1970, much has been done to high-light the differential impact of development on women. Yet, the persistence and, in some cases intensification, of old problems such as poverty exemplifies the insufficiency of this approach. Policy makers and practitioners must consider both the material realities in which women and men are immersed and the ways in which institutions and ideologies (political, economic, cultural, and religious) position women and men and impact their lives differently. Thus, using Michelle Barrett's terminology, it is important to analyse "words" as well as "things" to understand the gendered dimensions of development in general and poverty in particular. This implies that our understanding of poverty as it is experienced by women must include factors attached to its *meaning* as well as the material elements with which it is interlinked.

Both factors (the meaning of poverty and its material elements) contribute to the perpetuation of poverty and need to be addressed. As Elson has stated:

> Overcoming male bias is not simply a matter of persuasion, argument, change in view-point in everyday attitudes, in theoretical reasoning, and in policy process. It also requires changes in the deep structures of economic and social life, and collective action, not simply individual action.

It is also critical to incorporate in this analysis an understanding of gender relations, understood as relations of power between women and men that partially determine the terms on which they interact. Gender relations are revealed in a range of practices, including the division of labour and resources, and through ideologies and representations, such as the ascribing to women and men different abilities, attitudes, desires, personality traits, and behavioural patterns. Policies that are informed by the analyses above will address gender-specific needs of both poor women and men.

Engendering Poverty Eradication Measures

Gender-transformative policy can hope to provide women with the enabling resources which will allow them to take greater control of their own lives, to determine what kinds of gender relations they want to live within, and to devise the strategies and alliances to help them get there.

To be successful, gender-sensitive poverty eradication measures must be specific to the country, region, and locality of the targeted community. The formulation of context-specific measures is possible following detailed analysis of a given community's internal and external relations. Additionally, as Kabeer has argued, gender-sensitive policies must reflect an understanding that gender-specific needs and interests between women and men who belong to the same country, race, and/or social class may conflict, despite their intersecting needs and interests and similar life experiences. [. . .]

Conclusion

One of the defining moments of the 20th Century has been the relentless struggle for gender equality [. . .]. When this struggle finally succeeds – as it must – it will mark a great milestone in human progress. And along the way it will change most of today's premises for social, economic, and political life.

Much has changed since the first 1975 United Nations Conference on the Decade for Women. As it has been said, "we have moved from seeing women as victims to needing them to save the world". During the past two decades, women's issues have been at the forefront of social change. Yet poverty, with its gender dimensions, has far from disappeared. In this paper we argue that to successfully eradicate poverty it is imperative to focus on gender as a category separate from the category "women" in poverty eradication measures. Consequently, it is important to look not only at women in isolation but at women in relation to men and institutions. This approach is implicit in the World Social Summit's "Copenhagen Declaration and Programme of Action".

The Social Summit took place during an historical period in which social policy has taken the back seat in development debates. In working towards social policies for the 21st Century, the Declaration's guidelines need to be operationalised and its principles taken seriously, beginning with its emphasis on democratic processes:

The eradication of poverty cannot be accomplished through anti-poverty programmes alone, but will require democratic participation and changes in economic structures in order to ensure access for all to resources and opportunities.

It will also require rethinking social policy at a time of shrinking government budgets and growing opposition to socially responsible taxation.

Given the current emphasis on democratisation and investment in civil societies, it is important to focus on the factors that can contribute to this process. Most countries face one of the most potentially explosive contradictions of our times, namely, increasing economic and social polarisation, partially as a result of the dynamics of the market within an increasingly global economy. This is happening at a time when emphasis on human rights, equality, higher levels of education, and expanding information systems are the cornerstones of "the new civil society" and of democratic institutions. A significant proportion of the literature focusing on growing inequalities indicates that gender, class, racial, and other types of inequalities must be addressed. We must therefore insist that true democracies promote both political and economic equality to ensure sustainable human development.

An agenda for change

An agenda for eradicating poverty, and its gendered dimensions in particular, requires the dismantling of the institutions and ideologies that maintain women's subordination and that justify inequality in terms of political, social, and economic resources. To this end, international development organisations can work with governmental, non-governmental, and private sector organisations to:

- insist on the importance of eliminating illiteracy among poor women as an urgent first step towards the improvement of women's entitlements, expansion of their choices, implementation of their rights, and enhancement of their socially acquired capabilities;
- encourage the removal of legal obstacles and cultural constraints to women's access to and control over productive resources such as land and credit;
- promote the use of both quantitative and qualitative research methods to analyse the gendered dimensions of relative and absolute poverty, to emphasise the links between economic production and social reproduction and to render unremunerated labour visible in order that it may be accounted for in economic planning and poverty eradication strategies;
- ensure that poverty eradication policies and programmes are based on gendered analyses of the nature and extent of women's and men's differential entitlements, choices, rights and capabilities;
- invest in strengthening the capacity of local, national, and regional organisations to understand and respond to the gendered dimensions of poverty;
- encourage international financial institutions to implement foreign debt cancellation, reduction and/or rescheduling programmes on condition that resources are directed towards eradicating poverty in general and its gendered dimensions in particular; and
- ensure that national poverty eradication strategies, which signatories to the World Summit on Social Development's Declaration and Programme of Action agreed to develop, are fully engendered.

25 Does Globalization Lower Wages and Export Jobs?

Matthew J. Slaughter and Phillip Swagel

Does Globalization Lower Wages and Export Jobs?

Globalization – the international integration of goods, technology, labor, and capital – is everywhere to be seen. In any large city in any country, Japanese cars ply the streets, a telephone call can arrange the purchase of equities from a stock exchange half a world away, local businesses could not function without US computers, and foreign nationals have taken over large segments of service industries. Over the past twenty years, foreign trade and the cross-border movement of technology, labor, and capital have been massive and irresistible. During the same period, in the advanced industrial countries, the demand for more-skilled workers has increased at the expense of less-skilled workers, and the income gap between the two groups has grown. There is no doubt that globalization has *coincided* with higher unemployment among the less skilled and with widening income inequality. But did it *cause* these phenomena, as many claim, or should we look to other factors, such as advances in technology? This paper seeks to answer that question.

Basic Facts

It is best to start with the facts. Are economies around the world becoming more integrated? Have increased unemployment and widening income disparity in fact coincided with increased economic integration?

Global integration

The share of imports and exports in overall output provides a ready measure of the extent of the globalization of goods markets. Although foreign goods are available in every country now more than ever before, the expansion of product market integration has not been continuous over time. World trade in relation to output grew from the mid-1800s to 1913, fell from 1913 to 1950 because of the two world wars and protectionist policies implemented during the Great Depression of the 1930s, and then burgeoned after 1950. Only in the 1970s, however, did trade flows reach the same proportion of output as at the turn of the century, a result of the easing of tariffs and quotas, more efficient communications, and falling transportation costs.

Original publication details: Slaughter, Matthew J. and Phillip Swagel, "Does Globalization Lower Wages and Export Jobs?" International Monetary Fund, 1997.

For many advanced economies the most important decade for globalization since World War II was the 1970s, when the ratio of trade to output rose markedly in both advanced and developing economies in the wake of the two oil shocks. In the developing countries, exposure to international trade picked up again in the late 1980s, coinciding with their movement toward trade liberalization.

The rise in the ratio of exports to total output likely understates the degree of product market globalization. More and more output in the advanced economies consists of largely nontradable services: education, government, finance, insurance, real estate, and wholesale and retail trade. Perhaps it would be more accurate to measure the importance of international trade by considering merchandise exports as a share of the production of tradable goods only. This alternative measure shows a much larger role for trade. However measured, globalization has occurred and gives no sign of slowing down.

Labor market developments

An important trend in labor markets in the advanced economies has been a steady shift in demand away from the less skilled toward the more skilled. This is the case however skills are defined, whether in terms of education, experience, or job classification. This trend has produced dramatic rises in wage and income inequality between the more and the less skilled in some countries, as well as unemployment among the less skilled in other countries.

In the United States, for example, wages of less-skilled workers have fallen steeply since the late 1970s relative to those of the more skilled. Between 1979 and 1988 the average wage of a college graduate relative to the average wage of a high-school graduate rose by 20 percent and the average weekly earnings of males in their forties to average weekly earnings of males in their twenties rose by 25 percent. This growing inequality reverses a trend of previous decades (by some estimates going back as far as the 1910s) toward greater income equality between the more skilled and the less skilled. At the same time, the average real wage in the United States (that is, the average wage adjusted for inflation) has grown only slowly since the early 1970s and the real wage for unskilled workers has actually fallen. It has been estimated that male high-school dropouts have suffered a 20 percent decline in real wages since the early 1970s.

In other countries, the impact of the demand shift has been on employment rather than on income. Except in the United Kingdom, the changes in wage differentials have generally been much less marked than in the United States. Countries with smaller increases in wage inequality suffered instead from higher rates of unemployment for less-skilled workers.

What explains the differences in outcomes for wages and employment across countries is differences in labor market structures. In countries with relatively flexible wages set in decentralized labor markets, such as the United States and, increasingly, the United Kingdom, the decline in relative demand for less-skilled labor has translated into lower relative wages for these workers. In contrast, in countries with relatively rigid wages set in centralized labor markets, such as France, Germany, and Italy, it has meant lower relative employment.

Two other facts about these labor market trends shed some light on the impact of trade. The first is that about 70 percent of the overall shift in US labor demand in manufacturing was a change in skill demands *within* industries, not *across* industries from less skill-intensive to more skill-intensive. At all levels of industrial classification, the majority of US manufacturing industries during the 1980s employed relatively more high-skilled workers than in the 1970s, even though wages of these workers had risen.

The second finding is that income gaps have widened in a number of developing countries as well as in the advanced economies, and evidence suggests that labor demand in developing countries has also shifted toward workers with high skill levels relative to the average. For example, research reveals that trade liberalization in Mexico in the mid-to-late 1980s led to increased relative wages of high-skilled workers. We might have expected trade liberalization to boost the demand for unskilled labor and raise unskilled wages, but in fact the opposite has happened in some developing countries.

Does Import Competition Affect Wages?

Not surprisingly, people often link increased globalization to the decline in relative wages of less-skilled workers in the advanced economies. But does increased international trade, especially with developing countries, in fact worsen income inequality? There are two approaches to answering this question. One focuses on the role of the price of imports in lowering the prices of products and thus lowering wages. The second uses the quantity rather than the price of imports as a measure of the intensity of import competition.

Effect of import prices on wages

Economic theory suggests that international trade affects the prices of products in both exporting and importing countries and this in turn affects the price of labor – that is, wages – within countries by influencing the demand for labor. Changes in product prices brought about by competition from imports alter the profit opportunities facing firms. Firms respond by shifting resources toward industries in which profitability has risen and away from those in which it has fallen. Trade flows thus give rise to shifts in the demand for labor, as more workers are needed in newly profitable sectors and fewer in unprofitable sectors. If the supply of labor is fixed, these demand changes lead to a rise in wages, since workers will demand a premium for switching into more profitable industries.

Theory also suggests that import competition lowers the price of products (such as apparel and footwear) made by low-skilled labor relative to the price of products (such as office machines) made by skilled labor, so that domestic firms shift toward producing skill-intensive goods. But have product prices in the advanced economies in fact changed in this way? If so, trade might have contributed to rising income equality, but it must first be shown that changes in product prices are the result of trade rather than other, purely domestic, influences.

A great deal of research has been done on this question, and although the conclusions are not robust, there appears to be little evidence of larger price increases in skilled-labor-intensive products in advanced countries; if anything, price increases were larger in the unskilled-labor-intensive industries. Rapid technology change seems to have led to relative price declines in skill-intensive industries rather than the price decreases in unskilled-labor-intensive industries one would expect in the face of import competition from developing countries. In most cases, trade with developing nations has played only a small role, if any, in raising income inequality in the advanced economies.

Effect of import volumes on wages

A second way of measuring how trade affects wages is to focus on the volume of trade and to analyze the factors embodied in these flows rather than the prices of imports. Trade can be viewed as effectively shipping from one country to another the services of the workers engaged in the production of traded goods. All else equal, imports add to the labor endowment of the recipient country and reduce the labor endowment of the shipping country.

Data on US trade flows have been analyzed to infer the quantities of labor embodied in trade flows. The United States tends to export skilled-labor-intensive products and to import unskilled-labor-intensive products, so that the growing importance of trade in the US economy has increased the effective supply of unskilled labor in that country relative to the supply of skilled labor. Analysis suggests that trade accounted for around 15 percent of the total rise in income inequality during 1980–85, but that effect diminished in later years. Further studies have shown, for the advanced economies as a whole, that trade with developing countries has led to about a 20 percent decline in the demand for labor in manufacturing, with the decline concentrated among unskilled workers. The results of these latter studies are subject, however, to some uncertainty because of the influence of labor-saving technology in the advanced economies. Other studies have estimated that shifts in product market demand, including the effect of imports, account for less than 10 percent of the increase in wage differential.

Synthesis

Whether analyzed in terms of import prices or of import volumes, nearly all research finds only a modest effect of international trade on wages and income inequality. The average estimate of the effect of trade on wages and employment is not zero – most research finds some role for trade – but it is certainly lower than what might be expected from purely anecdotal evidence, and certainly far from the claim that import competition makes a "giant sucking sound."

This conclusion might seem puzzling in light of the presumption that the advanced economies have become more open to international trade since the 1970s. There are at least two explanations. First, it is possible that on balance the advanced economies have *not* become substantially more open to trade because, although tariffs have fallen, they have been replaced with nontariff barriers (for example, voluntary export restraints in autos and steel). Second, firms in the advanced economies might have upgraded their product mix – producing higher value-added goods – in the face of low-wage foreign competition. If this is true, foreign competition has been blunted and need not lead to large changes in relative product prices.

26 Globaphobia: Confronting Fears about Open Trade

*Gary Burtless, Robert Z. Lawrence,
Robert E. Litan and Robert J. Shapiro*

Not much sophistication is needed to rebut the claim that trade lowers total employment. Even as the United States has become more global during this decade, the economy has grown steadily, and in the process has generated more than 14 million additional jobs. The result is the lowest national unemployment rate in over twenty-five years.

Is the same true over a longer period? Figure 26.1 unequivocally answers yes. The figure shows that as a percentage of national output, the sum of imports and exports rose from 9 percent in 1960 to over 24 percent by the mid-1990s. Yet the fraction of Americans of working age who have a job has continued to grow, rising to new highs in every recent business expansion. Whereas only 55 percent of adults were employed in 1950, nearly 64 percent held jobs in 1997.

We do not make the bold claim that employment has risen because of closer integration of the US economy with the rest of the world. Most of the increase has come about because American women increasingly have wanted to work. Yet it is noteworthy that the big jump in women's employment occurred at the same time as US trade expanded – increased trade did not prevent women from getting jobs.

Some American workers do lose their jobs as a result of the inroads of foreign producers. But at the same time, as just described, jobs are created in other sectors of the economy, whether in industries making goods and services for export or in firms producing output for domestic consumption. As a result, there is no long-term relation between the national unemployment rate – which is determined by the health of the overall economy rather than of the firms in competition with foreign producers – and the volume of imports. This fact is demonstrated by figure 26.2. While imports' share of the national income more than tripled between 1960 and 1996, the unemployment rate fluctuated but showed very little overall trend. The jobless rate was roughly 5.5 percent in both 1960 and 1996.

Equally significant, neither trade nor its absence can shelter a country from wide cycles in unemployment. The longest and most severe contraction of the twentieth century was the Great Depression, when imports and exports represented a very small percentage of the US economy. Economic historians believe that the severity, duration, and worldwide scope of the Great Depression was partly the result of a sharp curtailment of global trade that resulted from greater protection, of which the Hawley-Smoot Tariff Act of 1930 was a prime and leading example.

Original publication details: Burtless, Gary, Robert Z. Lawrence, Robert E. Litan and Robert J. Shapiro, *Globaphobia: Confronting Fears about Open Trade*, Brookings Institution, 1998.

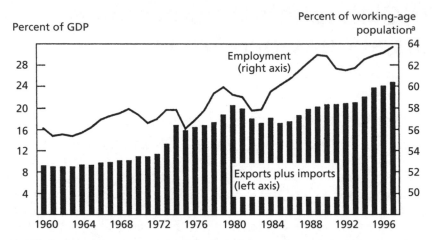

Figure 26.1   Growth of US trade and employment, 1960–97
Source: Data from Bureau of Economic Analysis and Bureau of Labor Statistics.
Note: (a) Ages sixteen years and older.

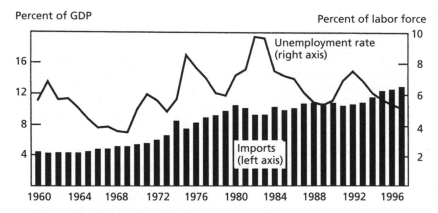

Figure 26.2   US imports and unemployment, 1960–97
Source: Data from Department of Commerce (National Income and Product
Accounts concept) and Bureau of Labor Statistics.

In recent years the relationship between imports, exports, and US employment
has been almost precisely the opposite of that predicted by critics of free trade, as
is shown in figure 26.3. The lower line in the figure shows that since the late 1970s,
net exports – the difference between the value of goods and services that US producers sell in overseas markets and the value of goods and services that foreign producers sell in the United States – as a share of total output has been consistently
negative, although since its sharp fall in the first half of the 1980s there has been
noticeable improvement. Yet the upper line of the figure illustrates that in all but
two years of this period, total employment increased. Indeed, the change in total
employment appears as the mirror image of the current account deficit.

The negative relationship between employment and the nation's trade performance may seem surprising to noneconomists. But if one stops and thinks about it

Percent

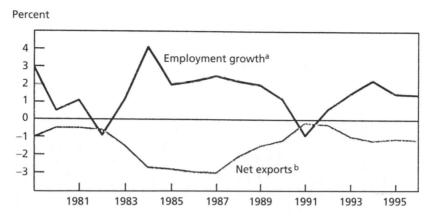

Figure 26.3 US net exports and growth in employment, 1979–96
Source: Data from Bureau of Economic Analysis and Bureau of Labor Statistics.
Notes: (a) Percent per year.
        (b) Percent of GDP.

for a moment, the relationship is easy to understand. Both the trade deficit and employment growth are linked to the American business cycle. When overall US demand rises strongly, consumers and businesses seek to increase their purchases from all available suppliers, both domestic and foreign. This tends to boost American companies' demand for workers, increasing the employment rate, and to push US imports up faster than exports. The process is reversed when US demand for goods and services contracts, as it does in a recession.

The demand for US exports in other countries is subject to a similar cycle. Strong overall demand in a particular country tends to lift US exports faster than imports. But the United States has dozens of important trade partners, each with a distinctive business cycle pattern. Consequently, the US cycle of rising and falling trade deficits tends to mirror the overall level of demand in the United States rather than that in any particular foreign economy. Figure 26.3 shows this typically means that the deficit increases when US employment soars, and shrinks when demand for new workers is weak or contracting.

Openness and Manufacturing Jobs

Even if trade does not reduce overall employment, many Americans worry that it destroys good jobs in the manufacturing industries that compete most directly with imports. A good job is easy to describe. It offers excellent wages and fringe benefits, healthy prospects of promotion, pleasant working conditions, and long-term job security. According to popular wisdom, manufacturing once offered such jobs to millions of workers, most of whom had no educational credentials beyond a high school diploma. Critics of free trade argue that imports have made such jobs unnecessary in the United States, thus blocking the traditional path to the middle class for Americans from modest backgrounds.

Statistics on job growth clearly support the claim that manufacturing's importance in employment has slipped. As shown by figure 26.4, in the 1950s manufacturing accounted for about one-third of all payroll jobs. It now provides only

Percent

Figure 26.4   Manufacturing as a share of the US economy, 1959–94
Source: Council of Economic Advisers (1997).

about one job in seven to workers on nonfarm payrolls. It is easy to exaggerate the importance of a shrinking manufacturing base in the loss of good jobs, however. The total number of payroll jobs in manufacturing has fluctuated between 18 million and 21 million since the mid-1960s, with the current level near the low end of that range. But manufacturing offers reasonably good jobs, especially to workers with average or below-average schooling. Hourly wages in manufacturing are about 9 percent higher than wages in other private sector jobs. If the manufacturing sector were larger, average wages would be somewhat higher, especially for workers with limited schooling.

The absolute level of manufacturing employment has declined much more slowly than the sector's share in total employment. A major reason for this relative fall in manufacturing employment is that manufactured goods account for a dwindling percentage of Americans' consumption. As people's incomes rise, they tend to spend an increasing percentage of their incomes on health, education, and other kinds of services and a smaller percentage on manufactured goods. Figure 26.4 also shows that the decline in the manufacturing employment share parallels the decline in manufacturing's share of total output. Short of forcing Americans to buy steel I-beams and household appliances and rationing their consumption of hospital services and restaurant meals, it is hard to see how this long-term trend can be reversed. Indeed, the same trends are visible in other countries, even those with a much lower living standard than the United States. Services – nonmanufactured output – have increased their share of overall output in both industrialized and developing or emerging market countries between 1980 and 1994. Clearly, the relative decline of manufacturing and the corresponding rise of services would occur with or without world economic integration.

The manufacturing share in employment also has declined because of the continued success of manufacturing industries in boosting worker productivity. In the early postwar period measured productivity in the entire business sector grew at approximately the same pace as productivity in manufacturing. However, since 1973 productivity growth has edged down in manufacturing, but it has plunged in other sectors of the economy, especially in the service sector.

Percent of payroll employment

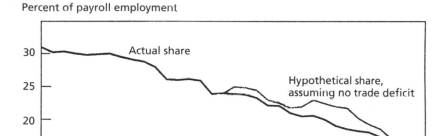

Figure 26.5 Manufacturing as a share of total US employment, 1960–94
Source: Authors' calculations based on Council of Economic Advisers (1997).

A simple comparison demonstrates the powerful impact on jobs of differential productivity in different parts of the economy. According to government statistics, steelworkers were 125 percent more productive in 1995 than in 1973. In contrast, the productivity of workers in the hotel and motel industry improved by just 11 percent over this period. These numbers mean that employment could only have grown at equal rates in the steel and lodging industries if the demand for steel had climbed at least ten times faster than the demand for hotel accommodations. However, the demand for lodging in fact nearly doubled between 1973 and 1995, while demand for steel remained roughly unchanged. Fast productivity growth combined with slow growth in demand meant that many jobs in the steel industry disappeared. In contrast, slow productivity growth combined with rapid growth in the demand for accommodations meant that hotels and motels added hundreds of thousands of workers to their payrolls.

These powerful domestic trends necessarily imply that any role played by international trade in the decline of manufacturing employment must have been small. Figure 26.5 confirms this to be the case. The bottom line illustrates the steep drop in the percentage of payroll workers employed in manufacturing. The top line in the chart shows, however, that only a very small portion of the decline in manufacturing employment would have been avoided if the entire trade deficit after 1975 had been eliminated through extra production of US manufactured goods. Under this very generous assumption, the payrolls of manufacturing companies would have been about 8 percent larger in 1994 than they in fact were; so that instead of falling 15 percentage points over the period 1960–94, manufacturing employment would have fallen 14 percentage points (to 17 percent of nonfarm payrolls).

The small change in the composition of employment, in turn, would have had a very small effect on average wages. Assuming the pay differential between manufacturing and nonmanufacturing workers were maintained, the average private sector wage would have risen just 2 cents an hour, or about one-tenth of a percent. Even if good jobs were disappearing in the American economy, which they are not, eliminating the trade deficit by restricting imports would not bring them back. [. . .]

Few of the globaphobic attacks on closer world economic integration have any merit. America's growing economic links with the rest of the world are not responsible for slower average income growth, higher unemployment, or the productivity slowdown. Closer economic integration accounts for at most a small fraction of the job loss in manufacturing and the increased disparity in US wages. The charge that American workers and companies must compete on an unlevel international playing field reflects a fundamental misunderstanding of what trade and exchange are all about. The point of trade is to exploit the advantages of differences between nations. The gains from trade would be vastly smaller if all countries were identical.

Globalization has not undermined US sovereignty. Pleas that the United States should negotiate trade agreements only with countries that meet minimum environmental and labor standards ignore the interests of US consumers and exporters. Even if negotiators heeded these pleas, they would not necessarily improve the welfare of low-income workers in the third world, the supposed beneficiaries of minimum labor standards. In many cases, US insistence on minimum standards would choke the expansion of the modern sector in third world countries, limiting poor workers' chances of improving their living standards.

If the intellectual case for globaphobia is weak, why does global competition continue to arouse so much fear among ordinary Americans? Why is globaphobia so attractive in the political marketplace? We believe the fundamental reason is that fear of global integration taps into a large reservoir of public anxiety about slow income growth, potential job loss, rising inequality, and a seeming loss of control of our economic destiny. Notwithstanding a twenty-five-year low in the national unemployment rate, many Americans remain fearful that, with little notice, they could be the victims of "downsizing" or be "reengineered" out of a job.

In spite of this fear, voters appear unwilling to pay higher taxes to cover major increases in government spending on assistance or tax relief for lower income workers, even though such spending might reduce workers' income insecurity and offset part of the effect of wider pay disparities. Voters' reluctance to fund such initiatives is not hard to explain. Slower economic growth has made Americans less willing to be taxed, and voters' experience with previous public initiatives has given them little confidence that a major expansion in government would in fact reduce their insecurity.

Throwing sand in the gears of globalization, by contrast, represents tangible action that politicians can take to change the situation. Even better, it requires no additional government spending. While economists may poke holes in protectionist theories and evidence, critics of global integration can point to apparently persuasive anecdotes and facts: anemic wage growth, identifiable workers thrown out of jobs, plants relocated to offshore sites, and claims by management that these unhappy steps are all necessary because of the evil effects of global competition. Elevating US barriers to foreign trade, or refusing to enter new trade deals with low-wage countries, if nothing else, offers the comforting illusion that these developments can be reversed or halted. [. . .]

27 AI on Human Rights and Labor Rights

Amnesty International

Our rallying cry for May Day is "labour rights are human rights". This reminds us that people traditionally look to unions to protect their rights and the unions have the largest force of "human rights defenders" in the world. Human rights embrace the whole spectrum of standards that every person should expect as a minimum entitlement in any decent society, and they include rights in every realm of life, civil, political, social and cultural – from social security to health, from education to sexual orientation rights.

The broad human rights movement and the unions still have a lot to learn from each other and both could benefit from working more closely together. Organising collectively into a union is one of the prime examples of action to prevent people's rights being violated and trade unions give us the models for mass action to respond to abuses of rights. Union solidarity action is a good illustration of organised activism by one branch of a movement to protect those at risk somewhere else. But apart from the campaigns of unions and rights organisations, what affects the state of labour rights and human rights are the same major social trends which are influencing every other aspect of life.

The theories of "neo-liberal economics" dominate current ideology and in reality, of the 100 largest economies in the world, 51 are now global corporations; only 49 are countries. The multi-nationals show the ever-increasing scope and power of globalisation. They work on a super-national scale and organise their business like a world-wide game of Monopoly, moving their operations, plant, finance and work-force around like pieces on the map. They fragment production to suit their interests. They continue to gain more control over each process, more control over the workforce and more control over the market, merging, acquiring, and garnering more power. Mitsubishi is now larger than Indonesia, with the fourth largest population on earth. General Motors is bigger than Denmark, Toyota is bigger than Norway. Philip Morris is larger than New Zealand.

With the latest computer technologies they hold extensive data and monitor the behaviour of millions of "citizen consumers"; with world-wide marketing and pin-sharp targeting, they manipulate and manage expectations, they penetrate our communities, our homes and our lives. They often push down wages and living standards, job-security and terms and conditions of employment.

Like super-powers, they have near-universal reach and supremacy and the rights of their staff, their suppliers, their customers and small businesses, have all been subordinated to the rules of the new big game. Governments court these corporations and compete in offering them inducements. The human consequences of this new order are seen in the erosion of rights in the "maquiladoras" and sweatshops

Original publication details: Amnesty International, "AI on Human Rights and Labour Rights," 1998, courtesy of Amnesty International.

of Latin America, the factory/storage/living blocks of the export processing zones in the far east. An alliance of women's organisations said: "While women who wear Nike shoes in the United States are encouraged to perform to their best, the Indonesian, Vietnamese and Chinese women making the shoes often suffer from inadequate wages, corporal punishment, forced overtime and/or sexual harassment." At the social and political level, the top 200 multi-national corporations have more economic power than the poorest four-fifths of humanity; the head of Microsoft has more money than twice the combined GDP of Uganda, Kenya and Tanzania. Through this sheer size, economic dominance and mobility, the multi-nationals can set the agenda for development, sway political decisions and have a major impact on the reality of human rights for very many people.

The global market means that governments have less control over economic matters. A lot of countries may look more social-democratic with the disappearance of many dictatorships, but the capacity and legitimacy of the state is in decline. At the same time traditional national governments are increasingly relinquishing power through privatising public services, including parts of the military, security and police services as well as their utilities, major industries etc. They have diminishing power to control mergers, take-overs and liquidations, may not know who plans to buy or sell a major industry or utility; a telephone, TV or water company may change ownership overnight.

"Peace-keeping" forces, prison detention and policing services are increasingly being privately run as corporations. AI and other NGOs have started developing techniques and learning from experience in exposing the involvement of corporations such as Shell, BP and Total in human rights violations in Nigeria, Colombia, Myanmar. This approach can effectively complement the efforts of unions and labour activists. Work on child labour exploitation, on apparel industries and sports goods have shown what is possible, although there is still much to be done to develop this area of work.

The sheer weight of national debt in many poor countries, alongside the power of IMF, large transnational corporations and overseas investors, leaves the governments with little power to make their own choices or control their nation's affairs. Rights and justice come very low on government priority lists compared to foreign debts. Human rights are undermined by extreme inequalities in power and wealth; injustice in access to food, fuel, shelter and the bare necessities of life go hand in hand with poverty and powerlessness leading to destitution, malnutrition, disease, illiteracy, unemployment.

The financial institutions like the IMF, the World Bank and the multi-national banks have a major impact on people's rights. More and more states have taken their loans and accepted the social policies they impose such as the infamous Structural Adjustment Programs which include cuts in public expenditure, unemployment, lower wages, reductions in welfare and public services – health, education, social security, transport etc.

International finance can move massive capital funds very quickly from one side of the world to the other, just to speculate, and people's rights suffer when the social fabric is torn apart by currency crises, national bank failure, government collapse. Let us hope that human rights will not be further eroded in the recently damaged "tiger economies" such as Indonesia and South Korea.

Thus overall, a new breed of world "super-bodies" seem to be emerging: the multi-national commercial corporations, the international banking and financial bodies and the regional inter-government economic organisations. These new super-bodies normally share the same outlook, the same analysis and culture. Human rights and labour rights are not a priority on their agenda.

In some countries in recent years there have remained no effective social structures at all to protect rights of any sort, when the normal machinery of government collapsed altogether as a result of armed conflicts. Human rights suffer in these conditions, whether the reason is resistance to oppression, competition among regional powers or "warlordism". Witness the effects on all human rights in former Yugoslavia, Somalia, Rwanda, parts of the former Soviet Union, in Zaire, Sierra Leone or Liberia, East Timor. Amnesty International's "concerns" arise in the increasingly widespread "limited", "internal" or "low intensity" wars around the world.

Across the world, unprecedented numbers of people whose rights have been denied are on the move, migrant workers looking for a better life with basic rights and refugees fleeing violence or conditions of oppression. But their freedom of movement and their most basic rights are at risk as more and more barriers are erected to keep them out.

Human rights and labour rights are being affected by the amazing capacities and spread of computer and communications technologies, and by the applications of new science – genetic engineering, biotechnologies, wonder drugs, artificial intelligence. So many "great leaps forward", but as ever, the question will be for whose benefit are they developed and who will have access to them? Who do they liberate and whose rights do they threaten?

Changes and threats to the environment and to eco-systems have major implications for all our rights as humans. Rights at work are threatened by toxic chemicals, new materials and waste products, rights to health services are threatened by pollution of the atmosphere, the right to life, liberty and security are put in jeopardy by meltdowns like Chernobyl, the Ogoni's rights to own property and to freedom of movement are put at risk by soil contamination. And no one can avoid the effects of global warming. The actual effects of the economic system can make a mockery of its alleged rationality and rob us of our rights.

AI has a tradition of emphasising the responsibilities of national governments, to "deliver" rights, to protect rights, to rectify violations. In the face of the decreasing functions and powers of governments, how should we respond, how can we globalise accountability?

Unions are familiar with the dilemma that the state is sometimes an ally, legislating or protecting norms, and sometimes the "enemy" sending police against demonstrations, demanding "registration" of unions, setting pay freezes etc. The key issue is surely about accountability, the right to participate in government and the right to change it.

Labour rights and human rights organisations need to find ways of working which are effective with power structures that lie outside the familiar context of the company or the nation state. We have to influence decision-makers in distant multinational company HQs, in board-rooms of management accountancy firms and investment analysts. We have to influence the decisions of technical experts and diplomats in the World Trade Organisation, the IMF, the World Bank and innumerable other remote, specialist agencies which are insulated from traditional democratic pressure. How should we adapt our campaigning to face this challenge?

With the intensive specialisation of human rights into separate topics from health issues to social security, from education rights to nationality issues, this field of interest risks becoming very "professionalised". The whole base of activism on labour rights and human rights issues is at issue. In order to retain people acting unpaid, out of conviction, our movements need to learn how to enable members to take up the particular causes which they identify with, feel passionately about and want to pursue very specifically. We also need to hold on to traditional principles of solidarity for when mass support is needed. But trends in trade unions and in voluntary organisations are tending to reflect noticeable changes in active participation; smaller, more flexible, specialised self-organised groups are playing a much more activist role than the traditional cohorts of uniform monolithic branches. Another set of issues we must study and adapt to.

The last decade has seen a big increase in the number of non-governmental organisations working on labour rights, human rights, international affairs, single issues, on themes or for specific sectors, or particular campaigns, but nothing on a scale to match the changes we have to face. We need to learn to work much more closely with each other in the different branches of human rights, recognising where we share, and where we differ over objectives, understanding differing specialist interests and strengths, differing structures and accountability.

As economic production, finance and control becomes more and more concentrated, it seems that when policies go wrong, they can lead to catastrophes on an ever increasing scale – massive economic crises, famines, environmental disasters, military conflicts, communal violence, mass killings and genocide erupt more suddenly and more disastrously than ever before. We need to adapt our movements to respond more quickly and more effectively to the massive scale of human rights violations and the sudden emergencies which arise today.

Historically there never was a period of halcyon days with equal rights in a society ruled by mutual respect: every age has been turbulent, beset with new risks and threats to people's rights. Those who care about rights face considerable challenges, we must adapt to reality or we'll be irrelevant.

Questions

1   What did Malaysia do to become more integrated into the world economy? Why does Greider expect that "convergence" between rich and poor will lead to a global "jobs auction"? How does Motorola's presence in Malaysia illustrate the "high drama of globalization"?

2   Think about the lessons you can draw from Korzeniewicz's case study of the Nike Corporation. What is a global "commodity chain"? What does the rise of such chains in many sectors tell you about the changing division of labor around the globe? Who benefits most from the work done in these chains?

3   How does Fishman demonstrate the dependence of middle-class Americans on other parts of the world economy? Do you find his argument about the "fruits of misery" convincing?

4   Why are women more at risk in periods of global change or crisis, according to Beneria and Bisnath? What does it mean to "engender" efforts to eradicate poverty?

5   How do Slaughter and Swagel answer their main question about the impact of globalization on wages and jobs? How do Burtless et al. confront "globaphobia" in the US? Do you think the kind of evidence presented in these articles will be sufficient to allay widespread fears about economic globalization, in the US and elsewhere?

6   How do Amnesty International's diagnosis of and solutions to workers' problems differ from those of traditional unions? What advantages and disadvantages does an international nongovernmental organization like AI have in addressing the problems of workers?

Part V

Political Globalization I: The Demise of the Nation-State?

Introduction

In a world made up of powerful and highly stable nation-states, political globalization might seem like a contradiction in terms. A state (more commonly called "government" in the USA) is the sovereign authority in a specified territory, with the right to use force both to maintain internal order and to defend its territory against aggression. Sovereignty, in turn, implies that the state is the ultimate authority in its territory, exercising jurisdiction over its citizens and the groups and organizations they form in the conduct of daily life. The sovereign state is not subject to any higher authority – no state has the right to expect compliance from any other state, and no all-encompassing world state has emerged with authority over all national states. Sometimes the United Nations is described as the potential nucleus of a world state, but it has no compelling authority over its member states and it relies entirely on the action of its members to enforce compliance with its resolutions and sanctions against misbehaving states.

In times past, world maps contained many different kinds of political units, from small dukedoms and principalities to large empires ruled by powerful states. Nearly all of the small units have been absorbed in larger nation-states, and all but a few of the colonies held by former imperial powers like Britain and France have become independent sovereign states. With the dissolution of the last great empire, the Soviet Union, in the 1990s, the world is now composed almost entirely of sovereign nation-states.

What sense does it make, then, to speak of political globalization? First, the very fact that the entire world, with the exception of the arctic areas and a few small colonies and dependencies, is organized by a single type of political unit, the nation-state, is a sign of globalization. Never before has the world been composed of only one type of political unit. The rapid decolonization of the twentieth century, when more than 130 colonies or dependencies became independent states, has been a great political surprise, since most of these new states are far too small and weak to defend themselves effectively from more powerful states. This indicates that the principle of state sovereignty itself has become a central feature of global society, and that a particular model of political organization, the sovereign state, has achieved global status as the most desirable, viable, and legitimate way of structuring political life.

Second, political globalization is indicated by the considerable uniformity exhibited by sovereign states in terms of their goals, structures, programs, and internal operations. Almost all states assume responsibility for a wide range of activities, including education, health care, management of the economy and finance, welfare programs, retirement pensions, environmental protection, and poverty alleviation, alongside the classic core concerns of states, foreign policy and military defense. Almost all states have elaborate bureaucratic structures to administer the many programs they operate to meet their responsibilities. And almost all states are formally structured (by constitutions and legislation) as democracies in which all citizens have an equal right to vote in elections that determine the holders of executive and legislative positions. Thus, a common basic model of the state is in place every-where in the world, though states vary considerably in how they implement the basic model in concrete terms.

A third dimension of political globalization is the emergence in the past hundred years of intergovernmental organizations (IGOs). IGOs are associa-tions of states created to deal with problems and manage issues that affect many countries at once or involve high levels of interdependence among countries. Of the approximately 300 global IGOs and more than a thousand regional or sub-regional IGOs, most are concerned with economic, technical, or political matters. Most prominent are the United Nations and its associated agencies (UNESCO, the World Health Organization, the International Labor Organization, ECOSOC, and so on), which constitute a central world political forum within which states conduct their international relations. Other promi-nent bodies include the World Trade Organization (WTO) and International Monetary Fund (IMF), which help manage the world economy; the Interna-tional Telecommunications Union and INTELSAT, which manage global telecommunications and satellite systems; the International Organization for Standardization (known as ISO), and the International Electro-Technical Com-mission (IEC), which develop and promote global standards for manufactur-ing, materials, product safety, and so on; and the Universal Postal Union, which manages international postal services.

As economic globalization has increased, as technology and technical systems have become more encompassing and complex, as problems like pol-lution and narcotics trafficking and terrorism have also become global, the adequacy of states to cope with the rapidly integrating world has increasingly been called into question. Many transnational corporations (TNCs) have larger sales revenues than the entire economies of most countries, and daily global financial transactions routinely surpass the $1 trillion level – so the world economy is beyond the control of states. Global warming and environmental degradation are inevitable by-products of economic development, and states are too much concerned with their own development to take serious action about such problems. Religious and ethnic groups within countries are increasingly militant and well-armed, threatening the viability of the states they oppose. These and numerous other factors have led many observers to speak of repeated "crises" of the state and to predict the breakdown or irrel-evance of states.

Other observers caution that the death of the state has been announced prematurely. Problems may be increasingly global and large-scale, but states are also larger and more capable than ever before. They take in a larger share of Gross National Product as tax revenues than ever before; they have larger and better trained bureaucracies than ever before; they are remarkably effec-tive in operating national health care systems, pension plans, postal services, road and air transportation systems, and many other programs, at least in the more developed countries. The demands on states are certainly growing, perhaps even faster than states can keep up with them, but it is by no means certain that states are as incapable of dealing with their responsibilities as many critics claim. Only in some poorer countries do we find clearly weak states that fall far short of global expectations for their performance.

Our selections on political globalization begin with Connie L. McNeely's analysis of the role of the UN in legitimating and, indeed, certifying the viability of nation-states in the postwar period. McNeely shows that no formal criteria for statehood are strictly necessary for membership in the United Nations as long as a plausible claim for statehood can be made. She also shows that UN membership confers a strongly egalitarian and juridically inviolate status on states, even those very small or weak states whose viability might seem quite dubious. Kenichi Ohmae, by contrast, expresses the more common view that the institutions and boundaries of the nation-state are becoming increasingly irrelevant. Ohmae argues that the "4 I's" (Investment, Industry, Information and Individual) render states powerless to do much more than stand by and watch as events spin out of their control.

Daniel Yergin and Joseph Stanislaw endorse Ohmae's view, arguing that faith in government to manage economies or provide for the general welfare of citizens has eroded badly. From a period when "market failure" was seen as the main cause of poverty, unemployment, and various social ills, they espy a growing consensus that government failure is the problem. The "commanding heights" of global development are now occupied by aggressive global production systems and capital markets, putting governments on the defensive and leading them to deregulate, downsize, and privatize much of the social management functions they had assumed over the past century.

Dani Rodrik provides evidence that economic globalization may indeed have undermined the capacity of states to give adequate support to citizens. The problem, Rodrik says, is that companies in the developed countries can move their operations to countries where labor costs are lower and unions are weaker, putting downward pressure on wages, weakening labor's bargaining power, and lowering government revenues so that welfare and social security programs become more difficult to support. The developed countries are also undercut by the low-cost imports available to consumers, which further intensifies this downward spiral. Rodrik argues that states should counteract the downward spiral by being more skeptical toward free trade and capital flows, so a balance can be struck between openness and social responsibility.

Geoffrey Garrett directly questions Ohmae's and Rodrik's claims. Garrett argues that expanded state action to cushion the negative impact of free flows of goods and capital can produce higher economic growth and more balanced economies than would be achieved if states passively succumbed to global openness. The key is the improved morale and motivation of the labor force that results from knowing that a strong social support system is always available, along with the willingness of labor organizations to cooperate with employers to reach mutually acceptable compromises about state support programs and thereby avoid the disruptions of strikes and lockouts when issues come to a head.

Finally, we include a statement by the World Trade Organization about the nature of its operations. Critics of globalization have castigated the WTO (formed in 1994 as a successor to the narrower General Agreement on Tariffs and Trade process, or GATT) as a global monster whose authority strips states of their sovereign control over national economies. However, the WTO statement depicts the WTO as an agent of and for states, operating solely in response to the wishes of its members. The WTO disclaims any interest in creating a supranational market governed by supranational organizations that would reduce states to mere shadows of their former selves.

28 The Determination of Statehood

Connie L. McNeely

Underlying our sociological explanation of the institutionalization and expansion of the nation-state is the notion that there are external social rules and requirements for statehood, that a state is supposed to look a certain way and do certain things. Yet, statehood, as a concept and as it applies to various political entities, is not necessarily self-evident; nor, apparently, is it the same in every application and at all periods in time. The increase in state formation has been a dominant feature of the modern international system since the end of World War II, with the emergence of a multitude of new states dramatically changing the character of the system and emphasizing the salience of this issue to a greater degree than ever before. When we look at the contemporary international order, we find a highly diverse array of entities claiming to be states, and recognized as such. Indeed, the concept of statehood is fundamental to the organization and structure of the international system: states are arguably the primary actors in the system, and statehood is the primary type of international personality. Thus, we are confronted with the crucial problem of ascertaining the criteria by which this statehood has been determined; we must ask ourselves whether identification or designation of states qua states in the global political system can be attributed to at least some type of general cultural rules or criteria. In short, how do we recognize a state? Moreover, given certain specifying criteria, the next issue that arises is the matter of how they are transmitted to (and imposed upon) the units in the system. I suggest that international organizations have played a crucial role on both these fronts.

The membership of international organizations, and international governmental organizations in particular, is composed primarily of states, and much of their importance derives from the fact that they are associations of states. Moreover, admission to international governmental organizations often turns on the issue of statehood, and statehood is typically required before any other eligibility considerations are made. Thus, it only follows that the rules and practices of international organizations must presume and prescribe certain accepted images of statehood, while proscribing others. More specifically, I argue that international organizations act not only to recognize, but also to define, enforce, and maintain these requirements. That is, international organizations operate as an institutionalizing mechanism in the sense of both setting and transmitting "requirements" for statehood, thereby framing and recognizing the nation-state as the primary unit in the global political system. This argument emphasizes the institutional and cultural conditions that create and structure the contemporary nation-state, while bringing attention to the role of international organizations in its construction. Thus, the criteria or standards that international organizations use to recognize a political entity as a sovereign state is the issue that emerges for investigation in this chapter.

Fundamentally, to restate the problem, the question is whether indeed there is some model or standard for statehood in the global political system, and whether this model has changed over time, particularly in the postwar period. This question has important theoretical implications for understanding the basic framework and development of the global political system. Most analyses of the international system begin with the assumption of organized states, as opposed to questioning the process by which those states are constructed and given meaning within the system. Yet, this meaning is fundamental to the very definition of that system, and this is the issue that we address here.

This understanding of statehood draws on concepts and principles that have traditionally arisen in international legal constructs and related discussion of the state, in keeping with institutionalist assertions. Expressed in terms of a "knowledge" discourse with a set of associated disciplinary devices, international law provides a generalized language, concepts, and mechanisms for the formal construction and characterization of nation-states and other international public entities. Moreover, international law, as a codified account of rights in world society, is the record of rights and obligations of states toward each other in the international system. As such, international law is more than a regime of rules in substantive issue areas; it is an important aspect of and issue in analyses of the world polity and nation-state relations.

In brief, the institutionalist account posits a general "operating set" of political-cultural norms and rules that emphasize the primacy and legitimacy of statehood and its institutionalization in the world system. In this sense, political status and statehood are matters of social definition and construction, and states are those entities so recognized in the system. Sovereign statehood does not mean the absence of external constraints on state action, but rather a claim to internal autonomy and external independence *recognized* as legitimate by other states that are constituted as sovereign in the same way. In other words, sovereign statehood is a socially defined political status of an entity in a system based on recognition by other sovereign states. Recognition implies acceptance of a claim to statehood, of a claim to final jurisdiction over a territory and population and of formal autonomy from any other political unit. Thus, statehood is an issue of membership – membership in the global political system, and recognition constructs and legitimates that statehood and membership.

More, statehood is an issue of membership in international organizations. Not only do international organizations symbolically represent the rules of the modern world polity, that is, the rules of a system in which states are the constitutive members, they also play an important role in the development and implementation of international legal forms and content. More to the point, international organizations are the primary instruments in the global political system through which formal state recognition and legitimation take place. Thus, analysis of the approach to statehood in international governmental organizations might help demonstrate the institutionalized rules by which nation-states are constructed in terms of wider system relations. By closely examining the requirements for membership and related issues over time, and the debates surrounding them, I attempt here to clarify and make explicit the international criteria for what constitutes a state. [. . .]

Subsequent Members

According to the Charter, those members admitted to the United Nations must satisfy five conditions. To be admitted to membership in the United Nations, an applicant must (1) be a *state*; (2) be peace-loving; (3) accept the obligations of the Charter; (4) be able to carry out these obligations; and (5) be willing to do so. Originally, the majority of the United Nations members simply thought of the primary purpose of the organization as peace and security, and were either against or unconcerned with universal membership. However, the rapid spread of independence in the postwar period changed the character and practice of international organizations. In general, there was a change in attitude in favor of universality and toward the notion that peace and security would be best served by a more universal participation. This shift was reflected in the pattern of United Nations membership growth. Before 1955, only nine new members were admitted to the United Nations. Between then and 1985, there were almost one hundred successful applications. By 1985, United Nations membership had expanded from the original 51 members to 159 members.

A major factor affecting admission policy, especially since the 1960s, has been this emphasis on universality, and United Nations membership has progressed to include nearly all of the states in the global political system. In 1945, approximately 68 percent of the entities with internationally recognized claims to statehood became the original members of the United Nations. By 1985, this figure had grown to 95 percent. [. . .]

New States and the Significance of Membership

In light of the rapid rise in United Nations membership the question arises as to why nations join in the first place. One important reason is legitimation; states must be able to legitimate themselves in order to survive in the global political system. Claude has convincingly argued that the function of legitimization in the international realm has been increasingly conferred upon international organizations, and that this is a particularly significant part of the political role of the United Nations. The United Nations, in its collective organizational identity, has acquired the role of granting recognition on behalf of the community of states, and it has come to be regarded, and used, as a dispenser of politically significant approval and disapproval of the claims of entities as independent members of the international system. Admission to the United Nations has become the formal acknowledgment of independence and statehood, to the extent that admission itself is the ultimate symbol of international recognition.

However, let me note here that recognition of a state should not be confused with recognition or accreditation of a government, as was the case with the recognition of China as a *state*, as opposed to legitimated recognition and accreditation of the *government* of the People's Republic of China versus that of Nationalist China. While recognition of the government was at issue, the existence of the state itself was undisputed. No one would argue that China itself did not exist. While on one level this notion of the state is admittedly abstract, we all still somehow have a sense of it, a cultural understanding of its existence. This refers to transcendent aspects of the state beyond, for example, concrete notions of bureaucracy and monopoly over the means of violence.

Furthermore, the Charter of the United Nations reaffirms "faith in the equal rights . . . of nations large and small" and declares that "the organization is based on the principle of the sovereign equality of all its members." It was determined during the planning and establishment of the United Nations that sovereign equality means that (1) states are juridically equal; (2) each state enjoys the rights inherent in full sovereignty; (3) the personality of the state is respected as well as its territorial integrity and political independence; and (4) the state should, under the international order, comply faithfully with its international duties and obligations.

In short, collective legitimization in support of the principle of sovereign equality was an important aspect of United Nations participation and membership, and is at least a partial explanation for the rush of applications for membership upon independence in many new states. Not including the Philippines and India (which gained independence in 1946 and 1947, respectively, but were among the original United Nations members), of the ninety-nine countries attaining independence or recognition between 1946 and 1985, all but four applied for membership and ninety-three of them had become members during that period. In fact, eighty-eight of those countries applied for membership within a year of independence, giving testimony to the importance of the collective legitimization function of the organization.

Furthermore, the United Nations principles of sovereignty and formal equality give small, weak, and poor states a platform that they might not otherwise have, and their application to and participation in the United Nations serve as reminders that even the smallest and weakest countries have interests and problems involving the world community and the right to assert themselves on the world scene. Many new states persist not so much by state or nation building per se, as by their status as members in the international state system, as represented by membership in the United Nations. [. . .]

Traditional international law has commonly relied on the criteria laid down in the 1933 Montevideo Convention when referring to a state. That is, "the State as a person of international law should possess the following qualifications: (a) a permanent population; (b) a defined territory; (c) government; and (d) capacity to enter into relations with other states." In addition, importantly, a discourse of independence and sovereignty was necessarily woven throughout these considerations, and was partly defined in them. These "classical" criteria rest upon the idea of effectiveness among territorial units, and are indeed reflected in the early discussions of statehood in the United Nations. However, they have been both supplemented and contradicted in United Nations deliberations over time. [. . .]

Population

No real problems have arisen in regard to population per se in United Nations practice. A population in a state is obviously assumed and there is apparently no prescribed minimum or maximum of inhabitants necessary to constitute a state – as long as somebody is there. United Nations members, internationally recognized as states by virtue of that membership, ranged in population from 42,000 in Saint Christopher and Nevis and 65,480 in the Seychelles to 754,387,000 in India and 1,084,924,000 in China. The issue of population could conceivably come into question, for example, only in the case of an entity such as Vatican City because of the official and nonpermanent nature of its population, or if Antarctica were to claim statehood. It has also been discussed in relation to the participation of mini-states in the United Nations, but the principle of sovereign equality for all nations "large and small" has discouraged its serious consideration as a factor affecting statehood. Also, other than as discussed previously, population "content" has not been a barrier to recognition, especially since there are few, if any, nation-states whose populations are entirely homogeneous, ethnically or culturally, to the exclusion of all others.

Defined territory and territorial integrity

Neither, apparently, does statehood have a minimum territorial requirement – as long as there is some recognized territory. Over time, United Nations members have ranged in area from 262 square kilometers in Saint Christopher and Nevis and 277 square kilometers in the Seychelles to 9,976,185 square kilometers in Canada and over 22,402,200 in the former Soviet Union. On the other hand, although the question of minimum territory has not been seriously considered in the United Nations and a member may be of any size, sovereign statehood is, in fact, predicated upon authority over some geographical area. Without at least a minimum recognized territory, there would be no recognition of statehood. [. . .]

The issue of territorial integrity has also been salient in the case of divided states. Following World War II, certain territorial entities found themselves divided into separate administrative units (Germany, Korea, and Vietnam). This situation raised questions of whether these entities constituted parts of a single state and whether the parts are bound to reunification and reabsorption into a single state. In these cases, over and above Cold War considerations, the United Nations position has reflected "national" considerations and has supported the objective of national unification, tying this objective to recognition of statehood and membership in the organization; informally at least, the integrity of nations has been taken quite seriously. Indeed, these cases demonstrate that an entity, though divided de facto into separate parts, can continue to be regarded as a single state. [. . .]

Although defined territory has been treated as important in United Nations practice, it has been interpreted rather liberally to the extent that even a substantial boundary or territorial dispute alone is not enough to challenge actual statehood. The requirement of territory is not a separate criterion; a territory is assumed, but beyond that it is more a constituent of government and independence.

Stable and effective government

The United Nations maintained a fairly consistent pattern of adherence to the requirement of a stable and effective government in United Nations practice until 1960 with the admission of the Republic of the Congo (Zaire). In fact, part of the normal admission procedure was an investigation into whether a government exercised effective authority within a state territory and was typically obeyed by the majority of its population. Cohen points out a tendency among members to have interpreted this criterion to mean democratic, rather than purely effective, government, and also indicates that the requirement of the existence of a government as a prerequisite to statehood often came near, and in part overlapped, the requirement of independence, which will be discussed later. These issues were particularly apparent in the applications of North and South Korea, North and South Vietnam, and Israel. However, given the existence of different government orientations and interpretations of what it means to be democratic, it became increasingly difficult to uphold this consideration as a prerequisite of statehood. The coming to independence of so many new and varied "states" further accentuated this point.

The situation of the Congo was such that its existence as a state was widely recognized, and it attained United Nations membership in 1960 without dissent, despite the fact that "the Assembly was unable or unwilling to choose among the warring Congolese factions to seat a representative of the new nation," suggesting "that there were considerable grounds to doubt the existence of a government that was either stable or effective at this crucial date." Similarly, while there was general agreement on the existence of an expanded Chilean state, there was conflict over the ruling group and the internal policies and external relations governing it; the existence of the state itself was not in question. [. . .]

Coups d'état, civil wars, and insurrections have upset the stability of many member governments without threatening their status as member states in the United Nations. In short, we can say that the state is not theoretically inevitably and integrally linked with the government apparatus (even though we may need to address it as such for empirical purposes). [. . .]

Diplomatic ties and interstate recognition

The issue of recognition as an indicator of statehood and condition for membership was discussed repeatedly in the United Nations, especially in Security Council "screening" sessions during the Cold War period. Over and above technical considerations, recognition of statehood is a political question. Although United Nations membership constitutes recognition of statehood, a distinction must be made between recognition by individual members and recognition by the United Nations acting in its collective corporate capacity representing the "world." The United Nations, as a corporate entity, in admitting a new member, recognizes a state above its role as a member; it recognizes it *as a state*. However, admission does not necessarily imply that each individual member is bound to recognize every other member.

The absence of diplomatic exchange and intercourse could not by itself bar United Nations admissions, and thus recognition of statehood, since states are under no international obligation to exchange diplomatic envoys. [. . .]

External affairs

More than any other factor, from the establishment of the United Nations to the present, control of external affairs has been discussed in relation to determining statehood and eligibility for United Nations membership. The legal department of the United Nations Secretariat has expressed the opinion that a criterion of sovereignty itself is that the government of a state should be solely responsible for its foreign affairs. In general, "where the claim has been for comprehensive participation, the United Nations has required a high degree of sovereignty in the conduct of foreign relations," and "in no case of virtually total limitation upon sovereign rights in this regard," as with Monaco and San Marino, "has an entity been admitted to membership." Formally speaking, a fundamental aspect of sovereignty is the absolute competence of a state to perform acts and make treaties and agreements in the international arena. Furthermore, a state is not subject to any international jurisdiction or settlement except by its own consent. [. . .]

Sovereignty and independence

International legal discourse has long maintained that an entity must possess independence and sovereignty before it can be acknowledged as a state, and United Nations practice has consistently upheld this condition. Yet, United Nations practice also reveals that there has been disagreement on what constitutes the requirements of independence and sovereignty and on when these requirements have been met.

The United Nations General Assembly has declared the right of all states to full and complete independence. However, as expressed by then United Nations Secretary General U Thant in 1966, "it appears desirable that a distinction be made between the right to independence and the question of full membership in the United Nations," or between "mere" independence and full statehood. Although independence may be generally acknowledged, it may be in fact seriously limited by the political and economic realities of international life. In other words, is "actual independence" as much a condition and issue of statehood as "legal independence" in the international system?

For example, in regard to Nepal's application for United Nations membership, the government of Nepal was requested to provide information concerning its sovereignty and independence. This question arose because of the close consultative relationship with India on Nepal's foreign policy, and the fact that India was kept very well informed of Nepal's relations with other states. Yet, the formal power to conduct external affairs rested solely within Nepal itself and, despite the relationship with India, Nepal still maintained substantial freedom to conduct its own foreign affairs. Bhutan's relationship with India is another example of the same issue. [. . .]

De facto and de jure independence are closely linked and the relationship between the two concepts in today's global political system is highly flexible. We can say that formal independence is the overriding prerequisite of statehood today, and actual independence would not become an issue except in the most extreme cases. Independence in general may be presumed where a territorial entity is formally independent, and where its creation was not attended by serious illegalities. [. . .]

Conclusion

The research here explores the concept of statehood in a way that is informed by, and speaks to, general models and understandings of the dynamics of the global system. Simply put, the world polity contains a particular model of statehood, reflected and supported in international organization discourse and practice, and it is this model to which nation-states aspire in the construction of their identities as such. Rates of transition to statehood intensified over time, particularly in the period after World War II, along with the increased international privileging of nation-state status. Independent states entered the international system at a progressively rapid rate, exemplified in applications for United Nations membership, and doing so implied a certain conformity with, or acceptance of and aspiration to, basic notions of nation-state form and function. However, the international scene of 1945 in which the United Nations was founded was vastly different from that of 1985 and today, in which a number of new states have emerged. Originally, wartime considerations aside, the United Nations membership was based on an image of the world more or less in the western tradition of statehood, determined by population, area, stable and effective government, and independence, especially as regards external affairs. However, the world has changed dramatically and the recognition of statehood has been modified accordingly. While the United Nations first formalized and endorsed the existing criteria, it is clear that in the course of United Nations history, the criteria for statehood have changed in subtle, but important ways – *toward increasing emphasis on the unconditional equality of all states, toward an underlying assumption that one criterion is self-determination or free choice, and toward the assumption that the ultimate destiny of every territory is that of statehood.*

The evolution of the concept of unconditional equality among states is a particularly fascinating and radical change, given the cultural, political, and economic diversity of states in the international system. While the system consists of unequally powerful and competing states, they are all still recognized as formally equal, sovereign, and independent. "A sovereign state in the modern world is one which is 'recognized' by other equally sovereign states. The sovereignty of the modern state is a partial, or qualified, sovereignty. The distinctive quality of the modern nation-state is not only the sovereignty that attaches to it, but the mutual and contingent quality of that sovereignty among existing states." Sovereignty, as a socially constructed principle, has always been at odds to varying degrees with reality, and it has been both threatened and intensified in recent decades. Yet, it is the basis on which the interstate system exists and is defined.

Clearly, we are speaking in terms of an ideal in which certain aspects of the state are discussed in order to illuminate them when empirically examining actual state existence in a system of states. Sovereignty occurs only as an intersubjective, relational value, the essence of which is mutual recognition of the right to exclusive political authority within territorial limits, and reciprocal sovereignty is at the heart of this process of social empowerment for nation-states. The geopolitical categorization, mapping, and valuation of the world in terms of sovereignty constitute a "moral geography," or set of ethical assertions that preorganizes explicit moral-political discourses, by which new states and those lacking in material power became inscribed in the society of states. The imagined state is given essentialist identity through the collective imperatives attached to state sovereignty and recognition. While spatial boundaries may be contested, the fact remains that it is only by virtue of reciprocal recognition that states have territorial rights. As Wendt argues, this recognition is a kind of social closure or boundedness that disempowers nonstate actors and empowers interaction among recognized sovereign states, supporting the dominant nation-state form and system.

Moreover, statehood is highly stable, indicating the independent effects of recognized status within the larger community, to the extent that the "life chances" of polities depend on formal political status. The stability and increase of statehood in the system is difficult to explain in terms of exchange and competition given the relative disappearance of unrecognized and dependent entities. Addressing cultural and ideological issues of statehood, we can use the world polity institutionalist perspective to better account for this by linkages and diffusion within and between the units in the system, mediated in large part by international organizations. This serves as a basis for the normative practices and views framing nation-state formation, integration, and legitimation in the international system. [. . .]

29 The End of the Nation State

Kenichi Ohmae

A funny – and, to many observers, a very troubling – thing has happened on the way to former US President Bush's so-called "new world order": the old world has fallen apart. Most visibly, with the ending of the Cold War, the long-familiar pattern of alliances and oppositions among industrialized nations has fractured beyond repair. Less visibly, but arguably far more important, the modern nation state itself – that artifact of the eighteenth and nineteenth centuries – has begun to crumble. [. . .]

In economics as in politics, the older patterns of nation-to-nation linkage have begun to lose their dominance. What is emerging in their place, however, is not a set of new channels based on culture instead of nations. Nor is it a simple realignment of previous flows of nation-based trade or investment.

In my view, what is really at stake is not really which party or policy agenda dominates the apparatus of a nation state's central government. Nor is it the number of new, independent units into which that old center, which has held through the upheavals of industrialization and the agonies of two world wars, is likely to decompose. Nor is it the cultural fault lines along which it is likely to fragment.

Instead, what we are witnessing is the cumulative effect of fundamental changes in the currents of economic activity around the globe. So powerful have these currents become that they have carved out entirely new channels for themselves – channels that owe nothing to the lines of demarcation on traditional political maps. Put simply, in terms of real flows of economic activity, nation states have *already* lost their role as meaningful units of participation in the global economy of today's borderless world.

In the first place, these long-established, politically defined units have much less to contribute – and much less freedom to make contributions. The painful irony is that, driven by a concern to boost overall economic well-being, their efforts to assert traditional forms of economic sovereignty over the peoples and regions lying within their borders are now having precisely the opposite effect. Reflexive twinges of sovereignty make the desired economic success impossible, because the global economy punishes twinging countries by diverting investment and information elsewhere.

The uncomfortable truth is that, in terms of the global economy, nation states have become little more than bit actors. They may originally have been, in their mercantilist phase, independent, powerfully efficient engines of wealth creation. More recently, however, as the downward-ratcheting logic of electoral politics has placed a death grip on their economies, they have become – first and foremost – remarkably inefficient engines of wealth distribution. Elected political leaders gain and keep power by giving voters what they want, and what they want rarely entails a substantial decrease in the benefits, services, or subsidies handed out by the state.

Original publication details: Ohmae, Kenichi, excerpt from *The End of the Nation State: The Rise of Regional Economies* (Free Press, New York, 1995).

Moreover, as the workings of genuinely global capital markets dwarf their ability to control exchange rates or protect their currency, nation states have become inescapably vulnerable to the discipline imposed by economic choices made elsewhere by people and institutions over which they have no practical control. Witness, for example, the recent, Maastricht-related bout of speculation against the franc, the pound, and the kronor. Witness, also, the unsustainable but self-imposed burden of Europe's various social programs. Finally, witness the complete absence of any economic value creation, save for those around the world who stand to benefit from pork-barrel excesses, in such decisions as the Japanese Diet's commitment – copied from the New Deal policies of Franklin Roosevelt – to build unnecessary highways and bridges on the remote islands of Hokkaido and Okinawa.

Second, and more to the point, the nation state is increasingly a nostalgic fiction. It makes even less sense today, for example, than it did a few years ago to speak of Italy or Russia or China as a single economic unit. Each is a motley combination of territories with vastly different needs and vastly different abilities to contribute. For a private sector manager or a public sector official to treat them as if they represented a single economic entity is to operate on the basis of demonstrably false, implausible, and nonexistent averages. This may still be a political necessity, but it is a bald-faced economic lie.

Third, when you look closely at the goods and services now produced and traded around the world, as well as at the companies responsible for them, it is no easy matter to attach to them an accurate national label. Is an automobile sold under an American marque really a US product when a large percentage of its components comes from abroad? Is the performance of IBM's foreign subsidiaries or the performance of its R&D operations in Europe and Japan really a measure of US excellence in technology? For that matter, are the jobs created by Japanese plants and factories in the Mississippi Valley really a measure of the health of the Japanese, and not the US, economy? The barbershop on the corner may indisputably be a part of the domestic American economy. But it is just not possible to make the same claim, with the same degree of confidence, about the firms active on the global stage.

Finally, when economic activity aggressively wears a national label these days, that tag is usually present neither for the sake of accuracy nor out of concern for the economic well-being of individual consumers. It is there primarily as a mini-flag of cheap nationalism – that is, as a jingoistic celebration of nationhood that places far more value on emotion-grabbing symbols than on real, concrete improvements in quality of life. By contrast, we don't hear much about feverish waves of Hong Kong nationalism, but the people in Hong Kong seem to live rather well. With much fanfare, Ukraine and the Baltic states have now become independent, but do their people have more food to eat or more energy to keep them warm during the winter or more electricity for light to see by?

An arresting, if often overlooked, fact about today's borderless economy is that people often have better access to low-cost, high-quality products when they are not produced "at home." Singaporeans, for example, enjoy better and cheaper agricultural products than do the Japanese, although Singapore has no farmers – and no farms – of its own. Much the same is true of construction materials, which are much less expensive in Singapore, which produces none of them, than in Japan, which does.

Now, given this decline in the relevance of nation states as units of economic activity, as well as the recent burst of economic growth in Asia, the burgeoning political self-consciousness of Islam, and the fragmentation, real or threatened, of such "official" political entities as Italy, Spain, Somalia, Rwanda, Canada, South Africa, and the former Yugoslavia, Czechoslovakia, and Soviet Union – given all this, it is easy to see why observers like Huntington should look to cultural, religious, ethnic, even tribal affiliations as the only plausible stopping point of the centrifugal forces unleashed by the end of the Cold War.

Once bipolar discipline begins to lose its force, once traditional nation states no longer "hold," or so the argument goes, visionless leaders will start to give in to the fear that older fault lines will again make themselves felt. And given the bloody violence with which many of these lines have already begun to reappear, these leaders will find it hard to see where this process of backsliding can come to rest short of traditional groupings based on some sort of cultural affinity. In other words, in the absence of vision and the presence of slowly rising panic, the only groupings that seem to matter are based on civilizations, not nations.

But are cultures or civilizations meaningful aggregates in terms of which to understand economic activity? Think, for a moment, of the ASEAN countries. In what sense is it useful to talk about them as a single, culturally defined economic area? As they affect local patterns of work, trade, and industry, the internal differences among their Buddhist, Islamic, Catholic (in the Philippines and the Sabah state of Malaysia), and Confucian traditions are every bit as large as, if not larger than, the differences separating any one of these traditions from the dominant business cultures of New York or London or Paris.

But in ASEAN, at least, differences of this sort do not provoke the same kinds of conflicts that often arise elsewhere. Most Western observers know, for example, that Spanish and Portuguese speakers can converse with each other, if with some minor degree of difficulty. Many fewer, however, know that the same is true of Indonesians and Malaysians. Or that, in border regions between Thailand and Malaysia, such as Phuket, there are peaceful, economically linked villages, some of which have mainly Buddhist and some mainly Islamic populations. These on-the-ground realities have made it possible for ASEAN leaders to accept and to reinforce, with little fear of internal friction, the development of cross-border economic ties like those stretching across the Strait of Malacca which are represented by the Greater Growth Triangle of Phuket, Medan, and Penang.

Even more important than such cultural differences within a civilization, and what Huntington's line of thought leaves out, is the issue of historical context. The particular dissolution of bipolar, "great power" discipline that so greatly affects us today is not taking place in the 1790s or the 1890s, but the 1990s. And that means it is taking place in a world whose peoples, no matter how far-flung geographically or disparate culturally, are all linked to much the same sources of global information. The immediacy and completeness of their access may vary, of course, and governments may try to impose restrictions and control. Even if they do, however, the barriers will not last forever, and leakages will occur all along the way. Indeed, the basic fact of linkage to global flows of information is a – perhaps, *the* – central, distinguishing fact of our moment in history. Whatever the civilization to which a particular group of people belongs, they now get to hear about the way other groups of people live, the kinds of products they buy, the changing focus of their tastes and preferences as consumers, and the styles of life they aspire to lead.

But they also get something more. For more than a decade, some of us have been talking about the progressive globalization of markets for consumer goods like Levi's jeans, Nike athletic shoes, and Hermès scarves – a process, driven by global

exposure to the same information, the same cultural icons, and the same advertisements, that I have elsewhere referred to as the "California-ization" of taste. Today,
however, the process of convergence goes faster and deeper. It reaches well beyond
taste to much more fundamental dimensions of worldview, mind-set, and even
thought process. There are now, for example, tens of millions of teenagers around
the world who, having been raised in a multimedia-rich environment, have a lot
more in common with each other than they do with members of older generations
in their own cultures. For these budding consumers, technology-driven convergence
does not take place at the sluggish rate dictated by yesterday's media. It is instantaneous – a nanosecond migration of ideas and innovations.

The speed and immediacy of such migrations take us over an invisible political
threshold. In the post-Cold War world, the information flows underlying economic
activity in virtually all corners of the globe simply cannot be maintained as the
possession of private elites or public officials. They are shared, increasingly, by all
citizens and consumers. This sharing does not, of course, imply any necessary similarity in how local economic choices finally get made. But it does imply that there
is a powerful centripetal force at work, counteracting and counterbalancing all the
centrifugal forces noted above.

The emotional nexus of culture, in other words, is not the only web of shared
interest able to contain the processes of disintegration unleashed by the reappear-
ance of older fault lines. Information-driven participation in the global economy
can do so, too, ahead of the fervid but empty posturing of both cheap nationalism
and cultural messianism. The well-informed citizens of a global marketplace will
not wait passively until nation states or cultural prophets deliver tangible improvements in lifestyle. They no longer trust them to do so. Instead, they want to build
their own future, now, for themselves and by themselves. They want their own
means of direct access to what has become a genuinely global economy. [. . .]

A Swing of the Pendulum

In the broad sweep of history, nation states have been a transitional form of organization for managing economic affairs. Their right – their prerogative – to manage
them grew, in part, out of the control of military strength, but such strength is now
an uncomfortably great burden to maintain. (It has also largely been exposed as a
means to preserve the positions of those in power, not to advance the quality-of-life
interests of their people.) Their right grew out of the control of natural resources
and colonies, but the first is relatively unimportant as a source of value in a
knowledge-intensive economy, and the second is less a source of low-cost resources
than a bottomless drain on the home government's treasury. It grew out of the
control of land, but prosperous economies can spread their influence through neighboring territories without any need for adjustment in formal divisions of sovereignty.
And it grew out of the control of political independence, but such independence is
of diminishing importance in a global economy that has less and less respect for
national borders.

Moreover, as it grew, the nation state's organizational right to manage economic
affairs fell victim to an inescapable cycle of decay. This should occasion no surprise.
It comes as close to being a natural law as the messy universe of political economy
allows. Whatever the form of government in power and whatever the political
ideology that shapes it, demands for the civil minimum, for the support of special

interests, and for the subsidization and protection of those left behind inexorably rise. In different circumstances, under different regimes, and during different eras, the speed of escalation varies. Good policy can slow the pace, bad policy can accelerate it. But no policy can stop it altogether. Nation states are political organisms, and in their economic bloodstreams cholesterol steadily builds up. Over time, arteries harden and the organism's vitality decays.

History, of course, also records the kinds of catastrophic, equilibrium-busting events that can stop or even reverse this aging process. Wars can do it, as can natural disasters like plagues, earthquakes, and volcanic eruptions. They have certainly done so in the past. But even for the most cold-blooded practitioners of *realpolitik*, these are hardly credible as purposeful instruments of economic policy.

Thus, in today's borderless economy, with its rapid cross-border [flows], there is really only one strategic degree of freedom that central governments have to counteract this remorseless buildup of economic cholesterol, only one legitimate instrument of policy to restore sustainable and self-reinforcing vitality, only one practical as well as morally acceptable way to meet their people's near-term needs without mortgaging the long-term prospects of their children and grandchildren. And that is to cede meaningful operational autonomy to the wealth-generating region states that lie within or across their borders, to catalyze the efforts of those region states to seek out global solutions, and to harness their distinctive ability to put global logic first and to function as ports of entry to the global economy. The only hope is to reverse the postfeudal, centralizing tendencies of the modern era and allow – or better, encourage – the economic pendulum to swing away from nations and back toward regions. [. . .]

30 The Commanding Heights: The Battle Between Government and the Marketplace that is Remaking the Modern World

Daniel Yergin and Joseph Stanislaw

All around the globe, socialists are embracing capitalism, governments are selling off companies they had previously nationalized, and countries are seeking to entice back multinational corporations that they had expelled just two decades earlier. Marxism and state control are being jettisoned in favor of entrepreneurship; the number of stock markets is exploding; and mutual fund managers have become celebrities. Today, politicians on the left admit that their governments can no longer afford the expansive welfare state, and American liberals recognize that more government may not hold the solution to every problem. Many people are being forced to reexamine and reassess their root assumptions. These changes are opening up new prospects and new opportunities throughout the world. The shift is also engendering, for many, new anxieties and insecurities. They fear that government will no longer be there to protect them as they become increasingly intertwined in a global economy that seeks to ignore national borders. And they express unease about the price that the market demands of its participants. Shocks and turbulence in international capital markets, such as those that roiled Latin America in 1995 and Southeast Asia in 1997, turn that unease into fundamental questions about the danger and even legitimacy of markets. But all these viewpoints need to be set in context.

Why the Shift?

Why the move to the market? Why, and how, the shift from an era in which the "state" – national governments – sought to seize and exercise control over their economies to an era in which the ideas of competition, openness, privatization, and deregulation have captured world economic thinking? This question, in turn, begets others: Are these changes irreversible? Are they part of a continuing process of development and evolution? What will be the consequences and prospects – political, social, and economic – of this fundamental alteration in the relationship between government and marketplace? These are the basic questions that this chapter seeks to answer.

Where the frontier between the state and market is to be drawn has never been a matter that could be settled, once and for all, at some grand peace conference.

Original publication details: Yergin, Daniel and Joseph Stanislaw, excerpt from *The Commanding Heights: The Battle Between Government and the Marketplace that is Remaking the Modern World* (Simon & Schuster, New York, 1998).

Instead, it has been the subject, over the course of this century, of massive intellectual and political battles as well as constant skirmishes. In its entirety, the struggle constitutes one of the great defining dramas of the twentieth century. Today the clash is so far-reaching and so encompassing that it is remaking our world – and preparing the canvas for the twenty-first century.

This frontier defines not the boundaries of nations but the division of roles within them. What are the realm and responsibility of the state in the economy, and what kind of protection is the state to afford its citizens? What is the preserve of private decision-making, and what are the responsibilities of the individual? This frontier is not neat and well defined. It is constantly shifting and often ambiguous. Yet through most of the century, the state has been ascendant, extending its domain further and further into what had been the territory of the market. Its victories were propelled by revolution and two world wars, by the Great Depression, by the ambitions of politicians and governments. It was also powered by the demands of the public in the industrial democracies for greater security, by the drive for progress and improved living conditions in developing countries – and by the quest for justice and fairness. Behind all this was the conviction that markets went to excesses, that they could readily fail, that there were too many needs and services they could not deliver, that the risks and the human and social costs were too high and the potential for abuse too great. In the aftermath of the traumatic upheavals of the first half of the twentieth century, governments expanded their existing responsibilities and obligations to their populaces and assumed new ones. "Government knowledge" – the collective intelligence of decision makers at the center – was regarded as superior to "market knowledge" – the dispersed intelligence of private decision makers and consumers in the marketplace.

At the extreme, the Soviet Union, the People's Republic of China, and other communist states sought to suppress market intelligence and private property altogether and replace them with central planning and state ownership. Government would be all-knowing. In the many industrial countries of the West and in large parts of the developing world, the model was the "mixed economy," in which governments flexed their knowledge and played a strong dominating role without completely stifling the market mechanism. They would reconstruct, modernize, and propel economic growth; they would deliver equity, opportunity, and a decent way of life. In order to achieve all that, governments in many countries sought to capture and hold the high ground of their economies – the "commanding heights."

The term goes back three-quarters of a century. In November 1922, half a decade after leading the Bolsheviks to victory, the already ailing Vladimir Illyich Lenin made his way to the platform of the Fourth Congress of the Communist International in St Petersburg, then called Petrograd. It was his penultimate public appearance. The year before, amid economic breakdown and out of desperation, Lenin had initiated the New Economic Policy, permitting a resumption of small trade and private agriculture. Now, communist militants were attacking him for compromising with capitalism and selling out the revolution. Responding with his old acerbity and sarcasm, despite his physical enfeeblement, Lenin defended the program. Although the policy allowed markets to function, he declared, the state would control the "commanding heights," the most important elements of the economy. And that, Lenin assured any who doubted him, was what counted. All this was before collectivization, Stalinism, and the total eradication of private markets in the Soviet Union.

The phrase found its way to Britain, via the Fabians and the British Labour Party, in the interwar years; it was then adopted by Jawaharlal Nehru and the Congress

Party in India, and spread to many other parts of the world. Whether or not the term was used, the objective was one and the same: to ensure government control of the strategic parts of the national economy, its major enterprises and industries. In the United States, government exerted its control over the commanding heights not through ownership but rather through economic regulation, giving rise to a special American brand of regulatory capitalism.

Overall, the advance of state control seemed to be inexorable. In the immediate post-World War II years, only governments could marshal the resources necessary to rebuild devastated and dislocated nations. The 1960s seemed to prove that they could effectively run, and indeed fine-tune, their economies. By the beginning of the 1970s, the mixed economy was virtually unchallenged and government continued to expand. Even in the United States, the Republican administration of Richard Nixon sought to implement a massive program of detailed wage and price controls.

Yet by the 1990s, it was government that was retreating. Communism had not only failed, it had all but disappeared in what had been the Soviet Union and, at least as an economic system, had been put aside in China. In the West, governments were shedding control and responsibilities. Instead of "market failure," the focus was now on "government failure" – the inherent difficulties that arise when the state becomes too expansive and too ambitious and seeks to be the main player, rather than a referee, in the economy. Paul Volcker, who conquered inflation as chairman of the US Federal Reserve System, explained the reason for the change in simple terms: "Governments had become overweening."

The Greatest Sale

Today, in response to the high costs of control and the disillusionment with its effectiveness, governments are privatizing. It is the greatest sale in the history of the world. Governments are getting out of businesses by disposing of what amounts to trillions of dollars of assets. Everything is going – from steel plants and phone companies and electric utilities to airlines and railroads to hotels, restaurants, and nightclubs. It is happening not only in the former Soviet Union, Eastern Europe, and China but also in Western Europe, Asia, Latin America, and Africa – and in the United States, where federal, state, and city governments are turning many of their traditional activities over to the marketplace. In a parallel process that is more far-reaching and less well understood, they are also overturning the regulatory apparatus that has affected almost every aspect of daily life in America for the last six decades. The objective is to move away from governmental control as a substitute for the market and toward reliance on competition in the marketplace as a more efficient way to protect the public.

This shift does not, by any means, signal the end of government. In many countries, governments continue to spend as large a share of national income each year as the year before. The reason, in the industrial countries, is social spending – transfer payments and entitlements – and almost everywhere, government remains the solution of last resort for a host of societal demands. Yet the scope of government, the range of duties it takes on in the economy, is decidedly receding. The world over, governments have come to plan less, to own less, and to regulate less, allowing instead the frontiers of the market to expand.

The decamping of the state from the commanding heights marks a great divide between the twentieth and twenty-first centuries. It is opening the doors of many formerly closed countries to trade and investment, vastly increasing, in the process, the effective size of the global market. Many new jobs are being created. Still, it is capital and technology that, in this new mobile economy, easily move around the world in search of new opportunities and markets and more favorable business environments. Labor, which does not travel as easily, could be left behind. The result for workers is a double anxiety – about global competition and about the loss of the social safety net.

The word *globalization*, minted not much more than a decade ago, has become the all-too-familiar description for the process of integration and internationalization of economic activities and strategies. Yet the term has already been overtaken by events. A new reality is emerging. This is not a process but a condition – a globality, a world economy in which the traditional and familiar boundaries are being surmounted or made irrelevant. The end of the Soviet Union and communism has redrawn the map of world politics and subdued ideology as a dominating factor in international affairs. The growth of capital markets and the continued lowering of barriers to trade and investment are further tying markets together – and promoting a freer flow of ideas. The advent of emerging markets brings dynamism and opportunity on a massive scale to the international economy. National firms are turning themselves into international operators; and companies, whether long experienced in international business or newcomers, are hastening to generate global strategies. Paralleling and facilitating much of this is a technological revolution of momentous but uncertain consequences. Information technology – through computers – is creating a "woven world" by promoting communication, coordination, integration, and contact at a pace and scale of change that far outrun the ability of any government to manage. The accelerating connections make national borders increasingly porous – and, in terms of some forms of control, increasingly irrelevant. [. . .]

Crisis of Confidence

Experience is a teacher, and what experience taught in the 1970s and into the 1980s was an increasing skepticism about the capabilities of what had become the traditional mixed economy. For some, it would result in an outright rejection of government's abilities. For others, there was unease and the growing sentiment that the economic structures of the postwar era no longer fulfilled the aims their founders had intended. In either case, the change of heart happened over time as, in one form or another, the confidence generated by the thirty glorious years began to dissipate. It was less a revelation than a process of learning about the limits of government's ability to run a modern economy.

For three decades the consensus held that achieving economic growth and improvements in the standard of life and human welfare required some form of central management. The extent of coordination was considered so great that only the state could provide it. This consensus rested upon trust. In order for it to work, the public and business enterprises would have to believe that political leadership – tested and recalibrated by elections, to be sure – could gather the knowledge required to look into the highly uncertain future and apply economic tools to improve a country's prospects and make that future more secure. The governments of the mixed economy did so by using some combination of five sets of tools – regulation, planning, state ownership, industrial policy, and Keynesian fiscal management. These tools could be augmented by a sixth – monetary policy. The actual mix varied considerably among countries, depending upon their traditions and history.

The basic rationale for government's role was the economists' concept of "market failure." Some desired outcomes required a degree of coordination that individual competitors in the marketplace could not muster. As a result of this failure, government would step in and provide that coordination. Time horizons and returns were often important concerns. Business alone could not provide investment; it either would take too long to come to fruition or would generate benefits that went to society at large, rather than the individual firm that had made the investment. Infrastructure was an example of something that took too long to develop, as were expenditures on basic research and development – a case in which the benefits might be quite diffused and thus not capturable by the firm that spent the money.

There was another sense to market failure as well – a failure of acumen, of knowledge. "Government knowledge" – what the government knew and was considered responsible for knowing – was different from "business knowledge." The latter was cultivated in different academies – in schools of law and policy, not business, and certainly not in the "trades." It was thought that the more an economic activity aimed toward the future and affected the broad population, the less sufficient was simple business knowledge to see it through. The instruments of intervention became the tools with which to apply government knowledge. Resources were directed and allocated by the state, by political and bureaucratic decision making, rather than by the elemental forces of supply and demand – forces shaped by the knowledge of those in the marketplace. Valéry Giscard d'Estaing, the former French president, was a star pupil at the École Nationale d'Administration, France's great repository of government knowledge, in the early 1950s. Looking back on his education, he recalled that he was taught about indicative planning and price controls, "but there was no reference, no discussion whatsoever of the market or about the market."

At first, government's assumption of the risks of economic activity seemed logical – and safe. No one could forget the 1930s. Thus government became a sort of national insurance company, guaranteeing growth while protecting the public from the risks of the market. Like vast insurers, governments collected premiums to pay for their outlays via direct and indirect taxes of all sorts. Unlike insurers, they also had at their disposal the prerogative of public authorities – deficit spending, on which they increasingly drew. But as government's role as insurer became entrenched, so too did the expectations of consumers, workers, and businesses. Once established, an interventionist government could only grow larger, not shrink. The expectation that government could and would guarantee growth and expanding benefits became part of the political culture.

Yet who could deny the success of the experiment? From the end of the Second World War until the oil crises of the 1970s, the industrial world enjoyed three decades of prosperity and rising incomes that sparked aspirations and dreams. It was an extraordinary achievement. The children of wartime and postwar rationing became the adolescents of economic recovery and growth and then the parents of the consumer society. Housing improved enormously. Families bought their first and then their second car; they acquired appliances and televisions. They shopped in supermarkets and department stores, they went on vacations and traveled to foreign countries, and they purchased products that had been turned into brand names and status symbols by advertising. And, most of all, they had jobs. Social critics bemoaned consumerism and materialism; they identified the gulf between "private affluence" and "public squalor." But the fundamental fact was that a quality of life had emerged that could not have been dreamed of at the end of World War II. It is no wonder that throughout the noncommunist, industrialized world, voters gave politicians the go-ahead to use that standard set of tools to guarantee a steadily growing economy – and, hence, full employment. In so doing, they deferred to government's superior knowledge of the national economic interest.

The warning flag was inflation. Throughout the 1960s, inflationary tendencies crept upward in the mixed economies, but never to the point of causing serious alarm. However, by the early 1970s, inflationary pressures were becoming more pronounced and visible. The tools governments had used to muddle through – to sustain consumer demand, to match inflation with wage increase – were now inadequate. Keynesian demand management assumed that low unemployment and a low, managed rate of inflation was a sustainable combination. That proved wrong.

The lesson took time to learn, for it challenged all that had been accepted as the received wisdom. The shortage of political will to tackle the problem head-on only gave conditions time to get worse. Inflation was becoming entrenched in many ways: by the growth of government deficits, by the expansion of the welfare state, by the barriers to competition, by the rigidities of the labor market, by the "social charges" added to the labor bill, and by the nature of the bargaining between labor and management over wages and the way they would be passed through the system. A good part of the inflation was a cost of the protection provided by the insurance state against uncertainties, volatilities, and competition. The adoption of wage and price controls became testament to the prevalence of the inflationary dynamics. But controls were no more than a stopgap. They could hold inflation at bay ever so briefly but could not disable its causes.

When the oil crisis of 1973–4 hit, the mixed economy was already straining. What made the dramatic rise in the price of oil truly a "shock" was the extent to which it upset the familiar patterns of costs in the economy. In the slump that followed the oil crisis, inflation and unemployment began to rise together in a deadly and unprecedented spiral. The phenomenon was christened stagflation. And between 1974 and 1980 governments of the left and the right alike learned that attempts to buy one's way out of the crisis by means of deficit spending would be futile and counterproductive. Keynesianism lost its cachet. The economic growth of the preceding decades, formerly much taken for granted, was now sorely missed.

Poor economic performance and the muddling and confusions of government policy engendered a loss of confidence in existing arrangements. Government knowledge was less powerful; governments, less all-knowing. By the end of the troubled 1970s, a new realization had gained ground: More than daily management, it was the entire structure of the economy that had reached its limits. It was imperative to rethink government's role in the marketplace. For the pioneers – the economists, politicians, and technocrats who shepherded the early programs of government withdrawal from the economy in various countries – the task was nothing short of revolutionary. For the first time in decades, governments would seek to reverse direction – to shed assets and to confront at least the idea of giving up some control. [. . .]

The New Consensus?

The market focus that had seemed radical and beyond the pale when Margaret Thatcher initiated her revolution has become the new consensus in less than two decades. Governments continue to be entrusted with a fundamental responsibility for welfare; but in the industrial world, the debate is now about how to define that responsibility, how broad or limited it should be, and how to deliver services – in short, how to reform the system.

But how much has really changed? How deeply rooted is this new consensus? Less than a month after Blair's election, the French Socialists, led by Lionel Jospin, sailed back into government, delivering a devastating defeat to the French right. But they did not sound like New Socialists. They presented plans that recalled the ill-fated *relance* policies of the early 1980s. With their agenda largely set by the reality of unemployment – twice the level of that in Britain – they promised to expand public-sector employment, increase labor charges, and slow privatization. Once in power, the government soon took a far more pragmatic stance in its economic policies. But the episode showed just how deep was the challenge to an idea of European unity that seemed founded on economic austerity alone. The difference was made clear when Blair and Jospin met at a socialist congress in Sweden just after their victories. The task of the left, Blair told the delegates, was "marrying together an open, competitive and successful economy with a just, decent and humane society." He served notice that "we modernize or die." Jospin made no secret of his disagreement: "Market forces," he said, "if there is no attempt to control them – will threaten our very idea of civilization." He went on to attack what he called "ultracapitalism."

Indeed, whatever the transformations in the world economy, an underlying mistrust of the market persists. Why? George Shultz pointed to one reason when he said, "Markets are relentless." As competition becomes more intense, there is no respite from its pressures. People turn to government to provide shelter from the constant demands of the market. The move to the market may bring a higher standard of living, better services, and more choice. But it also brings new insecurities – about unemployment, about the durability of jobs and the stress of the workplace, about the loss of protection from the vicissitudes of life, about the environment, about the unraveling of the safety net, about health care and what happens in old age. Workers – both white- and blue-collar – fear, and sometimes find, that employers, in order to please financial analysts, will break the social contract and cut salaries, benefits, and jobs of employees who have given fifteen or twenty irretrievable years of their life to the company. Further, the global nature of the marketplace disrupts traditional values and familiar forms of organization, amplifying the sense of a loss of control and generating a nostalgia for the past and its settled order. While there are gains, there are also losses, all of which are given a special edge by the undercurrent of millennial anxiety. There is an ambivalence and an uneasy balance. It is heard when a senior official in the Clinton administration talks about the battle between "the free marketeer in me and the liberal in me." It is encountered in the conviction in some countries that the process of privatization has meant the movement of government assets into the hands of those who are friends of the government, massively enriching them in the process. Even with an expertly executed privatization program, the results mean a redistribution of wealth, power, and status within a society, all of which can be highly unsettling.

Yet despite the doubts and the discontents, the move to the market is being driven by a shift in the balance of confidence – a declining faith in the competence of government, offset by a renewed appreciation of the workings of the market. One's parents and grandparents, so deeply traumatized by the Great Depression, may have lived with the permanent fear of another slump. In the United States, suspicion and criticism of the market historically focused on the tendency toward collusion – the

Progressives' critique – and the risk of market failure – the New Deal's preoccupation. Yet over the half century since World War II, market systems have demonstrated extraordinary vitality, enormously enhancing their credibility. One has to pause to grasp the extent of the shift in outlook. In 1975, the economist Arthur Okun – a chairman of the President's Council of Economic Advisers and, of course, a child of the Great Depression – would say, "The market needs a place, and the market needs to be kept in its place. . . . Given the chance, it would sweep away all other values, and establish a vending-machine society. I could not give it more than two cheers." In the two decades since, real GDP in the United States has almost doubled; and that tone, and the mistrust that underlies it, sounds archaic. The contrast is made all the more stark by examining the 1997 annual report of the Council of Economic Advisers, the main theme of which is the "advantage of markets." Indeed, the Council's focus on what it called the "insufficiently appreciated property of markets" – "their ability to collect and distribute information" – is vintage Hayek. And the report criticized the New Deal for having "crystallized" the belief in "the omniscience and the omnipotence" of the government "into a new kind of liberalism." All this is a very different view of the world.

The Woven World

Today, there is a resumption – a relinking – of a global economy after the disruptions of world wars, revolutions, and depression. As the steam engine and the telegraph shrank the dimensions of the nineteenth-century world, so technology today is once again eroding distance and borders. But this time the effects are much more comprehensive, for they leave virtually no country or community untouched. The pattern is evident in a host of measures. The number of international air passengers rose from 75 million in 1970 to 409 million in 1996. Between 1976 and 1996, the cost of a three-minute phone call from the United States to England dropped in real terms from about eight dollars to as low as thirty-six cents – and the number of transborder calls has increased from 3.2 billion in 1985 to 20.2 billion in 1996. Today, the world shares the same images from film and entertainment; the same news and information bounces down from satellites, instantaneously creating a common vocabulary for events.

Amid all this, the decisive new force is computers: Information technology is creating a woven world of distant encounters and instant connections. Knowledge and information do not have to wait. Within, outside, and across organizations and national boundaries, people are tied together, sharing information and points of view, working in virtual teams, bartering goods and services, swapping bonds and currencies, exchanging chatter and banalities, and passing the time. Information of every kind is available. With the establishment of the US government data Web site in 1997, a ten-year-old could gain access to more and better data than a senior official could have done just five years earlier. Libraries are open for business on the Internet. Researchers share their results in real time. Activists band together to promote their causes. Would-be terrorists surf for weapon designs. All this is increasingly heedless of the nation-state and outside the traditional structure of organizations. If the Internet is the new commanding heights, it is also beyond the reach of the state. While governments can promote the Internet, they cannot control it.

The hallmark of this new globality is the mobile economy. Capital sweeps across countries at electron speed; manufacturing and the generation of services move flexibly among countries and are networked across borders; markets are supplied from a continually shifting set of sources. Ideas, insights, techniques all disperse among countries with increasing ease. Access to technology across national boundaries continues to grow. Borders – fundamental to the exercise of national power – are eroded as markets are integrated. International trade between 1989 and 1997 grew at an annual rate of 5.3 percent – nearly four times faster than global output (1.4 percent). Over the same years, foreign direct investment rose even faster – at a rate of 11.5 percent per year. One indicator of the rapidity of change is the transformation of more and more firms into multinationals that provide the world market with goods and services that are conceived, produced, and assembled in several countries. The criterion of "national origin" has given way to "local content," which in turn is becoming harder and harder to pin down. The spread of fast, reliable information and communications technology pushes companies to draw on people and resources the world over. [. . .]

The integration of financial markets is particularly significant. Information and communications technology has, of course, provided the architecture for globally connected capital markets, but that is only part of the explanation. The big British privatizations in the mid-1980s were the first true global offerings of equity, and they changed the orientation and widened the ken of investment managers throughout the world. Not long after, European companies began to offer their shares. Increasingly, investors around the globe are using the same approach and criteria to make their decisions, and they are looking at the same pool of companies. The distinctions among national markets have become lost. In not so many years, a few national stock exchanges could well become global exchanges, opening for business not long after the sun rises and not closing until well after dark – all in order to deal in the equity of world-class companies, irrespective of their domicile. In turn, shares of leading firms will be traded on a twenty-four-hour basis.

When Harold Wilson was Britain's prime minister in the 1960s, he would blame the "gnomes of Zurich" for the pound's recurrent weakness, suggesting a cabal of a few hard-faced Swiss bankers cynically betting against the British currency. Conspiracy theories die hard: no less colorful allegations – against the "rogues" and "highwaymen" of the international economy – surfaced with the 1997 currency crisis in Southeast Asia. But, in fact, today thousands and thousands of traders drive a foreign-exchange market that has grown from a daily turnover of $190 billion in 1986 to an estimated $1.3 trillion in 1997. Analysts and brokers and strategists see the same information at the same moment and compete in their response time. Performance – whether it is a company's quarterly earnings or a country's inflation or trade balance data or the outcome of a national election – sets off an immediate chain reaction. While the publics vote only every few years, the markets vote every minute. And it is private capital – the pensions and accumulated retirement savings of the first world – that is being courted and lured by what used to be called the third world. But this financial integration comes with a price. National governments, whether in developed or developing countries, must increasingly heed the market's vote – as harsh as it sometimes can be. [. . .]

31   Has Globalization Gone Too Far?

Dani Rodrik

The process that has come to be called "globalization" is exposing a deep fault line between groups who have the skills and mobility to flourish in global markets and those who either don't have these advantages or perceive the expansion of unregulated markets as inimical to social stability and deeply held norms. The result is severe tension between the market and social groups such as workers, pensioners, and environmentalists, with governments stuck in the middle. [. . .]

While I share the idea that much of the opposition to trade is based on faulty premises, I also believe that economists have tended to take an excessively narrow view of the issues. To understand the impact of globalization on domestic social arrangements, we have to go beyond the question of what trade does to the skill premium. And even if we focus more narrowly on labor-market outcomes, there are additional channels, which have not yet come under close empirical scrutiny, through which increased economic integration works to the disadvantage of labor, and particularly of unskilled labor. This book attempts to offer such a broadened perspective. As we shall see, this perspective leads to a less benign outlook than the one economists commonly adopt. One side benefit, therefore, is that it serves to reduce the yawning gap that separates the views of most economists from the gut instincts of many laypeople.

Sources of Tension

I focus on three sources of tension between the global market and social stability and offer a brief overview of them here.

First, reduced barriers to trade and investment accentuate the asymmetry between groups that can cross international borders (either directly or indirectly, say through outsourcing) and those that cannot. In the first category are owners of capital, highly skilled workers, and many professionals, who are free to take their resources where they are most in demand. Unskilled and semiskilled workers and most middle managers belong in the second category. Putting the same point in more technical terms, globalization makes the demand for the services of individuals in the second category *more elastic* – that is, the services of large segments of the working population can be more easily substituted by the services of other people across national boundaries. Globalization therefore fundamentally transforms the employment relationship.

The fact that "workers" can be more easily substituted for each other across national boundaries undermines what many conceive to be a postwar social bargain between workers and employers, under which the former would receive a steady

Original publication details: Rodrik, Dani, excerpt from *Has Globalization Gone Too Far?*, Institute for International Economics, 1997.

increase in wages and benefits in return for labor peace. This is because increased substitutability results in the following concrete consequences:

- Workers now have to pay a larger share of the cost of improvements in work conditions and benefits (that is, they bear a greater incidence of nonwage costs).
- They have to incur greater instability in earnings and hours worked in response to shocks to labor demand or labor productivity (that is, volatility and insecurity increase).
- Their bargaining power erodes, so they receive lower wages and benefits whenever bargaining is an element in setting the terms of employment.

These considerations have received insufficient attention in the recent academic literature on trade and wages, which has focused on the downward shift in demand for unskilled workers rather than the increase in the elasticity of that demand.

Second, globalization engenders conflicts within and between nations over domestic norms and the social institutions that embody them. As the technology for manufactured goods becomes standardized and diffused internationally, nations with very different sets of values, norms, institutions, and collective preferences begin to compete head on in markets for similar goods. And the spread of globalization creates opportunities for trade between countries at very different levels of development.

This is of no consequence under traditional multilateral trade policy of the WTO and the General Agreement on Tariffs and Trade (GATT): the "process" or "technology" through which goods are produced is immaterial, and so are the social institutions of the trading partners. Differences in national practices are treated just like differences in factor endowments or any other determinant of comparative advantage. However, introspection and empirical evidence both reveal that most people attach values to processes as well as outcomes. This is reflected in the norms that shape and constrain the domestic environment in which goods and services are produced – for example, workplace practices, legal rules, and social safety nets.

Trade becomes contentious when it unleashes forces that undermine the norms implicit in domestic practices. Many residents of advanced industrial countries are uncomfortable with the weakening of domestic institutions through the forces of trade, as when, for example, child labor in Honduras displaces workers in South Carolina or when pension benefits are cut in Europe in response to the requirements of the Maastricht treaty. This sense of unease is one way of interpreting the demands for "fair trade." Much of the discussion surrounding the "new" issues in trade policy – that is, labor standards, environment, competition policy, corruption – can be cast in this light of procedural fairness.

We cannot understand what is happening in these new areas until we take individual preferences for processes and the social arrangements that embody them seriously. In particular, by doing so we can start to make sense of people's uneasiness about the consequences of international economic integration and avoid the trap of automatically branding all concerned groups as self-interested protectionists. Indeed, since trade policy almost always has redistributive consequences (among sectors, income groups, and individuals), one cannot produce a principled defense of free trade without confronting the question of the fairness and legitimacy of the practices that generate these consequences. By the same token, one should not expect broad popular support for trade when trade involves exchanges that clash with (and erode) prevailing domestic social arrangements.

Third, globalization has made it exceedingly difficult for governments to provide social insurance – one of their central functions and one that has helped maintain social cohesion and domestic political support for ongoing liberalization throughout the postwar period. In essence, governments have used their fiscal powers to insulate domestic groups from excessive market risks, particularly those having an external origin. In fact, there is a striking correlation between an economy's exposure to foreign trade and the size of its welfare state. It is in the most open countries, such as Sweden, Denmark, and the Netherlands, that spending on income transfers has expanded the most. This is not to say that the government is the sole, or the best, provider of social insurance. The extended family, religious groups, and local communities often play similar roles. My point is that it is a hallmark of the postwar period that governments in the advanced countries have been expected to provide such insurance.

At the present, however, international economic integration is taking place against the background of receding governments and diminished social obligations. The welfare state has been under attack for two decades. Moreover, the increasing mobility of capital has rendered an important segment of the tax base footloose, leaving governments with the unappetizing option of increasing tax rates disproportionately on labor income. Yet the need for social insurance for the vast majority of the population that remains internationally immobile has not diminished. If anything, this need has become greater as a consequence of increased integration. The question therefore is how the tension between globalization and the pressures for socialization of risk can be eased. If the tension is not managed intelligently and creatively, the danger is that the domestic consensus in favor of open markets will ultimately erode to the point where a generalized resurgence of protectionism becomes a serious possibility.

Each of these arguments points to an important weakness in the manner in which advanced societies are handling – or are equipped to handle – the consequences of globalization. Collectively, they point to what is perhaps the greatest risk of all, namely that the cumulative consequence of the tensions mentioned above will be the solidifying of a new set of class divisions – between those who prosper in the globalized economy and those who do not, between those who share its values and those who would rather not, and between those who can diversify away its risks and those who cannot. This is not a pleasing prospect, even for individuals on the winning side of the divide who have little empathy for the other side. Social disintegration is not a spectator sport – those on the sidelines also get splashed with mud from the field. Ultimately, the deepening of social fissures can harm all. [. . .]

The Role of National Governments

Policymakers have to steer a difficult middle course between responding to the concerns discussed here and sheltering groups from foreign competition through protectionism. I can offer no hard-and-fast rules here, only some guiding principles.

Strike a balance between openness and domestic needs

There is often a trade-off between maintaining open borders to trade and maintaining social cohesion. When the conflict arises – when new liberalization initiatives are under discussion, for example – it makes little sense to sacrifice social concerns completely for the sake of liberalization. Put differently, as policymakers sort out economic and social objectives, free trade policies are not automatically entitled to first priority.

Thanks to many rounds of multilateral trade liberalization, tariff and nontariff restrictions on goods and many services are now at extremely low levels in the industrial countries. Most major developing countries have also slashed their trade barriers, often unilaterally and in conformity with their own domestic reforms. Most economists would agree that the efficiency benefits of further reductions in these existing barriers are unlikely to be large. Indeed, the dirty little secret of international economics is that a tiny bit of protection reduces efficiency only a tiny bit. A logical implication is that the case for further liberalization in the traditional area of manufactured goods is rather weak.

Moreover, there is a case for taking greater advantage of the World Trade Organization's existing escape clause, which allows countries to institute otherwise-illegal trade restrictions under specified conditions, as well as for broadening the scope of these multilateral safeguard actions. In recent years, trade policy in the United States and the European Union has gone in a rather different direction, with increased use of antidumping measures and limited recourse to escape clause actions. This is likely because WTO rules and domestic legislation make the petitioning industry's job much easier in antidumping cases: there are lower evidentiary hurdles than in escape clause actions, no determinate time limit, and no requirement for compensation for affected trade partners, as the escape clause provides. Also, escape clause actions, unlike antidumping duties, require presidential approval in the United States. This is an undesirable situation because antidumping rules are, on the whole, consistent neither with economics principles nor, as discussed below, with fairness. Tightening the rules on antidumping in conjunction with a reconsideration and reinvigoration of the escape clause mechanism would make a lot of sense.

Do not neglect social insurance

Policymakers have to bear in mind the important role that the provision of social insurance, through social programs, has played historically in enabling multilateral liberalization and an explosion of world trade. As the welfare state is being pruned, there is a real danger that this contribution will be forgotten.

This does not mean that fiscal policy has to be profligate and budget deficits large. Nor does it mean a bigger government role. Enhanced levels of social insurance, for better labor-market outcomes, can be provided in most countries within existing levels of spending. This can be done, for example, by shifting the composition of income transfers from old-age insurance (i.e., social security) to labor-market insurance (i.e., unemployment compensation, trade adjustment assistance, training programs). Because pensions typically constitute the largest item of social spending in the advanced industrial countries, better targeting of this sort is highly compatible with responsible fiscal policies. Gearing social insurance more directly toward labor markets, without increasing the overall tax burden, would be one key step toward alleviating the insecurities associated with globalization.

There is a widespread feeling in many countries that, in the words of Tanzi and Schuknecht, "[s]ocial safety nets have . . . been transformed into universal benefits with widespread free-riding behavior, and social insurance has frequently become an income support system with special interests making any effective reform very difficult." Further, "various government performance indicators suggest that the growth in spending after 1960 may not have brought about significantly improved economic performance or greater social progress." However, social spending has had the important function of buying social peace. Without disagreeing about the need to eliminate waste and reform in the welfare state more broadly, I would argue that the need for social insurance does not decline but rather increases as global integration increases. So the message to reformers of the social welfare system is, don't throw the baby out with the bath water.

Do not use "competitiveness" as an excuse for domestic reform

One of the reasons globalization gets a bad rap is that policymakers often fall into the trap of using "competitiveness" as an excuse for needed domestic reforms. Large fiscal deficits or lagging domestic productivity are problems that drag living standards down in many industrial countries and would do so even in closed economies. Indeed, the term "competitiveness" itself is largely meaningless when applied to whole economies, unless it is used to refer to things that already have a proper name – such as productivity, investment, and economic growth. Too often, however, the need to resolve fiscal or productivity problems is presented to the electorate as the consequence of global competitive pressures. This not only makes the required policies a harder sell – why should we adjust just for the sake of becoming better competitors against the Koreans or the Mexicans? – it also erodes the domestic support for international trade – if we have to do all these painful things because of trade, maybe trade isn't such a wonderful thing anyhow!

The French strikes of 1995 are a good case in point. What made the opposition to the proposed fiscal and pension reforms particularly salient was the perception that fundamental changes in the French way of life were being imposed for the sake of international economic integration. The French government presented the reforms as required by the Maastricht criteria, which they were. But presumably, the Maastricht criteria themselves reflected the policymakers' belief that a smaller welfare state would serve their economies better in the longer run. By and large, the French government did not make the case for reform on its own strengths. By using the Maastricht card, it turned the discussion into a debate on European economic integration. Hence the widespread public reaction, which extended beyond just those workers whose fates would be immediately affected.

The lesson for policymakers is, do not sell reforms that are good for the economy and the citizenry as reforms that are dictated by international economic integration.

Do not abuse "fairness" claims in trade

The notion of fairness in trade is not as vacuous as many economists think. Consequently, nations have the right – and should be allowed – to restrict trade when it conflicts with *widely held* norms at home or undermines domestic social arrangements that enjoy *broad* support.

But there is much that is done in the name of "fair trade" that falls far short of this criterion. There are two sets of practices in particular that should be immediately suspect. One concerns complaints made against other nations when very similar practices abound at home. Antidumping proceedings are a clear example: standard business practices, such as pricing over the life of a product or pricing over the business cycle, can result in duties being imposed on an exporting firm. There is nothing "unfair" about these business practices, as is made abundantly clear by the fact that domestic firms engage in them as well.

The second category concerns cases in which other nations are unilaterally asked to change *their* domestic practices so as to equalize competitive conditions. Japan is frequently at the receiving end of such demands from the United States and the European Union. A more recent example concerns the declaration by the US Trade Representative that corruption in foreign countries will henceforth be considered as unfair trade. While considerations of fairness and legitimacy will guide a country's own social arrangements, even by restricting imports if need be, such considerations should not allow one country to impose its own institutions on others. Proponents of fair trade must bear this key distinction in mind. Thus, it is perfectly legitimate for the United States to make it illegal for domestic firms to engage in corrupt practices abroad (as was done with the Foreign Corrupt Practices Act of 1977). It is also legitimate to negotiate a multilateral set of principles with other countries in the Organization for Economic Cooperation and Development (OECD) with broadly similar norms. It may also be legitimate to restrict imports from a country whose labor practices broad segments of the domestic population deem offensive. But it is not acceptable to unilaterally threaten retaliation against other countries because their business practices do not comply with domestic standards at home *in order to force these countries to alter their own standards*. Using claims of fairness to advance competitive aims is coercive and inherently contradictory. Trying to "export" norms by asking other countries to alter their social arrangements to match domestic ones is inappropriate for the same reason. [. . .]

32 Partisan Politics in the Global Economy

Geoffrey Garrett

> Throughout the world today, politics lags behind economics, like a horse and buggy
> haplessly trailing a sports car. While politicians go through the motions of national
> elections – offering chimerical programs and slogans – world markets, the Internet and
> the furious pace of trade involve people in a global game in which elected representa-
> tives figure as little more than bit players. Hence the prevailing sense, in America and
> Europe, that politicians and ideologies are either uninteresting or irrelevant.
>
> Roger Cohen, "Global Forces Batter Politics," *The New York Times Week in
> Review*, November 17, 1996, p. 1.

This book challenges the conventional wisdom about the effects of globalization on
domestic politics in the industrial democracies. There is a glut of research claiming
that the international integration of markets in goods, services, and above all capital
has eroded national autonomy and, in particular, all but vitiated social democratic
alternatives to the free market. In contrast, I argue that the relationship between
the political power of the left and economic policies that reduce market-generated
inequalities has not been weakened by globalization; indeed, it has been strengthened in important respects. Furthermore, macroeconomic outcomes in the era of
global markets have been as good or better in countries where powerful left-wing
parties are allied with broad and centrally organized labor movements ("social
democratic corporatism") as they have where the left and labor are weaker.

These findings have broader implications for the relationship between democracy
and capitalism in the contemporary period. People who propose dire scenarios based
on visions either of the inexorable dominance of capital over labor or of radical
autarkic and nationalist backlashes against markets overlook the ongoing history
of social democratic corporatism. There is more than one path to competing successfully in the global economy. The impact of electoral politics has not been
dwarfed by market dynamics. Globalized markets have not rendered immutable the
efficiency–equality trade-off. These lessons from the industrial democracies should
hearten advocates of social democracy throughout the world.

The conventional wisdom about the globalization of markets claims that the ever-
increasing capacity of firms and investors to move production and capital around
the world has precipitated a sea change away from the halcyon days of the postwar
mixed economy. In this new environment of deep trade interdependence, multinational production regimes and global capital markets, government attempts to intervene in the economy are thought to be doomed to fail if they extend beyond minimal
"market friendly" measures. The lesson for all governments is supposedly clear: The

Original publication details: Garrett, Geoffrey, "Introduction" from *Partisan Politics in
the Global Economy* (Cambridge University Press, 1998).

imperatives of the market impose heavy constraints on the bounds of democratic choice. Good government is market friendly government, and this effectively rules out most of the "welfare state" policies that the left labored long and hard to establish in the forty years following the Depression.

From this perspective, the age-old debate about the relative power of the capitalist economy and the democratic polity as social forces has been definitively settled in capital's favor. From the Depression until the 1970s, it was widely argued that government could (and should) intervene in the economy to reduce inequality without adversely affecting the macroeconomy. In the contemporary era of global markets, however, the trade-off between efficiency and welfare is considered to be harsh and direct. Even left-wing governments that would like to use the policy instruments of the state to redistribute wealth and risk in favor of the less fortunate have no choice but to bow to the demands of the market.

My portrayal of the globalization thesis is anything but a straw man. Consider the following gloomy predictions from recent and influential scholarly research on the future of social democracy. Paulette Kurzer concludes:

> [T]his book does not hold great promise for social democracy. . . . [L]eft-wing parties will continue to seek election and occasionally win power. However, these parties have little in common with their predecessors in terms of articulating progressive options and pursuing programs different from the conservative, or establishment view. . . . In the past decade, growth has been sluggish, and investments have stagnated. Unemployment and declining wages marked the 1980s. Governments could combat such situations by spending money on public programs, increasing public employment, or raising social transfer payments, but no governments can afford to do this today.

Fritz Scharpf's bottom line is very similar:

> Unlike the situation in the first three postwar decades, there is now no economically plausible Keynesian strategy that would permit the full realization of social democratic goals within a national context without violating the functional imperatives of the capitalist economy. Full employment, rising real wages, larger welfare transfers, and more and better public services can no longer all be had simultaneously. . . . For the foreseeable future . . . social democracy has a chance to influence economic policy only if it explicitly accepts the full harshness of world economic conditions and hence the constraints on domestic policy options.

The globalization thesis can, of course, be taken much further than claims about the demise of social democracy. Some have pointed to the rise of xenophobic nationalism as a profoundly destabilizing consequence of globalization. For example, Ethan Kapstein argues that there are disturbing similarities between the 1990s and the 1930s:

> While the world stands at a critical time in postwar history, it has a group of leaders who appear unwilling, like their predecessors in the 1930s, to provide the international leadership to meet economic dislocations. . . . Like the German elite in Weimar, they dismiss mounting worker dissatisfaction, fringe political movements, and the plight of the unemployed and working poor as marginal concerns compared with the unquestioned importance of a sound currency and balanced

budget. Leaders need to recognize the policy failures of the last 20 years and respond accordingly. If they do not, there are others waiting in the wings who will, perhaps on less pleasant terms.

Others argue that the nation-state itself, irrespective of how it is governed, is a dinosaur that is very poorly adapted to the global economy. Management theorist Kenichi Ohmae's description of the anachronistic and embattled nation state provides a vivid portrayal of this view:

> [T]he glue holding traditional nation states together, at least in economic terms, has begun to dissolve. Buffeted by sudden changes in industry dynamics, available information, consumer preferences, and flows of capital; burdened by demands for the civil minimum and for open-ended industrial subsidies in the name of the national interest; and hog-tied by political systems that prove ever-less responsive to new challenges, these political aggregations no longer make compelling sense as discrete, meaningful units on an up-to-date map of economic activity.

I, however, challenge the reasoning and conclusions that underpin all of these studies and many others like them. I do not wish to argue that analysts have exaggerated the extent to which goods, services, and capital markets are internationally integrated today. Others have made this case, but it is not necessary for my argument. Rather, I argue that existing studies have significantly underestimated the effects of domestic political conditions both on the way governments react to globalization and on their impact on the national economy. Posed in its starkest terms, my argument is that there remains a leftist alternative to free market capitalism in the era of global markets based on classic "big government" and corporatist principles that is viable both politically (in terms of winning elections) and economically (by promoting strong macroeconomic performance).

The first element of this argument concerns domestic political dynamics. Proponents of the globalization thesis focus almost exclusively on the increased "exit" threats of mobile asset holders. Despite and because of the reality of this phenomenon, market integration has also increased demands on government ("voice") to mitigate the insecurities, instabilities and inequalities it has generated. As Robert Keohane and Joseph Nye argued twenty years ago, globalization heightens the vulnerability of countries to the international economy – in terms of both the portion of society subject to global competition and the speed with which changes in market conditions are transmitted across borders. Even the OECD is well aware of this relationship:

> Reduced wage and employment security has extended to sectors and population segments that have been historically considered "safe", such as public sector employees and executive and managerial workers. In all countries the nature of employment is changing, with an increasing share of total employment accounted for by part-time work and temporary contracts . . . the share of involuntary part-time employment has been increasing in almost all countries.

These conditions have proved fertile ground for left-wing parties and for economic policies that ameliorate market-generated inequality and risk. Some conservative parties – notably in the Anglo-American countries – have chosen not to cultivate voters who benefit from government efforts to mitigate the dislocations of globalization. But most left-of-center parties have concentrated their efforts on this constituency.

The consequences of government efforts to compensate short-term market losers, however, are not necessarily benign. Indeed, most people would argue that they are bad for competitiveness and can only result in greater capital flight. Dani Rodrik makes this argument eloquently. He contends that the twin domestic consequences of globalization – increased exit options for mobile asset holders ("footloose capital") and increased voice among the less mobile (most citizens) for policies that cushion market forces – may be on a collision course that will do great harm to all. According to Rodrik:

> [T]he cumulative consequence of (globalization) will be the solidifying of a new set of class divisions – between those who prosper in the globalized economy and those who do not; between those who share its values and those who would rather not; and between those who can diversify away its risks and those who cannot. This is not a pleasing prospect even for the individuals on the winning side of the divide with little empathy for the other side. Social disintegration is not a specta-tor sport – those on the sidelines also get splashed with mud from the field. Ulti-mately, the deepening of social fissures can harm all.

The second element of my argument is that social democratic corporatism pro-vides a way to avoid this collision course. Rodrik's argument makes explicit the common perception that government policies reducing inequality and social risk are antithetical to the interests of mobile asset holders. This view contends that when-ever footloose capital sees powerful left-wing parties, strong labor market institu-tions, and interventionist big government, it will exercise its exit options. Not only will this make it increasingly difficult for government to tax business to fund its spending objective, but capital flight will also deal a body blow to economic performance.

There are numerous reasons to be skeptical of this argument. One, ultimately limited, reason follows from "new growth" theory. In recent years, many economists have argued that the ambit of market friendly government should be broadened to include policies that produce growth-enhancing collective goods undersupplied by the market. The clearest example of such goods is public educa-tion and training, but the label can also be applied to physical infrastructure. These collective goods are not only beneficial to citizens in terms of jobs and improving future life chances; they are also attractive to capital in terms of increasing invest-ment returns. There are nonetheless clear limits to the types of government policies sanctioned by new growth theory. Most government spending, for example, is con-sidered unproductive.

Indeed, it would be very hard to make the case that income transfer programs or in-kind benefits for the unemployed, the sick, or the old are "good for growth" in a direct sense. But this is precisely the argument I wish to make by taking a broad view of the positive externalities of big government. I contend that the types of redis-tributive economic policies associated with strong left-wing parties are compatible with strong economic performance in the global economy, provided labor market institutions are sufficiently "encompassing" to facilitate collective action among the bulk of the workforce.

Social democratic corporatist regimes are based on a virtuous circle in which government policies that cushion market dislocations are exchanged for the regulation of the national labor market by the leaders of encompassing trade union movements. The products of this virtuous circle include predictable patterns of wage setting that restrain real wage growth in accordance with productivity and competitiveness constraints, highly skilled and productive workers, cooperation between labor and business in the work place, and low levels of social strife more generally. These economic "goods" are attractive even to mobile asset holders in the volatile global economy, offsetting the disincentives to investment generated by big government and high labor costs highlighted by neoclassical economics. I thus contend that there is no good reason to believe that in the global economy, capital flight will be the knee-jerk response of mobile asset holders to social democratic corporatism.

This doesn't mean, of course, that contemporary social democratic corporatism doesn't face important challenges. For example, the graying of society in the context of generous public health and pension entitlements to retirees and the power of public sector trade unions are both significant problems that must be confronted. But there are solutions to these problems that do not violate the fundamental tenets of social democracy. More importantly for my purposes, these challenges have very little to do with globalization. Rather, they are better thought of as inherent products of the success of the social democratic project in the postwar period.

My primary claim is that globalization and national autonomy are not mutually exclusive options. The benefits of globalization can be reaped without undermining the economic sovereignty of nations, and without reducing the ability of citizens to choose how to distribute the benefits – and the costs – of the market. The experience of the social democratic corporatist countries should provide succor, not spawn regret, among advocates of social democracy as an equitable and efficient means for reconciling markets and democracy.

The Argument

The dominant view about the domestic effects of globalization accords a *deus ex machina* quality to market forces. If business occupies (in Charles Lindblom's famous terms) a "privileged position" in all capitalist economies, its position is even stronger where markets are global but politics is national. Capital can simply choose to exit the national economy if government pursues policies that business people disapprove of. The rubric of bad economic policies is presumed to cover all market "distortions," including government spending on goods and services that could be provided more efficiently by the market, and taxes to pay for them that treat different income sources unequally.

The notion that mobile asset holders in the industrial democracies today have credible exit threats is indisputable. Many firms have production regimes that cross national boundaries, and strategic alliances are increasingly common. The growth of international portfolio investment in equity, bond, and currency markets has been explosive in the past twenty years. Do these developments represent the death knell of social democracy? The conventional wisdom makes two implicit assumptions about the political economy of capitalist democracy. First, the state of the macroeconomy is considered the primary – if not the sole – determinant of a government's prospects for reelection. Second, government interventions in the economy beyond explicitly capital friendly measures precipitate downward spirals in economic performance. When combined with capital's exit options, these two assumptions lead to the conclusion that social democracy is incompatible with global markets.

I argue that both of these assumptions are inappropriate. There is ample evidence that macroeconomic outcomes significantly influence elections. But presiding over an expanding pie is not the only path to electoral success. Political parties can also attract support by distributing the social pie in ways that favor certain groups over others. Indeed, the short-term nature of democratic politics creates a bias in favor of distributional strategies: Governments cannot afford to do what is good for the economy in the long run if this immediately hurts their core electoral constituencies.

The most important distributional cleavage in the industrial democracies has long been between those who support the market allocation of wealth and risk – the natural constituency of right-wing parties – and those who favor government efforts to alter market outcomes – the left's core base of support. The welfare state – broadly construed to include not only income transfer programs such as unemployment insurance and public pensions but also the provision of social services such as education and health – is the basic policy instrument for redistribution. Left-wing and centrist Christian democratic parties have long been more willing to expand the welfare state than their counterparts on the right. Some have claimed that the electoral appeal of the welfare state has declined apace with the shrinking of the manufacturing working class. But even in the Anglo-American democracies, popular support for the welfare state grew at the same time as the traditional working class shrank. Broader cross-national surveys of public opinion also show that public support for the welfare state continues to be very strong in most countries.

The key to understanding the popularity of welfare programs in the global economy is recognizing that although market integration may benefit all segments of society in the longer run through the more efficient allocation of production and investment, the short-term effects of globalization are very different. Indeed, perhaps the most important immediate effect of globalization is to increase social dislocations and economic insecurity, as the distribution of incomes and jobs across firms and industries becomes increasingly unstable. The result is that increasing numbers of people have to spend evermore time and money trying to make their future more secure. Whatever the portion of the labor force that is directly affected by market dislocations, perceptions of growing economic insecurity will always be considerably more widespread. In the contemporary period, this constituency obviously extends well beyond the traditional manufacturing working class.

Given this nexus between globalization and economic insecurity, it is not surprising that government policies that cushion market dislocations by redistributing wealth and risk are at least as popular today as they have ever been. This does not mean that parties across the political spectrum will choose to expand the welfare state; ideological concerns will also play a role. Nonetheless, globalization has provided new and fertile ground for the social democratic agenda (and for more populist and xenophobic appeals for economic closure).

Critics might accept this part of my argument but dismiss it as irrelevant, claiming that the political incentives to pursue interventionist economic policies are overwhelmed by the macroeconomic costs of doing so in the global economy. If such policies only lead to disinvestment and recession, even voters who benefit in the short term from a large public economy will ultimately abandon governments that preside over its expansion. From this perspective, it is only a question of when, not whether, the left bows to the power of the market.

Careful analysis of the evidence about the macroeconomic consequences of big government, however, prompts more caution and less dogmatism. Joel Slemrod concludes in an exhaustive review of the empirical literature, for example, that there is no overall nor consistent relationship between the size of government and rates of economic growth. In a similar study on unemployment, Charles Bean argues that there is no clear link between government-generated rigidities in labor markets and rising unemployment in the industrial countries since the early 1980s.

The underlying message of these studies is that although it is easy to point to specific costs of discrete interventionist policies, big government seems to produce positive externalities that are overlooked by its critics. These externalities may take two forms. The first is quite specific and relates to new growth theory. Many economists now believe that government investments in infrastructure – from bridges and roads to research and development to education and training – are beneficial to the economy. Thus, government spending on human and physical capital is unlikely to provoke capital flight in global markets.

The second type of externality generated by big government is more general. It is also central to claims about the economic efficacy of social democratic corporatism. Where powerful left parties are allied with encompassing labor movements, policies that redistribute market allocations of wealth and risk are unlikely to provoke capital flight among mobile asset holders.

Consider the following hypothetical example of a left-wing government's decision to increase the duration of unemployment benefits. Even economists who argue that appropriately constructed unemployment insurance schemes are desirable look dimly on increasing the duration of benefits. The wages acceptable to those in employment, and especially those organized into trade unions, increase with declines in the material costs of unemployment. The government must borrow money or raise taxes to fund its new scheme. Thus, increasing the duration of benefits must slow output growth and job creation.

The flaw in this logic is that it ignores the impact of labor market institutions on the behavior of workers. I argue that where national labor market institutions are sufficiently encompassing to overcome labor's collective action problem, the benefits of leftist policies that mitigate the distributional asymmetries inherent in the market allocation of resources and risk offset the costs highlighted by the neoclassical perspective. In contrast, interventionist economic policies are likely to have deleterious macroeconomic consequences where labor movements are not encompassing, precisely because isolated groups of workers can be expected to take advantage of reduced market constraints to push up their wages.

In the scenario outlined above, the government's enhanced unemployment insurance policy helps all those at risk in the labor market. The direct effect of this policy reform is that the threat of unemployment is now less disciplining on the labor market, which could be detrimental to overall economic performance. Those currently in work could push up their wages, reducing demand for the currently unemployed. The result of this "insider–outsider" problem would be higher inflation and higher unemployment.

The leaders of encompassing labor movements, however, care about the welfare of the whole labor force, and they have the institutional clout to ensure that the behavior of certain groups of workers does not reduce the welfare of others. In my example, labor leaders have both the incentive and the capacity to mitigate the insider–outsider problem. They appreciate that the best path to increasing total employment at the highest possible level of disposable incomes (both wages and work-related benefits) is to constrain wage growth among those currently employed in accordance with productivity improvements. In so doing, labor as a whole can reap the benefits of the government's policy without incurring the costs that it might otherwise generate.

This argument can be made more general. Indeed, it is at the core of the vast literature on social democratic corporatism. All government programs that alter the market allocation of wealth and risk in favor of labor should prompt the leaders of encompassing organizations to "internalize" the costs of decentralized militancy for the economy as a whole. In addition to upward pressures on wages, these externalities comprise all types of inefficiency and instability associated with groups of workers who have the organizational capacity to voice effectively their grievances. These range from the threat of strikes to unwillingness to cooperate with management at the workplace to more general social agitation.

The combination of left government and encompassing labor market institutions reduces these sources of inefficiency and instability. In turn, the strategic decisions of mobile asset holders will be affected not only by the direct costs of social democratic corporatism – a bigger public economy and higher total labor costs – but also by the benefits – higher productivity and economic, political, and social stability. A price must be paid for these desirable outcomes, but the return is considerable. There is thus no good a priori reason to think that mobile asset holders will choose to exit from social democratic corporatist regimes.

Let me now summarize the structure of the argument. I have suggested that the "class compromise" of capitalist democracy – in which asset holders accept redistributive government policies and governments accept the primacy of market mechanisms – is at least as important in the global economy as it has ever been. Globalization increases the potential long-run social benefits of markets, but it also heightens political opposition to them in the short run. Governments face the daunting task of reconciling these two forces. Where the left is allied with encompassing labor markets, it is possible to reap the benefits of market integration without increasing the risk of damaging popular backlashes in the form of economic, political and social instability. Farsighted capital can be expected to understand the upside of social democratic corporatism and hence to forgo the temptation to use the threat or reality of exit. [. . .]

The Evidence

The empirical core of this argument can be distilled into three basic propositions about the interrelationships among globalization, partisan politics, and the economy that track the progression of the theoretical argument:

- Globalization has generated new political constituencies for left-of-center parties among the increasing ranks of the economically insecure that offset the shrinking of the manufacturing working class. As a result, enduring cross-national differences in the balance of power between left and right remain. So, too, do marked differences in labor market institutions.
- Globalization has increased the political incentives for left-wing parties to pursue economic policies that redistribute wealth and risk in favor of those adversely

affected in the short term by market dislocations, especially in countries where organized labor is also strong. Thus, the historical relationship between left-labor power and big government has not weakened with market integration.

* Globalization has increased the importance of economic, political and social stability to the investment decisions of mobile asset holders. Because the combination of powerful left-wing parties and encompassing labor market institutions promotes stability in the wage-setting process and in society more generally, macroeconomic performance under social democratic corporatism has been as good as – if not better than – that under any other constellation of political power and labor market institutions.

33 Seven Common Misunderstandings about the WTO

World Trade Organization

1 The WTO Dictates Governments' Policies

Not true.

The WTO does not tell governments how to conduct their trade policies. Rather, it's a "*member-driven*" organization. That means:

- the *rules* of the WTO system are agreements resulting from negotiations among member governments, and they are ratified by members' parliaments, and
- *decisions* taken in the WTO are generally made by consensus among all members.

The only occasion when a WTO body can have a direct impact on a government's policies is when the Dispute Settlement Body (which consists of all members) adopts a ruling by a disputes panel, or an appeal report.

Even then, the scope of these rulings is narrow: they are simply judgements or interpretations of whether a government has broken one of the WTO's agreements – agreements that the infringing government had itself accepted. If a government has broken a commitment it has to conform.

In all other respects, the WTO does not dictate to governments to adopt or drop certain policies.

As for the WTO Secretariat, it simply provides administrative and technical support for the WTO and its members.

In fact: it's the governments who dictate to the WTO.

2 The WTO is for Free Trade at any Cost

Not true.

Yes, one of the principles of the WTO system is for countries to lower their trade barriers and to allow trade to flow more freely. After all, countries benefit from lower trade barriers.

But just how low those barriers should go is something member countries bargain with each other. Their negotiating positions depend on how ready they feel they are to lower the barriers, and on what they want to obtain from other members in return.

The WTO provides the forum for negotiating liberalization. It also provides the rules for how liberalization can take place.

Original publication details: World Trade Organization, "10 Common Misunderstandings about the WTO," 1998.

The rules written into the agreements allow barriers to be lowered gradually so that domestic producers can adjust.

They also spell out when and how governments can protect their domestic producers, for example from dumped or subsidized imports. Here, the objective is fair trade.

Just as important as freer trade – perhaps more important – are other principles of the WTO system. For example: non-discrimination, and making sure the conditions for trade are stable, predictable and transparent.

3   The WTO is only Concerned about Commercial Interests. This takes Priority over Development

Not true.

Developing countries are allowed more time to apply numerous provisions of the WTO agreements. Least developed countries receive special treatment, including exemption from many provisions.

The needs of development can also be used to justify actions that might not normally be allowed under the agreements, for example giving subsidies.

At the same time, underlying the WTO's trading system is the fact that freer trade boosts economic growth and supports development.

4   In the WTO, Commercial Interests take Priority over Environmental Protection

Not true.

Many provisions take environmental concerns specifically into account. A range of subsidies are permitted for environmental protection. Environmental objectives are also recognized specifically in provisions dealing with product standards, food safety, intellectual property protection, etc.

What's important in the WTO's rules is that measures taken to protect the environment must not discriminate against foreign goods and services. You cannot be lenient with your own producers and at the same time be strict with foreigners.

Also important is the fact that it's not the WTO's job to set the international rules for environmental protection. That's the task of the environmental agencies and conventions.

An overlap does exist between environmental agreements and the WTO – on trade actions (such as sanctions or other import restrictions) taken to enforce an agreement. So far there has been no conflict between the WTO's agreements and the international environmental agreements.

5   The WTO Dictates to Governments on Issues such as Food Safety, and Human Health and Safety. Again Commercial Interests Override

Not true.

Remember, the agreements were negotiated by WTO member governments.

Key clauses in the agreements (such as GATT Art. 20) specifically allow governments to take actions to protect human, animal or plant life or health.

But these actions are disciplined, for example to prevent them being used as protectionism in disguise.

Some of the agreements deal with product standards, and with health and safety for food and other products made from animals and plants.

The purpose is to defend governments' rights to ensure the safety of their citizens.

At the same time, the agreements are also designed to prevent governments setting regulations arbitrarily in a way that discriminates against foreign goods and services. Safety regulations must not be protectionism in disguise.

One criterion for meeting these objectives is to base regulations on scientific evidence or on internationally recognized standards.

Again, the WTO does not set the standards itself. In some cases other international agreements are identified in the WTO's agreements. One example is Codex Alimentarius, which sets recommended standards for food safety and comes under the FAO and WHO.

But there is no compulsion to comply even with internationally negotiated standards such as those of Codex Alimentarius. Governments are free to set their own standards provided they are consistent, are not arbitrary, and do not discriminate.

6   The WTO Destroys Jobs, Widens the Gap Between Rich and Poor

Not true. But take a closer look at the details.

Freer-flowing and more stable trade boosts economic growth. It creates jobs and helps to reduce poverty. When a country lowers its trade barriers, it is itself the biggest beneficiary. The countries exporting to it also gain, but less.

Clearly, producers who were previously protected face new competition when trade barriers are lowered. Some survive by becoming more competitive. Others don't. But that's not the end of the story.

Freer trade creates more jobs than are lost. And the boost it gives to the economy allows adjustments to be made (such as preparing people for new jobs) more easily. That's why the trade agreements allow changes to be made gradually – to give governments and producers time to make the necessary adjustments.

There are also many other factors behind recent changes in wage levels. Why for example is there a widening gap in developed countries between the pay of skilled and unskilled workers?

According to the OECD, imports from low-wage countries account for only 10–20 percent of wage changes in developed countries. Much of the rest is attributable to "skill-based technological change". In other words, developed economies are naturally adopting more technologies that require skilled labour.

In fact protection is expensive because it raises costs and encourages inefficiency. According to another OECD calculation, imposing a 30 percent duty on imports from developing countries would actually *reduce* US unskilled wages by 1 percent and skilled wages by 5 percent. One of the costs of protectionism is lower wages in the protectionist country.

At the same time, the focus on *goods* imports distorts the picture. In developed countries, 70 percent of economic activity is in *services*, where the effect of foreign competition on jobs is different – if a foreign telecommunications company sets up business in a country it will naturally employ local people, for example.

Finally, while about 1.5 billion people are still in poverty, trade liberalization since World War II has contributed to lifting an estimated 3 billion people out of poverty. [. . .]

7   The WTO is Undemocratic

Not true.

Decisions in the WTO are generally by consensus. In principle, that's even more democratic than majority rule because everyone has to agree.

It would be wrong to suggest that every country has the same bargaining power. Nevertheless, the consensus rule means every country has a voice, and every country has to be persuaded before it joins a consensus. Quite often reluctant countries are persuaded by being offered something in return.

Consensus also means every country accepts the decisions. There are no dissenters.

What is more, the WTO's trade rules, which were the result of the Uruguay Round negotiations, were ratified in members' parliaments.

Questions

1   Identify several aspects of globalization that make it more difficult for states to manage their societies.

2   What happens to the territory of an empire when it collapses? Think about the case of the Soviet Union after 1989, when many new states appeared. Did any former Soviet republics choose not to become independent states? Can you explain why?

3   How can intergovernmental organizations (IGOs) help solve the problems states face in dealing with globalization?

4   McNeely argues that UN membership is not strictly dependent on any particular criteria, such as defined territory or a stable and effective government. Who, then, is eligible to join the UN? To answer this question, start by identifying types of organizations that cannot be considered for membership.

5   Ohmae says that "nation states have become little more than bit actors" with respect to the global economy. Explain what he means by this. Then discuss a variety of measures taken by states to ensure that they are not just "bit actors" on the global economic stage.

6   According to Yergin and Stanislaw, faith in government has declined severely while faith in the market has grown. Rodrik, on the other hand, suggests that globalization may have gone too far. In your opinion, should business and markets be totally free of government regulation and oversight? How large a role should government play in managing the economy and seeking solutions to social problems?

7   Garrett challenges the claim that expanded government interferes with economic growth. What are some of the "positive externalities" of expanded government that may help economic growth, despite the higher taxes and lowered flexibility that government expansion often entails?

8   Pick any two of the "common misunderstandings" about the World Trade Organization. Make an argument against the position presented by the WTO, thinking especially from the perspective of small and weak countries that belong to the organization.

Part VI

Political Globalization II: Reorganizing the World

Introduction

The selections in this part turn to the impact of international nongovernmental organizations (INGOs), global social movements, and the United
Nations on world politics and global governance. While most work on world
politics sees states as the primary actors, stressing their jockeying for power
as the driving force behind world development (or, as we saw in part V, raising
doubts about the capacity of states to meet the challenges posed by globalization), in these selections states are not so much "in the driver's seat"
regarding world affairs. Instead, states are only one among many types of
global actors, and they often are influenced substantially by other actors in
ways they may hardly themselves recognize. In addition, in many sectors of
global development states are only marginally involved, and the past decade
has witnessed a growing insistence on the importance and value of non-
governmental organizations and social movements as mechanisms for satisfying the needs and desires of the world's population, rather than the desires
of often corrupt or power-hungry elites.

Until quite recently, researchers approached the study of social movements
on a country-by-country basis, with movements in the USA receiving the lion's
share of attention. Case studies have traced in great detail the origins,
growth, and successes and failures of the civil rights movement, the women's
movement, gay and lesbian rights organizations, environmentalism, and so
on. Sometimes, a broader perspective has been added by bringing together
case studies of, say, the anti-nuclear movements in the USA, Germany, and
Japan, comparing the cases to identify common and dissimilar elements.
Often unnoticed or little discussed is the striking fact that a great many social
movements have emerged and flourished in a large number of countries
simultaneously. This simultaneity, and the tendency of movements to form in
countries of highly varied social conditions, leads some researchers to conclude that movements often are global in character, not simply national. Correspondingly, scholars have begun to identify the global and regional
structures underlying social movements in many sectors.

These global and regional structures, it turns out, usually take the form of
INGOs. INGOs are voluntary associations of individuals (and, sometimes, of
other associations or corporations) banding together for specific purposes on
a worldwide or regional basis. The best known INGOs are human rights organizations like Amnesty International and Human Rights Watch, environmental bodies like the World Wildlife Fund (now called the Worldwide Fund for
Nature) and Greenpeace, and relief organizations like the Red Cross and
CARE. Human rights and environmental INGOs are good examples of global
social movement organizations, working to improve conditions in countries
all around the world and drawing on members from all continents and many

countries. Many other global movements are also driven by INGOs, almost always in conjunction with domestic nongovernmental organizations (NGOs) – movements for women's rights and equality, for democracy and free elections, for the rights of indigenous peoples, for improved labor practices by global corporations like Nike or The Gap, for homosexual rights, and so on.

Social movement INGOs stand out because they interact extensively with states, trying to change state policies or prompt state action on specific problems. To a large extent, they have little choice but to work through states because their own resources are usually meager and states are the only actors capable of and responsible for solving broad social problems. Many other types of INGOs pay little attention to states, however. Sports federations, professional associations, technical and standardization bodies, science and knowledge associations, and medical INGOs, among others, usually resist state participation and carry out their global governance activities quite autonomously. They may rely on state subsidies to some extent, but for the most part they draw on member fees, the sale of documents and publications, and individual donations to finance their work.

INGOs interact not only with states and other INGOs but also with intergovernmental organizations (IGOs), which were introduced in part V. Of special importance are the United Nations and its agencies, which formally involve INGOs in their work through what is known as "consultative status." Thousands of INGOs now have consultative status with UN bodies, and they are key participants in many UN programs. Indeed, the UNAIDS Programme has even placed INGO representatives on its governing board, the first time an IGO has permitted such direct INGO involvement.

The most important IGO, the United Nations, was formed after World War II as the successor to the League of Nations. Unlike the League, which the USA never joined, the UN mandate from the beginning was much broader than the issues of security and peace. Very quickly the UN became the focal point for global governance in many domains, and by the 1960s it had assumed a major role in promoting decolonization, the formation of new states in the former colonies, and the development of education, health care, and other modern systems in the less developed world. One of the UN's more striking activities has been its sponsorship of major world conferences on emerging issues, such as the three world conferences on women's issues during the UN Decade for Women (1975–85) and the more recent Beijing conference in 1995, as well as global conferences on the environment, including the highly publicized "Earth Summit" in Rio de Janeiro in 1992. In every instance, the official UN conferences, attended by delegates from states, have been overshadowed by parallel and much larger INGO/NGO conferences that speak not for governments but, in the broadest sense, for humanity as a whole.

As we enter the twenty-first century, we therefore find a complex and highly decentralized global governance structure that involves much cooperation among INGOs, IGOs (led by the UN), and states – but also much divisiveness, disagreement, and controversy about specific policies, programs, and lines of development in many domains. Global consensus is often hard to reach, but the globalization of issues – the degree to which issues and policies are debated and settled at the global level – is continually on the rise.

In the first of our selections, Larry Diamond documents the domestic and global forces that have brought about the strong shift toward democratic political institutions in many countries that previously were ruled by authoritarian or dictatorial regimes. The democratic state has become the one legitimate model for national governance, mobilizing groups and classes internally to work for democracy and generating much external support for these forces, especially from the strong older democracies of the West. Diamond also illuminates the limits of democratization, arguing that there are no guarantees that the twenty-first century will remain as resolutely democratic as the world has become at the end of the twentieth century.

Nitza Berkovitch's work focuses on the global women's movement, which originated in the late nineteenth century and became an increasingly coherent and effective social movement after World War I as it concentrated its efforts on the International Labor Organization, a new IGO set up to promote and standardize labor law and policy. Berkovitch analyzes the rise of new sets of global rules and expectations pertaining to women, crystallizing after World War II in a powerful ideology calling for women's full equality with men. Sparked by the UN Decade for Women in 1975 85, women's INGOs have proliferated rapidly, making the movement both more global and more divided as the voices of Third World women have become increasingly prominent. Our next selection, the Beijing Declaration from the Fourth World Conference on Women in 1995, provides a good encapsulated statement of the current demands of the world women's movement. It also neatly sidesteps some of the more controversial women's issues, such as female circumcision.

In the next selection, John Boli and George Thomas present a high-level overview of the entire population of international nongovernmental organizations since 1875. After charting the enormous increase in INGO formation and its ups and downs with the two world wars, they set INGOs in a world cultural context by showing how they foster and enact increasingly widespread global principles. Their article finds considerable evidence that INGOs can and do influence IGOs and states, though the extent of such influence varies greatly from issue to issue.

Adam Roberts and Benedict Kingsbury address the significant role of the world's chief intergovernmental organization, the UN, in shaping international relations. The UN helps promote shared values and norms, protect human rights, dampen violent conflicts between and within countries, and encourage dialogue rather than threat and the use of force. Roberts and Kingsbury also outline some of the constraints on UN effectiveness. Our last selection in this section, by Sadako Ogata, the UN High Commissioner for Refugees, turns to a specific dimension of UN engagement, the care and repatriation of refugees from political repression and civil war. Ogata describes the global thrust of her work both in cooperation and in confrontation with states, giving us a sense of how much the UN has accomplished for refugees and how difficult the problems are in aiding the victims of power politics.

34   The Globalization of Democracy

Larry Diamond

The 1980s, and particularly the final stunning years of that decade, recorded extra-ordinary progress for democracy around the world. It could even be argued that the decade saw the most widespread diffusion of democratic forms of governance since the inception of the nation-state. By the end of 1990, more independent countries could be rated democratic or "free" – 65, by the count of Freedom House – than at any time in the history of the modern world. Using the same annual data from Freedom House, one could claim that more people, and a higher proportion of the world's people, were living under democratic forms of government by the end of the decade than ever before. Freedom House counted over two billion for the first time in 1989.

With some important exceptions and reversals, this progress has continued into the 1990s. Freedom House rated 75 countries (including the three newly independent Baltic states) "free" at the end of 1991 – an increase of 10 in one year. And by a more generous standard for classifying "democracies," it counted 89 at that time, well over half the 171 independent countries it rated, and twice the number 20 years ago. Considering as well "another thirty-two countries in some form of democratic transition," 70 percent of the world's countries had democracy or were moving toward it by the end of 1991.

In his book, *The Third Wave*, Samuel Huntington argues that we are now in the midst of a "third wave" of democratic expansion in the world. "A wave of democratization is a group of transitions from nondemocratic to democratic regimes that occur within a specified period of time and that significantly outnumber transitions in the opposite direction." He dates the first "long" wave of democratization back to 1828, with the expansion of democratic suffrage in the United States. It began to expire in the early 1920s with the coming to power of Mussolini in Italy, giving rise to a "first reverse wave." A second, shorter, democratic wave began with the Allied victory in World War II and continued until around 1962, incorporating a number of Latin American and newly independent (primarily former British) colonies. But by then a second reverse wave had begun, bringing widespread military and one-party rule and leaving only two states in South America democratic. The third wave, which began with the overthrow of the Caetano dictatorship in Portugal in April 1974, became a truly global phenomenon during the 1980s, doubling by 1990 the number of democracies in countries with populations exceeding one million.

Original publication details: Diamond, Larry, "The Globalization of Democracy" reprinted from *Global Transformation and the Third World*, edited by Robert O. Slater, Barry M. Schutz and Steven R. Dorr. Copyright © 1993 by Lynne Rienner Publishers, Inc. Reprinted with permission of the publisher.

Democrats around the world have been exhilarated by this widespread democratic progress – what could be called the "globalization of democracy" – in terms of the nearly universal diffusion of popular demands for political freedom, representation, participation, and accountability. However, the gross numbers and almost miraculous developments disguise a much more complex and variegated picture. An important element in that complexity has been the more subtle erosion of democratic institutions and norms in many developing countries in recent years. Another is the vexing economic and social problems, including the resurgence of virulent nationalist passions, that stand in the way of democratic consolidation in Eastern Europe and the republics of the former Soviet Union, as well as in the Third World. [The chapter goes on to describe the democratic trend and its domestic causes.]

International Factors

International influences and pressures have interacted with and often quickened all processes of authoritarian breakdown. Specific responses to human rights violations and democratic pressures from powerful established democracies, especially the United States, have sometimes served to narrow the domestic support of authoritarian regimes and to aggravate the divisions within them. The pressure exerted by the Carter administration on Uruguay and especially Argentina, through sanctions such as cutoffs in military and economic aid, had this kind of effect, while bringing significant improvement in those human rights situations. Carter administration human rights policies, along with specific diplomatic initiatives, also supported democratic transition in Peru, "prevented an authoritarian relapse" in Ecuador in 1978, and, in that same year deterred electoral fraud in the Dominican Republic's presidential balloting. Reagan administration diplomatic and economic pressure on the authoritarian regimes in Chile and South Korea significantly contributed to democratic transitions in those two countries, while preventing planned military coups in El Salvador, Honduras, and Bolivia in the early 1980s and in Peru in January 1989. Increasing, and increasingly open, dissatisfaction with Ferdinand Marcos in the US Congress and administration, and in US public opinion, undermined his support base in Manila and led him toward the ultimately disastrous step of calling a presidential "snap election." US military intervention (in the form of overflights by US planes based near Manila) helped defeat the 1989 coup attempt in the Philippines, while US invasions restored constitutional democracies in Grenada in 1983 and Panama in 1989. US pressure, both coercive and diplomatic, also figured prominently in the decision of the Sandinistas to hold early and free elections, as did a mix of other domestic and international factors (the desperate state of the Nicaraguan economy, the uncertainty of continued Eastern bloc aid, the promise of new Western aid after free elections).

Overall, as Huntington concludes, "US support was critical to democratization in the Dominican Republic, Grenada, El Salvador, Guatemala, Honduras, Uruguay, Peru, Ecuador, Panama, and the Philippines," and "it was a contributing factor to democratization in Portugal, Chile, Poland, Korea, Bolivia and Taiwan." Sikkink, however, points out that US human rights pressure has not been particularly effective in Guatemala. He cautions that even superpower pressure for democratization may be ineffective unless it is applied in a comprehensive and forceful manner – clearly conveyed through multiple channels and utilizing a wide range of policy instruments – and unless there exists a moderate faction within the authoritarian regime prepared to be receptive to such pressure.

Both governments and societies do respond to international sanctions, as well as to anticipated rewards. In Taiwan, "the political reform movement was initially triggered" in the early 1970s, when the "forced severance of its formal ties with many Western countries and its loss of membership in the United Nations" catalyzed a wave of new intellectual concern with domestic politics. Sophisticated Taiwanese began to realize that democratization was the only way their country could become politically reintegrated into the world and ultimately accepted as a full partner among the advanced industrial nations. In fact, this is a lesson that is increasingly discerned by East Asian business and professional elites, whose countries are so dependent on international trade. It played an important, if intangible, role in the transition to democracy in South Korea, as Sung-joo Han has noted:

> For a country such as South Korea, which has placed the utmost importance in the promotion of exports, expansion of external relations is an inevitable consequence as well as a requirement of economic growth. In due course the government and the people realize that democratization is the necessary ticket for membership in the club of advanced nations. This provides a strong incentive for political, as well as economic, liberalization at home.

Of course, such conditionality will be more effective the more explicit it is and the more tangible are the rewards at stake. The fact that "democratic practices and respect for fundamental rights and freedoms" are explicitly a requirement for membership in the European Community has been "an important incentive for the consolidation of democratic processes in the Iberian Peninsula," Greece, and now Turkey.

Specific sanctions can also work, especially when reinforced by international demonstration effects and domestic factors. Years of stiffening international sanctions and opprobrium, along with other dramatic changes in the international environment, have been instrumental in inducing key elites in South Africa's business establishment and ruling National Party to abandon apartheid and opt for a negotiated transition to democracy. Economic sanctions and disinvestment by the Western powers – "as much a psychological as a financial blow" – merged with the decline in global gold prices and domestically generated debt and inflation to produce "protracted recession, capital flight, and a profound sense of isolation. . . . Whites began to realize that unless they came to terms with the political demands of the black population, the economic noose would not loosen." At the same time, the collapse of communism in the Soviet Union and Eastern Europe "removed a perceived external threat, undermining hardliners in the security establishment," while raising concerns among state officials "about South Africa's long-term vulnerability to popular upheaval." That a political system so different from communism would draw such a direct lesson underscores the potency of international demonstration effects, especially in the contemporary world of instant and highly visual communications.

One should also not discount the capacity for authoritarian leaders to read the international environment and learn from comparative experience, however cynically they may be motivated by the sheer instinct for survival. The movement toward a more democratic and constitutional monarchy in Nepal has been facilitated not only by mass pressure from below (stimulated by international demonstration effects) but by the realization of King Birendra that massive repression would ruin the international standing he needs in his aid-dependent country.

Demonstration and diffusion effects

The pressure for democratic change in South Africa has also been stimulated by political changes in the region, which have added both to the reduction in security threats (with the withdrawal of Cuban troops from Angola) and to the sense of isolation on the part of the administration (with the passage of Namibia to independence under Black majority rule). Yet Black Africa as a whole has in turn been affected by developments in South Africa in the past decade. Since the late 1980s, Africans themselves have been exposing the hypocrisy of demanding political liberties in South Africa that are routinely trampled elsewhere in Black Africa. In condemning the authoritarian abuses and intransigence of the Doe regime in Liberia, for example, a prominent Nigerian newspaper editorialized, "The very same reprehensible practices, which the world has persistently condemned in South Africa, are being daily replicated by the government of an independent African country." Declared Roger Chongwe, chairman of the African Bar Association, "All Africa demands: if South Africa is to have one man, one vote, why not us?" African leaders themselves finally began to concede, as they put it in a statement at their Organization of African Unity summit meeting in July 1990, that they would need "to democratise further our societies and consolidate democratic institutions."

Significantly, the OAU statement on the need for human rights, political accountability, and the rule of law was titled, "The Political and Socio-Economic Situation in Africa *and the Fundamental Changes Taking Place in the World.*" Africans have shown an acute responsiveness to the democratic wave sweeping through Eastern Europe and across the globe. International diffusion effects have contributed heavily to the eruption of pressures in virtually every country on the continent for more liberal, accountable, responsive, popularly based forms of government. As Nigeria's UN ambassador Ibrahim Gambari (who is also an astute political scientist) observed, Africans "listen to the BBC, the Voice of America, Radio Moscow, sometimes in their local language. They're fully aware [of what's been happening in Eastern Europe] and they ask, 'Why not here?'" Indeed, "Many young African protesters, inspired by television images showing Eastern European crowds demonstrating against communism, are seeking to emulate the success of Poles, Hungarians, East Germans, Czechoslovakians, Bulgarians and Romanians in throwing off unpopular one-party governments and demanding multiparty democracy." Even one of the architects of the African one-party state, Tanzania's Julius Nyerere, conceded that his country could learn a "lesson or two" from Eastern Europe.

Of course, the East European democracy demonstrations themselves spread like a wave from one country to the next. What Huntington calls the "snowballing" effect – the phenomenon of earlier transitions "stimulating and providing models for subsequent efforts at democratization" – was clearly evident in 1990 in Bulgaria, Romania, Yugoslavia, Albania, Mongolia, Nepal, much of Africa, and several Arab countries, such as Egypt, Jordan, Tunisia, and Algeria, where the Eastern European upheavals "prompted leaders . . . to open up more political space for the expression of discontent."

As Huntington observes, demonstration effects "remain strongest among countries that [are] geographically proximate and culturally similar." Thus, the impact of Poland's democratic transition spread most rapidly and intensely to its neighbors in Eastern Europe, and their collective transformation has probably had the greatest impact on the countries of the former Soviet Union. As noted earlier, the strongest and most immediate impact of the "people power" democratic revolution in the Philippines was in South Korea. "A month after Cardinal Sin played a central role in the regime change in the Philippines, Cardinal Kim for the first time called for constitutional change and democracy in Korea," and a month after that (in April 1986), Korean democratic opposition leader Kim Dae Jung declared (with specific reference to the Philippines), "This is the time of people's power in the developing countries of Asia. We have never been so sure before."

Diffusion effects also resonate deeply from history; the fact that virtually all of the democratic countries in Asia, Africa, and the Caribbean are former British colonies is striking testimony to the potency of cultural and institutional diffusion, and the current mobilizations against authoritarian regimes in Africa draw in part from this same reservoir of values and institutions that took (fragile) root during colonial rule.

Finally, diffusion effects are typically, by their nature, widespread and long-term. They involve the spread not only of specific models, strategies, and tactics for democratization, but more profoundly, of generic preferences for personal liberty, pluralism, political voice, and market competition. In Taiwan, most of the leaders of the democratic movement that emerged in the 1970s were educated abroad, in law and the social sciences. They returned "ready to apply at home" the "ideas and institutions of a reference society" in the West. "They adopted Western democratic ideals as well as democratic procedures, institutional design, political techniques, and legal frameworks." Through overseas study, economic exchange, and especially the international communications revolution, democratic and antiauthoritarian values, norms, and ways of life have slowly been seeping into the cultures of many undemocratically ruled countries. While the points of contact and influence are initially through elites, the broader diffusion of Western culture, ideas, and information – not only news and opinion but music and entertainment – has had a big impact on mass thinking in many countries.

Technological progress has sharply accelerated the speed and widened the spread of this diffusion. Large proportions of many Third World populations now have access to television, and even more have access to radio. By 1985 there were about 14 radios per 100 people, on average, in Asia and Africa. Given the size of the typical family in many poorer developing countries and the communal character of radio listening in village and urban slum settings, such proportions can translate into some access for over half the adult population. Satellite television and telephone linkages convey news with stunning speed; CNN is now watched routinely by elites in every region of the world. All of these increasingly dense international communication linkages feed a global democratic "zeitgeist" of unprecedented scope and intensity.

The diffusion of democratic values, models, and ideologies is also heightened by the relative absence of alternative visions. This is not just linked to the waxing and waning of intellectual fashions but is grounded in objective realities. Communism, state socialism, and one-party mobilizational regimes have shown themselves to be miserable failures at even the rapid material progress they promised, not to mention the nourishing of the human spirit. As news has spread of these developmental failures, and of the nearly universal corruption and cynicism of party elites and nomenklaturas, peoples living in these countries have been able to place their own national experiences in a wider context. They "could and did ask the relevance for themselves of political events in far-off countries." The failures of individual regimes now appear as systemic flaws in principle and design, not the perversion of an individual experiment gone wrong. State socialism as a system has now been discredited as thoroughly as was fascism in World War II. The only systemic alternative to democracy that remains viable in world politics is the still largely untested Islamic State, but its record of accomplishment in Iran hardly inspires confidence. This does not mean that the democratic alternative can and will succeed everywhere; it does mean that it is the only *systemic* alternative that is empirically and normatively attractive to a broad range of peoples today.

All of these types of diffusion and demonstration effects have helped to divide authoritarian regimes, undermine their legitimacy, erode their support bases, disillusion and embolden their populations, and thus foster transitions to democracy. As indicated above, however, even more forceful and deliberate forms of international pressure have also been at work.

Democratic assistance

For the past two years, talk has been escalating among international aid donors of the need for greater political accountability, participation, and consensus building if recipient countries are to use aid effectively for development. The United States has moved explicitly to establish political democratization as a third condition for assistance (in addition to human rights and economic reforms), and Britain and France have also begun to signal that their aid may favor countries moving toward democracy. Just as political conditionality is likely to induce political openings (however superficial at first), sanctions can undermine dictators, and indeed did so in Benin in 1989–1990. Because of their economic destitution and political fragility, most African regimes are heavily dependent on international support. During the past two years, even such longstanding dictators as Mobutu Sese Seko in Zaire have been losing economic and security assistance and the external legitimacy they need to sustain their rule.

Of course, while economic, political, and military dependence does render developing countries more susceptible to pressure from abroad, this does not necessarily have democratic consequences. To the extent that powerful external actors pursue economic and strategic goals compatible with, or even requiring, repressive regimes abroad, external intervention may prop up dictators and undermine popular struggles for democracy, as it often did during the Cold War.

In recent years, international assistance has increasingly interacted with and strengthened democratizing changes in civil society. Although they are primarily indigenous phenomena, the proliferations of autonomous and largely democratic associations around the world have been aided and abetted by foreign influence and assistance. Organizational models have spread across borders, including alternatives to the styles and strategies used by Western civic and interest groups. The women's civic movement, *Conciencia*, founded in 1982 by 20 Argentine women "to transform a passive citizenry accustomed to authoritarian governments," now has affiliated movements in 14 other Latin American countries, forming a cooperative network to educate for democracy and to motivate and train women to organize for democracy. And as democrats around the world establish communications and face-to-face links with one another, such models spread across even regional boundaries (inspiring, for example, a similar effort in the Philippines).

Financial and technical assistance from the industrialized democracies has played an important and sometimes critical role in the expansion of autonomous democratic organizations and media. For some three decades the four (West) German party foundations (*Stiftungen*) have channeled large amounts of aid and exchange activity to democratic organizations and parties abroad; they continue to spend more money for this purpose than any other network of nongovernmental organizations from the industrialized democracies. A more recent example is the US National Endowment for Democracy (NED), which has had a significant impact since its establishment in 1983. Its extensive efforts in Poland, Chile, and Nicaragua provided critical support to the democratic movements that brought down those dictatorships. Throughout Eastern Europe it helped to build the independent civic infrastructure that undermined communism in the late 1980s, and it is now doing the same in Russia and other post-Soviet states, through more than 20 projects aiding democratic movements, independent publications and research institutes, modern information systems, and (through the Free Trade Union Institute) democratic trade unions. NED efforts were also credited with a major role in facilitating the transitions to democracy in Namibia and Haiti, in part through international projects to observe elections there. NED programs also help to strengthen new and troubled democracies. They provide support to civic education efforts such as that of *Conciencia*; to new democratic political parties, legislatures, judicial systems, electoral systems, and local governments; and to independent trade unions, business associations, and human rights groups. They also advance innovative efforts in many countries to demonstrate the need for economic reform, advise legislatures on economic issues, and promote the teaching of private enterprise principles and techniques.

The globalization of the resource bases of democratic movements is a significant dimension of the global democratic trend. NED's annual budget increased from $17 million to $25 million in fiscal year 1991 and to $27.5 million the following year, despite an unprecedented budget crisis in the United States. If one considers the efforts of the US Agency for International Development, current US spending for democracy promotion is probably about $200 million (or twice that if the relevant programs of the US Information Agency are included). In proportional terms, the German party foundations spend considerably more of their budgets than do US institutions and agencies to promote democratic civic and political life in new, prospective, and struggling democracies (about $100 million on such overseas projects in 1988). There is also a growing network of foundations, both governmental and nongovernmental, in the other established democracies to support democratic initiatives and institutions abroad; Britain established in 1992 a Westminster Foundation for Democracy modeled on NED, and now the Japanese too are showing interest in developing a similar type of political assistance program. By providing resources and technical assistance to nascent democratic institutions, and to democratic groups in civil society, the established democracies are playing an increasingly aggressive, sophisticated, and long-term role in helping to initiate and consolidate democratic transitions.

As we have seen, international factors influencing democratizing movements can be identified in a wide range of forms, styles, and processes. Sometimes these factors can be elusive; often, they may overlap with and amplify each other. In Nicaragua, the democratic opposition triumphed only because it was able to unite almost completely in the broad front of the National Opposition Union (UNO) and its single presidential candidate, Violeta Chamorro. We will probably never know to what extent official and unofficial US actors encouraged those forces to coalesce and remain united, but pressures and inducements were probably considerable. In the

Philippines, the challenge of defeating Ferdinand Marcos was similarly threatened by intense factionalism among the opposition, especially between supporters of Corazón Aquino and Salvador Laurel. Although Cardinal Sin appears to have been the decisive force in producing unity around the Aquino candidacy, the "US embassy also played a part by ensuring that the two sides kept talking to one another," and some US citizens, acting privately, also became involved in mediation between the two camps.

Yet another dimension of the internationalization of the democratic struggle is also reflected in Nicaragua's democratic transition: the role of international election monitoring. In circumstances where democracy is just beginning to emerge after years of oppression or violent conflict, both international observation and international mediation of the electoral process have made a critical contribution to its credibility and hence success. At a minimum, a well-organized team of international observers can help to verify the election results so as to enhance the credibility and legitimacy of the declared victor in a polarized contest, as in South Korea in 1987 and Bulgaria in 1990. In some countries, the presence of observers has deterred an authoritarian or incumbent government from rigging the election or forging or canceling the result, as with the 1988 plebiscite that ended Pinochet's rule in Chile. Where fraud does occur, as in Panama under Noriega and the Philippines under Marcos, observers can demonstrate it and deny it domestic and international acceptance. In all of these cases, international election observers bolster participation and confidence in the electoral process, "by ensuring that the election will either be free or denounced as fraudulent." At times, observers can also go much further, helping bitterly opposed sides to negotiate mutually acceptable terms of the electoral game, and even mediating the implementation of "a collectively guaranteed process of national reconciliation and democratization." This was the formula that ended the civil war in Nicaragua and appears likely to do so in Angola, El Salvador, and Cambodia as well. Official diplomacy – particularly within the context of multilateral organizations such as the OAS and the UN – may also help to bring hostile parties to the bargaining table and guarantee an agreement. Many times, the international role is truly indispensable, since mediation and observation of elections requires impartial arbiters whom all sides can trust.

Two other dimensions of the international variable in democratization require mention. First, democratic movements in some countries have drawn significant financial assistance, international political support, and intellectual and strategic counsel from their compatriots working, studying, or living in exile overseas. Taiwanese democratic opposition leaders made an important breakthrough in a 1982 trip to the United States when they discovered not only the salience of US congressional concern for democracy and human rights in Taiwan but a whole network of "overseas Taiwanese organizations, several of whom were already active in the lawful lobbying business." With Taiwan dependent on US trade and security assistance, this discovery helped to establish democratic publics abroad, and especially the US Congress, as an important arena of bargaining and maneuver for Taiwan's democratic activists (an arena where they held the upper hand). Exile communities from countries as diverse as Poland, Nicaragua, Haiti, and Zaire have played important roles in generating US and European pressure for democratization and in aiding democratic movements with their own financial resources. A single Hungarian emigré, Wall Street financier George Soros, contributed more than $15 million in 1990 alone to democratic dissidents and organizations throughout Eastern Europe. He has been assisting such groups for years.

Finally, transnational organizations have strengthened civil society and thereby fostered democratization, wittingly and unwittingly. The most powerful force here has been the Catholic church, which underwent a striking shift in doctrine, "manifested in the Second Vatican Council of 1963–1965," that transformed "national Catholic churches from defenders of the status quo to opponents of authoritarianism." The international democratizing role of the Catholic church gathered momentum with the accession of Pope John Paul II, who spoke out eloquently for human rights, and whose papal visits lent powerful symbolic support at strategic moments to movements for democracy in Poland, Brazil, the Philippines, Argentina, Central America, South Korea, Chile, and Paraguay. Other types of international nongovernmental organizations – for example, the Asia Foundation, the African-American Institute, and Freedom House – have played a more subtle role by supporting the long-term development of independent organizations and think-tanks in civil society. [. . .]

35 The Emergence and Transformation of the International Women's Movement

Nitza Berkovitch

The Interwar Period: Lobbying for Expansion of the World Agenda

The world polity after World War I differed markedly from that of the previous period. Earlier dreams of establishing permanent international cooperative bodies were realized with the creation of the League of Nations and the International Labor Organization (ILO), which ushered in a new phase of world-polity construction. The League and the ILO, both created at the Paris Peace Conference of 1919, constituted the first stable organizational basis for inter-state cooperation. They opened a new arena for women's mobilization by offering a central world focal point that theretofore had been lacking. In so doing, they changed the context in which women's organizations operated, consequently provoking changes in their modes of operation as well. Their main effort now targeted the newly created international bodies.

By turning their attention to the new world bodies, women's organizations conferred legitimacy on them and thus helped institutionalize their centrality. At the same time, the degree of organization and cooperation among women's groups increased. Many women's organizations moved their headquarters to Geneva to facilitate contacts with the various bodies of the League, while others established specialized bureaus expressly to deal with the League. In addition, a new type of organization emerged, the multi- or supra-international organization consisting of representatives of a number of international organizations. For example, in 1925 the Joint Committee of Representative Organizations was founded, and in 1931 ten of the largest women's groups formed the Liaison Committee of Women's International Organizations. Members of the Committee established close contacts with high officials in the League Secretariat, cooperating with the League on various welfare-related and other activities.

The increased global mobilization of women within the formally organized global arena sharpened tensions within the international women's movement. Bitter conflict emerged between those who supported action on behalf of women's equality and those who favored laws that gave women special protection, especially in the area of work. Both camps focused their efforts on getting the League and ILO to take action on women's issues, but with quite different emphases.

Original publication details: Berkovitch, Nitza, "The Emergence and Transformation of the International Women's Movement" excerpted from *Constructing World Culture: International Nongovernmental Organizations Since 1875*, edited by John Boli and George Thomas with the permission of the publishers, Stanford University Press. © 1999 by the Board of Trustees of the Leland Stanford Junior University.

The League's limited mandate did not allow women's issues to be considered in full; regulation of the relationships between states and their respective citizens was not included in its jurisdiction. Instead, the League concentrated on regulating relations among states. Individual "rights," a construct that had mobilized social movements for more than a century, were not considered an international concern that could be regulated by international standards. It was only through a sustained effort lasting almost two decades that women's international organizations were able to place the heart of their social concerns, the legal status of women, on the League's agenda.

The exclusion of the issue of women's rights from the League's jurisdiction was explicitly stipulated by officials during the Paris Peace Conference. Facing continuous pressure from women's organizations, however, and after much hesitation and deliberation on the part of the politicians, Conference officials agreed that "women's organizations could be heard," but only "by commissions occupying themselves especially with questions touching on women's interests." The women's delegation to the Conference presented seven resolutions covering moral, political, and educational issues. For the most part, they were ignored. [. . .]

Development Ideology

During the 1970s, the discourse of women's rights encountered that of development. This encounter was the result of the most significant event in global organizing on women's issues: the United Nation's Decade for Women (1976–1985). The Women's Decade coincided with the Second United Nations Development Decade, during which development started to dominate global discourse and activity. The two events melded into each other in the sense that a core dimension for grappling with women's issues became the concern for "incorporating women into development"; women's issues came to the fore in many development documents and projects. Framing women's issues in the context of development brought about qualitative and quantitative changes on both national and international fronts. It led to an intensification of world activity on women's issues that in turn had an enormous impact on nation-states, while it stimulated the establishment of women's movements in many countries and led most governments in the world to create an official state agency for the promotion of women's issues. Women's issues became a state concern.

Before discussing these interrelated developments, I should note that the catalyst for the Decade for Women is believed to have been a women's organization, not any of the UN bodies. Hilkka Pietila, who was herself involved in some of the activities she documents, refers to "an oral tradition in the UN family" that identifies the Women's International Democratic Federation (WIDF) as the source of the proposal for an International Women's Year. As observers on the UN Commission on the Status of Women, the WIDF's president and a number of other WINGO leaders drafted a proposal that the Commission recommended to the General Assembly. Despite initial resistance, the Assembly eventually endorsed the idea in 1972, proclaiming 1975 as International Women's Year (IWY) with the themes of equality, development, and peace.

In 1975 the World Conference of the International Women's Year was held in Mexico City. One hundred and thirty-three states participated, endorsing two major documents: the "Declaration of Mexico on the Equality of Women and Their Contribution to Development and Peace" and the "World Plan of Action for the Implementation of the Objectives of IWY." The conference designated the 1976–1985 period as the UN Decade for Women. Representatives from 145 countries attended the 1980 Mid-Decade Conference in Copenhagen, covened as a "mid-point review of progress and obstacles in achieving the goals of the Decade," and adopted a Programme of Action. The end of the Decade was marked by the 1985 World Conference to Review and Appraise the Achievements of the UN Decade for Women, held in Nairobi. Drawing representatives from 157 countries, the conference adopted a document titled "The Nairobi Forward-Looking Strategies for the Advancement of Women."

It was during the Women's Decade that the status of women was linked to the development of their countries. As a result, both the form and content of global organizing has changed. Official bodies and the international women's movement shifted their focus from legal standards and international law to concrete projects, further organizational expansion, greater research efforts, and network enhancement to coordinate these numerous endeavors.

Within the new framework, elevating women's status and achieving equality between the sexes were conceptualized as necessary conditions for full national – economic and social – development. Women were now considered important human resources essential to comprehensive rationalization. Eradicating discrimination was an integral part of the global plan to improve the well-being of national societies and of the world as a whole. "Human rights" as a leading concept lost its prominence, though it did not disappear. Thus, for example, the sweepingly broad Convention for the Elimination of All Forms of Discrimination Against Women (adopted by the General Assembly in 1979) incorporates, side by side, the principles of abstract social justice and a more "instrumental" principle of development. In 1982, a commission under the same name was established to monitor the Convention's implementation. By 1990, this convention had been ratified by 101 countries, one of the highest rates of ratification of any UN convention. [. . .]

Summary

The story of "united womanhood" must be understood within the larger framework of the changing world polity. The existence of the international women's movement as such, its huge conferences, its plethora of documents and resolutions, and its ubiquitous lobbying visibly enact the concept of transnationalism and thus boost our tendency to see the world as a single global social system. As Roland Robertson notes: "Indeed this is one among many movements and organizations which have helped to compress the world as a whole." Thus, the international women's movement did not only reflect world culture but also helped shape its content and structure.

What started in earlier periods as moral crusades led by women's groups eventually culminated in highly legitimized and rationalized actions enacted by official world bodies on behalf of women. Around the turn of the century, the women's movement, being part of the transnational reform movement, reflected and reinforced the emphasis on moral reform and universalism. However, these early groups also promoted elements of equality, rights, and suffrage. One way of resolving the tension between the notions of individual rights and moral regeneration was subsuming the former in the latter. The international women's movement promoted women's rights as a necessary condition for enacting and bringing about desired changes in society. However, in the early period there were no world bodies to act on behalf of women.

With the establishment of the ILO as a global organization with the mandate to set international standards, the women's movement found a central target for its advocacy of the principle of equality alongside the principle of "protection," with growing tension between the two principles. The League of Nations also helped shape the mode of action and agenda of the women's groups when it became the focus for their lobbying efforts for and against an international equal rights treaty. However, it was only after World War II, when world-level organizing intensified and a more authoritative world center was established, that the principle of equality began to guide world activities regarding women. The changing agenda of the ILO regarding women's employment is striking. The sole focus on protective legislation was widened to include binding standards on equality in employment. Nation-states joined the campaign, and the majority of them revised their national labor codes to be consistent with the new spirit of women's rights.

In the 1970s another layer was added: an instrumental discourse of development that brought with it further rationalizing and organizing of world activities on women's issues. The encounter between the two discourses shaped much of the activity and spirit of the UN Decade for Women (1976–1985). The international women's movement began to operate in a much more complicated environment, with more options but also more constraints. Thanks to the initiatives of women's organizations, regular world women's conferences were held both during the Decade and after, the latest in Beijing in 1995.

The three UN conferences indicate a great deal about the worldwide construction of women's issues. First, official world organizing and activities regarding women's issues have expanded tremendously in comparison with previous periods. Second, the effects are not limited to the international level. Nation-states put "women" on their agenda, altering existing laws and establishing official bureaus and departments to deal with women's issues. Third, world-cultural ideas about women have penetrated developing countries as well, leading to the emergence of women's movements in almost every country in the world.

All the while, the international women's movement has expanded in size and transformed in content and composition. It became truly global as it grew to incorporate women from the Third World, with their specific concerns and perspectives. This process, however, was not unproblematic. Rather, it was accompanied by rising tension between women from the South and women from the North. This shows that, in contrast to conventionally held wisdom, transnational movements in general and the women's movement in particular cannot be reduced to the interests of one hegemonic region. National and regional factors can affect international organizing agenda, but the wider context affects, to large degree, the legitimacy and effectiveness of international organizing. Once international organizing emerges and gains a degree of legitimacy and operational capacity, however, new organizational dynamics are set in motion that reshape the wider context itself.

Women everywhere have been integrated into the ongoing global campaign. The international women's movement has emerged as a visible and viable global force. The overarching result is, indeed, a reconceptualization of feminism as

a movement of people working for change across and despite national boundaries, not of representatives of nation states or national governments . . . we must be global, recognising that the oppression of women in one part of the world is often affected by what happens in another, and that no woman is free until the conditions of oppression of women are eliminated everywhere.

36 Beijing Declaration

UN Fourth World Conference on Women

Resolutions Adopted by the Conference

Resolution 1

Beijing Declaration and Platform for Action

The Fourth World Conference on Women,

Having met in Beijing from 4 to 15 September 1995,

1. Adopts the Beijing Declaration and Platform for Action, which are annexed to the present resolution;

2. Recommends to the General Assembly of the United Nations at its fiftieth session that it endorse the Beijing Declaration and Platform for Action as adopted by the Conference.

Annex I

BEIJING DECLARATION

1. We, the Governments participating in the Fourth World Conference on Women,

2. Gathered here in Beijing in September 1995, the year of the fiftieth anniversary of the founding of the United Nations,

3. Determined to advance the goals of equality, development and peace for all women everywhere in the interest of all humanity,

4. Acknowledging the voices of all women everywhere and taking note of the diversity of women and their roles and circumstances, honouring the women who paved the way and inspired by the hope present in the world's youth,

5. Recognize that the status of women has advanced in some important respects in the past decade but that progress has been uneven, inequalities between women and men have persisted and major obstacles remain, with serious consequences for the well-being of all people,

6. Also recognize that this situation is exacerbated by the increasing poverty that is affecting the lives of the majority of the world's people, in particular women and children, with origins in both the national and international domains,

7. Dedicate ourselves unreservedly to addressing these constraints and obstacles and thus enhancing further the advancement and empowerment of women all over the world, and agree that this requires urgent action in the spirit of determination, hope, cooperation and solidarity, now and to carry us forward into the next century.

We reaffirm our commitment to:

8. The equal rights and inherent human dignity of women and men and other purposes and principles enshrined in the Charter of the United Nations, to the Universal Declaration of Human Rights and other international human rights instruments, in particular the Convention on the Elimination of All Forms of Dis-

Original publication details: Beijing Declaration, United Nations Fourth World Conference on Women, 1995.

crimination against Women and the Convention on the Rights of the Child, as well as the Declaration on the Elimination of Violence against Women and the Declaration on the Right to Development;

9.   Ensure the full implementation of the human rights of women and of the girl child as an inalienable, integral and indivisible part of all human rights and fundamental freedoms;

10.   Build on consensus and progress made at previous United Nations conferences and summits – on women in Nairobi in 1985, on children in New York in 1990, on environment and development in Rio de Janeiro in 1992, on human rights in Vienna in 1993, on population and development in Cairo in 1994 and on social development in Copenhagen in 1995 with the objective of achieving equality, development and peace;

11.   Achieve the full and effective implementation of the Nairobi Forward-looking Strategies for the Advancement of Women;

12.   The empowerment and advancement of women, including the right to freedom of thought, conscience, religion and belief, thus contributing to the moral, ethical, spiritual and intellectual needs of women and men, individually or in community with others and thereby guaranteeing them the possibility of realizing their full potential in society and shaping their lives in accordance with their own aspirations.

    We are convinced that:

13.   Women's empowerment and their full participation on the basis of equality in all spheres of society, including participation in the decision-making process and access to power, are fundamental for the achievement of equality, development and peace;

14.   Women's rights are human rights;

15.   Equal rights, opportunities and access to resources, equal sharing of responsibilities for the family by men and women, and a harmonious partnership between them are critical to their well-being and that of their families as well as to the consolidation of democracy;

16.   Eradication of poverty based on sustained economic growth, social development, environmental protection and social justice requires the involvement of women in economic and social development, equal opportunities and the full and equal participation of women and men as agents and beneficiaries of people-centred sustainable development;

17.   The explicit recognition and reaffirmation of the right of all women to control all aspects of their health, in particular their own fertility, is basic to their empowerment;

18.   Local, national, regional and global peace is attainable and is inextricably linked with the advancement of women, who are a fundamental force for leadership, conflict resolution and the promotion of lasting peace at all levels;

19.   It is essential to design, implement and monitor, with the full participation of women, effective, efficient and mutually reinforcing gender-sensitive policies and programmes, including development policies and programmes, at all levels that will foster the empowerment and advancement of women;

20.   The participation and contribution of all actors of civil society, particularly women's groups and networks and other non-governmental organizations and community-based organizations, with full respect for their autonomy, in co-operation with Governments, are important to the effective implementation and follow-up of the Platform for Action;

21.   The implementation of the Platform for Action requires commitment from Governments and the international community. By making national and international commitments for action, including those made at the Conference, Governments and the international community recognize the need to take priority action for the empowerment and advancement of women.

We are determined to:

22.   Intensify efforts and actions to achieve the goals of the Nairobi Forward-looking Strategies for the Advancement of Women by the end of this century;

23.   Ensure the full enjoyment by women and the girl child of all human rights and fundamental freedoms and take effective action against violations of these rights and freedoms;

24.   Take all necessary measures to eliminate all forms of discrimination against women and the girl child and remove all obstacles to gender equality and the advancement and empowerment of women;

25.   Encourage men to participate fully in all actions towards equality;

26.   Promote women's economic independence, including employment, and eradicate the persistent and increasing burden of poverty on women by addressing the structural causes of poverty through changes in economic structures, ensuring equal access for all women, including those in rural areas, as vital development agents, to productive resources, opportunities and public services;

27.   Promote people-centred sustainable development, including sustained economic growth, through the provision of basic education, life-long education, literacy and training, and primary health care for girls and women; [. . .]

We are determined to:

35.   Ensure women's equal access to economic resources, including land, credit, science and technology, vocational training, information, communication and markets, as a means to further the advancement and empowerment of women and girls, including through the enhancement of their capacities to enjoy the benefits of equal access to these resources, inter alia, by means of international cooperation. [. . .]

37 World Culture in the World Polity: A Century of International Non-Governmental Organization

John Boli and George M. Thomas

For a century and more, the world has constituted a singular polity. By this we mean that the world has been conceptualized as a unitary social system, increasingly integrated by networks of exchange, competition, and cooperation, such that actors have found it "natural" to view the whole world as their arena of action and discourse. Such a conceptualization reifies the world polity implicitly in the often unconscious adoption of this cultural frame by politicians, businesspeople, travelers, and activists, and explicitly in the discourse of intellectuals, policy analysts, and academicians.

Like all polities, the world polity is constituted by a distinct culture – a set of fundamental principles and models, mainly ontological and cognitive in character, defining the nature and purposes of social actors and action. Like all cultures, world culture becomes embedded in social organization, especially in organizations operating at the global level. Because most of these organizations are INGOs, we can identify fundamental principles of world culture by studying structures, purposes, and operations of INGOs. By studying INGOs across social sectors, we can make inferences about the structure of world culture. By studying the promotion of world-cultural principles that INGOs are centrally involved in developing, we can see how INGOs shape the frames that orient other actors, including states. [. . .]

An Historical Overview of the INGO Population

Data

Since 1850 more than 25,000 private, not-for-profit organizations with an international focus have debuted on the world stage. They include the Pan American Association of Ophthalmology, International Exhibitions Bureau, Commission for the Geological Map of the World, International Catholic Child Bureau, International Tin Council, and Tug of War International Federation. Most are highly specialized, drawing members worldwide from a particular occupation, technical field, branch of knowledge, industry, hobby, or sport to promote and regulate their respective areas of concern. Only a few, such as the Scout Movement, International Olympic Committee, International Red Cross, and World Wildlife Fund, are widely known.

Original publication details: Boli, John and George Thomas, "World Culture in the World Polity: A Century of International Non-Governmental Organization," *American Sociological Review* (April 1997), courtesy of American Sociological Association, Washington D.C.

We analyze data on 5,983 organizations founded between 1875 and 1988. They constitute the entire population of INGOs classified as genuinely international bodies by the Union of International Associations (UIA) in its *Yearbook of International Organizations*. [. . .]

Data quality and coding issues

The UIA limits INGOs to not-for-profit, non-governmental organizations (TNCs and IGOs are excluded). They vary in size from a few dozen members from only three countries to millions of members from close to 200 countries. About half of the INGOs in our data base have members from at least 25 countries, 20 percent have members from 50 or more countries, and only 11 percent have members from fewer than eight countries. [. . .]

Basic historical patterns

Figure 37.1 presents the number of INGOs founded and dissolved in each year between 1875 and 1973. Not-for-profit international organizing grew rapidly in the latter part of the nineteenth century, with about 10 new organizations emerging each year during the 1890s. The population burgeoned after the turn of the century, reaching a peak of 51 foundings in 1910. The severe collapse after that point led to a low of four foundings in 1915. Swift recovery after World War I yielded a period of fairly steady growth followed by some decline during the 1930s that preceded another steep fall going into World War II.

Following the war, international organizing exploded. By 1947 over 90 organizations a year were being founded, a pace that was maintained and even surpassed through the 1960s. The pattern for dissolved INGOs is similar, indicating a generally steady proportion of INGOs that eventually dissolved, but revealing peaks of fragility among organizations founded just before each of the wars.

INGO foundings and dissolutions thus match the general "state of the world" rather well, rising in periods of expansion and declining rapidly in times of crisis, with the declines beginning shortly before the outbreaks of the world wars. [. . .]

World Development, INGOs, and Capitalist and Interstate Systems

Global organizing proceeds in mutually reinforcing tension with the expansion of the nation-state system. INGOs began to proliferate during the heyday of nationalism and European imperialism; bringing the last "unclaimed" regions of the globe into the world economy and under the jurisdiction of states made the notions of "one world" and "one history" structurally compelling.

This dialectic is further evident in the effects of the world wars. The precipitous decline in INGO foundings after 1910 reflects the dominance of states for most of that decade, but the war also strengthened the conception of the world as a single polity and prompted expanded INGO (and IGO) efforts to organize the world polity. After a similar cycle in the 1930s and 1940s, a much broader discursive space for INGOs opened up as global technical and infrastructural resources increased exponentially. World-polity organizing jumped to a higher level than ever before,

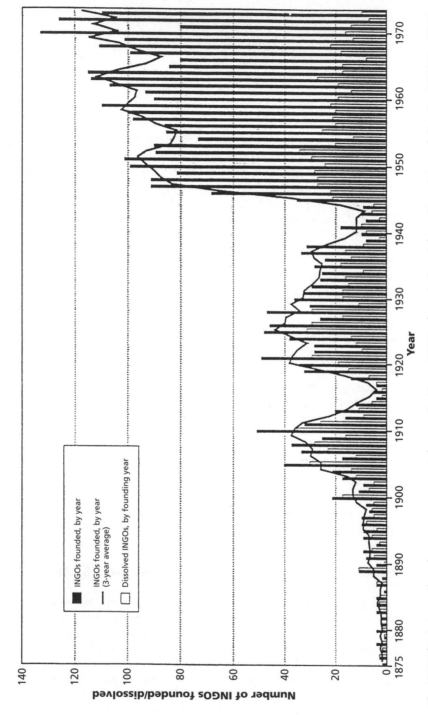

Figure 37.1 International non-governmental organizations: INGOs founded and founding dates of dissolved INGOs, 1875 to 1973

Source: Yearbook of International Organizations (UIA 1985, 1988).

just as the independent nation-state form was adopted by or imposed on the rest of the world.

The dialectic between world-polity and national-level organization is also evident in the relationship between IGOs and INGOs. Many IGOs were founded as INGOs and later co-opted by states, including such major bodies as the World Meteorological Organization, the International Labor Organization, and the World Tourism Organization. Moreover, INGOs have often been instrumental in founding new IGOs and shaping IGO activities. Thousands of INGOs have consultative status with agencies of the United Nations – over 900 with the Economic and Social Council alone – and most IGOs engage relevant INGOs as providers of information, expertise, and policy alternatives. IGO authority is not relinquished to INGOs, but IGO decisions are heavily influenced by INGO experts and lobbyists. [. . .]

INGOs as Enactors and Carriers of World Culture

Almost all INGOs originate and persist via voluntary action by individual actors. INGOs have explicit, rationalized goals. They operate under strong norms of open membership and democratic decision-making. They seek, in a general sense, to spread "progress" throughout the world: to encourage safer and more efficient technical systems, more powerful knowledge structures, better care of the body, friendly competition and fair play. To achieve their goals they emphasize communication, knowledge, consensual values and decision-making, and individual commitment. Following are five basic world-cultural principles that underlie INGO ideologies and structures: universalism, individualism, rational voluntaristic authority, human purposes of rationalizing progress, and world citizenship.

Universalism

Humans everywhere have similar needs and desires, can act in accordance with common principles of authority and action, and share common goals. In short, human nature, agency, and purpose are universal, and this universality underlies the many variations in social forms. Most INGOs are explicit about this – any interested person can become an active member, and everyone everywhere is a potential beneficiary of INGO activity.

Universalism is evident also in the breadth of INGOs' claims about what they do. Physics and pharmacology are presumed to be valid everywhere. Techniques for playing better chess are not country-specific. Red Cross aid will alleviate suffering in Africa as well as Asia. Across every sector, the purposes and means of action promoted by INGOs are assumed to be useful and meaningful everywhere.

A world not characterized by universalism does not coalesce as a singular polity; rather, it develops distinct subworld polities (societies, civilizations, empires) across which joint mobilization is unlikely. At the opposite extreme, a world state would thoroughly incorporate and regulate individuals and organizations – universalism would prevail but it would be bureaucratically absorbed.

The present world polity lies between these two extremes. Neither segmental nor ad hoc, neither is it *étatisée*; legal-bureaucratic authority is partitioned among multiple states. The principle of universalism that INGOs embody remains culturally autonomous because INGOs operate in the interstices of this decentralized structure.

Individualism

Most INGOs accept as members only individuals or associations of individuals; the main exceptions are trade and industry bodies, which often have firms as members. Individualism is also evident in their structures: INGOs use democratic, one-person–one-vote decision-making procedures, they assess fees on members individually, and they downplay national and other corporate identities in their conferences and publications. In the world-view embodied by INGOs, individuals are the only "real" actors; collectivities are essentially assemblages of individuals.

The combination of universalism and individualism may undermine traditional collectivities like the family or clan, but it also strengthens the one truly universalistic collectivity – humanity as a whole. INGOs habitually invoke the common good of humanity as a goal. The cultural dynamic at work parallels that characterizing national polities: As cultural constructs, the individual and the nation reinforce one another. In recent times, this centuries-old dynamic has shifted to the global level.

Rational voluntaristic authority

INGOs activate a particular cultural model when they organize globally, debate principles and models, and attempt to influence other actors. This model holds that responsible individuals acting collectively through rational procedures can determine cultural rules that are just, equitable, and efficient, and that no external authority is required for their legitimation. Such "self-authorization" runs counter to Weber's analysis of authority as forms of domination because INGOs cannot dominate in the conventional sense. INGOs have little sanctioning power, yet they act as if they were authorized in the strongest possible terms. They make rules and expect them to be followed; they plead their views with states or transnational corporations and express moral condemnation when their pleas go unheeded.

INGO authority is thus informal – cultural, not organizational. It is the agency presumed to inhere in rational individuals organizing for purposive action. Its basis can only be the diffuse principles of world culture, for INGO authority does not flow from any legal-bureaucratic or supernatural source.

Rational voluntarism is encouraged by the decentralized character of formal authority; at the world level, it is practiced by states and transnational corporations as well. For example, because sovereignty implies that no state has authority over any other, collective actions by states can occur only via rational voluntarism. This is why most IGOs, like INGOs, have resolutely democratic formal structures. It also helps explain why the legal-bureaucratic authority of states is brought into play to enforce INGO conceptions and rules.

Human purposes: dialectics of rationalizing progress

The rational character of INGOs is evident in their purposive orientation, formalized structures, and attention to procedures. INGOs in science, medicine, technical fields, and infrastructure activities are engaged in purely rationalized and rationalizing activity; almost all other INGOs rely on science, expertise, and professionalization in their operations and programs. What INGOs seek is, in essence, rational progress – not the crude nineteenth-century idea that steam engines and railroads would lead to heaven on earth, but the more diffuse and embedded concept of "development" that now prevails. This concept includes not only economic growth but also individual self-actualization, collective security, and justice.

At all levels, progress is assumed to depend on rationalization. Rational social action is the route to equality, comfort, and the good life. Rational production and distribution achieve all sorts of collective purposes. The scientific method, technique, monetarization, logical analysis – these are the favored *modi operandi*. These instruments of progress may often be criticized, but they are built into worldwide institutions and the ideology of development.

Rationalization, however, has another face. A tension operates between the rational and the irrational that strengthens both. Disenchantment of the world via rationalization endows the agents of disenchantment with increasing substance and sacredness; the apparent failure of actors to behave entirely rationally leads to theorizing about actors' irrational selves or cultures. Rationalized actors are thus culturally constituted as having complex "non-rational" subjectivities that are more primordial than objectified rationality. À la Nietzsche, the irrational becomes the arena of authenticity. Moreover, this face of rationalization launches widespread movements claiming to be anti-science, anti-Western, or postmodern: Western science, capitalism, and bureaucracy are imperialistic, dehumanizing forces against which authentic peoples must struggle to maintain their true, nonrational natures.

The rational/irrational tension thus generates conflict, but the irrational and subjective are continually channeled into rationalized activities and forms (e.g., revolution, UFO cults). Movements of self-exploration and expression, though rhetorically rejecting rationalism, also are rationalized (transcendental meditation becomes a test-improvement technique). Thus we find sports, leisure, spiritual, and psychological INGOs in abundance.

World citizenship

The principles discussed so far come together in the construct of world citizenship. Everyone is an individual endowed with certain rights and subject to certain obligations; everyone is capable of voluntaristic actions that seek rational solutions to social problems; therefore, everyone is a citizen of the world polity. World citizenship rules infuse each individual with the authority to pursue particularistic interests, preferably in organizations, while also authorizing individuals to promote collective goods defined in largely standardized ways.

World citizenship is strongly egalitarian. Individuals vary in their capacities, resources, and industry, but all have the same basic rights and duties. Correspondingly, only fully democratic governance structures are consistent with world citizenship. "Autocratic" tendencies are decried even within some INGOs (e.g., Greenpeace and the International Olympic Committee).

World citizenship is prominently codified in the Universal Declaration of Human Rights, which depicts a global citizen whose rights transcend national boundaries. The Declaration insists that states ensure the rights of their citizens and even that every human has the right to a national citizenship. In the absence of a world state, however, these obligations cannot be imposed on states. Acting as the primary carriers of world culture, INGOs translate the diffuse global identity and authority of world citizenship into specific rights, claims, and prescriptions for state behavior.

Here again we observe that states sometimes act as agents of informal world-polity authority. World citizens must turn to national states for protection of their rights, and INGOs back them up in the process. Increasingly, individuals need not be national citizens to make claims on the state; noncitizen residents of many countries have extensive rights almost equivalent to those of citizens, simply because they are human.

The cultural principles *re*-presented by INGOs are also integral to the world economy and state system, but INGOs push them to extremes. Their discourse is often critical of economic and political structures, stigmatizing "ethnocentric" (nonuniversalistic) nationalism and "exploitative" (inegalitarian) capitalism. INGOs dramatize violations of world-cultural principles, such as state maltreatment of citizens and corporate disregard for the sacredness of nature. Such examples illustrate the contested nature of these principles; they are widely known but by no means uncontroversial. [. . .]

Conclusion

INGOs are built on world-cultural principles of universalism, individualism, rational voluntaristic authority, progress, and world citizenship. Individuals and associations construct rationalized structures with defined goals, some diffuse (world peace, international understanding), but most quite specific and functional. Some INGOs, including sports, human rights, and environmental bodies, dramatically reify the world polity; human rights and environmental INGOs are especially prominent because of their conflicts with states over world-cultural principles. But most INGOs unobtrusively foster intellectual, technical, and economic rationalization that is so thoroughly institutionalized that they are hardly seen as actors, despite the enormous effects they have on definitions of reality, material infrastructure, household products, school texts, and much more.

The decentralization of authority among states facilitates transnational organizing (because centralized barriers to rational voluntarism are weak) and forces transnational organizations to focus their attention on states. Contrary to the claims of global neo-realist theories, states are not always leaders of social change; they can also be followers. In mobilizing around and elaborating world-cultural principles, INGOs lobby, criticize, and convince states to act on those principles, at least in some sectors and with respect to some issues.

How extensively this model of global change applies we cannot say. One of the central tasks for world-polity research is the development of a general theory about the conditions under which INGOs are able to take the initiative *vis-à-vis* states. A related task is the study of INGO relationships with the other major sets of reified world-polity actors, IGOs and transnational corporations. The literature contains many case studies touching on these relationships but little systematic analysis.

If a legal-rational world state emerges, much of the INGO population is likely to be co-opted to staff its bureaucracy and advise on policy decisions. To this point, we think of the operation of the world polity only as a world proto-state. A singular authority structure is lacking, states monopolize the legitimated use of violence, and states jealously guard their sovereignty. Nevertheless, the world as a proto-state has shared cultural categories, principles of authority, and universally constructed individuals who, as world proto-citizens, assume the authority to pursue goals that transcend national and local particularisms. More often than is commonly acknowledged, the resulting organizations prove to be effective. If they are absorbed in a formal global authority structure in the future, it may well be said that the road to a world state was paved by the rational voluntarism of INGOs.

38 The UN's Roles in International Society since 1945

Adam Roberts and Benedict Kingsbury

In the half century since its foundation in 1945, the United Nations has been a central institution in the conduct of international relations. This is an assessment of the UN's many roles in a world which has remained obstinately divided: roles which have changed over time, and have been the subject of different interpretations, fears, and hopes. It is a study of how, in the era of the UN, international society has been modified, but not totally transformed. It examines the UN's opportunities and difficulties in the new and confused circumstances of the post-Cold War era. Behind all these issues lurks the fear that the UN has by no means overcome the range of problems which have in the past bedevilled efforts at collective security and global organization.

The international system over which the UN in some sense presides is historically unique. For the first time in human history, the world has come to consist of nominally equal sovereign states; almost all of them are members of one world organization and subscribe to a single set of principles – those of the UN Charter; there is a functioning global organization which has the capacity to take important decisions, especially in the sphere of security – as was done in the Gulf crisis of 1990–1. Yet despite these elements of uniqueness which distinguish the UN era from earlier times, international society remains "anarchical" in the sense that, even though there is order of a kind and a wide range of international institutions, there is no central authority having the character of a government.

The UN era has also been notable for the continuing – and in many respects burgeoning – role in international society of actors other than states. The UN itself has provided a political space for non-governmental organizations, especially in such fields as human rights and environmental protection, and it provides fora in which all manner of non-state groups can articulate demands and pursue their interests. More generally, some have argued that a transnational civil society is beginning to emerge, constructed upon the growing density and ease of cross-border interactions, and characterized by the diffusion or contagion of multi-party democracy, market liberalism, and related political and social values. In this view, power is shifting from increasingly enmeshed states to cross-state groupings or to international institutions; territoriality is declining as a central principle of organization; and state sovereignty is being recast to accommodate human rights, economic aspirations, and internal and external conceptions of legitimacy. Perceptions of national interest are broadening, and normative convergence at the domestic, transnational, and international levels is gathering pace to the extent that these levels are themselves beginning to

Original publication details: Roberts, Adam and Benedict Kingsbury, "Introduction: The UN's Roles in International Society since 1945" from *United Nations, Divided World: The UN's Roles in International Relations* (Clarendon Press, Oxford, 1993).

merge. The European Community has been a popular model for proponents of the thesis that state sovereignty is gradually being transcended and that international civil society is being established by progressive enlargement from a liberal heartland.

International society is indeed changing, as are the issues and forms of its politics. Particular states or societies cannot easily remain outside the core institutions of economic, social, and political interaction. There are changes in the nature, forms, and uses of power, some of which result from interdependence or from the asymmetries which frequently accompany interdependence. There are shared norms and values, which the UN both reflects and projects. Not all states work well, and the state is perhaps not quite sacrosanct as the building block of international society in the way it was thought to be at other times during the twentieth century. Nevertheless the state remains the principal institution for achieving domestic order, and the inter-state system continues to provide the skeletal ordering framework for international society. The UN as an organization created and maintained by states is built upon an inter-governmental framework which some find unrealistic or unsatisfactory. Proposals for reshaping the framework, for instance by establishing a nationally-elected parliamentary assembly alongside the General Assembly, may attract greater interest in the future. But for the time being the structures and activities of the UN, while in some tension with the changing circumstances and needs of international society, necessarily continue to reflect the essential role of states and the difficulties of the contemporary states system.

In the post-Cold War era the international system is beset by a bewildering multitude of problems, many of which derive from ancient and enduring features of international politics. Although the East–West divide of the Cold War period has largely disappeared, the world is still divided into separate sovereign states, with their own interests, types of government, and differing world-views. There are other fundamental divisions: North vs. South; regional animosities; and communal cleavages which in many cases cut through states and across frontiers, raising challenges for the existing domestic and international order. Power still counts, whether in the decision-making processes of the UN or in the wider and messier realities beyond. The spectre of war, both civil and international, has not been banished. Many urgent crises which crowd the UN's agenda today derive from these divisions.

Global international organizations which proclaim as their goal the radical restructuring of the unsatisfactory condition of international relations inevitably attract high hopes – and subsequent disappointment. This has been true of the various communist internationals since the First International was founded in 1864, and of the League of Nations founded in 1919–20. The UN has had its fair share of such disappointed hopes, and will do so again. Yet it has achieved a utility, an institutional durability, even a degree of permanence, that eluded its predecessors.

In the immediate aftermath of the Cold War, an attractively teleological view of the UN's place in the international order gained some currency. In this view, the UN, for over four decades in which the world had been divided between East and West, had been unable to act effectively; indeed, in matters relating to war and peace it had been almost completely powerless due to frequent threat or use of the veto in the Security Council. Then, with the end of the Cold War in the late 1980s, it was at last in a position to act more or less as its founders had intended, taking a decisive role in many crises, including in the Gulf in 1991. It now had an opportunity to advance, if not to world government, at least towards a centrally regulated and well ordered international system.

This view was always open to challenge. First, the UN's performance in the long decades of the Cold War was much more impressive than the picture of a stymied organization suggests. It was in the years of East–West hostility that the UN became the world's first truly universal organization of states; helped to develop international standards on a wide range of matters, including human rights; and built up peacekeeping and diplomatic services which proved useful in addressing several conflicts. Secondly, since the end of the Cold War, the UN has faced some problems of a kind which have since time immemorial defeated the best efforts of the international community, and can be expected to do so again.

Many of the divisions within and between states have become more serious in the UN era than before – not least because the UN, somewhat paradoxically, has presided over a further phase in the triumphant advance of the idea of the "sovereign state". In the wake of European decolonization and the collapse of the Soviet Union, the total number of such states has more than tripled. Many conflicts of our time have their origins in partitions and disputes following upon the end of empires, and the attendant uncertainties about the legitimacy of new post-colonial states, regimes, institutions, and frontiers. Such problems have been especially marked following the disintegration of the USSR and Yugoslavia: indeed, the newly emerging regimes and frontiers were called into question more quickly there than in most former European colonies. The world is, and is likely to remain, divided into separate sovereign states, which have a capacity for making war, and many of which are conscious of their internal fragility and external vulnerability. Processes of integration and disintegration, cooperation and competition, liberation and domination, understanding and incomprehension, which have always characterized the system of states, will continue even if in new forms. [. . .]

When the United Nations was established in the immediate aftermath of the Second World War, it was viewed similarly as being concerned above all with the maintenance of peace. However, in the years of East–West rivalry its role in this area sometimes seemed marginal. In the field of international security, while some major developments took place wholly or partly within a UN framework, many did not. For example, many fundamental issues between the USA and USSR, and also between countries of eastern and western Europe, were addressed outside UN institutions. The same is true of most security issues involving the People's Republic of China; and of many elements of the Arab–Israeli conflict. In such cases, more private bilateral or multilateral frameworks were preferred from which unwelcome states could be excluded, and in which there was less pressure to follow some established UN principles and practices. However, the UN did maintain an effective involvement in many security issues, including in regional conflicts in southern Africa and the Indian sub-continent. The UN involvement in regional security issues has increased dramatically since the late 1980s. Even in this period of heightened activity, the UN remains only part of the wider international framework for addressing security concerns.

Against this background, it is not surprising that the UN's contribution came to be seen by many as being less in the field of peace between the major powers than in other areas: defusing certain regional conflicts, advocating self-determination, assisting decolonization, codifying international law, protecting human rights, and providing a possible framework for social and economic improvement, even for redistribution of wealth on a global scale. [. . .]

Role in Proclaiming International Priorities and Principles

Despite all its failings, the UN has by no means lost its importance as a proclaimer of international standards. This is a complex role, which is central both to the maintenance of a viable international order and to the communication, consolidation and development of shared values within international society.

The centre-piece of the UN's proclamation of international principles and standards remains even today the Charter of 1945. The Charter, or at least the Charter order, proclaims such principles as sovereign equality; territorial integrity and political independence of states; equal rights and self-determination of peoples; non-intervention in internal affairs except under Chapter VII; peaceful settlement of disputes; abstention from threats or uses of force; fulfillment in good faith of international obligations; international cooperation; and respect for and promotion of human rights and fundamental freedoms without discrimination. Inevitably there are differences in interpretation of terse statements of principle drawn up by a limited group of states in a somewhat different world. Nevertheless the dominant diplomatic view has been that the Charter principles are an exemplary basis for the conduct of international relations, and that the need is not to rethink any of them but to focus, as the UN has done, on elaborating them and developing new principles where necessary. There are, however, fundamental tensions between some of the principles, as between territorial integrity and self-determination, or non-intervention and human rights. Where revisionist pressures have become very strong there has been controversy about relations between values of order and of justice, expressed for instance in debates about the relations of the principles of peaceful settlement and non-use of force on the one hand and human rights and self-determination on the other. There has also been criticism of the state-centric nature of the set of Charter principles, occasionally because of fundamental dissatisfaction with the Charter scheme as a foundation for global order, but more often with a view to adding further principles directed towards re-distributing wealth or power, to empowering non-state groups (especially "peoples"), or to reorienting priorities toward, for example, developmental or ecological concerns.

Another view of the Charter principles is that they are incorrigibly idealistic. In many ways, however, the Charter is a distinctly hard-headed document. For example, it is extremely cautious in what it says about disarmament; and it refers not to the long-asserted but highly problematic principle of "national self-determination", but to the much vaguer formulation "equal rights and self-determination of peoples", which was less haunted by ghosts from Europe's history between the two world wars. To some extent the Charter anticipated the growth of concern with economic and social matters and with human rights, the advent of regional security organizations, and the process of decolonization.

In addition to these different interpretations of the Charter's actual provisions, there are different views of its whole ethos. Some, particularly those steeped in constitutionalist domestic polities such as the USA, are inclined to find the solution to questions of all sorts in the interpretation and reinterpretation of the Charter provisions. This tendency has often coincided with organic views of an expanding and diversifying UN, founded on an ethos of continuous progress, and sustained by teleological interpretations of the original Charter language. The Charter embodies the architecture of a dynamic organization, but it is not a complete constitution for international society. The Charter's foundational principles do not contain prescriptions for all problems of international public order, let alone for all issues of international justice. The UN has thus been concerned both to elaborate existing principles and to formulate new standards, a task it has shared with many other international institutions.

The UN serves an important function in shaping the international agenda, and in both facilitating and conditioning the articulation of new political demands. It has contributed to global awareness of numerous issues, including racial discrimination, torture and disappearances, rights of children, illiteracy, international dimensions of poverty, problems relating to refugees, and protection of cultural heritage. It has got deeply involved in a wide range of environmental issues: Patricia Birnie points both to the UN's contribution and to the problems of simultaneous and sometimes uncoordinated action in areas of environmental policy by a multitude of UN subsidiary bodies and specialized agencies. The UN has roles in areas such as the control of the production, trade, and consumption of narcotics, where international coordination of national policies and actions is more effective if accompanied by collective legitimation of otherwise controversial measures. More generally, UN endorsement lends legitimacy to doctrines and ideas, as with those concerning development assistance, the "common heritage of mankind" in the deep sea-bed and outer space, and the unacceptability of colonialism. UN endorsement may also legitimize compromise solutions reached in particular international disputes and crises.

UN and regional standard-setting instruments, and the bodies charged with their implementation, have prompted a convergence of the public pronouncements of states in a common international rhetoric of human rights. To a much smaller extent this convergence is mirrored in domestic practice. It remains the case that, despite the existence of many purportedly definitive agreements on the subject, different societies have and will continue to have very different conceptions of the nature, content, and importance of human rights. Nevertheless, the growth in importance attached to human rights in most states is in significant measure a product of the extensive activity stimulated by the UN: international standards and institutions have provided a basis for domestic human rights activism and resistance to governmental oppression as well as for international pressure.

There are signs, albeit limited, that the UN may be becoming more closely associated with the promotion of multi-party democracy. Since the late 1980s it has been involved in election-monitoring activities in many independent countries, including Nicaragua, Haiti, El Salvador, Angola, Cambodia, and Mozambique. While several of these operations have related to international peace and security and been undertaken under the auspices of the Security Council, there is also noticeably less opposition in the General Assembly to such activities than in earlier periods. Boutros-Ghali has put great emphasis on democracy and its significance both for economic development and for international peace. However, many states continue to emphasize the principle of non-interference in internal affairs, and there is no consensus on the universal desirability of particular democratic models. Moreover, the vast problems of transition from authoritarian to democratic systems, and of establishing democratic structures in the face of severe communal division, involve much more than the UN and other international agencies can realistically provide, as developments in some successor states of the former Yugoslavia and the former Soviet Union make clear. Nevertheless, the legitimizing effect of pro-democratic incantations and international observation, and such practical contributions as electoral aid and voter education, may well be important for emerging democracies and for vulnerable existing democracies. [. . .]

The UN has had particular difficulty in enunciating effective principles for tackling perhaps the most basic and fundamental division of international life – the division between the largely affluent societies of the North and the largely poor societies of the South. Conscious of a link between economic disruption and war, those who framed the UN Charter placed much emphasis on economic and social progress; after a long period of virtual silence on the subject, the Security Council began to return rhetorically to the theme of the connection between development and international peace in the early 1990s, although with little in the way of immediate results. The UN General Assembly began to proclaim an ideology of development, couched increasingly in terms of rights or entitlements, from the mid-1960s. However, in this area more than in many others there has been a huge gulf between the UN rhetoric and the progress actually achieved in large parts of the South. Expectations that the UN could play a central role in development issues have had to yield to a more cautious and nuanced view of its actual and potential role, and indeed of the nature of the development process itself. The rhetorical and programmatic UN commitment to development has nevertheless continued, although it has proved increasingly difficult to integrate this commitment to other UN priorities. A long-running debate on the real relations between human rights against the state and state-supervised development has never been effectively resolved beyond superficial agreement on the formula that they are mutually interdependent. The debate on relations between environment and development has similarly produced a verbal commitment to "sustainable development", but without an underlying reconciliation of the very different agendas. The backdrop of the general unwillingness of the North to make the sacrifices necessary to finance the development urged by the South has not changed greatly throughout the UN period, but the UN has contributed to improved understanding of the issues. [. . .]

39 Peace, Security, and Humanitarian Action

Sadako Ogata

Humanitarian Action and International Political Structure

My start as High Commissioner for Refugees in early 1991 coincided with the break down of the Cold War structure on the global political scene. While the East–West confrontation has been directly or indirectly responsible for many conflicts in the developing world, the bipolar "structure", if I may call it that way, also meant a certain degree of clarity and predictability for my Office. Although our work has never been easy, we knew what to do. For long periods we protected and assisted refugees fleeing from communist regimes, proxy wars and decolonization conflicts. Solutions were envisaged only in relation to regime changes, however remote.

In those days, international refugee protection, which is at the heart of our mandate, was less complicated and far less disputed than it is today. The 1951 Convention relating to the Status of Refugees, which having been ratified by 133 states remains the basic universal instrument in this domain, was based upon and heavily influenced by the Cold War structure. Receiving refugees was often both a political and humanitarian corollary of the ideological divide. Our work was also premised on the theoretical predictability of the Westphalian state system. Although the increasingly vocal human rights movement began attacking the absoluteness of sovereignty and non-interference deriving from the Westphalian adagium *eius regio, cuius religio*, we operated, in principle, only in countries of asylum.

In the contemporary world, however, the nature of conflicts affecting international peace and security has changed. As we all know, rather than nation state warfare we see more internal conflicts. Although many have regional dimensions, external aggression is not perceived or major powers cannot agree on its relevance. Increasingly these conflicts are ethno-political group confrontations beyond familiar patterns of democracy versus dictatorship, either left or right. Invariably they result in massive and extremely rapid displacement, both internally and externally. After the guns fall silent, as in Bosnia, reconciliation proves to be another battle, an uphill one, rendering early refugee repatriation elusive. Let me be frank. We have not established any solid international approach and regime to deal with these increasingly intractable problems. Although many lives have been saved, the international response to the mega-crises of the nineties has been mostly selective, ad hoc and improvised, whether the UN or regional multilateral actors were involved. I am afraid that the response is too often subject to the vicissitudes of the strategic interests – or their absence – of major powers and countries adjacent to the theatre of conflict.

Original publication details: Ogata, Sadako, "Peace, Security and Humanitarian Action," United Nations High Commissioner for Refugees, 1997.

The changing nature of conflicts has profoundly affected the work of my Office. It has been expanded and diversified, and it has become far more complex and dangerous. In 1996 we were protecting not only 13.2 million refugees who had crossed international borders, but we also tried to enhance the protection and material security of 3.3 million repatriating refugees in the early stages of their re-integration, 4.7 million internally displaced people and 4.9 million other victims of conflict. The global figure of internally displaced persons is unknown but estimated to outnumber the refugee total. Their fate is often as dismal as that of refugees, yet no international agency has been mandated to cover them. Concrete action on their behalf may be barred by states on grounds of national sovereignty, except when undertaken in the context of Chapter VII action. UNHCR's [UN High Commissioner for Refugees] engagement with the internally displaced has been flexible, based upon specific requests of the Secretary-General or the principal organs of the UN. While we want to help as many people as possible, the link with our mandated activities, resources and staff security need to be taken into account. Humanitarian agencies cannot always bear the burden of humanitarian intervention on their own, when indispensable political and security actions are not undertaken. Far too frequently I feel we are making up for political inaction.

Humanitarian action has indeed become an even more pronounced instrument of politics, and of foreign policy in particular, than in the past. Some manifestations of this are benign, for example when humanitarian negotiations on access, prisoner exchanges or refugee return help to build confidence during stalled political talks. By showing dividends to all sides, impartial humanitarian action can help bring them together to a certain extent. It can also help restore the perception of the UN as an evenhanded political mediator in situations where UN forces have been deployed to peace keep, or even threaten to use force. But there are also more worrisome manifestations. Humanitarian and human rights issues are constantly exploited by conflicting parties and their protagonists to pressurize the other side through the media. I am also extremely concerned about the diversion of aid by armed elements, who in many conflicts are barely distinguishable from ordinary civilians. The mixing of political objectives in humanitarian interventions is another aspect of the blurring of humanitarianism and politics.

Turning back to refugees, the relative predictability of their protection has evaporated as a result of asylum fatigue, confusion about mixed migratory and refugee movements in rich countries and the emphasis on adverse consequences of refugee flows in poor countries. Growing democratization and press freedom in the latter, for example in Africa, are leading to increasing pressure from domestic public opinion. International burden sharing is not working in the industrialized world, and is insufficiently divided between rich and poor countries.

Addressing Humanitarian Crises

You may perhaps feel that I am lamenting too much about my problems and worries. The question is how to tackle them. Needless to say, the causes for refugee outflows are by nature political. Many of today's ugly group conflicts, while ignited by political oppression in the absence of democratic governance, are the product of deeper social inequality and injustice. If the sense of injustice is generated or manipulated along ethnic or other communal lines, then disputes may be further aggravated. Hegemonic political power confrontations, as we see them in Rwanda and Burundi, reflect therefore the lack of a complex mixture of political and socio-economic rights of people. The argument in some quarters that economic development, or vast post-war reconstruction, would eliminate the refugee problem, is clearly too simplistic. Not all poor countries produce refugees. I wish to underline this, because a proper understanding of these causal relationships is essential in advancing prevention and solution-oriented strategies.

Both the prevention and solution of contemporary refugee problems requires the settlement of political conflicts. The need for military interventions in the course of conflict resolution depends on the intensity with which obstructive forces must be overcome and political or humanitarian objectives must be pursued. I am talking here about military intervention by UN peace keeping forces or by a coalition of several states in the context of today's internal conflicts as compared to the all-out international wars we have seen in the past. For humanitarian actors, cooperation with the military even in this limited mission has always posed uncertainties. Would military protection of the provision of assistance compromise the neutrality and impartiality of humanitarian action? Can military action remain neutral when wars intensify?

During the turbulent years of conflict in Bosnia and Herzegovina, UNHCR's initial hesitation to receive military protection of its convoys gradually changed, as it could no longer carry out its mission without the cooperation of UNPROFOR [UN Protection Force]. It was indeed thanks to UNPROFOR's military support that UNHCR and its partners could sustain one of the largest and most complex relief operations in history. While human suffering and perhaps even a spreading of the conflict were contained, we also witnessed painfully the impossibility of an over-charged peace keeping mission where there was no peace to keep and when the protection of "safe areas" began to undermine the neutrality of its mission.

When NATO came in and force was used against the Bosnian Serbs, our relationship with the military became delicate in terms of our humanitarian neutrality and impartiality. Our task became almost impossible by the summer of 1995. Enforcement is indeed a critical issue. It may complicate the arduous efforts of conflict mediators preferring to operate in a "neutral" environment, and it may lead to retaliations against humanitarian staff and the blocking of life saving access to populations of the opposing side. On the other hand, strict neutrality and ineffective protection could not lead to political settlement. Nor could humanitarian responses ensure the security of people. The relief operation became an excuse to avoid resolute military and political action.

With intensifying military action, Sarajevo in August 1995 demonstrated that a people and their city can be saved when the major powers agree to act. Determined political leadership both in Europe and across the Atlantic stepped in, out of compassion but perhaps even more out of a shared political interest in halting tensions in the Atlantic alliance. The combination of enforcement action and leadership also delivered the push necessary to arrive at the breakthrough in Dayton in November 1995. Dayton put us all back on the peace track. Military intervention four years earlier, in Vukovar, might well have done the same. Yes, I am a bit bitter as so many others, having lived through the devastation of ethnic cleansing and now being charged to help reverse it by organizing the return of 2.1 million refugees and internally displaced to their homes. Could the international community have prevented the debacle had it taken more resolute action earlier? Or was it inevitable for humanitarian and political efforts to run their course?

Post-Dayton Bosnia is a vivid example of the symbiotic relationship between political, military and humanitarian action to solve refugee problems and establish

278 POLITICAL GLOBALIZATION II: REORGANIZING THE WORLD

durable peace and security. With 250,000 people having returned – and far more expected to follow them in the coming months, we are making progress. In addition to the occupation and destruction of houses, political obstruction, most notably on the Bosnian Serb and Croat side, remains however the biggest stumbling block for inter-ethnic returns and hence for the re-integration of Bosnia. Bosnia shows that there can be no lasting military peace without civilian peace. We are extremely worried that the future of the Dayton accord is at stake. Regarding refugees, Dayton leaves open the choice between return to one's place of origin and relocation, thus giving room for policies of ethno-political inclusion as well as exclusion. The Dayton formula was probably the only one possible through political negotiations, but it does not indicate a real compromise about the multi- or mono-ethnic make-up of society and leaves humanitarian actors like my Office to grapple with essentially political issues. The pressure in some European countries to repatriate refugees regardless of their place of origin or where they can re-establish themselves, does not help and may lead to a dangerous "pressure cooker" effect in Bosnia. As far as UNHCR is concerned, we are committed to make inter-ethnic returns possible, but we need the close security involvement of NATO forces, targeted progress in reconstruction and concerted political backing.

In terms of our close collaboration with the political and military actors, Rwanda and Zaire have been rather painful. In fact such a relationship has not materialized, except for the military assistance during the initial outflow of 1.1 million Rwandan refugees to Zaire in the summer of 1994 during and after the genocide in their country. Without the military airlift capacity and emergency assistance, my Office could not have coped with the disastrous situation in Goma when thousands of people died. However, the military assistance quickly pulled out, amidst speculation about the possible revival of armed conflict between the ousted Hutu and new Tutsi leadership. There was no intention among major powers to use their military or to engage in intensive efforts to solve the complex political and ethnic problems in the region.

Very quickly, security in the refugee camps in Zaire and Tanzania worsened. Under control of the ex-political leadership, former Rwandan army and militias, refugee repatriation was often violently obstructed. In close consultation with my Office, the UN Secretary-General proposed various options to the Security Council to mobilize security support to halt this situation. The response was negative and nothing happened. As a minimum stop-gap measure, my Office then created a security contingent with the Zairean government, recruiting both Zairean soldiers and a small number of foreign security personnel. Their task was to ensure a minimum of law and order in the camps in Zaire, which they did. Humanitarian agencies were left alone, then criticized for protecting and feeding those who had committed genocide. Our dilemmas have been agonizing, but as the large majority in the camps were innocent and needy civilians, did we have another choice?

The failure of Zaire and of the international community to separate military elements from the refugees has contributed to the spreading of insecurity and conflict. The Rwandan militias in exile compounded inter-ethnic tension in eastern Zaire, whereas cross-border incursions in both directions aggravated tension between Rwanda and Zaire. Two essentially domestic conflicts became overlapped and internationalized, leading eventually to the war in Zaire.

I will not go into detail about the attempt in late '96 to build a humanitarian coalition force for eastern Zaire. Authorized under Chapter VII, the force was to assist in the repatriation of refugees and the protection of relief operations.

However, the participating states clearly did not intend to separate the military elements from the refugees. While the MNF was wavering how far it would step into the conflict, the turn-around of 500,000 Rwandan refugees triggered by the attacking rebel forces quickly reduced the interest of most contributing nations in military intervention. In December my Office was even accused of exaggerating the remaining refugee population chased and dispersed in the Zairean bush. It seemed rather clear who favoured deployment of the Force and who did not. Each country had its own, not necessarily humanitarian objective. As in the case of Bosnia, effective humanitarian action suffered from the absence of a convergence of views and interests among the major powers. Having fled in chaos from one place to another, the number of identified refugees has now dwindled sharply. Many are dying from exhaustion and hunger. While we have finally obtained access to them to provide emergency care and to help them repatriate to Rwanda, humanitarian staff continue to face enormous security risks and logistical constraints. Peaceful settlement in Zaire is far from certain, and reconciliation between Hutus and Tutsis in Rwanda is a long way from being realized. We must recognize that the problems are eminently political rather than humanitarian. [. . .]

Questions

1   How can a social movement be global rather than national? Identify some of the factors that have made it easier since World War II for movements to coordinate their activities and pursue common goals in many countries simultaneously.

2   What international nongovernmental organizations (INGOs) can you name? Do they receive much attention in the media? Why are you more likely to hear about an organization like the Red Cross than the International Council for Science or the World Federation of Advertisers?

3   The United Nations and its agencies have given consultative status to thousands of INGOs. Would you expect INGOs always to support UN projects and programs? How might INGOs be critical of what UN agencies do?

4   In Diamond's view, further democratization of the governments of the world, though promising, is not inevitable. What signs do you see that democracy may be in trouble in various places around the world? Could democracy be threatened in the developed countries as well?

5   For Berkovitch, the women's movement has become more complex and conflictual as Third World women have become more active participants in the movement. Does this mean that the status and role of women are becoming less globalized issues? Does globalization imply consensus, or is it more likely to lead to disagreement and controversy?

6   In the Boli and Thomas selection, five principles that undergird most INGOs are identified. Explain these principles. Then identify at least two types of INGOs that are not likely to embrace these principles as fully as most INGOs do.

7   Describe the strengths and weakness of the UN in global governance, drawing on the Roberts and Kingsbury analysis and the specific issues raised by Ogata about UN efforts to aid refugees.

Part VII

Cultural Globalization I: The Role of Media

Introduction

Cultural globalization is probably the most familiar form for most people. Everyone knows that prominent icons of popular culture, like Coca-Cola, blue jeans, rock music, and McDonald's Golden Arches, can be found "everywhere." We are also all aware of the seeming sameness engendered by the diffusion of such cultural objects and genres. Add to the list Hollywood movies, French philosophizing, and Japanese organizational techniques that have been widely adopted by American and European companies, and it is easy to believe that cultural globalization inevitably acts as a universal solvent that will dissolve all cultural differences in a dull and colorless homogeneity throughout the world.

Call it "Americanization," call it "westernization," call it cultural imperialism (and many have, both within and outside the West) – the driving forces behind this homogenization, critics claim, are the mass media. Controlled mainly by American and European companies, spreading their ethereal tentacles through the airwaves to the farthest reaches of the globe, the media impose their powerful images, sounds, and advertising on unprepared peoples who succumb meekly to their messages, which are designed to increase the profits of capitalist firms. Such is the kernel of one side of the debate on the role of the media in world society. But contrary voices can also be heard, and changes in the structure of the global news, television, radio, music, and film industries have changed much of the received wisdom about cultural imperialism.

The cultural imperialism debate picked up speed soon after decolonization had begun to produce dozens of new states in Africa, Asia, and the Pacific. Though colonialism was dead or dying, in its place scholars identified a new form of capitalist subjugation of the Third World (the latter term itself comes from the 1960s), more economic than political, more ideologically than militarily supported: neo-colonialism. As the argument goes, because direct politico-military control could no longer be practiced, neo-colonialist powers turned to symbolic and psychological means of control, conveniently facilitated by the rapid integration of global telecommunications systems and the proliferation, especially, of television. Pushing mainly American culture that promoted ideologies of consumption, instant gratification, self-absorption, and the like, the expanded mass media fit neatly with the further extension of global capitalism in its struggle with the Communist-dominated "Second World" led by the Soviet Union.

One prominent outcome of the cultural imperialism thesis was the strident call for a "New World Information Order [NWIO]." Less developed countries pleaded their case against the domination of western media in UNESCO and other UN forums, arguing that restrictions should be placed on western cultural propagation and that aid should flow to the former colonies to improve their nascent communications systems. A related issue was the purportedly biased view of the world presented by the major global news organizations, Associated Press (AP) and United Press International (UPI) from the USA, Agence France-Presse (AFP), and British-owned Reuters, which together accounted for the vast majority of stories entering the newsrooms of the world's major newspapers and television stations. The NWIO debate led to few concrete actions, in part because the less developed countries lost interest as many new states took direct control of the broadcast media in their countries and turned radio, television, and major newspapers into mouthpieces of official government policy.

While the press wire services (AP, UPI, AFP, Reuters), all with their roots in the nineteenth century, represent a long-standing form of news globalization, it was only in the 1970s and 1980s that electronic media globalization assumed serious proportions. Mergers and acquisitions by aggressive media companies like Rupert Murdoch's News Corporation yielded massive conglomerates with truly global reach. Ted Turner's upstart Cable News Network (CNN) survived the struggles of its early days to become a ubiquitous, 24-hour news provider watched almost religiously by global business and political elites. At the same time, however, a steady process of decentralization of global media industries was underway, as major countries in different world regions became regional production centers: Mexico for Spanish-language television, India for film, Hong Kong for East Asian film and television, and so on. Alongside this development has been the "indigenization" of many television formats and genres that originated in the West. The once hugely popular "Dallas" has given way to local equivalents with local twists – Brazilian soaps, Mexican telenovellas, and so on. The net result is an undeniable global increase in the degree to which people's everyday lives are experienced through the media, but the homogenizing effects of media globalization are much less clear than was once supposed.

The first of our selections in this part, by Sean MacBride and Colleen Roach, presents the cultural imperialism thesis and an argument in favor of global governance structures to reduce western media domination. MacBride chaired the UNESCO International Commission for the Study of Communications Problems, appointed in 1976 to investigate global communications and information. He became a western spokesman for the mostly Third World countries that were demanding changes in global media industries. The Commission's MacBride Report of 1980 led UNESCO to call for a restructuring of global media along more egalitarian lines. The report also, however, was critical of restrictions on freedom of the press and broadcast media in many of the very countries that were demanding an end to cultural imperialism.

Lewis Friedland's article investigates how the world information order has actually developed by tracing the growth and increased prominence of CNN. Friedland gives us a close look at crucial events that boosted CNN's reputation and reach: the Tiananmen Square massacre of human rights activists in China in 1989 and the Gulf War against Iraq in 1990–1. He then reviews the expansion of CNN to become a truly ubiquitous news source, the first fully global integrated network.

The next two selections challenge the cultural imperialism thesis. Referring to the growing variety of media content and the emergence of new regional centers for media production, John Sinclair, Elizabeth Jacka, and Stuart Cunningham question whether the "peripheral visions" of the media in the less developed countries are rightly described as the product of imperial western design. As regional centers gain market share in exports to their regions, the authors are also led to question whether US media dominance has ever been as great as the cultural imperialism thesis supposed. The excerpt from John Tomlinson's book on the issue, which provides a thorough analysis and critique of the cultural imperialism argument, leads to considerable doubt about the degree to which US television shows and pharmaceutical advertising in the Third World actually carry US values and improve the profits of US companies. Cultural homogenization is growing in some respects, Tomlinson suggests, but local transformations and interpretations of imported media products imply that cultural diversification is hardly at an end in global society.

40 The New International Information Order

Sean MacBride and Colleen Roach

Resolutions, meetings, and manifestos calling for a "new order" in international information structures and policies became a feature of the world scene in the early 1970s and often generated intense dispute. The original impulse came from the non-aligned nations, many of which had gained independence in the postwar years. To many the euphoria of independence was turning to a sense of disillusionment. In spite of international assistance programs, the economic situation in many developing countries had not improved, and in some it had actually deteriorated. For certain countries foreign trade earnings could not cover interest due on foreign loans. These same years witnessed the rapid development of new communications media, and the era was constantly characterized as the Information Age – one in which information would be a key to power and affluence. To the developing countries it was increasingly clear that the "flow of information" (a term that seemed to subsume ideas and attitudes and followed a one-way direction from rich to poor countries) was dominated by multinational entities based in the most powerful nations. The resulting disparities tended to set the framework for discussion even within developing countries. Clearly political independence was not matched by independence in the economic and sociocultural spheres. A number of nonaligned countries saw themselves as victims of "cultural colonialism." The imbalances it involved, and what might be done about them, became the focus of debate for the nonaligned countries.

Evolution of the Debate

The nonaligned nations movement took form in 1955 at a meeting in Bandung, Indonesia, that brought together world leaders from Asia and Africa. Subsequent meetings – in some cases, summit meetings of nonaligned leaders – were held in Bangkok, Algiers, Tunis, Havana, and elsewhere. During the 1970s the membership grew to more than 90 countries plus several regional groups and represented a majority in various United Nations bodies, with strong influence over their agendas. These UN agencies embraced a "development ideology," meaning that high priority would be given to the development needs of the Third World.

A nonaligned summit held in Algiers in 1973 adopted a resolution calling for a "new international economic order," which was endorsed the following year by the UN General Assembly. This served as precedent and model for a similar resolution

Original publication details: MacBride, Sean and Colleen Roach, "The New International Information Order" from *International Encyclopedia of Communications*, 4 volumes, edited by Erik Barnouw. Copyright © 1989 by Trustees of the University of Pennsylvania. Used by permission of Oxford University Press, Inc.

focusing on information, which was articulated at a 1976 nonaligned news symposium in Tunis. A leading figure at this meeting was Mustapha Masmoudi, Tunisian secretary of state for information, who demanded a "reorganization of existing communication channels that are a legacy of the colonial past." This "decolonization" of information, he said, must lead to a "new order in information matters." In subsequent meetings this phrase evolved into a *new international information order* and, at a later stage, into a *new world information and communication order*.

That same year UNESCO's General Conference in Nairobi also discussed information issues, in a context that produced sharp confrontation between the interests of developed and developing countries. The focus was on the free-flow-of-information doctrine. UNESCO's mandate in the area of communications is explicit in its constitution, adopted in 1946, which enjoined the agency to "collaborate in the work of advancing the mutual knowledge and understanding of peoples, through all means of mass communication and to that end recommend the free flow of ideas by word and image." The free-flow doctrine was developed by the United States and other Western nations after World War II. As viewed by supporters, the unhampered flow of information would be a means of promoting peace and understanding and spreading technical advances. The doctrine had ties with other Western libertarian principles such as freedom of the press. However, critics of the doctrine came to view it as part of a global strategy for domination of communication markets and for ideological control by the industrialized nations. They saw it as serving the interests of the most powerful countries and transnational corporations and helping them secure economic and cultural domination of less powerful nations. A rewording of the doctrine was urged by nonaligned spokespersons calling for a free *and balanced* flow of information. The suggestion stirred deep suspicion in developed countries. If it meant that Third World nations would ordain a proper balance, and control or limit the flow, this would be – according to Western spokespersons – the very antithesis of a free flow. "Free and balanced flow" and "free flow" seemed at this meeting to be irreconcilable concepts.

An important outcome of this 1976 UNESCO meeting was the appointment by Amadou-Mahtar M'Bow, Director-General of UNESCO, of a 16-person commission – broadly representative of the world's economic and geographic spectrum and headed by Sean MacBride of Ireland – to study "the totality of communication problems in modern societies." Its members held different opinions about what sort of new order was needed, but all were in agreement that the existing information order was far from satisfactory. They began their work late in 1977 and, after two years of fact-gathering, committee hearings, and debate, submitted their final report – known as the MacBride Report – to the 1980 UNESCO General Conference in Belgrade. Published in English as *Many Voices, One World*, it has been translated into many languages. Along with a resolution adopted at the same conference confirming UNESCO's support for a *new information and communication order* (see table 40.1), the report became the focus of debate during the following years – a rallying point as well as a target for attack.

Themes

The debate had at first centered on the news-flow question. The major Western international news services – AP and UPI of the United States, the French Agence France-

Table 40.1　Resolution 4/19 adopted by the Twenty-first Session of the UNESCO General Conference, Belgrade, 1980

The General Conference considers that
(a)　this new world information and communication order could be based, among other considerations, on:
  (i)　elimination of the imbalances and inequalities which characterize the present situation;
  (ii)　elimination of the negative effects of certain monopolies, public or private, and excessive concentrations;
  (iii)　removal of the internal and external obstacles to a free flow and wider and better balanced dissemination of information and ideas;
  (iv)　plurality of sources and channels of information;
  (v)　freedom of the press and of information;
  (vi)　the freedom of journalists and all professionals in the communication media, a freedom inseparable from responsibility;
  (vii)　the capacity of developing countries to achieve improvement of their own situations, notably by providing their own equipment, by training their personnel, by improving their infrastructures and making their information and communication media suitable to their needs and aspirations;
  (viii)　the sincere will of developed countries to help them attain these objectives;
  (ix)　respect for each people's cultural identity and for the right of each nation to inform the world about its interests, its aspirations and its social and cultural values;
  (x)　respect for the right of all peoples to participate in international exchanges of information on the basis of equality, justice and mutual benefit;
  (xi)　respect for the right of the public, of ethnic and social groups and of individuals to have access to information sources and to participate actively in the communication process;
(b)　this new world information and communication order should be based on the fundamental principles of international law, as laid down in the Charter of the United Nations;
(c)　diverse solutions to information and communication problems are required because social, political, cultural and economic problems differ from one country to another and, within a given country, from one group to another.

Presse, and Reuters of the United Kingdom – were consistently described as having *monopoly* control over the flow of news to and from developing countries, and exercising it from a limited perspective reflecting the economic and cultural interests of the industrialized nations. Expressions such as "coups and earthquakes" were frequently used to describe reporting of Third World events. In 1976 Indira Gandhi, the prime minister of India, expressed the prevailing view: "We want to hear Africans on events in Africa. You should similarly be able to get an Indian explanation of events in India. It is astonishing that we know so little about leading poets, novelists, historians, and editors of various Asian, African, and Latin American countries while we are familiar with minor authors and columnists of Europe and

America." The need for policies and structures to develop communications between developing nations (sometimes referred to as "South–South dialogue") was constantly stressed.

The flow of television programming, including *entertainment* programming, was soon incorporated into the debate, in large measure owing to a study conducted by two Finnish researchers, Kaarle Nordenstreng and Tapio Varis, and published by UNESCO in 1974. The study demonstrated that a few Western nations controlled the international flow of television programs, with the United States, the United Kingdom, France, and the Federal Republic of Germany accounting for the largest shares. The implications of this domination, in both financial and ideological terms, received increasing attention.

The integration of television with new technologies such as the communications *satellite* – including direct broadcast satellites – and telecommunications networks that were channels for an increasing volume of transborder data flow difficult or impossible to control, extended the range of topics covered in the debate. Here the questions also included imbalances in the assignment of spectrum frequencies and of orbital slots for future satellites.

The international flow of *advertising*, under similar multinational controls, was another issue that entered the debate. It was described by many as furthering not only products and services but also a way of life, generally centered on the acquisition of consumer goods. Some saw this as diverting attention from necessities to luxuries, and others saw it as a serious threat to indigenous culture.

In 1978 a new element was added to the debates with the passage of a UNESCO Declaration on the Mass Media. It was the result of six years of negotiation to achieve a consensus text, which finally carried the title *The Declaration of Fundamental Principles concerning the Contribution of the Mass Media to Strengthening Peace and International Understanding, to the Promotion of Human Rights and to Countering Racialism, Apartheid and Incitement to War.* Regarded by the nonaligned nations as furthering the *new order* movement, it was the first international instrument referring directly to moral, social, and professional responsibilities of mass media in the context of "the universally recognized principles of freedom of expression, information, and opinion." Hovering over the debate once again was the issue of the role of government. The final version of the resolution did not include – because of Western demands – proposals to make national governments responsible for the actions of communications companies working within their jurisdictions.

Collision Course

In the early 1980s the nature of the debate underwent decisive changes. Nonaligned nations were no longer as unified as they had been; amid a widespread economic recession some leaned toward a more militant, others toward a more conciliatory, stance. Differences in political systems came more sharply into focus. In the developed nations a trend toward *deregulation* of information media and privatization of public-sector enterprises was gaining momentum. The industrialized nations were increasingly attentive to information markets, including those in the Third World. Because the continued growth of the private sector seemed vital to this strategy, "government-controlled media" were viewed as particularly ominous.

The importance of this issue was evident at a 1981 UNESCO-sponsored meeting on the protection of journalists. For two decades attempts had been made by international organizations of journalists and publishers – such as the International Federation of Journalists, the International Federation of Newspaper Editors, and the International Press Institute – to draft and have adopted an international convention for the protection of journalists. At the UNESCO meeting the concerns of the journalists' organizations were quickly obscured by the recurring issue of the role of governments, this time revolving around licensing. Most governments were prepared to recognize the importance of safeguarding journalists, even though few seemed to cherish the activities of "investigative reporters." The status of journalists and the special protections proposed for them would presumably be based on professional credentials – but issued by whom? In raising this issue, Third World leaders were accused of wishing to license journalists, an idea that was anathema to Western nations.

Nonetheless, attempts were made during the early 1980s to steer the *new order* debates away from such divisive issues. This was especially evident in the creation of a new organization based on an earlier initiative of the United States: the International Program for the Development of Communication (IPDC). The IPDC was designed to be a key instrument for organizing international technical cooperation, helping in the creation and implementation of operational projects, and mobilizing the resources needed for those purposes. Although officially launched in 1980, its first meeting was not held until June 1981. It soon became apparent, however, that contributions from donor countries were much more limited than had been expected. The IPDC was faced with the same dilemma confronting a number of international development agencies: a necessary curtailment of expectations and plans.

The 1982 and 1983 UNESCO General Conferences, held in Paris, did not witness the heated polemics of similar meetings held in 1978 and 1980. At the 1983 conference the call for a new information and communication order was formally designated as "an evolving and continuous process" – a concession to Western interests intent on ensuring that the new order should not be viewed as requiring a sudden and radical transformation of existing communication structures.

A 1983 United Nations–UNESCO Round Table on a New World Information and Communication Order held in Igls, Austria, was another promising sign of dialogue. At the first official United Nations–UNESCO meeting on the issue, the Austrian round table was noteworthy for the absence of political rhetoric and the determination of participants to establish specific mechanisms for assisting the developing countries. Communications technology, rather than news flow alone, was now the primary concern of developing countries.

The year 1983 was to end with two paradoxical but not unrelated events. In early December the nonaligned nations movement held in New Delhi its first Media Conference. It opened with a call to intensify efforts to promote the proposed new order. Weeks later, as December came to a close, Secretary of State George P. Schultz of the United States sent a letter to the director-general of UNESCO informing him that, after the required one-year notification period, in December 1984 the United States would withdraw from UNESCO. An indirect reference to the *new order* campaign was evident in a passage referring to the necessity of maintaining "such goals as individual human rights and the free flow of information." The US decision to withdraw from UNESCO surprised observers who had taken note of the apparent absence of conflict in 1982 and 1983. However, it was clear that throughout the early 1980s there was significant bipartisan congressional opposition to UNESCO, not only because of its efforts to promote a new information order but also because of disputes relating to Israel, UNESCO's examination of the issues of peace and disarmament, and a new generation of "people's rights," as well as various financial and organizational reasons. This opposition was widely backed by the US press and other groups.

Challenges

Two decades of debates and resolutions had done little to solve underlying problems of the international flow of information, although they had made the world community more aware of the issues involved. Those issues would be a continuing presence, posing a diversity of challenges, many of which had been spelled out in the MacBride Commission's report. A notable aspect of the report was that it went beyond immediate needs and brought to the fore the overall significance of communications in modern society and the implications of media policies for the world's future.

Meanings of technology

The commission noted that technological needs had been a central concern at many meetings but urged that they not be allowed to overshadow the social, political, and economic implications. The importance of the new communications technologies was seen to lie to a large extent in the fundamental transformations they impose on society. Governments and private companies alike have long been inclined to think of technology as a means available to serve their particular needs without consideration of the impact on humanity at large. Use of technical developments cannot and should not be slowed, in the view of the commission, but their implications should be constantly assessed. Technology "is seldom neutral – its use is even less so" – for use is influenced by political, financial, and other considerations. Therefore, decisions about communications policies and priorities should not be made solely by technocrats but should involve wide public participation and discussion. "We must beware of the temptation to regard technology as an all-purpose tool capable of superseding social action." The commission noticed a widespread feeling that "technological progress is running ahead of man's capacity to interpret its implications and direct it into the most desirable channels," and cited the fear expressed by Albert Schweitzer that humankind has "lost the capacity to foresee and forestall the consequences" of its actions.

Ways of freedom

The commission noted the perilous status of freedom of expression around the world. The fact "that there is said to be freedom of expression in a country does not guarantee its existence in practice." The commission further noted that "even where freedom is not openly attacked by authority, it may be limited by self-censorship on the part of communicators themselves. Journalists may fail to publish facts which have come into their possession for several reasons: sheer timidity, an excessive respect for the power structure or in some instances lest they give offence to officialdom and thus risk losing access to their sources of information." Self-censorship, like censorship itself, was seen by the commission as a constantly distorting factor in the flow of communication.

The commission emphasized its view that the exercise of freedom in the communications field involves responsibilities. "We need to ask, moreover, on what grounds a claim for freedom is being made. The freedom of a citizen or social group to have access to communication, both as recipients and contributors, cannot be compared to the freedom of an investor to derive profits from the media. One protects a fundamental human right, the other permits the commercialization of a social need."

The report observed that because of the overwhelming importance of communication today, the state imposes some degree of regulation in virtually all societies. It can intervene in many diverse ways – through the allocation of broadcast licenses and newsprint and through visa policies, import restriction, and many other procedures. "Some governments find it natural to assume total control over the content of information, justifying themselves by the ideology in which they believe. Even on purely pragmatic standards, it is doubtful if this system can be called realistic."

Democratization of communication

Surveying the "spectrum of communication in modern society," the commission found that it almost defies description because of its immense variety. Barriers could readily be seen: monopolistic controls, technical disparities, restrictive media practices, exclusion of disadvantaged groups, blacklist, censorship. Nevertheless, a tendency toward democratization seemed to be taking place – for example, in the growing role of public opinion. Governments throughout the world were becoming increasingly aware that they must take into account not only national opinion but "world public opinion," because today's media are capable of diffusing "information on international questions to every part of the world." Occasionally opinion crystallizes on some issue with enough force to compel action. This happened, as the commission saw it, on the issues of colonialism, apartheid, and nuclear proliferation. But a meaningful process of opinion formation will in the long run require richer media fare, development of widespread "critical awareness," assertion of the "right to reply," the establishment of "alternative channels of communication," and public participation in decision making on media policies. The goal, the commission felt, should be that everyone would be both "producer and consumer of communication." [. . .]

41 Covering the World

Lewis A. Friedland

It was not until the late 1980s and early 1990s that CNN gained international prominence during a series of crises, including the Tiananmen Square Massacre in China and the Persian Gulf War. CNN pushed the boundaries of world news: No longer did the network merely report events, but through its immediate reportage, CNN actually shaped the events and became part of them. This power not only attracted new viewers to CNN, it also forced American networks to revise their approach to the news. In essence, coverage of the events demonstrated how an international network could function, and stimulated the British Broadcasting Corporation (BBC), Nippon Hoso Kyokai (NHK), and others to consider starting their own international television networks. And it became a laboratory for new uses of news technology.

To better understand just what a sea change this was, let us first look at the coverage of the two incidents.

Tiananmen Square Massacre

By the time of the prodemocracy movement in China in 1989, world television had come of age. Every major country in Europe, Asia, and Africa received CNN, including China and the former Soviet Union. And the world's heads of state and foreign offices had begun using CNN as a medium of diplomatic exchange.

The Beijing Spring – which came to be known as the Tiananmen Square Massacre – was a turning point in the development of the world news system. The most important news story to be covered by international satellite television to that date, it was the first story in which the world television news system directly affected events themselves, while they were occurring, at three specific levels: within national boundaries, throughout the world diplomatic system, and on the stage of international public opinion. It was also a testing ground for comparing CNN's handling of the story with that of its major American network competitors. Finally, coverage of China in 1989 shaped the world news system for years to come: "It was after Tiananmen Square that we really redefined how we do television," according to Susan Zirinsky, a senior producer at CBS. "Berlin Wall falling live on television; bombs over Baghdad, live; scud missiles in Israel, live, live . . . it is a new universe."

The death of proreform Politburo member Hu Yaobang on April 15, 1989, set off the democracy movement on Chinese campuses around Beijing. In a round of unprecedented bargaining between leaders of the Chinese government, headed by Premier Deng Xiaoping, and student groups, the students raised demands for "democratic reform." This process reached a crisis point with the visit of Soviet

Original publication details: Friedland, Lewis A., excerpt from *Covering the World*, Twentieth Century Fund, 1992.

president Mikhail Gorbachev on May 15. The international media converging on Beijing for the visit focused a spotlight on the students' demands, which in turn escalated the crisis for the Chinese government, as the occupation of Tiananmen Square continued through Gorbachev's visit. Live satellite transmissions were cut off on May 19, with Gorbachev's departure. The confrontation between the government and students deepened, culminating in the events of June 3–4, the Tiananmen Square Massacre.

The students skillfully used the Western media in several ways. First, they adopted American symbols including "The Goddess of Democracy"; they carried signs with quotations from Abraham Lincoln and Patrick Henry, all in English for the benefit of the Western audience. Although the students were portrayed by American television as having a somewhat naive understanding of these symbols, in fact the student leadership was quite sophisticated. The Beijing students were the future elite of China. Many had been abroad and understood American media. They knew that keeping the cameras on them would be a powerful tool in their struggle, and they also understood that appealing to Americans' traditional belief in the United States as a beacon of democracy would further this goal. In fact, the Big Three (ABC, CBS and NBC) all adopted a "prodemocracy" frame for the student movement, despite evidence that the movement's definitions of democracy were extremely broad, and that its stated and actual goals were reform of the Communist system. CNN was a partial exception, using more specific descriptions than its network counterparts. However, according to a study by Harvard's Joan Shorenstein Barone Center, "Turmoil at Tiananmen," ABC, CBS, and CNN all portrayed the story in confrontational terms as a direct student challenge to the Chinese leadership.

The reporting in Beijing also offers a comparison of the various methods of coverage. Typically, the major networks claim to provide depth and perspective that CNN does not, through more experienced anchors, reporters, and producers. CNN counterclaims that the luxury of time allows it to offer fuller treatment of issues. China offers a contrast. Only CNN ran excerpts from official government speeches, press conferences, and CCTV. This coverage reflected CNN's wire-service-like commitment to bring viewers all significant statements from all sides, regardless of whether there were "good pictures." CNN's feature pieces, on the other hand, included descriptions of biking in Beijing and a montage of natural street sounds intercutting traditional dragon dancing and dragon images. In contrast, at the beginning of Gorbachev's visit on May 15, CBS's Bruce Morton filed a background piece in which he effectively portrayed the poverty of student lives as one major element in their political frustration. For CNN, perspective resided in the breadth of its coverage, and the commitment that all significant stories and points of view would be aired. For CBS, perspective came from the background it provided.

The China story also marked the first time a major breaking story was covered twenty-four hours a day for a worldwide television audience. This meant, in essence, that traditional deadlines were telescoped. Until China, the traditional print wire services had the relative luxury of holding a story until it could be checked out to editors' satisfaction. With the presence of CNN, the wire services had live competition. Because government-run news agencies are widely understood by the Chinese people to be political conduits, news in the streets travels by rumor. Rumor is easily manipulated by political factions, and the students understood that, as significant sources for reporters, they could sometimes get unconfirmed stories aired that would reflect very unfavorably on the government. Before the night of June 3, waves of rumors swept Beijing concerning impending troop movements on Tiananmen Square, and the fall of either Zhao Ziyang or Deng Xiaoping. When CNN was forced to decide whether to report these rumors or not, it chose to do so. CNN International editor Eason Jordan said: "We know we're on the air twenty-four hours a day. But we don't put information on the air that might be construed as irresponsible. . . . [CNN correspondent Mike] Chinoy was reporting information from sources, some of which some people might say was rumor. When rumor is that big a part of the story, you just have to say so. But we never billed rumor as fact."

What CNN reported became more significant because it was a primary source for other news organizations. Editors at the *Washington Post* and Associated Press used CNN as a video wire throughout the crisis. Some reporters, especially from the wire services, complained that their editors would see reports on CNN and then send them out to check on stories that the reporters in the field thought were unlikely. Others, like UPI's David Schweisberg, said that CNN was "more right than wrong." CNN's Vito Maggioli, then a producer in China, explained the problem this way: "There is this twenty-four-hour machine. . . . You have to constantly be thinking about what do we have here, what are we going to do with it, can we wait, should we wait?"

CNN's coverage often set the news agenda for other news organizations. Any reported rumors had to be checked out, and sometimes those rumors gained political and diplomatic force that reverberated long after they were disproved. On June 5, for instance, immediately after the massacre, a "US intelligence" estimate of the death toll was widely reported as 3,000; the background source was Secretary of State James Baker. Four US government sources anonymously told the writers of the Harvard study that the 3,000 figure was an extrapolation of the 2,600 figure released by the Chinese Red Cross and reported by CNN and ABC. The figures were later revised downward to between 400 and 800.

The coverage had a clear effect both within and outside of China. For the Chinese people themselves, radio was much more important than television. Both the Voice of America (VOA) and BBC World Service were readily available, and VOA broadcasts were regularly translated into posters and placed on walls. Although CNN had achieved the most significant television presence in Beijing, it was mostly accessible in hotels with an overwhelmingly foreign audience. However, according to Mark Hopkins, VOA's Beijing bureau chief, hundreds of young English-speaking Chinese staff did watch CNN in the hotels. There is anecdotal evidence that word of CNN's telecasts also got out into the streets. According to CNN's Alec Miran, who was executive producer in China at the time, "People were coming up to us in the street, telling us to 'Keep going, keep broadcasting, that they won't come in while you're on the air.' That turned out to be true. The troops went in after our cameras were shut down."

New technology was thrown into the breach during the China story, and old technology was used in new and innovative ways. While satellite news gathering was not new, CNN pioneered the use of "fly-away packs," portable satellite news-gathering gear that could be packed in a number of crates and set up at virtually any site. CNN also used cellular telephones to feed voice reports, "phoners," from Tiananmen Square to Atlanta. CNN had ordered the cellular connections before the crackdown, and they were left in place. (CNN remembered its use of telephone lines in Beijing when planning for Baghdad; perhaps the Big Three did not.) On June 12, after the crackdown, CNN also flew in "handicams," miniature 8 mm video cameras, after it was no longer safe to use regular-sized field gear. Handicams were used surreptitiously by CNN crews riding bicycles around Beijing to get footage.

This was not a case of a new technology being available to CNN. Rather, perhaps because of its unorthodox operating methods, CNN was willing to use the smaller cameras – often scorned as "toys" – on a breaking story.

The Chinese government clearly grasped the link between satellite transmission and its world standing. Both CBS and CNN had obtained permission to operate their satellite uplinks only during the week of Gorbachev's visit. CNN brought in its own portable satellite fly-away dish; both CBS and CNN transmitted their pictures from Tiananmen Square via cable to CCTV, and from there back to their hotels. Two separate, dramatic confrontations occurred, the first between Dan Rather and CCTV officials, the second between CNN's Alec Miran and government officials. The shutdown of live transmissions visually personified government repression for American and world audiences. Shortly after the satellite shutdowns, the US government issued a formal protest – via CNN – about what President Bush had just witnessed in China while watching CNN from his summer home in Kennebunkport, Maine.

The traditional relation between US public opinion and diplomacy was inverted during the Tiananmen Square Massacre. While the crisis unfolded on television, US policymakers were forced to take what the nation's people were seeing into account *while* creating policy. The tension of the crisis was heightened, shortening the time for acceptable diplomatic response. When American viewers could see troops moving into Tiananmen Square, it became impossible for the Bush administration to avoid a public condemnation of the Chinese government, however much it may have wished to do so, and despite its conviction that quiet diplomacy would have been more effective. According to *Time*, State Department spokesperson Margaret Tutweiler dragged Secretary of State Baker to watch CNN's coverage of the Tiananmen crackdown. Moreover, *Time* quotes a "senior official" on CNN's coverage: "It demanded a solution we couldn't provide. We were powerless to make it stop."

Indeed, CNN became the primary source of information for much of the US government. According to one Capitol Hill staff member, "The [New York] Times and the evening newscasts were a day late . . . [and] there was not much time to read or watch media. It was CNN that determined the base of events, throughout the beltway. The images of that night were the primary stimulus for the feeding frenzy that took place here in Congress immediately afterward."

CNN's presence in Beijing intensified the interaction between the American public and the American government; that call and response would likely have been there had only CBS been present. But CNN was viewed worldwide, at least by elite audiences. The Chinese government knew precisely what US leaders were seeing and the kind of pressure it would place on them. Likewise, US officials knew that the same events were being seen in London, Paris, Tokyo, and Moscow, and this also pressured them to act on a newly emerging stage of world diplomatic opinion. The events in China did not attain the full wiring of the diplomatic circuit that would occur during the Persian Gulf War, but they did forcefully demonstrate that world events could no longer be restricted to exchanges among one or several nations at a pace dictated solely by the leadership of the superpowers.

The War in the Persian Gulf

If the China crisis established CNN and world television as a legitimate force, the Gulf War placed CNN in the forefront of the broadcast world and increased the pressure on other players to enter the global news competition.

The Gulf War demonstrated the strengths of international television as a medium of diplomacy and as a witness to events. At the same time, it demonstrated how world television could be bent to follow lines favorable to the dominant Western nations that were the base of that system.

CNN's function as a diplomatic news wire was well established by the time of Iraqi president Saddam Hussein's invasion of Kuwait in August 1990. Speaking at a Stanford University symposium on global communication in 1990, George Shultz, former secretary of state, described how the officer at the State Department operations desk always had a television tuned to CNN. While this did not seem unusual, Shultz said he was surprised that when he visited the foreign ministries of other nations, their operations officers were also watching CNN. During the events leading up to the war, CNN operated as a diplomatic seismograph. Immediately after the August 1990 invasion of Kuwait, President Bush publicly referred to CNN on several occasions. Tariq Aziz, Iraqi foreign minister, made reference to President Bush's news conferences televised on CNN; during subsequent formal diplomatic exchanges, Kuwait's foreign minister referred to comments that reflected Aziz's prior CNN comments. The use of CNN as a diplomatic party line became almost comical at times. During the Gulf buildup, President Turgut Ozal of Turkey was watching a CNN telecast of a news conference given by President Bush. He heard a reporter ask Bush whether Ozal would cut off Turkey's oil pipeline into Iraq. Bush said he was about to ask Ozal the same question. When Ozal's telephone rang, he told Bush he was expecting the call. As Richard Haass, National Security Council aide to President Bush, told *Time*: "You end up hearing statements for the first time, not in diplomatic notes, but because you see a foreign minister on the screen. By television, I really mean CNN. It has turned out to be a very important information source."

As the crisis moved closer to war, CNN became an unofficial line of communication within the US government. President Bush reportedly told other world leaders, "I learn more from CNN than I do from the CIA." After the start of the air war, Secretary of Defense Richard Cheney said at a press conference, "The best reporting I saw on what transpired in Baghdad was on CNN." In *The Commanders*, Bob Woodward recounts the regular monitoring of CNN in the period leading up to the war. After the air war was launched, in secret, Cheney went back to his office and turned on CNN. "He thought the first leak or hint that the air operation was underway would most likely come from the twenty-four-hour news service." When CIA Director William Webster received word that an Iraqi missile had been launched, he reportedly told National Security Council Adviser Brent Scowcroft "turn on CNN to see where it lands." Indeed, in place of the standard "no comment," State Department, Pentagon, and military spokespersons would regularly respond to questions with "I don't know anymore than what you saw on CNN."

This was, of course, not true. There was information available to government officials of which the public was never informed, and the standard CNN disclaimer served as a convenient excuse for nondisclosure, a part of the government's propaganda war. What was remarkable, however, was the extent to which government officials *did* appear to rely on CNN as their primary source of breaking news.

During the Gulf crisis, both sides saw CNN as part of an international battleground for public opinion. Beyond its role in diplomacy, CNN was the staging ground for massive public opinion campaigns. President Saddam Hussein of Iraq used CNN several times. Shortly after the invasion of Kuwait, he seized a group of predominantly American and British hostages and moved them to military installations as "human shields." As Western public opinion turned against Saddam Hussein, he went on Iraqi television to "visit" with the British hostages. The meeting was carried around the world by CNN. Clearly Saddam Hussein believed his "visit" was an effective propaganda move; CNN was widely condemned for airing the meeting. Nevertheless, the staged quality of the meeting, and its international distribution, only served to discredit Saddam as a clumsy propagandist. At the end of January, after the start of the air war, Hussein again appealed to international public opinion in an exclusive interview with CNN's Peter Arnett, the only Western correspondent then operating out of Baghdad. Hussein threatened to use chemical warheads and expressed regret at letting his hostages go. Arnett sent out the interview via a flyaway satellite uplink, with the single comment: "Chilling."

Arnett's reporting from Baghdad was attacked by the Bush administration and its supporters as "Iraqi propaganda." However, the US military also used CNN to its advantage in the public opinion war. The daily US military briefings, televised in full as they occurred on CNN, were staged news events. American military public affairs officers and briefers skillfully used the briefings to convey sanitary images of the war to the American people – for example, the smart bomb videos – and sometimes to send messages to the Iraqis. When transports of the 82nd Airborne Division arrived in Saudi Arabia in August 1990, General Norman Schwartzkopf made sure they were covered by television, because he knew Saddam Hussein was watching CNN. In February, after Iraqi command and control was presumably shattered by US bombing, a high-ranking US intelligence officer said of Hussein: "CNN may have been the only accurate source of information that he had. So we knew what he was getting. We were able to pass information to him."

CNN, as is widely known, was the only network to send news out of Baghdad on January 16, 1991, the night US air attacks were launched. CNN obtained permission from the Iraqi government to place an uninterruptable "four-wire" telephone hookup in Baghdad. The result was the riveting Shaw-Holliman-Arnett reporting during the air attacks. ABC, CBS, and NBC news staffers groused (without evidence) that CNN had to do special favors for the Iraqi government, some implying that bribes were paid. CNN executives say they simply planned better, worked harder, and were more persistent. Stuart Loory, a former newspaperman and now a CNN vice president, points to CNN's ongoing relation with Iraqi television: "When Iraq's invasion of Kuwait took place, we were probably the only American network that had good contacts with Iraqi television. The year before, we had the director general of Iraqi television right here in Atlanta at a 'World Report' contributors conference. We had spent hours trying to arrange Iraq's contributions for the 'World Report,' going back probably three years before that happened." The Big Three's complaints paled alongside CNN's obvious scoop, and the night of January 16 has since entered journalism lore.

The networks and some critics complained further that CNN was a loose cannon, diluting traditional network depth and perspective, airing unsubstantiated live reports. When Tom Shales of the *Washington Post* criticized CNN's live reporting, saying "liveliness is not next to godliness" and that "CNN pulled some tremendous scoops, but also lots of blunders," he was widely understood to have been reflecting the viewpoint of network insiders, especially at CBS. Shales contrasted his criticism of CNN with praise of network professionalism.

The criticism that CNN lacks depth angers CNN executive producer Robert Furnad. "First of all they can't outdo our analysis when they are doing a half an hour a day and we are doing eighteen hours a day. Where we have been weaker is in compiling at the end of the day, the packaging, but we have made great gains." Furnad says that it is absurd to say "when CNN offers an eight-minute interview and the networks a fifteen-second clip that the nets have greater depth and analysis." He in turn criticizes the networks: "What amazes me about the networks and all the creative geniuses is that they don't know how to do live television."

During the Gulf War, CNN's perspective showed up in places other than the anchor desk. One was the regular appearance of foreign journalists on CNN, the only unfiltered, non-American viewpoints, and certainly the only unmediated views from the Arab world, to appear regularly on American television. The two regular fora were "World Report" and "International Correspondents," a roundtable discussion of journalists from countries other than the United States. "World Report" offered the only uncensored world public opinion on the war accessible to the American public in a significant viewing time slot. "World Report" included stories from US allies, opponents, and Third World nations, many of which were critical of the United States' conduct of the war. "World Report" executive producer Donna Mastrangelo noted, "Iran contributes to 'World Report' regularly, Saudi Arabia does, Kuwait does, they all do in the Gulf region. . . . Getting reports helped form a different perspective." "International Correspondents" featured regular discussions with world journalists. The most striking programs featured Arab journalists from Egypt, Lebanon, Jordan, and Syria, as well as Palestinians. By presenting the unmediated views of journalists who were not recognized as experts by the three networks and PBS, "International Correspondents" presented the most openly critical discussion of America's actions in the war from an Arab point of view to a mass American audience.

Another innovation during the war was introduced on the "Larry King" show, a talk radio show brought to television: an international call-in line. This turned the King show into the first international call-in show on television. The King show functioned as a kind of nightly town-hall meeting of the air, in sharp contrast with CBS's "America Tonight" with Charles Kuralt and Leslie Stahl. CBS launched the program during the Gulf War, perhaps hoping for a repeat of "Nightline's" success a decade earlier. "America Tonight" consciously developed the image of a folksy town meeting, reflected in a patriotic format and the choice of Kuralt. In actual content, however, the program relied on the same narrow range of experts as other network programs.

By the traditional standards of the television news battles, CNN demonstrated during the early days of the war that it could "out-cover" the Big Three, even though CBS and ABC eventually caught up (NBC never did). And ABC and CBS brought some perspective through their anchors and field correspondents that CNN did not have. However, CNN remained the first source for news. For all practical purposes it became the newswire for other news organizations. CBS analyst retired general Michael Dugan said of his work for CBS during the war: "What CBS did during the Gulf War was watch CNN." And *New York Times* foreign editor Bernard Gwertzman commented, "Like everyone else, we're thankful for CNN. It's become the unpaid news service for papers. We rely on it an enormous amount."

CNN's success and influence during the Tiananmen Square Massacre, the Gulf War, and the attempted Soviet coup has established it as the preeminent global television news service. Today, CNN International (CNNI) reaches a global audience of fifty-three million viewers in 138 nations; in the United States, CNN reaches about sixty million households. As a twenty-four-hour service, it has changed the way television can be used. At any given moment less than 1 percent of the

American viewing audience is watching CNN. During any week, however, about 25 percent of the viewers will have checked in with CNN. In contrast, viewers watch the Big Three nightly newscasts in numbers ranging from 11 to 15 percent every night. The networks provide the day's headlines in twenty-two minutes. CNN is there twenty-four hours a day, to be taken as needed. Robert Ross, Turner Broadcasting System's vice president for international business development, says: "I think people buy CNN not because they want to watch it at this particular point in time, but they buy it for the option to watch it when they want to, which is to say when something important happens which is worth watching. And this is how you explain that CNN has such low ratings, and yet so many people have bought it."

It is precisely this twenty-four-hour option that distinguishes CNN from its domestic and international competitors. CNN is now capable of feeding news from virtually any point on the globe to Atlanta, and from there sending it back out to any point on the globe. This point-to-point structure is the hallmark of the emerging international television system. [. . .]

42 Peripheral Vision

John Sinclair, Elizabeth Jacka, and Stuart Cunningham

Instead of the image of "the West" at the centre dominating the peripheral "Third World" with an outward flow of cultural products, we see the world as divided into a number of regions which each have their own internal dynamics as well as their global ties. Although primarily based on geographic realities, these regions are also defined by common cultural, linguistic, and historical connections which transcend physical space. Such a dynamic, regionalist view of the world helps us to analyse in a more nuanced way the intricate and multi-directional flows of television across the globe.

New Patterns of Television Flow

Public discourse about television and the media-studies literature are both replete with anxiety about the supposed cultural effects of the global spread of programmes like *Dallas* or, more recently, *Beverly Hills 90210*. The unquestioned basis for this anxiety is expressed in the orthodox critical paradigm for analysing the connection between international power relations and the media, the thesis of "cultural imperialism", or more particularly, "media imperialism". According to this view, world patterns of communication flow, both in density and in direction, mirror the system of domination in the economic and political order. Thus, world centres like New York, Los Angeles, London, and Tokyo are major nodes for international telecommunications traffic, as well as for other kinds of flows, such as television programmes. The media imperialism perspective more particularly sees that the major world sources for programme exports are located in the USA and secondarily in Europe, mainly the UK, and that these centres act as nodes through which all flows of cultural products must pass, including those from one peripheral part of the world to another.

The *locus classicus* of the cultural imperialism thesis is found in the work of Herbert Schiller. As recently as 1991, in an article tellingly entitled "Not Yet the Post-Imperialist Era", he has restated his position in the following way: "The role of television in the global arena of cultural domination has not diminished in the 1990s. Reinforced by new delivery systems – communication satellites and cable networks – the image flow is heavier than ever. Its source of origin also has not changed that much in the last quarter of the century". The classic study for UNESCO by Nordenstreng and Varis in 1974 documented the dominance of the USA in world television programme exports at that time. Television programme

Original publication details: Sinclair, John, Elizabeth Jacka and Stuart Cunningham, "Peripheral Vision" from *New Patterns in Global Television: Peripheral Vision*, John Sinclair et al. (eds.) (Oxford University Press, Oxford, 1996).

flows became an integral issue for the New World Information Order movement and its debate within UNESCO. As this continued into the 1980s, the cultural imperialism view of international domination stood challenged only by those who were seen as apologists for the USA and its demand for a "free flow" international regime for trade in cultural products. Neither critics nor apologists questioned the oft-quoted factoid that entertainment is second only to aerospace as an export industry for the USA.

Indeed, as long as the flows of television programme exports seemed to continue along the "one-way street" from the West (and the USA in particular) to the rest of the world, the critical discourse of cultural imperialism was a plausible theoretical response, at least in its more subtle variations, notably that of "cultural dependence", and "media imperialism". In an essential respect, the cultural imperialism perspective was the then-current neo-Marxist analysis of capitalist culture projected on to an international scale: the "dominant ideology" thesis writ large. As such, it had the all-embracing appeal of a comprehensive theory, and also provided the high moral ground from which the international activities of USA networks and the ideological content of their television programmes could be analysed, and then denounced.

However, by the mid-1980s it became evident that the cultural imperialism discourse had serious inadequacies, both as theory and in terms of the reality which the theory purported to explain. Actual transformation of the world television system made it less and less sustainable on the empirical level, and shifting theoretical paradigms, including postmodernism, postcolonialism, and theories of the "active" audience, made its conceptual foundations less secure. To take the empirical aspect first, Jeremy Tunstall had long since pointed out that the "television imperialism thesis" of such writers as Schiller and Wells was based on the quite incorrect assumption that the high levels of USA programme imports into Latin America in the 1960s were a permanent condition rather than a transitional stage in the development of television in these regions. The other empirical development which ought to have given pause to theorists of cultural imperialism was the research reported by Varis as an update of the original "one-way street" project, in which he noted "a trend toward greater regional exchanges", in spite of continued USA and European dominance in television programme flows. This finding was reinforced by other studies around the same time which, although absurdly exaggerated in their estimation of how far the flows had formed new patterns, were able nevertheless to document just how one such regional market was taking shape, in the case of Latin America.

Thus, even in Latin America, virtually the cradle of the theorization of cultural imperialism, USA imports were prominent only in the early stages. As the industry matured in Latin America, and as it developed "critical mass", USA imports were to some extent replaced by local products, a pattern that can be found repeated many times over around the world, and which is currently shaping Europe's new privately owned services. Of course, not all countries in Latin America have the capacity to develop sizeable indigenous television production industries. Rather, the pattern in Latin America, as in Asia and the Middle East, is that each "geolinguistic region", as we shall call them, is itself dominated by one or two centres of audiovisual production – Mexico and Brazil for Latin America, Hong Kong and Taiwan for the Chinese-speaking populations of Asia, Egypt for the Arab world, and India for the Indian populations of Africa and Asia. The Western optic through which the cultural imperialism thesis was developed literally did not see these non-Western systems of regional exchange, nor understand what they represented. Yet by the late 1980s, Tracey could observe that the "very general picture of TV flows . . . is not a one-way street; rather there are a number of main thoroughfares, with a series of not unimportant smaller roads".

We have noted how, as theory, the cultural imperialism critique tended to identify the USA as the single centre of a process of mediacentric capitalist cultural influence which emanated out to the rest of the world in the form of television programmes. It also assumed that these programmes had an inevitable and self-sufficient ideological effect upon their helpless audiences in the periphery. Although this rationale established a theoretical connection between US television programmes and "consumerism", it did not address the question of just how such a mechanism of effect might work, nor how it could be observed in action upon actual audiences. In the discourse of cultural imperialism, the mystique of television entertainment's multivalent appeal for its audiences, and how specific audiences responded to it, were never on the agenda.

Other shortcomings arose from the theory's emphasis on external forces from the USA, and the corresponding disregard for the internal sociological factors within the countries seen to be subject to them. In its eagerness to hold US companies, and behind them, the US government, responsible for regressive sociocultural changes in the "Third World", the cultural imperialism critique neglected the internal historical and social dynamics within the countries susceptible to their influence. This left out of consideration the strategic social structural position of the individuals and interest groups who benefited from facilitating US market entry or even from taking their own initiatives. Some of these have subsequently built up their own international media empires, such as Mexico and Brazil. Other players have more recently joined the game, such as some Saudi investors, while investment in the new channels in India by expatriates shows that media entrepreneurism also can be widespread on a small scale. The cultural imperialism theory failed to see that, more fundamental than its supposed ideological influence, the legacy of the USA in world television development was in the implantation of its systemic model for television as a medium – the exploitation of entertainment content so as to attract audiences which could then be sold to advertisers. American content may have primed this process, but as the experience of many parts of the peripheral world shows, it is not required to sustain it.

We should also note that with its dichotomized view of "the West" versus the "Third World", the cultural imperialism theory was unable to give an adequate account of semi-peripheral settler societies such as Australia and Canada, where the experience of colonialism, and postcolonialism, has been quite distinct from that of nations in other former colonized zones, a distinctiveness manifest in the television systems which they developed.

The basic assumption of Western domination via television is worth further comment. Paradoxically, even though the cultural imperialism thesis has been articulated in the name of defending the "Third World" against domination by audiovisual products from the USA, it is more inclined to reinforce Western cultural influence by taking it as given, when it should be challenging it. A more postcolonial perspective in theory has forced us to realize that USA domination always was limited, either by cultural or political "screens", or both. A related weakness or "blind spot" of the cultural imperialism thesis has been its over-emphasis on the significance of imported *vis-à-vis* local television. Television has always been more of a local than a global medium, and remains so, although the increasingly multichannel and globalized nature of the industry may alter the balance at the margin in the longer term. According to figures from 1989, the volume of purely domestic material in national markets is twenty-nine times higher than that which is traded. Television is still a gloriously hybrid medium, with a plethora of programming of an inescapably and essentially local, untranslatable nature.

Although US programmes might lead the world in their transportability across cultural boundaries, and even manage to dominate schedules on some channels in particular countries, they are rarely the most popular programmes where viewers have a reasonable menu of locally produced material to choose from. And even where there is imported content, it is no longer acceptable to read off from that fact alone any presumed effects of a cultural or political kind. Hamid Naficy captures this vividly in his brilliant study of television amongst Iranian exiles in Los Angeles. Describing how his exclusively English-speaking Iranian daughter, Shayda, and his exclusively German-speaking Iranian niece, Setarah, communicated through the Disney film *The Little Mermaid*, he goes on to comment:

> The globalization of American pop culture does not automatically translate into globalization of American control. This globalized culture provides a shared discursive space where transnationals such as Setarah and Shayda can localize it, make their own uses of it, domesticate and indigenize it. They may think with American cultural products but they do not think American. [. . .]

"Gatekeepers" and Cultural Industry Factors in Television Flows

Many cross-cultural studies emphasize the diverse, localized character of inter-national audience responses, and are imbued with a sense of the viability and integrity of the cultures of peripheral or "small" nations. So it is somewhat ironic, because of the dominance of American programmes at highly visible though only provisionally premium places in schedules, that such studies should focus on US programmes almost exclusively. As Ellen Seiter argues strongly with regard to the theoretical field from which this position draws, "in our concern for audiences' pleasures . . . we run the risk of continually validating Hollywood's domination of the worldwide television market".

Far more than for the USA, the success or otherwise of peripheral nations' exports is contingent on factors other than those captured by established modes of audience study. This explains why so little audience reception research has been able to be conducted on their products in international markets, and why we need instead middle-range analysis to do so. In the middle range between political economy approaches and reception analysis, a number of factors are mediating. How are programmes acquired overseas? Who engages in their appraisal and acquisition and what perceptions have they formed of peripheral programming? This "primary audi-ence" is the major source of informed "gatekeeping" which regulates (in the widest sense) the flow of peripheral programming in international markets. And what are the characteristics of the major territories which influence the success or failure of such programmes internationally? All these mediating factors embody legitimate, indeed central, aspects of cultural exchange, as virtually all the significant research on non-dominant nations' television production and reception indicates.

The actual structure of major international television trade markets is central to middle-range analysis. There is an ever-wider variety of modes of contracting for international programme production and exchange: offshore, co-production, official co-production, co-venture (including presales), and straight purchase of territorial rights for completed programmes in the major trade markets such as MIP-TV and MIPCOM. These run on annual cycles suited to the programming and scheduling patterns of the major northern hemisphere territories, but a notable shift in the patterns of global television traffic was indicated in 1994 when the first MIP-Asia was held, a trade market specifically for the Asian region. At such events, programming is often bought (or not bought) on the basis of company reputation or distributor clout, in job lots and sight-unseen. Very broad, rough-and-ready genre expectations are in play; judgements may seem highly "subjective" and arbitrary.

Universalist explanations may prove useful in accounting for the international successes of historically universal forms like US series drama, but there is solid evidence that cultural specificities, along with other middle-range industrial factors, are unavoidable and, at times, enabling factors for international success in peripheral countries' export activity. Studies which compare viewers' engagement with US as against other sources of television programming confirm that there tends to be a more distanced realm of "pure entertainment" within which US programmes are processed – as markers of modish modernity, as a "spectacular" world – compared to more culturally specific responses made to domestic and other sources.

The capacity for peripheral countries to export their programmes across diverse markets is to some extent based on their substitutability or non-substitutability for US material, although this also depends in part on the type of channel they are purchased for. Australian productions have provided useful models from which the protocols of commercial popularity may be learnt in rapidly commercializing European broadcasting environments, but the fact that Australian programmes are perceived as imitations of US formats constitutes a problem for both commentators and regulators in Europe.

To be sure, the structure of content and the form of internationally popular serial drama in particular are widely shared and may even be "borrowed" from US practice, as the *telenovela* was decades ago. But the "surface" differences, nevertheless, almost always are consequential, and contribute to the acceptance or rejection of non-US material, depending on whether the "primary audience" of gatekeepers and the viewing audience respond positively or negatively to those differences. As Anne Cooper-Chen has shown, even that most transparently internationalized of television formats, the game show, contains significant differences in the widely variant cultures in which it is popular. After looking at popular game shows in fifty countries, she regards them as having at least three structural variants – the East Asian, Western, and Latin models – and innumerable surface particularities. Hamid Mowlana and Mehdi Rad show that the Japanese programme *Oshin* found acceptance in Iran because its values of perseverance and long suffering were compatible with cultural codes prevalent in what might appear a distinctly different society. The evidence for the popularity of *Neighbours* in Britain demonstrates that, while Australian soaps arguably were brought into the market as substitutes for US material, their popularity built around textual factors based on projections and introjections of Australian "life-style". Australia has served in many ways as a kind of "other" to Britain – the younger, more upstart and hedonistic vision of how the British might like to see themselves.

The "export of meaning" is not just a matter of viewer reception. Many nations, both core and peripheral, place special importance on the international profile they can establish with their audiovisual exports. These are fostered both as a form of cultural diplomacy, and for intrinsic economic reasons, although national cultural objectives and audiovisual industry development are not always compatible, as Australia and Canada have long been aware, and some Asian countries are now learning. In the case of the Middle East, one commentator has observed that the popularity of Egyptian television exports in the Arab states has a number of cultural and even political "multiplier effects". This popularity was preceded by the success of Egyptian films, and carries with it a potential acceptance and recognition of Egyptian accents and performers that can operate as "a soft-sell commercial for Egyptian values" which then carries over into indirect political leverage. While it might be difficult to isolate and measure them, it is not unreasonable to infer cultural, trade, and political multiplier effects from what can be seen of peripheral nations' products on the world's television screens. [. . .]

Even amongst the globalization theorists, it is becoming a commonplace to observe that the globalizing forces towards "homogenization", such as satellite television, exist in tension with contradictory tendencies towards "heterogenization", conceived pessimistically as fragmentation, or with postmodernist optimism, as pluralism. Thus, "identity and cultural affiliation are no longer matters open to the neat simplifications of traditional nationalism. They are matters of ambiguity and complexity, of overlapping loyalties and symbols with multiple meanings". To the extent that we can assume that television is in fact a source of identity, and that audiences for the same programme derive similar identities from it, it becomes possible to think of identities which are multiple, although also often contradictory, corresponding to the different levels from which the televisual environment is composed in a given market. An Egyptian immigrant in Britain, for example, might think of herself as a Glaswegian when she watches her local Scottish channel, a British resident when she switches over to the BBC, an Islamic Arab expatriate in Europe when she tunes in to the satellite service from the Middle East, and a world citizen when she channel surfs on to CNN. [. . .]

43 Cultural Imperialism

John Tomlinson

"Watching *Dallas*": The Imperialist Text and Audience Research

For many critics, the American TV series *Dallas* had become the byword for cultural imperialism in the 1980s. Ien Ang's study, *Watching Dallas* takes as its central question the tension between the massive international popularity of the Texan soap opera:

> ... in over ninety countries, ranging from Turkey to Australia, from Hong Kong to Great Britain ... with the proverbial empty streets and dramatic drop in water consumption when an episode of the series is going out ...

and the reaction of cultural commentators to this "success":

> *Dallas* was regarded as yet more evidence of the threat posed by American-style commercial culture against authentic national identities. In February 1983 for instance, Jack Lang, the French Minister for Culture ... had even proclaimed *Dallas* as the "symbol of American cultural imperialism".

Ang detects amongst European cultural critics an "ideology of mass culture" by which she means a generalised hostility towards the imported products of the American mass culture industry, which has fixed on *Dallas* as the focus of its contempt.

Ang quotes Michelle Mattelart:

> It is not for nothing that *Dallas* casts its ubiquitous shadow wherever the future of culture is discussed: it has become the perfect hate symbol, the cultural poverty ... against which one struggles.

The evident popularity of *Dallas* juxtaposed with its hostile critical reception amongst "professional intellectuals" and the linked charges of cultural imperialism poses for us nicely the problem of the audience in the discourse of media imperialism. For the cultural critics tend to condemn *Dallas* with scant regard to the way in which the audience may read the text.

Cultural imperialism is once more seen as an ideological property of the text itself. It is seen as inhering in the images of dazzling skyscrapers, expensive clothes and automobiles, lavish settings, the celebration in the narrative of power and wealth and so on. All this is seen to have an obvious ideological manipulative effect on the viewer. As Lealand has put it:

Original publication details: Tomlinson, John, excerpt from *Cultural Imperialism: A Critical Introduction* (Pinter Publishers, 1991).

> There is an assumption that American TV imports do have an impact whenever and wherever they are shown, but actual investigation of this seldom occurs. Much of the evidence that is offered is merely anecdotal or circumstantial. Observations of . . . Algerian nomads watching *Dallas* in the heat of the desert are offered as sufficient proof.

However, encouraged by developments in British critical media theory, some writers have attempted to probe the audience reception of "imperialist texts" like *Dallas*. Ien Ang's study, although it is not primarily concerned with the issue of media imperialism, is one such.

Ang approaches the *Dallas* audience with the intention of investigating an hypothesis generated from her own experience of watching *Dallas*. She found that her own enjoyment of the show chafed against the awareness she had of its ideological content. Her critical penetration as "an intellectual and a feminist" of this ideology suggested to her that the pleasure she derived from the programme had little connection with, and certainly did not entail, an ideological effect. In reacting to the ideology in the text, she argues, the cultural critics overlook the crucial question in relation to the audience: "For we must accept one thing: *Dallas* is popular because a lot of people somehow *enjoy* watching it."

Ang saw the popularity of the show, which might be read as a sign of its imperialist ideological power, as a complex phenomenon without a single cause, but owing a good deal to the intrinsic pleasure to be derived from its melodramatic narrative structure. The show's ability to connect with "the melodramatic imagination" and the pleasure this provides were, Ang thought, the key to its success, and these had no necessary connection with the power of American culture or the values of consumer capitalism. What the cultural critics overlooked was the capacity of the audience to negotiate the possible contradictions between alien cultural values and the "pleasure of the text".

Ang's study was based on a fairly informal empirical procedure. She placed an advertisement in a Dutch women's magazine asking people to write to her describing what they liked or disliked about *Dallas*. Her correspondents revealed a complex set of reactions, including evidence that some did indeed, like Ang herself, manage to resolve a conflict between their distaste for the ideology of the show and a pleasure in watching it. For example:

> *Dallas*. . . . God, don't talk to me about it. I'm hooked on it! But you wouldn't believe the number of people who say to me, "Oh, I thought you were against Capitalism?" I am, but *Dallas* is just so tremendously exaggerated, it has nothing to do with capitalists any more, it's just sheer artistry to make up such nonsense.

Ang found such a high level of disapproval for the cultural values of *Dallas* in some of her correspondents that she speaks of their views being informed by the "ideology of mass culture" of the cultural critics. These viewers, she argues, have internalised what they perceive as the "correct" attitude towards mass-cultural imports – that of the disapproving professional intellectuals. They thus feel the need to justify their enjoyment of the show by, for example, adopting an ironic stance towards it. Alternatively, she suggests, an opposing "anti-intellectual" ideological discourse of "populism" may allow the *Dallas* fan to refuse the ideology of mass culture as elitist and paternalist, and to insist (in such popular maxims as "there's no accounting for taste") on their right to their pleasure without cultural "guilt".

Ang's analysis of the ideological positioning and struggle around the text of *Dallas* is not without its problems. But her empirical work does at the very least suggest how naive and improbable is the simple notion of an immediate ideological effect arising from exposure to the imperialist text. The complex, reflective and self-conscious reactions of her correspondents suggest that cultural critics who assume this sort of effect massively underestimate the audience's active engagement with the text and the critical sophistication of the ordinary viewer/reader.

The same message comes from most recent studies of audience response. Katz and Liebes, for instance, also looked at reactions to *Dallas*, but in a rather more formal empirical study than Ang's. Their work involved a large-scale cross-cultural study of the impact of *Dallas*, comparing different ethnic groups in Israel with a group of American viewers. Katz and Liebes situate themselves within the growing perspective in media research which sees the audience as active and the process of meaning construction as one of "negotiation" with the text in a particular cultural context. They argue that this perspective:

> raises a question about the apparent ease with which American television programmes cross cultural and linguistic frontiers. Indeed, the phenomenon is so taken for granted that hardly any systematic research has been done to explain the reasons why these programmes are so successful. One wonders how such quintessentially American products are understood at all. The often-heard assertion that this phenomenon is part of the process of cultural imperialism presumes, first, that there is an American message in the content and form; second, that this message is somehow perceived by viewers; and, third, that it is perceived in the same way by viewers in different cultures.

Katz and Liebes, like Ang, are generally dubious about the way in which the media imperialism argument has been presented by its adherents:

> Since the effects attributed to a TV programme are often inferred from content analysis alone, it is of particular interest to examine the extent to which members of the audience absorb, explicitly or implicitly, the messages which critics and scholars allege they are receiving.

Their study of *Dallas* thus represents perhaps the most ambitious attempt so far to examine the media imperialism argument empirically from the perspective of audience response. In order to do this, they organised fifty "focus groups" consisting of three couples each to watch an episode of *Dallas*. The idea of watching the programme in groups was essential to one of their guiding premises, that the meanings of TV texts are arrived at via a *social* process of viewing and discursive interpretation. They believe, in common with other recent views, that TV viewing is not essentially an isolated individual practice, but one in which social interaction – "conversation with significant others" – is a vital part of the interpretative and evaluative process. This may be even more significant when the programme in question is the product of an alien culture and, thus, potentially more difficult to "decode".

The groups that Katz and Liebes arranged were all from similar class backgrounds – "lower middle class with high school education or less" – and each group was "ethnically homogenous":

> There were ten groups each of Israeli Arabs, new immigrants to Israel from Russia, first- and second-generation immigrants from Morocco and Kibbutz members. Taking these groups as a microcosm of the worldwide audience of *Dallas*, we are comparing their "readings" of the programme with ten groups of matched Americans in Los Angeles.

The groups followed their viewing of *Dallas* with an hour-long "open structured" discussion and a short individual questionnaire. The discussions were recorded and formed the basic data of the study, what Katz and Liebes refer to as "ethno-semiological data".

The groups were invited to discuss, first, simply what happened in the episode – "the narrative sequence, and the topics, issues and themes with which the programme deals". Even at this basic level Katz and Liebes found examples of divergent readings influenced, they argue, by the cultural background of the groups and reinforced by their interaction. One of the Arabic groups actually "misread" the information of the programme in a way which arguably made it more compatible with their cultural horizon. In the episode viewed, Sue Ellen had taken her baby and run away from her husband JR, moving into the house of her former lover and his father. However, the Arab group confirmed each other in the more conventional reading – in their terms – that she had actually gone to live in her *own* father's house. The implications of this radical translation of the events of the narrative must at least be to undermine the notion that texts cross cultural boundaries intact.

More importantly, perhaps, Katz and Liebes found that different ethnic groups brought their own values to a judgement of the programme's values. They quote a Moroccan Jew's assessment:

> *Machluf*: You see, I'm a Jew who wears a skullcap and I learned from this series to say, "Happy is our lot, goodly is our fate" that we're Jewish. Everything about JR and his baby, who has maybe four or five fathers, who knows? The mother is Sue Ellen, of course, and the brother of Pam left. Maybe he's the father. . . . I see that they're almost all bastards.

This sort of response, which seems to be not just a rejection of Western decadence, but an actual reinforcement of the audience's own cultural values, extended from issues of interpersonal and sexual morality to the programme's celebration of wealth: "With all that they have money, my life style is higher than theirs." However, here, at the "real foundations", Katz and Liebes found a more typical response to be an agreement on the importance of money:

> *Miriam*: Money will get you anything. That's why people view it. People sit at home and want to see how it looks.
> [. . .]
> *Yosef*: Everybody wants to be rich. Whatever he has, he wants more.
> *Zari*: Who doesn't want to be rich? The whole world does.

It scarcely needs saying that responses like these demonstrate no more than agreement with aspects of the perceived message of *Dallas* and cannot be taken as evidence of the programme's ideological effect. All cultures, we must surely assume, will generate their own set of basic attitudes on issues like the relationship between wealth and happiness. *Dallas* represents, perhaps, one very forceful statement of such an attitude, informed by a dominant global culture of capitalism. But it would be absurd to assume that people in any present-day culture do not have developed attitudes to such a central aspect of their lives quite independent of any televisual representations. We clearly cannot assume that simply watching *Dallas* makes people want to be rich! The most we can assume is that agreement here, as with disagreement elsewhere with the programme's message, represents the outcome of people's "negotiations" with the text.

Katz and Liebes are careful not to draw any premature conclusions from this complex data. But they do at least suggest that it supports their belief in the active social process of viewing and demonstrates a high level of sophistication in the discursive interpretations of ordinary people. They also make the interesting suggestion that the social and economic distance between the affluent denizens of the Southfork Range and their spectators around the globe is of less consequence than might be thought: "Unhappiness is the greatest leveller." This thought chimes with Ang's argument that it is the melodramatic nature of the narrative and its appeal to the "tragic structure of feeling", rather than its glimpses of consumer capitalism at its shiny leading edge that scores *Dallas*'s global ratings.

The general message of empirical studies – informal ones like Ang's and more large-scale formal projects like Katz and Liebes's – is that audiences are more active and critical, their responses more complex and reflective, and their cultural values more resistant to manipulation and "invasion" than many critical media theorists have assumed. [...]

Multinational Capitalism and Cultural Homogenisation

Critics of multinational capitalism frequently do complain of its tendency towards cultural convergence and homogenisation. This is the major criticism made in the discourse of cultural imperialism which takes capitalism as its target. A good example is Cees Hamelink's book, *Cultural Autonomy in Global Communications*. Hamelink, who acknowledges the co-operation of both Schiller and Salinas, places the issues of cultural autonomy and cultural homogenisation – or what he refers to as "cultural synchronisation" – at the centre of his analysis. He is broadly correct in identifying the processes of "cultural synchronization" (or homogenisation) as unprecedented in historical terms and in seeing these processes as closely connected to the spread of global capitalism. But he fails to show why cultural synchronisation should be objected to and, specifically, he fails to show that it should be objected to on the grounds of cultural autonomy.

In his opening chapter Hamelink lists a number of personal "experiences of the international scene" to illustrate his thesis. For example:

> In a Mexican village the traditional ritual dance precedes a soccer match, but the performance features a gigantic Coca-Cola bottle.

> In Singapore, a band dressed in traditional Malay costume offers a heart-breaking imitation of Fats Domino.

> In Saudi Arabia, the television station performs only one local cultural function – the call for the Moslem prayer. Five times a day, North American cops and robbers yield to the traditional muezzin.

> In its gigantic advertising campaign, IBM assures Navajo Indians that their cultural identity can be effectively protected if they use IBM typewriters equipped with the Navajo alphabet.

The first thing to note about these examples is precisely their significance as *personal* observations – and this is not to make any trivial point about their "subjective" nature. Hamelink expresses the cultural standpoint of the concerned Westerner confronting a perplexing set of global phenomena. We have to accept, at the level of the personal, the sincerity of his concern and also the validity of this personal discourse: it is valid for individuals to express their reaction to global tendencies. But we need to acknowledge that this globe-trotting instancing of cultural imperialism shapes the discourse in a particular way: to say "here is the *sameness* that capitalism brings – and here – and here . . ." is to assume, however liberal, radical or critical the intention, the role of the "tourist": the problem of homogenisation is likely to present itself to the Western intellectual who has a sense of the diversity and "richness" of global culture as a particular threat. For the people involved in each discrete instance Hamelink presents, the experience of Western capitalist culture will probably have quite different significance. Only if they can adopt the (privileged) role of the cultural tourist will the sense of the homogenisation of global culture have the same threatening aspect. The Kazakhstani tribesman who has no knowledge of (and, perhaps, no interest in) America or Europe is unlikely to see his cassette player as emblematic of creeping capitalist domination. And we cannot, without irony, argue that the Western intellectual's (informed?) concern is more valid: again much hangs on the question, "who speaks?"

This said, Hamelink does draw from these instances an empirical conclusion which is, I think, fairly uncontroversial:

> One conclusion still seems unanimously shared: the impressive variety of the world's cultural systems is waning due to a process of "cultural synchronisation" that is without historic precedent.

For those in a position to view the world as a cultural totality, it cannot be denied that certain processes of cultural convergence are under way, and that these are new processes. This last is an important point, for Hamelink is careful to acknowledge that cultures have always influenced one another and that this influence has often enriched the interacting communities – "the richest cultural traditions emerged at the actual meeting point of markedly different cultures, such as Sudan, Athens, the Indus Valley, and Mexico". Even where cultural interaction has been in the context of political and economic domination, Hamelink argues, there has been, in most cases a "two-way exchange" or at least a tolerance of cultural diversity. There is a sharp difference for him between these patterns and modern "cultural synchronization":

> In the second half of the twentieth century, a destructive process that differs significantly from the historical examples given above threatens the diversity of cultural systems. Never before has the synchronization with one particular cultural pattern been of such global dimensions and so comprehensive.

Let us be clear about what we are agreeing. It seems to me that Hamelink is right, broadly speaking, to identify cultural synchronisation as an unprecedented feature of global modernity. The evaluative implications of his use of the word "destructive", however, raises larger problems. It is one thing to say that cultural diversity is being destroyed, quite another to lament the fact. The latter position demands reasons which Hamelink cannot convincingly supply. The quotation continues in a way that raises part of the problem: "Never before has the process of cultural influence proceeded so subtly, without any blood being shed and with the receiving culture thinking it had sought such cultural influence." With his last phrase Hamelink slides towards the problematic of false consciousness. As we have seen more than once before, any critique which bases itself in the idea that cultural domination is taking place "behind people's backs" is heading for trouble. To acknowledge that a cultural community might have thought it had sought cultural influence is to acknowledge that such influence has at least *prima facie* attractions.

This thought could lead us to ask if the process of cultural homogenisation itself might not have its attractions. It is not difficult to think of examples of cultural practices which would probably attract a consensus in favour of their universal application: health care; food hygiene; educational provision; various "liberal" cultural attitudes towards honesty, toleration, compassion and so on; democratic public processes etc. This is not to say that any of these are indisputable "goods" under any description whatever, nor that they are all the "gifts" of an expanding capitalist modernity. But it is to say that there are plenty of aspects of "culture", broadly defined, that the severest critic of cultural homogenisation might wish to find the same in any area of the globe. Critics of cultural homogenisation are selective in the things they object to, and there is nothing wrong in this so long as we realise that it undermines the notion that homogenisation is a bad thing *in itself*. But then we enter a quite separate set of arguments – not about the uniformity of capitalist culture, but about the spread of its pernicious features – which require quite different criteria of judgement.

Engaging with the potentially attractive features of homogenisation brings us to see, pretty swiftly, the problems in its use as a critical concept. But there are other ways of approaching the issue, and one of Hamelink's arguments seems on the surface to avoid these problems. He argues that cultural synchronisation is to be deplored on the grounds that it is a threat to cultural autonomy. I would argue against both the notion of autonomy as applied to a "culture" in the holistic sense and against any logical connection between the concept of autonomy and any particular *outcome* of cultural practices. Autonomy, as I understand it, refers to the free and uncoerced choices and actions of agents. But Hamelink uses the notion of autonomy in what strikes me as a curious way, to suggest a feature of cultural practices which is necessary, indeed "critical", for the actual survival of a cultural community.

Hamelink's reasoning appears to be based on the idea that the cultural system of any society is an *adaptive* mechanism which enables the society to exist in its "environment", by which he seems to mean the physical and material features of its global location: "Different climatic conditions, for example, demand different ways of adapting to them (i.e., different types of food, shelter and clothing)." Again, there is nothing particularly controversial about this, except in the obvious sense that we might want to argue that many of the cultural practices of modernity are rather more "distanced" from the function of survival than those of more "primitive" systems. But from this point he argues that the "autonomous" development of cultural systems – the freedom from the processes of "cultural synchronization" – are necessary to the "survival" of societies. Why should this be so? Because "the adequacy of the cultural system can best be decided upon by the members of the society who face directly the problems of survival and adaptation".

There are a number of difficulties arising from this sort of argument. First, what does Hamelink mean by the "survival" of a society? In his reference to very basic adaptations to environmental conditions he seems to trade on the idea that a culture allows for the actual physical survival of its members. At times he explicitly refers to the physical survival of people. For example, he claims that the intensive promotion of milk-powder baby food in the Third World by companies like Nestlé and Cow and Gate is a practice that can have life-threatening consequences:

Replacing breast-feeding by bottle feeding has had disastrous effects in many Third World countries. An effective, adequate, and cheap method has been exchanged for an expensive, inadequate and dangerous product. . . . Many illiterate mothers, unable to prepare the milk powder correctly, have not only used it improperly but have also inadvertently transformed the baby food into a lethal product by using it in unhygienic conditions.

There *are* important issues having to do with the "combined and unequal development" produced by the spread of capitalism of which this is a good example. But the incidence of illness and death Hamelink refers to here, deplorable though it is, will obviously not carry the weight of his argument about cultural synchronisation affecting the physical survival of whole populations in the Third World. He cannot, plausibly, claim that cultural synchronisation with capitalist modernity carries this direct threat. It is probably true that capitalist production has long-term consequences for the global environment, thus for physical survival on a global scale, but this is a separate argument.

At any rate, Hamelink's notion of survival seems to slide from that of physical survival to the *survival of the culture itself*. But this is a very different proposition, which cannot be sustained by the functional view of culture he takes as his premise. For the failure of a culture to "survive" in an "original" form may be taken itself as a process of adaptation to a new "environment" – that of capitalist industrial modernity. A certain circularity is therefore introduced into the argument. Hamelink claims that unique cultures arise as adaptive mechanisms to environments, so he deplores heteronomy since it threatens such adaptation. But what could cultural synchronisation mean if not an "adaptation" to the demands of the social environment of capitalism?

The incoherences of this account arise, I believe, from the attempt to circumvent the problems of autonomy in cultural terms by referring the holistic view to a functional logic of adaptation. Autonomy can only apply to agents, and cultures are not agents. Hamelink seeks to bypass these problems with an argument that reduces the ethical-political content of "autonomy" to make it a mere indicator of social efficiency – the guarantor of the "best" form of social organisation in a particular environment. His argument is incoherent precisely because autonomy cannot be so reduced: in cultural terms, "best" is not to be measured against a simple index of physical survival. Things are far more complicated than this. Cultural autonomy must address the autonomous choices of agents who make up a cultural community; there is no escaping this set of problems by appeal to functionality. Hamelink gives the game away in his reference, cited earlier, to a form of cultural "false consciousness" and elsewhere where he speaks of cultural synchronisation as cultural practices being "persuasively communicated to the receiving countries".

I do not believe the appeal to autonomy grounds Hamelink's critique of cultural synchronisation. Even if it did, this would be an objection to the inhibition of independence by manipulation, not to the resulting "sameness" of global culture. But Hamelink does want to object to "sameness": this is implicit in his constant references to the "rich diversity" of cultures under threat. What are the grounds for such an objection?

Adaptation to physical environments has, historically, produced a diversity in cultural practices across the globe. However, the *preservation* of this diversity – which is what Hamelink wants – seems to draw its justification from the idea that cultural diversity is a good thing in itself. But this depends on the position from which you speak. If the attractions of a uniform capitalist modernity outweigh the charms of diversity, as they well may for those from the outside looking in, it is difficult to insist on the priority of preserving differences. Indeed, the appeal to variety might well be turned back on the critic of capitalism. For it might be argued that individual cultures making up the rich mosaic that Hamelink surveys are lacking in a variety of cultural experience, being tied, as Marx observed, to the narrow demands of the struggle with nature for survival. Cultural synchronisation could in some cases increase variety in cultural experience.

It must be said immediately that arguments exist that the *nature* of such experience in capitalist modernity is in some sense deficient – shallow, "one-dimensional", "commodified", and so on. But this is not a criticism of homogenisation or synchronisation as such: it is a criticism of the sort of culture that synchronisation brings. It is quite different to object to the spread of something bad – uniform badness – than to object to the spread of uniformity itself. This demands quite separate arguments about capitalism as a culture. [. . .]

Questions

1   Discuss ways in which media globalization contributes to both homogenization and diversity in the countries of the world.

2   It is common to speak of the "Americanization" of countries influenced by the USA. What evidence do you see of "Japanization," "Africanization," and similar constructs in your culture – the borrowing and adaptation of cultural elements derived from other parts of the world?

3   Should the UN or UNESCO have the authority to regulate the global media, as the MacBride Report suggested? Identify positive and negative consequences of such regulation.

4   Thanks to its global reach, CNN speeds up the political reaction process, according to Friedland. Consider the consequences of this "speeding up" for the resolution of disputes among two or more states. Does it make resolution more likely, or is it setting the stage for greater misunderstanding among political leaders?

5   In the selection by Sinclair and colleagues, we see that media companies in less developed countries are producing "peripheral visions" ever more prolifically. Explain what this implies for the cultural imperialism argument about western domination. Does it suggest that we are now witnessing Mexican, Brazilian, and Indian cultural imperialism in some regions of the world instead?

6   For Tomlinson, any culture is a mélange of many other cultures. Does this mean that cultural imperialism is a meaningless concept? In responding, consider Tomlinson's emphasis on the survival of cultures as compared to their transformation and adaptation.

Part VIII

Cultural Globalization II: Constructing Identities

Introduction

In 1979, conservative clerics and their followers established an Islamic Republic in Iran. This was the outcome of a long battle to depose the Shah of Iran, a battle clerics interpreted as an effort to vindicate the true Islamic faith and restore the rule of Islamic law. The Shah, they claimed, was an illegitimate tyrant who had tried to "modernize" the country in violation of Islamic norms. Supported by the evil, alien power of the United States, he had suppressed the social role of Islam. He had been an instrument of "Westoxication," the intrusion of foreign ideas, symbols, goods, and lifestyles that were infecting Iranians. To the victors, the overthrow of the Shah was a blow against a secular vision of society and against an American-influenced conception of the world. Indeed, the Islamic Republic aspired to become a platform for a broader revolution to slay the Great Satan. By returning to fundamentals of an indigenous tradition, it would be able to transform the world.

The success of the Islamic Revolution was a major world event. In Iran itself, which had long-standing ties to the West, the policies of the new Republic abruptly changed the course of public life, refashioning the national community along traditional lines. To western audiences, the event announced the puzzling arrival of a new cultural force that deliberately dissociated itself from western views. When Iranian students took hostages at the American embassy in Teheran in 1979, the cultural resistance turned into political defiance. To Muslim audiences, even those who did not share Iran's dominant Shi'ite faith, the revolution reversed years of Islamic decline. Iran showed that it was possible to build an ostensibly Islamic Republic under modern circumstances. Active "Jihad" – in the sense of religiously-motivated opposition to a secular, liberal global order – became a live option. Symbolic of this jihad's global thrust was the Iranian response to the publication of Salman Rushdie's *Satanic Verses*: the book's fanciful treatment of the prophet Mohammed, justified as free expression, earned the author a death sentence.

The Islamic Revolution thus put "fundamentalism" on the world map. The term became a controversial concept signifying a collective attempt to establish identity by restoring a sacred tradition in its original form. But what did it have to do with globalization? Our sketch of the impact of the Revolution already indicates some connections. While globalization was by no means the sole cause of Iranian fundamentalism, it helped set the conditions for its mobilization and provided targets for the Islamic program. Fundamentalists also took a stand on two questions raised by globalization as challenges for any society: What does it mean to live in world society? What is any one group's place in it? Globalization, in other words, challenges groups and societies to "identify" themselves. Fundamentalism is one, but only one, solution to this global predicament. It signals that globalization is unlikely to lead to a single western-inspired culture that would prove universally satisfying. The Iranian model and its offspring, in short, indicate that, while all must engage in deliberate identity construction, the process of reimagining communities is bound to take different forms around the world.

We use the fundamentalist case to illustrate what happens to collective identity under globalization. Globalization creates an identity "problem," but it also produces a common mold within which to address it, namely, the nation-state. Collective identity generally takes the form of a national culture linked to a state. Globalization also gives rise to common models and reference points that all societies now must take into account. Societies are further exposed to many cultural influences – transnational popular culture and religious movements, the culture of business, the cultures of migrants and of international organizations. Globalization makes difference problematic: as cross-cutting cultural ties and influences increase, any traditional understanding of tradition becomes tenuous. At the same time, globalization accentuates difference: each group must define its particular place, fashion its particular interpretation of universal precepts. Globalization, in short, unifies and separates, creates similarity and difference.

The selections in this section help to make sense of this dimension of globalization. Appadurai, in this excerpt from his influential article, points to the intense cultural interactions globalization entails. They are marked by a tension between homogenization and heterogenization. To chart the ways in which this tension unfolds, Appadurai distinguishes between five "scapes" – distinct but intersecting global cultural flows. He sketches a picture of disjuncture: while the technoscape may create a common infrastructure, the mediascape creates varied repertoires of symbols and the ideoscape makes different images of social order globally available. These disjoint flows collide within particular societies, where identity construction becomes a matter of making local sense of the collision. To Appadurai, sameness and difference do not just happen together; they actually cannabilize each other. Hannerz complements this analysis by sketching a "scenario" for peripheral cultures that calls into question the notion that globalization refers to a one-way cultural flow from core to periphery, from North to South. As his observations of a Nigerian market town show, particular places achieve a distinct identity by mixing and matching elements from different cultural flows. Hannerz uses market, state, form of life, and movement to describe such flows. As peripheries "mature," they become "creolized."

Lechner draws on such ideas to describe fundamentalism as an ostensibly "antimodern" movement that is inevitably compromised by the very things it opposes. The search for the authentically sacred cannot be purely authentic. It is a distinctly modern project to create identity deliberately out of presumed fundamentals. But even as fundamentalisms become coopted, they nevertheless articulate a powerful oppositional stance within global culture. Even if they cannot reshape the world in their image, they sustain the ongoing contention about the direction of globalization.

The three next selections examine the Iranian case as an instructive and complex instance of collective identity-construction. Ann Elizabeth Mayer provides details about the actual purposes of Islamization in Iran. Islamization, she argues, was a by-product of the clerical takeover, not a conscious goal of a popular movement. Once initiated, it gave new authority to the clerics and to precepts derived from Islamic law; it also made Iran firmly oppose "foreign devils." Yet the program had limited success: many western ideas and institutions remained in place, "moderate" opposition emerged in the late 1980s, and the effect on other Muslim countries was minimal. In one respect, Islamization had a significant impact – in the new government's treatment of women. As Shahla Haeri shows, even as many Iranians supported the "plunge into an idealized past," the very mobilization of women in the revolution made it difficult to relegate them to second-class status. Fundamentalism sought to remove women from positions of authority and restrict their public roles, but Haeri argues that this inevitably provoked resistance. Majid Tehranian adds that Islamization also depended on the use of modern media to propagate Islamic values. The clerics' aim is, in part, to establish an integrated, national identity. A cleansed national self, created by a new educational system as well as the media, would be able to make Iran immune to "Westoxication." Yet such immunity is difficult to achieve. Tehranian gives the example of non-Islamic messages that seep in through the media, for example, via imported Japanese programs.

The impact of Islamization, therefore, is real enough. But the Iranian identity it has created is hardly the restoration of a world-transforming tradition. Iran is subject to multiple cultural flows and its brand of fundamentalism has run into global as well as local obstacles. In the way it deals with its dilemmas, Iran has carved out a distinct cultural stance. Yet for most other societies, it does not serve as an exemplar. They must create an identity of their own, fashioning their particular response to a universal predicament.

44 Disjuncture and Difference in the Global Cultural Economy

Arjun Appadurai

It takes only the merest acquaintance with the facts of the modern world to note that it is now an interactive system in a sense that is strikingly new. Historians and sociologists, especially those concerned with translocal processes and the world systems associated with capitalism, have long been aware that the world has been a congeries of large-scale interactions for many centuries. Yet today's world involves interactions of a new order and intensity. Cultural transactions between social groups in the past have generally been restricted, sometimes by the facts of geography and ecology, and at other times by active resistance to interactions with the Other (as in China for much of its history and in Japan before the Meiji Restoration). Where there have been sustained cultural transactions across large parts of the globe, they have usually involved the long-distance journey of commodities (and of the merchants most concerned with them) and of travelers and explorers of every type. The two main forces for sustained cultural interaction before this century have been warfare (and the large-scale political systems sometimes generated by it) and religions of conversion, which have sometimes, as in the case of Islam, taken warfare as one of the legitimate instruments of their expansion. Thus, between travelers and merchants, pilgrims and conquerors, the world has seen much long-distance (and long-term) cultural traffic. This much seems self-evident.

But few will deny that given the problems of time, distance, and limited technologies for the command of resources across vast spaces, cultural dealings between socially and spatially separated groups have, until the past few centuries, been bridged at great cost and sustained over time only with great effort. The forces of cultural gravity seemed always to pull away from the formation of large-scale ecumenes, whether religious, commercial, or political, toward smaller-scale accretions of intimacy and interest.

Sometime in the past few centuries, the nature of this gravitational field seems to have changed. Partly because of the spirit of the expansion of Western maritime interests after 1500, and partly because of the relatively autonomous developments of large and aggressive social formations in the Americas (such as the Aztecs and the Incas), in Eurasia (such as the Mongols and their descendants, the Mughals and Ottomans), in island Southeast Asia (such as the Buginese), and in the kingdoms of precolonial Africa (such as Dahomey), an overlapping set of ecumenes began to emerge, in which congeries of money, commerce, conquest, and migration began to create durable cross-societal bonds. This process was accelerated by the technology transfers and innovations of the late eighteenth and nineteenth centuries, which created complex colonial orders centered on European capitals and spread through-

Original publication details: Appadurai, Arjun, "Disjuncture and Difference in the Global Cultural Economy," *Public Culture*, Vol. 2, No. 2 (Spring 1990).

out the non-European world. This intricate and overlapping set of Eurocolonial worlds (first Spanish and Portuguese, later principally English, French, and Dutch) set the basis for a permanent traffic in ideas of peoplehood and selfhood, which created the imagined communities of recent nationalisms throughout the world.

With what Benedict Anderson has called "print capitalism," a new power was unleashed in the world, the power of mass literacy and its attendant large-scale production of projects of ethnic affinity that were remarkably free of the need for face-to-face communication or even of indirect communication between persons and groups. The act of reading things together set the stage for movements based on a paradox – the paradox of constructed primordialism. There is, of course, a great deal else that is involved in the story of colonialism and its dialectically generated nationalisms, but the issue of constructed ethnicities is surely a crucial strand in this tale.

But the revolution of print capitalism and the cultural affinities and dialogues unleashed by it were only modest precursors to the world we live in now. For in the past century, there has been a technological explosion, largely in the domain of transportation and information, that makes the interactions of a print-dominated world seem as hard-won and as easily erased as the print revolution made earlier forms of cultural traffic appear. For with the advent of the steamship, the automobile, the airplane, the camera, the computer, and the telephone, we have entered into an altogether new condition of neighborliness, even with those most distant from ourselves. Marshall McLuhan, among others, sought to theorize about this world as a "global village," but theories such as McLuhan's appear to have overestimated the communitarian implications of the new media order. We are now aware that with media, each time we are tempted to speak of the global village, we must be reminded that media create communities with "no sense of place." The world we live in now seems rhizomic, even schizophrenic, calling for theories of rootlessness, alienation, and psychological distance between individuals and groups on the one hand, and fantasies (or nightmares) of electronic propinquity on the other. Here, we are close to the central problematic of cultural processes in today's world.

Thus, the curiosity that drove Pico Iyer to Asia (in 1988) is in some ways the product of a confusion between some ineffable McDonaldization of the world and the much subtler play of indigenous trajectories of desire and fear with global flows of people and things. Indeed, Iyer's own impressions are testimony to the fact that, if a global cultural system is emerging, it is filled with ironies and resistances, sometimes camouflaged as passivity and a bottomless appetite in the Asian world for things Western.

Iyer's own account of the uncanny Philippine affinity for American popular music is rich testimony to the global culture of the hyperreal, for somehow Philippine renditions of American popular songs are both more widespread in the Philippines, and more disturbingly faithful to their originals, than they are in the United States today. An entire nation seems to have learned to mimic Kenny Rogers and the Lennon sisters, like a vast Asian Motown chorus. But *Americanization* is certainly a pallid term to apply to such a situation, for not only are there more Filipinos singing perfect renditions of some American songs (often from the American past) than there are Americans doing so, there is also, of course, the fact that the rest of their lives is not in complete synchrony with the referential world that first gave birth to these songs.

In a further globalizing twist on what Fredric Jameson has called "nostalgia for the present," these Filipinos look back to a world they have never lost. This is one of the central ironies of the politics of global cultural flows, especially in the arena of entertainment and leisure. [. . .]

The central problem of today's global interactions is the tension between cultural homogenization and cultural heterogenization. A vast array of empirical facts could be brought to bear on the side of the homogenization argument, and much of it has come from the left end of the spectrum of media studies, and some from other perspectives. Most often, the homogenization argument subspeciates into either an argument about Americanization or an argument about commoditization, and very often the two arguments are closely linked. What these arguments fail to consider is that at least as rapidly as forces from various metropolises are brought into new societies they tend to become indigenized in one or another way: this is true of music and housing styles as much as it is true of science and terrorism, spectacles and constitutions. The dynamics of such indigenization have just begun to be explored systemically, and much more needs to be done. But it is worth noticing that for the people of Irian Jaya, Indonesianization may be more worrisome than Americanization, as Japanization may be for Koreans, Indianization for Sri Lankans, Vietnamization for the Cambodians, and Russianization for the people of Soviet Armenia and the Baltic republics. Such a list of alternative fears to Americanization could be greatly expanded, but it is not a shapeless inventory: for polities of smaller scale, there is always a fear of cultural absorption by polities of larger scale, especially those that are nearby. One man's imagined community is another man's political prison.

This scalar dynamic, which has widespread global manifestations, is also tied to the relationship between nations and states. For the moment let us note that the simplification of these many forces (and fears) of homogenization can also be exploited by nation-states in relation to their own minorities, by posing global commoditization (or capitalism, or some other such external enemy) as more real than the threat of its own hegemonic strategies.

The new global cultural economy has to be seen as a complex, overlapping, disjunctive order that cannot any longer be understood in terms of existing center–periphery models (even those that might account for multiple centers and peripheries). Nor is it susceptible to simple models of push and pull (in terms of migration theory), or of surpluses and deficits (as in traditional models of balance of trade), or of consumers and producers (as in most neo-Marxist theories of development). Even the most complex and flexible theories of global development that have come out of the Marxist tradition are inadequately quirky and have failed to come to terms with what Scott Lash and John Urry have called disorganized capitalism. The complexity of the current global economy has to do with certain fundamental disjunctures between economy, culture, and politics that we have only begun to theorize.

I propose that an elementary framework for exploring such disjunctures is to look at the relationship among five dimensions of global cultural flows that can be termed (a) *ethnoscapes*, (b) *mediascapes*, (c) *technoscapes*, (d) *financescapes*, and (e) *ideoscapes*. The suffix *-scape* allows us to point to the fluid, irregular shapes of these landscapes, shapes that characterize international capital as deeply as they do international clothing styles. These terms with the common suffix *-scape* also indicate that these are not objectively given relations that look the same from every angle of vision but, rather, that they are deeply perspectival constructs, inflected by the historical, linguistic, and political situatedness of different sorts of actors: nation-states, multinationals, diasporic communities, as well as subnational groupings and movements (whether religious, political, or economic), and even intimate face-to-face groups, such as villages, neighborhoods, and families. Indeed, the individual actor is the last locus of this perspectival set of landscapes, for these landscapes are eventually navigated by agents who both experience and constitute larger formations, in part from their own sense of what these landscapes offer.

These landscapes thus are the building blocks of what (extending Benedict Anderson) I would like to call *imagined worlds*, that is, the multiple worlds that are constituted by the historically situated imaginations of persons and groups spread around the globe. An important fact of the world we live in today is that many persons on the globe live in such imagined worlds (and not just in imagined communities) and thus are able to contest and sometimes even subvert the imagined worlds of the official mind and of the entrepreneurial mentality that surround them.

By *ethnoscape*, I mean the landscape of persons who constitute the shifting world in which we live: tourists, immigrants, refugees, exiles, guest workers, and other moving groups and individuals constitute an essential feature of the world and appear to affect the politics of (and between) nations to a hitherto unprecedented degree. This is not to say that there are no relatively stable communities and networks of kinship, friendship, work, and leisure, as well as of birth, residence, and other filial forms. But it is to say that the warp of these stabilities is everywhere shot through with the woof of human motion, as more persons and groups deal with the realities of having to move or the fantasies of wanting to move. What is more, both these realities and fantasies now function on larger scales, as men and women from villages in India think not just of moving to Poona or Madras but of moving to Dubai and Houston, and refugees from Sri Lanka find themselves in South India as well as in Switzerland, just as the Hmong are driven to London as well as to Philadelphia. And as international capital shifts its needs, as production and technology generate different needs, as nation-states shift their policies on refugee populations, these moving groups can never afford to let their imaginations rest too long, even if they wish to.

By *technoscape*, I mean the global configuration, also ever fluid, of technology and the fact that technology, both high and low, both mechanical and informational, now moves at high speeds across various kinds of previously impervious boundaries. Many countries now are the roots of multinational enterprise: a huge steel complex in Libya may involve interests from India, China, Russia, and Japan, providing different components of new technological configurations. The odd distribution of technologies, and thus the peculiarities of these technoscapes, are increasingly driven not by any obvious economies of scale, of political control, or of market rationality but by increasingly complex relationships among money flows, political possibilities, and the availability of both un- and highly-skilled labor. So, while India exports waiters and chauffeurs to Dubai and Sharjah, it also exports software engineers to the United States – indentured briefly to Tata-Burroughs or the World Bank, then laundered through the State Department to become wealthy resident aliens, who are in turn objects of seductive messages to invest their money and know-how in federal and state projects in India. [. . .]

It is useful to speak as well of *financescapes*, as the disposition of global capital is now a more mysterious, rapid, and difficult landscape to follow than ever before, as currency markets, national stock exchanges, and commodity speculations move megamonies through national turnstiles at blinding speed, with vast, absolute implications for small differences in percentage points and time units. But the critical point is that the global relationship among ethnoscapes, technoscapes, and financescapes is deeply disjunctive and profoundly unpredictable because each of these landscapes is subject to its own constraints and incentives (some political, some informational, and some technoenvironmental), at the same time as each acts as a constraint and a parameter for movements in the others. Thus, even an elementary model of global political economy must take into account the deeply disjunctive relationships among human movement, technological flow, and financial transfers.

Futher refracting these disjunctures (which hardly form a simple, mechanical global infrastructure in any case) are what I call *mediascapes* and *ideoscapes*, which are closely related landscapes of images. *Mediascapes* refer both to the distribution of the electronic capabilities to produce and disseminate information (newspapers, magazines, television stations, and film-production studios), which are now available to a growing number of private and public interests throughout the world, and to the images of the world created by these media. These images involve many complicated inflections, depending on their mode (documentary or entertainment), their hardware (electronic or preelectronic), their audiences (local, national, or transnational), and the interests of those who own and control them. What is most important about these mediascapes is that they provide (especially in their television, film, and cassette forms) large and complex repertoires of images, narratives, and ethnoscapes to viewers throughout the world, in which the world of commodities and the world of news and politics are profoundly mixed. What this means is that many audiences around the world experience the media themselves as a complicated and interconnected repertoire of print, celluloid, electronic screens, and billboards. The lines between the realistic and the fictional landscapes they see are blurred, so that the farther away these audiences are from the direct experiences of metropolitan life, the more likely they are to construct imagined worlds that are chimerical, aesthetic, even fantastic objects, particularly if assessed by the criteria of some other perspective, some other imagined world. [. . .]

Ideoscapes are also concatenations of images, but they are often directly political and frequently have to do with the ideologies of states and the counterideologies of movements explicitly oriented to capturing state power or a piece of it. These ideoscapes are composed of elements of the Enlightenment worldview, which consists of a chain of ideas, terms, and images, including *freedom, welfare, rights, sovereignty, representation*, and the master term *democracy*. The master narrative of the Enlightenment (and its many variants in Britain, France, and the United States) was constructed with a certain internal logic and presupposed a certain relationship between reading, representation, and the public sphere. But the diaspora of these terms and images across the world, especially since the nineteenth century, has loosened the internal coherence that held them together in a Euro-American master narrative and provided instead a loosely structured synopticon of politics, in which different nation-states, as part of their evolution, have organized their political cultures around different keywords. [. . .]

This globally variable synaesthesia has hardly even been noted, but it demands urgent analysis. Thus *democracy* has clearly become a master term, with powerful echoes from Haiti and Poland to the former Soviet Union and China, but it sits at the center of a variety of ideoscapes, composed of distinctive pragmatic configurations of rough translations of other central terms from the vocabulary of the Enlightenment. This creates ever new terminological kaleidoscopes, as states (and the groups that seek to capture them) seek to pacify populations whose own ethnoscapes are in motion and whose mediascapes may create severe problems for the ideoscapes with which they are presented. The fluidity of ideoscapes is complicated in particular by the growing diasporas (both voluntary and involuntary) of intellectuals who continuously inject new meaning-streams into the discourse of democracy in different parts of the world.

This extended terminological discussion of the five terms I have coined sets the basis for a tentative formulation about the conditions under which current global flows occur: they occur in and through the growing disjunctures among ethnoscapes, technoscapes, financescapes, mediascapes, and ideoscapes. This formulation, the core of my model of global cultural flow, needs some explanation. First, people, machinery, money, images, and ideas now follow increasingly nonisomorphic paths; of course, at all periods in human history there have been some disjunctures in the flows of these things, but the sheer speed, scale, and volume of each of these flows are now so great that the disjunctures have become central to the politics of global culture. The Japanese are notoriously hospitable to ideas and are stereotyped as inclined to export (all) and import (some) goods, but they are also notoriously closed to immigration, like the Swiss, the Swedes, and the Saudis. Yet the Swiss and the Saudis accept populations of guest workers, thus creating labor diasporas of Turks, Italians, and other circum-Mediterranean groups. Some such guest-worker groups maintain continuous contact with their home nations, like the Turks, but others, like high-level South Asian migrants, tend to desire lives in their new homes, raising anew the problem of reproduction in a deterritorialized context.

Deterritorialization, in general, is one of the central forces of the modern world because it brings laboring populations into the lower-class sectors and spaces of relatively wealthy societies, while sometimes creating exaggerated and intensified senses of criticism or attachment to politics in the home state. Deterritorialization, whether of Hindus, Sikhs, Palestinians, or Ukrainians, is now at the core of a variety of global fundamentalisms, including Islamic and Hindu fundamentalism. In the Hindu case, for example, it is clear that the overseas movement of Indians has been exploited by a variety of interests both within and outside India to create a complicated network of finances and religious identifications, by which the problem of cultural reproduction for Hindus abroad has become tied to the politics of Hindu fundamentalism at home.

At the same time, deterritorialization creates new markets for film companies, art impresarios, and travel agencies, which thrive on the need of the deterritorialized population for contact with its homeland. Naturally, these invented homelands, which constitute the mediascapes of deterritorialized groups, can often become sufficiently fantastic and one-sided that they provide the material for new ideoscapes in which ethnic conflicts can begin to erupt. The creation of Khalistan, an invented homeland of the deterritorialized Sikh population of England, Canada, and the United States, is one example of the bloody potential in such mediascapes as they interact with the internal colonialisms of the nation-state. The West Bank, Namibia, and Eritrea are other theaters for the enactment of the bloody negotiation between existing nation-states and various deterritorialized groupings.

It is in the fertile ground of deterritorialization, in which money, commodities, and persons are involved in ceaselessly chasing each other around the world, that the mediascapes and ideoscapes of the modern world find their fractured and fragmented counterpart. For the ideas and images produced by mass media often are only partial guides to the goods and experiences that deterritorialized populations transfer to one another. In Mira Nair's brilliant film *India Cabaret*, we see the multiple loops of this fractured deterritorialization as young women, barely competent in Bombay's metropolitan glitz, come to seek their fortunes as cabaret dancers and prostitutes in Bombay, entertaining men in clubs with dance formats derived wholly from the prurient dance sequences of Hindi films. These scenes in turn cater to ideas about Western and foreign women and their looseness, while they provide tawdry career alibis for these women. Some of these women come from Kerala, where cabaret clubs and the pornographic film industry have blossomed, partly in response to the purses and tastes of Keralites returned from the Middle East, where their diasporic lives away from women distort their very sense of what the relations between men and women might be. These tragedies of displacement could certainly be replayed in a more detailed analysis of the relations between the Japanese and German sex tours to Thailand and the tragedies of the sex trade in Bangkok, and in other similar loops that tie together fantasies about the Other, the conveniences and seductions of travel, the economics of global trade, and the brutal mobility fantasies that dominate gender politics in many parts of Asia and the world at large. [. . .]

One important new feature of global cultural politics, tied to the disjunctive relationships among the various landscapes discussed earlier, is that state and nation are at each other's throats, and the hyphen that links them is now less an icon of conjuncture than an index of disjuncture. This disjunctive relationship between nation and state has two levels: at the level of any given nation-state, it means that there is a battle of the imagination, with state and nation seeking to cannibalize one another. Here is the seedbed of brutal separatisms – majoritarianisms that seem to have appeared from nowhere and microidentities that have become political projects within the nation-state. At another level, this disjunctive relationship is deeply entangled with various global disjunctures: ideas of nationhood appear to be steadily increasing in scale and regularly crossing existing state boundaries, sometimes, as with the Kurds, because previous identities stretched across vast national spaces or, as with the Tamils in Sri Lanka, the dormant threads of a transnational diaspora have been activated to ignite the micropolitics of a nation-state. [. . .]

States find themselves pressed to stay open by the forces of media, technology, and travel that have fueled consumerism throughout the world and have increased the craving, even in the non-Western world, for new commodities and spectacles. On the other hand, these very cravings can become caught up in new ethnoscapes, mediascapes, and, eventually, ideoscapes, such as democracy in China, that the state cannot tolerate as threats to its own control over ideas of nationhood and peoplehood. States throughout the world are under siege, especially where contests over the ideoscapes of democracy are fierce and fundamental, and where there are radical disjunctures between ideoscapes and technoscapes (as in the case of very small countries that lack contemporary technologies of production and information); or between ideoscapes and financescapes (as in countries such as Mexico or Brazil, where international lending influences national politics to a very large degree); or between ideoscapes and ethnoscapes (as in Beirut, where diasporic, local, and translocal filiations are suicidally at battle); or between ideoscapes and mediascapes (as in many countries in the Middle East and Asia) where the lifestyles represented on both national and international TV and cinema completely overwhelm and undermine the rhetoric of national politics. In the Indian case, the myth of the lawbreaking hero has emerged to mediate this naked struggle between the pieties and realities of Indian politics, which has grown increasingly brutalized and corrupt.

The transnational movement of the martial arts, particularly through Asia, as mediated by the Hollywood and Hong Kong film industries is a rich illustration of the ways in which long-standing martial arts traditions, reformulated to meet the fantasies of contemporary (sometimes lumpen) youth populations, create new cultures of masculinity and violence, which are in turn the fuel for increased violence in national and international politics. Such violence is in turn the spur to an increasingly rapid and amoral arms trade that penetrates the entire world. The worldwide spread of the AK-47 and the Uzi, in films, in corporate and state security, in terror, and in police and military activity, is a reminder that apparently simple technical uniformities often conceal an increasingly complex set of loops, linking images of violence to aspirations for community in some imagined world.

Returning then to the ethnoscapes with which I began, the central paradox of ethnic politics in today's world is that primordia (whether of language or skin color or neighborhood or kinship) have become globalized. That is, sentiments, whose greatest force is in their ability to ignite intimacy into a political state and turn locality into a staging ground for identity, have become spread over vast and irregular spaces as groups move yet stay linked to one another through sophisticated media capabilities. This is not to deny that such primordia are often the product of invented traditions or retrospective affiliations, but to emphasize that because of the disjunctive and unstable interplay of commerce, media, national policies, and consumer fantasies, ethnicity, once a genie contained in the bottle of some sort of locality (however large), has now become a global force, forever slipping in and through the cracks between states and borders.

But the relationship between the cultural and economic levels of this new set of global disjunctures is not a simple one-way street in which the terms of global cultural politics are set wholly by, or confined wholly within, the vicissitudes of international flows of technology, labor, and finance, demanding only a modest modification of existing neo-Marxist models of uneven development and state formation. There is a deeper change, itself driven by the disjunctures among all the landscapes I have discussed and constituted by their continuously fluid and uncertain interplay, that concerns the relationship between production and consumption in today's global economy. Here, I begin with Marx's famous (and often mined) view of the fetishism of the commodity and suggest that this fetishism has been replaced in the world at large (now seeing the world as one large, interactive system, composed of many complex subsystems) by two mutually supportive descendants, the first of which I call production fetishism and the second, the fetishism of the consumer.

By *production fetishism* I mean an illusion created by contemporary transnational production loci that masks translocal capital, transnational earning flows, global management, and often faraway workers (engaged in various kinds of high-tech putting-out operations) in the idiom and spectacle of local (sometimes even worker) control, national productivity, and territorial sovereignty. To the extent that various kinds of free-trade zones have become the models for production at large, especially of high-tech commodities, production has itself become a fetish, obscuring not social relations as such but the relations of production, which are increasingly transnational. The locality (both in the sense of the local factory or site of production and in the extended sense of the nation-state) becomes a fetish that disguises the globally dispersed forces that actually drive the production process. This generates alienation (in Marx's sense) twice intensified, for its social sense is now compounded by a complicated spatial dynamic that is increasingly global.

As for the *fetishism of the consumer*, I mean to indicate here that the consumer has been transformed through commodity flows (and the mediascapes, especially of advertising, that accompany them) into a sign, both in Baudrillard's sense of a simulacrum that only asymptotically approaches the form of a real social agent, and in the sense of a mask for the real seat of agency, which is not the consumer but the producer and the many forces that constitute production. Global advertising is the key technology for the worldwide dissemination of a plethora of creative and culturally well-chosen ideas of consumer agency. These images of agency are increasingly distortions of a world of merchandising so subtle that the consumer is consistently helped to believe that he or she is an actor, where in fact he or she is at best a chooser.

The globalization of culture is not the same as its homogenization, but globalization involves the use of a variety of instruments of homogenization (armaments, advertising techniques, language hegemonies, and clothing styles) that are absorbed into local political and cultural economies, only to be repatriated as heterogeneous dialogues of national sovereignty, free enterprise, and fundamentalism in which the state plays an increasingly delicate role: too much openness to global flows, and the nation-state is threatened by revolt, as in the China syndrome; too little, and the state exits the international stage, as Burma, Albania, and North Korea in various ways have done. In general, the state has become the arbitrageur of this *repatriation of difference* (in the form of goods, signs, slogans, and styles). But this repatriation or export of the designs and commodities of difference continuously exacerbates the internal politics of majoritarianism and homogenization, which is most frequently played out in debates over heritage.

Thus the central feature of global culture today is the politics of the mutual effort of sameness and difference to cannibalize one another and thereby proclaim their successful hijacking of the twin Enlightenment ideas of the triumphantly universal and the resiliently particular. This mutual cannibalization shows its ugly face in riots, refugee flows, state-sponsored torture, and ethnocide (with or without state support). Its brighter side is in the expansion of many individual horizons of hope and fantasy, in the global spread of oral rehydration therapy and other low-tech instruments of well-being, in the susceptibility even of South Africa to the force of global opinion, in the inability of the Polish state to repress its own working classes, and in the growth of a wide range of progressive, transnational alliances. Examples of both sorts could be multiplied. The critical point is that both sides of the coin of global cultural process today are products of the infinitely varied mutual contest of sameness and difference on a stage characterized by radical disjunctures between different sorts of global flows and the uncertain landscapes created in and through these disjunctures. [. . .]

45 Scenarios for Peripheral Cultures

Ulf Hannerz

The twentieth century has been a unique period in world cultural history. Humankind has finally bid farewell to that world which could with some credibility be seen as a cultural mosaic, of separate pieces with hard, well-defined edges. Because of the great increase in the traffic in culture, the large-scale transfer of meaning systems and symbolic forms, the world is increasingly becoming one not only in political and economic terms, as in the climactic period of colonialism, but in terms of its cultural construction as well; a global ecumene of persistent cultural interaction and exchange. This, however, is no egalitarian global village. What we see now is quite firmly structured as an asymmetry of center and periphery. With regard to cultural flow, the periphery, out there in a distant territory, is more the taker than the giver of meaning and meaningful form. Much as we feel called upon to make note of any examples of counterflow, it is difficult to avoid the conclusion that at least as things stand now, the relationship is lopsided. [. . .]

The shaping of world culture is an ongoing process, toward future and still uncertain states. But perhaps one conceivable outcome has come to dominate the imagery of the cultural future, as a master scenario against which every alternative scenario has to be measured. Let us call it a scenario of global homogenization of culture. The murderous threat of cultural imperialism is here rhetorically depicted as involving the high-tech culture of the metropolis, with powerful organizational backing, facing a defenseless, small-scale folk culture. But "cultural imperialism," it also becomes clear, has more to do with market than with empire. The alleged prime mover behind the pan-human replication of uniformity is late Western capitalism, luring forever more communities into dependency on the fringes of an expanding world-wide consumer society. Homogenization results mainly from the center-to-periphery flow of commoditized culture. Consequently, the coming homogeneous world culture according to this view will by and large be a version of contemporary Western culture, and the loss of local culture would show itself most distinctively at the periphery.

This master scenario has several things going for it. A quick look at the world today affords it a certain intrinsic plausibility; it may seem like a mere continuation of present trends. It has, of course, the great advantage of simplicity. And it is dramatic. There is the sense of fatefulness, the prediction of the irreversible loss of large parts of the combined heritage of humanity. As much of the diversity of its behavioral repertoire is wiped out, Homo Sapiens becomes more like other species – in

Original publication details: Hannerz, Ulf, "Scenarios for Peripheral Cultures" from *Culture, Globalization and the World-System*, Anthony D. King (ed.) (State University of New York, Binghamton, 1991).

large part making its own environment, in contrast with them, but at the same time adapting to it in a single, however complex way.

There is also another scenario for global cultural process, although more sub-terranean; thus not so often coming out to compete openly with the global homo-genization scenario. We may call it the peripheral corruption scenario, for what it portrays as a recurrent sequence is one where the center offers its high ideals and its best knowledge, given some institutional form, and where the periphery first adopts them and then soon corrupts them. The scenario shows elected heads of state becoming presidents for life, then bizarre, merciless emperors. It shows Westmin-ster and Oxbridge models being swallowed by the bush. The center, in the end, cannot win; not at the periphery.

Biases

The peripheral corruption scenario is there for the people of the center to draw on when they are pessimistic about their own role in improving the world, and doubt-ful and/or cynical about the periphery. It is deeply ethnocentric, in that it posits a very uneven distribution of virtue, and in that it denies the validity and worth of any transformations at the periphery of what was originally drawn from the center. There is little question of cultural difference here, but rather of a difference between culture and non-culture, between civilization and savagery. [. . .]

It is a more general familiarity with, as well as specific research experiences in, West African urban life that have done most to provoke my interest in the center–periphery relationships of world culture and to shape my gut reactions to the sce-narios I have pointed to.

In a Nigerian Town

Let me therefore say just something about the modest middle Nigerian town which I know best, its people and the settings in which meaning flows there. Some sixty years ago this town was just coming into existence, at a new junction of the rail-road built by the British colonial government. It is a community, then, which has known no existence outside the present world system. The inhabitants are railroad workers, taxi drivers, bank clerks, doctors and nurses, petty traders, tailors, shoe shiners, teachers and school children, policemen, preachers and prostitutes, bar owners and truck pushers, praise singers and peasant women who come in for the day to sell produce in the market place. Apart from attending to work, towns-people spend their time in their rooms and yards, managing household affairs; going up and down the streets to greet one another; shopping; arguing and drinking in the beer and palmwine bars; or especially if they are young men, taking in a show at the open-air movie theater. Since about fifteen years ago, when electricity finally came to town at a time when the Nigerian oil economy was booming, they might watch TV – all of a sudden there were a great many antennae over the rusting zinc roofs. People had battery-operated record players long before, and there were several record stores, but a number of them have since closed down. The listeners now prefer cassettes, and there are hawkers selling them, mostly pirate editions, from the backs of their bicycles. People also go to their churches or mosques. (A couple of years ago, actually, a visiting preacher chose his words unwisely, and

Christians and Muslims in the town proceeded to burn down a number of each other's houses of worship.)

Where Meaning Flows: Market, State, Form of Life, and Movement

Now let me take a round of collective human existence such as this apart, to see how culture is arranged within it. Culture goes on everywhere in social life, organized as a flow of meanings, by way of meaningful forms, between people. But it does so along rather different principles in different contexts. For a comprehensive account-ing of cultural flow, it is useful, I think, to distinguish some small number of typical social frameworks in which it occurs; frameworks which in part because of global-ization recur in contemporary life north and south, east and west; in an African town as well as in Europe or America. The frameworks are recurrent, that is, even as their cultural contents are different. The totality of cultural process, then, can be seen within these frameworks and in their interrelations. To begin with, one may look at these frameworks in synchronic terms. But time can be made to enter in, and we can then return to the problem of scenarios, as a matter of the cumulative consequences of cultural process. All this, obviously, I can only hope to sketch roughly here.

I see primarily four of these typical frameworks of cultural process. Whatever culture flows outside these four, I would claim, amounts to rather little. The global homogenization scenario, as I have described it, is preoccupied with only one of these, that of the market, so if anything significant at all goes on in the other three, that scenario would obviously have to be marked "incomplete." But let us begin there. In the market framework, cultural commodities are moved. All commodities presumably carry some meaning, but in some cases intellectual, esthetic or emo-tional appeal is all there is to a commodity, or a very large part of it, and these are what we would primarily have in mind as we speak of cultural commodities. In the market framework, meanings and meaningful forms are thus produced and dis-seminated by specialists in exchange for material compensation, setting up asym-metrical, more or less centering relationships between producers and consumers. The market also attempts expansively to bring more and more of culture as a whole into its framework, its agents are in competition with one another, and they also keep innovating to foster new demand. There is, in other words, a built-in tendency toward instability in this framework.

The second framework of cultural process is that of the state, not as a bounded physical area but as organizational form. The state is engaged in the management of meaning in various ways. To gain legitimate authority state apparatuses nowa-days tend to reach out with different degrees of credibility and success toward their subjects to foster the idea that the state is a nation, and to construct them cultur-ally as citizens. This involves a degree of homogenization as a goal of cultural engi-neering. On the other hand, the state also takes an interest in shaping such differences among people as are desirable for the purpose of fitting categories of individuals into different slots in the structure of production and reproduction. Beyond such involvements in cultural process, some states more than others engage in what one may describe as cultural welfare, trying to provide their citizenry with "good culture"; that is, meanings and meaningful forms held to meet certifiable intellectual and esthetic standards. Not least would this cultural welfare provide the instruments people may use in developing constructive reflexive stances toward themselves and their world.

The state framework for cultural process again involves a significant asymmetry between state apparatus and people. It concentrates resources at the center for long-term cultural work, and the flow of meaning is mostly from the center outward. In at least one current of the cultural flow which the state sets in motion the tendency may be toward a stability of meaning – the idea of the nation is usually tied to conceptions of history and tradition. But then again, we should know by now that such conceptions may in fact be spurious and quite contestable.

The third framework of cultural process I will identify, for lack of a more precise term, as that of "form of life." It is surely a framework of major importance, in that it involves the everyday practicalities of production and reproduction, activities going on in work places, domestic settings, neighborhoods, and some variety of other places. What characterizes cultural process here is that from doing the same things over and over again, and seeing and hearing others doing the same things and saying the same things over and over again, a great deal of redundancy results. Experiences and interests coalesce into habitual perspectives and dispositions. Within this framework, too, people's mere going about things entails a free and reciprocal cultural flow. In contrast with the market and state frameworks, there are no specialists in the production and dissemination of meaning as such who are to be materially compensated for cultural work. While every form of life includes some people and excludes a great many others, there are not necessarily well-defined boundaries between them, and people may develop some conception of each other's forms of life through much the same kind of everyday looking and listening, although probably with less precision. As a whole, encompassing the variety of particular forms of life, this framework involves cultural processes which are diffuse, uncentered. The "commanding heights" of culture, as it were, are not here. As the everyday activities are practically adapted to material circumstances, there is not much reason to bring about alterations in culture here, as long as the circumstances do not change. In the form of life framework, consequently, there is a tendency toward stability in cultural process.

In contemporary complex societies, the division of labor is the dominant factor in shaping forms of life, providing material bases as well as central experiences. But as the reciprocity and redundancy of the flow of meaning between people involved with one another at work, in domesticity and in sociability seem similar enough, I think of this as a single framework.

Looking now at my Nigerian town, or at peripheral societies generally, one can see that the variety of forms of life are drawn into the world system in somewhat different ways, as the local division of labor is entangled with the international division of labor. There are still people, fairly self-sufficient agriculturalists in the vicinity of the town, who seem only rather incompletely integrated into the world system in material terms: who just barely make it into the periphery. On the other hand, there are people like the railroad employees whose mode of existence is based on the fact that the desire arose, some time early in this century, to carry tin and groundnuts from inland Nigeria to the world.

But then also some forms of life more than others become defined, with precision and overall, in terms of culture which has flown and continues to flow from center to periphery. It is true that through their livelihoods at least, the peasant women who come to market in the Nigerian town, or the praise singer who performs for local notables, are not very much involved with metropolitan meaning systems; the railroader, the bank clerk and the doctor are rather more. Yet there is no one-to-one relationship either between the specificity of such cultural definition and degree of world system material involvement. In many places on the periphery, there are forms of life owing their material existence, such as it may be, very immediately to the world system – forms of life revolving around oil wells, copper mines, coffee plantations. And yet the plantation worker may earn his living with a relative minimum of particular technological or organizational skills originating at the center.

To the extent that forms of life, or segments of the daily round which they encompass, are not subjected to any higher degree of cultural definition from the center, by way of the international division of labor or otherwise, there is room for more cultural autonomy. And of course, the strength of the culture existing in such reserves may be such that it also reaches back to penetrate into segments more directly and more extensively defined by the center. This is putting things very briefly; we come back to the implications.

For the fourth and final framework of cultural process in contemporary life I would nominate that of movements, more intermittently part of the cultural totality than the other three, although it can hardly be gainsaid that especially in the last quarter-century or so, they have had a major influence – examples of this being the women's movement, the environmental movement, and the peace movement. In the present context of considering center–periphery links of culture, I will say less about the movement framework, however, and mention it here mostly for the sake of completeness. It is undoubtedly true, as Roland Robertson notes, that globalization often forms an important part of the background for the rise of contemporary movements. Yet it seems to me that the great transnational movements of recent times have not in themselves seemed to become fully organized in a reach all the way between center and periphery. Some rather combine center and semi-periphery, others parts of the periphery.

Market, state, form of life and movement can be rather commonsensically distinguished, but we see that they differ in their centering and decentering tendencies, in their politics of culture and in their cultural economies. They also have their own tendencies with respect to the temporal dimension of culture. At the same time, it is true that much of what goes on in culture has to do with their interrelations. States, markets and movements are ultimately only successful if they can get forms of life to open up to them. States sometimes compete in markets; nationalist movements have been known to transform themselves into states; some movements create internal markets, and they can be newsworthy and thus commoditizable in the market; forms of life can be selectively commoditized as life style news; and so on, indefinitely. These entanglements, involving often mutually contradictory tendencies, keep the totality alive, shifting, continuously unstable. [. . .]

I propose that it may be useful to identify two tendencies in the longer-term reconstruction of peripheral cultures within the global ecumene. One might think of each (although I prefer not to) as a distinctive scenario of future cultural history, and in these terms they would bear some resemblance to the global homogenization scenario and the peripheral corruption scenarios respectively.

I will call one the saturation tendency, and the other the maturation tendency. The saturation tendency is that which may be seen as a version of the global homogenization scenario, with some more detailed interest in historical sequence. It would suggest that as the transnational cultural influences, of whatever sort but in large part certainly market organized, and operating in a continuously open structure, unendingly pound on the sensibilities of the people of the periphery, peripheral culture will step by step assimilate more and more of the imported meanings and forms, becoming gradually indistinguishable from the center. At any one time, what is considered local culture is a little more penetrated by transnational forms than what went before it as local culture, although at any one time, until the end point is reached, the contrast between local and transnational may still be drawn, and still be regarded as significant. The cultural differences celebrated and recommended for safeguarding now may only be a pale reflection of what once existed, and sooner or later they will be gone as well.

What is suggested here is that the center, through the frameworks of cultural process within which the transnational flow passes most readily, and among which the market framework is certainly conspicuous, cumulatively colonizes the minds of the periphery, with a corresponding institutionalization of its forms, getting the periphery so "hooked" that soon enough there is no real opportunity for choice. The mere fact that these forms originate in the center makes them even more attractive, a peculiar but undeniable aspect of commodity esthetics in the periphery. This colonization is understood to proceed through relentless cultural bombardment, through the redundancy of its seductive messages. As the market framework interpenetrates with that of forms of life, the latter becomes reconstructed around their dependence on what was initially alien, using it for their practical adaptations, seeing themselves wholly or at least partially through it. [. . .]

The inherent cultural power of the form of life framework could perhaps also be such that it colonizes the market framework, rather than vice versa. This is more in line with what I see as the maturation tendency; a notion which has its affinities with the peripheral corruption scenario, although probably with other evaluative overtones. The periphery, it is understood here, takes its time reshaping metropolitan culture to its own specifications. It is in phase one, so to speak, that the metropolitan forms in the periphery are most marked by their purity; but on closer scrutiny they turn out to stand there fairly ineffective, perhaps vulnerable, in their relative isolation. In a phase two, and in innumerable phases thereafter, as they are made to interact with whatever else exists in their new setting, there may be a mutual influence, but the metropolitan forms are somehow no longer so easily recognizable – they become hybridized. In these later phases, the terms of the cultural market for one thing are in a reasonable measure set from within the peripheral forms of life, as these have come to be constituted, highly variable of course in the degree to which they are themselves culturally defined in the terms drawn from the center.

Obviously the creativity of popular culture in much of the Third World, and not least in West Africa, fits in here. Local cultural entrepreneurs have gradually mastered the alien cultural forms which reach them through the transnational commodity flow and in other ways, taking them apart, tampering and tinkering with them in such a way that the resulting new forms are more responsive to, and at the same time in part outgrowths of, local everyday life. [. . .]

This, then, is the local scene which is already in place to meet the transnational culture industries of the twentieth century. It is not a scene where the peripheral culture is utterly defenseless, but rather one where locally evolving alternatives to imports are available, and where there are people at hand to keep performing innovative acts of cultural brokerage.

The Periphery in Creolization

I should begin to pull things together. It is probably evident that I place some emphasis on the theme of maturation, and that I continue to resist the idea of saturation, at least in its unqualified form, which is that of global homogenization. In fact, in that form, it has suspiciously much in common with that 1940s or 1950s imagery of mass culture within the metropole which showed a faceless, undifferentiated crowd drowning in a flood of mediocre but mass-produced cultural commodities. Since then, metropolitan scholarship at home has mostly moved away from that imagery, toward much more subtle conceptions of the differentiation of publics, and the contextualized reception of culture industry products. Exporting the older, rather wornout and compromised notion to the periphery, consequently, looks suspiciously like another case of cultural dumping.

It is no doubt a trifle unfortunate that there seems to be no single scenario to put in the place of that of global homogenization, with similarly strong – but more credible – claims to predictive power. But then prediction is not something the human sciences have been very good at, and in the case of the global ordering of culture, what I have said may at least contribute to some understanding of why this is so. The diversity of interlocking principles for the organization of cultural process involves too many uncertainties to allow us to say much that is very definite with regard to the aggregate outcome. [. . .]

If there is any term which has many of the right associations by which to describe the ongoing, historically cumulative cultural interrelatedness between center and periphery, it is, I think, "creolization," a borrowing from particular social and cultural histories by way of a more generalized linguistics. I will not dwell on the potential of a creolization scenario for peripheral cultures very long here, and it may be that what I take from a rather volatile field of linguistic thought is little more than a rough metaphor. Yet it has a number of components which are appropriate enough. I like it because it suggests that cultures, like languages, can be intrinsically of mixed origin, rather than historically pure and homogeneous. It clashes conspicuously, that is to say, with received assumptions about culture coming out of nineteenth century European nationalism. And the similarities between "creole" and "create" are not fortuitous. We have a sharper sense than usual that creole cultures result as people actively engage in making their own syntheses. With regard to the entire cultural inventory of humanity, creolization may involve losing some, but certainly gaining some, too. There is also in the creolization scenario the notion of a more or less open continuum, a gradation of living syntheses which can be seen to match the cultural distance between center and periphery. And just as it is understood to involve a political economy of language, so the creolization continuum can be seen in its organization of diversity to entail a political economy of culture.

Furthermore, there is the dimension of time. Looking backward, the creolist point of view recognizes history. Creole cultures are not instant products of the present but have had some time to develop and draw themselves together to at least some degree of coherence; generations have already been born into them, but have also kept working on them. Looking forward, the creolization scenario is open-ended. This is perhaps an intellectual copout, but again, probably an inevitable one. It suggests that the saturation and maturation tendencies are not necessarily alternatives, but can appear in real life interwoven with one another. When the peripheral culture absorbs the influx of meanings and symbolic forms from the center and transforms them to make them in some considerable degree their own, they may at the same time so increase the cultural affinities between the center and the periphery that the passage of more cultural imports is facilitated. What the end state of all this will be is impossible to say, but it is possible that there is none. [. . .]

46 Global Fundamentalism

Frank J. Lechner

Fundamentalism is fashionable – as a problem for social analysis more than as a form of religious faith and activism. To be sure, the reemergence of a certain kind of religious traditionalism in the public arenas of some countries was sufficiently surprising to justify a major scholarly effort to account for it. For Western scholars, the puzzle to be solved went beyond the apparent influence and success of some seemingly archaic cultural movements. The very way in which those labeled "fundamentalist" tried to bring a sacred tradition to bear on the public affairs of their societies compelled scholars to reexamine their assumptions about the "normal" role of religion in modern societies and about the continued viability of religious traditions themselves. By virtue of its public character, fundamentalism seemed to point to a different future for religion from what many scholars had assumed. [. . .]

Global Perspectives

The "global turn" in sociology consists of sustained efforts by a number of researchers over the past few decades to treat the world as a social system in its own right. These efforts were obviously inspired by the simple realization that societies were becoming highly interdependent. Moreover, it became clear that the very processes in which sociologists were interested had an inherently global dimension. Nettl and Robertson argued, for example, that modernization consisted not of processes that simply occurred in similar fashion across the globe but rather of deliberate attempts by societal elites to place their society in a global hierarchy. Wallerstein saw this hierarchy as the product of long-term changes in the capitalist world economy, which had brought about not only a global division of labor but also a dominant world culture. This world culture became the primary concern of Meyer and his associates, who argued that modern institutions function according to global standards that are part of a "world polity." Robertson described such phenomena as aspects of "globalization" and specifically called attention to the importance of religious reactions against this process, brought forth by the tensions it has produced. An early attempt to link sociocultural movements to world-level changes was made by Wuthnow.

Given these scholarly precedents, what does it mean to speak of "global fundamentalism"? It means first of all that the predicament addressed by fundamentalist movements is a global one. Modernity is no longer a societal phenomenon, if it ever was. A reaction *against* modernity therefore necessarily has global implications: It entails a world-view in the literal sense of advocating a distinct view of "the world." For Islamic militants this includes an obligation to spread the Islamic revolution and

Original publication details: Lechner, Frank J., "Global Fundamentalism" from William H. Swatos (ed.), *A Future for Religion?*, pp. 27–32. Copyright © 1993 by Sage Publications Inc. Reprinted by permission of Sage Publications.

defeat the dominant Western satan. A global culture, not simply local circumstances, becomes the target of fundamentalist movements. The defenders of God aspire to bringing the kingdom of God to the earth as a whole, and in this sense they become important actors on the global scene. As global antisystemic movements, they attempt to resolve literally worldwide problems in global fashion – changing both the actual balance of power in the world and the cultural terms on which global actors operate. The struggle in which they are engaged is not, or not only, against modernity abstractly defined, but also for a particular shape of the globe. The extent to which they pursue this ambition depends in large part on variations in global change, on the extent to which particular societies or regions are socially or culturally unsettled by forces beyond their control.

The changing global condition not only becomes a context and target of fundamentalism, but also serves as its primary precipitating factor. Yet apart from globally induced variations in the strength of fundamentalism, the very attempt to restore a sacred tradition as a basis for a meaningful social order is globally significant, as one effort among others to preserve or achieve a certain cultural authenticity in the face of a greedy, universalizing global culture. It is, in other words, a particular, albeit radical and problematic, form of striving for communal and societal identity under circumstances that make such deliberate identification a global expectation – a point Robertson has repeatedly emphasized. Indeed, fundamentalism itself has become a global category, part of the global repertoire of collective action available to discontented groups, but also a symbol in a global discourse about the shape of the world. For liberal Westerners concerned about further "progressive" change, fundamentalism is the global Other, that which "we" are not; for those taking issue with the meaning and structure of current, Western-inspired global culture, fundamentalism becomes a most radical form of resistance, a symbolic vehicle. Interpreting fundamentalism in this global fashion is to subsume, not to discard, the treatment of fundamentalism as a form of antimodernism. Indeed, of all the conventional approaches to fundamentalism, this may well have the most lasting value; global culture, after all, is still (though not only) the culture of modernity. Standard criticisms of this approach as ethnocentric appear increasingly misplaced, for it is one that touches on crucial features of the global condition and represents a form of sociological realism rather than Western wishful thinking. To see fundamentalists locked in a struggle about the shape of the world is to recognize part of their actual predicament, not to deny their particularity in imperialist fashion. In fact, those advocating a less analytical, more subjective approach to fundamentalism as well as other manifestations of religiosity or cultural difference now face the difficulty that doing justice to the other in his or her particularity forces one to take into account the other's relation to universal structures, the other's reaction to alien penetration, the other's distinctly modern assertions of particularity.

In other words, the otherness of the other is increasingly problematic as a consequence of globalization; fundamentalism, to put it most simply, is inevitably contaminated by the culture it opposes. Just as in any pluralistic culture, the other is always already within us, we are also already in the other, even when she or he puts forth a grand display of antipluralist authenticity. In the modern world system, no fundamentalist can simply reappropriate the sacred and live by its divine lights. The very reappropriation is a modern, global phenomenon, part of the shared experience of "creolization." To see it as such is to include the other as full participant in a common discourse, a common society, rather than to relegate him or her to the iron cage of otherness.

The global perspective on fundamentalism also makes comparisons in the conventional sense problematic. Such comparisons, after all, presuppose that one can isolate the units to be compared, in order to examine the differential effects of similar but independently occurring processes. Often carried out for the sake of historical sensitivity, such an exercise increasingly comes to seem artificially abstract. Societies are now inherently oriented toward each other; they are involved in processes that encompass all; even the object of the comparison, namely the propensity to engage in fundamentalism, is no longer an indigenously arising phenomenon. Of course, careful comparisons can still help to determine the causal weight of particular factors in social movements. But, beyond that, the new global condition has changed the terms of scholarly analysis as much as it has the terms of actual social action.

A Future for Fundamentalism?

The global turn in the study of fundamentalism was partly inspired by the concern about the possible public influence of fundamentalism mentioned at the outset. In the end, the scholarly and the public interest in fundamentalism converge on the question about the likely extent of this influence. I will briefly offer grounds for judging this influence relatively minor and for skepticism about the overall future of fundamentalism as we know it.

Of course, assessing the future of fundamentalism, a hazardous undertaking in any case, by no means exhausts the question of the future of religion as a whole. Indeed, from the point of view of nonfundamentalist believers, it may well be the case that the demise of fundamentalism is a condition for the revitalization of serious religiosity. Expressing skepticism about the future of fundamentalism also does not imply that there is no future for research about fundamentalism. There is work to be done, if only because the trends in social analysis sketched above have improved our understanding but not answered all questions. And precisely because its future is problematic and conflicted, fundamentalism will remain a fruitful subject for research.

Turning to substance: As I and others have argued over the years, fundamentalism is a quintessentially modern phenomenon. It actively strives to reorder society; it reasserts the validity of a tradition and uses it in new ways; it operates in a context that sets nontraditional standards; where it does not take decisive control, it reproduces the dilemmas it sets out to resolve; as one active force among others, it affirms the depth of modern pluralism; it takes on the tensions produced by the clash between a universalizing global culture and particular local conditions; it expresses fundamental uncertainty in a crisis setting, not traditional confidence about taken-for-granted truths; by defending God, who formerly needed no defense, it creates and recreates difference as part of a global cultural struggle. So compromised, fundamentalism becomes part of the fabric of modernity.

Being compromised in this way portends a problematic future for fundamentalism – problematic, that is, from a fundamentalist point of view. It indicates one of the ways in which fundamentalism, like any other cultural movement, engages and must engage in creolization, juxtaposing the seemingly alien and the seemingly indigenous into a worldview and identity that combine both in new seamless wholes. Of course, upon inspection traditions often display a hybrid character. But if Robertson is right, such hybridization now becomes a normal feature of globalization, robbing cultures of easy authenticity while making the search for the authentic a virtual obligation. If the point of fundamentalism is to restore an authentic sacred tradition, this means that fundamentalism must fail.

This failure is exacerbated by the modern circumstances fundamentalism must confront. In some respects, modernity does act as a solvent, undermining the thrust of fundamentalist movements. Insofar as a society becomes structurally differentiated, religion loses social significance; once that happens, restoration is difficult if not impossible. In differentiated, specialized institutions engaged in technical control of the world, religious distinctions have little role in any case; the very conception of infusing a perceived iron cage with religious meaning necessarily remains nebulous. If a culture becomes pluralistic and tears down its sacred canopy, those who would restore it are themselves only one group among others. Making claims for a fundamentalist project requires wider legitimation, except where there is overwhelming popular support; such wider legitimation entails watering down the message. Trying to act globally with some effectiveness presupposes the use of global means, technological and institutional; but satellite dishes and fighter planes and nation-states draw the would-be opposition farther into the culture it claims to disdain. Although its relative success varies according to the conditions sketched above, fundamentalism is inevitably coopted.

But being modern and becoming coopted presuppose that there is a viable modern order to be coopted into. The future of fundamentalism is thus closely linked to the future of modernity. One advantage of the analytical view of fundamentalism, starting by conceptualizing it as one form of antimodernism among others in order to expose its modern character, is that it draws research on the subject into the larger discourse about modernity, central not only to the social sciences but in the public arena as well. If modernity in anything like the liberal version I adopt here can be sustained, albeit transformed through globalization, then the life chances of large-scale public fundamentalism are correspondingly diminished. How strong, then, is the fabric of modernity? Contrary to conventional assertions of the imperialism inherent in modernization or the emptiness of liberal culture or the loss of meaning in advanced societies, liberal modernity offers a wide variety of cultural meanings. The usual jeremiads about the ills and weaknesses of imperially secular modernity notwithstanding, the latter offers considerable room for free religious expression and experience. In the actual struggles about the future direction of world society, it appears to this biased observer, the liberal-modern view of social order thus far has prevailed against challenges issued by various kinds of antimodern movements and regimes. Even after two world wars, the crises and conflicts of modern societies have not brought about the demise of the liberal modern project.

And yet, fundamentalism has its origins in real discontents experienced by real people; the mobilization factors that account for its relative strength in particular places have not disappeared everywhere; the tensions inherent in the globalization process cannot be resolved in any permanent fashion; in modern global culture, fundamentalism has found a place as part of a movement repertoire, to be activated when conditions are right. This does not enable us to make any clear-cut predictions about the reemergence of fundamentalism in the twenty-first century. It does enable us to say, more modestly if less informatively, that fundamentalism has a future – albeit one less bright than that of liberal modernity. [. . .]

47   The Fundamentalist Impact on Law, Politics, and the Constitution in Iran

Ann Elizabeth Mayer

The Goals of Islamization in Iran

Any examination of the goals of fundamentalism in Iran entails an analysis of the goals of the Iranian Revolution of 1978–9, a complex phenomenon beyond the scope of this paper. At the very least, however, it should be noted that in Iran fundamentalist leaders and the fundamentalist program were linked in a variety of ways to a strong popular movement that culminated in a broad-based revolution. (This was not the case either in Pakistan or in the Sudan, where Islamization was imposed from above by military dictators.)

Iranian fundamentalists insist that the Iranian Revolution was led by them and fought on behalf of their cause, so that Islamization can be said to have been the goal of the revolution. It seems more accurate, however, to say that there was a fundamentalist takeover of a revolution that was fought primarily for secular political and economic goals. There was doubtless popular support for some of the broader fundamentalist goals, particularly among the lower middle and lower classes in urban areas, but it would be hard to establish that the Iranian Revolution was widely understood to have been waged on behalf of the specifics of the legislative program that emerged after powerful clerics seized control. Indeed, Ayatollah Khomeini, before consolidating his control, was evasive and vague in pronouncements about his objectives. It is possible that he realized that a candid revelation of the details of his fundamentalist agenda might weaken his position and undermine his popularity.

After the revolution the early focus of Iran's official Islamization program was on establishing an Islamic government, and one of the first tasks of the new regime was writing an Islamic constitution. This was a natural priority because of the prominence of Ayatollah Khomeini's leadership role in the struggle against the shah and his own preoccupation with setting up an Islamic government according to his model of *wilayat al-faqih*, or rule by the Islamic jurist. Khomeini's ideas for the Iranian constitution provoked much criticism by Iranians, including some prominent Shi'ite *ulama* who remained convinced that clerics should not play a role in governance. After a drafting process that was replete with disputes, in late 1979 Iran did succeed in promulgating a new constitution, in which the faqih was placed at the apex of the government (articles 5 and 107) and Islamic law was established

Original publication details: Mayer, Ann Elizabeth, "The Fundamentalist Impact on Law, Politics, and Constitutions in Iran, [Pakistan, and the Sudan]" from Martin E. Marty and R. Scott Appleby (eds.), *Fundamentalisms and the State* (University of Chicago Press, Chicago, 1993).

as the supreme law of the land (article 4), which meant the law of the majority Twelver Shi'ite sect (article 12).

Once firmly ensconced in power, Ayatollah Khomeini and his allies worked toward a goal that they had not advertised prior to the revolution or even in its immediate aftermath: implementing a theocratic model of government in which Shi'ite clerics would play a dominant role in all important spheres and particularly in the legal domain. Shi'ite clerics allied with Khomeini proved eager to take political positions and to supplant the Western-trained or Western-oriented judges and lawyers who had come to dominate the legal establishment under the Pahlavis, under whom law and the legal profession had been largely reformed along French lines. The revolution gave clerics the opportunity to assume the central roles that they had played in the courts and in legal education prior to the secularizing reforms of the 1920s. In addition, clerics began to play a new and unfamiliar role, that of the dominant force in the Majlis, or parliament, which had been a thoroughly secular institution during the reign of Muhammad Reza Shah.

One could see the clerics' dislodging of Westernized professionals and secular-minded technocrats from the dominant positions that they had occupied under the shah as just one facet of the populist, anti-elitist dynamic of the revolution. The Westernized elite of the shah's era had grown estranged from Iranian traditions and had little in common with the values and outlooks of less affluent Iranians. Clerics were more in touch with the traditional culture of the average Iranian than the elite of the Pahlavi era. Nonetheless, this does not mean that the Iranians would have chosen a theocratic form of government had they been given the opportunity to choose between theocracy and democracy in free elections.

As a result of clerical ascendancy, postrevolutionary fundamentalist policies in Iran have been articulated by Shi'ite clerics. Iran's fundamentalist clerics had two bêtes noires on the domestic scene. Not surprisingly, these were the groups most dramatically affected by the Islamization program. The first target was Iranian women who rejected their traditional cloistered and subjugated role and demanded full equality with men. As Shahla Haeri points out in volume 2 of this series, clerical ire had been aroused by the 1963 reform which granted women the right to vote and by the Iranian Family Protection Act of 1967, which significantly improved women's rights in the area of family law. The growing prominence of women in public roles and the professions in the last decades of the shah's regime was also profoundly disturbing to the clerics. A prime goal of the clerical regime was to discredit emancipated women as traitors to Islam, or "Western dolls," as they were often labeled. Once the clerics were in power, Islamic precepts were interpreted in ways that promoted sexual segregation and the exclusion of women from areas of education, employment, and public activity. Harsh criminal penalties were imposed to punish and deter any conduct by females that conservative clerics found indecent or immoral. Violating rules of modest dress was treated as a serious offense, with penalities such as seventy-four lashes being imposed on women if they appeared in public without proper veiling.

The other nemesis of the clergy was the sizable Baha'i community, which, not coincidentally, was ecumenically oriented, espoused liberal and humanistic values, and accorded full equality to women. Baha'ism had originated in Iran in the nineteenth century and had won many converts among Iran's Muslims. Clerics deemed that converts to Baha'ism and their descendants were apostates from Islam and deserving of capital punishment, the apostasy penalty set in premodern Shari'a jurisprudence. Under the shah, despite intermittent persecutions, Baha'is had been able to achieve a measure of equality with Muslims. By neglecting to mention Baha'is as a recognized minority religion, the 1979 constitution denied them the measure of religious toleration that was accorded Zoroastrians, Jews, and Christians in article 13. To destroy Baha'ism and the values it stood for, the regime undertook persecutions, imprisonments, and executions of Baha'is and Baha'i institutions were dismantled. Enormous pressure was exerted on Baha'is to repent of their theological errors and return to the Islamic fold. The reasons for the persecution of the Baha'is are complex, but some may relate closely to the kinds of reactions fundamentalists have to the modern world in general. One of the most distinguished scholars of Shi'ism and modern Iran has opined that Baha'is are seen by Iranians much as Jews were seen by European anti-Semites and that anti-Baha'ism is comparable to anti-Semitism. Like Jews they are viewed as being cosmopolitan types. "Baha'is are seen to symbolize threatening aspects of modernity. . . . They adopt modern education and modern science with alacrity, producing large numbers of intellectuals, physicians, engineers, and business people. If modernity menaces Iran's identity, they are surely accomplices."

How Islamization Was Pursued

In Iran Islamization proceeded as a by-product of the clerical takeover of the government and the courts. The process entailed the unseating and eventual defeat of secular forces that were disposed to resist clerical rule. The regime was intolerant of criticism by dissident Shi'ite clerics, who risked being censored, harassed, and even placed under house arrest when they questioned the legitimacy of clerical rule or criticized the official Islamization line. Claiming to represent "Islam," the regime treated its foes as if their opposition to the government was tantamount to declaring war on the Islamic religion. Ruthless persecution, incarceration, torture, and mass execution of the regime's critics withered the opposition. About two million Iranians, actual and potential opponents of the regime, fled to foreign havens and wound up as exiles in the West and in neighboring Turkey.

There was no way to challenge the regime's oppressive scheme of Islamization in the courts, which meted out an arbitrary form of summary justice from which any semblance of due process was banished. Among other secular institutions, the Iranian Bar Association was destroyed and with it the modern legal profession and its members' commitment to legality.

Khomeini's Islamization policy was directed against various foreign devils, among which the United States was singled out for particularly strong vilification due to American support for the shah. In Khomeini's program the pursuit of Islamization became closely associated with a strident anti-Americanism, with the United States incessantly excoriated as the Great Satan and presented as the enemy of Islam. (This stands in remarkable contrast to the situation in Pakistan, where the United States was the primary backer of the Zia regime, and to the situation in the Sudan, where the United States was the sole foreign prop in the final stages of Numayri's regime.) Khomeini's demonizing of the regime of Iraqi president Saddam Hussein served a similar role within his Islamization program; the war with Iraq was in part a prolonged demonstration of revolutionary zeal against infidels on the doorstep. And once that war ended in the 1988 ceasefire, Khomeini kept the fires stoked by calling for the execution of Salman Rushdie as an apostate from Islam, while Iran's propagandists sought to tie Rushdie's work to an American and Israeli plot against Islam.

It is thus ironic that, while these battles were being fought, strikingly little lasting progress was made toward eradicating Western influences on the fundamental structure and institutions of the legal system. For example, in the 1979 Iranian constitution one finds borrowed Western institutions that lack Islamic antecedents such as the republican form of government, the division of the government into three separate branches, a directly elected president who functions as chief executive, a prime minister and a cabinet, the ideas of the independence of the judiciary and judicial review, the concept of legality, the notion of an elected legislative body, the need for the cabinet to obtain votes of confidence from the legislative branch, and the concept of national sovereignty. Even the distinctive institution of the faqih, as set forth in the 1979 constitution, is embedded in a matrix of relations with other, conventional Western governmental institutions. For example, according to article 110 the faqih's duties include appointing the chief of staff of Iran's armed forces, declaring war, organizing the Supreme Council for National Defense (the president, prime minister, minister of defense, and others), confirming the appointment of the president after his election, and dismissing the president in the interests of the country after a Supreme Court ruling that the president has violated his legal duties. Such principles have counterparts in Western political systems, but they have no relation to the traditional function of a Shi'ite faqih.

In many facets and in its general format, the Iranian constitution resembles the 1958 French constitution. The way Islamic content has been injected into provisions with French antecedents can be illustrated by comparing the treatment of national sovereignty in article 56 of the Iranian constitution with article 3 of the French constitution. The French version establishes that sovereignty rests on the will of the people as expressed through referendums and enjoins interference with the exercise of popular sovereignty. It begins: "National sovereignty belongs to the people, which shall exercise this sovereignty through its representatives by means of referendums. No section of the people, nor any individual, may attribute to themselves or himself the exercise thereof." In chapter 5 of the Iranian constitution under the heading "The Right of National Sovereignty and the Powers Derived from It" one sees in article 56 the Islamized version of the same provision, in which the theological tenet that God is the Supreme Ruler is inserted and the French provisions enjoining interference – this time with Divine Sovereignty – have been incongruously retained: "Absolute sovereignty over the world and mankind is God's and He alone has determined the social destiny of human beings. None shall take away this God-given right from another person or make use of it to serve his special personal or group interests." Wanting to retain the provision for popular referendums, the authors of the Iranian constitution relegated it to article 59, by which placement the clash between the idea that national sovereignty is exercised by the people via referendums and the idea that sovereignty is the exclusive province of the deity has been rendered less obvious. The incongruity remains: there is no room for popular sovereignty exercised via referendums in a system based on the theological premise of divine rule, which at the very least should mean that God's laws are binding and not subject to modification by any human agency, such as popular referendums involve.

A similar pattern of borrowing Western constitutional principles and then modifying them can be seen in chapter 3 of the Iranian constitution, where there are provisions for rights principles that are of Western derivation but with Islamic qualifications added to circumscribe them. Thus, for example, article 20 provides for human rights, a Western concept, but Islamizes them by indicating that they are to be enjoyed "according to Islamic standards." Again, there is a resultant incongruity, since the philosophy of human rights precludes curbing rights by reference to the standards of a particular religion.

Even though the making of laws via human agency is barred under traditional Islamic legal theory, according to which all laws are to be found in and derived from the Islamic sources, Iran's Islamic constitution provided for lawmaking by the Majlis in article 58, and laws continued to be enacted by the Majlis just as they had been under the shah.

The Iranian approach to legislation thus differed markedly from the approach to law in Saudi Arabia, where, in deference to Islamic tradition, there was officially no man-made law. Ayatollah Khomeini seems to have originally aspired to return to a similar system of jurists' law, asserting in 1970 in a speech: "The entire system of government and administration, together with the necessary laws, lies ready for you. There is no need for you, after establishing a government, to sit down and draw up laws, or, like rulers who worship foreigners and are infatuated with the West, run after others to borrow their laws. Everything is ready and waiting. All that remains is to draw up ministerial programs." However, modern legal institutions on Western lines proved firmly rooted and survived the Islamic revolution largely intact.

The ultimate guarantee that laws would be in conformity with the Shari'a lay in the provision in article 4 that Islamic law would be supreme, overriding not only any laws in conflict with it but even the constitution itself. The article also provided that clerics on the Council of Guardians would make the decisions in this regard. This represented the achievement of a goal of Iran's clerics, who had been determined to ensure that there would be effective clerical review of proposed legislation in order to ensure conformity with Shari'a requirements.

In practice, the Council of Guardians reviewed and invalidated proposed laws with such stringency and zeal that acute embarrassment resulted at times for the government. For example, economic reforms such as land reform laws enacted by the Majlis were needed to retain the political support of the poorer classes but were repeatedly nullified by the Council of Guardians on the grounds that they violated Islamic law. For nine years Khomeini avoided challenging these "Islamic" vetos of legislation that the regime deemed politically essential. However, Khomeini finally ruled on 7 January 1988 that the Islamic state had absolute power – like the power enjoyed by the Prophet Muhammad – and was permitted to adopt such measures as it deemed necessary for the interests of the Islamic state *even where these might conflict with Islamic law or a fundamental religious obligation like the pilgrimage to Mecca*. This ruling seemed to mean that measures passed by the Majlis and acceptable to the faqih would henceforth go into effect even if the Guardians believed that they contravened the requirements of the Shari'a. This ruling proved that fundamentalists were not actually concerned with restoring Shari'a law per se. As the Iranian experience showed, the commitment was actually to reinstate Shari'a rules insofar as they served fundamentalists' political agendas. Conversely, Shari'a rules could be discounted when they stood in the way of programs that served the fundamentalists' own political interests.

Thus, considerations of *raison d'état* were officially permitted to override Islamic criteria. This was, ultimately, embarrassing for a government officially committed to the implementation of Islamic law. A constitutional amendment adopted on 28 July 1989 attempted to deal with this problem by endorsing the establishment of a council that would mediate and consult when conflicts occurred between the Majlis and the Council of Guardians. Since the new council's members were to be appointed by the faqih, it seemed unlikely that they would be disposed to contradict his views. It is too early to say what role the council will actually be able to play in resolving conflicts between legislation and Shari'a law, but its establishment suggests that the position of the Council of Guardians has been downgraded.

How Successful has Islamization Been?

Islamization has gone far enough in Iran that it is destined to have a long-term impact. The government itself has been reconstituted, and the constitution rewritten to institutionalize clerical authority and the supremacy of Islamic law (however it might be interpreted). In the 1980s and early 1990s fundamentalist clerics were firmly ensconced in powerful positions and dominated the country's legal system. Laws were enacted that embodied the fundamentalists' policies of combating the erosion of the traditional social structure and value system. Even if the application of criminal laws to enforce Islamic morality was relaxed somewhat, as it appeared to be in 1991, the impact of these laws on Iranian society remained considerable. Pre-revolution advances in women's status were rolled back, the 1967 Family Protection Act repealed, and women relegated to subservient roles caring for their husbands and children. The Baha'i religion has been virtually persecuted out of existence in Iran.

At the same time, there have been detrimental side effects of fundamentalist policies that were not intended by the policymakers. In the wake of official efforts to confine women to domestic roles and encouraged by the regime's initial pronatalist policies, the birthrate soared to 3.9 percent a year. The population growth became so alarming that in 1990 fears were being publicly expressed in official circles that it could pose an obstacle to Iran's development. In a dramatic reversal, the regime began to support birth control measures. Another obstacle to development was the brain drain resulting from the mass exodus of highly trained professionals and technocrats who were alienated by the fundamentalist policies of the regime. By 1989 there was growing evidence that leaders of the regime felt that a policy of liberalization was essential to woo back members of the educated elite from exile. In hopes of attracting foreign investment and trade from Europe and Japan, a major project for a free-trade zone on Qeshm Island at the entrance to the Persian Gulf was approved by the Parliament in February of 1990, despite conservatives' vocal opposition to the plan for granting foreigners on Qeshm exemptions from Iranian law. In the prevailing climate of pragmatism, it was possible to hear a cleric, Hojjatulislam Hassan Ruhani, say openly in Parliament: "To install Islamic codes on Qeshm is in contradiction with reality. The more freedom we provide for investors, the more of them we can attract." Thus, to attract badly needed foreign capital, the regime was prepared to lift the application of its version of Islamic law. Ironically, this meant replicating the kind of scheme of extraterritorial treatment for foreign nationals that had been negotiated by Americans under the shah, which Ayatollah Khomeini had excoriated in a famous speech in 1964 as the work of traitors. Moreover, there were even some indications of official sentiment favoring liberalization of the veiling requirements for women.

Iran's clerics remain uneasy with Iranian nationalism, which has been generally espoused by secular-minded politicians and intellectuals unsympathetic to clerical interests. The late shah gave Iran's clerics special reasons for opposing Iranian nationalism, since his version of Iranian nationalism sought to revive pride in Iran's pre-Islamic heritage as a means of denigrating the Islamic contribution to Iranian culture. In consequence, clerics have at various points since the revolution advocated measures like destroying the ancient ruins at Persepolis, banning the distinctive Iranian Nowruz (New Year) celebrations as pagan, and promoting Arabic as a replacement for Persian. That is, Iran's character as a nation-state, which survived the revolution, did so despite clerical and fundamentalist antipathy to aspects of Iranian nationalism. The failure of the fundamentalists to carry out their plans for eradicating a separate Iranian national identity and setting up a supranational polity on a religious basis was due to the great resistance from Iranians, who are for the most part profoundly nationalistic and proud of their distinctive culture.

The Iranian model has not been emulated by other countries. In the eyes of many fundamentalists, the Islamic Republic of Iran is a failure as an Islamic polity, because it has a specific, Iranian national character. Islamic fundamentalists, including some in Iran, have tended to favor the concept that in Islam the only legitimate political entity is the *umma*, or community of believers, and that the nation-state and nationalism are inherently un-Islamic. One of the issues that had proved contentious during the drafting of the constitution was whether or not it was permissible for a self-proclaimed Islamic state to have a national territory, a national language, and citizenship requirements like those of other nation-states. Although the final version of the Iranian constitution affirms Iran's character as a nation-state, Islamic fundamentalists have persisted in challenging its legitimacy.

The Iranian fundamentalist version of Islam is not an inclusive, ecumenical one but is fraught with distinctive Twelver Shi'ite characteristics, and this bias in favor of Twelver Shi'ism may eventually have an untoward effect on the political loyalties of the Sunni Baluchis, Kurds, and Turkomans inside Iran. Outside Iran this same Shi'ite bias has sharply limited the appeal of Iran's Islamic revolution, which was originally intended to be a model that would be emulated throughout the Muslim world but which has inspired scant emulation except in Twelver Shi'ite communities in places like Lebanon.

Future Prospects

The fortunes of fundamentalism in Iran will be strongly affected by which factions are ultimately successful in the power struggles that ensued after Khomeini's death. Politically active clerics in 1990 and 1991 differed significantly in the degree to which they were actually committed to the fundamentalist cause.

Before the Rushdie affair of Fubruary 1989 there were indications that powerful figures in the government were ready to adopt more moderate and conciliatory policies toward the opposition and the West and that they had become disenchanted with fundamentalist extremism. After the Rushdie affair exploded, the moderate Ayatollah Hossein Ali Montazeri, long Khomeini's chosen successor, came under siege. He was finally obliged to resign on 28 March after being attacked for having criticized government repression and for urging toleration of dissent. These manifestations of liberal sympathies led Montazeri to be characterized as one who had moved away from the Islamic system.

The June 1989 death of Ayatollah Khomeini placed the viability of his concept of governance by the leading jurist in jeopardy. No successor of equivalent prestige and charisma was available to serve as faqih. After the disgrace of Ayatollah Montazeri and his elimination from the succession, no distinguished, high ranking clerics remained who could be trusted to follow Khomeini's political line. Articles 107 and 109 of the constitution were amended in July of 1989 to downgrade the requirements for serving the office of faqih in order to accommodate Ayatollah 'Ali Khamene'i, a far less eminent cleric than Ayatollah Khomeini had been. In the aftermath of these changes, the importance of the office of faqih seemed destined to dwindle.

Constitutional amendments adopted in July of 1989 eliminated the office of prime minister and concentrated power in the presidency, a secular office, even though currently occupied by a cleric. Hojjatulislam Ali Akbar Hashemi Rafsanjani was able to win a pro forma election as president in July 1989. Rafsanjani's subsequent consolidation of his power signaled at least a temporary victory by a relatively moderate and pragmatic faction in the government at the expense of the fundamentalist hard-liners. The original Islamic scheme of government seemed to be in the process of being transformed into a mundane presidential one.

Under the leadership of President Rafsanjani it seems that Iran's policies are being significantly liberalized in the political, economic, and social domains. One suspects that, if he did not have to fear a backlash from militant fundamentalist forces and could follow his own personal inclinations, Rafsanjani might be moving even faster toward liberalization. In a brave move for a cleric, he has supported the idea of allowing women greater freedoms and participation in public life and the professions than they enjoyed under Khomeini.

Like Prime Minister Nawaz Sharif of Pakistan, Rafsanjani seems to have little personal enthusiasm for the cultural dimensions of Islamization and appears primarily concerned with bold reforms to end his country's economic deterioration and to promote rapid development along free-market lines. This liberalization program entails improving Iran's relations with Europe and Japan and institutions like the IMF, which in turn necessitate hewing to a moderate political line. The trends justified a tentative conclusion that under President Rafsanjani and the pragmatists allied with him, and in the face of overwhelming need to extricate the country from an economic morass, the fundamentalist impulse faded in the early 1990s – at least at the governmental level, where it would shape politics, laws, and the constitution.

48 Obedience versus Autonomy: Women and Fundamentalism in Iran and Pakistan

Shahla Haeri

Islamic societies from Morocco to Indonesia were radically affected in the 1980s and early 1990s by movements advocating a return to the Islamic ideals, to the fundamentals, particularly in the area of family relations, marriage, and divorce. This chapter is set, however, within the broader context of an ongoing dialectical relationship between Islamic secular reformers of the 1950s and 1960s, and Islamic fundamentalists of the late 1970s and 1980s in Iran and Pakistan. The former, who initiated legal and social reforms, came under strong criticism by the latter who have argued that the laws and the ensuing reforms are un-Islamic and hence illegal. The fundamentalists contested the legitimacy of these reforms, claiming them to be inspired (or imposed) by the West rather than guided by Islamic law. The tension between the secularist governments and fundamentalists has mirrored the alienation from and disillusionment with ideals and promises of "modernity" in many Muslim societies.

Much of the debate between fundamentalists and secularists has centered on the issues of status of women, marriage, and family law. Islamic laws and commandments are spelled out in the Qur'an, the hadith, and other classical legal sources. They are believed to be divine and unchanging, and are understood to be central to the texture of social life in an Islamic society. Changes in Islamic marriage law were initiated by the colonial powers in the late nineteenth century in India and Egypt, setting the stage for later protests by Islamic groups, including the fundamentalists in Iran and Pakistan. On the whole, however, Islamic family law itself remained unchanged well into the twentieth century, and relative unanimity has existed among different schools of Islamic law regarding the contractual form of marriage (*nikah*), the reciprocal rights and obligations of the spouses, divorce, and child custody.

Ironically, after centuries of resistance to changing Islamic family law, the Muslim reformers of the 1950s and 1960s adopted elements of Western law and applied them within an Islamic framework. They referred to the sources, to the Qur'an and Sunna of the Prophet Muhammad, to find an "Islamic rationale" for such adoptions, and an "Islamic methodology" to implement them. Nonetheless, a number of the ulama and their followers, including Maulana Maudidi in Pakistan and Ayatollah Khomeini in Iran, perceived such "reforms" as a form of capitulation to the West, as a thinly veiled apologetic, and as an all too eager attempt to find an "Islamic justification" for an essentially Western approach to the issue of interpersonal relations.

Original publication details: Haeri, Shahla, "Obedience versus Autonomy: Women and Fundamentalism in Iran and Pakistan" from Martin E. Marty and R. Scott Appleby (eds.), *Fundamentalisms and Society* (University of Chicago Press, Chicago, 1993).

Within this context I discuss the interaction and exchange between fundamentalists, who continue to advocate structured gender relations, and Iranian and Pakistani urban middle-class women, who are articulating their own interpretations of personal laws as their knowledge of religious, legal, and political discourses grows. In the 1980s these women added a new voice to the decades-old debates between the fundamentalists and secularists.

The theoretical concepts underpinning my argument are those of *obedience* and *autonomy*, both of which are inextricably associated with the reciprocal rights of the spouses and derived from the contractual form of marriage in Islam. Though seminal to the historically dominant worldview of Islamic countries, both concepts are subject to new interpretations due to a heightened tension between secularists and fundamentalists. Whereas the former are more inclined to break through or improvise on the predetermined boundaries of the marriage contract, the latter are determined to return to a literal meaning of such concepts.

We must look to the broader logic of an Islamic marriage contract, and the historically maintained perception of its immutability, to understand some of the specificities of gender relations in Iran and Pakistan, historical resistance to the reform of personal laws, and hence the basis for the fundamentalists' objection to women's legal autonomy. Contracts constitute the dominant metaphor, or model, for marital relations in Islamic societies and belong to that category of concepts referred to as "root paradigms," that is, "as distinct from what is probably in each culture a wide range of quotidian or situational models for behavior under the sign of self or factual interest," and are "concerned with fundamental assumptions underlying the human bonds." Root paradigms provide people with "cultural maps" that can guide them through specific social "territories." Accordingly, the logic of a marriage contract necessitates a woman's obedience to her husband, while limiting her autonomy.

My concern is with the legal structure of the Islamic marriage contract. Wedding rituals, of course, vary greatly from one Islamic society to another, they take on local coloring and flavor, but the legal form of the Islamic marriage contract, nikah, is the same in almost all Islamic cultures. Moreover, although my focus is on women in Iran and Pakistan, the model of contractual marriage I am proposing is theoretically relevant to other Islamic cultures. Although both are Muslim societies, Pakistan is predominantly a Sunni and Iran mainly a Shi'ite society. Whereas Pakistan is within the South Asian cultural sphere, Iran shares the cultural area of the Middle East. Unlike the fundamentalists who represent the state in Iran and have appeared to be omnipotent within their domain, Pakistani fundamentalists are only a part of the ruling coalition and must compete for political and electoral power with other parties and interest groups. Their interpretation of the role and status of women, marriage, and family law is more contested than that of their counterparts in Iran, at least publicly. Despite years of apparent prosperity under Zia ul-Haq and their renewed prominence in the early 1990s, the fundamentalists' impact in Pakistan has been more limited, indirect, selective, and uneven than the Shi'ite fundamentalists' impact in Iran.

Obedience is a cornerstone of the Islamic vision of a just social order; the term "Islam" means, among other things, submission and obedience. The Qur'an enjoins believers to "Obey God, His Prophet, and those in authority among you." Like the concept of contract, the concept of obedience is paradigmatic in an Islamic culture. Obedience maintains the status quo, making the hierarchy of social relations culturally meaningful. In the context of family life and marriage, the observance of obedience *(tamkin)*, and avoidance of disobedience *(nushuz)*, are not just obligations with far-reaching legal and social ramifications for women; they are also a wife's divine obligation. A disobedient wife is known as *nashizih*, a rebellious one, who should be admonished because her action transgresses the divine command, and brings about discomfort to the husband and disorder to the family. She also sets a bad example for her own children and others. Within such a worldview, a wife cannot legally be autonomous; a man cannot be obedient to a woman; a woman cannot be the leader of a Muslim state.

Islamic Worldview: The Marriage Contract

The marriage contract maintained its legal form until the passage of the Family Law Ordinance (1961) in Pakistan and the Family Protection Law (1967) in Iran. These acts were intended to give women some judicial relief by granting them certain rights and minimizing a man's unilateral right to divorce. In legal form, an Islamic marriage is a contract of sale *('aqd)*, although contemporary Islamic legal scholars generally shy away from specifying the category of contracts to which it actually belongs. Such reluctance, or "misrecognition," is more pronounced in the case of the contemporary ulama, who have become increasingly conscious of the implications of the concepts of ownership and purchase that are embedded in a contract of marriage. There are nonetheless significant similarities between a contract of marriage and a contract of sale.

Like a contract of sale, an Islamic marriage involves an exchange of goods and services, each meticulously tied in with the proper functioning of the other. In exchange for brideprice *(mahr)* and daily maintenance *(nafaqih)*, which the wife receives, the husband gains exclusive ownership right *(tamlik)*, over his wife's sexuality and reproductive activities and, by extension, over her person. Significantly, Islamic marriage does not involve the purchase or exchange of women, at least not in the sense conceptualized by Lévi-Strauss. Initially, Islamic law upholds the right of a woman as partner, albeit an unequal one, to the marriage contract; this provision assumes she has some degree of autonomy and volition. According to Islamic law, the woman is to give her consent, however nominally, and it is the woman, not her father, who is to receive the full amount of brideprice (custom aside). However, the moment a woman agrees to a marriage contract, she is understood to relinquish "voluntarily" all control and autonomy she may have had over her own legal and social persona. Prior to signing the contract of marriage, an adult Muslim woman is accorded a degree of legal autonomy (though the extent differs among the Sunnis and the Shi'ites), but after the conclusion of the contract she is legally and conceptually associated with the object of exchange, and hence she comes under the jural authority of her husband.

Conceptually, within the structure of a marriage contract, a woman's sexual and reproductive organs are viewed as an object, a fetishized "commodity" – actually and/or symbolically – that is separated from her person and is at the core of an individual, social, and economic transaction. Though conceptually isolated from a woman's body, a woman's sexuality is in practice identified with her whole being. In this gender ideology, woman as person is conflated with woman as object. Furthermore, women are perceived not only as sexual beings but as the very embodiment of sex itself. In this sense veiling is an expression of the concealment of sexuality itself. This cultural/religious ideology leads to a particular pattern of interpersonal relations. Men view women as objects to be owned and jealously controlled; as objects of desire to seclude, to veil, and to discard; and, at the same time, as objects of indispensable value to men's sense of power and virility. This association of women with objects of exchange is at the heart of an ideological ambivalence toward women, inspiring a sustained resistance against granting women independent rights.

Within this ideological scheme, a man is legally empowered to engage in a dual relationship with his wife; in the one she is considered a person, and in the other a sexual and reproductive object. The woman, too, assumes the dual characteristics of a person and an object – characteristics that, though often subjectively blurred, nonetheless color her sense of self-perception. Theoretically, the relationship between husband and wife is mediated through the object of exchange, an object that has become a highly charged cultural symbol, a gift that bestows power on the woman who has it and authority on the man who has legal control over it.

The logic of this particular form of contract dictates a wife's obedience to her husband, while limiting her autonomy. The legal structure of a marriage contract obliges a wife to be obedient, while the divine verses in the Qur'an and the socio-cultural beliefs regarding the "nature" of man and woman further entangle a wife in a web of obedience and surrender.

The comments of Ayatollah Khomeini and his Sunni counterparts in Pakistan are indicative of shared legal conceptualizations of the sexes, and the reciprocal rights and obligations of the spouses. "A permanent wife," argued Ayatollah Khomeini, "must not leave the house without her husband's permission, and must submit *(taslim)* herself for whatever pleasure he wants. . . . In this case her maintenance is incumbent upon her husband. If she does not obey him, she is a sinner *(gunahkar)* and has no right to clothing, housing, or sleeping." Similarly, citing a hadith, Maulana Maududi (1903–79), the founder of the most vocal fundamentalist movement in Pakistan and a renowned Sunni scholar, wrote: "When a woman steps out of her house against the will of her husband, she is cursed by every angel in the heavens and by everything other than men and jinn by which she passes, till she returns." Citing Bukhari and Muslim (two major sources of Sunni collections of hadith), Muhammad Imran, a member of the Jamaat-i-Islami, wrote in a similar vein: "As a rule, no wife should refuse her husband what he wants from her except on legitimate grounds, i.e., at the time of menstrual flow or fasting. Some theologians regard even this refusal unlawful as the husband may get enjoyment from his wife in other ways – embracing, kissing, etc. The duty of the wife to her husband is to give him pleasure in his bed whenever he wants her. . . . No woman should, therefore, cause anxiety or give trouble to her husband. If she acts otherwise, she will not be able to be his mate in Paradise. There the pure-eyed virgin maids will be his consorts."

The general secretary for the women's division of the Jamaat-i-Islami in Lahore, though not expressing her interpretation of marital obligations in exactly the same terms, reflected on the issue from a broader perspective shared by the public: "A man's primary duty is to 'provide' (or 'protect') for his family, and that of the wife's is to raise children, take care of her husband, and be obedient to him at all times."

A woman's obedience to her husband and to the larger social order is reciprocated with financial security in the family and prestige in society. A wife's disobedience, however, has legal ramifications that may lead to a severing of her daily support and maintenance, if not to her repudiation. "Women are sometimes murdered by their husbands," wrote Justice Javid Iqbal from Pakistan, "for being rude or disobedient. In such cases the man is not sentenced to death, he usually gets off with a sentence of ten years or life imprisonment." A disobedient wife is guilty of a double violation: reneging on her contractual promise by denying her husband access to that which he legally possesses, and transgressing God's will.

The underlying assumption here is twofold. First, as "purchasers" in a contract of marriage, men are "in charge" of their wives because they pay for them, and naturally they ought to be able to control their wives' activities. Second, women are required to submit that for which they have been paid – or promised to be paid. It follows, therefore, that women ought to be obedient to their husbands. The issue of child custody and the expectation of their unquestioned obedience to their father should be seen within this context as well. Given that a contract of marriage creates "some sort of ownership," it follows that any issue of this contract should automatically belong to the father. Although different schools of Islamic law have different minimum-age requirements, the custody of children is nonetheless a legal/divine right of a father.

By the same rationale, it is woman's autonomy and independence that pose a "problem" for the status quo within the family and the proper functioning of marital relations, and ultimately a challenge to the social order. Any expression of female autonomy can be construed as disobedience and an infringement on male prerogative, and by extension a deviation from the divinely ordained, legally upheld, and historically enforced duties of a wife. The ulama's fierce resistance to any legal/political changes in the status of women in Islamic societies and the moral and cultural ambivalence felt toward empowering women proceed from the assumptions undergirding the logic of the marriage contract.

Of course the legal requirement and cultural expectation that women obey their husbands does not mean that women always do so. Nor does it mean that marital relations necessarily lack partnership and romance. They do mean, however, that the contractual form of marriage provides the basis for a range of specific patterns of gender relations and expectations in Islamic societies. For example, the preoccupation with virginity and the obsession with veiling assume a certain coherence within the framework of the marriage contract and the worldview it enacts. And the potential insecurity embedded in marital relations, which can be manipulated at the moment of conflict, also stems from the set of rights and assumptions on which the contract rests. Recent ethnographic data emerging from the Middle East underscore the often subtle forms through which many women negotiate their wants and desires. Using the potential power that is tacitly perceived to be inherent in their being in possession of the object of desire, women exercise a degree of autonomy and self-assertion. The logic of the marriage contract sets the context, framing the outer boundaries for marital obligations and duties. Having contained the boundaries of marital relations accordingly, this same structure allows for a range of negotiated and improvisational social behavior by means of which both husband and wife, though departing from different junctures, can exercise control, negotiate power, "bargain reality," use or abuse each other.

Muslim women are intimately aware of the reciprocal implications of obedience and financial support: if they do not oblige their husbands' wishes, their very livelihood is in danger. At the same time they are aware, however vaguely at times, of the potential power inherent in their possession of an object that is tied to a man's sense of history and continuity, honor and virility. Theoretically, therefore, women have the power to be obedient (or disobedient) to their husbands; they can use that power judiciously, situationally, and strategically as leverage. A woman has little authority to force her husband to support her, however, should he decide to punish her for insubordination.

Fundamentalism Consolidated: The Case of Iran

The decade of the 1970s was a period of dramatic change and restlessness in Iran and Pakistan. Even though they were following different historical paths, both societies seemed poised for an upheaval. In the end, the financial deluge of the petrodollar brought about more destruction than development in Iran. It widened the gap between the haves and have-nots; disrupted the traditional patterns of social relation, expectation, and propriety; distorted the fabric of moral order; and created crises of identity. Personal privileges were abused and public trust was betrayed. The economic, political, and moral corruption that followed in the wake of the economic boom and development left many citizens disoriented, dislodged many from their physical environment and ideological beliefs, and perplexed others as to where the nation was heading and where they stood in the overall scheme of things. A sense of moral chaos prevailed, particularly in cities and urban centers.

As confusion and uncertainty in all spheres of public and private life intensified, the need to reassert oneself and hang on to the familiar also increased. Many Iranians were unable to internalize the "unveiling" of gender relations, or to tolerate the vagaries associated with modern life in Iran, or to focus on any one of the many voices that dictated new directions and orientations for citizens almost daily. An overwhelming majority of Iranians took a collective plunge into an idealized past, hoping to retrieve what they thought they could agree on, namely, an Islamic identity. The stunning victory of Ayatollah Khomeini is attributed, among other causes, to his unambiguous call for an Islamic identity that presumably once existed but had been seriously undermined by the policies of successive ruling monarchies, particularly by Muhammad Reza Pahlavi (1941–79).

Ayatollah Khomeini portrayed the latter as a usurper, an impostor, and a "false god," a *taghut*, who sold his soul and that of his nation to the "Great Satan." Khomeini regarded the shah's policies as inimical to a "genuine" Islamic society, and contrary to "God's purposeful creation to further the establishment of ethical order on earth." In the area of family and personal law Khomeini objected in particular to the Unveiling Act of 1936 and the Family Protection Law of 1967 that granted women some autonomy and rights in the family.

The most immediate and noticeable change in the status of women after the revolution was the requirement of veiling. The Islamic regime made wearing a veil (optional since 1941) mandatory and required all women to wear an "Islamic veil" while appearing in public. Despite this, however, a significant degree of continuity in the legal status of women and in the social beliefs associated with their role and status endured the revolutionary changes. What changed significantly was the rhetoric of the Islamic regime (matched at times by the "emancipation" rhetoric of the Pahlavi regime) regarding the high status accorded veiled women in an Islamic society. Caught in the exuberance of the moment, women initially donned the veil and participated en masse in the anti-shah demonstrations. Many women's reasons for wearing the veil were symbolic (a protest against its forced removal in the 1930s) or pragmatic (fear of recognition by the SAVAK, the shah's secret police) rather than motivated by religious conviction.

In response, the fundamentalists encouraged women to participate in demonstrations against the Pahlavi regime, to fight against oppression and demand justice in the spirit of Zainab, the Prophet Muhammad's granddaughter who defended her martyred brother, Imam Husain, in the aftermath of the tragedy of Karbala in 680 C.E. The Iranian revolution thus ushered in a new role model for women, one that proved to have widespread appeal to urban women, and also one that the regime began to retract soon after consolidating its power. Although for political purposes the Zainab model is still publicly supported, in the privacy of marital relations and in relation to men, the Fatimah model is the privileged one and the one encouraged by the government. However, the representation of Zainab as a patron saint of women sowed the seed of a new consciousness in the minds of many urban Iranian women. Here lies a locus of tension between the Islamic regime and women.

The Islamic fundamentalist regime found itself challenged to fulfill its revolutionary promises, made during the mobilization of 1978–9, to provide social justice, welfare, equal access to education, jobs, and other resources to women. For their part, with increasing sophistication, Iranian women have engaged the fundamentalist regime in frequent dialogues and debates during the 1980s and early 1990s, articulating their own interpretations of various Qur'anic commandments and injunctions, and sayings of the Prophet Muhammad. Individually and collectively, be they women leaders such as Mrs Zahra Rahnavard and Azam-i Taliqani or members of the editorial board of a popular weekly magazine (such as *Zan-i Ruz*), women have criticized and even scolded the regime, demanding that it live up to its promises and allow Iranian Muslim women to develop their full potential in a just and equitable Islamic state. They call for full participation of women in the public sphere and in education, demand the creation of opportunities for divorced and widowed women, and seek to curb men's unilateral right to divorce and polygamy.

The fundamentalists thus have been confronted with an unintended consequence of their success as revolutionaries – the heightened awareness and increased expectations of small but vocal segments of the urban female population. The fundamentalists responded by attempting to negotiate "new" boundaries of male–female relationships, rights, reciprocal obligations, and duties with an old "adversary" who is determined to assert herself – to be the Zainab of her time – and take her place on the sociopolitical hierarchy. The fundamentalists' dilemma has been how to deal with this "new woman" without themselves being dislodged from their traditional position of power and privilege, yet without appearing to undermine their own revolutionary Islamic rhetoric.

Although disgruntled women have not been able to challenge the legitimacy of the regime, they have endeavored to counter the cultural images and perceptions detrimental to its view of women in family and society. Having acquired knowledge of the Shi'ite Islamic discourse, educated urban Iranian women have engaged the fundamentalists in frequent debates, questioning publicly the images of "nagging," "weak," or "dependent" women portrayed on Iranian National Television. For example, a public debate occurred in 1989 between the editorial board of *Zan-i Ruz* (Modern woman) and Hashemi Rafsanjani (the present Iranian president and then Speaker of the Parliament). Mr Rafsanjani apparently feared popular discontent with the high casualty rate of young men in the Iran–Iraq War, and the consequent frustration of many families with delays in arranging suitable marriages for their children. In one of his Friday sermons, Rafsanjani called on men to marry several wives (permanently or temporarily), telling women to put aside their inhibitions and selfishness. His recommendations prompted swift response from the editorial board of *Zan-i Ruz*, leading him to revise and modify his comments. "Only in a true Islamic society," argued the editorial board of *Zan-i Ruz*, "can a man be a good enough Muslim to maintain justice between his wives. Until then, polygamy leads to more misery for women. That is why we object to polygamy [and recommend monogamy]."

The tension between the fundamentalist regime in Iran and the women who helped bring them to power is exacerbated by a number of issues affecting daily life.

Veiling

Veiling in the Islamic world is not monolithic and uniform, even within individual Islamic societies. Rather, veiling is a multifaceted and polysemic institution, involving a multiplicity of forms and meanings both domestically and internationally. Unlike in Iran, veiling is not universally prescribed in Pakistan. It is much more diverse in Pakistan than in Iran, ranging from the very thin and attractive scarf casually worn by female television newscasters (under Zia ul-Haq's regime, use of the scarf became mandatory for them), to the facial veils worn by some, to the *burqa* which covers all parts of the body except for a narrow rectangular "window" over the eyes (particularly worn by female beggars in urban areas). The particular garment prescribed for women in Iran after the revolution came to be known as "Islamic veiling" *(hijab-i Islami)*.

Despite the Islamic regime's attempt at uniformity, many urban women have learned to assert their "individuality" by improvising on the theme of Islamic veiling. Some reverted to wearing the traditional long black veil *(chador)* because underneath they can dress anyway they like. Others, rather than using the dull colors of black, brown, maroon, or gray prescribed by the government, use colorful scarfs interwoven with gold and silver threads; some wrap their scarves differently, and others show a few strands of highlighted hair. These variations of veiling have consistently provoked the ire of the more radical elements within the Islamic regime, toward whom the "moderates," such as President Rafsanjani, have had to defer.

Notwithstanding the differences of perception on veiling among the ruling fundamentalists themselves, the issue in Iran is no longer to veil or not to veil. It is, rather, to "veil well" or to "veil bad" *(bad hijabi)*, the former a sign of a good woman, one who obeys the regime's teachings and directives, and the latter a sign of a bad (autonomous) woman, one who holds on to the remnants of the old "decadent" and "Westoxicated" Pahlavi regime. In April 1989 the regime passed laws forbidding once again the "bad veiling" of women and threatening disobedient women with seventy-four lashes and internment for "rehabilitation." A woman's family would also be punished by being forced to pay all her expenses during internment.

That the Islamic regime found it necessary to pass yet another set of directives with harsh punishments is indicative of the regime's continued intolerance of any expressions of autonomy by women. It also indicates that there is a relentless, though submerged, struggle against the veiling directives of the Islamic regime. Although the veil itself is not subject to negotiation, what emerges from this continuous and subtle subversion of authority is a public and highly politicized debate about the particular way the veil is worn, the specific colors chosen, or the arena within which women can appear and work.

Iranian history is replete with unilateral orders and edicts issued by autocratic rulers. In 1936 Reza Shah Pahlavi (1925–41), responding to a growing ideology of modernity that was rapidly spreading across the globe, dramatically ordered Iranian women to appear in public unveiled. Any form of veiling was banned. Women caught disobeying the law were severely punished. The impact of law was felt strongly in the Iranian urban centers where traditionally women wore a chador, or long black veil.

Then as now some women obeyed the law. Some, though resenting it, did not take any action, but others felt obliged to challenge such unilateral laws. Many refused to leave their homes, not even to go to the public bath; some defied the regime and paid a heavy price for their insubordination. Only women who obeyed the law and packed their veils in their trunks could hope for any public recognition in the form of access to education, professional training, and employment. Similarly, after the Islamic revolution, only women who wore the veil were permitted to leave their homes, to enter government premises and agencies, and to have limited access to sociopolitical and economic resources.

In both situations obedience to the authorities was the key to access. The relationship between the dominant regime (in its autocratic as well as theocratic form) and women operates on two interconnected levels. On a more obvious level, women who obey the law are accorded certain concessions and given limited privileges. On a more subtle level, however, women quietly yet consistently challenge the premises of their oppression, while asserting a degree of their own will, however minimal, at times. In the early 1980s some women were openly defiant, which led to their punishment or incarceration. Later they changed their tactics to quiet resistance: while wearing the veil they attempted to subvert the law. Women disobey the law not only to defy the male authority, but also to protest their exclusion from decision-making processes, from having a choice in a matter so directly involving their lives. [. . .]

49   Islamic Fundamentalism in Iran and the Discourse of Development

Majid Tehranian

The Islamic Revolution of 1979 signaled the triumph of the "alternative media" and the beginning of a new era in cultural and communication policies. The revolution was achieved through the mobilization of mass protests that employed both the traditional and modern media of communication. Ayatollah Khomeini's messages were transmitted via long-distance telephone calls from Najaf and Paris to his supporters throughout the country, courtesy of sympathetic telephone operators and at His Majesty's expense. The messages were recorded on cheap transistor tape recorders; they were then transcribed, photocopied (often at government offices), and distributed through the oppositionist, religious networks within hours of their reception. The cassette and photocopy revolution thus multiplied the power of the traditional channels by using modern, accessible, inexpensive, and elusive (to the government censors) media.

The revolution, however, became heir to a much more highly sophisticated telecommunication system. Faced with the necessity of governing the newly established Islamic Republic and consolidating and disseminating the Islamic discourse that had brought them to power, the revolutionaries were confronted with the challenge of integrating the traditional and modern cultural and communication systems in a much more sophisticated and systematic way than had been attempted in the years leading up to the revolution.

In meeting this challenge in the 1980s, the revolutionary ideology itself passed through three distinct phases, each of which featured a distinctive role for the media. In the first phase, lasting for about a year during Dr. Mehdi Bazargan's tenure as prime minister (February–November 1979), a *liberal Islamic* ideology allowed a multiparty and competitive media system. The taking of American hostages on 4 November and the resulting resignation of Dr. Bazargan's government signaled a shift of power from the liberal, secular politicians to the clerics led by Ayatollah Khomeini. The hostage crisis thus represented a coup by the clerical leadership to seize power and initiative from the secular liberals. It used to clerical advantage the historical memories of the coup d'état of 1953 and the powerful anti-American sentiments it had created.

In the second phase, lasting until Ayatollah Khomeini's death in June 1989, a neotraditionalist Islamic ideology expelled its liberal, communist, and Marxist Islamic rivals from the political arena. During this period, Dr. Bazargan came under fire, President Hasan Bani-Sadr was ousted and fled the country, the communist Tudeh party leaders were arrested on charges of espionage for the Soviet Union,

Original publication details: Tehranian, Majid, "Islamic Fundamentalism in Iran and the Discourse of Development" from Martin E. Marty and R. Scott Appleby (eds.), *Fundamentalisms and Society* (University of Chicago Press, Chicago, 1993).

and a bloody battle was waged against the Marxist Fadaiiyan Khalq and the Islamic Marxist Mujahidin Khalq. The latter managed to put up strong military resistance through urban guerrilla warfare before their leader, Massoud Rajavi, had to flee the country. Rajavi established his headquarters first in Paris, where he made common cause with Bani-Sadr, then moved to Baghdad where he came under the protection of Saddam Hussein. In the Iran–Iraq War, the Mujahidin made a few unsuccessful skirmishes over the border into Iran but in the meantime lost much of their political credibility as an autonomous political force.

A third phase in the Islamic Republic, which might be labeled as pragmatic Islamic, began in 1989 with the dual leadership of Ayatollah Sayyid Ali Khamanei as Supreme Faqih and Hojjatolislam Ali Akbar Hashemi Rafsanjani as President of the Islamic Republic. This phase has thus far featured less ideological and more pragmatic policies in order to consolidate the revolution's political gains during its first decade, to pursue the country's economic reconstruction after the devastating war with Iraq, and to reform the social and educational foundations of the country. The new pragmatic policies include an opening to the West, even to the United States, a focus on economic reconstruction, and a softening of the social and cultural strictures.

Media programming has shifted from strictly Islamic to more diversified, entertainment-oriented content. Given the flight of some two million Iranians after the revolution, an active campaign to lure some back started in 1990, including a significant rise in the salaries of the faculty of the universities and invitations to the Iranian investors and managers to consider returning to their homeland.

Following the ascendancy of the clerical factions to power, the Islamic regime followed a dual mobilization policy. The repression or expulsion of the liberal Islamic, Marxist Islamic, Tudeh Communist, and ethnic and religious minority parties and media required some measure of demobilization, but the war with Iraq (1980–8) necessitated a high level of social and economic mobilization. In 1981 the number of officially licensed newspapers in the country was reduced to eight. The two major dailies, *Kayhan* and *Ettela'at*, were taken over by the government, as was Amir Kabir, the country's major publishing house. Liberal and Marxist literature which enjoyed freedom of publication during the first brief phase of the revolution was curtailed. Former Prime Minister Mosaddeq's memoirs, for example, which had reached the status of best-seller, were banned again. And in order to ensure a high degree of self-censorship by the publishers before encumbering the expenses of printing, the old procedure of submitting printed copies of books to the government censors was reinstated: the pre-revolutionary Ministry of Information became the Ministry of Islamic Guidance after the revolution. Except for a period of revolutionary enthusiasm when daily newspaper circulation reached one million and beyond, print runs gradually declined in the 1980s to the vicinity of 150,000. Aside from books of poetry and religious devotion, the highest selling volumes reached 100,000 copies for well-publicized, subsidized, religious titles, 10,000 for popular titles, and 2,000 for scholarly titles. Overall annual title production was back to 2,500. Censorship, price increases, paper scarcity, subject repetition, and declining interest by readers were given as the main reasons for the decline. The print media were still largely an elitist affair, while broadcasting assumed the status of true mass media with a far more sensitive political role.

To mobilize internal and external support under Khomeini's reign, the Islamic Republic developed a powerful broadcasting network both inside and outside the country. To reflect its new image, the name of the broadcasting agency was changed from NIRT to the Voice and Vision of the Islamic Republic of Iran (VVIRI). While the operation of the national news agency (the Islamic News Agency or IRNA), the press, publishing, and film are under the Ministry of Islamic Culture and Guidance, the operation of broadcasting has been put under the direct supervision of the Republic's leadership.

The (unintended) similarities with the overthrown regime and its discourse survived Khomeini. In a country in which family ties represent the most politically reliable bond of loyalty, the head of NIRT under the shah's regime had been a cousin to Queen Farah. Under President Rafsanjani, the head of VVIRI is the president's brother. However, to ensure some degree of collective leadership in media control, a revised and supplementary constitution adopted in 1990 placed VVIRI under a council composed of two members from each of the three branches of government, while reserving to the leader of the revolution or members of the Leadership Council the right to appoint the managing director.

In 1990 there were two national television channels, one predominantly devoted to light, popular programming and the other to educational programming, corresponding to the division of labor between TV1 and TV2 under NIRT's management. Television broadcast hours ran from 5:00 P.M. to about midnight. Children's programming had an extra two hours on Friday, the Islamic Sabbath. In 1990 there was also a daily two-hour program of news, features, and commentaries in Arabic, directed at the Arab population of Khuzistan Province and the Persian Gulf region as well as Iraqi refugees and prisoners of the Iran–Iraq War. With an estimated audience of twenty million (out of a total population of over fifty million), Iranian television had established itself as a mass medium. Its two channels covered 628,000 square miles, more than three times the area of Spain, larger than the whole of Western Europe, and equal to more than one-fifth of the United States. Its signals could spill over the 1,200-mile border with the Soviet Union to the north and along almost the entire coastline of the Persian Gulf. A mammoth new television house under construction in northern Tehran promised to be the largest broadcasting center of its kind in the Middle East.

To mobilize its foreign communication networks, the regime committed considerable resources to IRNA and foreign radio broadcasting. IRNA established bureaus in some twenty capitals of the world, producing 54,150 words of news daily by 1988. In the print media, the official cultural periodicals (*Soroush, Adineh, Nashr-i-Danesh, Andisheh*, and *Kayhan Farhangi*) showed a new balance between Islamic, Iranian, and foreign themes. The regime also developed an active publication program in other Muslim languages (notably Arabic), including a quarterly journal *Al-Tawhid*, which competes with those of Egypt and Saudi Arabia. Foreign radio broadcasting expanded significantly to 323 hours per week by 1990, making Iran one of the top twenty major world broadcasters.

With the voluntary or forced exile of the opposition as well as the immigration of two million Iranians to the United States and Western Europe since the revolution, an expanding exile media also came into existence in the 1980s. Some of this opposition media may be viewed as countermobilization against the Islamic regime, but some are clearly media serving a high-status immigrant community with its own networks of radio, television, and publishing. In such major concentrations of Iranians as those in Los Angeles and Washington, D.C., Farsi radio and television programs as well as special Yellow Pages and bookshops serve fairly prosperous Iranian communities. In distant Honolulu, which has no more than a few hundred Iranian immigrants, there is now a Farsi radio program with two hours of broadcasting per week. Due to a constantly fluctuating situation, the number of Farsi periodicals pub-lished outside the country cannot be accurately ascertained, but it seems that the emergence of new ones has generally outstripped the demise of the old. The highest circulation (about twenty thousand) probably belongs to *International Iran Times* (in English and Farsi), which in 1970 started to publish out of Washington, D.C. This newspaper, published privately, has grown considerably in size, coverage, and circulation since the revolution. By borrowing from all sources, including the government and opposition inside and outside the country, the newspaper has main-tained a relatively neutral and professional standard. By comparison, the opposi-tion newspapers in exile cannot claim high circulations. Their fate has often been tied to the political group to which they belong. A number of literary and political journals have also appeared in exile. There is considerable richness and diversity in the Iranian exile media, which may be setting a new tradition in exile discourse.

Following the dislocating effects of the revolution, Iran appears once again to be returning to its historic path of a distinctly Islamic-Iranian cultural and political development. The excessive entanglement with inter-Islamic and Arab politics, caused in part by a reaction against the shah's anti-Islamic policies, is gradually coming to an end. The failures of the Islamic regime in its war with Iraq and involve-ment in the Lebanese civil war seem to have taught it a lesson. Iranian nationalism is once again on the rise. Appeals to Iranian nationals abroad to return home, a rapprochement with the West, a greater focus on internal rather than external affairs, a revival of Iranian cultural traditions, and a softening of the Islamic image are the most apparent signs of this change of direction. A new phase of involve-ment with the former Soviet Muslim republics began in 1991–2 with the formation of the Economic Cooperation Organization, which includes Iran, Pakistan, Turkey, and five former Soviet Muslim republics; and the Caspian Council, consisting of Iran, Turkmanestan, Kazakhstan, Azerbaijan, and Russia. As the regime's agents of legitimation and socialization, the media and educational systems are also reflecting this change.

Integration and the Discourse of Identity

Cultural integration in Iran, with its heterogeneous population and high rate of illit-eracy, has faced serious obstacles. Before the Islamic revolution the Iranian popu-lation was increasingly divided between the modern, urban, and secular populations and the traditional, rural, semi-urban, and religious sectors. Against this back-ground, the religious unity of Iran with its 98 percent Muslim population (with a majority of Shi'a) has proved to be an integrating factor.

The modern media before and after the revolution played an important role in increasing cultural and linguistic integration. Iran, like most other developing coun-tries, moved from the oral to the visual stage of communication history without experiencing the literacy revolution. Illiteracy is believed to have increased or stag-nated at some 50 percent in the late 1970s. Women's illiteracy rate is probably as high as 80 percent. Rapid population growth in the 1980s (an increase from 2.7 percent to one of the highest rates in the world, 3.3 percent), the abolition of the shah's Literacy Corps, the ideological purge of the school system, and a decline in the quality of instruction contributed to the stagnation in literacy.

Whereas the monarchical regime had followed largely elitist cultural policies, propagating Western-style cultural forms, the Islamic regime in the 1980s pursued an active program of Islamization of culture, media, education, and social conduct. Accordingly, the content of the media changed radically. Television broadcasting hours were considerably reduced, and the new program policy excluded all Western imports and domestic productions that indulged in sex, violence, and "indecent" moral behavior such as holding hands with members of the opposite sex. The new programs included war and revolutionary movies, civil defense instructions (particularly during the war with Iraq), news, public events, audiences with religious leaders, talk shows, and more talk shows. Because of its rural setting and propagation of simple virtues, "Little House on the Prairie" was one of the few American television serials to survive. All the other pre-revolutionary serials, including all westerns, "Kojak," "Charlie's Angels," "Loves of Napoleon," "Days of Our Lives," and domestic and foreign variety shows and musicals (all representing the "decadent" lifestyle of an urban elite) were eliminated. The American popular television series of the 1980s, "Dallas" and "Dynasty," never reached Iran but seem to have overwhelmed some other parts of the world. Imported movies from the Soviet Union, Eastern Europe, and the Third World, dealing with revolutionary struggles, took their place. The attire of television announcers also dramatically changed from coat and tie to revolutionary fatigues or open-neck shirts for men, and from the latest Parisian fashions to Islamic head-cover for women. Female announcers are increasingly conspicuous by their absence.

Like the monarchical regime, however, the Islamic regime of the 1980s faced tenacious problems in their cultural policies of homogenization. Modern communication programs in every society entail some intended consequences such as information, persuasion, education, entertainment, but also many unintended consequences such as the dominance of either visual or print literacy, the reinforcement of either loyalty or opposition to the government, and the promotion of either modern or neotraditional values. Where audience feedback has been weak or conspicuous by its absence, the mass media have often created illusions of power at the centers, while cultural resistance has developed in a variety of ingenious forms at the peripheries. For example, broadcasting before the revolution fostered Iran's emerging consumer industries through commercials that earned as much as 20 percent of NIRT's revenues. Television programs and commercials were particularly seductive in their demonstration of the new standards of living of an emerging, acquisitive society. Items such as new consumer durables, banking services including travelers' checks, and cosmetics were particularly conspicuous in advertising. They demonstrated the chasm between elite consumer behavior and the deprivation of the masses. The flaunting of this affluence brought to the remotest regions of Iran a sense of alienation and outrage that undermined the monarchical regime. Rising expectations and frustration thus seemed destined to lead to a revolution characterized by regression and aggression.

The media policies of the Islamic Republic carried their own unintended consequences. During the 1980s the regime placed a high value on the role of broadcasting in propagating Islamic values. The Islamic Constitution of Iran is perhaps the first of its kind to have a special article devoted to the duties of the mass media. The duty of propagation *(tabligh)* of the faith is a well-recognized Islamic principle; encouraging virtue and discouraging vice *(amr-i-be-m'aruf wa nahy-i-az-munkar)* is also the duty of every Muslim. Accordingly, article 175 of the Constitution maintains that "freedom of publicity and propaganda in the mass media, radio and television, shall be ensured on the basis of Islamic principles." And, although the first director of broadcasting, Sadeq Qotbzadeh, argued that television is bad for the family, President Rafsanjani has gone so far as to suggest that entertainment programs are as important as mosques in the proper education of the people. In his last testament made public immediately after his death, Ayatollah Khomeini made at least fifteen references to the role of the mass media, including the following:

> Television films depicting Eastern or Western products made young men and women stray from the normal course of their work, throwing life and industry into oblivion in respect of themselves and their personalities. It also produced pessimism *vis-à-vis* their own being, their country, and culture and about highly valuable works of arts and literature, many of which found their way into art galleries and libraries of the East and West through the treachery of the collectors.

> My advice to the Islamic Consultative Assembly [Parliament], to the Guardianship Council, to the Supreme Judicial Council, and to the government now and in the future is to maintain the news agencies, the press, and the magazines in the service of Islam and in the interest of the country. We must all know that the Western-style freedom degenerates the youth, [and] is condemned in Islam's view and by reason and intellect.

Unintended consequences arose from the emphasis on media, however; facing limited technical and financial capacity for production, the Islamic regime has had to import almost as many programs as the monarchical regime, albeit from non-Western sources. Japanese television has provided one such important source for program imports. In November 1987, Iranian television started to dub into Farsi and broadcast the most popular of these programs – a Japanese television serial called "Oshin." "It was believed, from a policy standpoint, that Oshin's spirit of self-sacrifice was what the Iranian people needed at the moment." In addition to the television broadcast, 168 episodes of the serial were also shown on Saturday evenings to packed houses at local movie theaters. The "Oshin" fad was further manifested through clothing, personal effects, and toys displaying Oshin's picture. As in other Asian countries, Oshin soon achieved such popularity that Tehran traffic fell to a minimum during its show time. According to the audience research department of Iranian television, during the three quarters of 1988, "Oshin" enjoyed the highest rating among a number of other television programs.

The effect of "Oshin" is, however, worthy of note. The hero of this serial, Oshin, is a poverty-stricken peasant woman who, through sheer stamina and perseverance, achieves human dignity and worldly success. The cultural impact of this show was so powerful that many parents gave their newborn daughters her name rather than a traditional Islamic one. The issue came to a boil when a young woman on a call-in radio program admitted that she took Oshin as a role model more readily than Fatimah Zahra, the Prophet Muhammad's daughter. Ayatollah Khomeini was so incensed by the broadcast that he ordered the head of radio imprisoned and the director of the broadcasting agency's ideology group sentenced to fifty lashes. Only on the intercession of the chief justice did the ayatollah pardon the participants.

Such instances document the cultural resistance the audiences might show toward officially sanctioned ideologies and norms. However, Mowlana and Rad posed another equally plausible interpretation of the popularity of Oshin in Iran: "The available data . . . provide the first glimpse of evidence on the thesis that television viewers, at least in the case of Iran, are less interested in what they cannot get [i.e., "Dallas"-style wealth, eternal youth, greed, power] and more concerned with what they might perceive as their own cultural setting. This is very well-illustrated in the viewers' absorption of Oshin's life as a tragedy and drama so well depicted within the Iranian cultural and religious setting."

By contrast to foreign imports, the domestic production of films and television serials focused on new historical series in the 1980s. Notable among these television series were "Bu-Ali Sina" (the biography of the tenth century Iranian philosopher and physician known in the West as Avecina), "Mirza Taqi Khan Amir Kabir" (the biography of Nasser ed-Din Shah's reformist prime minister who was put to death by him), and "Hezar Dastan" (about life under Reza Shah in the 1930s). All these programs have commanded respectable audiences.

Iranian cinema seems to have made progress during the first decade of the revolution. Filmmaking techniques greatly improved in all areas, although screenwriting and dialogue were still weak. Dubbing, prevalent despite the technical possibility of live recording, detracts from the credibility of the films. From 31 March to 10 April 1990, a festival of Iranian cinema covering the first decade of the revolution was held at the University of California at Los Angeles. In the presence of such well-known Iranian film directors as Dariush Mehrjou'i and Abbas Kia-Rostami and a large andience, twenty feature films were screened at this festival. Mahasti Afshar commented:

All the [Iranian] Directors exercised caution in dealing with religious and political issues, a sensibility that the films themselves reflected. With one or two exceptions, the films could have been products of pre-revolution days in that they concentrated on abiding social and personal problems, staying clear of political issues. Even Makhmalbaf's *Marriage of the Blessed*, a film highly critical of the general public's abandonment of the "ideals" of the Islamic Revolution, never pointed to the ruling powers.

Despite this measure of caution, the degree of realism, sincerity, and autocriticism in these films underscored a new strength in Iranian cinema. The films showed a greater interest in portraying urban society, and to a lesser extent, the impact of international politics on Iran. The roots of this movement go back to the television productions of Nasser Taqvaii and Ali Hatami [among others] in the mid-seventies. Mehrjuii's *Dayere-ye Mina*, a popular film of those years that supplanted stereotypical portrayals with real problems and personalities, was a turning point in Iranian film history. Mehrjuii's latest film *Hamoun*, which Nafici managed to screen virtually the minute it came off the editing machine, continues this probing look by being the first film to focus on the dilemmas of the educated and intellectual classes in contemporary Tehran.

The role of women in society and in film production was only minimally explored. To be sure, restrictions applied to the showing of women with bare heads, sometimes leading to comical results: Female characters in Ebrahimifar's *Nar-o Ney*, a film based on the poetry of Sohrab Sepehri and set in the 60s or 70s, appeared (anachronistically) clad in veils that have become widespread only after 1979! Nonetheless, female directors were surprisingly independent and aggressive in handling their subject matter.

The Islamic regime has embarked on a challenging road to the cultural restoration of Islamic values in a predominantly secular world. Despite the regime's efforts to insulate Iran from the Western world, an oil economy, permeable borders, and a deeply urbanized and internationalized population have undermined such efforts. Sale of audio and video cassettes of Western cultural imports have soared. The sale of VCRs, however, were soon curtailed by government confiscation and a ban on imports. Literature is increasingly popular but also censored if lacking in Islamic values. Several classical poets such as Omar Khayyam (extolling wine, women, song, and skepticism) have been removed from bookshops. However, others such as Ferdowsi (glorifying the pre-Islamic past) and Hafez (castigating clerical hypocrisy) enjoy a new popularity. Fiction, both Persian and foreign, are also enjoying good sales. And sales of foreign translations such as *Ghorresh-i-tufan* (*Wuthering Heights*) and *Bina-vayan* (*Les Misérables*) are also on the rise. Following the end of the war with Iraq, Khomeini's death, and the beginning of the presidency of Rafsanjani in 1989, a more relaxed cultural policy seems to be forming.

Education in the Islamic Republic

To achieve cultural integration in the field of education, the regime has attempted to revamp the entire educational system into an Islamic mold. These reforms have taken two major routes, including textbook and structural reforms. A revolution in the educational system was considered so urgent that only nine days after the victory of the revolution, on 20 February 1979, Ayatollah Khomeini demanded fundamental change in the primary, secondary, and tertiary textbooks to purify them of all past secular and foreign influences. The task of rewriting textbooks was practically complete by 1981. After that time, except for some minor additions or omissions, no major rewriting has taken place. By 1986, seven hundred topics from 636 textbooks had been changed at the elementary and secondary school levels, especially in the social sciences, humanities, and religious studies. By 1989, 10 percent of the textbooks had been written in the post-revolutionary period, while the remaining 90 percent were new editions of pre-1979 ones.

Analyzing the new textbooks from the perspective of socialization of schoolchildren, Golnar Mehran has divided the values they attempt to inculcate into four major categories: (1) the attributes of a New Islamic Person; (2) political beliefs; (3) cultural values; and (4) role models. Martyrdom seems to be the central unifying theme in the socialization of Islamic children into a New Islamic Person. Aside from the traditional Islamic attributes of belief in God, love of nature, piety and chastity, honesty, trustworthiness, thrift and frugality, knowledge, sense of responsibility and dependability, loyalty and devotion, modesty, simplicity, and passion for equality and justice, it is argued that the New Islamic Person must be ready to martyr herself or himself for the cause of the revolution. Schoolchildren are inculcated with the belief that a society based on martyrdom can never be conquered, since surrender and defeat come about only as a result of fear of death. "A nation that believes in martyrdom," declares a chapter on martyrdom in the social science textbook of secondary schools, "will never be enslaved." The idea of martyrdom is then extended to relations between the individual and the state. According to the new textbooks, these relations must be based on unity, support, trust, and mutual assistance. The individual must assist the state in every conceivable way by obeying the laws and acting as "the eyes and ears of the state." Since government is based on the laws laid down by God and the Prophet and government belongs to the people, this is entirely natural. By contrast to dictatorial regimes in which elaborate security organizations are required, in the Islamic Republic people must be the intelligence service of the state.

With respect to political beliefs, the new textbooks teach children that in Islam, religion and politics are not separate. The mosque is presented as a community center in which religious and political matters are jointly discussed. However, before the revolution, the textbooks point out, this cardinal principle of Islamic polity had been undermined by the secular tendencies from two sources of external as well as internal threat: Westoxication *(gharbzadegi)* and Eastoxication *(sharqzadegi)*. Westoxication is a concept borrowed from the modern Iranian novelist and social critic Jalal al-Ahmad, whose book under the same title became a major source of ideological inspiration for the revolution. As a critic of the developmentalist policies of the shah's regime, al-Ahmad argued that Western neocolonialism often penetrated the minds and souls of the nations of the Third World through a pathology called "Westoxication," a total and irrational fascination with everything Western at the expense of the indigenous cultural heritage. His remedy for this disease was a return to the national self. Similarly, the Islamic textbooks argue, Eastoxication is a pathological obsession among intellectuals with Marxist and communist ideologies. Negating religion as "the opiate of the masses," these intellectuals wittingly or unwittingly have detached themselves from the masses and served the interests of the colonial powers in the Soviet camp. "Neither East nor West, Islam is best" is therefore the proud slogan of the Islamic Republic.

With respect to cultural values, cultural imperialism has been the chief target of the new textbooks. This has been defined primarily as neocolonialism, a new form of dependency that operates mainly through cultural dependence by "brainwashing" and humiliating Third World nations, leading them to blind imitation of the West and complete denial of their own values, beliefs, and traditions. Cultural autonomy is not possible, however, unless one rejects alien ideologies and returns to an indigenous cultural self. Franz Fanon is one of the few non-Iranian and non-Islamic sources used to substantiate these views. Both the diagnosis and proposed therapy have been largely inspired by Fanon's psychoanalytical view of the problem. Fanon had argued that to exorcise their colonial oppressors from their psyche, the oppressed need to reject their "white" Western masks and return to their own "black" faces. In the case of Iran, the new textbooks teach, cultural independence can be attained by totally rejecting Western models and returning to an Iranian-Islamic identity.

With respect to role models, the new textbooks provide a hierarchy of the Shi'a Islamic saints and heroes ranging from Imam Hussain and Imam 'Ali to the oppositionist ulama as exemplary lives to be emulated. In this pantheon of heroes, however, a dark corner is reserved for the countermodels to be abhorred, that is, the Westoxicated intellectuals. They are introduced as the "fifth column of imperialism and neocolonialism," the main agents of economic, political, and cultural dependence. The new textbooks have thus undertaken a major rewriting of Iranian history, in which kings and their underlings are castigated while Islamic Imams and ulama are portrayed as true heroes. [. . .]

Questions

1   What views of cultural globalization does Appadurai challenge when he describes the process as an "infinitely varied contest of sameness and difference" in a complex, "disjunctive order"? How can (or must) any group draw on the flows in different "landscapes" to construct its identity?

2   What view of cultural globalization does Hannerz challenge when he argues that cultural change in the periphery often takes the form of "maturation" and "creolization"? What building blocks do the people in the Nigerian town he studied use to construct their identity?

3   What makes fundamentalism a distinctly global phenomenon? How does Lechner assess its likely impact?

4   What were the goals and methods of Islamization in Iran? What impact did it have, according to Mayer? What effects on Iranian women does Haeri describe, and what tensions did these create? How did the media and the educational system promote the cultural integration of Iran under "restored" Islamic ideals, according to Tehranian? Overall, what did the Islamic Republic find most threatening about "Westoxication" and the West's "cultural imperialism"? What are its strengths and weaknesses as the core of a global antisystemic movement?

Part IX

Changing World Society:
Environmentalism and the
Globalization of Social Problems

Introduction

Over the past three decades, it has become routine to think of problems as being global in nature. Obviously, we tell ourselves, environmental degradation in the form of air pollution, acid rain, tropical deforestation, and the thinning of the ozone layer affect the entire globe, so it makes no sense for states or environmentalists to attempt anything less than a global approach to such problems. In historical perspective, though, it is difficult to avoid the conclusion that nothing inherent in a given problem, whether related to environmental degradation, human rights violations, inequality, authoritarian political regimes, or the oppression of women, automatically qualifies it as a global concern.

Take air pollution as an example. During the heyday of unregulated industrial capitalism in the nineteenth century, air pollution was far worse in most major cities than it was in the 1960s, when global environmentalism first became a major social movement. The reason the air was so bad is simple: in the days before electric heaters, natural gas furnaces, and centralized delivery of hot water to radiators, factories and homes directly burned enormous quantities of coal. Unlike today, however, the smoke belching from factory stacks often evoked not horrified criticism but almost lyrical praise as a sign of the glorious progress that industrialization was bringing to the blessed peoples of the ever-richer West. Not only was pollution not a global problem; for the most part, it was not a problem at all.

The same analysis applies to human rights violations, inequality, authoritarianism, and women's oppression: though the "problems" have long been widespread and often severe, either they have not been interpreted as problems or they have been treated primarily as local or national issues requiring only local or national responses. The sovereign authority of the state to manage its own society meant that critics and activists from outside the country were more likely to be told to mind their own business than to be heard or allowed to spread their critical views. Each state was to "put its own house in order," but international cooperation was neither needed nor desired.

By the end of the twentieth century, of course, much has changed. On the one hand, social problems of all sorts have proliferated wildly. No longer can inequality, oppression, or violations of rights be justified as "in the natural order of things" or "divinely ordained," and modern societies are filled with specialists of many stripes who make it their business to identify and publicize never-before-imagined problems. On the other hand, the ongoing integration of world society, and the thickening web of international organizations and social movements that cover the globe, have made it increasingly likely that social problems, new or old, will be cast in global terms and lifted up to the global agenda of major IGOs and INGOs. Many INGOs in particular are dedicated to searching out problems and publicizing them so that IGOs, states, and other INGOs will pay attention to them and begin to work toward global approaches to solving them.

What has emerged, then, is a global "civil society" largely analogous to the national civil societies that identify, publicize, and attempt to solve a growing array of social problems. By "civil society" we mean the vast network of organizations that are neither profit-oriented businesses nor government agencies. Operating "between states and markets," and often deliberately outside them, these organizations are usually voluntary associations with democratic structures and specific programs of action intended to meet the needs and interests of their members or effect change and improvement in some aspect of social life. They include charities, sports clubs, advocates for the homeless, women's rights groups, hobby associations, churches, endangered species protectors, and much more. Local and national organizations concentrate on local and national issues, but increasingly they are linked to INGOs and thereby to their counterparts in other countries. They thus form complex networks of ties, sharing information about problems, tactics, solutions, and coordinated action that can attract global attention to problems that appear to affect the entire globe or some large portion of it.

In this part we have chosen readings from a single sector of global civil society, environmentalism. By concentrating on environmentalism, we can reveal some of the complex issues that arise when a social problem with far-reaching ramifications – for economic development, for the quality of life, for inequality, foreign investment, and interstate relations – enters the global arena and assumes a prominent place on the agenda of many global organizations. To a large extent, the messages these readings convey are applicable to many other global civil society sectors, such as those mentioned above dealing with human rights violations, inequality, political repression, and the oppression of women. Important differences will be found across these and other sectors, of course, and researchers are busily studying a great many sectors to learn more about the role of global civil society organizations in global governance.

It is tempting to believe that global civil society groups, most notably INGOs, hold out the promise of considerable progress in solving major social problems. Some successes are striking, such as the ability of two small but highly professional INGOs to win a 50-year moratorium on mineral exploitation in the 1991 revision of the Antarctic Treaty, or the remarkable achievement of the International Campaign to Ban Landmines, a coalition of many INGOs and NGOs, in getting most countries of the world to agree to stop using or making anti-personnel mines. Yet many problems are so large and so much built into the structure of global economic and political development that even modest improvements can come only over a period of decades. One critical issue is whether the global activists who make up the INGOs and NGOs working to ameliorate these stubbornly intractable problems will be able to sustain their efforts long enough to make a substantial difference. An equally critical issue, however, is whether world society will be able to avoid widespread catastrophes and collapses if they do not.

Our selections on world environmentalism begin with a statement from the influential World Commission on Environment and Development, established by the UN in 1983 as a body independent of states and even of the UN itself. The statement describes the successes and failures of global environmental action and the severe problems facing the world at the end of the twentieth century, making a plea for a model of "sustainable development" that balances economic growth with careful environmental management. We then present the final declaration from the 1992 Earth Summit, the world's largest IGO conference to date, that was accompanied by the largest parallel nongovernmental conference ever. Though the principles enunciated in the declaration are stated in general and abstract terms, they spell out a high degree of responsibility for states and citizens to protect the natural environment from unregulated or careless development.

The selections by Paul Wapner, by Margaret Keck and Kathryn Sikkink, and by Jackie Smith analyze the impact of various nongovernmental groups in creating global concern about, and pressing for action on, the degradation and pollution of the natural world. Wapner discusses Greenpeace, which grew from a small band of activists protesting against the nuclear bomb tests in Alaska in 1969 to a massive transnational organization that can call on the contributions of millions of supporters to carry out a wide range of attention-grabbing actions all over the globe. Keck and Sikkink emphasize the growth and operation of environmental "advocacy networks" that link local NGOs and global INGOs in the effort to preserve the rainforests. We have chosen their discussion of the campaign in Sarawak, which was able to achieve some success but ultimately could not put an end to logging in this part of Borneo, because of the fine detail they provide about this case. Finally, Smith reviews the work of EarthAction, a social movement organization founded in 1991, as its attempts to ensure that the principles and programs outlined in the agreement at the Rio Earth Summit will have real and meaningful effects. Smith discusses efforts with respect to maintaining biological diversity, particularly in rainforest areas, and resisting desertification, which many expect to be one of the inevitable consequences of global warming (itself a controversial matter). Smith finds some progress on these matters, but she underscores the slow rate at which states have moved in living up to the agreements they have signed.

50 From One Earth to One World

World Commission on Environment and Development

In the middle of the twentieth century, we saw our planet from space for the first time. Historians may eventually find that this vision had a greater impact on thought than did the Copernican revolution of the sixteenth century, which upset the human self-image by revealing that the Earth is not the centre of the universe. From space, we see a small and fragile ball dominated not by human activity and edifice but by a pattern of clouds, oceans, greenery, and soils. Humanity's inability to fit its doings into that pattern is changing planetary systems, fundamentally. Many such changes are accompanied by life-threatening hazards. This new reality, from which there is no escape, must be recognized – and managed.

Fortunately, this new reality coincides with more positive developments new to this century. We can move information and goods faster around the globe than ever before; we can produce more food and more goods with less investment of resources; our technology and science gives us at least the potential to look deeper into and better understand natural systems. From space, we can see and study the Earth as an organism whose health depends on the health of all its parts. We have the power to reconcile human affairs with natural laws and to thrive in the process. In this our cultural and spiritual heritages can reinforce our economic interests and survival imperatives.

This Commission believes that people can build a future that is more prosperous, more just, and more secure. Our report, *Our Common Future*, is not a prediction of ever increasing environmental decay, poverty, and hardship in an ever more polluted world among ever decreasing resources. We see instead the possibility for a new era of economic growth, one that must be based on policies that sustain and expand the environmental resource base. And we believe such growth to be absolutely essential to relieve the great poverty that is deepening in much of the developing world.

But the Commission's hope for the future is conditional on decisive political action now to begin managing environmental resources to ensure both sustainable human progress and human survival. We are not forecasting a future; we are serving a notice – an urgent notice based on the latest and best scientific evidence – that the time has come to take the decisions needed to secure the resources to sustain this and coming generations. We do not offer a detailed blueprint for action, but instead a pathway by which the peoples of the world may enlarge their spheres of cooperation.

Original publication details: World Commission on Environment and Development, excerpt from *Our Common Future* (Oxford University Press, Oxford, 1987).

The Global Challenge

Successes and failures

Those looking for success and signs of hope can find many: Infant mortality is falling; human life-expectancy is increasing; the proportion of the world's adults who can read and write is climbing; the proportion of children starting school is rising; and global food production increases faster than the population grows.

But the same processes that have produced these gains have given rise to trends that the planet and its people cannot long bear. These have traditionally been divided into failures of "development" and failures in the management of our human environment. On the development side, in terms of absolute numbers there are more hungry people in the world than ever before, and their numbers are increasing. So are the numbers who cannot read or write, the numbers without safe water or safe and sound homes, and the numbers short of woodfuel with which to cook and warm themselves. The gap between rich and poor nations is widening – not shrinking – and there is little prospect, given present trends and institutional arrangements, that this process will be reversed.

There are also environmental trends that threaten to radically alter the planet, that threaten the lives of many species upon it, including the human species. Each year another six million hectares of productive dryland turns into worthless desert. Over three decades, this would amount to an area roughly as large as Saudi Arabia. More than 11 million hectares of forests are destroyed yearly, and this, over three decades, would equal an area about the size of India. Much of this forest is converted to low-grade farmland unable to support the farmers who settle it. In Europe, acid precipitation kills forests and lakes and damages the artistic and architectural heritage of nations; it may have acidified vast tracts of soil beyond reasonable hope of repair. The burning of fossil fuels puts into the atmosphere carbon dioxide, which is causing gradual global warming. This "greenhouse effect" may by early next century have increased average global temperatures enough to shift agricultural production areas, raise sea levels to flood coastal cities, and disrupt national economies. Other industrial gases threaten to deplete the planet's protective ozone shield to such an extent that the number of human and animal cancers would rise sharply and the oceans' food chain would be disrupted. Industry and agriculture put toxic substances into the human food chain and into underground water tables beyond reach of cleansing.

There has been a growing realization in national governments and multilateral institutions that it is impossible to separate economic development issues from environment issues; many forms of development erode the environmental resources upon which they must be based, and environmental degradation can undermine economic development. Poverty is a major cause and effect of global environmental problems. It is therefore futile to attempt to deal with environmental problems without a broader perspective that encompasses the factors underlying world poverty and international inequality.

These concerns were behind the establishment in 1983 of the World Commission on Environment and Development by the UN General Assembly. The Commission is an independent body, linked to but outside the control of governments and the UN system. The Commission's mandate gave it three objectives: to re-examine the critical environment and development issues and to formulate realistic proposals for dealing with them; to propose new forms of international co-operation on these issues that will influence policies and events in the direction of needed changes; and to raise the levels of understanding and commitment to action of individuals, voluntary organizations, businesses, institutes, and governments.

Through our deliberations and the testimony of people at the public hearings we held on five continents, all the commissioners came to focus on one central theme: many present development trends leave increasing numbers of people poor and vulnerable, while at the same time degrading the environment. How can such development serve next century's world of twice as many people relying on the same environment? This realization broadened our view of development. We came to see it not in its restricted context of economic growth in developing countries. We came to see that a new development path was required, one that sustained human progress not just in a few places for a few years, but for the entire planet into the distant future. Thus "sustainable development" becomes a goal not just for the "developing" nations, but for industrial ones as well.

The interlocking crises

Until recently, the planet was a large world in which human activities and their effects were neatly compartmentalized within nations, within sectors (energy, agriculture, trade), and within broad areas of concern (environmental, economic, social). These compartments have begun to dissolve. This applies in particular to the various global "crises" that have seized public concern, particularly over the past decade. These are not separate crises: an environmental crisis, a development crisis, an energy crisis. They are all one.

The planet is passing through a period of dramatic growth and fundamental change. Our human world of 5 billion must make room in a finite environment for another human world. The population could stabilize at between 8 billion and 14 billion sometime next century, according to UN projections. More than 90 percent of the increase will occur in the poorest countries, and 90 percent of that growth in already bursting cities.

Economic activity has multiplied to create a $13 trillion world economy, and this could grow five- or tenfold in the coming half-century. Industrial production has grown more than fiftyfold over the past century, four-fifths of this growth since 1950. Such figures reflect and presage profound impacts upon the biosphere, as the world invests in houses, transport, farms, and industries. Much of the economic growth pulls raw material from forests, soils, seas, and waterways.

A mainspring of economic growth is new technology, and while this technology offers the potential for slowing the dangerously rapid consumption of finite resources, it also entails high risks, including new forms of pollution and the introduction to the planet of new variations of life forms that could change evolutionary pathways. Meanwhile, the industries most heavily reliant on environmental resources and most heavily polluting are growing most rapidly in the developing world, where there is both more urgency for growth and less capacity to minimize damaging side-effects.

These related changes have locked the global economy and global ecology together in new ways. We have in the past been concerned about the impacts of economic growth upon the environment. We are now forced to concern ourselves with the impacts of ecological stress – degradation of soils, water regimes, atmosphere, and forests – upon our economic prospects. We have in the more recent past been forced to face up to a sharp increase in economic interdependence among nations. We are now forced to accustom ourselves to an accelerating ecological interdependence among nations. Ecology and economy are becoming ever more interwoven – locally, regionally, nationally, and globally – into a seamless net of causes and effects.

Impoverishing the local resource base can impoverish wider areas: Deforestation by highland farmers causes flooding on lowland farms; factory pollution robs local fishermen of their catch. Such grim local cycles now operate nationally and regionally. Dryland degradation sends environmental refugees in their millions across national borders. Deforestation in Latin America and Asia is causing more floods, and more destructive floods, in downhill, downstream nations. Acid precipitation and nuclear fallout have spread across the borders of Europe. Similar phenomena are emerging on a global scale, such as global warming and loss of ozone. Internationally traded hazardous chemicals entering foods are themselves internationally traded. In the next century, the environmental pressure causing population movements may increase sharply, while barriers to that movement may be even firmer than they are now.

Over the past few decades, life-threatening environmental concerns have surfaced in the developing world. Countrysides are coming under pressure from increasing numbers of farmers and the landless. Cities are filling with people, cars, and factories. Yet at the same time these developing countries must operate in a world in which the resources gap between most developing and industrial nations is widening, in which the industrial world dominates in the rule-making of some key international bodies, and in which the industrial world has already used much of the planet's ecological capital. This inequality is the planet's main "environmental" problem; it is also its main "development" problem.

International economic relationships pose a particular problem for environmental management in many developing countries. Agriculture, forestry, energy production, and mining generate at least half the gross national product of many developing countries and account for even larger shares of livelihoods and employment. Exports of natural resources remain a large factor in their economies, especially for the least developed. Most of these countries face enormous economic pressures, both international and domestic, to overexploit their environmental resource base.

The recent crisis in Africa best and most tragically illustrates the ways in which economics and ecology can interact destructively and trip into disaster. Triggered by drought, its real causes lie deeper. They are to be found in part in national policies that gave too little attention, too late, to the needs of smallholder agriculture and to the threats posed by rapidly rising populations. Their roots extend also to a global economic system that takes more out of a poor continent than it puts in. Debts that they cannot pay force African nations relying on commodity sales to overuse their fragile soils, thus turning good land to desert. Trade barriers in the wealthy nations – and in many developing ones – make it hard for Africans to sell their goods for reasonable returns, putting yet more pressure on ecological systems. Aid from donor nations has not only been inadequate in scale, but too often has reflected the priorities of the nations giving the aid, rather than the needs of the recipients. The production base of other developing world areas suffers similarly both from local failures and from the workings of international economic systems. As a consequence of the "debt crisis" of Latin America, that region's natural resources are now being used not for development but to meet financial obligations to creditors abroad. This approach to the debt problem is short-sighted from several standpoints: economic, political, and environmental. It requires relatively poor countries simultaneously to accept growing poverty while exporting growing amounts of scarce resources.

A majority of developing countries now have lower per capita incomes than when the decade began. Rising poverty and unemployment have increased pressure on environmental resources as more people have been forced to rely more directly upon them. Many governments have cut back efforts to protect the environment and to bring ecological considerations into development planning.

The deepening and widening environmental crisis presents a threat to national security – and even survival – that may be greater than well-armed, ill-disposed neighbours and unfriendly alliances. Already in parts of Latin America, Asia, the Middle East, and Africa, environmental decline is becoming a source of political unrest and international tension. The recent destruction of much of Africa's dryland agricultural production was more severe than if an invading army had pursued a scorched-earth policy. Yet most of the affected governments still spend far more to protect their people from invading armies than from the invading desert.

Globally, military expenditures total about $1 trillion a year and continue to grow. In many countries, military spending consumes such a high proportion of gross national product that it itself does great damage to these societies' development efforts. Governments tend to base their approaches to "security" on traditional definitions. This is most obvious in the attempts to achieve security through the development of potentially planet-destroying nuclear weapons systems. Studies suggest that the cold and dark nuclear winter following even a limited nuclear war could destroy plant and animal ecosystems and leave any human survivors occupying a devastated planet very different from the one they inherited.

The arms race – in all parts of the world – pre-empts resources that might be used more productively to diminish the security threats created by environmental conflict and the resentments that are fuelled by widespread poverty.

Many present efforts to guard and maintain human progress, to meet human needs, and to realize human ambitions are simply unsustainable – in both the rich and poor nations. They draw too heavily, too quickly, on already overdrawn environmental resource accounts to be affordable far into the future without bankrupting those accounts. They may show profits on the balance sheets of our generation, but our children will inherit the losses. We borrow environmental capital from future generations with no intention or prospect of repaying. They may damn us for our spendthrift ways, but they can never collect on our debt to them. We act as we do because we can get away with it: future generations do not vote; they have no political or financial power; they cannot challenge our decisions.

But the results of the present profligacy are rapidly closing the options for future generations. Most of today's decision makers will be dead before the planet feels the heavier effects of acid precipitation, global warming, ozone depletion, or widespread desertification and species loss. Most of the young voters of today will still be alive. In the Commission's hearings it was the young, those who have the most to lose, who were the harshest critics of the planet's present management.

Sustainable development

Humanity has the ability to make development sustainable – to ensure that it meets the needs of the present without compromising the ability of future generations to

The World Commission on Environment and Development first met in October 1984, and published its report 900 days later, in April 1987. Over those few days:

- The drought-triggered, environment-development crisis in Africa peaked, putting 35 million people at risk, killing perhaps a million.
- A leak from a pesticides factory in Bhopal, India, killed more than 2,000 people and blinded and injured over 200,000 more.
- Liquid gas tanks exploded in Mexico City, killing 1,000 and leaving thousands more homeless.
- The Chernobyl nuclear reactor explosion sent nuclear fallout across Europe, increasing the risks of future human cancers.
- Agricultural chemicals, solvents, and mercury flowed into the Rhine River during a warehouse fire in Switzerland, killing millions of fish and threatening drinking water in the Federal Republic of Germany and the Netherlands.
- An estimated 60 million people died of diarrhoeal diseases related to unsafe drinking water and malnutrition; most of the victims were children.

The Commission has sought ways in which global development can be put on a sustainable path into the 21st century. Some 5,000 days will elapse between the publication of our report and the first day of the 21st century. What environmental crises lie in store over those 5,000 days?

During the 1970s, twice as many people suffered each year from "natural" disasters as during the 1960s. The disasters most directly associated with environment/development mismanagement – droughts and floods – affected the most people and increased most sharply in terms of numbers affected. Some 18.5 million people were affected by drought annually in the 1960s, 24.4 million in the 1970s. There were 5.2 million flood victims yearly in the 1960s, 15.4 million in the 1970s. Numbers of victims of cyclones and earthquakes also shot up as growing numbers of poor people built unsafe houses on dangerous ground.

The results are not in for the 1980s. But we have seen 35 million afflicted by drought in Africa alone and tens of millions affected by the better managed and thus less-publicized Indian drought. Floods have poured off the deforested Andes and Himalayas with increasing force. The 1980s seem destined to sweep this dire trend on into a crisis-filled 1990s.

meet their own needs. The concept of sustainable development does imply limits – not absolute limits but limitations imposed by the present state of technology and social organization on environmental resources and by the ability of the biosphere to absorb the effects of human activities. But technology and social organizations can be both managed and improved to make way for a new era of economic growth. The Commission believes that widespread poverty is no longer inevitable. Poverty is not only an evil in itself, but sustainable development requires meeting the basic needs of all and extending to all the opportunity to fulfil their aspirations for a better life. A world in which poverty is endemic will always be prone to ecological and other catastrophes.

Meeting essential needs requires not only a new era of economic growth for nations in which the majority are poor, but an assurance that those poor get their fair share of the resources required to sustain that growth. Such equity would be aided by political systems that secure effective citizen participation in decision making and by greater democracy in international decision making.

Sustainable global development requires that those who are more affluent adopt lifestyles within the planet's ecological means – in their use of energy, for example. Further, rapidly growing populations can increase the pressure on resources and slow any rise in living standards; thus sustainable development can only be pursued if population size and growth are in harmony with the changing productive potential of the ecosystem.

Yet in the end, sustainable development is not a fixed state of harmony, but rather a process of change in which the exploitation of resources, the direction of investments, the orientation of technological development, and institutional change are made consistent with future as well as present needs. We do not pretend that the process is easy or straightforward. Painful choices have to be made. Thus, in the final analysis, sustainable development must rest on political will. [. . .]

51 Rio Declaration on Environment and Development

UN Conference on Environment and Development

The UN Conference on Environment and Development,

Having met at Rio de Janeiro from 3 to 14 June 1992,

Reaffirming the Declaration of the United Nations Conference on the Human Environment, adopted at Stockholm on 16 June 1972, and seeking to build upon it,

With the goal of establishing a new and equitable global partnership through the creation of new levels of cooperation among States, key sectors of societies and people,

Working towards international agreements which respect the interests of all and protect the integrity of the global environmental and developmental system,

Recognizing the integral and interdependent nature of the Earth, our home,

Proclaims that:

Principle 1

Human beings are at the centre of concerns for sustainable development. They are entitled to a healthy and productive life in harmony with nature.

Principle 2

States have, in accordance with the Charter of the United Nations and the principles of international law, the sovereign right to exploit their own resources pursuant to their own environmental and developmental policies, and the responsibility to ensure that activities within their jurisdiction or control do not cause damage to the environment of other States or of areas beyond the limits of national jurisdiction.

Principle 3

The right to development must be fulfilled so as to equitably meet developmental and environmental needs of present and future generations.

Principle 4

In order to achieve sustainable development, environmental protection shall constitute an integral part of the development process and cannot be considered in isolation from it.

Principle 5

All States and all people shall cooperate in the essential task of eradicating poverty as an indispensable requirement for sustainable development, in order to

Original publication details: United Nations Conference on Environment and Development, excerpt from "Rio Declaration on Environment and Development", 1992.

decrease the disparities in standards of living and better meet the needs of the majority of the people of the world.

Principle 6
The special situation and needs of developing countries, particularly the least developed and those most environmentally vulnerable, shall be given special priority. International actions in the field of environment and development should also address the interests and needs of all countries.

Principle 7
States shall cooperate in a spirit of global partnership to conserve, protect and restore the health and integrity of the Earth's ecosystem. In view of the different contributions to global environmental degradation, States have common but differentiated responsibilities. The developed countries acknowledge the responsibility that they bear in the international pursuit of sustainable development in view of the pressures their societies place on the global environment and of the technologies and financial resources they command.

Principle 8
To achieve sustainable development and a higher quality of life for all people, States should reduce and eliminate unsustainable patterns of production and consumption and promote appropriate demographic policies.

Principle 9
States should cooperate to strengthen endogenous capacity-building for sustainable development by improving scientific understanding through exchanges of scientific and technological knowledge, and by enhancing the development, adaptation, diffusion and transfer of technologies, including new and innovative technologies.

Principle 10
Environmental issues are best handled with the participation of all concerned citizens, at the relevant level. At the national level, each individual shall have appropriate access to information concerning the environment that is held by public authorities, including information on hazardous materials and activities in their communities, and the opportunity to participate in decision-making processes. States shall facilitate and encourage public awareness and participation by making information widely available. Effective access to judicial and administrative proceedings, including redress and remedy, shall be provided.

Principle 11
States shall enact effective environmental legislation. Environmental standards, management objectives and priorities should reflect the environmental and developmental context to which they apply. Standards applied by some countries may be inappropriate and of unwarranted economic and social cost to other countries, in particular developing countries.

Principle 12
States should cooperate to promote a supportive and open international economic system that would lead to economic growth and sustainable development in all countries, to better address the problems of environmental degradation. Trade policy measures for environmental purposes should not constitute a means of arbitrary or unjustifiable discrimination or a disguised restriction on international trade.

Unilateral actions to deal with environmental challenges outside the jurisdiction of the importing country should be avoided. Environmental measures addressing transboundary or global environmental problems should, as far as possible, be based on an international consensus.

Principle 13

States shall develop national law regarding liability and compensation for the victims of pollution and other environmental damage. States shall also cooperate in an expeditious and more determined manner to develop further international law regarding liability and compensation for adverse effects of environmental damage caused by activities within their jurisdiction or control to areas beyond their jurisdiction.

Principle 14

States should effectively cooperate to discourage or prevent the relocation and transfer to other States of any activities and substances that cause severe environmental degradation or are found to be harmful to human health.

Principle 15

In order to protect the environment, the precautionary approach shall be widely applied by States according to their capabilities. Where there are threats of serious or irreversible damage, lack of full scientific certainty shall not be used as a reason for postponing cost-effective measures to prevent environmental degradation.

Principle 16

National authorities should endeavour to promote the internalization of environmental costs and the use of economic instruments, taking into account the approach that the polluter should, in principle, bear the cost of pollution, with due regard to the public interest and without distorting international trade and investment.

Principle 17

Environmental impact assessment, as a national instrument, shall be undertaken for proposed activities that are likely to have a significant adverse impact on the environment and are subject to a decision of a competent national authority.

Principle 18

States shall immediately notify other States of any natural disasters or other emergencies that are likely to produce sudden harmful effects on the environment of those States. Every effort shall be made by the international community to help States so afflicted.

Principle 19

States shall provide prior and timely notification and relevant information to potentially affected States on activities that may have a significant adverse transboundary environmental effect and shall consult with those States at an early stage and in good faith.

Principle 20

Women have a vital role in environmental management and development. Their full participation is therefore essential to achieve sustainable development.

Principle 21

The creativity, ideals and courage of the youth of the world should be mobilized to forge a global partnership in order to achieve sustainable development and ensure a better future for all.

Principle 22

Indigenous people and their communities and other local communities have a vital role in environmental management and development because of their knowledge and traditional practices. States should recognize and duly support their identity, culture and interests and enable their effective participation in the achievement of sustainable development.

Principle 23

The environment and natural resources of people under oppression, domination and occupation shall be protected.

Principle 24

Warfare is inherently destructive of sustainable development. States shall therefore respect international law providing protection for the environment in times of armed conflict and cooperate in its further development, as necessary.

Principle 25

Peace, development and environmental protection are interdependent and indivisible.

52 Greenpeace and Political Globalism

Paul Wapner

> There are forces in the world which work, not in an arithmetical, but in a geometrical ratio of increase. Education, to use the expression of Plato, moves like a wheel with an ever multiplying rapidity. Nor can we say how great may be its influence, when it becomes universal.
>
> Benjamin Jowett

Nonstate-oriented politics is nothing new. Since the dawn of social life, human beings have worked to shape and direct collective affairs independent of formal government. In recent years, however, scholars have begun thinking theoretically about this type of activity and, in so doing, have provided a degree of conceptual clarity to it. In particular, the contributions of social movement theory, post-structuralism, feminism, and critical thought have broadened understandings of power and thus have heightened our sensitivity to how politics takes place in the home, office, and marketplace, as well as in the halls of congresses and parliaments. Politics, in this sense, is much more subtle to notice than the conduct of governments but, according to proponents of these orientations, no less significant for political affairs.

It is with a more comprehensive notion of power that I wish to begin investigating the ways in which transnational environmental groups engage in world civic politics. By suspending judgment about what constitutes real politics, one can focus on diverse forms of agency that actually shape world environmental affairs. In this chapter, I describe the ways in which activists work outside of, around, or at the margins of governmental activity in their efforts to alleviate global environmental problems. This descriptive element will sensitize readers to genuinely alternative forms of political activism.

In addition to describing forms of nonstate environmental politics, one must still ask the political question about them: namely, do they make a difference? Does all the time, money, and human energy involved actually contribute to addressing and partly alleviating environmental problems? Specifically, in what ways does a nonstate-oriented type of political action actually affect world environmental affairs? That activists employ such a politics is, as I will demonstrate, true; but does it really matter in terms of world politics? In this chapter, in addition to describing the work of transnational activists, I furnish evidence to suggest that their efforts actually do matter in world political events. They create conditions that direct the actions of others within a world context.

Original publication details: Wapner, Paul, "Greenpeace and Political Globalism." Reprinted by permission of the State University of New York Press, from *Environmental Activism and World Civic Politics* by Paul Wapner. © 1996, State University of New York. All rights reserved.

To begin, I want to draw attention to a level of analysis that has a long history in the study of world politics but which is, at present, still underdeveloped and underappreciated. This is the level at which norms, values, and discourse operate in the global arena outside the domain of states. It is that dimension of world experience where widespread, shared understandings among people throughout the globe act as determinants for present conditions on the planet. It is part of, for want of a better phrase, the *cultural* school of thought which believes that ideas within societies at large structure human collective life. Working within this tradition, the key argument of this chapter is that transnational environmental groups contribute to addressing global environmental problems by heightening worldwide concern for the environment. They persuade vast numbers of people to care about and take actions to protect the earth's ecosystem. In short, they disseminate what I call an *ecological sensibility*. This serves an important political function in coming to terms with the environmental threat.

A sensibility operates as a political force insofar as it constrains and directs widespread behavior. It works at the ideational level to animate practices and is considered a form of *soft law* in contrast to the *hard law* of government directives, policies, and so forth. Scholars make it a habit of differentiating between hard and soft law insofar as they distinguish legal and cultural factors in their understanding of social change. On the one hand, there are those who claim that governmental action is the key to social change. Laws, policies, and directives drive social norms, and thus as they change, the entire configuration of social life will shift. Those who share this perspective see governmental action as the "base" with cultural and social life being the "superstructure." On the other hand, there are those who claim that social norms are central to social change. Governmental decrees, from this perspective, are not the source of change but merely reflections of it. Laws and policies arise out of, or give authoritative expression to, norms that already enjoy widespread acceptance. Scholars sharing this view see social norms as the "base" and governmental directives as the "superstructure."

Differentiating legal and cultural factors, while analytically helpful, is misguided when it forces a thinker to choose between them. When it comes to such large categories of social analysis, it is a mistake to assume that one dimension of social change is definitively more significant than the other. The obvious response to such differentiation is that both factors are important. Indeed, some argue that they are in dialectical relation to each other. As Christopher Stone writes, "in general, laws and cultural norms are mutually reinforcing. Formal laws arise from cultures, and command obedience in proportion to their coherence with the fundamental beliefs of the culture. Cultures, however, are not static. Law, and especially the activities of law making and legal reform, are among the forces that contribute to cultural evolution."

In this chapter, I do not weigh in on the ideational side and argue for its primacy nor celebrate the dialectical relationship. Rather, I simply emphasize the degree to which widely held conceptualizations animate large-scale practices and use this to show how efforts to disseminate an ecological sensibility have world political significance. What makes such efforts political, it should be clear, is not that they are ultimately codified into law or governmental decree but that they represent the use of power to influence and guide widespread behavior. An ecological sensibility, then, is not itself an answer to global environmental threats nor *the* agent for shifting one state of affairs to another. It is, however, an important part of any genuine response to environmental harm. Put simplistically for the moment, it creates an ideational context which inspires and motivates people to act in the service of environmental well-being and thus constitutes the milieu within which environmentally sound actions can arise and be undertaken. While not solely responsible for the *existence* of this sensibility, transnational environmental groups deserve substantial credit for *spreading* it throughout the world. [...]

Since 1972, Greenpeace has grown from having a single office in Vancouver to staffing offices in over thirty countries and, until recently, a base in Antarctica. Greenpeace has offices in the developed as well as the developing world, including Russia and Eastern Europe. Its eco-navy consists of eight ships, and it owns a helicopter and a hot-air balloon. It employs over 1,000 full-time staff members, plus hundreds of part-timers and thousands of volunteers. As of July 1994, it had over 6 million members worldwide and an estimated income of over $100 million. All money comes from voluntary donations, 90 percent of which is in the form of small contributions from individual members. Additionally, Greenpeace sends hundreds of canvassers out each night to raise funds and educate the general public about current environmental issues. Finally, it has expanded its area of concern. While originally focused on nuclear weapons testing, it is now concerned with all threats to the planetary ecosystem. In short, from 1972 to the present Greenpeace has grown into a full-scale, transnational environmental organization.

Transnational Organizational Structure

Greenpeace sees the bulk of global environmental problems falling into four categories: toxic substances, energy and atmosphere, nuclear issues, and ocean and terrestrial ecology. Greenpeace works for environmental protection by dividing its attention among these four issue areas, also called campaigns. Within each of these, Greenpeace works on numerous subissues. For example, under the rubric of its nuclear campaign, Greenpeace focuses on reprocessing and dumping of nuclear material, sea-based nuclear weapons and nuclear testing. Under the rubric of ocean ecology, Greenpeace concentrates on whales, sea turtles, fisheries, and dolphins.

As a transnational environmental group concerned with threats to the entire planet, Greenpeace undertakes its campaigns and projects worldwide. The problems associated with toxic substances, energy, and atmosphere and so forth are not limited to individual countries. Almost all parts of the world are vulnerable to the environmental consequences involved. Greenpeace is organized to allow it to address these dilemmas on a global scale.

The top tiers of the organization are made up of the Greenpeace Council, an executive board, and regional trustees. The council is made up of representatives from all the countries where Greenpeace has offices and meets once a year to decide on organizational policy. The council is one of the ways Greenpeace coordinates its diverse activities. The council sets guidelines for the general operation of Greenpeace, approves the international budget, and develops long-term goals. Because council members come from around the world, decisions can reflect a sensitivity to differing regional and local aspects of environmental problems. To provide greater efficiency in day-to-day operations, and to emphasize coordination among campaigns and projects, there is an executive board that ratifies all council resolutions and makes significant decisions for Greenpeace throughout the year when the council is not in session. The board consists of both voting and nonvoting members and is elected by the Greenpeace Council.

In addition to the council and the executive board, there are regional trustees that provide the final stamp of approval for Greenpeace's overall operations. Trustees are representatives of the areas of the world where Greenpeace has offices. These include Latin America, the Pacific, North America, and Europe. While the trustees generally approve all decisions put forward by the council and the executive board, it serves as the final arbiter of Greenpeace policies. Because individual trustees represent diverse regions of the world, as a whole the trustees advance a global rather than a national or even regional orientation within Greenpeace.

Aside from the council and executive board, Greenpeace organizes itself world-wide along the lines of its four campaign areas. Heading each campaign is an international coordinator. He or she designs the way specific campaigns play themselves out in different regional and national contexts. For example, the campaign coordinator of toxic substances orchestrates all Greenpeace projects that contribute to achieving the aims of the toxics campaign. She or he provides the global perspective to different projects.

Underneath international campaign coordinators are project directors. Project directors are scattered across the globe and work on subissues of the larger campaigns. For example, there are nine projects currently being undertaken by the toxics campaign. One of these focuses on the pulp and paper industry. The pulp and paper industry is responsible for 50 percent of all organchlorine discharges into the earth's waterways. Organchlorine is dangerous to both humans and the natural environment; it is known to cause sterility and cancer in mammals. The project's aim is to change the production process of the industry away from bleaching procedures that use chlorine. The bulk of the pulp and paper industry is located in a number of countries, and Greenpeace pursues the project in each of them. The project director oversees all these efforts. Project directors, like campaign coordinators, take a global perspective on their respective projects. They make sure that separate Greenpeace activities throughout the world support each other and fit together to advance the cause of their specific project.

Working under the project coordinators are regional and national campaigners. Campaigners devise specific Greenpeace activities. They identify what they take to be the most effective ways to communicate with people and change environmentally destructive practices. For purposes of this chapter, one should think of campaigners as organizers of concrete activities that aim to alter people's perceptions of particular environmental threats. To use the pulp and paper example, there are campaigners in a number of countries including the United States, Canada, Sweden, and Germany. Campaigners focus on the pulp and paper industries in their respective countries, taking into account the governmental, cultural, and industrial attributes of each country to address the problem. Regional and national campaigners are key to Greenpeace's global efforts because they understand the particular contexts within which environmental damage is being caused and fashion appropriate responses. They take the general intentions of projects and overall campaigns and translate them into concrete actions that are tailored for specific geographical and political contexts.

Working with campaigners are a host of assistants and volunteers who help carry out specific activities. There are literally thousands of these people throughout the world. They paint banners, circulate petitions, research issues, organize protests, and take part in direct, nonviolent actions. All levels of activity are designed, at least in theory, to advance the goals of specific campaigns.

Greenpeace's Politics

Key to all Greenpeace's efforts is the insight that people do not damage the ecosystem as a matter of course. Rather, they operate in an ideational context that motivates them to do so. People are not machines; they do not respond directly to situations. In the words of Harry Eckstein, people are moved by "predispositions which pattern behavior." In the language of social science, human behavior is a matter of "oriented action." People process experience into action through general conceptions or interpretations of the world. At the most general level, but also the most important, then, an important step toward protecting the earth is to change the way vast numbers of people understand the world. It involves persuading them to abandon their anti-ecological or non-ecological attitudes and practices, and to be concerned about the environmental well-being of the planet. In short, it requires disseminating an ecological sensibility.

People respond to situations through interpretive categories that reflect a particular understanding of everyday circumstances. Such mediating orientations are cultural in character. They reflect customary, socially transmitted understandings that are embedded in the prevailing values, norms, and modes of discourse. Greenpeace targets and tries to alter these dispositions. It literally attempts to manipulate values, norms, and modes of discourse; it seeks to alter people's conceptions of reality. Greenpeace hopes that in so doing, people will undertake actions that are more respectful of the ecological integrity of the planet.

Central to Greenpeace's efforts is the practice of "bearing witness." This is a type of political action, originating with the Quakers, which links moral sensitivities with political responsibility. Having observed a morally objectionable act, one cannot turn away in avoidance. One must either take action to prevent further injustice or stand by and attest to its occurrence. While bearing witness often works to stop specific instances of environmental destruction, in general, it aims simply to present ecological injustice to the world. This offers as many people as possible an alternative understanding of contemporary affairs and sets them in motion against such practices. One way Greenpeace does this is by engaging in direct, nonviolent action and advertising it through the media worldwide.

Direct, nonviolent action is a form of political practice that shares much with the passive resistance of Mahatma Gandhi and Martin Luther King. It is a vehicle for confrontation and an outreach to other citizens. For Greenpeace, such action includes climbing aboard whaling ships, parachuting from the top of smokestacks, plugging up industrial discharge pipes, and floating a hot-air balloon into a nuclear test site. Such actions create images that can be broadcasted through the media to spark interest and concern of the largest audience.

Greenpeace is able to capture media attention because its actions are visually spectacular. According to political theorist J. Glenn Gray, human beings have what the New Testament calls "the lust of the eye." This is a primitive urge for visual stimulation; it describes the aesthetic impulse. The urge is lustful because it requires the novel, the unusual, the spectacular. The eye cannot satiate itself on the familiar, the everyday, the normal. Greenpeace actions excite the eye. They portray people taking dangerous risks. These grab attention and thus receive media coverage. By offering spectacular images to the media, Greenpeace invites the public to bear witness; it enables people throughout the world to know about environmental dangers and tries to pique their sense of outrage.

A number of years ago it was difficult to use direct, nonviolent action to change political conditions around the globe. While direct action has always been a political tool for those seeking change, the technology did not exist to publicize specific actions to a global audience. Recent innovations in communication technologies have allowed information to whip around the globe within seconds, linking distant corners of the world. Greenpeace plugs into this planetwide communication system to advertise its direct actions.

For example, in the 1970s Greenpeace ships used Morse code to communicate with their offices on land. Information from sailing expeditions would be translated in a central office and then sent out to other offices and onto the media via the telephone. This was cumbersome and expensive and compromised much of the information that could prove persuasive to public audiences. After weeks at sea, ships would return with still photographs, and these would be the most convincing images Greenpeace could use to communicate about environmental destruction taking place on the high seas.

With the advent of affordable innovations in the field of communications, Greenpeace has been able to update its ability to reach diverse and numerous audiences. Instead of Morse code, Greenpeace ships now use telephones, fax machines, and satellite uplinks to communicate with home offices. This allows for instantaneous information to be communicated and verified. Moreover, Greenpeace uses video cameras to capture its actions. Footage can be taken of whaling expeditions, ocean dumping of nuclear wastes, and discharging of toxic substances into streams and waterways. This documents more accurately actual instances of environmental destruction and the risks that Greenpeace members undertake to protect the environment. Once Greenpeace has footage and photographs of such abuse, it sends them into peoples' homes across the world through the planetwide mass communication system. Greenpeace has its own media facilities and uses these to get its information out to the public. Aside from attracting journalists and television crews to their actions, Greenpeace provides its own photographs to picture editors and has facilities to distribute edited, scripted, and narrated video news spots to television stations in eighty-eight countries within hours.

To see how Greenpeace uses direct, nonviolent action to make the world bear witness, consider its whale campaign. For years, Greenpeace has been trying to preserve whale populations and guard them from extinction. This is part of a larger campaign to generate more awareness and concern for the mass depletion of species currently taking place throughout the world. One technique Greenpeace uses to do this is direct action on the high seas. In one of its early expeditions, for instance, Greenpeace sent a ship to pursue a Russian whaling fleet. One of Greenpeace's first actions was to document the fleet's activities. Greenpeace found that the Russians were killing whales that were smaller than the official allowable size, as designated by the International Whaling Commission. To record this, Greenpeace filmed the killing of an undersized whale and took still photographs of a human being perched over it to demonstrate that it was merely a whale calf. Greenpeace noticed, moreover, that the sheer size and capability of the fleet enabled it to take large catches and thus threaten the sperm whale population in the area. To dramatize this, Greenpeace members boarded inflatable dinghies and positioned themselves between harpoon ships and pods of whales. In essence, they tried to discourage harpooners from firing by threatening to die for the cause. This proved effective as numerous times Russian whalers did not shoot their harpoons for fear of killing Greenpeace members. What turned out to be crucial was that Greenpeace captured this on film.

Footage was broadcasted on television stations and still photographs were reproduced in newspapers and magazines worldwide. Greenpeace has engaged in numerous similar actions since then and continues to use such strategies.

A second example of direct action is Greenpeace's campaign to stop ozone depletion. In 1989, Greenpeace members infiltrated a DuPont manufacturing plant in Deepwater, New Jersey. Activists climbed the plant's 180-foot water tower and hung a huge, blue-ribbon banner awarding DuPont a prize for being the world's number-one ozone destroyer. (At the time, DuPont produced half of the chlorofluorocarbons (CFCs) used in the US and 25 percent of world annual production.) The following day, Greenpeace bolted a steel box – with two people inside – onto the plant's railroad tracks and blocked the export of CFCs from the plant. Greenpeace draped the box with a banner that read, "Stop Ozone Destruction Now," with a picture of the earth in the background and used it to stage an 8-hour blockade holding up rail cars carrying 44,000 gallons of CFCs.

What is curious is that, according to Greenpeace, within minutes of removing the blockade, business proceeded as usual. The plant continued to function, producing and sending out substances that are proven to erode the stratospheric ozone layer. Nonetheless, something had happened in those brief 8 hours; something had changed. While DuPont workers continued to manufacture CFCs, they now did so knowing that others knew about and were concerned with the environmental effects. Moreover, because Greenpeace captured its actions on film and distributed video news spots to television stations throughout the world, vast numbers of people were now able to understand the connection between the production of CFCs and ozone depletion. In short, the utility of Greenpeace's activity in this case had less to do with the blocking action and more to do with the message that was conveyed. Greenpeace gave the ozone issue form and used the image of disrupting DuPont's operations to send out a message of concern. As Paul Watson, an early member of Greenpeace put it, "When you do an action it goes through the camera and into the minds of people. The things that were previously out of sight and out of mind now become commonplace. Therefore you use the media as a weapon."

Political Strategies

Greenpeace obviously does more than perform direct actions. It also lobbies government officials, gathers information, organizes protests and boycotts, produces record albums and other educational merchandise, and carries out scientific research. While many of these endeavors, especially lobbying, are directed specifically at states, a large percentage of Greenpeace's work is not meant to change states' policies per se but is aimed at changing the attitudes and behavior of the more general public. It seeks to change prevailing, and at times internationally shared, values, norms, and modes of discourse. It strives to "sting people with an ecological sensibility regardless of occupation, geographical location, or access to government officials. [. . .]

53 Environmental Advocacy Networks

Margaret E. Keck and Kathryn Sikkink

The Campaign against Deforestation in Sarawak

A case of deforestation that began to receive considerable attention in the late 1980s was the extremely rapid logging of tropical timber in the Malaysian state of Sarawak, on the island of Borneo. Logging had already decimated the forests of neighboring Sabah, but received little public attention. Sarawak was different, for three reasons: (1) a change in the international institutional context for discussion of tropical forestry issues, with establishment of the International Tropical Timber Organization, provided a new campaign focus, following upon a relatively successful effort to target a similar organization on the whaling issue; (2) strong connections between deforestation and native land rights issues brought environmental and indigenous rights campaigners together, especially in Europe, and the actions of Bruno Manser, an amateur anthropologist who had lived with a nomadic people in Sarawak called the Penan, dramatized their plight; and (3) the case was taken up vigorously by a Malaysian organization, Sahabat Alam Malaysia, that was already a member of Friends of the Earth International as well as several other mainly southern, transnational networks.

Background

Sarawak and Sabah are the two Malaysian states located on the northern coast of Borneo. They enjoy significant autonomy under the country's federal system, with the ability to control customs, civil service, and immigration (Sarawak requires a passport for visitors from peninsular Malaysia). Sarawak also controls the revenues from timber concessions, the result of an agreement at the time of joining the federation that gave peninsular Malaysia, in return, control over oil revenues. As a result of this deal, the federal government in Kuala Lumpur has been able to deny responsibility for logging practices in Sarawak.

With the exception of a severe recession in 1986, Malaysia's GNP has grown at 6–8 percent per annum since the early 1970s. A series of five-year plans have worked toward the goal, articulated in Prime Minister Mahathir Mohamad's "Vision 2020" program, of being a fully industrialized economy by the year 2020. Industry currently represents around 70 percent of the nation's exports. Timber is second to oil as a revenue producer in the primary sector.

Original publication details: Keck, Margaret E. and Kathryn Sikkink, "Environmental Advocacy Networks" from *Activists Beyond Borders: Advocacy Networks in International Politics.* Used by permission of Cornell University Press, 1998.

The country is a multi-ethnic state. The shadow of ethnic conflict has hung heavily over Malaysia since an explosion of violence in 1969. Although preferential treatment is given to Malays, the benefits of development are very widely distributed. Given the image of rapid modernization which is currently a central component of Malaysia's political identity, the idea that Dayak (indigenous) land rights should be secured in part to preserve traditional lifeways commonly portrayed as backward does not fit with the image of a country racing toward the twenty-first century. Malaysia has been ruled by a large multi-party coalition headed by the UMNO-Baru (United Malays National Organization), a Muslim–Malay party, since independence in 1957, and overtly ethnic politics is seen by dominant groups as potentially destabilizing.

Logging in peninsular Malaysia declined significantly between 1975 and 1985 as a conservationist National Forestry Policy (which does not affect Sarawak and Sabah) came into effect. At the same time, log output in Sarawak increased from 4.4 million cubic meters in 1976 to 12.2 million in 1985. Although in theory logging in Sarawak was tightly controlled from the outset, enforcement has been practically nonexistent; both the geographical constraints of hill logging and the economic incentives for cutting beyond the targets are very strong. Briefly, timber concessions under the control of state politicians are granted (sold) for short-term logging licences to timber companies, whose motivation to log selectively and with care in areas designated for protection is virtually nil.

Logging decimated traditional forms of livelihood, meanwhile accelerating the integration of Dayak communities into the state's cash economy. Although logging brought short-term jobs to native communities, it eroded soils, polluted rivers and reduced fish stocks, eliminated wildlife formerly hunted for food, and increased flooding. Employment benefits ended when the logging companies moved on to the next area. Attempts by Dayak communities to gain the rights to log in their own areas have been unsuccessful, as have most attempts to have areas declared communal forests and thus protected from the loggers. Making land rights effective has been a losing struggle in the state. Logging hit especially hard for the still partially nomadic Penan people of the Baram region, for whom the forest provided food and home.

Dayak resistance came to international attention beginning in March 1987, when the Penan set up barricades on logging roads in the Upper Baram. Use of this tactic quickly spread throughout the region to other Dayak groups (the Kenyah, Kayan, Lambawang, and Kelabit). Activities in at least sixteen logging camps were halted. Although this is not the first time that barricades were used against loggers, it is the first time they were part of a sustained campaign, and the first time the resistance received so much attention.

What elements projected the Sarawak conflicts onto a broader stage in 1987? First, interrelated political crises at the national and state levels amplified their importance. Malaysia had undergone a severe recession in 1986, with per capita income declining by 15.7 percent. Criticism of the government became pervasive both in the governing coalition and the opposition, mainly concerning access to decision-making. Within Sarawak, rising Dayak nationalism since 1983 had spawned the first explicitly ethnic political party in the state (Parti Bansa Dayak Sarawak – PBDS). Prime Minister Mahathir began to fear for his coalition. In addition, by early March 1987 Sarawak was in the midst of its own political crisis, significant for the present story because of revelations about official corruption in granting timber concessions. This multifaceted crisis formed the backdrop for the logging blockades.

Second, tropical forests had become increasingly visible on the international agenda by the mid-1980s. In March 1983 sixty-four countries had agreed to establish an International Tropical Timber Organization (ITTO). Composed of producers and consumers of tropical timber, the new group was given a mandate to consider global resource management issues. Then in 1985, declared the International Year of the Forest, the UN Food and Agriculture Organization, the World Bank, and the UN Development Program, working with the World Resources Institute, produced the Tropical Forestry Action Plan and published "Tropical Forests: A Call for Action." The resulting International Tropical Forest Timber Agreement and Action Plan, passed in June 1986 in Geneva, was to be implemented by the International Tropical Timber Organization, headquartered in Yokohama, Japan. The ITTO council met for the first time in March 1987, at the same time that the blockades of logging roads began to spread throughout the Baram region of Sarawak. [. . .]

The third factor that brought Sarawak logging wide attention was that local protests were linked to international publics through two different network nodes. One was the charismatic (and enigmatic) Bruno Manser, a Swiss national who had lived with the Penan for a number of years and who apparently helped to organize the blockade; and the other was Sahabat Alam Malaysia, one of a set of interrelated organizations based in Penang. Involved in a variety of environmental campaigns in peninsular Malaysia, SAM had an office in Marudi, Sarawak, run by Harrison Ngau, a Kayan from the Baram region. SAM was also the Malaysian member of Friends of the Earth International. SAM provided logistical support for the blockades, and arranged for twelve native representatives to go to Kuala Lumpur, where they met with the acting prime minister and a variety of high government officials. Although Dayak customary rights to land were recognized in law, the state government continued to violate them.

Before the blockades in 1987, forest campaigners had already begun to mount an international campaign involving deforestation in the region. At a meeting of FOE International in Penang in September 1986, everyone was looking for a way to influence the tropical timber trade, especially with regard to Japan. FOE–UK promoted the view that a campaign needed an institutional lever such as International Tropical Timber Organization. Experience with the International Whaling Commission in the antiwhaling campaign was undoubtedly a factor in that assessment. Others preferred to work for export bans and timber boycotts. Although organizations in the network concentrated on different aspects of the campaign, these were not seen as mutually exclusive. [. . .]

Despite passages of a forest amendment bill in late 1987 that made interfering with logging operations a criminal act punishable with a heavy fine and imprisonment, the blockades were repeated. From 1988 into the 1990s, they offered a powerful symbol of resistance and a continuing stimulus to network activities though they were of little value in producing concessions from state officials. Although the Penan Association and longhouse organizations continued to try to gain land titles or communal forest designations, the logging went on.

Framing the Sarawak conflict

The Sarawak campaign has different meanings for different groups of proponents. For people influenced by the experiences of Bruno Manser, who emerged from his hiding place in the forest and somehow returned to Europe in 1990, the nomadic Penan tribesmen were the symbolic center of the story. Organizing with the Penan at the center has created powerful images of an exotic and lost people fighting a heroic battle for the forest in the interest, it is implied, of all of us. Not surprisingly, this vision of the conflict has generated the most powerful media images. Film-makers, journalists, and photographers have in the main placed the Penan at the center of their accounts. Although the Penan are indeed an important part of the Sarawak story, several other frames have produced different kinds of strategies and engaged different constellations of actors.

Some organizations, including the World Rainforest Movement's Forest Peoples' Program, SAM, Survival International, and *The Ecologist*, have placed primary emphasis on indigenous land rights, which is also a central issue in Evelyne Hong's influential book *Natives of Sarawak*. Without secure land title, they argue, the struc-tural inequalities that prevent Dayak populations from resisting timber interests can never be addressed. This cogent vision of the problem is less resonant internation-ally than the Penan story, and one with which transnational networks have more difficulty organizing. The causal chain is fairly long, and the remedies difficult to devise.

The other main transnational strategy that emerged from the Sarawak case was its embedding in a broader campaign around tropical or rainforest timber (and in some cases temperate and boreal timber as well). This decentralized strategy has allowed space for considerable variation in organizational activities. Its main com-ponents have been consumer boycotts, targeting corporations and particular kinds of businesses (Mitsubishi, Do-it-Yourself stores, for example), persuading local or state governments to refrain from using tropical timber in construction projects, pressuring national governments and the European Union for tropical timber bans, pressuring ITTO members to develop sustainability requirements, and, increasingly, "eco-labeling." A large number of organizations have adopted these strategies, shared information, and collaborated on certain activities, though sometimes dis-agreeing over where to direct energies at particular stages.

This campaign involves a number of loosely connected subcampaigns with dif-ferent organizational sponsors. A central role, though not always a coordinating one, has belonged to the constellation of organizations headquartered in Penang—SAM, the Asian-Pacific People's Environmental Network, the Third World Network, and the World Rainforest Movement. By the early 1990s the campaign was focused on logging in Papua New Guinea, Guyana, and Brazil (in all of which Sarawak logging companies have expanded their operations). [. . .]

Campaign strategies around Sarawak's forests

The Sarawak campaign's efforts to set in motion a boomerang strategy had some effect, but fell far short of success. From taking Dayak representatives to meet with officials in Kuala Lumpur and foreign capitals to contesting the information Malaysian representatives presented in international forums, the network mobilized vast quantities of information and testimony. Repeated barricades of logging roads were powerful symbols of resistance. Demanding that the Malaysian federal gov-ernment intervene to control or block log exports from Sarawak, the network hoped to exert moral leverage. No effective material leverage was available – no World Bank loans in relevant areas, for example, or strategically placed aid programs.

However, because Malaysia aspired to leadership in the Southeast Asian region, the idea that it would respond to moral leverage seemed a credible one. Moral leverage proved insufficient, however, to overcome Prime Minister Mahathir's dependence on the votes of Sarawak's political elites to maintain his broad coalition government. Moreover, there is some evidence that Mahathir's willingness to stand up to US and European critics on this issue may even have enhanced his regional prestige.

Beyond the matter of leverage, however, the tropical timber campaign implicitly proposed a different kind of relationship between north and south than existed in the Brazilian case. From the perspective of most of the Sarawak campaigners, the blame for overexploitation of timber in the region belonged even more to importers than it did to the exporter. Without demand, went the argument, there would be no supply. Thus the campaign was framed and focused quite differently from those waged around World Bank projects; instead of focusing the energies of activists in developed countries on a developing country target, it asked them to target their efforts at home.

The reasons for the difference were both ideological and logistical. First, there was no single source of leverage that provided the same purchase over the Sarawak situation that the World Bank seemed to offer in Rondônia. The central government's insistence that it had no authority over timber extraction in Sarawak was not a fiction; the tradeoff between centralizing oil revenues and leaving timber revenues to the states of East Malaysia had been a crucial compromise at the time of federation. For Sarawak's politicians, growing rich from timber concessions, there was simply no incentive – positive or negative – to stop logging. Because of Mahathir's dependence on a very broad coalition, the political costs of attempting to intervene might have been very high. Furthermore, the Malaysian NGOs that provided the bridge between the Dayak populations in Sarawak and the transnational network were not anti-development – though they wanted to see development's fruits distributed more justly – and believed that first-world governments and NGOs should not use the environmental issue as a weapon to prevent third-world countries from developing autonomously. This argument was especially salient in international debates during the preparatory process for the 1992 UN Conference on Environment and Development in Rio de Janeiro. The tropical timber campaign therefore focused attention on the industrialized world, that rabidly consumed Sarawak's tropical hardwoods.

The tropical timber campaign and its effects

Campaigning around tropical timber had the advantage of decentralization, which allowed for a variety of activities and styles – from Rainforest Action Network activists climbing Mitsubishi office buildings to hang boycott banners and parading with huge Godzilla figures to protest Japanese tropical hardwood imports, to WWF's more sober negotiations over sustainability guidelines with corporations.

Organizations in Germany, the United Kingdom, and the Netherlands launched boycotts in 1988. On a motion from a Dutch Green party delegate, the European Parliament voted in 1988 to recommend Malaysian timber bans to European Union (EU) members until its logging became sustainable. The EU Commission subsequently overturned that recommendation, but as a symbol of protest it garnered much publicity. In May 1989 Australia's Rainforest Action Group, which had already called for a boycott, deployed swimmers and kayaks to Malaysian timber-bearing ships. The Rainforest Action Network in the United States declared a boycott of Mitsubishi, and Friends of the Earth did the same in Europe.

In addition to corporate boycotts, environmental organizations organized hundreds of local government boycotts of the use of tropical timber in municipal construction. This strategy was very successful in Europe; by November 1990 local boycotts had so incensed Malaysians and Indonesians that they threatened trade retaliations. In 1993 and 1994 Japanese activists stepped a similar local campaign.

These protests had little effect on logging. In 1990, timber operators in Sarawak cut a record eighteen million cubic meters of tropical hardwood logs. In early 1990, angry at foreign pressure, the Malaysian government had asked the ITTO to assess the question of sustainability. The ITTO team reported in May 1990 that Sarawak was logging at eight to ten times a sustainable level. The report recommended a reduction in log output by 1.5 million cubic meters a year. In 1992 the Sarawak government claimed it would comply with the recommendation, but regulations continued to be weakly enforced, and illegal logging is common.

But the trade issue had clearly become a serious one. In October 1991 Prime Minister Mahathir gave the keynote address at the meeting of the Association of Southeast Asian Nations (ASEAN) economy ministers, saying that ASEAN countries must speak with one voice against campaigns linking trade and environmental issues, and that the threats these posed to development had reached serious proportions. [. . .]

Measuring the impact of the tropical timber campaign requires that we define clearly the goals the campaign intended to reach. For those who wanted to preserve the nomadic lifeways of the Penan and the forest in which they lived, the campaign failed. Only a few hundred Penan remain in the forest. The rest live in longhouses, many work in timber camps and others suffer from the chronic unemployment that has beset communities throughout the region as the loggers move on. For those who wanted to fuel a struggle for land rights, the campaign continues. SAM has helped to organize several hundred community associations, for which security of tenure remains the precondition for any kind of community development activity. Although the transnational network does not exert direct leverage over this question, the campaign nonetheless provides some degree of protection to local efforts. For those who wanted to stop tropical timber logging in Sarawak, the campaign also failed. Sarawak will be logged out in five years, and Sarawakian timber companies are now repeating the process in Guyana and Papua New Guinea. The substantive goals of the Sarawak campaign, in other words, were not met.

In some respects, though, the efforts of the NGO networks and activists were remarkably successful. The Malaysian newspaper *Business Times* reported in October 1995, "Malaysia's timber exports to Europe have fallen by half since 1992 due to pressures from environmental groups on local and municipal governments in Europe to boycott or ban tropical timber products." Tropical timber imports into the Netherlands fell by 50 percent between 1990 and 1995, "mainly as a result of an NGO boycott campaign." Everyone seems to agree that the campaign succeeded in reducing consumption of tropical timber in some of the major importing countries.

If we see the tropical timber campaign as pursuing procedural rather than substantive goals, that is, a change in the international timber trading regime, then it has had some limited success. Campaign activities raised the salience of the issue and eventually placed it on the trade agenda. Unlike subsequent environmentalist attempts to use the trade agenda, as in the dispute over the effects of tuna fishing on dolphins, a forum was in place in which the issues could be ajudicated – the ITTO. Within the ITTO, beyond pressuring the institution to send investigative missions to logging areas and holding states accountable to their commitments, activists in the network have forced debates on the social dimensions of logging and on customary and common property arrangements. However, the new international tropical timber agreement negotiated in 1994 was far weaker than expected. [...]

Conclusions

More than other network campaigns, rainforest campaigns are built on the tensions between recognizing structural causes and designing strategies that seek remedies by placing blame on, and influencing the behavior of, particular actors. Furthermore, the struggles they entail over meaning, power, and access to resources highlight the north–south dimension found in many network campaigns. The campaigns include participants whose understandings have been changed by their ongoing conversation with what anthropologist Anna Tsing calls people in out-of-the-way-places. And, since these are stories about the real world, the campaigns include participants whose understandings have not been changed at all.

Environmental advocacy networks have not so much gotten the tropical forest issue onto the agenda – it was already there – as they have changed the tone of the debate. To the frequent consternation of the epistemic community of scientists and policymakers who had succeeded in placing it on the agenda initially, the advocacy networks deliberately politicized the issues. While the epistemic community had sought to design sound policies and tried on the basis of their authoritative knowledge to persuade governments to adopt them, advocacy networks looked for leverage over actors and institutions capable of making the desired changes. Advocacy networks also insisted on different criteria of expertise. Although they did not deny the expertise of the scientists, they demanded equal time for direct testimony about experience. And within the networks they also cultivated the strategic expertise of good organizers. The issue, especially for the multilateral bank campaigners, was not ultimately forests, or dams, or any other particular environmental issue, but leverage over institutions that make a difference.

The advocacy networks helped to broaden the definition of which information and whose knowledge should shape the agenda on tropical forest issues. In the process, they won seats at the bargaining table for new actors. Their campaigns created a new script for sustainable forest management projects, with roles for "local people," "NGOs," and so forth. We must be careful not to exaggerate the power of the individuals and groups that play these roles, relative to that of states, economic actors like corporations, or multilateral organizations (the Planafloro deliberative council is a good example). Nonetheless, once these roles have been legitimized, organizations like the World Bank must address them.

How much change have transnational advocacy networks produced in the tropical forest issue? Because the networks are not the only reform-minded actors engaged, exact attributions of influence are difficult. The multilateral development bank campaign would certainly not have had much success without the collaboration of network members inside the bank. At the levels of both discursive and procedural change the network has been remarkably successful. Multilateral development banks increasingly claim to be addressing environmental objectives in loans, and there is some evidence that they have begun to eliminate high-risk projects much earlier in the project evaluation cycle. Besides having adopted the discourse of sustainable development, the bank has also implemented important procedural changes, including the information policy. Under increased pressure from the United States after the 1989 Pelosi amendment, all of the multilateral banks are taking the environmental assessment process more seriously.

Similarly, though less dramatically, the tropical timber campaign has had considerable success in promoting discursive change and some success with procedural change as well. Malaysia, as well as other tropical forest states, has begun at least to use the discourse of sustainable forestry, whether or not much has changed in practice. Malaysia has also adopted action plans phasing out unsustainable logging, and has begun to encourage local wood processing. The ITTO has adopted somewhat more stringent standards for movement toward demonstrably sustainable forestry practices. Green labeling, about which forest campaign advocates are quite divided, has not yet proved itself; should it change behavior in the ways that its proponents hope, this may stimulate further steps from the ITTO.

Among the people whose testimony generated the sharpest images of the impact of deforestation on lives, signs of success are harder to find. In Sarawak the transnational advocacy campaign has had very little impact. Logging goes on with its ecological and human impacts. [. . .]

54   Building Political Will after UNCED: EarthAction International

Jackie Smith

Abstract

Some transnational social movement organizations (TSMOs) intervene directly in intergovernmental conferences to try to influence the language of particular treaties and to help implement multilateral agreements. But many more elements of transnational movements work to educate national and local organizations and individuals about global problems and the political systems designed to address these. EarthAction is a TSMO that works to integrate its affiliate organizations into multilateral policy processes by informing them about the issues at stake and by suggesting tactics that encourage local mobilization around global issues. For example, EarthAction helped to sustain pressure on governments to adhere to declarations they made during the 1992 UN Conference on Environment and Development (UNCED). Such TSMO efforts, however subtle their results, may be critical to advancing concrete policy change to protect the environment.

Although many scientists and activists are increasingly convinced of the urgency of international action to counter many global environmental problems, national leaders often lack the political will to generate multilateral cooperation that effectively addresses these problems. Where problems are recognized, governments often prefer to take minimal steps towards their mitigation rather than to act decisively for their prevention or reversal. In democracies, one reason for such a choice is that politicians' electoral mandates lead them to think in terms of two- to six-year periods, whereas the consequences of environmental degradation may not be manifest for decades or centuries. Political leaders are, therefore, unlikely to have strong interests in supporting multilateral responses to global crises with only subtle, ambiguous, and long-term implications for their own constituencies. Nevertheless, in the past two decades, states have advanced multilateral cooperation for the environment in dramatic ways. Environmental transnational social movement organizations (TSMOs) have contributed to this development.

EarthAction's Mobilization to Advance UNCED Goals

Founded in 1991, EarthAction is a TSMO that mobilizes local, national, and international nongovernmental organizations (NGOs) around issues of peace, human

Original publication details: Smith, Jackie, "Building Political Will after UNCED: Earth-Action International" from *Transnational Social Movements and Global Politics: Solidarity Beyond the State*, Jackie Smith, Charles Chatfield and Ron Pagnucco (eds.) (Syracuse University Press, Syracuse, 1997). By permission of the publisher.

rights, and sustainable development. Its more than 1,500 partner organizations in over 140 countries are linked around common campaigns through routine mailings and telephone contacts from EarthAction's regional international offices. Earth-Action attempts to make global issues matter for politicians' short-term (e.g., electoral) interests. It has sought in particular to advance the goals outlined in Agenda 21, the final declaration of the UN Conference on Environment and Development (UNCED). UNCED was held in Rio de Janeiro in 1992 to address growing concerns, particularly among Northern governments, about continued environmental degradation and to reconcile these with Southern governments' urgent development needs.

Between late 1992 and early 1995, EarthAction initiated more than twenty global campaigns focused on environment, development, peace, and human rights issues. Nearly half of these campaigns sought explicitly to further goals specified in Agenda 21. EarthAction's environmental campaigns have aimed to generate pressure on governments to strengthen their commitments to more equitable and sustainable development. These campaigns supported multilateral negotiations on the two major conventions that resulted from UNCED – the biological diversity and the climate change conventions – and EarthAction has also supported the development of the Desertification Convention, which was another goal of the Agenda 21. Earth-Action's treaty-oriented campaigns are complemented by its efforts to support institutional reform and treaty implementation.

EarthAction's strategy

EarthAction works as a catalyst for global political change primarily by building the infrastructures for a politically active, global civil society. Believing that global change will occur only when political leaders face sufficient pressure from their constituencies, EarthAction's leadership attempts to make global issues matter for local and national elections by helping inform citizens and their legislators about global problems and about government attempts to resolve these problems. Providing detailed information about the timing of negotiations, the terms of debate, and expert assessments of what is needed to resolve a crisis, EarthAction enables partners, their members, and elected officials (parliamentarians) to become more involved in multilateral political processes than they could be otherwise. Its editorial advisories, moreover, provide media producers with tools they need to cover complex global issues that they may find difficult or that may not be part of their routine reporting.

Both directly and through its network of NGOs, EarthAction also monitors global political processes, informing partners about how and when effective pressure can be applied. Partners that hope to influence their government's policies on the rights of indigenous peoples, for instance, may have been unaware of an International Labor Organization (ILO) convention on indigenous peoples' rights before receiving EarthAction's Alert on the subject. And few citizens' organizations are able to attend international negotiations in order to identify which governments need to be pressed on what issues.

In addition to providing informational tools, EarthAction serves to aggregate global environmental interests. Its communications links with partner organizations foster communication among NGOs and the identification of common interests and possibilities for cooperation. In other words, EarthAction helps develop and reinforce transnational movement frames, that is, interpretations of global environmental problems and the steps needed to remedy them. [. . .]

Protecting biological diversity

The second major agreement signed at UNCED was the Convention on Biological Diversity, which called upon its signatories to develop and advance national plans for protecting biological diversity while encouraging the transfer of technological and financial resources from Northern to Southern countries. Although lacking legally binding commitments, this convention specified concrete aspects of national conservation plans while seeking to mitigate inequalities caused by the exploitation of national resources. EarthAction's campaigns on the Biological Diversity Convention included two Action Alerts to promote this convention and the Alert, described above, on restructuring the GEF. An "Editorial Advisory" on the convention was issued just before the October 1993 meeting of the signatories. Sent to a list of reporters compiled by EarthAction, the advisory provided the international news media with background on the convention and on the problem of biological diversity. It recommended reading matter, prerecorded radio and television material, and questions to ask policymakers, in addition to notifying journalists about a media briefing and workshop to be held near the negotiation site. This editorial campaign provided critical information for the news reports of several media outlets, and it was used by World Environment News to produce a video news clip that was rebroadcast by CNN and other large networks worldwide.

A key to reaching agreement on the Biological Diversity Convention and to its ultimate success was the commitment of Northern governments to provide financial and biotechnological support for less developed, Southern countries that lack the means to develop the biological resources within their boundaries. EarthAction sought to reinforce these redistributive commitments and to otherwise mitigate tensions between Northern and Southern governments through its campaign to strengthen the GEF. It also explicitly addressed North–South tensions in its campaign against Canadian logging policy. This EarthAction Alert argued, "[i]f affluent British Columbia is unable to save its rainforests, how can we expect other countries, under tremendous pressures of poverty and debt, to save theirs?" Through this campaign, EarthAction focused international citizen pressure on bringing the environmental policy of a single, Northern government in line with global interests. Using a single Action Alert and two follow-up notices, EarthAction helped to bring *sustained* pressure on the Canadian government to protect its remaining forests, just as it and other Northern governments were asking Southern governments to do. An EarthAction partner in Canada, Friends of Clayoquot Sound, reported that

> [t]he Canadian Government is clearly feeling the international pressure. Last week Canada's ambassador to the UN, Arthur Campeau, said "I believe that the Clayoquot conflict has gone on far too long. It is causing us damage greater than we are prepared to admit. Abroad, Canada's envied image of world leader in protection of the environment is being eroded and replaced by one of an environmental outlaw."

Thus EarthAction's international citizen pressure highlighted for Canadian officials the potential international costs of the continued destruction of its forests.

EarthAction's "Forests Campaign" of March 1995 tried both to advance the formal commitments made at UNCED and to promote other initiatives to protect the earth's resources. In this campaign EarthAction used a Parliamentary Alert and Editorial Advisory in addition to the regular citizens' alert to reach government officials through their constituents, national legislators, and media. The campaign addressed the broad problem of losing plant and animal species, citing two main ways to curb further environmental destruction. Recognizing that governments were currently in the process of negotiating a Forest Convention, EarthAction pointed out that such a treaty would take years to realize and that other multilateral steps could address this increasingly urgent crisis.

EarthAction emphasized the need for the 157 state signatories to the Convention on Biological Diversity to carry out their pledges to protect vanishing species and ecosystems. Partners were asked to hold their governments to their pledges to identify and protect endangered species. Moreover, believing that "[t]he indigenous people who inhabit many of the world's forests make far better forest stewards than distant bureaucrats," EarthAction promoted the rights of indigenous people to control the land they have traditionally occupied.

The International Labor Organization's Tribal People's Convention (ILO Convention 169) protects the rights of indigenous peoples to own and control the use of their traditional land. This convention not only reaffirms indigenous peoples' territorial rights but also protects indigenous lands from destructive business and government practices. However, as an EarthAction Alert informed partners, although ILO Convention 169 promised to protect endangered forests, only seven countries had signed the convention. Northern governments, the Alert stated, should be urged to sign it, to provide financial support for indigenous peoples' efforts to protect their territorial rights, and to increase their financial support of developing countries trying to implement the Convention on Biological Diversity. By relating this ILO initiative to the Convention on Biological Diversity, EarthAction helped both to advance UNCED's general aims and to link the UNCED process to other multilateral efforts.

Resisting desertification

Also resulting from UNCED was the International Convention to Combat Desertification. Formal negotiations for the convention originated with Agenda 21, although it remained secondary in importance, behind the Conventions on Biological Diversity and Climate Change. EarthAction's campaign sought to generate more widespread awareness of and support for the Convention to Combat Desertification, as the negotiations for it proceeded.

EarthAction's first antidesertification effort was to issue an Action Alert and Editorial Advisory in December 1993. These materials informed partners and journalists about the causes and consequences of global desertification and about the status of intergovernmental negotiations to address the problem. The Alert provided background information for partners interested in attending the negotiations or in becoming more involved with the Intergovernmental Negotiating Committee for a Convention to Combat Desertification (the international agency charged with organizing the negotiations and implementing their decisions) or with other NGOs. It sought to help partners influence intergovernmental negotiations at the early stages, when the form of the convention was still open for modifications.

EarthAction issued toolkits on the Desertification Convention again in April and October of 1994 to increase the awareness of both the general public and politicians of the issues at stake and the steps to which governments were committing themselves. EarthAction partners and parliamentarians were urged to press governments to increase financial support for efforts to combat desertification and to uphold their treaty commitments by "ensur[ing] that decisions on the . . . programmes to combat desertification and/or mitigate the effects of drought are [under]taken with the participation of . . . local communities." Throughout the treaty negotiations, governments of industrialized countries resisted increasing funds devoted to combating desertification, even though such funds were less than $1 billion per year, in contrast to what UNEP estimates is a need for between $10 billion and $22.4 billion annually.

To facilitate journalists' coverage of the signing of the convention, an Editorial Advisory was sent to several thousand editorial writers around the world. It included suggested "news hooks," local angles on the issue, a background summary of desertification and efforts to prevent it, questions journalists could ask policymakers, "key facts and quotes" to include in stories on the issue, expert sources, and a camera-ready map locating desertification problems. As a result of EarthAction's work on the Desertification Convention, numerous news stories were written that otherwise might not have been. EarthAction helped draw journalists' attention to the materials by following the initial mailing with telephone calls to hundreds of writers and producers to remind them about the toolkit and to answer questions about desertification or the negotiations to combat it.

EarthAction's staff used these calls to help journalists tailor stories on global desertification to their particular regions or locales. As a result of EarthAction's media work, National Public Radio in the United States was prompted to send a team of reporters to five African countries to produce a series of broadcasts on desertification, and major news outlets, such as *The Times* (UK), the *Independent* (UK), the Canadian Broadcasting Company, and *Berlingske Tidende* (Denmark), reported on desertification negotiations.

Conclusions

Although the road from Rio has been disappointing because some of the world's governments have failed to take more decisive environmental action, it clearly has led to some progress. Perhaps most important, UNCED – including the preparation for the conference and the follow-up work done by EarthAction and other TSMOs – has generated increased public and governmental awareness of global environmental issues. Efforts by transnational environmental movements have helped advance transnational mobilizing frames that amplify the prominence of environmental issues on many governments' policy agendas and reinforce multilateral solutions to environmental problems. Another important consequence of UNCED is the new global institutions it helped spawn, most notably, the GEF and the Commission on Sustainable Development. These institutions, although largely failing to address the core obstacle to global North/South equity concerns, have created new forums through which EarthAction and other TSMOs and NGOs can press governments to develop more environmentally sustainable policies. EarthAction's persistent work to reinforce the goals of Agenda 21 is an important part of the political processes surrounding global environmental policy. And the UNCED conference process itself provided both a focal point and political legitimacy for EarthAction's efforts.

As UNCED Secretary-General Maurice Strong observed, "Inertia is as powerful a force in human affairs as it is in the physical world." As a result, the political processes structured by intergovernmental institutions are far from automatic. States typically resist infringements on their own sovereignty by intergovernmental agencies. By nurturing transnational mobilizing frames and by drawing citizen groups into multilateral decision-making processes, EarthAction nudges governments to act.

By monitoring government progress in and commitment to resolving environmental crises, EarthAction provides its partners with information they need to be active in global policy processes. In short, EarthAction's work helps articulate and focus shared interests of its partners, amplifying the needs and demands of local populations and empowering them to act on global issues. These functions of Earth-Action help shape the contexts in which national, multilateral, and transgovernmental decisions are made. Specifically, such TSMO activities alter decision makers' perceptions of the costs and benefits (both political and environmental) of different policy choices.

UN conferences and review sessions provide opportunities for TSMO action, and they also represent important steps in the international community's adaptation to newly identified problems. They are used to mobilize public and official attention to issues, to develop or cultivate support for particular responses to problems, and to generate (and, increasingly, to help implement) mechanisms for ongoing problem management. TSMO participation in these events and their aftermaths is, however, vital to their realization of the tasks of drawing public attention to global problems and of sustaining institutions that effectively respond to such problems. Moreover, the work of TSMOs like EarthAction can help governments reach agreements in multilateral negotiations by expanding policy options, altering the political costs of multilateral cooperation, and enhancing the transparency of international negotiations and institutions. Over the long term, TSMOs' work helps improve the effectiveness and responsiveness of multilateral institutions.

Questions

1 What makes a social problem global? Discuss features of the contemporary world that make it increasingly likely that problems will be considered global rather than national or regional in character.

2 Given that global civil society organizations have no formal authority and, often, not much money either, why do states and IGOs pay any attention to them? What is it about INGOs and similar organizations that makes them influential with respect to global issues?

3 Are global environmental organizations necessary? How do you think transnational corporations would act if they were not being constantly scrutinized by groups like EarthAction, Greenpeace, and the World Wildlife Fund (now called the Worldwide Fund for Nature)? Is there reason to believe that corporations would try to limit the environmental damage they do if there were no environmental INGOs?

4 In light of the selection from the World Commission on Environment and Development, explain what the concept of "sustainable development" means. Do you feel that the way of life in your country is consistent with this concept? Give examples to amplify your response.

5 Despite the participation of almost all governments in the Earth Summit in Rio, tropical deforestation continues, waterways remain badly polluted, and smog plagues many cities. Is the Rio Declaration therefore a meaningless document? Give arguments suggesting that it is; then give arguments suggesting that the Declaration will have important long-term effects.

6 Wapner says that Greenpeace depends on "visually spectacular" actions to get attention and put environmental problems on the global agenda. Do such actions have any drawbacks? Think about how they may both promote environmentalism and hurt the environmentalist cause.

7 The anti-logging campaign in Sarawak was not able to protect the rainforests there, according to Keck and Sikkink. What lessons can you draw from this case about how environmental action becomes effective? What else could have been done that might have led to more success for this movement?

8 Smith's article about EarthAction shows that environmental groups depend on states to enforce measures to protect the natural world. Explain why the media attention EarthAction generates, and its efforts to mobilize public opinion, are likely to be more effective with respect to democratic states than non-democratic states. Does this mean that sustainable development is achievable only if most countries of the world are democratic?

Index